Travellers **S**urvival **K**it

SIMON CALDER & EMILY HATCHWELL

Published by
VACATION WORK, 9 PARK END STREET, OXFORD

TRAVELLERS SURVIVAL KIT: CUBA

by Simon Calder and Emily Hatchwell

Copyright © Vacation Work 1996

ISBN 1 85458 144 9

Cover Design
Mel Calman
Miller Craig and Cocking Design Partnership

Illustrations by William Swan

Maps of Cuba, Havana and Santiago de Cuba district by Lovell Johns Ltd

Town maps by Andrea Pullen

Printed by Unwin Bros, Old Woking, Surrey, England

Contents

Acknowledgments

In order to present an impartial and realistic view of Cuba, this book has been written without the collaboration of the authorities there. The authors have received no free facilities from the travel industry inside or outside Cuba. Many Cuban people, and a number of US citizens, have provided a great deal of help with this book — but they must, for the time being, remain anonymous.

Numerous travellers have made contributions to this revised edition, including Jean-Pierre Bou, Neville Chanin, Laura Druce, Jonathan Glancey, Martin Godfrey, Duncan Hunt, Iain Macfarlaine, Fred Mawer, Andy Mitchell, Randy Montgomery, Cleo Paskal, Sanjeen Payne-Kumar, William Simmonds, David Stanley, Keith Strickland, David Thornhill, Brigit Van Hout and Sue Wheat. The updated section on Cuba's natural history was contributed by Andy Mitchell of the North Ronaldsway Bird Observatory in Orkney; he has asked for his fee to be donated to the Threatened Birds of Cuba Project, to help preserve species in the Zapata peninsula.

This book is dedicated, with respect, to all those who have contributed to it — and to the people of Cuba.

The authors and their friends

In the six years since this book first appeared, some people have been reported to be passing themselves off as close personal friends of the authors — even to one or other of the authors themselves. The authors are indeed fortunate to have a number of good friends on the island, some of whom will be pleased to mention the fact and may ask you to bring a letter home with you. But someone who offers to change money and says he is a special friend of "Emeely Hashwill", is probably not on our Christmas card lists.

All the research for this book is conducted anonymously and without requesting any special privileges. It follows that anyone seeking free facilities on the grounds of preparing the next edition is fibbing.

Every effort has been made to ensure that the information in this book was accurate at the time of going to press in February 1996. Nevertheless some details are bound to change during the lifetime of this book. If in the course of your travels you encounter errors or omissions, please write to Simon Calder and Emily Hatchwell at Vacation Work Publications, 9 Park End Street, Oxford OX1 1HJ. Those whose contributions are used will receive a complimentary copy of the next edition.

Preface

Cuba is like nowhere else on earth. Whether or not you sympathize with Fidel Castro's brand of state socialism, you are guaranteed to find the Caribbean's largest island fascinating. On the most basic level Cuba is attractive purely physically, with some of the best beaches and landscapes in the Caribbean. The Republic has a deep sense of history and culture. Cuban society, the product of complex internal and external pressures, is unique.

Yet compared with the rest of the region, few foreigners visit Cuba. It does not have a good reputation for catering to the whims of Westerners; it is hard to reach, and when you get there the chances of finding a decent meal or a fully-functioning bathroom are slim. But travellers prepared to put up with a little inconvenience are guaranteed the adventure — and education — of a lifetime. You might be a *capitalista*, but the people who are presently offered a choice between *socialismo o muerte* ('socialism or death') will treat you with generosity, respect and good humour.

'Eastern Europe-on-Sea' is one face of Cuba, an outdated Iron Curtain nation transplanted to the Caribbean, with all the discredited trappings of the old Soviet bloc: queues for the most basic goods, black marketeers, and ugly office blocks whose faded net curtains conceal faceless bureaucrats maintaining a harsh, undemocratic regime. A different view is of an heroic experiment in social reform which transcends economic and political sabotage by a powerful neighbour, the USA. Mixed with the influences of Spanish colonialism and the rhythms and religions of West Africa, Cuba is entrancing.

Preface to the Third Edition

The changes which have taken place in the past three years have been traumatic for the people of Cuba, but their prospects as the island approaches the Millennium are more promising than in the early 1990s. And for the visitor, life is both easier and more exciting.

Some things remain the same, such as the US regulations designed to prevent American citizens visiting Cuba — restrictions which increasing numbers are circumventing. Much of the stress and repression that led to the riots and mass exodus of August 1994 still remains. But tourism is doing its bit to help lift Cuba from the socio-economic morass.

If you are planning a trip to Cuba for the first time, we hope you find what you are looking for. Certainly the clichés about fine cigars, exquisite automobiles and beautiful people are true. Equally present, though sometimes harder to see, is a sense of community that long ago evaporated in more materialistic nations. Cuba is both astonishing and addictive.

Simon Calder and Emily Hatchwell
Oxford
February 1996

CUBA AND ITS PEOPLE

Cuba is the largest, most diverse and most beautiful island in the Caribbean. It has some of the most charming, cultured and friendly people in the world, and enormous potential for economic development. It could be a reasonable approximation to perfection. Yet it is a country struggling to recover from national economic breakdown. Cuba's political system has survived the collapse of state socialism elsewhere in the world, but has been continually assailed by the United States — nine US presidents have been confronted by a fiercely independent nation on their doorstep, and have been increasingly energetic in trying to eliminate the source of irritation. Cuba is a thorn in the side of American foreign policy, and is subject to stringent economic sanctions. Coupled with decades of toeing the Communist Party line, the result is an island far from Utopian, but one which is utterly fascinating.

Fidel Castro's name hits a raw nerve in the USA, but the leader of the Cuban revolution in the 1950s has hung on to life, power and a measure of popularity. He still commands a degree of loyalty which any democratic politician would envy, though in a country without freedom of speech there is a great deal that must remain unexpressed. Who succeeds him is probably the subject of the greatest speculation in Cuba and in Miami — where tens of thousands of exiled Cubans dream of returning home one day.

It is remarkable that Cuba's communist system should be endeavouring to take state socialism into the new millennium while the rest of the world order has changed so radically. The uniqueness of Cuba is a result of its location and human history. The first part of this chapter explains the elements and accidents of history and geography which have produced this bizarre and beguiling state of affairs.

GEOGRAPHY

The Cuban mainland is the large island at the western end of the Antilles chain, a broad scar 90 miles (144km) beneath the Florida coast. At their closest, Haiti is 48 miles (77km) distant and Jamaica 86 miles (140km) away. Cubans refer to their island as the 'sleeping alligator' because of its shape. The island is the same size as England or the state of Pennsylvania. It stretches 750 miles (1,200km) end to end: the same distance as between London and Vienna. The Republic of Cuba includes more than 1,600 offshore islands and keys, the largest of which is the Isle of Youth (Isla de la Juventud) dangling off the south coast; few other islands are inhabited. Coral reefs skirt the mainland, the longest extending for some 250 miles (400km) along the north coast of Camagüey province.

The terrain is largely low-lying, the rural landscape a curious blend of sugar plantations, forest, swamp and rolling hillsides. The most spectacular mountain chain is the Sierra Maestra in the far east of Cuba, parts of which consist of dense forest and are largely inaccessible. The tallest peak in the range is Pico Turquino at 6,476ft (1,974m). The highest point in the Escambray mountains, in the centre of the island, is Pico San Juan (3,465ft/1,056m). A smaller range, the Cordillera de Guaniguanico, is in the region of Pinar del Río, west of

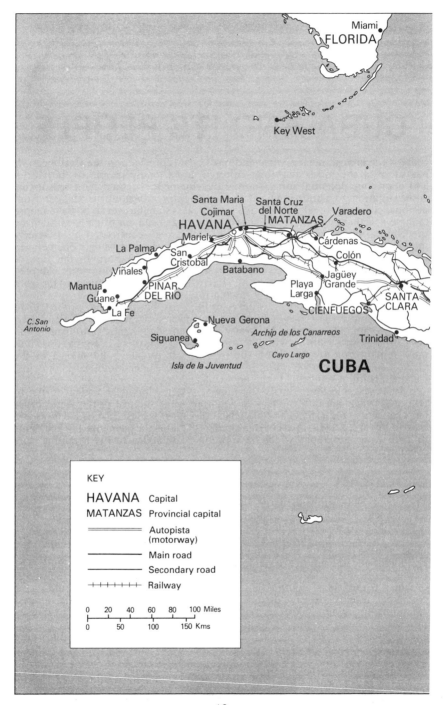

Miami
FLORIDA

Key West

Santa Maria
Cojimar
HAVANA
Mariel
La Palma
San
Cristobal
Viñales
Mantua
Guane
La Fe
PINAR
DEL RIO
C. San
Antonio
Siguanea

Santa Cruz
del Norte
MATANZAS
Varadero
Cárdenas
Colón
Batabano
Playa
Larga
Jagüey
Grande
CIENFUEGOS
SANTA
CLARA

Nueva Gerona
Archip de los Canarreos
Trinidad
Cayo Largo
Isla de la Juventud
CUBA

KEY

HAVANA   Capital
MATANZAS   Provincial capital
━━━━━━   Autopista
           (motorway)
━━━━━━   Main road
━━━━━━   Secondary road
++++++++   Railway

0   20   40   60   80   100 Miles
0   50   100   150 Kms

12

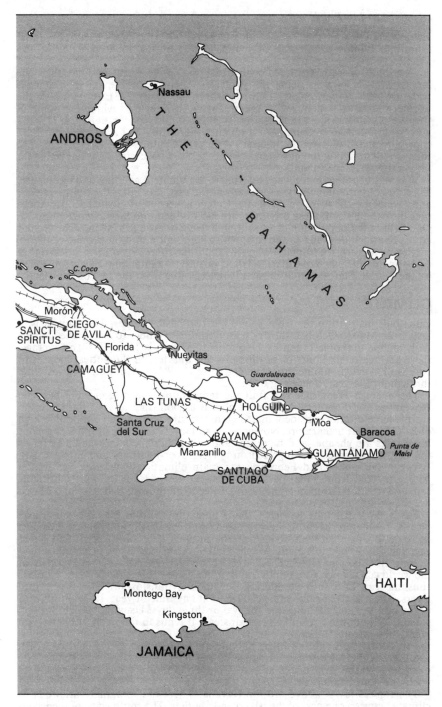

ANDROS

Nassau

T H E

B A H A M A S

C. Coco

Morón

CIEGO
DE ÁVILA

SANCTI
SPÍRITUS

Florida

Nuevitas

CAMAGÜEY

Guardalavaca

Banes

LAS TUNAS

HOLGUÍN

Santa Cruz
del Sur

Moa

Baracoa

BAYAMO

GUANTÁNAMO

Punta de
Maisi

Manzanillo

SANTIAGO
DE CUBA

HAITI

Montego Bay

Kingston

JAMAICA

13

Havana. It includes the Sierra de los Organos with the bizarre *mogotes*, large limestone humps which rise dramatically out of the tobacco fields of the Viñales valley.

The south coast is scattered with dense mangrove forest and marshes, the largest area of swamp being the protected Ciénaga de Zapata in Matanzas province; this is particularly rich in birdlife (see page 243). By contrast, the northern coast is largely rocky, except for the central part which has some of the island's finest white sand beaches — most famously at Varadero near Havana and Santa Lucía near Camagüey. Cuba has more than 200 rivers, but most are short and shallow. Even the longest — the Río Cauto, which stretches for 230 miles (370km) along the northern edge of the Sierra Maestra — is navigable for only a tiny distance inland.

You may hear regions of Cuba referred to as Oriente, Las Villas and Occidente. These are old provincial titles: Oriente was the east, Las Villas the central region, and Occidente the west. In 1974, the Cuban government created 13 provinces plus the capital itself; these provinces are sub-divided into *municipios* (counties). One-fifth of the population of 11 million lives in or around Havana. The second city is Santiago de Cuba in the east, with about half a million people.

It came as surprise to many who saw the film *A Few Good Men* to learn that a 45-square mile patch of Cuba is a US naval base; Guantánamo Bay is controlled by the United States, and at present is inaccessible from the rest of the island.

CLIMATE

Cuba falls just within the tropics, and has two basic seasons. The rainy season lasts from May to October, the dry season from November to April. The average daily high in the coolest months, December to March, is 26°C (79°F); on average, there are nearly six hours of sunshine in this quarter. In the hottest months of July and August, temperatures average 32°C (89°F). Humidity varies little throughout the year, averaging 62%.

The average Westerner will find the temperatures most congenial between November and February. Late November is a good time to visit since autumn storms have usually subsided and the temperature drops to a comfortable high of 27°C (81°F). Furthermore, November is still low season in Cuba, which means hotel rates are cheaper and museums and other sights less crowded. (As far as tourism is concerned, the high season is December-February and July-August). Between December and February, the main climatic disturbance are *frentes fríos*, the 'cold fronts' that occasionally sweep down from the north, bringing rain and a sudden drop in temperature. In general, though, February and March are the driest months of the year.

Easily the worst time to visit Cuba is in summer. From May the wet season begins. Temperatures climb sharply, reaching a peak in July and August. Tempers increase too, as even the Cubans find the summer heat hard to bear and spend as much time as possible on the beach. Your days are most likely to be interrupted by rain in June and October, the wettest months. The weather in this part of the world can change very rapidly, and in the space of a couple of hours glorious sunshine can turn into thundering downpours, transforming the streets into rivers. These kind of rainstorms can occur at any time of year. It is not unheard of for rain to continue non-stop for two or three days. Usually, though, the wet season does not have relentless rain; instead, it tends to fall in short bursts with plenty of sunshine in between. In September and October, however, not only is the humidity and rainfall high, but the skies are often heavy and overcast, resulting in the lowest average sunshine per day — less than five hours. The hurricane season also peaks around October, providing one more reason to postpone your trip a little.

The figures given above are for Havana. There are marginal variations in climate between one part of the island and another. The south coast of the island tends to be warmer, and the north and western half wetter, particularly in the hills. Santiago de Cuba is noticeably hotter: the city lies about 250 miles (400km) south of Havana's latitude, and temperatures are higher by almost five degrees. To cool off, the nearby Sierra Maestra is the best place to head for the hills.

Cuba lies in the path of 'Hurricane Avenue', a broad swathe across the Caribbean. Since 1800, the island has been hit by about 15 devastating hurricanes, including Hurricane Flora in 1963, that killed 4,000 people. Unless a hurricane is in the offing, Cubans don't bother much with weather forecasts — though projections are given in the national daily newspaper, *Granma*. For fuller details, tune in to a Florida or Jamaican radio station; see page 70 for suggested frequencies. The weather prospects in Cuba are usually broadly similar to the Florida Keys and the north of Jamaica.

Whatever time of year you go to Cuba, take a light jacket or sweater. Temperatures cool off in the evening and the air conditioning in hotels and restaurants can be viciously cold.

HISTORY

To understand Cuba at the turn of the millennium, you need to consider its history over the past 500 years. Little trace remains of the original Indian people who migrated to Cuba from either South or Central America from around 1000BC onwards. The first to settle were the Siboneys, but they were later forced into the western corner of the island by the more forceful Taínos — Arawak Indians originally from the Orinoco basin in what is now Venezuela. These people were still arriving in Cuba as late as 1460. This tribe was more sophisticated than the Siboneys, engaging in farming and making pots, though for all Cuban aborigines the sea remained a vital source both of food and raw materials for making tools, jewellery and so on.

The only significant trace that remains of the indigenous peoples of the island is the name that they used for it: 'Cuba'. They lived relatively peacefully together, and were ill-suited to providing effective resistance to the invasion by the Spanish *conquistadores* despite an heroic struggle. The first European to arrive was Christopher Columbus, who landed near Gibara on the north coast on 27 October 1492, on his first transatlantic voyage. He was convinced he had discovered the East Indies. The *Santa María* spent several weeks sailing along the coast without its captain realising Cuba was an island. Two years later he called in again on his way to Jamaica. Cuba was found to be an island only in 1508 when another explorer, Sebastián de Ocampo, circumnavigated it.

Colonisation. In 1510, the conquistador Diego Velázquez landed with a small army at Guantánamo Bay in the southeast. His attempt to take the island met considerable initial resistance. The Indians, not normally a warlike people, grouped around a fearsome leader called Hatuey, who had already encountered the Spanish on his native island of Hispaniola. The invaders retreated to a wooden fortress on the coast (in what is now the town of Baracoa), and were besieged there for three months before they were able to capture Hatuey and burn him at the stake. Resistance from the Indian population then crumbled. Hatuey is commemorated by a statue in Baracoa's main square and, more prominently, in the name of one of Cuba's beers.

Velázquez established seven villas (garrison towns) along the island — Baracoa, Santiago, Bayamo, Puerto Príncipe (now Camagüey), Trinidad, Sancti Spíritus, and Batabanó — and these became important stopping-off points for other Spanish conquistadores heading towards Central and South America. All except Batabanó are still substantial settlements. Batabanó, now just a small port on the south coast, became Cuba's first capital in around 1515. It has a natural harbour with a narrow entrance ideal for keeping out marauders, but a still better harbour was soon identified due north on the Atlantic coast. Thus it was that Havana became capital of Cuba. The new city became a flourishing trading post. Tobacco and sugar were grown in increasing quantities. Ships returning from the Americas docked in Havana or one of Cuba's other ports to load up before the journey back to Europe. In common with the pattern of economic development elsewhere in the Caribbean, slaves were brought to Cuba from West Africa. They helped to satisfy the increasing demand for labour on the sugar and tobacco plantations.

Cuban Nationalism. Considerable anti-Spanish feeling built up over the years against the colonising nation — not least from those of Spanish origin who had been born in Cuba and were known as creoles. Many islanders felt they were being exploited by their masters in Europe. Resentment against the *peninsulares,* the colonialists from Spain who held all the positions of power in Cuba, increased to the point where self-determination was just a matter of time.

Meanwhile the Europeans were squabbling amongst themselves over foreign possessions. In 1762 the British navy captured Havana. Less than a year later they exchanged it for Spanish-occupied Florida, but during their brief tenure they turned the city into a free port. The easing of trade barriers between Cuba and the British colonies in North America gave an enormous boost to the export trade in the colony, which in turn had a huge impact on the island's semi-dormant economy. Once back in control, the Spanish reinstated their monopoly on commerce, but not for long. In the early 19th century Cuban ports were opened up to international trade, and immediately began to capitalise on problems on the neighbouring island.

Cuba became the centre of the sugar trade in the Caribbean almost overnight at the end of the 18th century. A slave revolt in the neighbouring French colony of St Domingue (now Haiti) in the 1790s resulted in the exodus of many French settlers and a collapse in the industry there. Cuba, to which many settlers fled, pressed still more Africans into service on the plantations. Consequently, living conditions for slaves became yet more wretched, while the plantation owners became extremely wealthy. The United States was by this time buying about 40% of the sugar produced in Cuba. It was showing increasing interest in the island, and at one stage the possibility of Cuba becoming an American state was seriously considered. It would have saved Washington countless problems if it had done so.

The Uprisings. In 1868 a plantation owner, Carlos Manuel de Céspedes, freed the slaves working on his small estate near Manzanillo, and launched Cuba's first war of liberation against the Spanish. Two charismatic figures — Antonio Maceo, a heroic mulatto (of mixed race) known as the 'Titan of Bronze', and Máximo Gómez, a defector from the Spanish army — took the lead in the military campaign and ten years of bitter struggle. By the end of it, Céspedes was dead, along with 250,000 Cubans rebels and 80,000 Spanish soldiers. The rebel army had been defeated not so much by the Spanish as by the creoles, who found it impossible to trust an army made up predominantly of peasants and black Africans.

The Ten Years' War virtually destroyed the sugar industry. Amid the devastation, American landowners seized the opportunity to buy up abandoned property at bargain prices. Slavery was officially abolished in 1886 (much later than in other countries in the region), but blacks continued to live in such misery that they might as well have been enslaved. Despite the latent hatred for the colonial power, Spain showed no sign of bestowing greater independence.

The first Cuban to make real headway in the quest for liberation was José Martí, who is regarded as the father of independent Cuba. Exiled because of his dissident views, Martí spent the greater part of his life in Florida, where he worked as a journalist, poet and philosopher, writing political articles which were published prominently in the American press. In 1892 he and a group of fellow exiles founded the Cuban Revolutionary Party, which led a new uprising against Spain in 1895. Martí managed to rally behind him not only the peasants and blacks who had formed the backbone of the Ten Years' War, but also urban workers and the increasingly frustrated middle classes.

Antonio Maceo and Máximo Gómez joined the military campaign, which began near Santiago de Cuba on 24 February 1895. Despite being outnumbered five to one, the *mambises*, as the rebels were known, forced the colonial army gradually westwards. The Spanish were on the brink of collapse by 1898, which is when the United States chose to intervene.

Unsettled by a continued Spanish presence so close to its shores, and seeking to extend its influence in the region, the US government sent the warship *USS Maine* to the Bay of Havana — ostensibly to provide protection for the numerous American citizens in the city. In February 1898 the ship was sunk, and virtually the entire crew lost. Washington blamed Spain and promptly declared war. The so-called Spanish-American War which followed was fought throughout that year, largely on Cuban soil. By Christmas the might of the world's newest great power had prevailed, and the Stars and Stripes flew over Havana. The Treaty of Paris, signed on 10 December 1898, transferred sovereignty over Cuba to the United States. As with previous international accords, the wishes of the Cuban people did not figure highly.

Independence. The Spanish pulled out officially on 1 January 1899, and three years later Cuba was declared a Republic. The Americans also stepped back from direct rule, but not without retaining a degree of influence that bordered on control. The 1902 Platt Amendment gave the USA the right to invade Cuba at any time 'for the preservation of Cuban independence'. The naval base in Guantánamo Bay, east of Santiago, was developed on a 99-year lease, signed in 1934, which continues unless both sides renounce it. The Isle of Pines (now the Isle of Youth) was retained as a US colony, largely for the benefit of affluent American tourists. American investors bought up large chunks of the Cuban economy. Sugar, the island's chief export, was granted preferential access to the US market. This move was portrayed as a gesture of benevolence, but it had the effect of tightening the economic chains on Cuba. While business bank accounts swelled, most Cubans lived in poverty and misery.

Any semblance of democracy soon collapsed. A series of ineffectual presidents came and went until General Gerardo Machado took power in 1925. He ruled harshly for eight years, and introduced the Cuban people to the 20th-century tradition of military dictatorship. The world economic depression of the Thirties hit Cuba hard, and social unrest increased steadily amongst a people angry at the blatant corruption of politicians and at the iniquity in Cuban society. A General Strike largely organised by the fledgling communist party succeeded in toppling Machado in 1933, but the mini-revolution that followed left a vacuum into which an army sergeant called Fulgencio Batista stepped deftly.

Cuban people today tend to spit, rather than say, Batista's name, but at the start of his rule he enjoyed a certain amount of popularity. He won the presidential elections in 1940 more or less fairly, but failed to repeat his success four years later. He went into 'voluntary exile', only to return in 1952 to stage a military coup. By now a self-proclaimed General, Batista rapidly developed a cruel and oppressive regime. He dissolved Congress, abolished the Constitution and suppressed any opposition. Havana, meanwhile, boomed as a result of growing US affluence. The Cuban capital was a playground for the American rich, who arrived by the thousand to splash cash around in the casinos and brothels. The Mafia arrived, too, and with the connivance of Batista took control of tourism in the city, building many of the ugly high-rise hotels that still dominate the Vedado district.

The Assault on Moncada. The name of a former barracks in the city of Santiago de Cuba is part of modern Cuban consciousness. The army's base at Moncada was the target of a guerrilla attack launched on 26 July 1953 by a young Fidel Castro and 125 other young dissidents opposed to Batista. Fidel Castro Ruz, born in 1927 in Oriente, was the second of five illegitimate children born to a Galician plantation owner. He attended a Catholic and then a Jesuit school, and in 1945 entered Havana University, graduating in law six years later. Politics, however, was Castro's passion. He tried conventional politics for a time, but after Batista's 1952 coup the young lawyer decided armed insurrection was the only means to the end of liberation.

The assault on Moncada would have been comic (some revolutionaries arrived by taxi) were it not so tragic. Many of the rebels died. Fidel Castro and the other survivors were captured and imprisoned. Even so, the event caught the imagination of disaffected Cubans and has remained the defining moment of Cuban nationalism and the most sacred date in the calendar. The black and red flag marked M26.7 (26th of July Movement) became the banner of revolutionaries, and crops up all over the country. Moncada, meanwhile, has been converted into a school and is the nation's number one revolutionary attraction.

After a couple of years in prison on the Isle of Pines (where you may today view his cell), Castro was sent into exile in Mexico. It was in Mexico City that he met Che Guevara, the Argentinian revolutionary who was to play a crucial part in the liberation of Cuba.

The Revolution. Following the success at Moncada, Batista tightened his grip on the country. Yet increased oppression triggered the 20th century's most improbable and heroic episode of successful guerrilla insurgency. In 1956, a group of 82 guerrillas landed on the southeast coast of Cuba in a cabin cruiser, the *Granma*. (The vessel is now encased in glass outside the Museum of the Revolution in central Havana.) Among them were Che Guevara, Fidel Castro, and his brother Raúl. Before the rebels could begin to build support, skirmishes with Batista's forces reduced their number to about a dozen. Yet these few swiftly established themselves in the Sierra Maestra mountains. Assisted by the underground movement in the cities, they gradually won the approval of the Cuban people. Relatively little blood was shed as the rebellion gained momentum, and territory fell easily into the revolutionaries' hands. An attack by Che Guevara on a troop train in Santa Clara (yet another tourist attraction) late in December 1958 persuaded Batista that the battle was lost. He finally abdicated power and fled to the Dominican Republic on New Year's Day 1959.

Batista's army surrendered, leaving a ragged, ill-educated and poverty-stricken population in the hands of a strange collection of revolutionaries. The name *Granma* was adopted for the main daily newspaper and for the province in which the revolutionaries first landed — even though it is merely a Mexican rendition of the abbreviation for grandmother.

Che Guevara. Intellectually, Ernesto 'Che' Guevara was a very different kind of revolutionary from the Cubans with whom he served. He was born in 1928 to left-wing middle-class parents in Buenos Aires. His whole life was plagued by chronic asthma and an allergy to mosquito bites (a real problem in Cuba). He studied to become a doctor, but felt he had a calling of the sort espoused by Simón Bolívar, the great 19th-century liberator of Latin America. After hitchhiking through South and Central America, he met up with Fidel Castro and his brother Raúl while they were in exile in Mexico. He joined their guerrilla cell, first as a medic but subsequently as a fully-fledged fighter. He earned the nickname 'Che' (meaning 'mate' or 'buddy') through his gregariousness.

Guevara was injured twice during revolutionary battles, but survived to become an important member of the new government. As head of the Cuban National Bank, Guevara arranged the oil-for-sugar swap with the Soviet Union that was to stand Cuba in good stead for three decades.

Motives for his departure after only a few years of power are a matter for speculation. Perhaps unhappy with the course adopted by Castro's government — especially the increase in bureaucracy — he set off in 1965 to find other causes to champion, in Africa and South America. While trying to spark off another revolution among peasants in Bolivia in October 1967, he was captured and summarily executed. He achieved revolutionary martyrdom, and the amount of coverage of an attempt by the Bolivian authorities to find his remains in 1995 demonstrated the hold that his image still has on the world. Although his radical ideas have been abandoned, the Cuban regime plays more strongly than ever on his popularity as the archetypal romantic hero.

After the Revolution. When he took power in 1959, Fidel Castro was the focus of overwhelming public support. His government inherited an economy near collapse, one which had been developed to satisfy American investors, gamblers and tourists rather than the Cuban people. One of Castro's first acts was to seize American assets without compensation, which enraged the USA and triggered economic retribution. The new leader cast around the world for new allies. The Soviet Union was delighted at the prospect of a friendly power so close to the USA, and offered Cuba unhesitating support. From the Soviet model of government, Castro took a centralised, bureaucratic political system and imposed it on a Caribbean people. Economic activity was brought under state control. Trade with the socialist bloc expanded as rapidly as commerce with 'capitalist' countries diminished. In 1959 Eastern Europe was the destination for barely 2% of Cuba's exports; by 1962 this had increased to a staggering 82%; imports rose almost as dramatically. This economic support was to continue for the next thirty years.

The USA severed diplomatic links with Cuba on 3 January 1961, in one of the last acts of the outgoing President Eisenhower. John Kennedy took over as head of state two weeks later and continued his predecessor's plans to destabilise Cuba. The CIA recruited a force of 1,400 anti-Castro Cubans who had fled to the USA, and gave them military training. On 17 April 1961 this ragbag army landed at the Bay of Pigs on the southern coast of Cuba, aiming to overthrow the government. It was a pathetic invasion, easily repulsed. Its main effects were to galvanise the Cuban people's support for Castro, and to provide his government with a propaganda weapon which is still being exploited, half a lifetime after the event.

It was after a bombing raid by the Americans in the run-up to the Bay of Pigs invasion that Fidel Castro first proclaimed Cuba to be a socialist republic. Months later, communists were included in the ruling political alliance from which the Partido Comunista de Cuba (PCC) was to emerge in 1965. The revolution had always been nationalist rather than socialist — it was never described as a left-wing struggle. Tellingly, one of Castro's guerrilla slogans, *libertad o muerte* ('liberty or death'), made an amended reappearance years later as *socialismo o muerte*. There has always been much debate as to whether Castro purposefully concealed his true political colours during the rebel campaign, but many observers suggest that his emergence as a communist was simply a pragmatic response to the need for economic support following the severing of links with Cuba's main trading partner, the United States. The current flirtation with capitalism gives this latter view more credence.

The Missile Crisis. On 22 October 1962, President Kennedy announced that the Pentagon had identified a build-up of military activity in Cuba. Reconnaissance aircraft had spotted a Soviet convoy heading for Cuba with a cargo of atomic weapons. The Soviet Union was planning to use the island as a base for a possible nuclear attack on the USA. The American Navy was mobilised to stop the missiles reaching the island. After six days of growing global tension Kennedy reached agreement with Nikita Krushchev, the Russian premier, on a withdrawal of Soviet armaments. It is now accepted that the world was on the brink of a nuclear holocaust. Soviet officers in Cuba were equipped with tactical nuclear weapons, and had authority to fire them unilaterally if they came under threat. The subsequent retribution from the USA could have meant all-out nuclear war.

American Retribution. The crisis embarrassed and infuriated President Kennedy, who ordered the CIA to increase its efforts against Castro and Cuba. Numerous assassination attempts — from *femmes fatales* (intended literally) to risible exploding cigars — were made on Castro. They even tried to make the Cuban leader's beard drop off by painting chemicals on his shoes, in the hope that his authority would also fall away if he lost his facial hair. More successful sabotage was achieved on civilian targets, such as the bomb attack on a Cubana DC-8 full of passengers.

The other tack was economic. Before the revolution more than 60% of Cuba's trade was with the United States. Following the Cuban Missile Crisis, President Kennedy tightened the economic embargo, declaring that the United States would 'build a wall around Cuba'. Trade between the two nations is still prohibited, although American goods reach Cuba via third countries. Coca-Cola, the *Miami Herald* and Levi jeans are easily available on the island. Thirty-five years of American economic sanctions have failed to bring about the political liberalisation the White House had envisaged, though this remains their main argument for continuing sanctions. It is a widely held view among both supporters and opponents of Castro that significant political change will come about in Cuba only after the embargo is ended.

The Revolution in Progress. As well as withstanding pressure from the USA, Castro had to deal with insurgents within Cuba. Counter-revolutionaries refused to give up without a struggle after the overthrow of Batista, and considerable effort was expended to quell these 'bandidos'. (Ironically, many were imprisoned in the same jail where Castro had been incarcerated.) A particularly fierce campaign was waged in the Escambray mountains of central Cuba; the last rebels weren't flushed out until 1965. As part of the campaign to sniff out opponents, neighbourhood Committees for the Defence of the Revolution (*Comités de Defensa de la Revolución*) were established. A large part of the work of these CDRs was to identify anti-revolutionary activity. Every street and block of flats still has a CDR, whose members *(CeDeRistas)* regard snooping on their neighbours as a duty.

With help from the Soviet bloc, Cuba made great social advances after the revolution. Schools were built, clinics opened, education and health care became available to all. Wealth was diverted from the capital to rural areas. Housing was improved, with huge construction projects carried out by micro-brigades — units of voluntary workers collaborating on building the apartment blocks that now skirt many Cuban cities. In Third World terms, the Republic performed a miracle by virtually eradicating poverty, disease and illiteracy.

Economic development was by no means smooth, however, and the people also suffered severe intellectual frustration. In 1980, there was a huge show of dissatisfaction with the political and economic state of the country when 125,000 Cubans fled to Florida during the so-called Mariel boatlift.

Cuba in the Nineties. The Cuban media chose to minimise news of the historic events in the Soviet bloc between 1989 and 1992. The authorities were concerned that Cubans would follow the example of the masses in Eastern Europe and rise up against state communism. After Gorbachev introduced the idea of change to the Soviet Union, Castro was at pains to emphasise that in Cuba *El Camino Corecto,* 'the right way', would continue.

The economic damage caused by changes in Europe was devastating to Cuba. The island's reliance upon the Eastern bloc had stifled the country's economic growth and brought disaster once its traditional trading partners left the communist fold. A subsidy of $5 billion a year from the Kremlin evaporated almost overnight, and trading links with Europe dwindled as the new democracies began insisting on payment in hard currency. In 1990, Castro implemented an austerity package known as the Special Period in Peacetime, which had an immediate effect on the quality of life of most Cubans. The conservation of energy was the top priority: factories and offices closed down, power cuts (known as *apagones*) became a feature of everyday life, bus services were reduced to a minimum, and oxen and carts took the place of tractors. Rationing, first introduced in the early 1960s, was intensified to a degree that left the majority of Cubans with barely enough to prepare even one decent meal a day.

Meanwhile, Washington was piling on the pressure, confident that Fidel Castro's days were at last numbered. The Torricelli Bill, approved by the US Congress in 1992, banned overseas subsidiaries of American corporations from trading with Cuba, and authorised the US president to cut off trade or economic aid to any country that assisted the island.

The situation in Cuba was critical, politically as well as economically. The execution in 1989 of Arnaldo Ochoa, a charismatic general accused of drug-smuggling and corruption, sent shock waves around the country. A popular figure, Ochoa was rumoured to be in favour of a form of *perestroika* (Gorbachev-style reform), and his execution was perceived by many as a warning to those who would attempt to undermine the course of the revolution. The 1991 Communist Party Congress reiterated the message that Cuba had no intention of following the example of its former Eastern European allies. Delegates discussed measures aimed at liberalising the economy, but the first of these were not introduced until two years later. At the time it was made clear that they had been approved simply because they represented the best means of ensuring the survival of Cuban socialism — not as an end in themselves.

Most important among the new measures was the depenalisation of the dollar, known colloquially as 'dollarisation'. Cubans were permitted to handle a currency that would previously have earned them a prison term; they could finally visit the dollar shops that before had been open only to foreigners and a few privileged officials. Dollarisation received a mixed reception amongst Cubans since it improved the lot mainly of black marketeers and those Cubans that received regular cash hand-outs from relatives in Miami; the majority, who did not have access to dollars, reaped little benefit.

Tension increased palpably, and the summer of 1993 saw an unprecedented spate of small demonstrations in Havana. The government responded by stepping up vigilance across the island and by locking up hundreds of Cubans considered to be a destabilising influence. The flow of people willing to risk their lives by fleeing covertly to the US across the Florida Straits rose dramatically. The situation finally erupted on 5 August 1994, when police stopped a boatload of would-be refugees from leaving Havana. Hundreds of people took to the streets of the capital and 30 people were injured in the worst rioting Cuba had seen since the triumph of the revolution in 1959.

As events in Cuba hit the headlines around the world, Fidel Castro took an extraordinary gamble. He called off the coastguards, inviting an exodus along the lines of the Mariel boatlift in 1980. At least 30,000 Cubans reached Florida, many rescued from their makeshift rafts and boats by US coastguard patrols; thousands more did not survive the perilous sea journey. Washington had always welcomed the sight of Cubans fleeing from communism, but not even the United States could handle such an influx. Fidel Castro had converted the anger against him into a refugee crisis for the United States, deftly inverting a home-grown problem into an issue of Cuban-American relations. President Clinton found himself forced to reverse his country's long-standing policy of granting automatic political asylum to Cubans, and to confer recognition upon the nation with which he was obliged to negotiate.

Many people still wish to leave Cuba, but they now know that anyone who arrives in the United States illegally, i.e. by boat, will no longer be welcomed with open arms. Instead, they must hope to be included in the quota of legal emigrés agreed in talks between the two sides.

The Future. Hopes were expressed that the Cuban-American talks in 1995 would extend to issues other than immigration, but no further discussions materialised. Instead, at the start of 1996 moves were made to implement further tightening of the embargo — the Helms-Burton bill. Its original extreme provisions were watered down, but it showed that the right-wing hawks were still ascendant in Washington. So there seems no immediate prospect of change, and the impasse remains: as far as Washington is concerned, the embargo will stay in place until Castro agrees to embrace a brand of democracy of which the US approves; as far as Havana is concerned, political change is inconceivable until the sanctions are lifted.

There does appear to be some kind of momentum behind economic liberalisation in Cuba; a recent British report to investors described Castro's reforms as 'cohesive, systematic and unstoppable'. But the regime needs to perform a delicate balancing act — introducing the right dose of change to save Cuban socialism without poisoning it. With every new reform, notably the legalisation of private markets and restaurants, expectations among the Cuban people rise, creating political pressure for yet more change. But as long as Castro can drip feed the people with measures designed to improve their standard of living, he probably remains safe from serious internal threat.

Whatever the reforms, however, the island remains in an appalling mess financially. The degree of material deprivation in Cuba is all too evident, in the form of long queues and ever-shrinking rations for those without access to dollars. Observers love to speculate about the ability of the people to tolerate the hardships. A report in 1995 revealing that Cuba has the highest suicide rate in the Western hemisphere, showed that some simply cannot take the strains of everyday life. However, in a country where people feel powerless to influence events, a general feeling of resignation is more typical. There is little appetite for insurrection. Dissatisfaction with the regime has risen dramatically during the Special Period, but few dare express open dissatisfaction with Fidel Castro himself. Given that the majority of Cubans know no other leader nor political system, fear runs deep. Some despise him, yet find the prospect of life without him unfathomable.

POLITICS

On one level, Cuban politics are all too simple. There is one political party — the Partido Comunista de Cuba (PCC) — presiding over a rigid centralised control structure that admits of no legitimate opposition. But the story of Cuba today is a complex tale of power and personalities. The story begins with modern Cuba personified: Fidel Castro — *El Comandante.*

Fidel Castro. The Cuban president has many names besides El Comandante, including *El Líder Máximo*, but most people refer to him simply as Fidel or *El* ('Him', with the deific overtones intended). Less complimentary titles also circulate, such as *El Diablo Rojo* (the Red Devil), *El Bárbaro* (The Barbarian) or *Terminador — El Ultimo Capítulo* (Terminator — The Final Chapter); don't expect to hear these names used in public. Whatever people say in private, public demonstrations of loyalty to the president are a feature of everyday life in Cuba.

Fidel Castro possesses astonishing determination and an extraordinary intellect; his success as a revolutionary leader, however, is due as much to his charisma and ability to arouse a crowd. The Cuban leader's voice is strangely gentle and high-pitched, but his stamina when making speeches is legendary. He set his own record in 1959 when he talked on television for seven hours without a break. Now approaching 70, the Cuban leader seldom performs such marathons these days (to the relief of his audience).

Castro's isolation since the fall of communism in Eastern Europe led one commentator to describe the Cuban president as the 'Last of the Mohicans', presiding over what some see as a living museum of socialism. His political shelf-life has been a favourite topic of conversation for a decade, and his staying power continues to fascinate observers. He has survived 35 years of American sanctions, the death of his Soviet sugar daddy and the political upheavals of 1994. Fidel Castro has been in power longer than any other head of state. His longevity and near-legendary status has made him centre-stage at every big international event, from the investiture of President Mandela to the 50th anniversary of the United Nations. Rumours circulate occasionally of assassination attempts or of coups, but no recent such incident has been substantiated. Castro is one of the most heavily guarded heads of state in the world, and is reported to have a double who acts as a decoy.

The Maximum Leader enjoys tantalising the world with conflicting statements as to his future plans. In 1994, for example, Castro announced that 'revolutionaries do not retire'. This was followed some months later by a statement suggesting that if the United States were to lift the embargo then he would resign. Perhaps he will take up the open invitation he has from King Juan Carlos to retire to Spain. The problem is that Fidel Castro has no obvious successor. Raúl Castro, currently Armed Forces Minister and his brother's deputy, has been talked of as a possible heir, but he is unpopular among Cubans. More likely candidates include Carlos Lage, Minister of Economic Planning (echoing the role played by Che Guevara); Ricardo Alarcón, president of the National Assembly; and Roberto Robaina, who became Foreign Minister in 1993 at the age of just 37. These figures have so far remained fiercely loyal (at least outwardly) to their leader, and none possesses a fraction of the character, charisma or courage of Fidel Castro.

Signs suggest that the youngest contender is manouvering for pole position in the eventual leadership race. Speaking to the BBC during a visit to Guyana, Roberto Robaina said that Cuba needed to combine 'the experience of the older generation with the ideas and enthusiasm of the young'. He said Cuba was looking for a collective leadership, where Fidel Castro would 'continue to contribute to the political process'.

The Party. The Cuban president stretches credibility by asserting — as he does from time to time — that Cuba is the most democratic country in the world. Few definitions of democracy would identify much evidence of the concept in Cuba. Human rights and political freedom that Westerners would regard as fundamental are hard to find in present-day Cuba.

Constitutionally, Cuba is described as a socialist republic of workers, farmers and other manual and intellectual labourers. Theoretically, power is exerted by the workers through the municipal and provincial assemblies of People's Power *(Poder Popular)*, which send delegates to the 589-member National Assembly. Elections are held every five years. Voters choose from a single list of officially approved candidates, the vast majority of whom are members of the same organisation — the Cuban Communist Party. Described in the Cuban constitution as the 'highest guiding force of society and the State', the Party influences every sphere of activity: each centre of work or study has its own nucleus of members.

The Central Committee *(Comité Central)* is the driving force of the Communist Party, with most power concentrated in the hands of a smaller group within it, the *Buró Político* or Politburo. Grassroots members can sit in on policy discussions at the party congress, held every five years, but the big decisions are made beforehand by the party leadership. The political influence of the assemblies of People's Power, which deal with the day-to-day administration of the country, is small by comparison. The National Assembly is officially the 'supreme organ of state power', but it meets just twice a year. At other times, decisions are made by Cuba's top government bodies, the Council of Ministers *(Consejo de Ministros)* and the Council of State *(Consejo de Estado)*. The big names in the Central Committee dominate both these councils. Fidel Castro, as president of the Council of State, is automatically head of state and head of the government. His full title is Commander-in-Chief of the Armed Forces, First Secretary of the Central Committee of the Cuban Communist Party and President of the Councils of State and Ministers. The title President of the Republic does not exist, though Castro is often referred to by that name.

Political Life Today. It is obvious from the posters and murals cluttering the countryside that the island is highly politicised. You will be constantly assailed with statistics showing the strides made since the revolution. Official guides describe the vast improvements since the Revolution of everything from health care to asphalt production. Certainly there have been massive social enhancements, but the combination of inflexible, inefficient production methods and American economic sanctions have stifled growth.

The structural problems inherent in a centralised economy run on Leninist lines were identified in the Soviet Union and Eastern Europe well before the collapse of communism. Yet Castro has shown much greater reluctance to dabble with the concepts of *glasnost* and *perestroika* with which Mikhail Gorbachev changed the USSR. The Cuban president has several substantial advantages over the leaders of the old communist regimes in Eastern Europe. Most importantly, he has a political legitimacy derived from his pivotal role in overthrowing a corrupt regime — in no sense was he imposed on an unwilling nation. Secondly, Cuba compares favourably with other Latin American nations in all manner of indices. The fearful discrepancy between rich and poor found in most countries of South and Central America does not exist in Cuba, though dollarisation has certainly been economically divisive. Thirdly and most practically, Cuba's status as an island means that isolation is relatively easy to sustain.

Relying upon public support (and the unwavering help of the Cuban media), Castro has so far kept his political opponents in check. With an economy underwritten by a large dose of Soviet finance, the Cuban leader was under great pressure from Moscow in the late 1980s to begin a radical restructuring. With the dismantling of the Soviet Union, that pressure diminished. Despite the introduction of some radical economic reforms, significant political changes have yet to emerge. Castro has said that a multi-party system is conceivable in Cuba at some time in the future, but the usual attitude of the Cuban Communist Party to multi-party politics is one of disdain. In 1995 Castro himself described elections as 'a popularity competition between political personalities', adding that he preferred not 'to get involved in that kind of competition.' He compared his own selection as leader to that of the Pope, who is elected by a ballot of cardinals.

The leadership has displayed increasing openness towards the West in its campaign to boost tourism and foreign investment. But rather than being an exercise in furthering international understanding and building political bridges, the motive is simply because Havana desperately needs hard currency. The tourist industry is designed to extract the maximum number of dollars from visitors. Resorts like Cayo Coco — an offshore island developed exclusively for foreigners — are examples of how far the country will demean itself to attract sun-seekers to beautiful beaches. A nation so proud of its egalitarian society now has a three-tier system which gives first priority to foreigners, second to dollar-holding Cubans, with people loyal to the tenets of the Revolution in a poor third place. The rise in the sex trade, which some see as condoned by the state, gives rise to an image of Cubans prostituting themselves individually and collectively to foreigners.

Opposition. Little has changed since the 1960s, when anyone who was not with the Revolution was by definition against it. Fidel Castro has cultivated his image as the defender of Cuban nationalism, enabling him to dismiss opponents as unpatriotic people who would undermine the country in its fight against the enemy, the United States. The regime goes further and maintains that its opponents are barely distinguishable from criminals: that the Cubans who whisper conspiratorially to you in a backstreet bar about the iniquities of life under Castro are the same black marketeers that undermine the country's economy or the petty thieves who make a living by robbing from tourists. This is the justification behind the authorities' assiduous attempts to keep perceived troublemakers off the streets. Since the early 1990s, thousands have been imprisoned under the charge of *peligrosidad* or 'dangerousness', a loose term used to describe 'anti-social behaviour' and directed against anyone who is perceived to threaten the social or political order in Cuba.

Many disaffected Cubans are not active politically, but covert dissident groupings committed to peaceful change and increased democracy do exist. In a nation without freedom of expression, where political graffitti and demonstrations are virtually unknown, the state of the domestic opposition is hard to gauge. Known dissidents are closely watched by the security forces, with the help of the CDRs, and dawn raids on suspects are commonplace; the usual charge is of *propaganda enemiga* or 'enemy propaganda'. The people which the government calls 'traitors to communism' are also known as *gusanos* ('worms'), a term coined originally to describe Cuban exiles in Miami.

There are said to be about 50 dissident movements in Cuba. Most of them have emerged since the United Nations Human Rights Commission sent a delegation to the island in 1988. In recent years, these small groups have sought to increase their clout by forming coalitions. One of the most influential of these is the Corriente Socialista Democrática, co-founded by Elizardo Sánchez, Cuba's best known dissident. Sánchez has spent many years in prison for his political views, but he has recently been allowed to travel abroad — in what many perceive as a skilful public relations exercise on the part of the Cuban government. Despite his harsh treatment, Elizardo Sánchez regards Castro as the only figure who can successfully steer the country towards democracy. In 1996, Sánchez was allowed to meet a visiting US Congressman in Havana's Hotel Nacional, an encounter that many observers took to signal a shift in the state's hard line against dissidents.

Staunch anti-Castroists criticise the message of national reconciliation advocated by Sánchez, but there is an increasing realisation among opposition groups that gradual change is the only way to ensure a bloodless transition to democracy. There is palpable fear of civil war. The cultivation of a huge military machine means Cuba is awash with weapons and people who are well trained in using them.

The other significant opposition alliance is the Concertación Democrática Cubana, which incorporates a small social democratic faction known as the Criterio Alternativo, led by Cuba's foremost living poet, Maria Elena Cruz Valera.

Cuba has 300 prisons, proportionately the highest number in the world. Leading dissidents estimate that 5,000 Cubans are in jail for their political beliefs, compared with the figure of 600 put forward by Amnesty International. Hard figures are impossible to obtain, but whatever the truth many more thousands of Cubans are scared of displaying their feelings because of the omnipotence of the government; it can take away a job, and therefore a person's livelihood, at will. In the 1990s there has been a trend for civilian mobs to attack dissidents' homes in so-called 'acts of repudiation', clearly with the connivance of the authorities. As the economy plummeted and discontent increased in 1992, the authorities created a force of Rapid Action Brigades *(Brigadas de Respuesta Rápida)* — vigilante-style groups to supplement the activities of the CDRs.

The lack of coherent opposition to Castro is due partly to intimidation, but mainly to the political structure in Cuba which does not readily allow for the possibility of dissent. Clumsy US intervention in the years immediately after the revolution has left the authorities with an unhealthy but understandable degree of paranoia. Castro uses the US actions to justify what some see as repression but others regard as a necessity given the attitude of the USA. Meanwhile, the suppression of democracy in Cuba is the weapon which the Americans use to justify further sanctions.

THE ECONOMY

The largest and most fertile island in the region, Cuba ought to have the strongest economy in the Caribbean. But the break-up of the Soviet Union, economic sanctions and a highly centralised command economy of the kind which lost credibility elsewhere years ago has left a country which can barely afford to feed itself. The austerity measures introduced as a temporary fix in the early 1990s, described as the 'special period in peacetime', are still in place.

The sugar industry, traditionally the lynchpin of the Cuban economy, has been badly hit by shortages of fuel and spare parts. Harvests have deteriorated dramatically: the yield in 1994-5 was just 3.3 million tons, the lowest for more than 50 years and less than half the previous yearly average of around 7 million. Furthermore, basic commodities like sugar are subject to wide price fluctuations on the world market. This is a disastrous state of affairs since Cuba has long been over-dependent on sugar and its derivatives. The country's gross national output is estimated to have fallen by one-third in the five years to 1993; manufacturing is running at below half capacity, and imports are also down by half.

Since 1989, Cuba has lost almost all its Warsaw Pact trading partners — which used to account for over 85% of the island's overseas trade. In its search for new markets, Havana has turned increasingly to Latin America. Imports from the region rose from 7% in 1990 to 47% in 1993. Cuba is hampered by $6.4 billion of foreign debt, the servicing of which devours much of the inflow of funds. Cuba's trade deficit in 1994 was $642 million, with imports 50% higher than exports. Domestically, a serious short-term problem is excess liquidity: around 10 billion pesos are in private hands, not least because of the absence of anything much to spend them on in the early 1990s. The potential for inflationary pressure is high, giving rise to fears of hyper-inflation.

Havana is taking careful note of the economic turmoil in Russia and its neighbours that followed the collapse of the Soviet Union. Cuba is pinning its hopes for economic growth not only on the import and export trade but also on direct foreign investment. Alterations made to the constitution mean that overseas companies now have the freedom to invest in virtually any sector of the Cuban economy, the only restriction being the denial of access to business connected with national security, defence, education and public health. Furthermore, foreigners are now allowed full ownership, instead of a 50% partnership with the state, and have certain guarantees on repatriation of profits.

Mexico is Cuba's leading foreign investor. Other countries with which the island trades significantly include Colombia, Canada, Spain, Japan, France, Germany and the UK. Problems remain (foreign companies dislike, for example, having to recruit their staff through the state employment agency), but overseas investors are showing interest in all areas of the economy, from biotechnology and the manufacture of pharmaceuticals to oil exploitation and nickel refinement. The Spanish firm, Tabacalera, has virtually taken over Cuba's tobacco industry, and Mercedes Benz is already investing in the sugar industry. On a smaller scale, Adidas has agreed to sponsor Cuban athletes, and for several years a Benetton billboard has been the first thing to greet you as you leave Havana airport.

Associations with foreign companies, known as joint ventures, have so far been most successful in the field of tourism. An industry that barely existed less than a decade ago, tourism has now taken over from sugar as the island's prime hard currency earner. In 1995, tourism grossed $1 billion, ten times as much as in 1990. The number of visitors rose by one-sixth in a year, from 630,000 in 1994 to an impressive 740,000. Predictions that this figure will rise to two million by the year 2000 are over-optimistic given the problems that still exist, but they do at least convey a level of confidence that is hard to find in any other sector of the economy. The fact that Cuba is once again on the lucrative Caribbean cruise circuit (thanks to an Italian line based in the Dominican Republic) shows how swiftly the country has re-joined the tourism mainstream.

The Economic Outlook. The term 'economic miracle' is normally used to describe Far East nations reporting rapid growth. In fact, the most miraculous economic performance of the 1990s is that Cuba managed to withstand double-digit decline for several years in succession without total collapse — and by 1995 had managed to turn in modest-but-positive growth of 2%. This would seem to back official claims that Cuba is over the worst. If you use the crude measure of activity on the streets of Havana, then the economy is certainly back on its feet. Furthermore, the nation's hard currency earnings in 1994 rose to $1.3 billion, a rise of 15.6% on the previous year. The improvement was attributed primarily to the recovery of nickel production, an increase in oil extraction and the improved generation of electricity. Increased remittances from Cuban expatriates in the USA, taking advantage of the 'dollarisation', have also helped. Even though President Clinton's tightening of the embargo in 1996 was aimed at reducing the flow of dollars to Cuba, plenty of routes exist to channel funds via Mexico or Panama.

A great deal of economic repair work still needs to be done. While the revenues from the tourist industry rise steadily, the future of the island cannot realistically be built on the back of tourists — a notoriously fickle breed. Cuba is essentially an agricultural nation, and even with increased yields of natural resources such as oil and nickel, the roots of future growth lie in the soil. The legalisation of private farmers' markets in 1995 has already had a beneficial effect, as have the so-called Basic Units of Cooperative Production, created in 1993 to allow workers to farm state-owned land and sell the resulting produce. But as long as the sugar industry remains in its current moribund state, a result of woefully low productivity, real economic stability will remain an elusive goal. The recent securing of $100 million worth of foreign investment in sugar may give the industry the kickstart it needs, but there is a marked reluctance to work in the industry; sugar mills have opened shops selling sought-after consumer goods to try to attract new workers and boost production.

Having created a whole new economic sector in which joint ventures and companies partly financed by foreign capital predominate, Cuba now needs to resolve the dual character of its economy; the traditional sector, consisting of purely state-owned enterprises, needs to be modernised too. For continued, stable growth, a single, integrated system is essential. Some Cuban economists are even calling for a national private sector, employing its own workers; new company laws are said to be under discussion. Others, worried by the traumatic experience of eastern Europe, advocate a more gradual process of reform.

The model that Cuba seems to be following most closely is that of Vietnam and China. In a speech in Santiago de Cuba in July 1995, Fidel Castro declared that the 'incredible disasters that have taken place in the countries of the former Soviet Union (in spite of its vast resources in energy and raw materials, as well as foreign aid) in contrast to the impressive successes in China and Vietnam, are a clear indication of what should and should not be done if we wish to save

Castro is by maintaining the embargo, which provides ample justification for the country's economic problems and for continued political repression. In addition, US business leaders are increasingly vocal about the investment opportunities that are being lost in Cuba to European and Latin American investors. Executives of US corporations have already paid visits to the island, and some have been wined and dined personally by Fidel Castro. In February 1996, a delegation of retired high-ranking US military figures visited the island, adding considerable weight to the campaign to normalise relations.

Whatever your view of the sanctions imposed on Cuba by the United States, they have demonstrably failed to have the desired effect. They have not forced political change in Cuba; indeed, their very existence has shored up Castro's legitimacy and increased the misery of most ordinary Cubans. Washington needs to devise a policy which will ensure a smooth transition to democracy rather than invite a chaotic change that could produce a refugee crisis far more serious than that seen in 1994.

THE PEOPLE

Ethnic Background. Cuba has the broadest racial mix in the Caribbean, so dividing the population into neat ethnic groups is not easy. Official statistics state that the population is 66% white/Hispanic (*blanco* or *criollo*), 12% black (*negro, moreno*), 21.9% mixed Hispanic and black (*mulato*) and 0.1% Asian (*asiático*). In reality, the majority of Cuban people — some say as much as 70% of the population — are of mixed race. Most pure black Cubans, the descendants of African slaves, live in Havana and nearby Matanzas province. The Asian community consists primarily of the descendants of Chinese contract labourers who were shipped to Cuba in the second half of the nineteenth century, as the slave trade from Africa began to collapse. Chinese blood has been diluted considerably (the old dictator Fulgencio Batista was a mix of white, black and Chinese), but a few of pure Chinese descent survive. Most live in Havana's small Chinatown (see page 182).

Cubans as a whole have become considerably darker-skinned since 1959, a result largely of the economic and social changes brought by the Revolution. This encouraged unprecedented movement within the population, between rural and urban areas and also between the social classes. But increased racial integration does not mean that racism has been eradicated, as Fidel Castro claimed in 1966. Following the Revolution, beaches, hotels and universities were opened up to black Cubans for the first time, and other laws were introduced to combat racism. In no country in the world, however, has racial discrimination been eliminated through legislation. Whites, blacks and mulattos seem to mix easily in Cuba, and the kind of racial violence that occurs in North America and Europe is virtually unknown. But few black Cubans reach top jobs. In hotels, for example, white Cubans tend to work as receptionists and waiters, while black women make up the bulk of the chamberstaff. In universities, the army and other important institutions, whites dominate. Music and sport are the only fields in which black Cubans lead.

Social marginalisation has forced blacks — particularly the young — to turn to the parallel economy and prostitution to survive. Prejudice against the Afro-Cuban community has worsened as a result. Young blacks endure constant harassment by the police, particularly in Havana; and if you are robbed, the first question you will be asked (and not just by the police) is 'was he black?'. Black Cubans are refused entry to bars and hotels simply because of their colour, even when they are accompanied by a tourist. On occasion, black tourists have been stopped from entering a hotel, until — amid much embarrassment — the doorman discovers the person in question to be a tourist and therefore immune from discrimination.

Women in Cuba. Gender discrimination has been combatted rather more success-fully than racial prejudice. Women comprise two-fifths of the Cuban workforce, compared with one-sixth in 1953. They have achieved considerable professional success, especially in the traditionally male-dominated fields of medicine and law. Even so, they rarely reach the upper echelons of their professions, and only one in nine management positions is held by a woman.

The Family Code introduced in 1974 gave men and women equal rights and responsibilities for child-rearing, education and even housework. But despite making considerable statutory progress towards sexual equality, the authorities admit that theirs is a society still struggling against male machismo; the mass media continues to promote the image of women above all as good wives and mothers. While 90% of Cuban women officially belong to the Federación de Mujeres de Cuba (FMC), women's groups exist primarily to mobilise their members politically rather than to campaign against gender discrimination.

Homosexuality in Cuba. Life for gay people in Cuba is considerably easier than it was in the early years of the Revolution, when many homosexuals were sent to labour camps along with other 'social deviants'. The film *Fresa y Chocolate* ('Strawberry and Chocolate'), a story about the friendship between a gay man and a young communist, was heavily promoted by the government following its release in 1993; it brought homosexuality into the public arena for the first time in years. In 1995, a conference on 'nudism, eroticism and transvestism' was held in Havana's National Art Gallery; and there have also been reports of a new gay association, that has been neither approved nor banned by the authorities. Yet at the same time, gay Cubans cannot be members of the Communist Party and it remains illegal to display homosexuality in public. There are no official venues where gay people can gather socially. In Havana, members of the gay community hold parties in their own homes — known as *fiestas de diez pesos* since guests pay ten pesos to get in; some people refer to them as *suda suda* ('sweat sweat') because they attract such a crowd.

While *Fresa y Chocolate* liberalised some people's attitudes to homosexuality, general prejudice in Cuban society remains a big aggravation for most gay men and women. The most common term for a gay man, *maricón*, is often used as an insult among heterosexual males.

Sex and Marriage. Having sex is a favourite occupation in Cuba. It is one of the few things on the island that cannot be rationed, though the cramped conditions in which most Cubans live mean that it is hard for couples to find much privacy. Rooms can be rented in short-stay establishments known as *posadas*, but these are deeply unromantic locations.

The regime has done much to encourage marriage since 1959, providing material incentives to those who take the plunge. As a result, the number of weddings each year has doubled. Given the Cubans' propensity for ending relationships and the ease with which a divorce is obtained, however, this has also meant a sharp rise in the number of separations: among Cubans aged 25-40, three out of five marriages end in divorce.

Religion

Article 8 of the Cuban constitution says 'the State recognises, respects and guarantees religious freedom'. In practice, the church is stifled by a combination of financial stringency and the denial of access to the media, education system, etc. The country has some beautiful churches; many are in use, but are in poor condition.

Catholicism is weaker in Cuba than in any other Latin American country. It has been thus ever since the Catholic Church and the Spanish colonists were perceived by the ordinary people to be in cahoots. The influence of the Church dwindled still further immediately after the Revolution, when it became a focus of opposition against the regime. In retaliation, the government closed many churches, the priesthood was reduced to one-fifth of its pre-revolutionary level and church schools were disbanded. Christmas was abolished in 1965, and other religious holidays have been replaced by celebrations of revolutionary events. The government has starved the church of funds, and many churches rely on foreign donations to survive.

Over the last few years relations between church and state have improved. In 1991, Catholics were allowed to be admitted to the Communist Party for the first time. However, the fragility of the relationship became only too clear in 1993, when an official letter published by the Cuban bishops attacked official ideology and accused the regime of denying civil rights. Such a foray into the political arena horrified Party officials, who were quick to condemn the bishops. The authorities are clearly concerned that the Catholic church will once more become a forum for dissent if the debate over the future of Cuba is allowed a degree of free discussion. Most church leaders seem reluctant to take on such a role. But Jaime Ortega, the Archbishop of Havana who was recently appointed a cardinal by the Pope, has urged greater freedom. While on a visit to Rome in 1995 he declared: 'The government has made great mistakes. It must make amends'. The Church has even started classes in democracy.

Church congregations have grown dramatically recently, with young Cubans making up the bulk of new worshippers. It is not uncommon for people to turn to religion during economic hardship, but church leaders deny that this is the reason for the growth in size of their congregations. They suggest it is more a response to the vacuum that people find in society. Whatever the cause, the security forces are said to be monitoring church services. And over in the United States, evangelical Protestant groups are waiting in the wings to swoop on a society that is seen as ripe for conversion.

Given the problems facing religion in Cuba, it is surprising how many functioning churches you see while travelling around the country. There is a sizeable number of Protestant congregations, particularly Pentecostalist, Baptist and Methodist. Havana has a synagogue, a small mosque and even a Quaker Meeting House.

Afro-Cuban Religions. While Christianity is weak, the influence of animism and ancestor worship is strong. African religious beliefs came across to Cuba with the thousands of slaves brought by the island's colonists. The Africans absorbed sufficient elements of Catholicism into their own religion to earn toleration of the sects by the Spanish, who seemed to think that Catholicism would in the end prevail. Most plantation owners were more concerned with their slaves' ability to work hard than with their degree of interest in Christianity. The fusion of African and Catholic beliefs is so complete that it is hard to tell where one ends and the other begins.

Santería: the 'rule of the saints', or *Santería,* is the most widespread of the Afro-Cuban religions. It is followed by perhaps 50% of Cubans, of all races and all walks of life — including members of the Communist Party. Known also as *Regla de Ocha,* Santería has its origins in the religion of the Yorubá people of Nigeria.

There are several hundred gods and goddesses, or *orishas,* though only about twenty feature regularly in religious rituals. Each *orisha* is paired up with a Catholic saint, according to shared attributes. Olofí is the closest Santería equivalent to a supreme god, but he would be powerless without Orula, through whom believers consult with Olofí and the other orishas. This is done by means of divination, performed by male priests called *babalawos* in their own homes. Santería has no public temples of worship, though some believers pray in church (much to the chagrin of some orthodox Catholics).

The most important orishas, with their Christian counterparts, are as follows:

Babalu-Ayé — San Lázaro
Changó — Santa Bárbara
Eleggua — San Antonio
Obbatalá — Virgen de las Mercedes
Ochún — Virgen de la Caridad del Cobre (Cuba's patron saint)
Orula — San Francisco
Yemayá — Virgen de Regla (patron saint of Havana)

Small coloured beads worn around the wrist and neck demonstrate to which orisha a person is affiliated: green and yellow are the colours of Orula, yellow the colour of Ochún, etc. Initiates into Santería (known as *santeros* or *santeras*) must abide by a strict code of rules, such as wearing white for the first six months after the initiation ceremony.

The anniversaries of gods and goddesses are celebrated in much the same way as Catholic saints' days, and Santería believers may attend mass at the church dedicated to the relevant saint. In many homes a small shrine is decorated, offerings of food are made, candles lit and music dedicated to that particular god or goddess is played. Necessary accompaniments to the celebration, if available and affordable, are sticky cakes and rum.

The authorities have realised that foreigners are intrigued by Afro-Cuban religion, and have begun to push Santería as a tourist attraction. Books about Afro-Cuban culture fill the shelves of hard-currency bookshops, museums in Havana have displays devoted to the Afro-Cuban cults, and you can even go on an organised trip to a religious ceremony. Whether or not it is due to this official promotion, Santería has never been more popular among Cubans. Some dismiss it merely as a craze, charging that the new young followers are attracted less by the faith than by the mystique and the prestige: the cost of the initiation ceremony means that to be a *santero* represents a certain financial status.

The two other most important Afro-Cuban cults — Palo Monte and Abakuá — lack the complexity of Santería, but they share a fundamental belief in the supernatural.

Palo Monte: known also as *Regla Mayombé,* this cult was brought by Bantu slaves originally from the African Congo; it has only a modest following in eastern Cuba. The sacrifice of small animals is an integral part of Santería ceremonies, but it is Palo Monte, with its cauldrons, skulls and spells, which has most in common with Haitian voodoo.

Abakuá: open to men only and dominated by white Cubans, the Abakuá secret societies are traditionally the most sinister of the island's Afro-Cuban cults. During the Republic, the members of these Mafia-style mutual protection societies earned a reputation for being Cuba's most ruthless killers. Nowadays the few thousand members in and around Havana and Matanzas are more like masons than mafiosi. Secrecy still breeds suspicion, however, and the authorities believe that many criminals and 'anti-social elements' join in order to seek protection from the law. Members are known as *abakuas* or *ñáñigos.*

MEETING THE PEOPLE

In a country where much happens out of the public eye, getting to know the local inhabitants can radically alter your view of Cuba. To understand the country it is essential: the Cubans themselves are the island's great virtue. Despite daily hardships, the people demonstrate amazing resilience and still have the energy to show charm and generosity to foreigners. They are among the friendliest people in the world, and no traveller comes away without stories of great kindness and often a string of new addresses too. Asking for directions in a town or city will frequently result in the local taking you some or all of the way; an enthusiastic music fan will give you exhaustive resumés of the best clubs to go to in town; and the briefest acquaintance may take you home for lunch or offer to put you up for the night.

If and when you make friends, you must be prepared to pay for any food or drinks you share together. You are infinitely richer than your host; in real terms, the average monthly wage of a Cuban is less than $10. (Don't invite someone to visit you back home if you wouldn't want them to take you up on it: having a written invitation from somebody living overseas is about the only way most Cubans can hope to apply for permission to travel.) That the Cubans are as welcoming as they are is all the more admirable given the existence of the tourist 'apartheid', which allows foreigners to jump restaurant queues, enter hotels that are off-limits to most locals and spend dollars in hard-currency shops stocked with goods that many Cubans can only dream of. In short, you have the run of the whole nation — Cubans are second-class citizens in their own country. Many people despise the system but rarely express any resentment against tourists personally. Adverse behaviour towards tourists is usually limited to petty theft.

Most Cubans enjoy talking to tourists. The thirst for conversation results partly from a feeling of isolation. Before the collapse of communism, many students, doctors and teachers travelled to the Eastern bloc or other friendly nations. Nowadays, however, few Cubans get to go abroad, so tourists are the only foreigners most local people ever meet. Many visitors are eager to quiz Cubans about their views of the regime, but you should never press anyone to talk about the political situation. Asking for a view on Fidel Castro is the fastest way to silence a Cuban, though some will discuss such matters happily in the privacy of their own homes. Many people will talk openly to visitors about the economic deprivations, but in public, topics of conversation are more likely to revolve around where you come from, your marital status, occupation, etc.

Most overseas tourists visit only Havana, Varadero and a handful of other towns, such as Trinidad and Santiago. Here, therefore, the foreign visitor is not regarded as an oddity. This is true above all in the capital, where local Cubans are so aware of the money to be made from tourists that some visitors find the atmosphere oppressive. It is by no means the case that everyone who approaches you will be more interested in your money than your friendship, but in the main tourist areas it is wise to be more circumspect than you need be in other areas. Certain groups of people will go out of their way to meet foreigners. For example, some Cuban children seem to have been programmed at birth to go up to tourists demanding chewing gum (*chicle*), sweets (*caramelos*), a pen (*bolígrafo*) or, increasingly, dollars (*fula*). It is hard to say 'no', but if you give something to one child, be warned that a whole gang of kids is likely to materialise from nowhere, demanding a similar gift. An unfortunate sign of the times is that a growing number of adult beggars have joined the younger generations in asking foreigners for money.

You are also likely to have several encounters with *jineteros*, a term used to describe Cubans whose main aim in life is to take advantage of tourists. Male *jineteros* exist most commonly as touts, who will offer to change money or sell you cigars. Their opening gambit is usually to ask for the time or enquire where you are from. Fending off unwanted approaches takes a little practice. If someone comes out with a direct question in Spanish or English, you can pretend to be from Norway, Greece, or some other country whose language is not spoken widely in Cuba. Most touts are fairly easy to shake off. Otherwise simply ignore them, cross the street or, in extremis, walk or point towards a policeman.

Some jineteros simply want to be treated to a few drinks and free meals. This is often the goal of their female counterparts, *jineteras*, though young Cuban women find themselves involved increasingly in more conventional prostitution. This is most visible in Havana and the resort of Varadero, where male tourists, either singly or in pairs, are prone to be pestered by both the prostitutes themselves and by pimps. Perhaps surprisingly, you are more likely to be approached in the lobby of your hotel than on the street. Prostitutes are about the only black people allowed freely into hotel lobbies; hotel doormen and security staff make money on the side by charging tourists to take prostitutes up to their room, and by taking a cut from the woman's earnings. Some say that the government turns a blind eye since prostitution is making a vital contribution to the earning capacity of the tourist industry. It is a sad fact that a growing number of Western men visit Cuba specifically to exploit the new 'service'. Some countries are even marketing sex in Cuba. One company in Spain provides potential customers with a catalogue of 'escorts' from which to choose, while an Italian travel magazine rates Cuba ahead of Thailand and Brazil as a destination for sex tourism.

Finally, you will find it impossible not to meet plenty of Cubans in official capacities. In a country where the people are so warm and friendly, it is surprising how unhelpful a Cuban can become once installed behind a counter — particularly when a problem arises, in which case no one likes to assume responsibility. The policemen and door staff that guard many hotel entrances are supposedly there to 'protect' tourists from jineteros and other supposedly unsavoury characters, but many visitors find their presence aggravating. If you make friends with local people, try to arrange a rendezvous away from your hotel.

Addressing People. If you are not sure how to address a local, use *Señor* (for men) and *Señora* or *Señorita* (for women). Otherwise, you can adopt the Cuban practice of using *compañero* (to men) or *compañera* (to women). Loosely translated, it means something between 'comrade' and 'friend'. If you are male and want to be more matey, you can impress your new friends by using one of the local terms, the most common being *socio, compadre* (or *compay*) and *hermano* (literally brother).

Names in Spanish have three components: the first or Christian name, the father's second name, and the mother's second name; thus the leader's full name is Fidel Castro Ruz. Women's names are changed after marriage by replacing the third component by 'de' followed by the husband's second name. The third component is rarely used except on formal occasions. One consequence is that it is difficult to tell whether or not couples are married.

The usual greeting between men and women is a kiss on both cheeks, even at the first meeting if you are introduced by a mutual friend. Otherwise, it is polite to shake hands and say your name simultaneously: 'Mucho gusto — Guillermo'. Note that hissing to attract attention in the street is not considered rude in Cuba.

Women Travellers. As in most Latin nations, female tourists can rarely walk along a street without being noticed by the local men. Foreign as well as local women will often be ogled at, hissed at or be on the receiving end of compliments, known as *piropos*. While not necessarily welcome, this behaviour is rarely threatening, and outside the bigger towns you are unlikely to be pestered by such overt demonstrations of machismo. Overt sexual harassment, as practised in Italy or Islamic countries, is minimal. In general, women need not feel that their freedom is unfairly restricted by their gender: Cuba is one of the few countries in the world in which it is easy and safe to hitch-hike alone. Most women find the kindness they encounter — from both sexes — overwhelming.

The Queue. Waiting has been elevated to an art form in Cuba. If a Cuban wants a plane ticket, pizza or a pair of shoes, he or she has to queue for it. So practised are they that it is rarely necessary to wait in a line; a gaggle of people standing randomly around a bus stop may well constitute a queue. The way you identify the queue and your place in it is to ask 'l'último?' (to a man) or 'l'última?' to a woman. Literally, you are asking if he or she is last in line. The respondent will either agree, or point to someone else. Through this process you yourself will become, until the next person comes along, último or última.

These queues are civilised, not least because everyone can relax without fearing that others might steal their place. Some queues in Cuba, though, are rigid lines which compare unfavourably with the crush for Space Mountain on a busy day at Walt Disney World. Fights can sometimes break out if someone is suspected of jumping the queue. The system has bred professional queue-standers: either middle-aged women who sell their places to people without the time or patience to wait, or young men who charge money for standing in line on somebody else's behalf.

Foreigners are usually unexposed to serious queuing, first because the worst queues are at small local shops where Cubans buy their rationed goods; secondly tourists are entitled to jump the queues that form outside hard-currency shops. If you do join a queue, you may find yourself bustled to the front of the line simply through Cuban generosity.

LANGUAGE

Travellers without at least a modicum of Spanish will find life in Cuba difficult. People will always try to help you, but they can't do much if you're unable to communicate with them. Do not assume that Cubans outside the hard-core tourist traps can speak English, though the young can usually speak at least some; indeed, enthusiastic language students anxious to try out their skills will often approach you. Other Cubans learn English as a tool for more effective black-market dealing, or simply in order to enjoy more in-depth conversations with visitors. And a small community of Jamaican immigrants has retained West Indian English as a first language.

Some older people have a grasp of English because a knowledge of the language was almost obligatory for anyone who wanted to make money from the American tourists before the revolution. A large number of Cubans trained or studied in the former Soviet Union, so Russian is widely spoken. It is of little use to them now. You may be able to communicate in French with some people too.

Learning Spanish. If you have neither the time nor the devotion to attend a regular evening class, then try to learn some Spanish at home. The BBC produces an excellent course for beginners in 'World Spanish', called *Sueños*. For £37.50 you get a book, five hours' worth of cassettes and an insight into how Spanish has evolved around the world. If time is short, try the BBC *Get By In Spanish* course — intended mainly for holidaymakers bound for Spain — which consists of a book and two cassettes for £12.99. An alternative, available worldwide, is the Berlitz *Latin American Spanish for Travellers* book and cassette. Learning a little more than the basics will add considerably to your enjoyment by enabling you to communicate with ordinary Cubans.

Spanish courses in Cuba: there are several courses up and running in Cuba. The Centro de Idiomas para Extranjeros José Martí at Calle 16 no. 109, between Avenidas 1 and 3 in Miramar, Havana (tel 22-1244, 23-5058; fax 33-1697) has courses for all ages and all levels. The number of hours you do per week is flexible; expect to pay $10 per hour.

Courses are also offered at Havana university. One-month courses begin on the first Monday of each month, with three hours of tuition per day, Monday to Friday. The course costs $150-200, depending on which level you choose (three levels are available), though there is no obligation to do the full month. To enrol, contact the Dirección de Posgrado, Calle J no. 556, Vedado (tel 32-4245; fax 32-2350, 32-2757), either in advance or once you are in Havana. To get a feel for what the classes are like, you might choose to go direct to the university and speak with some of the students already on the course — the classes take place in the Varona Building on the main site, near the Habana Libre Hotel. The best time to go is at 10.30am, when you should find the students in the cafeteria on the first floor. A lot of students come from Sweden, Switzerland and Germany, but there are usually one or two from each of the UK, Italy, Japan, Canada, etc.

One-to-one tuition is available at Santiago University. There is a plenty of flexibility to arrange what suits you: expect to pay $80-100 per week for an average class load.

Both universities will try to arrange accommodation for you, either in a hotel or university apartment. Try to assert your right to find your own lodgings, which will almost certainly work out cheaper.

Some linguists have expressed concern about the idea of beginners learning Spanish in Cuba, where — as the section below explains — the language is distinct from forms spoken elsewhere in the world. If you want to learn Latin American Spanish somewhere more conventional, then Guatemala and Ecuador are possibilities.

Pronunciation. Latin Americans pronounce Spanish very differently from the pure Castillian mostly taught in England. In particular, the soft 'th' sound corresponding to the letters ce, ci or z is rendered as 's'; the use of the 'th' will cause great amusement and lead the locals to assume that you have a lisp. The Cuban accent is harder to understand than in most other parts of Latin America. Words run into each other, with final letters either merely hinted at or swallowed completely.

Unless an accent indicates otherwise, Spanish words which end in a vowel or *n* or *s* are always stressed on the last-but-one syllable: so, for example, Matanzas is pronounced Ma*tan*zas (though the 's' often disappears). Words ending in any other consonant are always stressed on the last syllable, e.g. Trini*dad*. If a word is to be stressed on any other syllable, an acute accent is written over the vowel which needs to be stressed: Batabanó. Unlike in some languages (e.g. French), an acute accent on a letter does not affect the sound of that letter; it merely indicates where the stress should fall on a multi-syllable word if it does not comply with the rules outlined above. Guantánamo has an accent, Guantanamero (a citizen of Guantánamo) does not.

The letter *h* is never pronounced, i.e. hola is pronounced ola. *J* is pronounced as an aspirated *h,* as is *g* when followed by *e* or *i;* so José should be spoken as Ho-*say,* and Girón should sound like Hi-*ron.* The letter *v* is almost indistinguishable from the letter *b,* so 'Varadero' sounds like 'Baradero'. The letter *s* at the ends of words is rarely pronounced in Cuba, presumably due to laziness. Thus *buenos* is spoken as 'bueno', and *dos* as 'do'. At the end of words *n* is pronounced more like 'ng', though this is merely hinted at.

Note that the wave above an *n* (ñ), known as a tilde, changes the letter *n* to *ny.* Thus *mañana* is pronounced man-*yana.* Accents other than the tilde are rarely used on capital letters, a practice followed in this book. In dictionaries, indexes and telephone directories, listings beginning with the dipthong *ch* (pronounced as in the word 'chair') are listed after *c*; words starting with *ll* follow *l* and *ñ* follows *n.*

Useful Words and Phrases

More specialised glossaries can be found at the start of the sections on Money, Communications, Getting Around, Driving, Accommodation, Eating and Drinking, Exploring, Entertainment, Shopping, Health and Hygiene, and Crime and Safety.

hello	*hola*	I am hungry	*tengo apetito*
goodbye	*adiós, hasta luego, ciao*	I am thirsty	*tengo sed*
yes	*sí*	a little	*un popquito*

no	*no*	more	*más*
please	*por favor*	less	*menos*
thank you	*gracias*	to go	*ir*
excuse me	*perdón, permiso*	help me	*ayúdeme*
how much	*cuánto*	quickly	*rapidamente*
where is	*dónde está*	slowly	*despacio*
good	*bueno*	stop	*párese*
bad	*malo*	here	*aquí*
good morning	*buenas días* (or *hola*)	there	*allí*
good afternoon	*buenas tardes*	is there any. . .?	*hay. . .?*
good evening	*buenas tardes*	no, there isn't	*no hay*
goodnight	*buenas noches*	school	*escuela*
don't mention it	*de nada*	garden	*jardín*
how are you?	*qué tal?*	house	*casa*
pleased (to meet you)	*mucho gusto, encantado, a*	town	*ciudad*
I don't understand	*no entiendo*	village	*pueblo*
I don't speak Spanish	*no hablo español (castellano)*	big	*grande*
do you speak English?	*habla usted inglés?*	small	*pequeño*
my name is. . .	*me llamo. . .*	hot	*caliente*
what is your name?	*como se llama?*	cold	*frío*
can I photograph you?	*puedo tomar su fotografía?*	queue	*cola*
I am. . . years old	*tengo. . . años*	don't touch	*no tocar*
I would like. . .	*quisiero. . .*	no smoking	*no fumar*
I need. . .	*necesito. . .*	no entry	*no pase*
I am well	*estoy bien*		

Weather

rain	*lluvia*	storm	*temporal*
sun	*sol*	hurricane	*huracán*
it's hot	*hace calor*	shower	*chubasco*
it's cold	*hace frío*		

Time

what time is it?	*qué hora es?*	Tuesday	*martes*
minute	*minuto*	Wednesday	*miércoles*
hour	*hora*	Thursday	*jueves*
day	*día*	Friday	*viernes*
week	*semana*	Saturday	*sábado*
month	*mes*	January	*enero*
year	*año*	February	*febrero*
yesterday	*ayer*	March	*marzo*
today	*hoy*	April	*abril*
tomorrow	*mañana*	May	*mayo*
morning	*mañana*	June	*junio*
afternoon	*tarde*	July	*julio*
evening	*tarde* (early); *noche* (late)	August	*agosto*
now	*ahora*	September	*septiembre*
never	*jamás*	October	*octubre*
Sunday	*domingo*	November	*noviembre*
Monday	*lunes*	December	*diciembre*

Numbers

1	*uno* or *una*	24	*veinticuatro*
2	*dos*	25	*veinticinco*
3	*tres*	26	*veintiséis*
4	*cuatro*	27	*veintisiete*
5	*cinco*	28	*veintiocho*
6	*seis*	29	*veintinueve*
7	*siete*	30	*treinta*
8	*ocho*	31	*treinta y uno*

9	*nueve*	32	*treinta y dos*
10	*diez*	40	*cuarenta*
11	*once*	50	*cincuenta*
12	*doce*	60	*sesenta*
13	*trece*	70	*setenta*
14	*catorce*	80	*ochenta*
15	*quince*	90	*noventa*
16	*dieciséis*	100	*cien* (before nouns) or
17	*diecisiete*		*ciento*
18	*dieciocho*	200	*doscientos* or *doscientas*
19	*diecinueve*		(before feminine nouns)
20	*veinte*	500	*quinientos* or *quinientas*
21	*veintiuno*	1000	*mill*
22	*veintidós*	10,000	*diez mil*
23	*veintitrés*	1,000,000	*un millón*

Nationality and Status

English	*inglés*	single	*soltero, a*
England	*Inglaterra*	widowed	*viudo, a*
Scotland	*Escocia*	mother	*madre*
Wales	*País de Gales*	father	*padre*
Great Britain	*Gran Bretaña*	sister	*hermana*
Ireland	*Irlanda*	brother	*hermano*
Germany	*Alemania*	wife, woman	*esposa, mujer*
Netherlands	*Paises Bajos*	husband	*esposo, marido*
Canada	*Canadá*	boy/girlfriend	*novio, a*
Australia	*Australia*	daughter	*hija*
New Zealand	*Nueva Zelanda*	son	*hijo*
United States	*Estados Unidos (EEUU)*	man	*hombre*
married	*casado, a*	children	*niños, hijos*

Cubanisms

There are many local terms which not even a Spaniard or fellow Latin American would understand. Learning a few Cubanisms will enable you to impress the locals greatly, or will simply help you recognise words you will inevitably hear in the street. Look out for the *Diccionario cubano de términos populares y vulgares* by Carlos Paz Pérez (published by the Editorial de Ciencias Sociales, Havana, 1994), which you should find in good dollar bookshops. What follows is a selection of some of the most commonly used Cubanisms, given in alphabetical order.

ahorita	'any minute', but could be five minutes or five hours
apagón	power cut
candela	terrible
chévere	good (often used to refer to a person)
chino, a	an affectionate term of address between friends (literally meaning 'Chinese')
chisme	rumour, gossip
coño	exclamation, used to emphasise a point or show surprise
descarga	a live music show, usually small and informal
estar apurado, a	to be in a hurry
fula	dollar
fulano	chap, 'geezer', so-and-so (tends to be disparaging)
kilos	cents
maceta	black marketeer
menudo	small change
oye	literally 'listen', used to attract attention
oíste?	'did you hear?', tacked on the end of phrases
pepino	tourist
piquete	band (musical)

pinchar	to work
prieto, a	dark (skinned), including suntanned
puro	old man, cigar
yuma	foreigner, tourist (usually Caucasian)

There are just as many non-verbal expressions that are unique to the island. If someone rubs their arm, they are probably indicating that they would like you to give them some soap. A circular motion of the hands is an invitation to change money.

FURTHER READING

Don't expect to find too much in the way of reading material in Cuba unless you speak Russian or Spanish. There is a series of bland official guides covering Cuba, Havana and Varadero, with more planned. Published in five languages (Spanish, English, French, German and Italian), these offer little practical help, but have some pretty pictures and give sometimes good historical detail and information about museums and so on. Each one costs $8-10. Other books on Cuban life are hard to find on the island itself, and most of those listed below are obtainable only abroad; those you are most likely to find on the island are marked with an asterisk.

History and Politics

Case 1, 1989, the translation of *Vindicación de Cuba,* the official account of the case against General Arnaldo Ochoa, including transcripts from the trial. Fascinating.
Castro's Final Hour: the secret story behind the coming downfall of communist Cuba by Andres Oppenheimer (Simon & Schuster, 1992). An account by a *Miami Herald* journalist of events in Cuba from 1989 to 1992. A highly critical view of the regime, focussing in particular on the execution of General Ochoa and the 1991 Communist Party Congress. The tone is rabid in places but this is a compelling read.
Che: A Memoir by Fidel Castro (Ocean Press, 1994).
Conflict and Change in Cuba by E. A. Baloyra and J. A. Morris (New Mexico, 1993). A rather dense collection of essays, covering all aspects of contemporary Cuba from youth culture to the role of the armed forces.
Constitución de Cuba: available in some dollar shops in Havana, price just $1.50. Very interesting, with certain sections veering alarmingly between reality and fantasy.
Cuba After Communism by E. Cardoso and A. Helwege (Massachussetts, 1992).
Cuba: A Short History edited by Leslie Bethell (Cambridge University Press, 1993). Exactly that.
Cuba: Between Reform and Revolution by Louis A. Pérez (Oxford University Press, 1988). A very readable history of the island. Its 'Selective guide to the Literature' lists books covering every aspect of Cuba, divided helpfully under headings such as Economics, Race and Women, and runs for almost 100 pages.
Cuba for Beginners by Rius (Pathfinder Press, 1970). An excellent history of Cuba to 1969, depicted in cartoons.
Cuba in Transition: Options for US policy by G. Gunn (New York, 1993). A succinct and clear assessment of the choices open to the US government.
The Cuban Revolution — Origins, Course and Legacy by Marifeli Pérez Stable (Oxford University Press, New York, 1993).
Cuba Roja: cómo viven los cubanos con Fidel Castro by Román Orozco (Madrid, 1993). A 950-page tome covering everything from the role of the armed forces to Cuban sexual mores. Woven around numerous interviews, this is an important read for any Cubaphile.

Fidel: a Critical Portrait by Tad Szulz (Hodder & Stoughton, 1986). Describes Castro's rise to power and his successes and tribulations in the first quarter-century of the Revolution.

Fidel Castro by Robert E. Quirk (W. W. Norton & Co, 1993). The latest lengthy biography of the Cuban leader.

In Defence of Socialism by Fidel Castro (Pathfinder Press, 1989). The Cuban leader's speeches are renowned for their verbosity: this is a collection of edited highlights.

Mea Cuba by Guillermo Cabrera Infante (Faber & Faber, 1994). The exiled author's distaste for Fidel Castro and his regime exudes from every paragraph in this book.

For books that are unwavering in their devotion to the regime, visit Pathfinder Books, 47 The Cut, London SE1 8LL (tel 0171-401 2409). As well as publishing its own books, the bookshop stocks others on the subject, including those published by the Melbourne-based publisher, Ocean Press, whose titles fill the shelves in Cuban dollar bookshops.

Society and Culture

Afrocuba by Pedro Pérez Sarduy and Jean Stubbs (Latin America Bureau, 1993). An anthology of Cuban writings, including poetry and non-fiction.

Cuba in Focus: A guide to the people, politics and culture (Latin America Bureau, 1995). Part of LAB's In Focus series: an illustrated introduction to Cuba by the authors of this book, Emily Hatchwell and Simon Calder, describing everything from the structure of government to the origins of Santería.

The Cuban Commission Report — A Hidden History of the Chinese in Cuba (1876), a facsimile of the original (Baltimore, 1993). A revealing account of the miserable existence of the Chinese contract labourers that were shipped by the thousand to Cuba in the 19th century.

Cubans by Lynn Geldof (Bloomsbury Press, 1992). Interviews with Cubans from all walks of life by Sir Bob's sister. Not as illuminating as it could have been.

Los Negros Curros by the late Fernando Ortíz (Editorial de Ciencas Sociales, Havana, 1986), the first Cuban to write seriously about Afro-Cuban culture in the early 20th century. New editions of this and other Ortíz titles have been issued to tap the revived interest in Cuba's African heritage, but you can also pick up old editions in the street.

Salsa — Havana Heat, Bronx Beat by Hernando Calvo Ospina (Latin America Bureau, 1995). Traces the roots and development of Latin America's most famous rhythm.

Santería from Africa to the New World by G. Brandon (Indiana, 1993).

Travel and Picture Books

Cuba, a collection of photographs by Adam Kufeld (W. W. Norton, New York, 1994). An essay of introduction by Tom Miller provides the context.

Cuba — a journey by Jacobo Timerman (Picador, 1994). A succinct and extremely perceptive account by the well-known Argentine journalist and socialist of a trip to Cuba in 1987. Ample evidence that Cuba was already in deep trouble before the collapse of the Eastern bloc.

Cuba: the Land, the History, the People, the Culture by Stephen Williams (Michael Friedman, New York, 1994). An even balance of pictures and text.

Driving Through Cuba: an East-West Journey by Carlo Gébler (Abacus, 1988). A mediocre 'travel novel'.

Havana — 1933, a collection of photographs taken by the American, Walker Evans (Thames and Hudson, 1989). A revealing glimpse of pre-revolutionary Havana.

Havana, Portrait of a City by Juliet Barclay (Cassell, 1993). Lovely photographs of Old Havana, accompanied by an interesting account of the history of the city.
Into Cuba by Barry Lewis and Peter Marshall (Zena Books, 1987). Well-written, with delightful photographs, but the fact that this is one of the few English-language books available in Cuba says a lot about the content.
La Habana Colonial (1519-1898): available only from the Dirección Provincial de Planificación Física y Arquitectura at Calle 25 no. 307 between L and M, next door to the Habana Libre (tel 32-8620). Published with assistance from Spain, this excellent book includes photographs of each building described. The emphasis is on the architecture rather than the history of the buildings, but this is still one of the few up-to-date books found on colonial architecture.
Return to Havana: The Decline of Cuban Society under Castro by M. Halperin (Nashville, 1994). No mystery as to the views of the author.
Trading with the Enemy: a Yankee travels through Castro's Cuba by Tom Miller (Atheneum, New York, 1992). An account of a seven-month trip to the island. Not a classic.
The Exile: Cuba in the heart of Miami by David Rieff (Vintage, 1993). An excellent insight into the state of the Cuban community in Florida.

Fiction

Cuba's most famous pre 20th-century novel is *Cecilia Valdés* by Cirilo Villaverde, which was first published in 1838 and remains one of the greatest works of Cuban literature. A novel of manners, it gives a colourful view of urban life in Havana in the early 1800s.

Alejo Carpentier (1904-1980) spent much of his life in Paris but is remembered as the finest writer Cuba has produced this century. His avant-garde imagery and magic realist style are not to everyone's taste, but *Explosion in the Cathedral* is well worth reading. A contemporary of Carpentier, Nicolás Guillén (1902-89), was a lifelong member of the Communist Party and supporter of the regime. His poetry shows a strong Afro-Cuban influence, most noticeable in the musical rhythm of his verse. *Patria o Muerte! The Great Zoo and Other Poems* includes some of his best works, such as *Tengo* ('I have'), with parallel text in Spanish and English.

Cuba's most famous living writer, Guillermo Cabrera Infante, lives in exile, residing mainly in London, and many of his modernist works have been translated into English. *Three Trapped Tigers* and *View of Dawn in the Tropics* (Faber & Faber) are both set in pre-revolutionary Havana. One of the few other contemporary Cuban writers to have had his work translated is Miguel Barnet. His 'testimonial novel', *Biografía de un Cimarrón*, first published in 1967 and translated as 'The Autobiography of a Runaway Slave', is still a bestseller. It is based on an interview given to Miguel Barnet by a former slave, Esteban Montejo, at the age of 104.

Two recent books are the autobiographical *Before Night Falls* by the late Cuban exile Reinaldo Arenas (New York, 1993), and *Cuba and the Night* by Pico Iyer (Quartet, 1995), about an American photographer who falls in love with a Cuban woman, highly evocative of Cuba in the 1990s.

Last but not least, two of the 20th century's most prominent writers lived in and wrote about Cuba. Ernest Hemingway resided, wrote and drank heavily in Havana, and produced classics such as the Nobel Prize-winning novel *The Old Man and the Sea*, set in the coastal village of Cojímar, *To Have and Have Not*, and the less famous *Islands in the Stream*. Graham Greene spent some time in the Cuban capital, and *Our Man in Havana* is both a charming read and a good picture of life in the city before the revolution.

Bookshops. Those living in London or other capital cities will have the greatest choice as far as travel bookshops are concerned. Many shops produce their own catalogue, however, and ordering a book by phone or post should present no problem. The pick of those in London are as follows:

Daunt Books, 83 Marylebone High Street, London W1M 3DE (tel 0171-224 2295; fax 0171-224 6893). This shop has taken the concept of a travel bookshop to its logical conclusion: as well as a good collection of guides and travelogues, related literature is also included — from novels to cookery books.

Stanfords, 12-14 Long Acre WC2E 9LP (tel 0171-836 1321). As well as guides and travel literature, this shop has the best stock of maps in the capital.

Travel Bookshop, 13 Blenheim Crescent, London W11 (tel 0171-229 5260). Adopts a similar approach to Daunt Books but has a smaller stock. Secondhand guides and literature are also available.

Travellers Bookshop, 25 Cecil Court, London WC2 (tel 0171-836 9132). New and secondhand books are given equal space.

PRACTICAL INFORMATION

Getting to Cuba has never been easier; the republic seeks tourists almost to the point of desperation. Even so, a trip to Cuba still requires a little more planning than a jaunt to the Isle of Wight. This section contains options for getting to Cuba, details of passport and visa requirements, suggestions of what to take, and what you can expect in terms of food, accommodation, entertainment and so on; it ends with a selection of useful contacts.

In the six years since the first edition of this book was published, the possibilities of reaching Cuba have multiplied. Whether you want to take an inclusive holiday (which smooths out the hassles of documentation, finding accommodation, etc.), or just buy a flight and make your own arrangements for internal travel and accommodation, the options are better than ever before.

TRAVEL FROM BRITAIN

Specialist Agencies. To get a broad view of the expanding opportunities, enlist the help of a travel agent. Many general agents lack the knowledge and experience to give sensible advice on Cuba; they may either create the misleading impression that it is just another Caribbean destination, or warn inappropriately that the island is somehow unsafe. So it is well worth dealing with a specialist. The following British travel agents will not regard you as eccentric for asking for a flight to Havana. They offer up-to-date advice on travel to and within Cuba, and can supply anything from a cheap flight to a tailor-made holiday. Even if your starting point is elsewhere in Europe, the UK is an excellent place to buy travel — with costs much lower than in most other countries.

Journey Latin America, 16 Devonshire Road, London W4 2HD (tel 0181-747 3108; fax 0181-742 1312). The company has a second office at 28-30 Barton Arcade, Deansgate, Manchester M3 2BH (0161-832 1441).

Progressive Tours, 12 Porchester Place, Marble Arch, London W2 2BS; (tel 0171-262 1676; fax 0171-724 6941).

Regent Holidays, 15 John St, Bristol BS1 2HR (tel 0117-921 1711; fax 0117-925 4866).

VE Tours, 37 Great Marlborough St, London W1V 1HA (tel 0171-437 7534; fax 0171-494 0199).

South American Experience, 47 Causton St, London SW1P 4AT (tel 0171-976 5511; fax 0171-976 6908).

The number of air routes to Cuba is expanding, providing several low-cost possibilities from the UK and Europe. Many flights require connections, offering the chance of a stopover en route at places such as Madrid or Caracas. All the options are described below, starting with the cheapest and easiest link from Britain.

Scheduled Flights. At the time of publication, a non-stop flight operates weekly between London Stansted and Havana. It is operated by Cubana, the national airline of Cuba, and uses a French-registered DC-10 in the colours of its owner, the private airline AOM. This is unlikely to be the most outstanding (or on-time) flight you have ever had, but at least it has the benefit of operating direct to the Cuban capital; when a Russian jet was used, it called at Gander in Newfoundland to refuel on the outbound journey and returned via Madrid to Stansted. The official flight departure from Stansted is noon on Thursday, but if you get away by the early afternoon you should consider yourself lucky. The flight time is ten hours outbound, nine hours back, but do not bank on making tight connections at either end of your journey — delays of several hours are common. Anything is possible on Cubana.

The airline's UK office is at 49 Conduit St, London W1R 9FB (0171-734 1165), but prospective passengers are encouraged to buy tickets through agents rather than direct from the airline. For much of the year, the fare is around £400 return. This increases to more like £550 at peak times during the Christmas and New Year period, and in July and August. It is well worth calling several of the agents listed above, since fares on the same flight can vary significantly from company to company.

Cubana claims to be 'safe, efficient and hospitable'. This is an imaginative motto, and don't expect anything other than a cheap, no frills flight. The food is dull but usually edible; a special meal will be prepared for vegetarians on request, but this is likely to consist just of extra fruit or a cheese sandwich. Beer, wine and rum are free with meals, but a charge is made for subsequent drinks. You can elect to travel in Tropical class or Club class, costing about 50% and 100% more than the economy fare respectively and offering a few extra degrees of comfort.

In 1996, Cubana was introducing a second service from the UK Havana via Varadero, at least during the summer months.

Indirect Routings: in the bad old days before direct flights, an exotic route was not optional. Although East Berlin and Prague are now off the agenda, there are still good reasons for choosing a connecting flight. In particular, the Iberia Group (comprising Spain's national airline, the Venezuelan carrier Viasa, and Aerolineas Argentinas) allows all kinds of stopover possibilities — notably in Madrid and Caracas. (If you wish to change the date of your ticket in Havana, note that Viasa's booking system is not computer-linked.)

Charter Flights. Various charter carriers operate from Gatwick and Manchester airports to Varadero, with some services also calling first at Holguín. One particularly attractive feature of this latter arrangement is that you can fly into Holguín, and back from Varadero — as long as you carry only hand luggage. This 'open-jaw' arrangement means that if you want to travel through the island, you only need to worry about transport in one direction.

These charter flights are mostly intended for people on inclusive holidays, but 'seat-only' arrangements are possible. Consult Airtours (01706 260000); Cosmos (0161-480 5799); First Choice (0161-745 7000); and Sunworld (0113-239 3020).

Package Tours. There are sound reasons for choosing to visit Cuba on an organised holiday, since making arrangements independently is not completely hassle-free. There is of course no obligation to stick with the group for the whole trip, and the cost of some tours compares favourably with the price of flights alone. Late in 1995, for example, it was possible to get a package of a week in Varadero plus transfers for around £400 — not much more than the charter flight alone. A Caribbean holiday in peak season for that sort of price represents extremely good value. As with most things in travel, it pays to phone around: some travel agents tell you that prices are high because it is high season, only for you to find on arrival that everywhere is half-empty and full of Canadians

on cheap off-season packages. Plenty of companies, including those listed immediately above, offer organised trips.

More substantial tours are available from specialists such as Gane & Marshall International (266 East Barnet Road, East Barnet, Herts EN4 8TD; tel 0181-441 9592; fax 0181-441 7376); Havanatur UK (Interchange House, 27 Stafford Road, Croydon, Surrey CR0 4NG; tel 0181-681 3613, fax 0181-760 0031 — the UK representative of Cuba's leading tour operator); Regal Holidays (22 High St, Sutton, Ely, Cambs CB6 2RB; tel 01353 778096, fax 01353 777897). Some more mainstream operators offer tours, such as Cox & Kings (0171-873 5001); Cricketer Holidays (01892 664242); Kuoni (01306 742222); Saga (0800 414383); Tropical Places (01342 825123); and Voyages Jules Verne (0171-616 1000).

Agents with experience of Cuba can stitch together more individual packages of flights, transfers and hotels. A range of basic tours can be tailored to your

needs, for example by adding a week or two on top of the standard packages — enabling you to spend some time travelling independently. For a wide range of options, consult Cubanacan UK (0171-537 7909). This organisation operates some tours itself, but will also be able to give an up-to-date list of travel companies that are currently serving Cuba.

Specialist Tours. Several other operators offer trips based on their particular specialism. Bike Tours (01225 480130) has considerable experience in arranging group cycling holidays around the island, which cost around £1,100 including flights. Birdspotters can join trips organised by companies such as Birdquest (01254 826317). Train enthusiasts organise regular visits to areas where steam locomotives are still used for the sugar harvest (February and March being the most promising months). Divers are catered for by Aquatours (0181-339 0040) and Scuba Cuba (01895 624100). And a company called Special Places (01892 661157) has a week-long cigar tour of the island, culminating in a cigar-tasting dinner organised by Habanos SA.

TRAVEL FROM EUROPE

Cubana has a skeleton network of scheduled flights linking Havana with Paris (Orly), Madrid, Brussels and Berlin (Schoenefeld). It is supplemented by services on AOM from Paris, on Iberia from Madrid and Aeroflot from Moscow, Stockholm, Luxembourg and Shannon in the West of Ireland.

From Germany, the holiday airline LTU flies from Düsseldorf to Havana, Holguín and the tiny island of Cayo Largo off the south coast of Cuba. Another carrier, Condor, flies from Frankfurt to Havana and Camagüey.

From Holland, Martinair flies from Amsterdam to Holguín and Varadero. The main purpose of the charter is to ferry Dutch package tourists to the beaches of Guardalavaca (on Cuba's north coast close to Holguín), but it also carries independent travellers.

Package Holidays. The range of holidays offered by operators in Western Europe is wide. The problem is that prices are much higher than the best deals available from Britain or Ireland. Travellers from continental Europe would do best to contact tour operators in Britain in order to save money. Those wishing to travel direct from Europe should contact one of the following; prefix each number with the international access code when calling from abroad.

France: Havanatur (Paris) +33 1 4742 5858
Spain: Viajes Guamá (Madrid) +34 1 411 2048
Switzerland: Jelmoli Reisen (Zurich) +41 1 211 1357

TRAVEL FROM CANADA

Frequent flights link Havana, Varadero, Holguín and Santiago with Toronto, Montréal and Québec City. Most are charters, sold almost exclusively in conjunction with package holidays; see below.

Package Holidays. The first holidays in Cuba after the revolution originated in Canada, and there are some competitive deals on offer. Prices start at about C$700 (£350) for a week including flights and accommodation. The leading operators are as follows (to call them from the UK, dial 001 followed by the number):

Albatours (Toronto): 416-746-2890; fax 416-746-0397.
Cubacán Tours (Montréal): 514-861-4444.
Fiesta Holidays (Toronto): 416-498-5566; fax 416-498-7303.
Magna Holidays (Toronto): 416-665-7330; fax 416-665-8448.
Mirabelle Tours (Montréal): 514-632-5330.
Paramount Holidays (Toronto): 416-485-1700, fax 416-485-0553.
Regent Holidays (Toronto): 416-673-3343; fax 416-673-1717 (this last company has no connection with Regent Holidays in Bristol, UK).

You might also find a cut-price last-minute holiday. It helps if you have a contact in Canada who can scan the newspapers looking for bargains, but listed below are some companies specializing in last-minute holidays which you could try direct:

Belair (Montréal) 514-871-8330   Belair (Toronto) 416-699-8833
The Traveller Inc 416-975-9339   Travel Deals 416-236-0125
Wholesale Travel Group 416-366-1000

You will be expected to pay over the phone by credit card, and will have to organize a flight to Canada.

TRAVEL TO AND FROM THE USA

According to the magazine *Condé Nast Traveler*, 50,000-60,000 Americans visited Cuba in 1995 — four out of five of them illegally. Although the US government attempts to prevent its citizens visiting the island, many travel via Mexico, Jamaica or the Bahamas.

The world's first international flight was between Florida (Key West) and Havana, but since the US blockade began the amount of air traffic across the Straits has diminished drastically. All the leading American airlines have already filed their flight plans for when the embargo is lifted. Miami is likely to be the hub for dozens of flights to points all over Cuba. Until such time as Washington relaxes the blockade, though, there are few links. Direct flights, of which there are about ten a week, are strictly controlled because of the US embargo. These flights are not listed in timetables nor displayed on departure boards at Miami airport. The Americans go to considerable lengths to pretend that they do not exist. The flights are assigned a distant gate at Miami International Airport for the short hop to Terminal 2 at José Martí airport in Havana. The flight lasts barely 30 minutes, and fares are ludicrously high: $196 single, $280 return, plus miscellaneous taxes which can add $25 to the journey.

Flights are open only to Cubans, US citizens officially permitted entry into Cuba, and journalists. This latter category is the only possible one in which Europeans will be carried. Some evidence of status — and, increasingly, this means a convincing press card — is required. This is strictly enforced when travelling from the USA, not so much so when departing Cuba. On the northbound flight, you will need a US visa, since European passengers on Cuban flights do not qualify for the US visa waiver scheme.

The flights are operated on behalf of several charterers based in Miami:

ABC Airline Brokers Co — tel 305-871-1260, fax 305-447-0965,
   e-mail tfre97a@prodigy.com.
CBT Charters — tel 305-876-7660.
Marazul Charters — tel 305-251-9748.
(prefix numbers with 001 when calling from Europe).

From Miami: you can book a seat ahead by telephone, and need not pay for it until you reach the airport. Then you buy the ticket with cash or travellers cheques and check in for the flight. Most of the passengers are Cuban expatriates from south Florida.

From Havana: tickets must be booked at the Celimar office at Calle 24 no. 4314, esquina 45, Playa (tel 33-2555, 33-2281, 33-2983; fax 33-2074; telex 512143/2613). The office opens Monday to Friday until 4.30pm (but closes for lunch). There is a special office for foreigners: smarter and with a shorter queue. You can pay for tickets in cash or by credit card, preferably at least a week in advance of your flight. If you choose to try your luck and turn up at the airport without a booking, you must pay in cash dollars. 'Journalists' will be required to show an approximation to a press card. If you need to speak to ABC (which runs the service from Havana) at the airport, dial 33-5177 or 79-8160 (the airport switchboard) and ask for 'Tráfico Internacional, Terminal 2'.

Via Nassau: at the start of 1996, there was an indication that some degree of price competition was about to start. The Cuban charter carrier Aerocaribbean was planning a daily service operating Havana-Nassau (Bahamas)-Miami. The interpolation of a third country means that restrictions on Cuban aircraft could be eased, and fares are likely to fall. Unless or until these flights get off the ground, then the easiest route for circumventing US regulations will still be via Nassau, with onward tickets to Havana available from Lionel Carey, Bahatours, PO Box N-522, Nassau, Bahamas (tel 809-356 4700).

Packages from the USA. One experienced operator is Marazul Tours, Tower Plaza, 4100 Park Avenue, Weehawken, NJ 07087 (tel 201-319-9670; toll-free 1-800-223-5334; fax 201-319-9009; e-mail marazult@aol.com). Marazul organises tours for US citizens, and is well used to dealing with Treasury Department regulations. The company uses charter flights from Miami operated by its associate company there.

The Center for Cuban Studies (124 West 23rd Street, New York NY 10011;

212-242-0559) organises visits for academics. Global Exchange Reality Tours (800-497-1994) operates one- or two-week study tours focusing on a particular cultural, social or environmental topic. Caribbean Music & Dance Programs (2017 Mission St, San Francisco CA 94110; tel 510-444-7173, fax 510-444-5412, e-mail globalexch*f*igc.apc.org) organises three or four trips each year.

The advantage of using a Canadian company such as Wings of the World (Manhattan office: 1636 Third Avenue, New York, NY; 800-465-8687) is that the legal requirement to provide proof that you are travelling within US legislation does not apply.

TRAVEL FROM THE CARIBBEAN AND LATIN AMERICA

Flights from Caribbean islands. AeroCaribbean, the Cuban charter company, has flights to Havana and Varadero from Montego Bay in Jamaica, Nassau in the Bahamas and Santo Domingo in the Dominican Republic. Most of these are aimed at tourists in Cuba who want to visit another island during their stay, and a range of package tours are available locally. If you just want the flight element, then the prices to or from either Havana or Varadero are as follows:

Montego Bay: one-way $135, fixed-date return $180, open return $210.
Nassau: one-way $120, fixed-date return $165, open return $195.
Santo Domingo: one-way $180, fixed-date return $260, open return $290.

There are also links to the Colombian island of San Andrés on the Colombian scheduled carrier Aerorepublica.

Flights and Packages from Mexico and Central America. The cheapest tours are offered by Cuba-Mex, Calle 63 no 500, Edificio La Literaria, Mérida, Yucatán (tel 23-91-99 or 23-97-25), using scheduled Mexicana flights from Mérida.

The Cuban charter airline, Aerocaribbean, has flights twice weekly from Mérida (one-way $120, fixed-date return $165, open return $195). Contact the airline at Merihabana, Hotel Reforma, Calle 59 £508, esquina 62, Merida, Yucatan CP 97000 (tel/fax 991-236612).

There are frequent links on both Cubana and Mexicana from Mexico City, and an extraordinarily protracted journey to and from Havana calling at Cancún, Mérida, Villahermosa, Tuxtla and Oaxaca three or four times a week.

Cubana flies to and from Panama City, while Aeroflot retains its politico-historical link with the Nicaraguan capital, Managua. San José in Costa Rica is accessible most days on Cubana, the Costa Rican carrier Lacsa and Ladeco of Chile.

Flights from South America. Ladeco's 737 service continues to Santiago de Chile. Cubana operates to Bogotá in Colombia, and Guayaquil and Quito in Ecuador. Aeroflot serves Lima, and Aerorepublica operates to Barranquilla and Cali in Colombia.

ONWARD OR RETURN TRAVEL

Try to get all the tickets you need before going to Cuba. One-way fares from Havana are high, with few of the special offers which are available in the West.

Anyone continuing to Mexico from Cuba must have all the necessary documentation before going to the airport, although if you are travelling on a package tour, Mexican tourist cards are issued at José Martí airport. Be sure to check in advance. If necessary, tourist cards can be obtained before departing the UK or at the Mexican embassy in Miramar, Havana.

Cubana occasionally offers inclusive short breaks to destinations in Mexico, the Caribbean or Central America, but these can only be obtained locally. Most are organized through the Cubana leisure subsidiary Sol y Son, in the same block as Cubana itself at Calle 23 number 64 (tel 70-0483; fax 79-3333).

TRAVEL BY SEA

Cruises. Few cruise ships call at Cuban ports, mainly because of the US rule which bars vessels which have visited Cuba from calling at Florida ports. In 1995, a European cruise line, Costa, located a vessel (the *Costa Playa*) at Puerto Plata in the Dominican Republic for regular one-week voyages around Cuba, calling at Santiago, Havana and the Nipe bay (close to Holguín) as well as Montego Bay in Jamaica. By removing the dual problems of accommodation and getting around, this could become a very popular option. In the UK, it is being sold by Cosmos in the tour operator's 'Distant Dreams' brochure.

By Yacht. You can enter officially at Havana, Varadero or Cayo Largo. See *Red Tape*. Vessels may use VHF channel 16 to communicate with the Nautical Base of the Cuban National Tourism Institute, the nearest port or coastguard unit from a distance of at least 12 miles to provide details of vessel, etc. Most of the country's 17 marinas are operated by Puerto Sol; there are plans for four times as many marinas.

To rent a yacht locally, see page 115.

Passports. A full ten-year passport is required by all except American visitors to Cuba. (US Citizens are, however, severely restricted in travelling to the Republic; see *American Visitors to Cuba,* below.) Note that your passport number and the date of issue must match exactly the details on the tourist card or visa issued by the Cuban embassy. So if your passport needs renewing before your departure, get it done before applying for the document to enter Cuba.

If your passport is lost or stolen in Cuba, contact first the police and then the consular department of your embassy. Obtaining replacement travel documents is easier if you have a record of the passport number and its date and place of issue, ideally a photocopy of the relevant pages.

TOURIST CARDS AND VISAS

Tourist Cards. For visits in transit of less than 72 hours just show your onward or return ticket to the immigration official. Most people, of course, wish to visit Cuba for longer than three days. Some Europeans require only a valid passport, but most nationalities require either a visa or 'tourist card' (*tarjeta de turista*).

For a normal holiday, the tourist card is sufficient and very easy to obtain. Whether or not you are going on an organised tour, the travel agent who sells you the flight will normally issue the tourist card. This costs around £14. It does not require any photographs and can be issued more or less instantly. The traveller need only fill in the form, which asks for little more than your name, address, occupation and travel details. In theory you can buy a tourist card on arrival at the airport in Cuba, but you are advised to make the arrangements before you leave home.

The tourist card can be used for one entry only and permits a stay of up to 30 days. For independent travellers the main problem with a tourist card is that it ties you to the return date shown on your ticket. On your arrival in Cuba, the immigration official will ask how long you wish to stay. He or she will grant you the maximum of one month only if your ticket matches the requested period or if you have an open ticket. The best way to ensure that you can stay as long as you choose is to book a return flight for as late a date as you might wish to stay, then change the reservation once your plans are clearer. This can be tricky with some airlines, however, so check before you buy your ticket; there may also be a fee to pay. You also run the risk, of course, that flights home will be fully booked on the dates when you want to return.

Losing your tourist card during your trip is not the end of the world. Pay $10 or $20 and a new one will be provided at the airport. If you have overstayed your welcome, however, you are likely to be fined for each extra day you have stayed beyond the expiry of your original tourist card.

Extending your tourist card. Travellers may extend their tourist card once. This can be done most easily at the tourist information desk in the Habana Libre hotel in Havana (see page 161), or at some other tourist hotels. You need to take your air ticket (which gives a departure date), hotel card, plus $8 (payable in cash or by credit card). The extension will be issued on the spot, up to the date of departure given on your ticket as long as this is not more than one month ahead. Note that if you were given a fortnight on first entering the country, you are likely to be granted only a further two weeks. They may require an explanation if you have no accommodation booked for the rest of your stay; sketch out a few theoretical travel plans, e.g. a tour of the island in a hired car. If you are not in Havana on the date of expiry of your tourist card, go to the nearest immigration office (*oficina de inmigración*), found in every town, often attached to the police station.

Anyone wishing to stay in Cuba for more than two months, will have to leave the country in order to apply for a new tourist card. The frequency of flights means you will usually have to stay at least two nights abroad. Cancún (Mexico) and Montego Bay (Jamaica) are the cheapest destinations for a short trip from Havana. Havanatur offers two-night packages to both places for around $300, and organises a new tourist card as part of the deal. You can usually successfully 'launder' your identity a couple of times this way.

Tourist visas. To stay with a Cuban family, you must apply for a tourist visa. This takes at least a week to come through but is otherwise surprisingly uncomplicated. As with a tourist card, the maximum stay given is 30 days, renewable once. You have to register at the local immigration office within 72 hours of your arrival, which must be done with your host. You need to return to this office in order to extend the visa. Holders of ordinary tourist cards are, in theory, not allowed to stay in private residences, but it is not at all clear if and how this rule could ever be enforced.

Other visas. Business travellers and those intending to work or study in Cuba require a visa specific to their category. The business visa requires two photographs and costs $40 or the equivalent; you will need to specify who your sponsor in Cuba is. Business, scientific and study visas are valid for one entry and one exit only. No exit permit is required prior to departure from Cuba.

North American visitors to Cuba. The US authorities restrict visits by American citizens through a series of regulations under the 1917 Trading with the Enemy Act. These are designed to prevent Americans spending money in Cuba. The Treasury Department enforces these rules through the Chief of Licensing, Office of Foreign Assets Control, Department of the Treasury, 1331 G Street, NW

Washington DC 20220 (tel 202-376-0922). This department produces a leaflet giving full details of both the restrictions and the exemptions. The categories of traveller who are free to visit Cuba are as follows:

Journalists with a long-standing interest in Cuba.
Close relatives of Cuban citizens.
Travellers for whom all land expenses in Cuba will be paid by Cubans.
Professional investigators.
Academic researchers with 'Cuba-specific expertise'.

These people are covered by a 'general license' which allows them to spend money freely. It might seem tempting, perhaps, to set yourself up as a journalist or academic in order to circumvent the regulations. In practice, however, you will succeed only if you can prove after a thorough investigation (to the full satisfaction of the Treasury Department) that you are a bona-fide Cuban specialist. It is easier to dodge the rules by entering Cuba via a third country, such as the Bahamas, Canada or Mexico. While offenders risk facing problems on re-entering the United States — having their passport confiscated, being sentenced to a jail term and fined $20,000 — such politically sensitive prosecutions are rare. The most significant recent case was of a game fisherman who led angling tours to the island and was jailed for three months on his return, back in 1990. Still, you may find it preferable to join a tour organised by an operator experienced in sending parties of Americans to Cuba; see page 51. You are restricted to a maximum of $100 per day, excluding the cost of getting to Cuba.

US citizens should take their funds in travellers cheques (not American Express) and cash. Credit cards issued in the USA are not accepted in Cuba. The good news is that US citizens visiting for up to 72 hours require only a driver's licence or voter registration card; but for longer stays you must have a passport and apply through the Cuba Interests Section of the Swiss Embassy in Washington, whose address is 2900 Cathedral Avenue, NW, Washington DC 20008 (tel 202-745-7900). Non-Americans can apply in the USA for a visa or tourist card through the same office.

Americans who enter Cuba illegally may panic if they have their passport stolen. In reality, however, the US Interests Section in Havana (see page 192) deals with such cases as any other consulate would. A new passport will be issued as a matter of course, and they may even help you get money sent from the USA.

CUBAN EMBASSIES

If you need to apply to a Cuban embassy, try to go to the consular deparrment in person. The procedure is quick so long as you produce all the documents for the members in your party, i.e. travel tickets, passports and completed application forms.

The Cuban Embassy and Consulate in the UK occupy the building next to the Shaftesbury Theatre in London's West End. Due to a quirk at the post office, the addresses of the two offices are quite different, even though they share the same premises. The Embassy is at 167 High Holborn, WC1V 6PA, while the entrance to the Consulate — where you obtain a tourist card or visa — is 15 Grape St, WC2H 8DR. The telephone number for both is the same: 0171-240 2488. The Consulate opens 9.30am-12.30pm from Monday to Friday, but note that it is closed on both British and Cuban public holidays.

Other Cuban Embassies/Consulates are located as follows:

Australia
9-15 Bronte Road, Suite 804
Bondi Junction,
Sydney NSW 2026
Tel (2) 9371-5766

Austria
Eitelbergergasse 24
A1130 Wien
Tel (1) 877 8198

Canada
388 Main St
Ottawa K1S 1E3
Tel (613) 563-0141
Fax 540-2066

France
16 rue de Presles
75015 Paris
Tel 4567-5535
Fax 4566-4635

Germany
Kennedy Allee 22-24
5300 Bonn 2, Godesberg
Tel (228) 885-733

Netherlands
Prins Mauritslaan 6
2582 LRR The Hague
Tel (70) 354-1417

Italy
Via Licinia 7
00153 Roma
Tel (6) 575-5984

Mexico
Presidente Masarik 554
Colonia Polanco, México 5 DF
Tel (5) 259-0045

Spain
Paseo de La Habana 194
Madrid
Tel (1) 458-2500

Switzerland
Seminarstr 29
3006 Bern
Tel (31) 444-834/835

IMMIGRATION

Your first encounter with Cuban bureaucracy is likely to be at José Martí airport in Havana or one of the provincial airports. Assuming your documents are in order, and that you are not trying to smuggle contraband, the process should be painless.

Arrival by Air. Immigration procedures for those with the right paperwork are reasonably swift and relaxed. The official checks your passport and tourist card. Sometimes only the latter is stamped, but you cannot rely upon your passport being unscathed. The bottom copy of the tourist card is placed inside your passport, where it should stay.

Complications are likely to arise only if you have no accommodation booked. For this reason alone it is worth booking at least two nights in a hotel, though for particularly obstructive officials even this is not enough. Unlike in the former Soviet Union, the Cuban authorities have never actively discouraged independent travel — you are free to travel where you like — but they have long preferred visitors who arrive on organised tours. An increasing number of independent travellers are staying in private houses rather than in the state-run hotels, which means that much-needed hard currency is ending up in the hands of private individuals rather than those of the government. Plus, strictly speaking, the tourist card does not allow visitors to stay in private accommodation. In some cases, the official may escort you to the tourism desk and force you to book (and pay in cash for) some accommodation on the spot.

Single travellers, in particular, are favourite targets. Certain officials seem to delight in suggesting that the only reason for your visit is the fact that you are having a relationship with a Cuban, implying thereby that you won't be staying in a hotel. In one case, an official threatened to allow a traveller a stay of just two days, a situation the woman in question could reverse only with tears rather than a reasoned argument. Having an open ticket and not much money will not help your case, whereas producing wads of travellers cheques or dollars to indicate how wealthy you are and what a boon you will be to the Cuban economy almost certainly will. If all else fails, try to enlist the help of the Cubatur representative.

Once through Immigration, those on package tours should look for the tour representative who will be waiting beyond Customs. Those not on a fully-fledged package, but with accommodation and transfers pre-paid, will normally be directed to the same representative: groups from different agencies are generally taken into town on the same bus. The representative will take your transport and accommodation vouchers issued by your agent back home, and you are unlikely to see them again. If you plan to travel around on your own and join the group at a later stage, make sure you have both the tour number and the names of the relevant hotels — it is not unusual for groups to be moved from the pre-designated hotel at the last minute.

By Sea. Cruise ship passengers can enter Cuba freely for the duration of the ship's stay. It is sufficient that your name is on the passenger manifest.

People intending to sail to Cuba in a yacht or other pleasure craft need to contact Cubatur at least 72 hours in advance, giving a full list of passengers and crew, details of the vessel (including colour, length, registration number, etc.), port of origin, port of arrival, and ETA. This information should be sent by telex (511 336 or 511 243 TURCU) or by fax (+53 7-33 3104). You can apply for a tourist card on arrival, when you can expect a full immigration and customs check.

CUSTOMS REGULATIONS

Forms exist for tourists to list any valuable items (cameras, cassette players, jewellery, etc.) in their possession, plus details of the amount of money they have with them. But since Cuba has no real system for ensuring visitors take out what they bring in, the use of these forms has more or less been abandoned. Customs officials are often surprisingly lackadaisical; they rarely do more than look at the label on your baggage and give you a slip confirming that your bags have been checked — keep a hold of this ticket and hand it to the person at the exit. While the above procedure is the norm, there are items which if discovered will arouse a certain amount of interest.

Duty-free Allowances. The duty-free limit for cigarettes is 200 (or 250g of tobacco), and for alcoholic liquor two bottles of spirits. In addition you are entitled to import personal effects consistent with your expected length of stay. The regulations also state that you may take in only one camera and five rolls of camera film. Additional rolls are unlikely to be confiscated if discovered (baggage is checked upon arrival by a filmsafe X-ray machine), but be prepared to answer leading questions — particularly if you have more than one camera and are indeed a professional photographer with only a tourist card. In practice, many photographers and journalists enter the country with bags overflowing with equipment and are rarely questioned.

Other permitted equipment includes one video camera (with five cassettes), a portable tape recorder, a typewriter or lap-top computer and a baby's pram.

Forbidden articles. If a Customs official does decide to search your luggage, he or she will be looking for any infringement of duty-free allowances, evidence that you are entering the country for purposes other than those stated on your visa, or for certain prohibited items. The Cuban authorities provide the usual list of forbidden imports, including fire arms and material construed as being immoral, such as pornography. Literature that is blatantly anti-Castro or 'counter-revolutionary' could be confiscated, but customs officials are only likely to give books much attention if they are suspicious of your motives for visiting the country. Previous editions of this book have been imported without problem.

Fruit: like many other countries, Cuba is keen to avoid its agriculture being harmed by imported foreign pests. Customs officials are particularly strong on confiscating fruit. If you've stocked up with nutritious oranges or apples before departing for Cuba, you will inevitably be relieved of them by Customs staff adept at identifying forbidden fruit on the X-ray screens. It will be cheerfully confiscated, and you are probably right in thinking that it is later used to supplement the diet of airport officials.

Such is the preoccupation with fruit that staff sometimes lose interest in the rest of a traveller's luggage. Among the items known to have been imported without question after fruit has been confiscated are a professional digital recording machine complete with microphones, draft manuscripts of this book and several hundred syringes.

Drugs: illegal drugs are not a huge problem for the Cuban authorities, but occasionally attention will be paid to medicines in tourists' luggage. Keep medicines in their original containers, and bring along copies of the relevant prescriptions. Be warned that any opiate derivatives — such as kaolin and morphine — are prohibited, even though they are sold openly in the West. It goes without saying that anyone caught importing marijuana or other illegal narcotics can expect to get into serious trouble.

Export Regulations. Cuban traders, legal or otherwise, may try to sell you products made from endangered species. These include tortoiseshell, black coral, various butterflies and items made from reptile skins. Quite apart from moral considerations, you would offend the Convention on International Trade in Endangered Species (CITES). This international agreement covers all animals at risk. About the only way you can legally export any animal product is by purchasing goods made from a crocodile bred at an official breeding station. You should obtain a certificate stating this which you present to the Customs officer upon arrival in your home country.

If you wish to take something out of the country which you think might arouse the curiosity of Customs, check with the cargo office near the Cubana office in Havana. This is unnecessary for anything that you can buy in a hard-currency store, from a stuffed duckling to a three-foot conga drum. Keep the receipts for all purchases made in Cuba, as you may be asked for them when you leave.

Tourists rarely have to pay for excess baggage on departure. If check-in staff do insist, a 'gift' of chocolate and cigarettes or a tip in dollars will usually persuade them to waive the charge.

There is a limit of 200 on the number of cigars which may be exported from Cuba — but this is higher than the number allowed in free of duty by most other countries.

Works of Art: you are not allowed to export a painting or other work of art unless it was bought from a state gallery or shop. Anyone buying a picture direct from the artist runs the risk of having it confiscated (without compensation) at customs. Make sure you have a certificate of purchase and the receipt, which any gallery should give you automatically.

Returning Home. US citizens who have visited illegally may encounter problems if the passport has been stamped. The good news is that Americans are now allowed to bring in up to 100 Cuban cigars, providing they travel direct from Cuba to the USA (i.e. not via a third country). Non-Americans transitting via the USA may import up to 50; the same limit applies in Canada and countries of the European Union, including the UK. Alternatively you could import 200 cigarettes to Canada or the EU, although it is hard to imagine anyone wanting to take home ten packs of Cuban 'Popular' cigarettes. The limit on liquor is one litre of spirits and two litres of wine. Other goods to a value of £150 can be imported free of duty into the EU; if you should manage to spend more than that on souvenirs (unlikely), excess items will have duty of 10% or more imposed, with VAT levied on the total.

billete	bank note	*esterlina*	pounds sterling
bolsa negra	black market	*medio*	5 centavo coin
cambio	currency exchange	*mercado negro*	black market
cheque de viajero	travellers cheque	*moneda efectivo*	hard currency (cash)
(pron. check-ay)		*moneda nacional*	Cuban currency
cuenta	bill		(pesos)
dinero	money	*recibo*	receipt
divisa	hard currency (i.e. dollars)	*tarjeta de crédito*	credit card

Dealing with money in Cuba is a struggle. By knowing the basics about how the system works, however, you can approach financial matters with greater confidence and possibly cut your costs too. It is perfectly possible for you to spend a fortnight on the island without handling a single Cuban peso. The authorities have been remarkably successful in diverting foreigners from using the local peso economy. As a result, Westerners must pay for most things with US dollars. Only if you dabble in the parallel market or frequent the new private markets are you likely to spend significant amounts of pesos, though you can equally well use hard currency in both cases. The dollar was legalised in 1993, enabling Cubans for the first time to use the currency that is infinitely more useful than their own.

Living Costs. In an average three-star hotel a single room costs $25 and a double $35. Breakfast is usually another four or five dollars. A meal out at a dollar restaurant should set you back $10-15 per person. Drinks in hard-currency bars are about $1-2, whether you have a beer or a cocktail. Travel costs are negligible if you manage to get a seat on an ordinary bus; but since tourists must rely increasingly on taxis, hired cars, flights and organised day trips to get around, travelling expenses can use up a sizeable proportion of your daily allowance. Independent travellers should expect to spend around $50 a day for basic expenses, though if you budget carefully, stay in private accommodation, buy food from markets, etc., you should be able to survive on about $35.

Be warned that most visitors spend more money than they planned to, particularly in Havana, where prices are higher than elsewhere. In addition, if you meet Cubans that you would like to spend time with, you will have to pay for everything; the price of a couple of beers to the average Cuban is the equivalent of a month's salary.

What Money to Take. The US dollar is the only hard currency worth taking to Cuba. Because of the problems in obtaining funds in an emergency, you should take plenty of dollars in several forms. Due to the economic embargo, American Express cheques and charge cards are not accepted in Cuba.

Cash: it is worth taking a larger proportion of dollars in cash than you might on a normal holiday. Take low denominations ($1, $5 and $10) to avoid the recurring problem of a shortage of change. Given the amount of counterfeit currency in circulation, many hotels and shops now have machines to test for false dollar bills. Many a visitor has traipsed around tourist shops and hotels trying to find somebody able (or willing) to break down a $50 or $100 bill. One place you can spend high-denomination bills is at a Cupet service station, but you will have your passport details laboriously copied out. The quality of the counterfeit notes is generally so bad that you shouldn't have too much trouble recognising them. If you're not happy with a bank note someone has given to you, ask for another.

Travellers Cheques: the safest way to carry money is in the form of travellers cheques, issued by Visa or Thomas Cook. The unfortunate traveller who forgets that American Express cheques are not accepted will have to make use of Asistur, a government agency that cashes Amex cheques for a heavy 10% commission.

You can use dollar travellers cheques to pay for most goods and services. Change should be provided in dollars, assuming the enterprise has some. This is the easiest way to generate cash from travellers cheques. Otherwise, tourist hotels should be able to cash travellers cheques for dollars, though some will plead shortage of cash and refuse to do so. To avail yourself of this facility you are supposed to be a guest of the hotel in question, but this is seldom checked. While most hotels charge 4% commission, at a bank the rate is more likely to be 2 or 3%. The international branches of the Banco Nacional de Cuba in Havana and Santiago de Cuba are most used to dealing with foreigners, but the Banco Financiero Internacional (BFI), with a growing number of branches throughout the island, also provides a money exchange service. Note that a torn travellers cheque will be refused wherever you try to cash it.

Most issuers of travellers cheques claim to be able to make refunds for lost or stolen cheques anywhere in the world, but this is not usually feasible in Cuba. You will have to wait until you return home or move on to another country before being reimbursed.

Credit Cards: take at least one credit or charge card to Cuba. Not only are cards now widely accepted in tourist establishments throughout the island, but you can also use your credit card to withdraw cash at branches of BFI. While cards issued in the United States, including American Express, are unusable, those issued in other countries, such as Diners Club, Access and Visa are welcome. Take a couple of pieces of plastic if you can, because some enterprises in Cuba impose a limit of $250 on the value of any one transaction.

All dollar hotels and tourist shops, and many restaurants catering for foreigners, theoretically accept credit cards. In practice, however, do not rely on this facility. Sometimes the supply of credit card vouchers may be exhausted, requiring you to pay with cash or travellers cheques. Even if vouchers are available, allow an extra 15 minutes to check out. The processing of a credit card still seems to baffle some staff. Furthermore Cuba's isolation means it has no access to on-line card authorisation services. Credit card transactions are processed through Mexico, and card numbers have to be checked laboriously against a printed list of stolen cards.

Emergency Cash. If your credit cards or travellers cheques are stolen, try to get in touch with your embassy in Havana. The British Embassy, for example, has a list of numbers for reporting stolen cards and cheques. The Asistur agency, which has branches in all the main tourist centres, is supposed to help tourists in emergencies, but in reality can offer only limited assistance. If you are in Havana, you can cancel your credit card at the BFI office in the Habana Libre Hotel.

The British Embassy will, with some reluctance, cash a cheque for up to £100 backed by a UK cheque guarantee card. This will not be enough to pay for a ticket out of the country, so if you're entirely destitute you'll have no option but to be repatriated and surrender your passport upon arrival back home; you won't get it back until you have paid the Foreign Office. Repatriation is unlikely, however, until all other avenues — such as finding someone at home to pay for your journey — have been explored. See page 137 for information on insurance.

If you need to have money sent out from home, it is best to do this via the Banco Financiero Internacional. Money from the UK should be sent in pounds sterling via either the Havana International Bank Ltd, 20 Ironmonger Street, London EC2V 8EY (0171-606 0781) or Midland Bank at 110-114 Cannon Street, London EC4N 6AA. The BFI branch most used to dealing with such transactions is in the Habana Libre hotel, Calles 25 y L, Vedado (tel 33-3429, fax 33-3795).

MONEY IN CUBA

As in many less developed countries, Cuba has a currency whose value is kept artificially high. The Cuban authorities maintain that the average foreign holidaymaker will have no need for Cuban pesos at all, the theory being that every enterprise that the Westerner is likely to encounter accepts hard currency. Most Cuban enterprises on the tourist circuit insist upon payment in US dollars at parity with the peso (US$1 = 1 peso). This means that for an air ticket from Havana to the Isle of Youth, for example, Cubans pay 16 pesos while you have to pay US$16.

Before tourism really took off in Cuba, foreigners could occasionally persuade Cuban enterprises to let them pay in local currency rather than US dollars. This is no longer the case and you will find it virtually impossible to use pesos to pay for 'tourist related services', including taxis, meals, hotels and most drinks. The re-introduction of private farmers' markets has increased the opportunities for spending pesos, although stall holders will also accept (and indeed prefer) dollars at roughly the equivalent price. If you try to use pesos elsewhere, you'll generally be asked politely but firmly to pay in dollars. You often have to make a special effort in order to use pesos. Many visitors simply can't be bothered.

Traditionally, the only things you can buy for pesos on a regular basis include stamps, a shave, ice cream, coffee, books and newspapers, records, a trip to the cinema and local bus fares — though any of these items bought in a hotel or tourist shop must be paid for in dollars.

Pesos. The local currency is the peso, divided into 100 centavos. The symbol used to represent a peso is $, the same as for the US dollar. To distinguish the two currencies, pesos are sometimes called *moneda nacional* (MN) and dollars *moneda efectivo* or USD. To confuse matters, however, most Cubans refer to both currencies as 'pesos'. To clarify what is being demanded, you should ask whether they mean 'pesos cubanos' or 'divisa'.

Prices in this book which are quoted in pesos are for items available for local currency; where prices appear in US dollars, you are expected to pay in hard currency.

Notes and coins: notes are issued in denominations of 1 peso (olive green), 3 pesos (red), 5 pesos (green), 10 pesos (brown), 20 pesos (blue) and 50 pesos (purple). Coins are as follows: 1 centavo, 2 centavos, 5 centavos, 20 centavos, 40 centavos, 1 peso and 3 pesos (there is no 10 or 50 centavo coin).

Most peso bills have been in circulation for years and are often in a terrible state. Cubans in the street may try to sell you red three-peso notes (discontinued) or the newer three-peso coins, both of which feature Che Guevara — not a bad present for a friend who's a fan. Hard currency shops sell these and other banknotes at even more outrageous prices.

The Convertible Peso. Don't be alarmed if you are given as change something which looks like Monopoly money. The government issues hard-currency convertible peso notes (in denominations of 1, 5, 10, 20 and 50) and coins denominated in centavos. These are on a par with US dollars and cents. Since Cuba has no economic links with the USA, it has problems maintaining a 'float' of American currency. Therefore it has made some of its own. These 'convertible' pesos are accepted in lieu of dollars but they are not as yet convertible on the world market and are valueless outside Cuba. Don't worry about the possibility of being stuck with them; you can change them back to dollars at hotel reception desks or the bureau de change at the airport on the way out.

At the time of going to press, convertible pesos were new enough to be easily distinguished from the ordinary (less valuable) kind. Given a few more months, however, and the two lots of banknotes are likely to look dangerously similar. Be sure to check your change carefully.

The Official Line. Cubans can change pesos for dollars at official Cadeca bureaux de change, but few bother; since 'dollarisation', the parallel currency market has become both stable and more or less legal. It is much quicker and easier for the average Cuban to change money with friends or a black-market trader than to track down a bureau de change while it is open and going through all the attendant bureaucracy.

Foreigners are encouraged to change money at the official (and ludicrous) rate of 1 ordinary peso to 1 dollar — at the airport upon arrival, at hotels or at branches of the Banco Nacional de Cuba. Bank opening hours are 8am-noon and 1-3pm from Monday to Friday. If you really want to change money legally then try not to use a bank. The service at hotel desks is much quicker and queues shorter; you may be asked to show your hotel identification card. Rates are identical at all official exchange desks. Some foreigners have succeeded in changing money at an exchange house, and it seems likely that this will become easier with time. Meanwhile, the parallel market (see below) will remain the main source of pesos for visitors. Since it became legal for Cubans to hold dollars, the need for local currency has diminished, but there are still people who refuse to accept foreign funds.

You cannot change more than 10 pesos back into hard currency at the end of your trip, even if your receipts show that you have acquired more than that officially. This presents an ideal opportunity to take home a novel — but illegal — souvenir: it is forbidden to import or export Cuban pesos, though checks are rare.

The Parallel Market. The government's recent economic strategies have managed to increase the value of the Cuban peso dramatically, so dealing on the parallel market is not nearly as profitable for travellers as it was in 1994, for example, when $1 could buy you 100 pesos. By the end of 1995, the value of the dollar had dropped to around 20 pesos. Travellers are no longer approached by young Cubans looking to change money; these days they concentrate on trying to flog black-market cigars or cassettes rather than pesos.

Opinions differ on the morality of using the parallel market. Some believe it is wrong to break the laws of a country you are visiting, and that changing money other than at the official rate adds to Cuba's economic woes. Other travellers feel strongly that they should make full use of the parallel market to try to ensure that some of their money benefits the Cuban people directly rather than letting it simply be swallowed up into the state economy. The majority of visitors just want to live as cheaply as possible. The distortions caused by an unrealistic exchange rate would disappear if the peso were made fully convertible for foreigners, and life would become a great deal simpler. The penalty for illegal currency transactions is a term in prison for Cubans, while foreigners are usually just given a telling off. In the history of this guidebook, however, no traveller to Cuba has ever reported being caught by the police.

If you are tempted to play the parallel market in foreign currency, choose carefully with whom you trade. Dealing with people that you have got to know (and trust) is the safest option. They should know the going rate and will get you the best deal. Markets are often a good place to change dollars for pesos, since stallholders should have plenty of local currency to spare.

If you do business with established street dealers, you cannot expect to be given the top rate, and there is also a danger that you will be ripped off. If you feel you have to deal on the street, choose an individual and try to make sure he has no accomplices. Ideally there should be two of you. The best transaction is as follows. Firstly, agree how much you are going to exchange and the rate. The dealer should give your companion the pesos to count. He or she should check them, then move slightly away (out of grabbing range). You then hand over the dollars. To further minimise the chances that you'll be conned, you should follow these rules:

1. Never try to change more than $10; if you are going to be ripped off, better that it is for a small amount. And trying to spend more that $10 in pesos in a fortnight, was, at the time of writing, quite a challenge.
2. Keep the amount that you want to change in a separate pocket. It is foolish to reveal where all your funds are kept.
3. If, after agreeing to change money, you feel threatened, don't hesitate to pull out of the transaction.
4. Avoid being lured into a dark alley to change money. Dealers routinely choose somewhere discreet for the handover, but some may be out to mug you.
5. Count the pesos carefully; in particular, check that you're not being fobbed off with one peso notes, which when grubby are difficult to distinguish from five peso bills.

With all the care in the world, you cannot always avoid being cheated. Favourite tricks include grabbing at the dollars as soon as you produce them (one hapless Westerner on the Malecón promenade in Havana held on tight, and was left clutching one worthless half of a $20 note); excessive haste, to make you panic and hand over the dollars before you've checked the pesos; and the old chestnut of shouting 'policía' and running off leaving you with insufficient pesos or perhaps none at all.

OTHER MONEY MATTERS

Bills. Some Cubans show worrying alacrity at creative accounting. Always check your bill carefully, whether in a hotel or restaurant. In hotels where you keep an account during your stay, ask to see all the bills before paying the final account at the end. In restaurants, stand your ground if the wrong order is brought: what they bring is almost invariably more expensive than what you originally ordered.

Tipping. Tipping is no longer illegal in Cuba and has become par for the course with the growth in tourism. There are no hard-and-fast rules except that you should only tip in dollars. If you leave a few excess pesos on the table after a meal in a dollar restaurant, your waiter is likely to be more insulted than grateful. In capitalist countries, it is common practice to pay at least 10% of the bill as a tip. This is generous in Cuba. Use your discretion, but remember that waiters should be rewarded according to the quality of service and not the food, which is hardly their fault. When drinking at a bar, it is usual to leave a little loose change for either the bartender or, if you are being served at a table, the waiter or waitress. If you eat in a private restaurant (see page 103), there is no need to to tip unless you wish to show particular gratitude for a good meal. You might also like to tip the musicians who entertain you while you eat. You may grow sick and tired of this uninvited entertainment by the end of your stay, but the musicians are often very good (too good to be doing what they do), and enjoy doing requests. Giving a tip is optional but will be greatly welcomed.

The other people most accustomed to being tipped are hotel porters and taxi drivers. With cab drivers, it is easiest simply to round up the fare to the nearest dollar. If you hand over a large bill in payment, make it clear that you expect change. Do not, as you might in the West, press a $20 note into their hands to settle a $5 ride with a courteous 'Thank you' since some drivers may interpret this as a particularly generous tip.

During your trip, you are also likely to pay out numerous informal tips, in the form of cash or gifts. Faced with severe financial problems, Cubans are forced to seek remuneration for many small services.

Begging. This is a fast-growing phenomenon in Cuba's main tourist centres. In Havana, schoolchildren gather outside the hotels, ready to pounce on anyone who ventures outside. They ask for money first, then ball-point pens or chewing gum if no change is forthcoming. Keep some coins handy, either to give to the most deserving or get rid of the most persistent. Otherwise, keep a supply of sweets or chewing gum. If you give Cubans local currency, they will probably just laugh at you and reject the offer.

Communications

apartado (de correos)	post office box	*pizarra*	switchboard
buzón	letter box	*por avión*	air mail
canal	channel (TV or radio)	*por palabra*	per word
centro telefónico	telephone exchange	*postal*	postcard
correo	post	*recogida*	(postal) collection
correos aérea	air mail	*revista*	magazine
larga distancia	long distance	*sello*	stamp
llamada por cobrar	collect (reverse-charge) call	*semanal*	weekly
allá, llamada a pagar		*sobre*	envelope
allá		*telefax*	fax
casa de correos	post office	*teléfono*	telephone
novella	soap opera	*telegrama*	telegram
paquete	parcel	*tarifa*	rate
periódico	newspaper		

All communications within Cuba are in the hands of the Ministerio de Comunicaciones, whose blue *MC* logo adorns mail boxes, post offices and telephone offices. It is not one of the world's most efficient post and telecommunications organisations. Most telephone lines, when you eventually get through, vary between tolerable and inaudible, which is why everyone shouts into the receiver. The phone service provided in hotels and other hard-currency enterprises makes life easy for tourists, but everyone must use the same postal system, which is amazingly slow and unpredictable. Cards posted to addresses abroad can take anything from three weeks to three months, particularly if sent from the provinces. Even telegrams, the best form of communication whether within Cuba or abroad, are unreliable when sent from anywhere but Havana.

TELEPHONE

Just as many Cuban motorists rely upon pre-revolutionary American vehicles, so the Republic's telecommunications depend largely upon a system installed before 1959. Technologically, much of the network is still in the Stone Age. It is difficult to make anything but local calls, and even these are fraught with problems. Storms can make the telephone network seize up more or less completely, since rainwater gets into the machinery and causes havoc. Repair and development work is painfully slow, though investment from abroad has brought some improvement, particularly in Havana. Many offices and institutions, including hotels and embassies, have two or three numbers to choose from. Numbers beginning with the digits 33, are those most likely to work, since these are operated on a separate 'hard-currency' telephone network specifically intended for business operating in dollars.

Calling Cuba from Abroad. At present foreign subscribers can dial direct only to Havana. To call a number in the capital, use the international access code (00 from the UK), the country code 53, plus the code for Havana, 7, and the number. Thus to call the British Embassy in Havana from the UK, dial 00 53 7 33-8071; from Canada, dial 011 53 7 33-8071. If you get a ringing tone it doesn't necessarily mean that a telephone is ringing somewhere in Cuba. After you've held on for a while, try again. To call anywhere outside Havana, add the dialling code shown on page 66 and the subscriber's number.

Time. Cuba maintains the same time as the rest of the Caribbean: Eastern Standard Time in winter and Eastern Daylight Time (one hour later) in summer. This is five hours behind British time, i.e. noon in London is 7am in Havana. However, because the clocks change on different days, there are periods between late March and late April, and between early and late October, when Cuba is only four hours behind.

The 24-hour clock is never used in Cuba; all times are quoted as 'am' or 'pm'.

Tones. Cuba's telephones use the same system of tones as the rest of the Caribbean and North America, i.e. a constant buzz or tone before you begin to dial, long rings with even longer pauses when you connect, or short, frequent beeps if the line is engaged. You will also hear the continuous 'number unobtainable' tone more often than you might care to. Alternatively, you can hang on for minutes hearing nothing but static. If a number seems to be permanently engaged, the most likely explanation is that the telephone is out of order.

Payphones. The older variety of public telephones take 5 centavo coins and, in the rare case that one still works, can be used only for local calls. They are fairly common in towns, often bolted to the walls of buildings. Sound insulation is poor. Pick up the receiver and insert a 5c coin before dialling. When the light starts flashing as you approach three minutes, insert another. Often the warning light is broken, so if you're in doubt put in more coins than you expect to use; unused coins are returned.

Newer payphones have three slots, one for 5c coins and the other two for 10c and 20c pieces. They may be used for local and long-distance calls, but not for international calls. For local calls, insert up to six 5c coins. Long-distance calls require 20c coins, again with a maximum of six in each slot. You can top up the coins once they start falling through.

To avoid potential frustration with a payphone, in Havana you can also try going to a newspaper kiosk. Most of these kiosks rarely have any periodicals to sell, but some remain open to provide a telephone service. In general, the telephones are good only for local calls, for which the normal charge is 5 centavos.

The latest revolution in communications has been the introduction of phone cards, which can be used for both national and international calls. The new phones, currently found in just a handful of hotels in Havana, are sure to appear all over the city and eventually nationwide. Telephone cards are available to the value of $10, $25 and $45. Calls to Europe cost $5.59 per minute.

Public Telephone Stations. Every town of any size has a *centro telefónico*. A typical one looks like a waiting room, with a number of poorly insulated booths where calls are made. In some small provincial towns you may be able to pay in pesos; as a foreigner, however, normally you will be asked to pay in dollars, or else you'll be sent to the nearest hotel.

Calling from a public telephone station can require huge reserves of patience, particularly if you are brave enough to try calling abroad, but is rewarding when you succeed. The operators rarely speak English, but this is not usually a problem since all you need do is write down the number and wait. Eventually you should be directed to a cubicle. Pick up the receiver and start shouting.

Private telephones. The cheapest option of all is to call from a Cuban home. Local calls from private phones are free in Cuba and even calling long-distance is very cheap. It is not always possible to make international reverse-charge calls from private phones.

Long-distance calls. Codes vary from one province to another, but the most common ones are as follows, listed by province alphabetically:

Camagüey	**Las Tunas**
Camagüey (city) — 332	Province — 31
Santa Lucia — 32	**Matanzas**
Ciego de Avila	Girón — 59
Ciego de Avila (city) — 33	Matanzas — 52
Moron — 5	Playa Larga — 59
Cienfuegos	Varadero — 5
Cienfuegos (city) — 432	Other cities — 51
Other cities — 43	**Pinar del Rio**
Granma	Pinar del Rio — 82
Province (Bayamo and Manzanillo) — 23	Vinales — 8
Guantánamo	**Sancti Spíritus**
Province (inc Baracoa) — 21	Trinidad — 419
Havana	Other cities — 41
Havana city — 7	**Santiago de Cuba**
Holguín	Santiago (city) — 226
Province (Banes, Moa, Guardalavaca) — 24	**Villa Clara**
Rest of province — 22	Santa Clara — 422
Isle of Youth	Other cities — 42
Island (Nueva Gerona) — 61	

Within Cuba you can call certain parts of the western half of the island direct. For areas not served by direct dialling, you have no choice but to go through the operator. If you are calling from outside a hotel, dial 155 for the operator. You can expect to wait anything from two minutes to two hours for the connection to be made and the operator to call you back. After the first thirty minutes, call again; a little friendly chivvying often helps.

Calls from Hotels. In reality, most people take the easy option and call from a hotel. You can sometimes dial direct from your room (dial 9 for an outside line), but in many places you must still go through the operator. If you are not a guest, go into any hotel and just ask someone at reception to get the number for you; they will direct you to a telephone in the lobby. A deposit of $20 or more will be requested for interational calls.

Local calls: hotels in Havana charge anything from $0.25 to $0.50 per minute for a local call, compared with just 5 centavos from a public payphone. If you have a string of local numbers to call, you should find a payphone in the street or look for the nearest kiosk.

International Calls: hotel operators can get international lines through in a matter of seconds, but the rates are high: $5.50 per minute to Europe, Africa, Australasia and most other destinations, $2.50 per minute to North America. Furthermore, the line sometimes cuts out, so if you have to redial several times during one call, the price escalates dramatically.

Most hotels will let non-residents make a call abroad. If all you want to do is ask someone to phone you back, having made the first call home, let the hotel operator or receptionist know that you are expecting someone to ring.

Calling Collect. The Cuban authorities like to benefit from the money made from international telephone calls, and it is therefore very difficult to make reverse charge calls. This facility is not permitted from any 'hard-currency' number (which begin with the digits 33), thereby eliminating most of the hotels at a stroke.

Useful Numbers. In theory, each province publishes a telephone directory (*Directorio Telefónico*), but none has been issued for years and few people have ever clapped eyes on one. Your best way to find out a number is to ask the operator, or dial directory inquiries on 113.

To summon the police, dial 116; for the fire brigade, 115. The number for the ambulance service varies, depending on location.

TELEX AND FAX

Hotel reservations, flight bookings and car rentals have a greater chance of materialising if you request them by telex and keep a copy. Telexes are most easily sent from hotels. Top hotels have fax facilities, but they are not nearly as widespread as the ubiquitous telex. Since fax transmissions use ordinary telephone lines, the service is not reliable except to or from '33' numbers. Charges are as for telephone calls, plus $1 extra, i.e. $6.50 per minute from most hotels.

TELEGRAMS

Telegrams are used by many ordinary Cubans as a cheap and effective means of communication. Every post office can handle them, although it is advantageous to know Spanish in order to decipher the complex *Solicitud de Telegrama* form.

Cables can be sent abroad from post offices at a rate of 49 centavos per word, with a minimum of twelve words. The rate for the USA is just 20 centavos per word. (Some post offices may oblige you to pay the equivalent in hard currency, and this is certainly the case if you go to a hotel.) The service to most destinations is swift if it works, which seems to be in about 50% of cases. Note that international cables sent to addresses in the UK are slowed up by being consigned to the regular mail service upon arrival in Britain.

MAIL

The long hours kept by post offices — often 8am to 10pm — used to be a boon for travellers. Such working hours have proved unsustainable during the Special Period, however, so avoid going on stamp-buying trips at twilight. As with other Cuban enterprises, queues are longest at weekends.

Larger offices have several counters. If you want to send a telegram or buy stamps, look for the signs *Telegramas* and *Sellos* respectively. Be warned, though, that post offices sometimes run out of stamps; buy all you think you might need as soon as you're able. Lick a stamp bought in a local (peso) post office and you'll try in vain to stick it onto your postcard. Instead you must use the glue provided in pots on the counter. You won't have this problem if you buy stamps from a hotel shop.

Posting a letter within Cuba costs 5 centavos. Addresses should carry a five-digit post code, just like an American zip code. Cuban cards and envelopes often have a box in which to write it. If you don't know the post code, you could go to a post office where the staff may or may not be able to find it for you. Frankly, though, mail takes an unseeming length of time to arrive whether it has a postcode or not.

An air mail letter to the UK or elsewhere in Europe costs 75 centavos, while a postcard is 50 centavos. Stamps sold in hard-currency shops cost the equivalent of the peso price in dollars, which is a very good reason for buying at an ordinary post office with cheap pesos — otherwise you could be paying around 20 times more than you need. Aerogrammes to anywhere cost 50 centavos, but they are hard to find. If you plan on writing long letters, take your own writing paper and envelopes, of which there is a national shortage in Cuba. As with the local mail, overseas delivery times are long, with some letters known to have taken nearly a year to reach Europe. In January 1996, this had shortened to two weeks, but it is not without reason that Cubans ask tourists to post letters for them when they get home. In theory, letters and postcards can reach Canada in ten days and Europe in 14 but these should be regarded as the minimum, and apply only to items posted in the capital. All foreign mail goes through Havana; from far-off or isolated parts of Cuba it can take a week to get that far. Even from one side of Havana to the other takes a good few days. The best bet is to post everything almost as soon as you arrive or shortly before your departure — preferably from a post box in a hotel or at the airport.

To increase the chances of your postcards arriving before the end of the millennium, use the Spanish version of the name of destination countries:

England	Inglaterra
Great Britain	Gran Bretaña (although it may be safer to use Inglaterra, even if the destination is Wales or Scotland)
Ireland	Irlanda
France	Francia
Germany	Alemania
Spain	España
Switzerland	Suiza
USA	Estados Unidos or EE.UU.
New Zealand	Nueva Zelanda

The Spanish names for Canada and Australia are unchanged (though strictly speaking the first should have an accent on the last syllable).

Parcels. Stringent rules govern the wrapping of parcels. Take whatever it is you want to despatch unwrapped to a post office, where the problem should be taken away from you in a flurry of hands, brown paper and string. However, given the temptation that a parcel inevitably provides for impoverished post office employees, consider sending parcels via a courier: see below. If you are determined to use the regular postal service, send only low-value goods — either to avoid problems with paying duty or so as not to be too disappointed if they go astray. The risk of parcels being 'lost' is even greater when sending a package into Cuba. This is not only because somebody may like the look of it, but because deliveries are decidedly unreliable: Cubans living in a smart part of town, such as Miramar in Havana, are more likely to receive their post than people with an address in a poor area such as Colón.

Couriers. DHL has operated in Cuba for some time and represents the most reliable method of sending parcels or documents to or from the island. It has its main office in Havana (Avenida 1era y 42, Miramar; tel 33-1578 or 29-0700; fax 33-1578), with provincial branches in Varadero (Avenida 1era y 64), Cienfuegos (Hotel Jagua), Guardalavaca (Hotel Atlántico), Holguín (Hotel Pernik), Nueva Gerona (Calle 39 no. 2201) and Santiago de Cuba (Hotel Santiago). Some sample rates for sending a packet to Britain are as follows: $73 for 1kg, $137 for 5kg, $197 for 10kg.

Poste Restante. There is no post office service for foreigners wishing to receive mail from abroad. Instead, ask people to write to a particular hotel — ideally one you're planning to stay at, though this is not essential. They should mark the letter *esperar* ('to await the arrival of') and address it as in this example:

Esperar PRESLEY, Sr. E.   (use Sra. if the addressee is female)
Hotel Habana Libre
Calle 23 entre L y M   (Street 23 between Avenues L and M)
Vedado   (district)
Ciudad de La Habana   (the city of Havana rather than the province)
Cuba

Alternatively your embassy may hold mail for you; see page 192 for addresses. Bear in mind that mail sent to Cuba takes at least as long to get there as cards sent in the opposite direction.

MEDIA

Newspapers. The shortage of materials coupled with minimal freedom of the press means that you are unlikely to spend much time engrossed in a paper. Newspaper kiosks rarely have anything to sell these days, and when they do receive a delivery they sell out in a flash. Even in Havana you'll find little for sale outside the hotels.

In what other country of the world would a newspaper called 'Grandma' be taken seriously? Yet *Granma*, the local equivalent of *Pravda*, toes the party line with an enthusiasm redolent of the Soviet press during the stagnant years under Brezhnev. You are much more likely to find Castro's speeches quoted verbatim than hard foreign news. Interviews in *Granma* are invariably published in question-and-answer form with no attempt at analysis. International news is comprised largely of agency reports; understandably it has a pronounced non-aligned/Third World stance, and news of Europe is scarce. *Granma* is published daily except Sundays and costs 20 centavos ($0.20 in a dollar shop). The paper shortage means that it rarely consists of more than eight pages, and on occasions is reduced to just four.

The trades unions' daily, *Trabajadores,* is little better than *Granma* and has an overdose of articles about the sugar industry and agriculture; but anything that costs just 15 centavos is worth a browse. Its editorial page has occasionally tackled thorny economic issues, but always tempered by great restraint. The other main paper is *Juventud Rebelde*, the organ of the Young Communists Party (UJC). Formerly daily papers, both now appear only once or twice a week.

All the forementioned newspapers are in theory circulated nationally, but they rarely reach the provinces; here you are more likely to see only a local paper, which will be cheaper and even worse than the national dailies. In the larger tourist centres, however, you may find the weekly international edition of *Granma,* published on Saturdays. This is a digest of the highlights of the week's news, with a bias towards foreign readers and an increasing preponderance of tourism or business-related articles. It appears in English, French and Portuguese as well as Spanish and costs $0.50.

Magazines. Given the shortage of paper, it is perhaps surprising that you can still find a choice of magazines. The best general read is *Bohemia,* with articles on a range of subjects including culture, society and current affairs. None of the journalism could be described as incisive, but it is considerably better than the turgid writing in *Cuba Internacional,* a monthly magazine containing dauntingly dull and fawning articles on political, social and economic matters. The bi-monthly magazine *Prisma* appears in English as well as Spanish and includes articles of more general interest to visitors. A recent edition included pieces on Old Havana, Cuba's search for oil, the National Assembly and Dulce Maria Loynaz (Cuba's most famous poetess). It also has a regular food column by Nitza Villapol, Cuba's answer to Britain's great television cook, Fanny Craddock, plus a few cartoons. For humour, however, you would do better to buy *Palante.* The most recurrent themes are bicycles, food and sex, some of the few issues considered safe subjects for satirical treatment.

Cuba boasted some excellent cultural periodicals before the Revolution, and these are still what the country does best. They are not always easy to get hold of, but are well worth reading for the insight they give into contemporary Cuban culture. Most easily available is *Revolución y Cultura,* a bi-monthly magazine devoted to the arts and literature. The *Gaceta de Cuba,* published by UNEAC (the Union of Writers and Artists), contains not only articles and reviews but also excerpts of new writing.

Somos Jovenes caters to a young readership. Printed on good quality paper and full of advertisements (mostly by Cuba's new joint ventures), it looks much more like a Western magazine than its grown-up equivalents. As well as featuring articles on Cuban youth's favourite rock stars, it deals with social issues such as Aids in a surprisingly frank manner.

Foreign Press. The Cuban government may have spent millions of pesos trying to block the transmission of North American propaganda via TV Martí (see below), but you'll have no difficulty in picking up North American newspapers. In the top-notch hotels, you can buy *USA Today* as well as a whole range of capitalist magazines from *Time* to *The Economist.* For lighter reading, you can choose from *Elle, Vogue* and many other North American and European fashion magazines. Spanish-speakers should look out for a magazine called *Contrapunto,* which is published in Miami and focusses on Latin America and particularly Cuba — from a surprisingly pro-Castroist standpoint.

Radio. Southern Florida's radio stations provide all the Western news and music networks you could wish for, although the signal deteriorates the further you get from the USA. Reception is best on the north coast around Havana. Try one of the following:

WOW-FM (92.5) or WAIL-FM (99.5) for rock
US-1FM (103.5) for oldies and news, WMRZ-AM (790) for oldies only
WCTH-FM (98.5) for easy listening
WTKN-AM (580) for news.

It can be an odd feeling to cruise the last bastion of Marxism in your rental car, listening to commercials for Domino's Pizza Delivery (and it may also make you feel hungry). You might also be able to pick up Radio Bahamas on 1540 AM; the International Hour, 6-7pm daily, includes a number of reports from BBC correspondents. Further southeast, you move into territory covered by Jamaican stations such as RKO (650 AM, oldies), RJR (580 AM, talk) and JVC

Radio 1 (700 AM, talk). Around the US naval base at Guantánamo, tune to the American Forces Network (AFN) on 1340 AM or 102.1 FM for rock music and AP network news on the hour.

An American radio station, Radio Martí, was set up in 1985 to beam criticism of the Castro regime to Cuba. The use of the name of the country's national hero (not to mention the propaganda) was regarded by the government as an insult. People in Cuba seem to appreciate the station mainly as a source of news about friends and relatives in Florida — there is a daily slot during which Miami Cubans can send messages to their families back home.

The main official radio stations in Cuba are as follows:

Cadena Habana: Cuban music and information (in Spanish and English).
Enciclopedia: classical, Latin and jazz music.
Havana Cuba: beams the Castro message to the world in nine languages, including English. Since transmissions are intended for audiences outside Cuba, it is easier to pick up programmes in Houston or Harare than in Havana.
Progreso: Cuban music, interviews and magazine programmes.
Rebelde: wide range of music, including American rock, news and interviews.
Reloj: 24-hour news channel made unbearable by the permanent ticking of a clock in the background.
Taíno: Cuba's own 24-hour tourism station (AM in Havana and Varadero, FM in Oriente). It plays predominantly schmaltzy middle-of-the-road material, interspersed with information and news, sometimes in English.

The best source of informed and impartial news from around the world is the BBC World Service. Broadcasts are beamed to Cuba and the Caribbean on short wave. The monstrous 1950s Soviet wirelesses found in some hotel rooms can usually pick up the signals adequately, but if you want to be certain then take a good short-wave receiver. The best time for reception is, inconveniently, in the early hours of the morning, Cuban time. For further information on frequencies, call the BBC Transmission Planning Unit in London on 0171-257 2685.

Television. Cuban television is surprisingly sophisticated, both technically and artistically. MTV could learn a thing or two from Cuba's music television. The Sunday night show *Mi Salsa* is a mix of breezy live performances and cleverly shot videos. Other music favourites are *Sabadazo* on Saturday night, in which a guest band — usually one of Cuba's top salsa groups — shares the studio with a group of comics skilled in the art of improvisation. Home-grown music programmes are generally a better prospect than the imported shows (a surprising number of which are pirated from the US) or worthy educational programmes. To ensure that Cubans do not waste working time watching the box, Cuban television is broadcast only after six o'clock in the evening. At weekends, the scheduling allows for a few morning shows.

The two national networks are Tele Rebelde and Cuba Visión. The former concentrates on educational and sports (especially baseball and boxing) programmes, while Cuba Visión broadcasts a whole mix of programmes: officially sanctioned news and documentaries, films, music shows, arts programmes (which are sometimes excellent), and the all-important soap operas. There are usually two soaps on the go at any one time — one imported (usually from Brazil) and one Cuban — which the local people follow avidly. The Saturday film, broadcast on Cuba Visión at 10pm, provides the best chance for non-Spanish speakers to enjoy Cuban television. The *película del sabado* is normally a US film, broadcast in the original language with subtitles. It is preceded by a Cuban critic providing an often hilarious ideological appreciation of the film about to be shown.

In the last couple of years Cuban television has expanded its repertoire by broadcasting a weekly news programme produced by the US news station CNN. The half-hour *World Report* bulletin is shown every Friday. Although its coverage tends to be uncontroversial, this show is a welcome alternative to the normal diet of government-approved news.

A special tourist network called Sun Channel (Canal del Sol) is available within some luxury hotels, mainly in Havana. Programmes, in both English and Spanish, are broadcast between 2pm and 2am. The channel churns out some risible travelogues, appalling cartoons and tacky folkloric videos, but also has good and comparatively new films, music and even English-language commentaries on South American soccer matches. Hotel rooms with the facility should also provide a full guide to programmes; if not, ask for one at reception.

Only diplomats, high-ranking officials and a small proportion of ordinary Cubans have access to satellite television. A few years ago, satellite dishes — sometimes ingenious contraptions made from old umbrellas — were seen all over Havana, but sporadic clampdowns by the authorities seem to have reduced the number considerably. Tourists staying in one of the smarter hotels, particularly in Varadero, may be able to choose from several satellite channels, including VH1 (Video Hits 1 — a competitor for MTV), the Movie Channel, TNT (Turner Network Television — popular programming) and the Disney Channel. Around Havana and the north coast, many residents have their aerials directed northwards to pick up TV services broadcast from Miami for Florida's large Spanish-speaking population. Therefore it is relatively easy to tune into the US English-language networks in a Cuban's home, but not in hotels where the channels (as with the radio) are usually fixed. Around Guantánamo, American forces TV is easily picked up.

TV Martí, like its radio counterpart, was designed to pump flagrant capitalist propaganda from Miami. However, it fails completely in its aim since the Cuban government goes to great lengths to jam the signal. These days the only place you'll see TV Martí is in the US Interests Section in Havana. In March 1996, a new Cuban channel called Multimedia Caribe was due to start broadcasting by satellite from Havana over much of the Americas — including the United States.

Getting Around

aeropuerto	airport	*moto*	motorbike
andén	platform	*muelle*	wharf
asiento	seat	*ómnibus*	bus, usually long-distance
a su hora	on time	*parada (de buses)*	bus stop
avenida	avenue	*parada oficial*	hitching point
barco	boat	*para camiones*	
bicicleta, ciclo	bicycle	*pasaje*	ticket, fare
boleto	ticket	*pasajero, a*	passenger
hacer botella	to hitch-hike	*punto de los*	hitching point
buey	ox	*amarillos*	
caballo	horse	*punto de recogida*	hitching point
calle	street	*de pasaje*	
camión	lorry, truck	*regreso*	the return segment of a
cancelado	cancelled		journey
cerca	near	*reparto, barrio*	district, quarter (of town
climatizado	air conditioned		or city)
coche	horse-and-cart, car	*salida*	departure
colectivo	collective taxi	*taquilla*	ticket office/booth
crucero ferrocarril	railway crossing	*terminal*	bus station

cuadra	block (of buildings)	*Intermunicipal*	for services within the
diario	daily		province
equipajes	luggage	*Interprovincial*	for long-distance services
esquina	corner	*terminal de tren*	railway station
estación	railway station	*vuelo*	flight
goma	tyre	*norte*	north
gua-gua	bus	*sur*	south
(pronounced *wha-wha*)		*este*	east
horario	timetable	*oeste*	west
ida	one-way	*izquierda (a la)*	left (on the)
llegada	arrival	*derecha*	right
malecón	seafront boulevard	*derecho, (di)recto*	straight on

First-time visitors are often surprised by the sheer size of Cuba and the tribulations of travelling around the island. It appears on maps as a slim slice of land in the Caribbean, but bear in mind that from east to west it measures nearly one thousand miles (1,600km).

The public transport system has always been slow, inadequate for the numbers wishing to travel and often irritatingly disorganised. But the shortage of fuel and spare parts now means that moving around can be fraught with difficulty. Bus and train services have been reduced drastically; horses and carts are used as a regular means of transport in towns; and Cuba has also become a nation of cyclists. Out in the country, if you haven't a bicycle or a horse, the only sure way to get around is to hitch-hike.

The authorities discourage tourists from using most kinds of public transport, preferring them to opt for guided coach trips, dollar taxis or a rental car. But while long-distance bus journeys are virtually out of the question, train journeys are still feasible and easily arranged, as are domestic flights. After severe cutbacks in the Cubana airlines network at the onset of the Special Period, the number of flights has increased again. Even so, try to book your flights as far in advance as possible, particularly at busy holiday times.

To think that you will spend a fair proportion of your time planning or worrying about your next journey is to take the gloomy view. Cubans demonstrate a touching concern for the welfare of those travelling independently, and you may find yourself hustled to the front of queues an embarrassing number of times. With a little know-how you can cover a lot of ground and minimise waiting time. The tourist board does not advertise the fact that you can book a seat on a train just an hour in advance, nor that Cuba is probably the safest place in the world in which to hitch, including for women travelling alone. Furthermore, you are more likely to enjoy and get to know the country and its people if you choose to crack the local transport systems.

Maps. The best map of Cuba available abroad is Freytag & Berndt's, which includes excellent street maps of Havana, Cienguegos, Camagüey, Santiago, Varadero and the Playas del Este. In Britain, the Cuba Holiday Map published by Bartholomew (£4.95) is not so good a road map but has reasonable city plans. Maps of Cuba available on the island vary greatly in their accuracy. If you plan to do any driving, you should be particularly careful about which you choose. Out of the three or four currently on the market, the *Automapa Nacional* (produced by Ediciones GEO in Havana) is by far the most reliable. It includes several important roads that seem to have eluded other cartographers.

If you arrive in Havana ahead of a tour of the island, then you can stock up with maps at El Navegante, in Old Havana at Mercaderes 115 (entre Obispo y Obrapia), tel 613625 or 623466. This excellent shop opens 8am-5pm daily, and sells a wide range of road maps and city plans. It also offers a good selection of nautical charts, and yachtmen and women can contact the shop direct on VHF Channel 16 (CMYP 3050).

In the main tourist centres you can find reasonably useful maps showing hotels, restaurants, museums and so on, but in smaller places all you are likely to find is a map of postal zones known as a *Mapa de Codificación Postal*, which shows streets, post offices and postal zones, but precious little else.

The maps in this book have been compiled using all available sources, but some are based solely on the authors' observations. An indication of the paucity of cartography in Cuba is that this book constitutes a more complete collection of maps than is available anywhere in the Republic.

Place Names. Abbreviations on timetables can be confusing: Santiago de Cuba is often abbreviated to Stgo de C, and you are expected to know from the context whether Sta C refers to Santa Clara or Santa Cruz.

The following pronunciations of place names run from west to east. Some might offend some Spanish-speaking purists, but are guaranteed to be understood by the locals. Letters in brackets may be left unpronounced or just hinted at.

Cuba = *Coo*-ba (not Queue-ba as pronounced in the West).
Pinar del Rió = Pin-*ar* del R*ee*-oh
Havana = La Ha*bana*
Nueva Gerona = N'*way*va He*roh*na
Varadero = Bara*dair*-oh
Matanzas = Ma*tanza*(s)
Santa Clara = Santa Cl*aa*ra
Cienfuegos = Syen-*fway*-go(s)
Trinidad = Trini*da(d)*
Ciego de Avila = S*yay*-go de *A*vila
Camagüey = Cama*gway*
Holguin = Ol-*geen*
Bayamo = Bay-*ah*-mo
Manzanillo = Manza*nee*yo
Santiago = San-tee-*yah*-go
Guantánamo = Gwan-*tan*-amo
Cayo Largo = *Kye*-o *Lar*go

AIR

Given the distances involved, flying is well worth considering. It is cheap by Western standards, and reliable in comparison with other public transport in Cuba. The official timetables are observed fairly closely. The national airline Cubana links the capital with all the main cities, and with the Isle of Youth. A second, smaller hub is the new airport near Varadero, which has flights to Santiago and the Isle of Youth. Flights on the busy route between Havana and Santiago cost $136 return, expensive compared with the cost by train or bus but low in comparison with the cost of a 600-mile air journey elsewhere in the world.

The Cubana fleet is an odd one, and could certainly do with some investment. The airline uses Soviet aircraft alomst exclusively, from the 22-seat YAK-40 to the Tupolev-154 seating 150+. They share common features such as discomfort (the heat is often stifling, seats rarely recline, etc.) and questionable airworthiness. Fortunately, Western aircraft such as the Fokker F-27 are gradually being introduced. Smoking is prohibited on all services. Inflight catering is modest; sometimes you might get a ham sandwich, coffee and a cold drink, at other times just a boiled sweet.

Aerocaribbean is a charter airline operating flights principally for tourists on excursions organised by other Cuban agencies such as Havanatur or Cubanacán. It operates predominantly on routes not served by Cubana, for example to Trinidad, Cienfuegos, Cayo Largo or to the Hotel Colony diving centre on the Isle of Youth. Aerocaribbean's motley collection of planes, including Antonov 24s, Ilyushin 18s and Yak-40s, can also be chartered direct for private use. A newer charter airline, Gaviota, run by the eponymous tourist agency, operates on a similar basis to Aerocaribbean.

Reservations. If you know exactly where you would like to go before you leave home, it is worth pre-booking in the UK. Note that during the months of August and December, when many Cubans take holidays, the demand for seats is much higher than usual; even out of the high season, flights may be fully booked a week in advance. If you book a domestic flight abroad, your agent should include it on the ticket for your international flight. It is worth noting that some minor domestic routes (e.g. Havana to Guantánamo) cannot be booked outside Cuba.

Once in Cuba, even fluent Spanish-speakers who are able to get through on the Cubana reservations numbers (see page 171) should not rely upon a verbal assurance of a booking having been made. To increase your chances of getting on a particular flight, go to a Cubana office to make your reservation and pay for your ticket. Foreign visitors are normally able to bypass the endless queues, and sometimes it is possible to make a reservation and get a ticket in five minutes flat. Note that to change an internal flight, you may have to pay eg $6 for the privilege.

The time shown on your ticket is the time you should check in, not the departure time (which is usually one hour later). It is a risk to turn up after the check-in time, since most flights have a long waiting list of hopeful travellers, to whom empty seats are assigned. If you do lose your place, the staff should get you on the next flight out. This is fine for those travelling on a busy route with plenty of flights, but a disaster if you're in somewhere like Baracoa (which has just two services a week).

Schedules. Cubana does not publish a schedule, and limited information provided in the ABC World Airways Guide is inaccurate. Late in 1995 the following departures from Havana were known to be operating:

Baracoa: Tuesday and Friday at 6am, via Varadero.
Camagüey: one flight daily at different times.
Ciego de Avila: flights on Tuesdays and Sundays.
Guantánamo: daily except Tuesday at 6am.
Holguín: one flight daily in the afternoon, departure time variable, sometimes via Varadero.
Manzanillo: flights on Mondays and Saturdays.
Nueva Gerona (Isle of Youth): twice daily at 7.15am and 7.55pm.
Santiago de Cuba: three flights daily at 7am, 8.55am and 5.30pm, with an additional afternoon flight on certain days.
Varadero: 8am on Tuesday, Thursday and Saturday.

Fares. Western visitors must pay in hard currency. There are no reductions for return tickets. One-way fares from Havana at the time of going to press were:

Baracoa — $78	Nueva Gerona (Isle of Youth) — $16
Camaguey — $51	Santiago de Cuba — $68
Guantánamo — $73	Varadero — $20
Holguín — $59	

TRAIN

Rail travel is an excellent introduction to the uniqueness of Cuba. Trains are mobile microcosms of society, full of life and bustle as they trundle through the slowly changing scenery. For some visitors, however, once is enough. A Cuban train which both leaves and arrives on time is a rare train indeed, and on many lines short-notice cancellations are frequent. Nevertheless, rail travel is guaranteed to be an interesting experience. In rural areas, particularly in the east of Cuba, trains are no more than bus bodies attached to a railway wagon chassis. They wind through difficult curves and scale impossible gradients, and are a great way to see the countryside and meet the people. On the best trains, particularly the express between Havana and Santiago de Cuba, you can expect positive comfort and a fairly punctual arrival. In general, however, if your principal concern is speed or reliability, you should probably fly.

Cuba's main line snakes across the middle of the island from Havana to Santiago via Matanzas, Santa Clara, Ciego de Avila, Camagüey and Las Tunas. Branches off the main line serve several of the island's main towns and cities, principally Cienfuegos, Bayamo and Guantánamo. From Havana there is an extension west to Pinar del Río, a notoriously slow line. The only electrified railway is the Hershey line from Casablanca in Havana to Matanzas. Its name derives from the plantations that it serves, which were used to produce sugar for the North American Hershey chocolate company.

Speeds are low; even the crack overnight express between the capital and Santiago takes nearly fifteen hours to cover the 535-mile (860km) run, an average speed of only 58km/h or 36mph. The express linking Havana with Guantánamo takes over twenty hours to cover 560 miles (900km).

Surprisingly for a supposedly classless society, there are no less than four official classes of service. Each individual train, however, has only one class, and in reality most trains are known simply as *regular*. The terminology used in official timetables is as follows:

Especial — applies only on the expresses between Havana and Santiago, and is indicated on timetables as E. This is luxury class for which reservations are essential. Carriages are air-conditioned with reclining seats *(sillas inclinables)*, more comfortable than most aeroplanes.

Primera especial — a notch down on the top class, with similar facilities.

Primera — first class only in name, its chief attribute being that the carriages are slightly more comfortable and less crowded than the lowest category.

Segunda — ridiculously cheap and the only class available on many branch lines.

Reservations. *Long-distance trains:* booking a seat on a long-distance train has been made comparatively easy for tourists with the creation of the Ferrotur agency. While this means that fares must be paid in dollars, the ability to turn up at the Ferrotur office just an hour in advance to book a seat is a real boon. Many foreign visitors have enjoyed the freedom this new system has provided.

In smaller cities the operations of Ferrotur are not always as reliable as in say Havana or Santiago. If you end up having to do as the Cubans do, begin by asking what the booking procedure is for a particular train, i.e. whether you need to reserve a place the day before or on the actual day. If you fail to make any headway, you should be able to enhance your chances of success by sweet talking the station master *(jefe)*, possibly offering a small gift of some cigarettes or chocolate. Alternatively, a fellow traveller may take pity on you and sort out a ticket for you.

It is theoretically possible to book an entire itinerary at a single station, but in most cases reservations do not work their way through what can only loosely be described as the bookings system. If you are touring by train, therefore, you should try to get into the habit of reserving your next sector immediately upon arrival at each stop. If you subsequently change your plans, you can try to change the reservation upon payment of a small fee.

Local trains: Ferrotur does not sell tickets for local (usually second class) services, but this is because reservations are not available. It is usually a question of turning up an hour or two before departure and queuing at the office marked *boletines*. Try to establish who is *último* or *última*, stand behind him or her and then do as they do. You may surprise yourself with how territorial you become, marking out and then defending your patch prior to jostling your way on board. Tickets for these local services should be paid for in local currency. If you get on without a ticket, you pay a 100% surcharge.

Facilities. On some services, part of the train is roped off to provide an impromptu buffet, selling sandwiches or some other snack. This is the exception to the rule, however, and you are advised to take provisions with you.

Smoking. There are no demarcations, though on local services open windows alleviate the worst effects. Air-conditioned carriages are effectively sealed, so smoke can be a real problem.

BUS

Buses used to constitute the backbone of Cuban transport, with long-distance coaches racing across the island and converted trucks lumbering up the steepest gradients to outlying villages. Services have dropped dramatically since the start of the Special Period, and it is increasingly difficult to travel long distances by bus. Tourists have the possibility of paying for rides on tour buses, which zip all over the country from the main towns, but this is by no means a cheap substitute.

Cuban buses are known colloquially as *gua-guas* (pronounced wha-wha), a term which applies especially to local buses. These monstrous machines, assembled locally from Hungarian parts, rumble through cities and the surrounding countryside; try to sit at the back to avoid being gassed and deafened simultaneously. Longer-distance buses are more comfortable, often with padded seats; not quite as good as those found elsewhere in Latin America, but at least they have reclining seats.

Before you can begin to think about buying a ticket, you need to establish which is the right bus station for your destination. Most large towns have two, one for services within the province (Terminal de Omnibus Intermunicipales) and the other for long-distance buses (Interprovinciales). Often these are miles apart, so if you turn up at the wrong one you face a long hike. Most locals have a good grasp of which one to go to for a particular destination, so just ask someone.

Long-distance buses. The state enterprise Omnibus de Cuba runs long-distance bus services. The bus network is more extensive than that for trains, and services are faster: Havana to Cienfuegos takes four hours, two hours less than the train. Timetables allow for both *regular* and *especial* buses (the latter costing twice the normal fare), but don't bank on the specified category turning up. And while most stations have schedules written up, most of these are purely fictional.

Cuba's buses simply cannot cope with the demand. The average Cuban living in one of the main cities needs to book a long journey often weeks in advance. You will find it extremely hard to travel on long-distance buses from Havana, Santiago and other big centres unless you make friends with a bus company employee, in which case you may be able to get an under-the-counter ticket for dollars. (Ticket sellers usually keep a few numbers aside for 'special cases', rather like dealing from the bottom of a pack of cards). First, however, you should reflect on whether it is justifiable to deprive a Cuban of a seat on a bus, when you as a tourist have many other forms of transport at your disposal.

Havana has a bus reservations office downtown, but in most towns and cities passengers must book in advance at the bus station itself. The staff will have a good idea as to the state of the waiting lists for a particular destination, and they will tell you whether or not it is worth putting your name down. As with trains, try to book your onward or return service immediately upon arrival.

If you have no reservation, you can rarely just turn up at a bus terminal and get onto a bus. The one reason to go to the station on the day you want to leave is to get a cancellation — it's likely to be a vain attempt, but worth trying if you're desperate. There is usually a special section dealing with *fallos* (returns), but you need to get there early and accept that there is no guarantee of success.

Rest Breaks: on long routes stops are made every two or three hours, enabling you to get off and, if your luck's in, have a coffee and something to eat. Make for the food and drink counters as rapidly as possible, as there are rarely sufficient supplies for an entire busload of people. Since food and drink are generally served from different counters, you must decide which you want most (unless you have a friend with whom you can split the queuing). In some places, you find independent traders selling snacks which are likely to be far more tasty than anything the state can provide.

If you wish to use the lavatory, you may have to sacrifice sustenance altogether. Move fast to the toilets because queues form quickly and the longer you wait the more disgusting the prospect. Make sure you re-board the bus when called to do so, since otherwise new passengers may take your place.

Intermunicipal buses. You have a much better chance of getting on a local bus than on a long-distance one. This is because reservations are not possible on local services and you must simply join the queue (or scrum) on the day and hope for the best. Bus services tend to both start and finish early. Typically buses to nearby towns start at 5 or 6am and stop at around 6 or 7pm. Don't expect great comfort: sometimes 100 passengers can be packed in to a vehicle designed for half as many people though some drivers are strict about every passenger having a seat.

Because of the problems involved in booking long-distance bus journeys, you may be tempted instead to use a series of local services to cover a long route. This is a slow and unreliable process. An added quirk is that you may have to change at provincial boundaries. Local services are run by provincial enterprises for the benefit of their citizens, and therefore you'll have to get off and hang around for the connecting service arriving from the other direction.

The procedure for queuing varies from place to place. In some towns you simply go to the waiting room (or bus stop) and ask for *l'último* or *l'última.* The effectiveness of this apparently orderly system breaks down as soon as the bus appears, resulting in a mad rush for the doors. More commonly, however, either you will be given a slip of paper *(tike)* with your destination and a number, or your name will be entered on a list. Then it is a question of patience while you wait to be called. Don't wander too far from the terminal — if you miss your turn, you go to the back of the queue. Your slip of paper is not a ticket (you pay on the bus), and the golden rule is never to presume you've made it onto the bus until you are finally in your seat. This at least avoids bitter frustration when you have queued in vain.

In some places the number on your 'ticket' will correspond roughly to the numbers displayed on a board by the gate for your bus. When a bus for your destination arrives, a teller will appear and begin to shout numbers in sequence (a good enough incentive to master Spanish numerals as soon as possible). Go for it when your number is called as you have only one chance — otherwise somebody else will take your turn. If you have put your name down on a list, the teller may shout out names instead — it's worth giving an easy Spanish rendition of your name so as to have some chance of recognising it.

To avoid complete panic, try to enlist the help of another prospective passenger.

LONG-DISTANCE TAXI

Petrol rationing has badly hit the long-distance taxis which over the years have become an integral part of the transport network — and a vital alternative to the state-run bus and train services. But *colectivos* — often pre-revolutionary American saloons — have not disappeared altogether, and where they exist comprise a fine way to travel.

Every town has a recognised departure point for long-distance taxis and more-or-less fixed prices (in pesos). The colectivos usually congregate around the inter-provincial bus terminal or the train station, and do business by carrying passengers who have been unable to get on bus services. Some colectivos operate along a fixed route (the destination may be painted on the bonnet, or else the driver will stand around shouting it out to passers-by). Be warned that some drivers leave only when they cannot squeeze any more people in. You might be persuaded to get into the car, only to hang around for an hour while he waits for other passengers.

In reality, the most reliable way to travel between towns by car is to hire your own private taxi; car owners hang out around the transport terminals touting for custom. Most drivers will be willing to take you to the destination of your choice as long as the price is right. Drivers are used to departing immediately, but there is nothing to stop you arranging the journey a day or two in advance. The only disadvantage with doing this is that you may be left in the lurch if the driver receives a better offer in the interim.

While you may like the idea of cruising around the island in a 50s Cadillac, you should save that treat for a short downtown trip. For long journeys, choose a Lada or another Eastern European model, since these cars are much more economical on petrol and are easier to fix in the event of a breakdown.

If you plan to explore Cuba by car for several days but don't wish to drive yourself, consider hiring a private car and driver on a more formal basis, paying a daily fee (e.g. $50) plus petrol. This means that you will have to pay all other expenses in terms of food and accommodation, but some drivers will be happy to stay in peso hotels keeping your extra costs down. Another possible deterrent is the fact that to hire a private individual let alone his car is illegal in Cuba, though this seems to worry tourists more than the drivers, most of whom are willing to take the risk if the price is right.

The expensive alternative is to hire an official tourist taxi. Panataxi in Havana (see page 156), for example, offers special rates for long-distance journeys. Recent sample fares were as follows:

	One way	Return (Day)
Varadero	$80	$120
Playas del Este	$25	$40
Sancti Spíritus	$200	$310
Cienfuegos	$130	$200
Pinar del Río	$85	$150

By contrast, a private cab would probably charge the one-way fare for a return journey. If you are contemplating day trips out of Havana, hiring a private cab-driver can work out cheaper (and certainly more relaxing) than renting your own car.

HITCH-HIKING

As in other Third World countries, hitching lifts is a way of life in Cuba; a cluster of hitchers has long been a familiar sight by the roadsides on the edge of towns. But since the fuel shortage began to bite, hitching has become the principal means of getting around the island. Diminished bus services and petrol rationing mean that the demand outstrips supply, but hitching remains an extremely valuable (and often the only) option for those travelling on a limited budget.

In good Cuban style, hitching has become an organised occupation overseen by the state. Each town has a recognised hitching point, close to the most important road junction. A system of queuing operates, supervised by officials of the Inspección Estatal, who are known as *los amarillos* ('the yellow ones'), after their mustard-coloured (and amusingly flared) trousers; they are also recognisable by their clipboard which they use to flag down vehicles. State vehicles (but not tourist buses) are obliged to stop, and the officials instruct the driver to take whatever number of passengers they deem possible: they might shout out 'Camagüey — primero cinco', i.e. the first five people going to Camagüey can get on board. Some hitching points actually have a waiting shelter, plus a set of steps with which to help passengers onto the back of lorries. The sight of 50 or more people clustered at an intersection can be disheartening, but it is surprising how many people can be squeezed into one vehicle and therefore how quickly the queue moves. Try to arrive at the hitching point early, ideally at dawn — the already low volume of traffic, particularly long-distance lorries, drops dramatically in the afternoon. Western tourists may face the embarrassment of being put to the front of the queue.

Foreign visitors can, of course, return the favour by picking up hitch-hikers when hiring a car. You are not obliged to stop to pick up hitchers, but if you do your generosity will be much appreciated — not least as a gesture of solidarity. One researcher for this book picked up 79 hitchers during a three-day hire. Quite apart from the interesting people you meet, giving rides can be of practical help — finding your way to and around strange towns is a lot easier if you have a Cuban on board.

Lorries and trucks provide the majority of hitchable traffic. Comfort is minimal, as you might expect being bounced around with 30 other passengers, their effects, children and animals. But a journey in the back of a truck will give you an insight into the day-to-day struggle of ordinary Cubans, many of whom rely on such a haphazard method of transport to get to and from work. Furthermore, such communal hitching can be recommended for single women travellers.

Away from the main junctions you must rely on more traditional methods of hitching, and there are few crossroads without at least a couple of hopefuls. Most vehicles with any room will stop — including, hopefully, cars rented by tourists, which make up a fair proportion of traffic in some areas. The coding of licence plates can give a good indication of the propensity to stop.

Yellow: *particular* — private   Brown: *turismo* — hire cars
Red: *estatal* or *empresa* — official   Blue: taxi

If you get a ride on a truck stopped by the inspectors, you should expect to pay a small fare upfront, usually about a peso for an hour's journey. It is the local custom to pay a few coins in return for a more informal ride too, though Westerners are sometimes excused payment.

Around tourist centres there is a chance you could be picked up by a black market spiv who may turn you out in the middle of nowhere unless you agree to do business. Fortunately this is rare and many foreigners hitch happily around the island. Hitching in Cuba is arguably safer than in any other country in the world.

TOUR BUS

Travelling on a tour bus is unlikely to appeal to everyone, but the possibilities are not to be sniffed at if your heart is set on seeing as much of Cuba as possible in a limited time. While not always a cheap option, it is certainly the most comfortable and can be blissfully easy to arrange at short notice.

Foreign tourists are ferried around Cuba in a fleet of modern, air-conditioned minibuses and coaches. Independent Western travellers stand a good chance of getting a ride on one of these. The most official way is by paying for a *transfer* (pronounced 'trans-fare'). For instance, if a group day trip is arranged from Havana to Pinar del Río, for which the cost per person is $40, you can choose to simply take the bus and be dropped off at the other end. For this you would be charged around $30 — hardly good value, but worth paying if you have no alternative. The less official and cheaper way to get a lift is to ingratiate yourself with a group's courier or bus driver and negotiate a lower fare.

To find out what buses are leaving and when, look in hotel lobbies for tour operators' notice boards. Details of departure times for the airport or the next destination on the group's itinerary are usually pinned up. Often the most effective way, however, is to simply ask around; making a friend of somebody working in reception can boost your chances, since they can keep you posted of what groups are travelling where.

EXCURSIONS

Even those opposed to the idea of joining an organised tour may be forced to admit that these excursions can constitute the most effective way of seeing as much of Cuba as possible in a short time. And the only way to reach the resort island of Cayo Largo, for example, is to join an organised trip. The price for tours can appear steep, but when you take into account the fact that a large (and often excellent) lunch is included, it becomes a much better deal. The cost for a day's excursion to Trinidad and Cienfuegos from Varadero, for example, costs around $60. The same day trip done by air (in a DC-3 Dakota or even an old Soviet single-engined biplane) costs about $20 more per person.

Tours operate daily from the main tourist centres. Several different agencies run these trips, but prices for most are identical. The tourism desk in any big hotel will fix you up with a trip. Do not put undue faith in the organisational skills of the person with whom you deal. Buses have a habit of turning up at your hotel an hour later than scheduled.

A trip to a town such as Trinidad allows you to have a modicum of freedom to wander about on your own if you prefer. Other trips include tours around cigar and rum factories, making it harder to explore on your own. Even so, you can usually leave the group for an hour or so as long as you arrange a rendezvous for later. Be prepared for stops at roadside cafés en route — tourist traps where you are expected to spend money on the same souvenirs you've already seen in every other dollar shop on the island.

Bus tours usually require a minimum of eight people. While this is not a problem in high season, at other times you may have to wait and see whether or not enough people have signed up.

BOAT

Until the mid-90s, water transport in Cuba was limited to a diminishing number of ferry services (diminishing for the simple reason that boats were occasionally pressed into service for the one-way run to Florida). Two improvements have occurred, both from outside. The *Costa Playa* cruise ship is calling regularly at the island, offering an alternative to surface or air transport between tourist centres. A more intriguing option is to charter a yacht: see page 115.

DRIVING

aceite	oil	*doble tracción*	four-wheel drive
alquilar	to hire	*goma*	tyre
alto	stop	*llene el tanque,*	please fill the tank
apagar	turn off (engine)	*por favor*	
arrancar	turn on (engine)	*mecánico*	mechanic
autopista	motorway	*multa*	fine
bache	pothole	*no adelantar*	no overtaking
cámara	inner tube	*no parqueo*	no parking
camino cerrado	road closed	*no hay paso*	road closed
carretera	highway	*pare*	stop
ceda el paso	give way	*parqueo*	car park
carro, coche	car	*peatones*	pedestrians
circumvalación	bypass, ringroad	*reduzca velocidad*	reduce speed
cruce	crossroads	*semáforo*	traffic lights
crucero ferrocarril	level crossing	*servi(centro)*	service station, which
cuidado	take care, warning		may have fuel
cuide	beware (usually followed by	*taller de*	repair workshop
	los animales or *los ciclos*)	*reparaciones*	
curva peligrosa	dangerous bend	*terre plan*	unpaved road
desviación, desvío	diversion, turn-off	*velocidad*	speed limit
dirección única	one way	*permitida*	

Many diverse challenges face the driver in Cuba, from unmarked road works and wandering wildlife to improbably bulky saloon cars lurching arrogantly along in the middle of the road. 'Speed is an ally of death' read slogans by the roadside, but many Cuban drivers take the view that one should drive as fast as the vehicle will permit. Fortunately, in many cases this is not very fast at all.

The standard Cuban conveyance is the Lada, the Soviet car which is still a subject of considerable mirth in the West (Q: What's the owner's manual for a Lada? A: A bus timetable; Customer: Have you got a windscreen wiper for a Lada? Mechanic: Hmmm . . . seems like a fair swap). Nevertheless, Ladas can cope with the tropical heat as adeptly as they do with the frozen wastes of Siberia. They are sufficiently hardy to withstand road surfaces that would cripple the axles of other vehicles, and are as happy when driven at high speed by the police in Havana.

Larger models are mostly immaculately maintained American saloons from the 1950s, preserved in a transportational time-warp. Huge Plymouths and Studebakers dating from 1959 or before cruise the streets, turning towns in Cuba into the set for a fifties Californian beach movie. These vehicles are surprisingly reliable considering their age. Sadly their numbers are diminishing — not only as they slowly give in to old age but also because the Cuban government is buying them up (offering their owners a brand-new Lada instead) and selling them abroad as collectors' items. A surprising number are turning up back in the USA, after being channelled through a third country such as Panama.

It is not feasible to bring a car into Cuba. If you insist upon the extra speed and independence offered by a car, you have no choice but to rent a vehicle. You will also have to cope with high-spirited local drivers, who show scant regard for the rules of the road. Defensive driving is called for at all times. Don't lose your temper even when a cyclist veers into your path or a horse and cart obstinately blocks your way. Such impediments are common. When estimating journey times, don't reckon on speeds over 90km/h (56 mph) on the freeway, 60km/h (38 mph) on rural roads. Be particularly careful when driving at night since bicycles, horse-drawn carriages and cars rarely have functioning lights.

Roads. Cuba has a strange collection of highways. Some rural roads are distinctly Third World and little better than dirt tracks, but there is also a limited network of freeways. Most of these were built in the 1950s (and are slowly crumbling), though the spine of the Cuban road system, the Ocho Vías, is more recent.

Literally 'eight ways', after the number of lanes, this motorway runs from Pinar del Río in the west, through Havana to just west of Ciego de Avila. Some maps show it reaching as far as Camagüey, but this is wishful thinking. Plans exist to extend it east to Santiago and eventually to Guantánamo, but these have been shelved. For most of its course the Ocho Vías is a six-lane highway with a hard shoulder, and has restricted access. The older Carretera Central (Central Highway), which runs roughly parallel, is a more interesting but much slower road. There is also the option of taking the road that runs parallel with much of the north coast, from Nuevitas across to Cárdenas and the Vía Blanca.

The Vía Blanca is near-motorway standard; it links the capital with Varadero, emerging from the tunnel east of Havana and running a short distance inland from the coast. It is pure Americana, built by US engineers and little changed since the Revolution. Other roads will be a disappointment to those used to fast driving, but are perfectly adequate for the low density of traffic found in most of Cuba — in many areas it is possible to drive for an hour and see only three or four other vehicles (most of which will be tractors).

The number of roadside bars is increasing along Cuba's main highways, but if you are going on a long journey you should take all the food and drink you think you might need.

Car Rental. Cuba imports a whole range of foreign cars to rent out to tourists, enabling you to travel in considerable comfort — though the quality of the car cannot make up for the poor state of some roads. In addition, the cost of hiring a car on the island has been radically reduced in the last few years, making it a much more viable proposition.

Your ordinary driving licence is sufficient to hire a car in Cuba; the minimum age for rentals is 21.

Cuba's two main car rental operators are Havanautos and Transautos (the latter run by Transtur, Cuba's main transport agency). There is scant difference between the two, and they offer similar types of car — mostly a choice between various models of Nissan, Daihatsu, Renault, Peugeot and Mercedes. Both have numerous agencies in the capital and all the main towns on the island, generally attached to a tourist hotel, as well as at Havana's José Martí airport. There are several other rental agencies, such as Cubanacán, but they have fewer outlets nationwide and tend to charge higher rates.

Book a car a day or two in advance if possible, but don't assume that there will necessarily be a car ready for you when you turn up. The booking system is less than perfect, and you may have to wait a few hours until a car is returned. The demand for cars by tourists has increased with the deterioration of public transport, and in high season vehicles are not always readily available. If you want to pick up a car on arrival at the airport, be sure to book it from abroad.

Even if the car is ready and waiting, allow at least an hour for the completion of forms, payment and final inspection of the vehicle. Only the main rental outlets will have a mechanic to hand, so if you pick up the car at a hotel and discover some problem with it, there will inevitably be some delay while a mechanic is located.

Rental rates: one reason why it is now so much cheaper to hire a car in Cuba is that the principle of charging for each kilometre above 100km per day has been abandoned. The previous charge of $0.30 per kilometre after the initial 100km used to make long journeys extremely expensive; limited mileage rates still exist but should be entered into cautiously. At the time of going to press, the cheapest car on the market was a Peugeot 205 hired through Transautos: $35 a day, with the price dropping to $30 or less for rental of a week or more. Daihatsu or Suzuki jeeps, which are usually available for a similar price, may look good value but they drink petrol. For a larger saloon car with air-conditioning (a serious consideration if you plan to do a lot of hard driving), such as a Toyota

Corolla, expect to pay $60-70 per day, depending on how many days you take it for.

To the standard rental charge you should add a further $5-$10 per day for insurance, depending on the policy and agency. You are strongly advised to opt for the higher rate, since this will cover you additionally for theft of parts from the car — an all-too-common problem in Cuba. You will also be expected to leave a deposit, generally about $200, and pay for the petrol in the tank; you should be reimbursed for any unused fuel when you return the car, but in practice the amount of fuel and refund are understated.

For a fee you can drop off the car at any outlet of the relevant rental agency on the island, the charge calculated according to the distance from the vehicle's base. The rates are high, e.g. $50 from Varadero to Cienfuegos, $180 from Havana to Santiago, but could be worthwhile compared with the cost in fuel and stress of driving all the way back.

If you merely want to rent a car for a few hours to do some local exploring, then ask Havanautos or Cubanacán rental outlets about renting a vehicle for six or 12 hours. (This also removes the problem of finding a safe place to park the car overnight).

Hazards: some travellers claim that it is only a slight exaggeration to suggest that Cuba's state car rental agencies are run by a bunch of crooks, and that this section of the book should carry a large warning that renters of cars will be ripped off. Every trick in the car hire book is used to extract dollars from visitors. A favourite ploy is to declare that a car half-full of petrol has, say, 30 litres in the tank; this is added to your initial bill. If you return the car with the petrol gauge in exactly the same position, you will be told that the tank has only 20 litres, and be charged for the ten litres of fuel which never existed. Although the money you pay goes straight to the company, the individual employee has effectively obtained ten free litres of fuel which can then be sold on the black market. For guidance, the Nissan Sunny or Peugeot 205 holds about 40 litres of fuel. But be warned that if you make too much fuss about the fuel scam, the representative might 'discover' some fault with the vehicle, and find some other way to charge you. Some travellers have been told that even though they paid for full insurance cover, stolen parts had to be paid for since the theft was not reported to the police. No agent specifies this in the conditions of hire, so stand your ground if a representative tries to pull that trick. If you do have something stolen and have an hour or two to spare, however, you could play safe and report it to the local police — if only to be able to wave a piece of paper under the nose of a hard-nosed rental agent.

Always look closely at the time stated on the rental agreement (which usually shows the moment you began negotiations, rather than when you drive away). If you don't return the vehicle on time, you will be charged one-fifth of the daily rate for every additional hour. In a final attempt to procure extra cash, the 'total' box on the credit card voucher is left blank in the hope that you will give a tip.

Tolls. Starting in 1996, tolls have been imposed on some sections of highway. The first 'victim' is the 25-mile (40km) road between Matanzas and Varadero, for which a toll of $2 is payable by foreigners and 2 pesos by Cubans. If the idea catches on, then driving could become a very expensive exercise once more.

Fuel. Foreigners must buy their fuel from the dollar petrol stations that have sprung up across Cuba in the last few years and continue to multiply. Cupet, the state oil enterprise, sells two grades of petrol — both leaded — but tourists will be served only the higher grade, *especial,* which costs $0.90 per litre, rather than the *regular,* which sells for $0.65. Occasionally you will land upon a friendly pump attendant who is willing to bend the rules. Rental cars can run happily on the lower grade. Motor oil is sold at $5 per quart.

The *Mapa Turístico de Cuba* (price $2.50) is by no means the best road map of the country, but it does at least give a list of Cupet's petrol stations. At the time of going to press, certain provinces — including Sancti Spíritus, Villa Clara and Pinar del Río — are badly off for petrol stations, but the situation is improving all the time. For example, there are already a couple of service stations along the Ocho Vías motorway. However, you can easily drive for 100km or more without glimpsing one dollar petrol pump, so a good rule is to fill up whenever you can. The smallest models of Nissan or Peugeot should deliver about 14km for each litre, though the stop-start nature of driving in Cuba means this will probably drop to only 9 or 10km.

If you run short of fuel, you will be dependent upon locating a peso station. You may have to drive around for some time to find one that is open, has fuel to sell, electricity to work the pumps and, after all that, is willing to serve you. It is not usually difficult to twist someone's arm, particularly if you can offer to pay in dollars. Indeed, some tourists manage to drive around for a whole week using petrol purchased entirely in this way. Normally, only *regular* will be available. Another method of buying what is effectively black market petrol is to approach the unofficial cab drivers that lurk around the transport terminals. They will have their own private source of black market petrol, which you may be able to take advantage of. The cost varies from place to place, but is likely to be at least half what you would pay officially. The risk lies in being given petrol diluted with water, though reports of this happening are few and far between and are almost unheard of outside Havana. As a general rule, any black market deal is less risky if you enlist the help of someone you already know and trust.

Petrol Stations. Glistening in red, white and green — the colours of Cupet — Cuba's petrol stations are a surreal sight amid Cuba's neglected urban landscapes. These *servicentros* (often known simply as 'servi') have become the social hub of small provincial towns such as Las Tunas or Colón that otherwise boast few trappings of the late 20th century. Every Cupet station is open 24 hours and has a dollar shop or bar that attracts a steady stream of customers — and can be useful for late night beers or snacks.

If you have been driving for a week or more your car may well be in need of a good wash before you hand it back. Cupet pump attendants will be only too pleased to oblige — for a small tip. Your windscreen is likely already to be sparkling clean, since screen washers pop up at many big intersections.

Rules and Regulations. Plenty of Cubans drive while under the influence either of rum or of an overdose of zeal, which goes some way to explaining the high accident statistics. The official blood/alcohol limit is the same as in the UK, i.e. 80mg of alcohol per 100ml of blood. The police have breathalyzers to detect offending motorists but rarely seem to use them. Penalties for infringement, however, are severe. A foreigner is unlikely to be locked up overnight, but you will certainly be made to pay a fine. Like other penalties imposed upon Westerners, this is payable in hard currency.

Lesser offences, such as breaking the urban speed limit of 50km/h or the national limit of 100km/h, are punishable by on-the-spot fines. Enforcement is sporadic, though traffic police are capable of installing highly effective speed traps and are not averse to picking on tourists. There are also sentry boxes guarding major intersections. If you are caught treating a *Pare* sign as a 'Give Way' rather than a 'Stop' sign — i.e. not coming to a full halt — you could face a fine of $10.

There is no law requiring seat belts (*cinturones de seguridad*) to be worn, which is just as well since in most Cuban vehicles they don't exist anyway. However, they are fitted in all officially rented cars, and you should, of course, wear them to enhance your chances of surviving an accident.

Road Signs. Standard international signs are used — sometimes. Otherwise there may be no sign at all, or one written in Spanish. Directional signs, where they exist, are mostly written in off-white letters on a grubby, pale blue background. This makes them difficult to read in daylight, and almost impossible at night. Be prepared for lots of wrong turning, and don't hesitate to ask. The standard motoring maps of Cuba should help, but the best idea is to pick up local hitch-hikers, who may not only express their gratitude by giving you fruit or some other treat, but also guide you along the correct road (and invite you for coffee breaks at their friends' houses en route). Note, however, that some local hitchers may try to push their luck and guide you towards their destination rather than where you actually want to go.

The approaches to Havana are the most problematic for motorists unfamiliar with the terrain; about 13 miles (20km) from the capital, direction signs for Havana disappear, to be replaced by indications for Plaza de la Revolución (the centre of 'new' Havana) or 'Túnel' (the harbour tunnel which takes you straight into Old Havana if you approach from the east).

While numbers inside blue rectangular signs are kilometre markers on motorways, distance indicators on both signposts and maps should be treated with caution, since they invariably indicate the distance to the edge of a town or city, giving a misleadingly optimistic idea of when you might arrive.

Highway Hazards. Even though largely devoid of other road users, Cuban highways present plenty of problems to the visiting motorist. Surfaces can be excellent for miles, but then suddenly deteriorate into a series of deep *baches* (potholes), which get worse each time a truck trundles over them. The dangers are worst after heavy rain, when water can conceal holes in the road. Railway crossings *(cruceros ferrocarriles)* never have gates and are found in the most unlikely places, e.g. in the middle of motorways. Everyone stops for them, not so much to look for trains (though these are becoming more prevalent these days) as to avoid breaking suspensions on the uneven surface.

Suspend all your preconceptions of what motorway driving should involve. The rules about the kinds of vehicles allowed on Cuban autopistas are widely disregarded: you are quite likely to find a tractor or bicycle on the carriageway, and pedestrians strolling across the autopista are not unusual. Years of neglect mean that the white lines between lanes have faded to nothing, encouraging vehicles to drift all over the road — though the central reservation does at least prevent cars from wandering completely off course. And forget about restricted access junctions, with a system of ramps and overpasses. Often intersections are ordinary crossroads, a potentially lethal hazard. Take great care at all times.

City driving can be equally hazardous. You should approach junctions with care, particularly those controlled by traffic signals. These can provide a rich source of confusion. A continually flashing amber light means that you can proceed with caution, but be prepared to encounter non-functioning traffic lights, in which case it becomes a free-for-all. In addition, the stop line is often some way in advance of the light and is often difficult to make out anyway, having been obscured by black oil dripping from countless leaky Russian engines. You can turn right against a red light when the sign *Derecha con Luz Roja* appears.

The regular street layout created by colonial urban planners ought to make it easy to find your way around Cuban town centres. But many streets are one-way, and you have to negotiate a junction at every block. It is not always clear who has priority, so play safe and drive defensively. In the absence of vehicular traffic, bicycles and people provide the main competition for space in the narrow streets; unless you are happy to travel snail-like behind cyclists or pedestrians proceeding leisurely up the road oblivious to traffic, you will need to be liberal with the use of your horn. The number of pedestrian precincts is increasing, restricting vehicular movement. Some city streets are being turned into bus-and-bicycle-only routes.

Night driving is something that you may wish to avoid altogether; Cuba has exactly the combination of problems to make it a nightmare: unmarked roads, unlit cyclists and undisciplined drivers. Drive with great care at night.

Parking. Even in the centre of Havana or in other large towns, you will have little problem finding somewhere to park, particularly if you follow Cuban drivers' practice of leaving the car anywhere (much to the inconvenience of other motorists, pedestrians, etc.). In one-way streets, park on the left. The most flagrant breaches are punished by having the vehicle removed — a rare occurrence but one that can cost hours (and up to $100) to sort out. Be especially careful to avoid spaces marked *Zona Oficial* from which removal is likely to be swift.

Most tourist hotels have car parks with attendants that charge $1 to look after your vehicle overnight. If you are staying in a small city centre hotel without a car park, leave your vehicle as near the main entrance as possible and pay the hotel doorman or guard (*custodio*) something to keep an eye on it. This is a small price to pay for the comfort of knowing that you will probably find your car in one piece the following morning. Some travellers have returned after a morning's sightseeing or evening out to find their car raised on blocks, with all the wheels missing. When parking your car during the day, leave nothing of value visible inside. Rental cars stick out a mile, not only because they are the smartest vehicles on the road but because each has a coloured registration plate prefixed TUR and cheerfully announcing the driver to be a *turista*.

Breakdowns. The car rental organisations will provide a list of their outlets nationwide, and in the event of a serious breakdown, contact the nearest one. Havanautos has breakdown numbers in Havana, 338176 or 338177, which should work from all over the country. You could wait several hours for assistance to arrive, and if you require a spare part there will inevitably be a further delay. If the problem seems fairly minor you would do well to start by enlisting local help. This is not as bad as it sounds since Cuba is a nation of car mechanics — on Sundays town and city streets are transformed into a huge open-air garage as men toil over their beloved cars. The fact that so many 40s and 50s cars are still on the road is a tribute to their ingenuity. If you ask around, you'll usually find someone who'll fix your car for a few dollars — though most Cubans will be more at home fiddling about with a Lada or a Cadillac than a brand new Nissan. If you are in a town or city, try asking at the Cupet petrol station, where there should be a resident mechanic familiar with the latest models.

Accidents. If you are involved in an accident (and still conscious), the first thing you notice is that a crowd gathers rapidly; a traffic accident is regarded as a spectator event. The police will turn up sooner or later, and will try to assign blame on the spot. Statements will be taken, and you will probably have to accompany the police to the nearest station. In the event that you are held responsible for the accident, the police may confiscate your passport as a surety that you will not leave the country. Contact your embassy, which will at least try to ensure that the proper rules are followed.

Be careful about whom you run into; an unfortunate foreigner whose car collided with that of the Interior Minister was allegedly arrested and beaten up by the police.

MOTORCYCLING

The police generally get given the best motorbikes, but Cuba has an impressive collection of bikes with sidecars — known as *motos con sidecar* (pronounced '*see*-daycar'). Some are great period pieces, and most are painted bright colours. Hitchers may be lucky enough to get a lift on or in one.

Anyone who has ridden a motorcycle around other Caribbean islands knows the joys of freewheeling around in the sun. Sadly there are few facilities for hiring motorbikes and, as with cars, it is impractical to import them. A growing number of resorts have silly little Argentinian scooters for hire, but there are no proper machines. Riders are not required to use a helmet.

CYCLING

Such has been the drive to get Cubans to cycle since the onset of the economic crisis that almost everyone seems to do it. Although the simple reality is that if they didn't cycle they simply wouldn't be able to go anywhere, bicycles have been absorbed remarkably smoothly into the Cuban way of life — you even see wedding parades proceeding on bikes. Facilities for cyclists are already an integral part of the urban landscape, with cycle lanes, special parking lots, puncture-repair workshops and even the odd cycle-bus.

While you still see a few of the old Soviet-made bikes, the most common model is the 'Forever Bicycle' (for men) and the 'Flying Pigeon' (for women). These sturdy creations come from China and are designed to carry at least one passenger on the back; they come with a footrest attached to the back wheel. What they lack in refinement (no gears, and most have an unreliable hub brake), the bikes make up for in what could be called rugged simplicity. And they are certainly effective in the hands of Cubans, who manage to pedal at a tremendous speed.

In view of the rising transport difficulties, cycling is an excellent way to get around Cuba — particularly if you plan to base yourself in Havana, which is within easy cycling distance of many interesting places. People wanting to explore further afield may have problems transporting their bikes around the island, though it's possible to load them onto a train, aeroplane, tour bus or even a taxi. You can hitch with a bike too, but the fact that it takes up precious space can be a nuisance. Alternatively, leave your bike at your hotel and go off without it for a few days.

A fairly strong nerve is needed to pedal around Havana (see page 156), but out in the country cycling can be a delight. Most of the terrain is flat, surfaces are good and the traffic light. You are sure to become something of a novelty, with people by the roadside waving and shouting madly as you speed past. Other cyclists will pedal alongside over both short and long distances, and this normally guarantees a most enjoyable journey.

When planning a long journey, always phone ahead to book a room — turning up at a hotel with no vacancies can be heartbreaking after a long and strenuous ride. Cycling in Cuba is hot at any time of year, and since there are few places by the roadside selling cool drinks or snacks, it is essential to carry a good supply of water and some food. People with experience of cycling around Cuba don't advise journeys of more than 70 miles (112km) in one day; and start early as it's already hot by 9am. It's also worth noting that Cuba is subject to strong winds, and that the prevailing wind is northeasterly.

Bike hire. Unfortunately, hire facilities in Cuba are poor, being confined largely to Havana and a few beachside hotels. Rental costs are usually $1 an hour and up to $10 a day. Only when you start negotiating the price for several days or a week does the price become vaguely reasonable. Alternatively, try to arrange to rent a bike privately from a Cuban, though do this carefully, since he or she can face a fine if caught. Or, if you were planning to hire a bicycle for a couple of weeks, buying your own may work out only marginally more expensive. Virtually every sizeable hard-currency shop stocks mountain-style bikes, which sell for around $150. Bicycles are now also manufactured in Cuba and cost about $80. At the end of your trip, you can give or sell the bike to a Cuban, or else take it home.

Bringing your own bicycle. Few European flights seem to arrive at Havana airport these days without at least one or two cyclists on board. Always check with the airline about bicycle carriage before you buy a ticket since different companies have different policies when it comes to the transporting of bikes. Most airlines allow you to take a bicycle free of charge providing your total luggage weight — including bike — is less than the airline's baggage allowance (usually 20kg per person). Maddeningly, the Stansted Express train from Liverpool Street in London to the airport from which the Havana flight leaves does not accept bicycles, and there is no alternative public transport.

When packing up the bike for transportation, you should ideally tape cardboard around the whole thing or, failing that, just around the gear and brakes levers and the rear wheel gear assembly; remove the pedals and deflate the tyres to avoid explosions at high altitude. Try to avoid removing the front wheel when stowing the bike — the front forks become extremely vulnerable to damage without an axle between them.

Take a rugged bike with good chunky tyres rather than a racer, whose slender tyres will be totally incapable of coping with the potholes. With so many cyclists circulating, many people have set themselves up to mend punctures — look out for signs saying *ponchera* (puncture-repair workshop) or *se coge ponche* ('punctures mended'). It isn't hard to find someone to do repairs, but few Cubans are familiar with Western models and there are no spare parts available for European multi-gear bicycles. You should take everything you may need, particularly spokes (these can be taped to the frame of the bike and forgotten about); gear cable (long), which can double as a brake cable if necessary; inner tubes; tyres; brake blocks (wheels get very hot and can wear brake blocks down surprisingly quickly); a small selection of nuts and bolts; and, of course, a puncture repair kit and a pump. Pumps are virtually non-existent in Cuba and most local cyclists must rely on service stations and on cycle workshops displaying the sign *se echa aire*. Note that European tyre valve fittings will not usually enable you to use these local facilities.

Sources of Information: the Cyclists' Touring Club provides members with general information sheets on cycling abroad, as well as trip reports; while it gives no specific advice on Cuba, the CTC remains a useful source. For further information contact the club at 69 Meadrow, Godalming, Surrey GU7 3HS (tel 01483 417217, fax 426994). The monthly magazine *New Cyclist* features articles on cycling trips abroad as well as more general advice about pedalling around foreign countries. It is available from newsagents or on subscription from New Cyclist, Freepost, Romford, Essex RM6 5NP.

Bike Events (tel 01225 480130) runs occasional tours to Cuba.

Security. Bicycle theft is a real problem in Cuba. Any bike which looks out of the ordinary is bound to attract attention, not all of it wanted, although in Havana mountain bikes are no longer the rarity they once were. Take a heavy chain and padlock, preferably a D-lock, and always attach the bicycle to a railing or put it in a bike park. (Simple chain locks are sold in some hard currency shops for $3-4 should you need to buy one in Cuba.) If you are visiting a friend, you will not be considered rude to take your bike into the house, and most hotels will let you leave it in a back room.

Foreign cyclists are often approached by well-meaning Cubans warning of the dangers of cycling at night, above all in Havana. The fact that few Cubans have the equipment to break a lock means that some specialise in ambushing cyclists instead. When travelling along a a quiet street at night, cycle in the middle of the road to make it more difficult for thieves to jump unseen from out of the shadows: this is less dangerous than it sounds because there are relatively few cars about.

CITY TRANSPORT

Cuba is unlike any other developing country, but in terms of its urban transport, the island looks increasingly like its Third World neighbours, with people clinging to overloaded buses and the arrival of a few bicycle rickshaws and even the odd Bangkok-style tuk-tuk.

Finding your way. Initially the style used for Cuban addresses can appear difficult, but in fact the system used is logical. Consider the address of Mexicana Airlines in the capital, as quoted in Spanish:

Calle 23 numero 74, esquina P, Vedado, Havana.

Translated, this means that the office is on Calle 23 (23rd Street) at number 74, on the corner *(esquina)* of Avenida P, in the district of Havana known as Vedado. Many other addresses are given in terms of bordering streets, so the Habana Libre hotel in the capital is on Calle 23 between Avenidas L and M. Its address may be written 23 e/ L y M; *e= entre* (between), *y* = and. Other symbols used to describe the same thing are ./. L y M; % L y M; and e/i L y M.

Cubans usually try to be helpful if you ask the way, but not many people know the street name even of the thoroughfare they are on. They also have a strange sense of distance, and generally over-estimate the time it will take you to walk somewhere. Just to confuse you, on other occasions they are wildly optimistic.

City Layout. Most Cuban cities are laid out on a regular grid pattern and are satisfyingly easy to get around on foot. The main scope for confusion lies in the survival of pre-revolutionary street names — on maps and colloquially — alongside those brought in to replace them after 1959. In some cities, as in the USA, streets have numbers rather than names. In Havana, numbered streets *(calles)* run parallel and are crossed by lettered streets or numbered avenues *(avenidas)*. In a further refinement, streets running east-west may be odd-numbered while those crossing north-south have even numbers.

Every town of any size has a main square, often named something like Plaza de los Trabajadores or Parque José Martí, but usually referred to simply as the Parque Central or Plaza Mayor.

Buses. Town buses are invariably overcrowded. They operate on a flat fare of 10 centavos, which you give to the driver or a conductor, or place in a box as you board. If you don't have the right change, don't worry too much. There are no recorded cases of Westerners being fined for fare evasion, but of course you should always endeavour to pay for your journey. If you board at one of the rear doors (technically breaking the rules, although everyone does it), you should pass your fare to the front.

While a queue might form at a bus stop, this doesn't always last when the bus actually arrives. Some buses also allow only a limited number to get on, so there are always a few disappointed people left behind.

Ruteros are minibuses that cruise on routes which are broadly fixed and known to the locals, if not to the temporary visitor. They are found mainly in Havana, and charge a fares of 40 centavos for any length of journey. The higher fare deters most local people from using them, which makes for a much more comfortable journey. You also see the odd *taxi bus*, which is similar to the rutero but charges one peso.

Taxis. In predictable Cuban style, there are taxis for tourists and taxis for Cubans. The former, of course, take dollars rather than pesos, the other main differences being that the tourist taxis are more numerous and more comfortable than the cabs designed for ordinary Cubans.

Dollar Taxis: air-conditioned vehicles known as *turistaxis* congregate outside large hotels and cater exclusively for tourists paying in hard currency. Most are run by Intur, but others are in the hands of Cubanacán or one of the tourist agencies. Major tourist areas, such as Havana, Varadero and Santiago de Cuba, have numerous turistaxis, while smaller centres such as Pinar del Río or Santa Clara may have just two or three.

For time-sensitive journeys, such as to a station or airport, you can ask your hotel desk to book you a car in advance. If you are staying in a downmarket hotel and have made friends with the staff, you may be able to persuade them to arrange for a private cab: see below.

Tourist taxis are willing to take you beyond town and city boundaries, but this is an uneconomic way to get around.

Peso Taxis: in contrast with the spanking new Toyotas and Nissans that ferry tourists around, ordinary peso taxis are mostly battered old Ladas. Many seem to have lost their rooftop 'Taxi' sign, but you may be able to make out the faded black checks on the side.

Finding any cab can be a nightmare, even for a Cuban. As with travelling by long-distance bus, you may find it distasteful to provide extra competition for Cubans who have far more problems than you do to get from A to B. Most peso cabs refuse to take foreigners and your best chance of using one will be to travel with a Cuban friend. Some peso cab drivers will expect a foreigner to pay in dollars, but these 'black market' cabs still work out cheaper than both the tourist taxis and the private cabs described below. The average peso cab functions these days as a collective taxi, with the driver picking people up until its full — though if you are the first on board and paying a special rate, he or she is less likely to do so. A Lada can take four passengers in relative comfort.

In smaller towns with fewer taxis, there are fixed locations from which taxis leave, and there is usually also a taxi despatcher; look for the person with a clipboard. Tell him or her where you want to go, and you will either be ignored or sooner or later packed into a taxi together with several other people. Understandably, the elderly and infirm, or those with young children, are given absolute priority, so if a succession of women with babes-in-arms turns up, your wait will be protracted.

Some taxis follow fixed routes. Others are confined to runs to and from a specific transport terminal or hospital, and are marked 'terminal de trenes' or 'hospital' accordingly. This might not seem much use unless you are travelling by train or seeking medical treatment, but in fact they are allowed to take passengers heading in the same direction.

Private taxis: you are far more likely to take a ride in a private cab than a peso cab. Virtually any town you visit in Cuba will have a supply of drivers looking for business, the same drivers that you can hire to take you on longer journeys: see *Long-Distance Taxi* above. Find a busy intersection and flag down anything that moves, or else ask around. If you want to visit a couple of museums or go on several errands, negotiate a round fee before you set off.

Horse-drawn Cabs. The predominant form of public transport in most towns is not the bus or the taxi but the horse-drawn cab, known as a *coche*. The horse can be pulling anything from a bare cart to an ornate carriage with leather seats. This is a lovely way to get around if you can bear to look at the ragged and overworked animals and witness the over-zealous use of a whip by the *cochero* (driver).

Most towns have fixed routes, and you can flag down a cab at any point along the route. A ride should cost no more than 1 or 2 pesos. It is feasible to charter a whole cart for journeys to somewhere off the normal route or to the local airport, etc.

Walking. As a pedestrian you have no rights. In every Cuban town, pavements are uneven and are obstructed by gaping holes, telegraph poles, small children and animals, obliging you to step into the road frequently. Furthermore they are often wet and slippery, since it is common practice for householders to slop out cleaning water into the street. Also keep your eyes peeled for maniacal drivers and cyclists.

Your lungs will not enjoy walking the streets in the larger Cuban towns, since cars, buses and lorries spew out all sorts of noxious fumes.

agua caliente	hot water	*gerente, jefe*	boss, manager
aire condicionado	air conditioning	*habitación*	room
alojamiento	accommodation	*huésped*	guest
ascensor	lift	*lavandería*	laundry
baños	toilets	*maletero*	bellboy
cabaña	(beach) cabin, bungalow	*matrimonio*	double (room) with double bed
caja de seguridad	safe deposit box	*piscina*	swimming pool (many dollar hotels have one)
cama	bed		
carpeta	reception desk	*media pensión*	half board
casa de campaña	tent	*piso*	floor (storey)
climatizado	air-conditioned	*planta baja*	ground floor
completo	full	*pulga*	flea
con baño	with bathroom	*rata*	rat
cucuracha	cockroach	*sencillo*	single (room)
desayuno	breakfast	*temporada alta*	high season
doble	double (usually twin) room	*temporada baja*	low season
		ventilador	fan

Pre-revolutionary Cuba boasted some of the finest hotels in the world, all of them rich men's ghettoes where US visitors were treated extremely well but locals were forbidden to stay. The American Mafia was heavily involved in the hotel industry, particularly during the building boom of the late 1950s. After the revolution many hotels were converted into apartments or left to decay, deprived of the dollars upon which they depended. Today the trend has gone full circle, with new beachside complexes being erected at a frenetic pace and older hotels undergoing massive refurbishment — all catering for foreigners who pay in dollars. Costs in Havana and the resorts are comparatively high. Elsewhere, rates are reasonable but rarely cheap. The tourist industry in Cuba is designed primarily for package tourists who will spend huge amounts of money in a very short time. Independent travellers who like to budget more carefully are not going to help the Cuban government out of its current economic crisis. Anyone living on a low budget will have to stay in peso hotels, run-down establishments catering mainly for Cubans, or in a private home. A growing number of Cubans rent out rooms to foreigners, providing by the far the cheapest and most entertaining form of accommodation. The government has harnessed this source of revenue by levying a monthly tax on proprietors. Unlike in the former Eastern Bloc countries, Cuba has never obliged visitors to account for where they spend each night.

HOTELS

In the early 1990s, when Cuba had only just started on its great tourism drive, the island had few of the facilities it needed to attract big-spending package tourists. Since then, considerable headway has been made in improving accommodation prospects, with the new breed of joint-venture hotels leading the way in providing world-class accommodation. Part financed by Western companies, these joint ventures have also spearheaded Cuba's drive to attract foreign investment. These high-class hotels have been built almost exclusively in the island's beach resorts, the state-of-the-art Meliá Cohiba (see page 162) being one of the few to have been built in the capital. Here, and in other towns and cities, the authorities have concentrated on refurbishing old hotels. Some of these occupy fine colonial or pre-revolutionary buildings, but on the whole Cuba is short of good quality, atmospheric hotels where you would happily spend your entire holiday. One of the exceptions is Los Jazmines in the Viñales valley (see page 220). If you are happy with simple facilities, the choice improves in places like Matanzas and Camagüey, but in general dollar hotels are drab, purpose-built, Soviet-style monstrosities situated some distance from the town centre. These seem to have been relegated to the bottom of the hotels waiting for refurbishment, although what most of them require is demolition.

Creature comforts vary dramatically, and never be taken in by a smart exterior. Although most hotels are untouched by the cost-cutting measures which affect most Cubans, in the provinces you may encounter power cuts; not all hotels have their own generators. Some hotels are adopting a positive attitude to customer care, so you may find such options as non-smoking rooms on offer — but don't count on it.

Hotel classifications run from one up to five stars, but most establishments fall into the top three categories. Many resort hotels are four or five-star and come with everything the Cubans think you could possibly need — down to aerobics classes and game shows. If you are happy with moderate comfort, you should be satisfied by the average three-star hotel, where rooms should come with a private bathroom, television, radio, air-conditioning and hot water. However, there is nearly always at least one thing wrong with the room, from a non-functioning radio to exposed electric cables. All the air-conditioning units are manufactured in Russia, a country not noted for its experience of hot weather, and rarely seem to function perfectly.

If there appears to be no hot water, there are several possible reasons. In the monolithic Soviet-style hotels it can take a long time for the water to get from wherever it's heated to your shower. Or there may simply be no hot water. That bathrooms in cheap hotels don't have bathplugs is often an irrelevance, since the plumbing may not work anyway; an all-purpose plug is essential if you aren't staying in Cuba's more modern establishments. If you refuse to believe that a socialist economy can fail to provide enough plugs, or you are forgetful, note that a handkerchief stuffed into the plughole or an upside-down tumbler should do the trick. This assumes, of course, that you can find your way around the bathroom. If you can't find the light switch, it's probably just below the mirror. A torch is useful in Cuban hotels even when there is no power cut.

Watch out for over-assiduous chamber staff, who tidy up rooms so effectively that you leave behind things that have been put away neatly into a drawer. A good ploy is to shove all your belongings in the wardrobe and leave tidy anything that is left visible. Don't be too surprised if the odd thing goes walkabout from your room, particularly soap and razors. Another favourite trick among chamber staff is to empty guests' bottles of shampoo and refill them with water.

If you have a serious complaint, take it up with the reception staff; a good bargaining point is to threaten to put your problem into writing in the complaints book labelled *Quejas y Surgerencias* which should be held at reception.

Room rates. The improvements to Cuba's hotel industry mean that double-booking has become less common, that elevators break down less often, and that water cuts are less frequent; but it has inevitably also brought higher prices. A two-star hotel that closes for renovation almost always jumps up a category or two on re-opening.

Cuba's dollar hotels are run by different agencies. The three main ones are Gran Caribe, which handles the top end of the market; Horizontes, which runs middle of the range and budget-priced hotels; and Isla Azul, which has taken over several peso hotels and made them accessible to more cost-conscious foreigners. Smaller groups, such as Cubanacán and Gaviota, tend to specialise in expensive, resort-style accommodation. Knowing which agency runs a hotel gives a good indication as to the quality and cost of a room.

Prices vary considerably according to location and also within the same category. The Caribbean, one of Cuba's few one-star hotels and an independent travellers' favourite in Havana, currently charges $25 per night for a single in high season. Most three-star hotels offer double rooms for about $30, while in the capital you can expect to pay $40-50. The cost of four-star rooms hover between $60 and $100 a night, the upper limit being characteristic in Havana and Varadero. The latter has the largest number of top-notch hotels outside the capital, including several luxury resorts where one night can cost well over $100 per person. Wherever you stay, singles are generally about 20% cheaper.

The official high seasons are December to February, and July and August. This creates a couple of extra peaks immediately before and after the high season; late November and early March are busy as people take advantage of low-season prices and good weather. Asking for a discount on the cost of your room in low season tends to be most successful by the beach, when the resorts are desperately quiet.

Breakfast is not usually included in the price paid, unless you have pre-booked accommodation. Some hotels may offer a discount on meals if you take half-board, and certain resorts that deal primarily with package tourists offer nothing but full-board. Most four-and five-star hotels have two restaurants: a buffet restaurant where you can buy breakfast, lunch and dinner at a fixed price, and a smaller restaurant with an à la carte menu. The buffet restaurants are designed primarily for package tourists, but are also open to individual travellers — whether or not you are a guest. See *Eating and Drinking* for a description of hotel food. Hotels may let you keep a tab during your stay, but be careful to check this carefully against the receipts that you have signed.

Finally, most hotels should be happy to look after your luggage while you travel around the country, though most will make a charge, e.g. $1 per piece per day.

All-inclusive Resorts. The worldwide trend towards holidays where everything from the flight to the food is included in one price has arrived with a vengeance in Cuba. Most of the resort areas have at least one or two such compounds. For those inside the fences, they have the advantage of solving the problem of finding palatable food and drink but the drawback of creating a thoroughly skewed image of Cuba. Outsiders will find these places closed to visitors.

Complaints. In theory, at least, guests can be compensated for poor facilities. Resolution number 52/89 of the State Prices Commission prescribes reductions in prices for shortcomings in room quality. For example, 'radio not working' earns a 2% discount; 'irregularities in the bathroom' (probably excluding a missing bathplug) gets 7% off; while 'mattress in a bad state' secures a 10%

reduction. There are no recorded cases of foreigners successfully negotiating a discount on this basis, but you're welcome to try.

Booking Accommodation. Prospective travellers to Cuba are advised by the Cuban authorities to book every night's accommodation in advance, the implication being that you are unlikely to get a room in the hotel of your choice, or indeed any hotel at all, if you leave it until after your arrival. The experience of the researchers for this book, however, is that finding a hotel room is hardly ever a problem; simply turning up at a hotel reception desk *(carpeta)* even late at night will normally secure you a room. If you encounter a hotel which claims to be full, try to persuade the receptionist to phone around to the other local hotels for you. In extremis you might try calling in at the police station; a phone call from the police to an uncooperative hotel may result in the miraculous appearance of vacancies (and on one occasion has resulted in a drop in price from $90 to $35 a night).

Nevertheless, if you plan to travel to only a couple of centres and are sure about the hotel in which you would like to stay, you can book ahead via any travel agent or tour operator that has links with the Cuban tourist agencies. You will be issued with vouchers, which you hand over to the hotel on your arrival. Note that rates will be slightly higher than those you would pay locally. On the other hand, if you enrol on an organised package deal, the accommodation costs can drop quite dramatically, though you will be unable to stay in the older, more characterful hotels.

Most independent travellers book their first two nights in Havana (the usual port of entry), then possibly a night or two back in the capital before leaving the country; this should ensure that you have easy passage through immigration and saves you the hassle of finding accommodation immediately on your arrival in Havana, where hotels do fill up in high season. This will also give you maximum flexibility; booking every night in advance ties you to an itinerary which you may regret once you have arrived. Booking even a single night's accommodation from abroad, however, renders you liable for a 'Representation Charge' of £14, which the booking agent will add to the bill.

In Cuba itself, the easiest way to book a room is to approach the tourism desk at your hotel and ask the clerk to book your next night's accommodation. There is usually no fee for this service, although you may be asked to pay for the room in advance. The clerk gives you a voucher which supposedly covers the cost of a room. Sometimes, though, you arrive at the next hotel where the staff say the price list was out of date and demand a supplement of, for example, $5. This is not a fiddle on the part of the management since you are given an official receipt. Alternatively, the clerk may simply reserve you a room over the phone, leaving you to pay directly. Spanish-speakers may opt to do this themselves, though of course there is no guarantee that they will hold the room for you. Faxing a confirmation will give you more clout.

When asking for a double room, remember to make the distinction between a *habitación doble* or *matrimonio.* The former will normally have twin beds, the second a double.

Peso hotels. Alongside the smart dollar hotels are the old peso hotels, no-frills establshments intended for privileged Cuban couples on honeymoon or touring musicians rather than for Westerners looking for somewhere cheap to stay. Some have already been converted into hotels suitable for comfort-demanding foreigners, however the old survivors are often worth seeking out since they are not only cheap (a double usually costs $10-15), but almost always centrally located and much more characterful than purpose-built tourist accommodation. Furthermore, you will be able to enjoy the company of Cubans rather than tourists. A room in even the most basic hotel has a bathroom with shower and provides towels and soap, though the plumbing and cooling systems are often unreliable. Unlike the standard tourist establishments, peso hotels are not immune to power cuts — still a feature of daily life at the time of going to press — and running water might be available only at certain times of day; in country areas, you might have to collect water in a bucket from a communal outdoor tap.

In the past, it was impossible to predict whether or not a peso hotel would permit you to stay. There are still a few that are not authorised to house tourists, but the majority automatically admit foreigners, simply charging them in dollars rather than local currency. Some peso hotels are now in the hands of the Isla Azul group and are reasonably well organised to deal with tourists, while for others the arrival of a foreigner is still a novelty, giving rise to discussions as to how much a room costs in dollars. Note that it is not possible to make an official reservation for a room in a peso hotels, but you can always try phoning ahead yourself.

It is common practice in peso hotels for someone to check your room before you leave — a measure designed to deter Cuban guests from stealing lightbulbs, towels and other much-needed items but which can prove embarrassing for unsuspecting tourists who left their room in a mess.

PRIVATE ACCOMMODATION

As a result of the economic crisis, Cubans have had to find ways of supplementing their meagre incomes simply in order to feed themselves. Those fortunate enough to live in a tourist centre can earn precious dollars by renting out a spare room or flat to tourists. Even Communist Party militants and officials of the Armed Forces get involved in this illegal business. The market is biggest in Havana, but private lodgings are not hard to find elsewhere. If someone doesn't approach you in the street offering a *casa particular* (private house), *habitación* (room) or *apartamento* (flat), just ask around.

Prices vary according to whether you live with a family or are in a self-contained flat. In Havana you should reckon on paying about $10 a night, less if you stay a week or more, and $100-150 if you stay a whole month. Those who take a room in a private home may have the option of eating with the family too, which can help reduce your costs considerably. Depending on where you are, the supplies of water and power may be erratic, but on the whole no worse than in a peso hotel. On the contrary, you are likely to live more comfortably than if you were in a cheap local hotel, and will leave the country with a far more vivid picture of what life in Cuba is really like. Most tourists who stay privately can't recommend the experience highly enough.

CAMPING

Cuba has about 100 campsites dotted over the island, created in the early 1980s to provide cheap holidays aimed particularly at the younger generations. The authorities haven't yet explored the full potential of its campsites as far as the foreign market is concerned. Cubamar runs a number of so-called *campismos*, but the term is a misnomer since these are complexes of bungalows rather than traditional campsites. There are currently just three international campismos — at Aguas Claras (Pinar del Río), El Abra (east of Havana) and Guaniguanico (between Trinidad and Cienfuegos).

There is nothing to stop you seeking out an old-style sites run by Campismo Popular, some of which are in fine and shady spots. The facilities are generally non-existent but most campsites have pre-erected tents and are very cheap, charging around $5 per person, payable in hard currency. The staff may tell you to go to the reservations office *(carpeta central)* in the nearest town, but they are equally likely to say that the site is for Cubans only. Rather than head off on a long trek after a reservation, try standing your ground at the site itself first.

If you have your own equipment, better still find somewhere else to pitch your tent, preferably near a house where you can ask politely for permission and for water and other essentials.

EATING

ahumado	smoked	*fritura*	fried snack
ajiaco	traditional Cuban soup	*garbanzo*	chick peas
ajo	garlic	*helado (heladería)*	ice cream (parlour)
almuerzo	lunch	*huevo*	egg
arroz	rice (invariably white)	*huevos revueltos*	scrambled egg
autoservicio	self-service cafeteria	*judia*	butter beans
bocadillo, bocadito	sandwich	*manis*	ground-nut snack,
caldo	soup		sometimes sugared
cena	supper		like halva
chiclé, goma	chewing gum	*mantequilla*	butter
cocido	cooked	*mermelada*	jam
combinación	set meal	*Mesa Sueca*	buffet
comedor	dining room	*moros y cristianos*	rice and beans
comida	food	*paladar*	private restaurant
congri	rice and beans	*pan*	bread
crema	creamed soup	*panadería*	bakery
cremería	ice cream parlour	*parrillada*	grill
cuchara	spoon	*pastel*	cake
cuchillo	knife	*plato fuerte*	main course
cuenta, cheque	bill	*potage*	soup (usually beans)
(chekay)		*revoltillo*	omelette
dulce	dessert, cake	*salsa*	sauce
enchilada	stew	*sin carne*	without meat
fabada	bean soup	*sopa*	soup
flan	crème caramel	*tenedor*	fork
frijoles	beans	*tortilla*	omelette
frito	fried	*(pan) tostada*	toast

Meat and Fish

albóndigas	meatballs	*ostiones*	oysters
asado	roast, grilled	*pescado*	fish
atún	tuna	*picadillo*	minced beef dish
camarrones	prawns	*pollo*	chicken
chicharrón	pork crackling	*puerco, cerdo*	pork
chuleta	chop	*rueda*	(fish)steak
cordero	lamb	*riñones*	kidneys
hamburguesa	hamburger	*tasajo*	horsemeat or dried
higado	liver		beef
jamón	ham	*ternera*	veal
langosta	lobster	*tortuga*	turtle
mariscos	seafood	*vaca*	beef

Fruit and Vegetables

boniato	type of sweet potato	*pepino*	cucumber
col (repollo in east)	cabbage	*piña*	pineapple

ensalada de estación	seasonal salad	*plátano*	plantain, banana
fruta bomba	papaya	*puré de papas*	mashed potato
fufú	mashed plantains	*quimbomba*	okra
guayaba	guava	*remolacha*	beetroot
lechuga	lettuce	*toronja*	grapefruit
limón	lemon	*tostones, chatinos*	fried plantains
malanga	fibrous root vegetable	*vianda*	(root) vegetables
naranja	orange	*vegetales, legumbres*	vegetables
papas	potatoes	*yuca*	root vegetable
papas fritas	French fries	*zanahoria*	carrot

The difficulty in finding a decent meal can be the most infuriating feature of a visit to Cuba. The island has all the natural attributes for producing plenty of fresh, wholesome food, but at times you may feel almost pathetically grateful if a meal is palatable. While visitors need not dread mealtimes as much as they used to, there is still some wear in the old saying 'if you want to lose weight go to Cuba'. Many travellers find it worthwhile to stock up at home with small and nutritious items such as muesli bars and dried fruit to supplement their diet when the going gets tough.

Before you think of complaining, however, reflect that you are likely to spend time with Cubans who have not eaten for 24 hours, not tasted cheese for a year and lost track of when they last had a beer. Food supplies in Cuba have been regulated since the early 1960s, but never have the ration books given the people so little. All staple foods are rationed. In 1995, the only regular items a Cuban received each month were 2kg of rice and a handful each of beans, sugar, salt and coffee, and one bread roll per day. Things like eggs, vegetables and fresh fish arrive occasionally, but are considered a bonus; fresh meat is a luxury for most Cubans. Characteristically, they are still able to laugh about the appalling deprivations. One of the jokes circulating recently was: 'Q: Why is Fidel Castro known as 'the onion'? A: Because he makes people cry in the kitchen'. The huge Soviet-built refrigerator in most Cuban homes rarely contains more than a few bottles of water keeping cool.

The main reason for the dearth of food in Cuba is the historic over-dependence on imports and the over-centralisation of agricultural production. The imports that sustained the island up to the 1990s dried up with the collapse of the Soviet Union, and while the government is loosening its grip on farming, it will take years for Cuba to recover. Families keep animals and chickens in their yards or even on a balcony to supplement their diets, and city dwellers are sent to the countryside to help grow the food that Cuba can no longer afford to import. The soil of this the Caribbean's most fertile island is a much under-exploited resource that only economic recovery and liberalisation is likely to correct. Poor distribution, exacerbated recently by fuel shortages, has also played its part, with many vegetables and fruits left to rot in the fields.

All this explains the difficulty chefs have in providing a decent meal. But perhaps the overriding reason is that while Marx espoused the principle of 'to each according to his need', he made no promises about the quality of the food. Cuba has more pressing problems to solve than dissatisfaction over restaurant meals. The sort of Cubans who demanded good food at restaurants mostly left when the Revolution triumphed.

Normal gastronomic standards simply do not apply in Cuba. There is little variety between restaurants, except in the quality of the food, which varies not only from one restaurant to another, but also from day to day at the same establishment — a result of the erratic supply of ingredients. The arrival of overseas companies with an insight into what foreign tourists expect to eat means that the standards in hotel restaurants are rising, but you must be prepared to set your sights a good deal lower when you travel away from the tourist centres. If your idea of a perfect holiday is spending long evenings over delicious dinners, you shouldn't venture too far from Havana or the resorts.

Before you despair, however, the economic liberalisation seen over the last couple of years has boosted greatly the availability of food. The re-introduction of private markets has at last made the marvellous array of tropical fruits that grow in Cuba accessible, and you can also buy prepared meals and snacks. Even two years ago, it was almost impossible for a tourist to find anything to eat in a small provincial town. Now, however, you can go to the local market and at least buy a snack. The legalisation of private restaurants has been another bonus, particularly in Havana. You are far more likely to eat your best meal in somebody's home than in a restaurant.

The new markets and restaurants have encouraged the reappearance of culinary traditions that were in danger of being lost permanently through the simple lack of food.

CUBAN CUISINE

Cuba's aboriginal inhabitants lived primarily on fish and seafood, together with native fruit and vegetables. These Taíno and Siboney Indians died out long ago, as did their cooking, the popular consumption of yuca and maize being one of the few legacies of Cuba's pre-Columbian inhabitants. The island's cuisine is largely an amalgam of foreign influences, particularly Spanish and African. The Spanish brought with them cows, pigs, rice, vegetables, citrus fruits and sugar, together with a rich variety of regional cuisines, and adapted local produce to suit their own tastes. Slaves could bring nothing with them, though some vegetables were brought over on the slave ships from Africa, but they brought their own customs and tastes, which gradually added an African flavour to the predominantly Spanish style of cooking. The staple dish of rice and beans is essentially an expression of this fusion.

Westerners tend to find traditional Cuban cooking, known as *comida criolla*, bland. Many dishes include garlic but rarely any spices. While this is partly due to the shortages, traditional dishes do tend to be very simple. The most typical meal you could expect to eat would be a mountain of rice and beans accompanied by a pork steak (*cerdo asado*) and an accompaniment such as fried plantains or a salad of whatever is in season at the time. You will be able to eat a variation on this theme in most restaurants, but note that the tastiest versions will almost certainly be cooked at home.

Rice and beans. This archetypal Cuban dish comes in two main versions, one made with kidney beans and the other with black beans. These are known respectively as *congri* and *moros y cristianos* (literally 'Moors and Christians'), though in Oriente the terms seem to be interchangeable. In private restaurants, you may sometimes be given plain white rice and a bowl of thick bean soup called *potage* — the idea is to mix the two, which is an excellent way of curing the dryness of the standard rice and beans. You sometimes see *potage* on restaurant menus, and it makes a cheap and satisfying lunch.

Meat and fish. Give a Cuban the choice between meat and fish, and they will go for the former almost every time. The favoured meat is pork, preferably an escalope simply fried. Fatty cuts might be added to *potage* to give extra flavour or else added to a stew, such as *ajiaco*. This classic country dish has many regional variations, but usually includes plenty of root vegetables. While meat almost always provides the flavour, in Guantánamo for instance it is sometimes prepared with fish. While not a common inclusion on a dollar restaurant menu, when well-prepared ajiaco is both delicious and filling. The traditional way to bring in the New Year is to roast a whole pig; families may keep a pig in their back yard or on the roof solely with this celebration in mind.

Chicken appears on most menus grilled or fried and is generally good. Beef rarely figures large on restaurant menus, and has all but disappeared from Cuban homes. Such is the state of the island's cattle industry that the cow has become something of a sacred beast. A Cuban can be sent to prison for eight or more years for killing a cow without authorisation; people joke that you can get fewer years for murdering a human being. What beef reaches the butchers' table mostly ends up on the plates of tourists. The poor state of the animals means that you won't often be offered steak, except in the top restaurants. One popular way to prepare beefsteak is to simply rub the meat with oil, garlic and lime, grill it and then serve with fried onions-known as *bistec palomilla*. More common, however, are the minced beef dish, *picadillo*, or the traditional *ropa vieja*, literally 'old clothes', which is a fairly apt way to describe this dish of shredded beef in a tomato-based sauce. Rather more unusual and well worth trying is *boliche mechado*, a fillet of beef stuffed with chorizo.

For a nation surrounded by sea, it is disappointing how little fish is served in Cuba. Private fishing is not permitted, which is a tragedy for an island with such rich waters lapping at its shores. Most of the 900-odd species that live in around the island are edible, but you are likely to see only one or two of them offered on a menu. On the other hand, you could live on lobster, prawns and other seafood. While clearly not for those on a strict budget, $20-30 for lobster is good value by international standards. Don't be too shocked to find restaurants selling turtle *(tortuga)*, several species of which are not endangered in Cuba. The most common types are *caguama*, a saltwater tortoise, or the freshwater *jicotea*. Both taste rather like fishy beef. Crocodile meat, which is like a cross between chicken and pork, is far rarer and found mainly in private restaurants.

Fruit and vegetables. One of the world's mysteries is what happens to all the fruit and vegetables which Cuba produces. Few restaurants offer anything but a disappointing choice of either. The former usually appear in the form of chips, while fruit is lucky to get a look in. A browse around a market reveals that there should be a great deal more on offer, though even here supplies are often small and erratic. If you are driving around the countryside — even along the motorways — look out for people selling fruit and other fresh produce by the roadside.

Most restaurants these days stretch to including plantains (green bananas) on the menu. *Plátanos maduros* are soft and sweet and are often simply fried whole, while the less ripe *plátanos verdes* are usually fried either as paper-thin chips or as thicker *tostones* (also called *chatinos*). Boiled and mashed, as *fufú*, plantains are much more of an acquired taste, but no dollar restaurant would dare risk serving tourists such a dish.

Unless you eat in a Cuban home, you will probably also miss out on the island's tastiest and most traditional root vegetables, though you find *yuca* (cassava) on some menus. This tuber is fibrous and fairly starchy, but has a distinctive and pleasant flavour which is greatly enhanced when served with a fried mixture of lemon and garlic known as *mojo*. In provincial markets, particularly in Camagüey, you may come across *casabe*, which is a kind of dry pancake made out of grated yuca that has been pressed (to extract poisonous juices) and then baked. Tourists don't seem to be considered ready for the delights of Cuba's other root vegetables. This is a great shame because *boniato*, a kind of sweet potato, is absolutely delicious. The *malanga*, a fibrous root also known as *ñame* and African in origin, is more of a challenge to the average Western palate.

You rarely find green vegetables, and in restaurants are more likely to be offered a salad, which will be whatever happens to be available. If you are lucky, this might be a mixed salad of lettuce, tomato and cucumber, but will more probably be a plate of just one of these three. And don't be shocked if the tomatoes are green; this is par for the course in Cuba.

Fruit is almost totally absent from menus. Hotels serve a limited selection — usually pineapple, banana, orange and occasionally papaya — but the ready-chopped fruit on offer is not a patch on what you can buy fresh. Cuba produces some wonderful fruits that are well worth scouring the markets for. Mangoes grow in such abundance that you can make yourself sick on them, and the bananas, including small and wonderfully sweet varieties, make a mockery of the versions you eat back home. Two unusual fruits to look out for are the *guanábana* and the *mamey*. The former has a rough green skin with brown specks and deliciously juicy white flesh. It is best eaten when small, about the size of an orange, but guanábanas can reach the size of a melon. The *mamey*, also known as *zapote*, is a more surprising fruit. The size of a small avocado, its dull brown skin reveals a fiery red inside. The flesh is dense and filling, and makes a wonderful fruit shake.

Snacks. The markets are the best place to go in search of a late breakfast, lunch on the hoof or just a snack. Almost invariably good are the pork sandwiches *(pan con puerco* or *pan con lechón)*, made with meat carved fresh from the pig's back. *Tamales*, mashed maize steamed in a corn husk, are popular with Cubans but are stodgy and not to everyone's liking. People also sell cakes and all manner of fried snacks, described generically as *frituras*. Sometimes you needn't seek out the market, but will find people selling snacks from stalls set up in the street in the town centre.

If you are reliant on a tourist restaurant, a good lunchtime meal is the ubiquitous ham and cheese sandwich *(sandwich de jamón y queso)*. Every tourist establishment seems to serve a version of it, the price — usually $3-$4 — varying as little as the appearance. Better still is the 'Cuban sandwich', which includes pork as well as ham and cheese, while the combination of cream cheese and strawberry jam in the 'Elena Rush' is rather startling. A more traditional way of mixing sweet and savoury foods in Cuba is to combine sweet guava paste *(dulce de guayaba)* with cheese, served as a pudding.

Vegetarian meals. The heavy Spanish influence on Cuban cooking is bad news for vegetarians, and even the harmless-sounding rice and beans often includes pieces of pork fat. Vegetarians are still a novelty and are rarely catered for. A few restaurants will (on request) prepare a special dish for vegetarians, but they are not renowned for their flexibility. Non meat-eaters will have a hard time away from the better-stocked hotel restaurants, where the buffets provide a wide range of dishes to choose from. Even so, many restaurants serve pasta or pizza in some form, and eggs feature on most menus in all the traditional forms, whether fried, scrambled or as an omelette.

Chinese food. During the 19th century, many Chinese were shipped to Cuba as labourers. Over the generations, they have been assimilated into the general population, but their descendants have not completely abandoned their heritage. Chinese restaurants are found all over the country and are very popular. Sadly, however, the shortage of supplies during the Special Period has meant that the oriental dishes often resemble the bland creations that you can eat anywhere else.

RESTAURANTS

You could probably count the number of 'good' restaurants (by Western standards) on the fingers of two hands, and the majority of these are in Havana. Most restaurants are mediocre in terms of food, service or ambience, and usually all three. Even if you plan to frequent Cuba's highest quality restaurants, you may find it useful to understand the phrase *no hay*, literally 'there is none' or 'it does not exist'. If you learn only two words of Spanish, go for those two.

All restaurants in Cuba are owned by the state and are split into seven categories. The top grade, 1, requires male guests to wear a jacket and tie and serves 'international' cuisine with a few local specialities thrown in. The clientele is restricted to rich (and well-dressed) tourists, diplomats and Party officials. Most travellers will eat in the second and third grade places. The majority of menus are depressingly predictable and a continual source of disappointment, but at least you have access to food which most ordinary Cubans can only stare at longingly through the window. This uncomfortable apartheid is still part and parcel of every day life in Cuba, though the situation has improved slightly since the dollar was legalised. Some travellers prefer to frequent the cheaper cafés simply to be able to enjoy the company of Cubans, for whom a meal in the more expensive dollar restaurants is simply out of the question.

Fourth class down to seventh class cafeterias are where most locals eat and drink if they go out. Outside Havana, however, where restaurants cannot survive purely on the tourist trade, Cubans can eat alongside visitors and pay in pesos. Reservations for local people are hard to come by, and are usually awarded as a privilege through the workplace. While the quality of the food is not as good, the ambience is often preferable. Even here, though, dollar-carrying Westerners are a privileged minority, able to jump the inevitable queues. Doormen at most places are under instructions to usher foreign tourists to the head of the line. While on principle most travellers would prefer to wait their turn, the temptation to queue barge can be hard to resist. Most provincial peso restaurants shut before 10pm, by which time they may well have run out of food anyway. You are advised to dine much earlier, between 7 and 8pm, which is when most Cubans will be eating. Some restaurants open only at lunchtime, and in some towns you will have no option but to eat your evening meal in the hotel.

Given the quality of the food, eating out in Cuba is expensive. In normal tourist restaurants main dishes cost $5-10 and rarely come with accompaniments, which you must order separately. You can keep your costs down by eating pasta and pizza, or by frequenting private or peso restaurants, where the price as well as the choice of food diminishes.

Hotel Restaurants. Few people will spend a holiday in Cuba without sampling a hotel buffet. The Soviet term 'Swedish Table' *(Mesa Sueca)* is often used to describe the eat-all-you-can buffet, though it is also known as *mesa buffet* or simply *buffet* (pronounced boo-*fay*). For ravenous travellers they can prove excellent value. Always have a look at what you're letting yourself in for before paying up. In the provinces you may have no choice, but in Havana there is always the option of trying another hotel down the road — most hotel restaurants are open to non-residents. All but the smallest hotels should serve a buffet, though some may revert to an à la carte menu during the low season. Most hotels have a separate restaurant designed for serving à la carte meals only.

In the average three or four-star hotel, breakfast, lunch and dinner will cost $5, $10 and $15 respectively. If you stay in the new Meliá Cohiba in Havana, breakfast alone will cost you $12, and prices are generally higher in Varadero too. But so is the quality. Whichever meal you go for, endeavour to go well before the end to avoid having to make do with the dregs, though replenishments are brought out regularly.

Breakfast: a good hotel breakfast in a hard-currency hotel is, relatively speaking, a delight. The prevalence of new hotels in Varadero means that here you can find treats such as croissants and bacon. Most hotels charge humbler prices and serve humbler food. The staples are fresh fruit, bread rolls, fruit juice, coffee, tea and several of many variables, from yoghurt and cakes to cold spaghetti salad and risotto. The latter are almost certainly the leftovers from dinner the night before. As a sop to the tastes of visiting Westerners, eggs may be available — sometimes in tasty omelettes, sometimes badly scrambled. Breakfast is usually served 7.30-10am.

If you plan to be out and about all day, a good eat-all-you-can breakfast will set you up for the day, and relieve the tension of having to find lunch. In hotels without a buffet, you can normally get coffee and toast (usually a slice of white bread which has merely been waved under a grill) or eggs. If you don't eat breakfast in your hotel, you won't get it anywhere else.

Eating out on pesos. No-frills pizzerias, burger bars and cafeterias are where most Cubans treat themselves to a meal out. These are fine providing they have food available. Often just one thing is on offer, whether it's soup, hamburgers or a bowl of boiled yuca (more tasty than it sounds). As elsewhere in the world, pizza is very popular. Most big towns have a pizzeria, and you find street corner pizza kiosks too. Their popularity means that these delicacies are available for only an hour or two each day, usually at lunchtime. Queues are always long. Don't expect a choice of topping, which is likely to consist simply of cheese and tomato.

If Cubans aren't queuing for a slice of pizza, they are likely to be waiting in line outside a hamburger bar. You are advised not to join them, since the average hamburger is a slab of grey, gristly and almost inedible junk, slung inside a dry white roll; forget about ketchup. As a tourist you would be advised to eat the more palatable version available in some dollar restaurants.

Most Cubans are resigned to the idea of waiting in line, sometimes for hours. The queueing procedure varies, but in the most popular places you must collect a ticket from the door and then wait in line until you are called. For once, Westerners do not receive special treatment, and you will actually find it much easier if you are with Cuban friends. The cheapest places won't even demand hard currency.

The typical lower-grade restaurant opens from 8am to 10pm, but food is available only sporadically, for an hour or so at midday and again in the early evening.

Service. In some restaurants pride is clearly taken, and in others natural Cuban hospitality to visitors may result in good service. But in most there is no obvious concept of service or meeting customers' wishes. Bear in mind that the average restaurant doorkeeper, waiter or chef has little incentive to make dining out a pleasurable experience. If you were a waitress or chef in an establishment which served either unappetising meals or food that was unavailable to the majority of the population, you too might become demoralised and disenchanted.

Don't expect a meal to arrive in the correct sequence or necessarily as you ordered it. And try to keep your cool when, having placed your order, you are told half an hour later that your chosen dish is not available. The concept of fast food ends at the Florida Keys. Getting lunch in some restaurants can require an investment of at least an hour, once waiting to order, waiting for your food and waiting to pay are taken into account. It might take only five minutes to eat the plate of meat or spaghetti plonked unceremoniously in front of you, but then you must wait another thirty to get out; telling the staff that you are in a hurry (*estoy apurado, a*) doesn't always work. Then, just as you've got the hang of timing your meals correctly, you choose a restaurant in which the bill is brought long before you are ready to leave and where the staff wait by the table impatiently until you have paid.

Private restaurants. One of the best things to happen in Cuba in 1995 was the legalisation of private restaurants, the legal requirement being that they should serve a maximum of 12 customers at any one time and should employ only family members (i.e. for no wages).

Known as *paladares*, these restaurants consist of just a few tables set up in the front room of a private home. Not only is the food likely to be more nutritious, tastier and hotter than in the average restaurant, but the ambience far more engaging. There is generally just one meal on offer — some version of the classic combination of rice and beans, meat, salad and trimmings — which will cost as little as $1. Most paladares take pesos or the equivalent in dollars, though some deal solely in local currency. Ask for a *cajita* and you will be given your meal in a small cardboard box to take away.

Private restaurants don't usually advertise their services with a sign, but ask around and the local inhabitants will know where to go. If you spend any time with Cubans, you are sure to end up eating in a paladar.

Cuban Restaurants Abroad. To find out what good Cuban cooking can be like, you might want to try a Cuban restaurant away from the island. In London, there are just two places to choose from: the Cuba Libre at 73 Upper St, Islington (Angel tube; tel 0171-354 9998) and Bar Cuba at 11 Kensington High Street (tel 0171-938 4137). The most authentic places for Cuban food are in Miami: in Little Havana (SW 8th St, between 1st and 27th Streets SW) you can find all sorts of places, though one of the best is actually across at Miami Beach: Lario's on the Beach at 820 Ocean Drive, reached by bus J from Miami Airport.

SHOPPING FOR FOOD

Markets. The new private farmers' markets are a great boon for tourists as well as those Cubans who can afford the high prices. For travellers they are the best source of fresh fruit, unavailable in dollar shops, and the good ones also have stalls selling prepared food, from whole meals to simpler snacks (see above). Even if you aren't hungry, it is worth seeking out these markets for the bustle and atmosphere. Every town has one, often located by the main bus or train station. The name differs between provinces but is usually some variation of *mercado campesino*, *mercado agropecuario* or *plaza campesina*. If you ask simply for *el mercado*, people will know what you mean. Most markets function daily, though are much depleted on a Sunday.

The size of the market reflects the size of the town and level of agriculture in that area. Santiago, Camagüey and Havana (which has several markets) boast particularly good ones. Stall holders accept pesos or dollars, though if you offer pesos you are more likely to pay the same price as a Cuban.

Shops. A glance at the shelves of a Cuban grocery store is an eye-opening and sobering experience. Shops are often bare, and those shelves which are full are likely to be taken up by just one or two products. Most food stores *(bodegas)* are now given over entirely to rationed goods (*productos normados* or *controlados*), with virtually nothing available on *libre venta* or 'free sale'.

Westerners must rely on hard currency shops to buy food not available in markets. Don't expect to be able to pick up the ingredients for a picnic; most of the food available is in tins or packets. Even bread is a virtual impossibility. Local bakeries dedicate themselves to providing Cubans with the one bread roll they are allowed every day. There are a couple of dollar bakeries in Havana and one in Varadero, but if you are in the provinces, forget it.

DRINKING

agua	water	*frío*	cold
carbonada, con gas	sparkling mineral water	*granizada*	crushed ice flavoured
natural	plain tap water		with sweet syrup
potable	drinking water	*hielo*	ice
azúcar	sugar	*infusión,*	herbal tea
batido	fruit shake	*manzanilla*	
bebida	drink	*jugo*	juice
borracho	drunk	*lata*	can (of fizzy drink)
café americano	black coffee	*licor*	liqueur

café con leche	white coffee	*malta caracas*	revolting non-alcoholic
café cubano (or	standard, small, black		malt drink
mezclado)	coffee	*refresco*	soft drink, including fizzy
caliente	hot	*sabor*	flavour
cerveza	beer	*ron*	rum
coctel	cocktail	*tomar*	to have a drink

If you are sometimes frustrated in your search for a good meal, you will at least be able to drown your sorrows. Cuba's hard-currency shops and tourist restaurants sell anything from American Coke to Spanish wine. The choice in any one establishment is often limited but varies surprisingly from place to place. The rows of bottles displayed in shops and restaurants look very different to those of a few years ago, when most alcohol on sale originated in Eastern Europe. You will hunt in vain for a bottle of Stolichnaya vodka or Armenian brandy, but may find instead Canadian beer or Scotch whisky.

Cubans enjoy their drink, particularly beer and rum. The Special Period has forced many people to quit the habit of drinking, though alcoholism appears to have increased in tandem with the economic crisis. Drive through any small town during the day and you are likely to see a gaggle of local men knocking back rum in the main square. Don't expect to find many local bars serving alcohol, though nightclubs usually serve low-quality rum or wine.

Rum. Brazilian cars run on a substance which has an almost identical chemical structure to Cuban rum, and indeed the cheapest versions smell peculiarly like petrol; this clear raw rum is what most Cubans make do with. If you are offered a *trago*, whether or not you accept may depend upon whether you are driving, how early it is in the morning, and the amount of persuasion applied — often you get the impression that your new friend will be mortified if you refuse to swill down a glass of highly unrefined rum at 10am. You will have to think of some good excuses. Take the first sip cautiously. One of the authors fainted on the spot after taking a careless gulp of home-made rum.

If you want to buy the proper stuff, then go to a hard-currency shop. The cheapest labelled rum available is three years old, known as *Tres Años* or *Carta Blanca* (because of the colour of the label); then come the five-year-old (*Cinco Años*) and the seven-year-old (*Siete*) versions. The most famous brand of rum in Cuba is Havana Club, of which Carta Blanca costs $5.70 a bottle — compared with $6.40 and $7.50 for the five and seven years respectively. If taste and quality are of little importance, try the 'imported' Havana Club, a white rum that costs just $3.15 a bottle. Should you want to take rum as a present for friends back home, don't go for anything less than the Siete Años, unless you'd like to splash out on one of the vintage 12-year rums.

Havana Club is more easily available than the other brands, but many Cubans seem to swear by Caribbean Club, which is slightly sweeter and cheaper: a bottle of five-year-old costs around $4.70, almost $2 cheaper than the equivalent bottle of Havana Club. The Bucanero, Añejo and Varadero brands are cheap but less tasty.

Cocktails. A good way to disguise the taste of cheaper brands of spirits is to mix them. Many Cuban bartenders are adept at creating good cocktails, though some palm tourists off with all kinds of tasteless and watery drinks. The most popular cocktails are as follows:

> *cubanito:* a Cuban Bloody Mary, made with rum (rather than vodka) and tomato juice.
> *daiquirí:* bears litle resemblance to the drink sold in American-style cocktail bars. The simple concoction of rum, sugar, lime and crushed ice, whizzed up together, was once described as 'a champagne glass full of snow'.

mojito: rum, lime juice, soda water, ice, sugar and mint leaves.
saoco: rum, coconut water and ice, a piñacolada without the pineapple juice; often served in a coconut shell.
Cuba libre: rum and Coke with a twist of lemon or lime.

The origins of the daiquirí, the most famous cocktail to have come out of Cuba, are a source of much discussion. It is said to have been 'discovered' by American troops when they disembarked at Daiquirí near Santiago during the War of Independence. What they encountered were local miners drinking rum with sugar and water, already common practice in Cuba. The Americans took the cocktail, which they called a 'daiquiri', to Havana, where it was first made famous by the barman at the Plaza Hotel. International fame came thanks to Constante, owner and cocktail-maker supreme of the Floridita bar. This was Ernest Hemingway's favourite haunt and the American novelist did much to promote the cocktail by taking his friends to drink there; he also describes daiquiris lovingly in one of his lesser-known novels, *Islands in the Stream*.

Other Spirits. Westerners can drink their favourite tipple without fear of ruin. Scotch whisky is cheaper in Cuba than in Scotland ($12 a bottle or $2 a shot) and most other popular spirits are sold. Native specialities include cacao, orange and coffee liqueurs, Menta (Crême de Menthe) and Anis (like ouzo) — sweet but good, and cheap for around $3 a bottle. Cuba's own whisky is vile, though worth a try if only for that reason.

Beer. The standard Cuban beer (*clara*) is adequate lager. Most provinces produce their own beer, the most widespread local brews being Bucanero, Cristal and Hatuey — refreshing, pleasant beers though with little to choose between them. Each province has its own brewery, and quality varies considerably; for example, Hatuey beer from the Havana brewery is far superior to that made in Santa Clara; the latter is much weaker and tastes it. Mayabe and Lagarto are not so widely available but are very popular. As a general rule, always go for bottled (rather than canned) beer if there is a choice.

If you are unimpressed by the local selection, you must make do with the imported varieties mainly from Canada, Mexico, Spain and Germany. Beers such as Heineken, Labatt and Miller are common, though you can also find more interesting brews, such as Atlas from Panama, or Bohemia from Mexico. Tecate, also from Mexico, is one of the best imported beers. A few Havana bars now offer draft (foreign) lager too. One sub-species of imported beer that may not appeal is cheap, nasty and strong brews (e.g. the beer that simply calls itself '8.6' — its name is its strength), whose sole purpose is to get you drunk quickly and cheaply.

Many towns used to have rollicking *cervecerías*, but now few Cubans can obtain, let alone afford, beer. What beer there is, is largely sold for dollars. The average price of beer is $0.80-$1 for a can in shops and $1.50 to $2 at a bar. A good source of cold beer at any time of the day or night are the shops attached to Cupet petrol stations.

Wine. The cheapest wines in a hard-currency shop cost about $5. In restaurants, wines are often exorbitantly priced, with little to choose from under $12. Most come from Spain and South America (particularly Argentina), though most labels are unrecognisable. Rioja is a favourite, but note that the cheapest Rioja on a restaurant menu will almost certainly be a rosé. French wines turn up occasionally at the best hard currency stores, such as the Diplotienda in Havana. If you have something to celebrate (or money to blow), you can spend $40 on a bottle of champagne.

If you share a bottle with some local people, the Cubans will demonstrate a trick on how to open bottles without a corkscrew; hold the bottle upside-down and hit the bottom firmly and repeatedly until enough of the cork is exposed to enable you to pull it fully out. Take care if you try it.

If you frequent a provincial nightclub or visit a private home, you may be offered Cuban wine, which tastes like nothing on earth. These local versions, often made from oranges or grapefruit, are an oenological outrage, but at least do less damage than some of the hardcore rums. If you get invited to a party and want to bring a bottle of something ethnic, a bottle of "wine" will cost around 10 pesos and not ingratiate you one bit with the host.

Soft Drinks. Coke and Pepsi were banned for years, but the Cubans have managed to bypass the US trade embargo by importing both drinks from third countries. Both are now common, though in some bars you must make do with the sweeter local version, Tropicola; the price is generally $0.80-$1.00 a can. Other well-known canned fizzy drinks such as Sprite and Orangina are available, as well as many unrecognisable brands, Cuban and otherwise. One such is Malta Caracas, imported from Venezuela and sold in distinctive brown and yellow cans; the malty contents are as dark as treacle, sugary and very popular among the sweet-toothed Cubans. Westerners may find it horrible.

Refresco is a general term for any kind of soft drink, from Coke to the sweet and watery concoctions that most Cubans make do with. The best place to look for these home-made refrescos is at the local market. The quality varies enormously, with most tasting only vaguely of fruit. Refrescos usually come in bottles but some vendors simply fill a glass from a bucket. Less common are the *granizadas* (sometimes known as *rallados*), consisting of crushed or shaved ice flavoured with hideously sugary syrup. In Oriente they serve a fizzy refresco called *pru* — made from vegetables and completely unpalatable. Ten times better than all these are *batidos*, still very sweet but made on the spot with fresh fruit. Milk, the essential ingredient of the batido, will either be powdered or tinned.

In a country where citrus fruits grow so effortlessly, it is remarkable that fresh orange juice is so hard to find. The best alternative are the boxed fruit juices, mostly imported. In a few places, you can enjoy fresh sugar cane juice or coconut milk. Bars known as *guaraperas*, that sell nothing but sugar cane juice, used to be a common sight in Cuba but nowadays function only erratically, according to supplies. Some tourist bars now serve *guarapa*. Mixed with rum, it is a lethal concoction.

Cuba possesses some exceedingly pure mountain springs and produces some excellent mineral water, both still and carbonated. This is ideal for quenching your thirst or diluting rum. You can sometimes buy water from kiosks for 10 or 15 centavos a glass, but you are advised always to carry a bottle of water with you.

Coffee and Tea. Coffee in Cuba is strong and sweet. Small bars devote themselves to dispensing tiny cupfuls of coffee to the public, and in the morning you see people queueing patiently for their daily fix of caffeine. Order two or three cupfuls if you feel in need of serious caffeine replenishment. A *café cubano* served in a dollar café will be similar to this, though some places now boast a proper espresso machine. The usual alternative to the traditional Cuban coffee is a longer, weaker version referred to as 'American' coffee. It will be served black unless you ask specifically for milk. A *café con leche* is generally a Cuban coffee topped up with hot milk, rather like the traditional Italian *caffelatte*. If you can make your own, buy locally-grown Cubita coffee from a dollar shop, which is excellent.

Brits might be appalled by the stuff served up as tea: you are presented with a cup of sugary, luke-warm water infused with a hint of something vaguely tea-like. You would do well to ask for the hot water, milk and teabag to be brought separately. Most hotel breakfast buffets allow you to make your own. Outside tourist establishments, normal tea is rare, but most towns have a Casa de las Infusiones specialising in herbal teas.

arrecife	reef	*jardín*	garden
ave, pájaro	bird	*lago, presa*	lake
bahía	bay	*laguna*	lagoon
bañarse	to swim	*manglar*	mangrove
bote	boat	*mirador*	viewpoint
buceo	diving	*montaña*	mountain
caminata, paseo	walk	*museo*	museum
caza	hunting	*naturaleza muerta*	still life
colina	hill	*pantano*	marsh
exposición	exhibition	*playa*	beach
galería	gallery	*retrate*	portrait
gratuito	free (no charge)	*río*	river
iglesia, templo	church		

Some people are lured to Cuba by its credentials as one of the world's last bastions of state communism; they spend their time touring around schools, hospitals and co-operatives and return home full of the achievements of the Revolution. Others are lured by pictures of limpid blue waters and palm trees; they spend two weeks on the beach and go home with a fine tan and a hangover. But there is much more to Cuba than socialism and beaches.

CUBAN ARCHITECTURE

Cuba's colonial architecture may not possess the refinement found in Peru and Mexico, for example, but it has a solid, tropical grace and an appealing simplicity. Once upon a time, Havana was one of the grandest and most beautiful cities in Latin America, and despite the ravages of time, Soviet influence and economic privation there is still ample elegance.

The overriding influence in Cuban architecture is hispanic. The Mudéjar style, which developed in Spain during the Middle Ages by the merging of Christian and Muslim traditions, dominated in Cuba throughout the early centuries of colonisation and lasted well into the 18th century. Most ships bound for the island from Spain left from Andalucía, so this was the main channel for architectural influence. Wood was the most popular material among the mudéjar craftsmen, traditionally great carpenters. Mahogany, cedar and other woods grew in abundance on the island and were used for everything from ceilings to balconies, to the extent that little now remains of once rich stocks of timber.

Colonial builders and craftsman achieved impressive results with the materials available to them, simplifying Spanish designs or adapting them to suit the local conditions. Their solutions to local problems — principally dealing with the heat and the need to create the maximum amount of shade and ventilation — provide some of the most distinctive aspects of Cuban colonial design; typical features of a colonial home include a central courtyard, an arcaded gallery and decorative wooden ceilings known as *alfarjes*. The greatest trademark of the mudéjar carpenters, these *alfarjes* were massive and complicated to build but eminently practical, being higher and therefore cooler than the more common flat ceilings, and infinitely more interesting. Carpenters had often trained as shipbuilders and the pitched ceilings spanned by parallel beams bear an uncanny resemblance to an upturned boat. The alfarjes are one of the few aspects of Cuban colonial design to feature carved decoration — usually consisting of simple geometric star patterns, a typical Moorish representation of the universe. The use of such ceilings persisted well into the 18th century. You find them in both domestic and religious buildings and they are often in a superb state of preservation. There are fine examples in Havana, Camagüey, Santiago and in the small town of Remedios near Santa Clara.

Another feature of many colonial houses are the high doors, with their own cooling device: a *postigo* or panel which could be opened to provide light and a breeze without the whole door having to be opened — thereby preserving the family's privacy. Coloured glass panels known as *medio puntos* or *lucetas* were often placed above windows and doors to filter the harsh sunlight. Another product of the obsession with keeping cool are the *mamparas*, glass-panelled swing doors that allow air to circulate easily between rooms. In Cuba's finest colonial mansions these can be highly decorative, with delicate woodcarving at the top and a painted landscape or other scene rather than the more usual plain coloured glass.

From the late 18th century, Baroque architecture began to flourish. It coincided with Cuba's first real economic boom and was perfect for expressing the sense of importance of the island's new rich, particularly in Havana. Many features of the mudéjar style were assimilated, and simplicity remained the overriding principle, partly because the local limestone was hard and very difficult to work with. Having arrived in Cuba late, the Baroque style barely had a chance to develop fully before the arrival of Neoclassicism from North America. This brought a more refined flavour, which dominated Cuba throughout the 19th century and beyond.

You could spend weeks in Havana exploring its architecture, which spans every era of Cuban history. The fortunes made after independence funded the construction of both the city's and the country's most ostentatious buildings, such as the Capitolio and the Presidential Palace (see page 179). Elsewhere, the most interesting architecture is almost exclusively colonial — as in Trinidad, which retains many of its original features and, like most of central Havana, is included on UNESCO's list of World Heritage Sites. Other towns worth seeing for their architecture are Santiago, Camagüey, and the little-visited treasures of Remedios and Gibara.

Restoration. The preservation of old architecture never featured on the list of Marxist priorities. Whatever your views of Castro's government, it is not hard to see its architectural legacy as anything but a tragedy. Buildings regularly collapse and many in Havana are fit only for demolition. Since the government woke up to the fact that Cuba's architecture is a major asset in its bid to attract international tourists, restorers have been working feverishly to make up for lost time. UNESCO and other international organisations are helping to finance the work.

To learn more about the conservation of architecture in Cuba, with a particular focus on Havana, contact one of the organisations listed below.

Centro Nacional de Conservación, Restauración y Museología: Santa Clara Convent, Cuba 610, entre Sol y Luz, Habana Vieja (tel 61-5043, 61-2877; fax 61-3335). Runs courses in conservation, attracting international audiences, and is also open to the public for tours: see page 177

Centro Internacional para la Conservación del Patrimonio: Mercaderes 116, entre Obispo y Obrapía (tel 62-2258). Partly funded by UNESCO, this group oversees restoration projects in Old Havana.

Empresa de Restauración de Obras de Monumentos: Muralla entre Mercaderes y Oficios, near Plaza Vieja. Involved with the restoration of buildings and monuments throughout Cuba.

Oficina del Historiador de la Ciudad: Palacio de los Capitanes Generales, Plaza de Armas, Habana Vieja. Run by Eusebio Leal, the City of Havana's chief historian, this organisation has done a lot to help raise foreign money for conservation projects in Cuba.

ART

Soon after the Revolution, Fidel Castro publicly rejected art as an end in itself ('Man is the end'). He stopped short of banning abstract painting as Khrushchev did in the Soviet Union. Some hardliners tried to impose a realist style, but without much success. Unlike in the Eastern Bloc, Cuban art has not been reduced to political propaganda. All art galleries are state-run, of course, and in the current drive to relieve tourists of their dollars, the government is pushing the nation's artistic achievements as never before. Even small provincial towns have at least one art gallery.

Modern Cuban art did not take off until surrealism and other avant-garde movements crossed the Atlantic from Paris. These were transported most effectively by Wilfredo Lam (1902-1982), a friend and pupil of Picasso, who exerted a heavy influence on the Cuban's work. Though Lam lived most of his life abroad, he remains the island's most renowned painter to date. The best artist of the next generation was René Portocarrero, who applied vivid oils to unmistakable pictures of women and cathedrals, two of his favourite themes.

Even if the Revolution has not produced another Lam or Portocarrero, a brief turn around the Museo Nacional de Bellas Artes in Havana (see page 182) demonstrates the kind of imaginative and eclectic work still being produced in Cuba. Primitivism shapes the work of Manuel Mendive, the island's most important living artist. Afro-Cuban mythology and folklore provide the background to his paintings, where people and animals are accompanied by mysterious shapes and earthy colours. Cuba's foremost female painter, Flora Fong (of part Chinese descent, like Lam) paints vigorous Caribbean landscapes infused with a delicate oriental touch.

MUSEUMS

Some of Cuba's best museums are old colonial homes and palaces that have been furnished in traditional style. Others are devoted to local or national history, or to a certain aspect of Cuban life — anything from music to pharmaceuticals. Every town has a Museo Provincial or Museo Histórico, which can vary dramatically in quality. Inevitably, a disproportionate amount of space is given to the local area's role in the struggle and achievements of the Revolution.

Opening hours are quoted in the book but cannot be guaranteed. You are sure to be disappointed occasionally, finding museums closed when they should be open. The favourite days for official closure are Monday or Tuesday. Admission used to be free, but now you must pay an entrance fee — usually $1 or $2, more in the case of some of Havana's big museums such as the Museum of the Revolution. There may be an extra charge for taking photographs. Student concessions apply only to those studying in Cuba. Local people pay a nominal amount in pesos. In some museums, a guided tour is part of the package, but you are usually free to stroll around on your own afterwards. Most rooms have their own attendant, who seems to be there mainly to turn the lights on (when you arrive) and off (when you leave). These employees are rarely in a position to answer detailed questions. If there is no official guide, you will have to ask for the 'director'. Signs describing exhibits are almost always in Spanish only.

THE GREAT OUTDOORS

Cuba is sufficiently thinly populated to leave plenty of wilderness. The problem lies in exploring it. If you want to go walking in the mountains, for example, you will find it impossible to get a decent map of the terrain and there are no signposted trails. A day's hike often involves a high degree of guesswork and requires an adventurous nature. With a few precautions, however, there is nothing to stop you enjoying the largely unspoilt natural beauty of Cuba and its flora and fauna. Take local advice and make sure you carry enough water.

Cuba has several national parks, but facilities within them are virtually non-existent. The situation is beginning to improve, though, with an emphasis being placed on providing accommodation and arranging horse-riding trips. For some of the best scenery in Cuba, go to the Sierra Maestra National Park, southwest of Bayamo (see page 305), where a villa now caters properly to visitors and from where you can go on guided walks or rides along mountain trails — including to Pico Turquino, the island's highest peak at 6,500ft (1,982m). Facilities are less developed in the Escambray mountains near Trinidad and in the hills of Pinar del Río province, though well-located hotels enable you to enjoy the tranquillity and views. The delightful country around Viñales provides particularly promising terrain for horse-riding, the Aguas Claras Campismo being a good place to arrange trips (see page 218). The lush forests around Baracoa provide much wilder territory. One possibility is to follow the River Tío upstream, where direct descendants of Cuba's aboriginal people still live.

WILDLIFE

Cuba's geographical position in the Caribbean and the fact that it has been an island for millions of years has allowed it to evolve a wide range of unique forms of flora and fauna. However, large areas have been cleared for agriculture, concentrating the more interesting forms in national parks, Faunal Refuges and other forms of protected area. As in most countries, farmers and country people in Cuba have a deep knowledge and interest in their land and they will be pleased to show you things if you ask. Visitors should not need to be reminded to treat the countryside with respect, and to avoid any souvenir that uses wild plants or animals.

Sources of Information. There is a severe shortage of field guides to the natural history of Cuba; this section hopes to give you a start. The most obvious animals are the birds: over 300 different species, of which 23 are found nowhere else in the world. The only guide to identifying these is James Bond's *Birds of the West Indies* published by Collins. This is woefully out of date but a new guide to the Caribbean, to be published by the Smithsonian, is in preparation. Bond's book does not include the North American migrants, so you will also need to buy a book on North American birds (the National Geographic *Guide to the Birds of North America* is good) to use as well.

A few Cuban books identify butterflies, bats and reptiles but these can be difficult to find. Other than that, there appear to be no guides to any other groups of animals. Even trees and plants are difficult — the guides being both selective in the species treated, and general to the whole Caribbean. So, you should travel in the knowledge that unless you are already an expert, you won't be able to identify most of what you see. However, this doesn't necessarily reduce the enjoyment at seeing the wealth of natural history on the island. The dry season (October to May) is the best time to see Cuba's wildlife. Access, particularly to the Zapata Swamp (see below) is much easier and there are far fewer mosquitos. You will also see many more species of birds as the numbers on the island are swelled by migrants from North America.

Flora: Cuba may not have lush vegetation to compete with Central and South

America, but there are small isolated pockets of tropical rainforest in the Sierra Maestra and Escambray mountains. The island boasts an estimated 70 million palm trees, among the highest such concentrations in the world. The elegant royal palm, with its smooth silvery trunk, is seen everywhere from sugar plantations to courtyards in the centre of Havana.

There is a great deal more besides. Even those with no interest in horticulture will notice that there are many beautiful flowers growing wild, including orchids. Over 8,000 species are native to Cuba. Among the best cultivated collections of plants are the orchid garden in Soroa, west of Havana, and the botanic gardens near Cienfuegos.

Fauna: Cuba has few large mammals living in the wild, though wild boar and deer are found in the remote Guanahacabibes Peninsula in Pinar del Río province, and monkeys live in some isolated areas. Freshwater crocodiles are found in the swamps of the protected Zapata Peninsula southeast of Havana and on the Isle of Youth. No land animal in Cuba is harmful.

Birdlife: visitors with no interest in birds may be content with observing the ubiquitous turkey vultures and equally common cattle egrets, but serious birdwatchers can have a field day. Species include the *tocororo*, a member of the quetzal family with red, white and blue plumage, and the bee hummingbird (*zunzuncito* or *pájaro mosca*), the smallest bird in the world: it is only two inches long and flaps its wings at an astonishing rate, producing a unique sound.

The Zapata Peninsula is the best place for birdwatchers. Go in February, March or early April to either Playa Larga or Playa Girón, where local guides take visitors on birdwatching tours into the swamp; see page 243. Specialist tours are organised from the UK by Island Holidays and Birdquest.

A Wildlife Tour of Cuba. The whole of the extreme western tip of the island, the Guanahacabibes Peninsula, is a National Park. It has been left wild for around a century because the regimes before the Revolution used it for hunting (mainly wild boar, which are still found there). Castro immediately declared it a national park in 1960. It is interesting for both resident and migratory birds as well as reptiles and amphibians. Unfortunately, it is also difficult to get permits to explore the area, and there is nowhere to stay except for a few tumbledown chalets at Las Tumbas (you must take your own food). Slightly further east, near Guane, is Laguna Grande — a tourist complex on a man-made lake (for fishing). It is a good place to see plenty of waterbirds close at hand, and the best location for snail kite. Nearby is Playa Colorada with plenty of seabirds and waders including black skimmer and brown pelican.

The remainder of the mountain areas in Pinar del Río province are both zoologically interesting and arguably the most beautiful parts of Cuba. The Viñales valley is a geologically fascinating area consisting of limestone caves and hills. There are many interesting plants and birds, including a species of palm thought to be one of the oldest plants in the world, and the Cuban solitaire with its haunting flute-like song. The numerous caves are home to a number of species of bat and the diversity of plantlife on the limestone provides food and egg-laying sites for many spectacular butterflies. It is worth spending some time exploring the area — a hire car is essential.

There are opportunities to get close to wildlife even if your stay confines you to Havana. Take a taxi to Parque Lenin on the south side of the city and you'll find plenty to see — particularly birds.

Matanzas province includes Cuba's finest wildlife area, the Zapata swamp. This is a must for anyone interested in natural history. As mentioned above, it is possible to see most of Cuba's endemic birds including the Zapata Wren and the smallest bird in the world, the bee hummingbird. Cuba's largest snake can also be found here: the Cuban boa or santamaria, beautifully marked and up to twelve feet long. There are miles of forest tracks alive with birds and butterflies.

The hotel management at Playa Larga can supply a knowledgeable guide for a reasonable price. The area is huge, and it is impractical to find your own way around.

The central section of Cuba is relatively uninteresting in terms of wildlife as well as scenery. It is mainly low-lying and fertile, and has therefore been extensively cleared for crop production. In Holguin province the Cuchillas de Toa comprise a remote wilderness area, the last-known site for the magnificent ivory-billed woodpecker as well as several other species of endangered bird. The last expedition to look for the woodpecker (in 1993) found no fewer than 12 species of frog new to science. If you get the opportunity to go to this area, take it.

RECREATION

The Old Man and the Sea by Ernest Hemingway bears witness to the excellent opportunities for deep-sea fishing off the coast of Cuba. A trip out in a boat usually costs $30 per hour, though you can charter an entire yacht for around $80 for four hours (six passengers) or a 17-seater for $120-150. If you are less ambitious, you might be able to persuade a local boatman to take you out for a couple of hours of inshore fishing.

In line with the militaristic ambitions of the government, every town has a shooting range. These *campos de tiro* are often overgrown nowadays and little used except on 'defence days', when volunteers do target practice. You are more likely to find a makeshift shooting range in a town park or in the ruins of an old building, where you can buy a handful of pellets for a few pesos and shoot at a few old tin cans. If you prefer to shoot live birds and animals, Cubatur has some limited facilities. The main venue is a ranch in the province of Pinar del Río; see page 215. Each year the INDER Anniversary Competition pits Cuba's best shots against each other.

For those who are happy to pit their skills against other people rather than animals, virtually every tourist hotel has a tennis court. Equipment can be hired but is below Western standards. Guests and outsiders alike are charged about $3 per hour. The big annual tennis championship is the Friendship Cup, but this does not attract players of international stature.

Cuba is not a golfer's paradise, the only decent course being the one in the outskirts of Havana (see page 189), though there are plans for several new ones.

Beaches. Someone has gone to the trouble of counting the beaches on the island of Cuba, and found there are 289. With their pure white sand and unbelievably blue water, they include some of the best in the Caribbean. The water temperature matches the air temperature fairly closely, around 25°C/77°F in winter, 28°C/82°F in summer. The water is noticeably warmer on the southern shores — washed by the Caribbean Sea — than on the Atlantic coast to the north. Compared with those elsewhere in the Caribbean, Cuba's beaches are undeveloped; this is a problem if you're keen on beachside bars and other side industries, but blissful if you want to escape commercialism.

Before 1959, Cuba's beaches were the preserve of the local rich and foreign tourists. At a stroke these millionaires' playgrounds were handed over to the people after the revolution, but the tourists are now returning. Long stretches of Cuba's best beaches are adjoined by luxury hotels and covered in swathes of peeling Canadians and Germans.

The island's finest white sand beaches are along the central part of the north coast, most famously at Varadero east of Havana, Santa Lucía near Camagüey and Guardalavaca northeast of Holguín. There are also fine beaches on Cayo Coco and Cayo Sabinal, part of a chain of offshore keys known as the Cayería del Norte, which spans the north coast of Ciego de Avila and Camagüey provinces. Both Coco and Sabinal have been developed comparatively recently and are both accessible by road.

Cayo Largo, off the south coast, has some of Cuba's best beaches. As a rule, however, the Caribbean coast has beaches that are fine for cooling down between sightseeing trips but are not ideally suited to a two-week seaside holiday. The one possible exception is the Ancón beach near Trinidad (see page 269), though the facilities are few compared with those of the northern resorts. Santiago province also has several new self-contained resorts designed for mostly Canadian and German package tourists.

If you are looking for a holiday by the sea with lots of choice in terms of hotels, restaurants and entertainment, Varadero is the best choice, though some people will prefer the smaller size of Santa Lucía or Guardalavaca, or the isolation of one of the offshore islands. If you wish to enjoy the company of Cubans — who flock to the seaside during the sultry summer months — you will have to make do with inferior beaches with little in the way of facilities.

It may come as a surprise that Cuba does not share neighbouring islands' enthusiasm for topless or nude sunbathing; try it only on clearly defined foreigners' beaches.

Safety: lifeguards are on duty at the more popular beaches most of the time, and their advice should be taken seriously; tides and currents in the Caribbean can be vicious. Flags are flown to indicate bathing conditions: red means 'no swimming', yellow indicates 'take care' and green means 'free swimming'.

Swimming pools. Almost every tourist hotel has a pool, which is open to non-residents as well as guests, usually for a fee of $3-5. The main obstacle to being able to spend a few relaxing hours by the pool arises from the common misconception among Cuban hotel managers that bathers like nothing better than to swim or sunbathe to the accompaniment of loud and distorted music. Another obstacle is the absence of water — due usually to 'maintenance', although there is rarely any sign of work being done. If there is water in the pool, you can expect it to be heavily chlorinated, or else decidedly murky and uninviting. The quality of Cuba's swimming pools is much more reliable in the resorts than at hotels in the interior.

Watersports. Cuba is a good place to learn to snorkel or windsurf, not least because fees are reasonably low. The hire of snorkelling equipment, for example, costs $10-15 for a three or four-hour session; if you want to go out a lot you should consider bringing your own gear from home or buying some once you've arrived; snorkelling and diving equipment is available from hard-currency shops in Varadero and some other resorts. Facilities for waterskiing are scarce, but this is also cheap, at about $30 per hour.

Diving: for qualified divers, the waters around Cuba are fascinating, with numerous reefs and wrecks, both in the Atlantic and the Caribbean. While the amount of fish is disappointing compared with that seen around the Cayman Islands or off Belize, the coral and sponges are impressive. Coral reefs skirt the main island, the longest stretching for some 250 miles (400km) along the north coast of Camagüey province; the water is very clear and perfect for diving. Off the south coast, the Jardines de la Reina archipelago and the Isle of Youth are both good diving areas; divers make up the majority of the guests at the Hotel Colony resort on the west coast of the Isle of Youth.

Several diving schools in Cuba offer qualifications recognised by the Professional Association of Diving Instructors (PADI). The Costa Sur Diving School in Trinidad and the Delphis Diving Centre at Guardalavaca on the north coast run training courses.

Yachting. Outside the hurricane season, the waters of the Caribbean are ideal for yacht cruising. Cuba does not have facilities to match those of the other nearby islands, though its old marinas are being revamped and in some cases expanded. The bonus is that the coastal waters are blissfully free of other yachtsmen, while still being sufficiently challenging for the keenest skipper. It is customary to fly the Cuban flag in addition to the flag from the yacht's country of registration.

The best marinas are located at Varadero, Havana and on Cayo Largo, with facilities in other locations being developed. For those without boats, excursions are available aboard seven-metre yachts. A Swiss businessman called Klaus-Peter Winter has established bases at Varadero (tel 66-7403) and Cayo Largo (tel 48221). The former is only for day charter, but at the latter you can rent an eight-berth sailing boat for between $2,730 and $4,620 a week, depending on season. This may appear expensive, but the per-person costs can be as little as $380 per week — considerably less than a luxury resort, and much more fun. For more information, contact K P Winter AG in Spain (+34 71 490900) or Havana (33-8939).

baile	dance	*espectáculo*	show
boleto	ticket	*fiesta*	festival
boletina	box office	*musica en vivo*	live music
casa de la trova	local music house	*orquesta*	orchestra
centro nocturno	nightclub	*película*	film
concierto	concert	*sala de video*	video room
desfile de moda	fashion show	*teatro*	theatre

Whatever material shortages there may be, the cultural wealth of Cuba is indisputable. The laudable achievement by the government in this field is reflected in the broadening of cultural life to reach the entire Cuban population. Every sizeable town has its own museum, cultural centre, theatre and cinema, to which access is either free or very cheap.

The state is the only sponsor of cultural activity on the island, most events being organised through the auspices of the National Ministry of Culture. This restricts the scope of performances, but the arts are still surprisingly innovative for a small, state-controlled country. The limits imposed by economic constraints or by censorship, however, have induced artists of all descriptions to seek work or asylum abroad. Most of Cuba's top musicians now do all their recording abroad. A more obvious effect of the economic hardship is the fact that many theatres, cinemas and other cultural centres now open only one or two nights a week. A cultural evening for most Cubans is a night in front of the television.

Don't be surprised to find art exhibitions staged in cinemas or classical concerts performed in museums; most facilities are shared. Tourist hotels are particularly versatile venues, with foreigners provided with all manner of entertainments on their doorstep — generally in the form of music, discos and cabaret acts. While some performances are simply appalling, others are by top quality musicians or singers. However much you might hate the idea of attending a show designed purely for tourists, it is always worth finding out the calibre of forthcoming performers.

One vice in which Westerners can no longer indulge is gambling. Although Cuba was formerly a punter's paradise — with the Mafia controlling most of

Havana's casinos — Castro banned gambling many years ago, describing it as a 'philosophy of capitalism'. It remains to be seen if this principle falls to pragmatism.

CINEMA

A trip to the cinema in Cuba is more exciting than you might expect. If your heart is set on seeing up-to-date foreign films you will almost certainly not agree. There is not a great deal of disposable money to pay for the latest films, and only in Havana's top cinemas are you likely to see films made in the last few years. Tourists staying in hotels with satellite television will have a better selection.

Most Spanish-language material is made in Latin America, and not a small amount in Cuba itself. Cuban film barely existed before the revolution. Suddenly the nation had to find itself a film industry, not least to churn out the official line on politics and morality. Thus a new film institute, ICAIC (Instituto Cubano del Arte y la Industria Cinematográficos), was established. In a move similar to the Soviet agitprop trains which toured the USSR after the 1917 revolution, taking propaganda films to the masses, one of the first actions after Castro's accession to power was to institute a programme of travelling projection units taking cinemas to the most remote areas of Cuba. Every town or village has a screen, whether a full-blown cinema or a *sala de video* — a small auditorium where video features are shown. Sometimes, makeshift cinemas are rigged up in the street, with films projected onto the wall of a building.

Cuban cinema has been uneven, veering unsteadily between poorly disguised government propaganda and a fresh, imaginative approach to film-making. But the island has produced films of undeniable interest, providing a fascinating reflection of contemporary Cuba. The most talented directors to have emerged since the revolution include Humberto Solás, José Massip, Santiago Alvárez, Juan Carlos Tabio and Tomás Gutiérrez Alea. The New Latin American Film Foundation in Havana, opened by Gabriel García Márquez in 1986, is a greatly respected institution. Every year, master classes are given by famous names which have included not only Márquez himself, but also Robert Redford and Francis Ford Coppola.

Cuban directors have managed to deal with issues which other artistic media rarely tackle head on. People still talk about the film, *Alicia en el Pueblo de Maravillas* ('Alice in Wonderland'), which was taken off the screens after just two weeks. In the more recent and internationally acclaimed *Fresa y Chocolate* directed by Tomás Gutiérrez Alea, the jibes at the system were described in the Cuban press as 'constructive criticism'. The authorities sold the film all over the world, and it won an award at the Berlin Film Festival in 1994.

The constraints brought by the Special Period mean that national investment in film is now minimal, with many of Cuba's film makers being forced by the hard times to concentrate on dubbing foreign films and soaps. The few movies that are made are achieved thanks to foreign money. These are often introduced to the public at the New Latin American Film Festival, the cinematic high spot of the year, held every December in Havana and attended by film buffs from around the world.

Listings of more mundane film showings are given in local newspapers and on posters in town centres. In Havana there are usually at least two or three performances per evening, while in the provinces there is more likely to be just one. Tickets for most shows are cheap, around 2 pesos for local films, Spanish-language imports or older American movies such as *Rambo*. Newer American releases cost 5 pesos. The classification system is *Todos* (all ages), *12* (twelve years or older) and *16* (sixteen years and over). Cubans love the movies and will queue for hours to see a new release. Tourists, of course, are not expected to stand in line.

THEATRE AND DANCE

Before the revolution, the authorities are pleased to point out, there were just 14 theatres in Cuba. Now there are 65. The Escambray Theatre, which once spread the news and ideas of the Revolution to the rural farmers of the central mountainous region, has lost its radical edge. Nowadays, more interesting work is performed in Havana by groups such as El Público and Teatro Buendía (see page 186 for details of theatre in the capital).

Tickets cost 2, 5 or 10 pesos according to the venue, type of performance, etc. In theory, foreigners must pay the peso price in dollars, but if you present pesos at the box office with enough conviction no one should quibble. In Havana you are likely to be charged in dollars only for important performances — at the Gran Teatro, for example — or if you book a ticket through a tourist information desk.

Ballet and Modern Dance. The National Ballet of Cuba has developed a remarkable reputation since 1959, thanks mainly to the work of its founder, Alicia Alonso, now in her 70s. The long association with the Bolshoi and Kirov of Russia also provided further impetus to an art that had little to offer before the revolution. Each November, Cuba fills with some of the world's best dancers for the annual Havana International Ballet Festival. Past festivals have featured the Dance Theatre of Harlem, London Festival Ballet and the Vienna Opera. Related events spill over into regional centres, so you might find the American Ballet Theater performing in Trinidad or the Kiev Ballet in Santiago.

The seat of the National Ballet is the Gran Teatro in Havana, which is where you can see the best dancers. Other good groups based in the capital are Danza Abierta and Grupo de Teatro Estudio. The Ballet of Camagüey is Cuba's best provincial company, though recently it has lost both its director, Fernando Alonso (husband of Alicia), and many of its best dancers, who have been lured either to Havana or abroad. The National Ballet has also lost some of its top performers, but has managed to maintain its high reputation.

Don't expect too much in the way of classical ballet, but those interested in the traditions of Caribbean dance will find plenty to enjoy. For more avant-garde dance, try to see a performance by the Danza Contemporánea de Cuba. The National Dance Group and the National Folklore Group (see below) are also recommended. The Danza de la Caribe and the Ballet Folklórico de Oriente, both based in Santiago, are worth seeing too.

If you are interested in learning to dance Cuban-style, the Danza Contemporánea de Cuba runs courses, both in traditional dance and more avant-garde choreography. Two weeks' tuition is good value at about $300 per person. For information contact Cubadanza, Teatro Nacional de Cuba, Calle Paseo y 39 (tel 79-2728, 79-6410) or ARTEX, 5 Avenida no. 8010, esquina 82, Miramar (tel 28426, 27693).

MUSIC

For many visitors the main attractions of Cuba are sun, rum and music. Sun and rum you can find elsewhere, but few places have such a rich musical heritage. Music is not just a passion, it's part of the Cuban temperament. It follows you wherever you go, blaring from someone's radio or from loud speakers in the street, or created there and then by a group rehearsing in somebody's front room or by a trio in a restaurant.

You should have ample opportunity to see live performances, though sadly the country's best musicians are often touring or recording overseas. The music industry, like every other sphere of activity in Cuba, is strapped for cash. Nowadays, the top bands play almost exclusively for foreign visitors who pay in dollars. When a major Cuban band plays to a local audience, it is often organised as a lever to attract young people to attend a political rally. Music is strictly controlled by the Ministry of Culture and EGREM, the state recording company. All professional musicians in Cuba are classified (A, B, C, etc.) and salaried by the state.

Young people have access to and enjoy a surprisingly wide range of foreign music, from Bob Marley to Whitney Houston and REM. But when it comes to dancing, Cubans almost invariably prefer their own music. In a world where the musical norms are defined by artists such as Michael Jackson and Madonna, the tenacity of Cuba's music is remarkable. Most of the musical rhythms to have emerged in the island over the last century, from *danzón* to *son*, are still popular and enjoyed across the generations.

Cuban Musical Styles

The *trova* ballad movement, which appeared in the second half of the 1800s, was the first distinctly Cuban music to emerge on the island. A strong home-grown style didn't really develop, however, until the turn of the century, when local music was given a new lease of life by the absorption of African rhythms and dances following the abolition of slavery. The white middle classes were almost schizophrenic in their music appreciation in the early twentieth century — fascinated by the rhythms produced by the blacks, yet resistant to abandoning their more formal dances such as the *danzón*. It was a case of mutual fusion, with the Africans and their descendents also adopting some of the instruments of their Spanish masters. Cuban music is derived, in the words of anthropologist, Fernando Ortíz, from 'the love affair of African drums and Spanish guitar'. Using mostly foreign ingredients, the Cubans have fashioned a music which is distinctly their own. In the process, they have adopted or developed a wide range of instruments, the most important of which are as follows:

> *batás:* hourglass-shaped drums that come in three different sizes and are usually played together. Originally from Nigeria, they are used primarily in Afro-Cuban music, but have also been adopted by salsa bands and other exponents of popular music.
> *bongo:* this small double drum, hit with the hands, first became part of the music scene in Oriente, with the development of *son*.
> *chekeré:* a large gourd enclosed in netting studded with beads, which rattles when shaken.
> *claves:* two wooden sticks, each about 8 inches (30cm) long, that make a hollow sound when knocked together. The beat of the *claves* governs son and salsa.
> *conga:* a narrow barrel-shaped drum hit with the hands.
> *güiro:* a gourd with a ridged side, along which a stick is wiped to create a rasping sound. Possibly of Amerindian origins, its closest Western equivalent is the washboard. The *güiro* is used a lot in popular Cuban music.
> *sincero:* a small, hand-held metal box, beaten with a stick.
> *tres:* a small guitar with three double strings, used mostly in *son*.

The following section gives a brief description of the musical rhytyms most prevalent in Cuba today.

Trova. A *trova* is a version of the old European ballad, traditionally sung to the accompaniment of a guitar. It developed in Oriente during the second half of the 19th century, when its most famous exponent was the Santiagüero, Sindo Garay (1967-1968). A modern version of the genre is *Nueva Trova*, described under *Popular and Rock Music* below.

Danzón. Incorporating elements from classical French ballroom dancing, notably the contredanse, the *danzón* was the most popular dance in Cuba in the early

20th century and dominated the dance salons until the 1920s. It was accompanied mainly by *charanga* orchestras, distinctive for their use of flutes and violins. These bands later took to playing the *cha-cha-cha*, whose heyday was in the 30s and 40s and which incorporates elements of danzón.

Bolero. The bolero, which emerged in Santiago in the late 1800s, evolved out of the trova movement and was the fruit of the first total fusion of Spanish and Afro-Cuban elements. This style of romantic song was often sung by trios, one of the most famous being the Trío Matamoros, formed in 1925.

It is not surprising that in a country that so loves romantic music, boleros remain popular. The 'Feelin' movement that hit Havana in the 40s and 50s was essentially a revival of the bolero, and you still find the odd club advertising 'Noches de feelin'. Boleros are also a favourite among the groups that serenade you in restaurants.

Guajira. There are strong Spanish elements in the *guajira* or 'country' music, in which the singer traditionally plays the guitar. The most famous song of this Country and Western-meets-Cuba style is *Guantanamera*, which was first sung by Joseito Fernández in the 40s and is sung to death by roving musicians.

Son and Salsa. One of the earliest manifestations of the fusion of Hispanic and African music, *son* has inspired Cuban musicians ever since it first emerged at the start of this century. It developed among the ballad singers of the *trova* movement in Oriente and hit Havana in around 1910, rapidly permeating the mainstream music scene. Early son groups centred around simply a singer and a *tres*, but later to this were added a guitar, double bass, trumpets, bongos, claves and maracas. Danzón orchestras also took up the new sound.

The Septeto Nacional of Ignacio Piñeiro was one of the first orchestras to make son famous in the 20s. Two decades later Benny Moré appeared on the scene. Nicknamed *El Bárbaro del Ritmo* ('The Barbarian of Rhythm'), he was a legend in his own time, a charismatic and much-loved figure. Without any formal training, he became the best son artist of his generation, and his orchestra, known as 'the tribe', was one of the finest in Latin America. Moré died of cirrhosis of the liver in 1965, at the age of just 43. You still see many of his records on sale.

The original son has spawned numerous variations, including the mambo and cha-cha-cha, all of which are still alive and kicking. Salsa (literally 'sauce'), a term first coined in the 1960s by a Venezuelan disc jockey, emerged in New York, but few would dispute its origins in Cuban son, which is how some musicians in Cuba still refer to it, in recognition of its roots. Salsa is essentially son mixed with other Latin and North American sounds; rhythms like merengue, bomba, cumbia and others have played a part in its development.

Salsa has gradually swept the world, but it is not without its critics, who dismiss it as simply a commercialised son. Cubans themselves are often critical of the sanitised versions of salsa that emanate from Colombia and Puerto Rico, for example. Most salsa bands in Cuba dabble in all kinds of rhythms, taking on elements from jazz or even Yorubá music, but they never lose sight of the essential ingredients of salsa, such as the brass section (*los metales*), syncopated percussion and catchy choruses. In Cuba, the use of the trumpet, flute and harmonised voices is particularly distinctive.

Cuban salsa has been rejuvenated by some excellent bands that are among the best in the field, and which are now frequently on tour in the West. Orchestras have been characteristic of the popular music scene in Cuba since the 40s, and there are at least a dozen people in a typical line-up. One of Cuba's oldest bands but still very popular is Los Van Van. Juan Formell, who formed the band in 1969, still directs the proceedings, accompanied by an impressive group of virtuoso musicians. The line-up of Los Van Van is basically that of a *charanga*, and the rhythmic use of violins is one of the hallmarks of the band. Cuba's other best known charanga orchestra is Charanga Habanera, which was hitting a real peak in 1995. Young Cubans also go wild for Issac Delgado (whose music some people have described as 'intellectual salsa'), and NG La Banda, which blends salsa with funk and streetwise lyrics; the album *Echalé limón* earned NG La Banda a cult following in the early 90s. A newcomer to the scene is the Médico de la Salsa — a medical student turned *salsero* who was such a new craze in 1995 that you couldn't even buy his records in the shops.

Other bands worth looking out for are Paulito y su Elite, Adalberto y su son, Dan Den and Pachito Alonso. Sierra Maestra, formed in the late 70s, stick more to traditional son than most contemporary salsa bands, but inject it with such energy that the result is eminently danceable. Their last album, *Dundunbanza!*, which includes classics by Arsenio Rodríguez (a big name in the 40s), was the group's best to date. Sierra Maestra spends much of the year on tour, appearing frequently in London, and as a result is not so well known in Cuba.

Afro-Cuban Music. Most music on the island could be described as Afro-Cuban, but the term is generally used to describe the purest kinds of black music. Rumba, which has been around since the end of the 19th century, first emerged among urban blacks in the slums and sugar mills of Havana and Matanzas. The religious music of the island's black communities has permeated most Cuban music — even salsa — over the last century, but rumba's links with religion are particularly strong. The three traditional rumba dances, described below, all evolved out of the ritual dances of the Afro-Cuban cults (see *Religion*).

Yambú — performed in pairs and sometimes known as the *baile de los viejos* ('old person's dance') because of the dancers' slow movements.
Columbia — a fast and almost acrobatic solo men's dance, based on the moves of the devils that feature in certain Abakuá ceremonies. It can involve the use of machetes, bottles and knifes; traditionally, the dancers are also blindfolded.
Guaguancó — a game of attraction and repulsion between two dancers, performed to a similar speed to the columbia.

You are most likely to see performances of rumba in Havana and Matanzas. Cuba's most famous rumba group is Los Muñequitos de Matanzas, which was largely responsible for the great rise in popularity of the rumba in the 1950s. They share no blame for the slick versions developed in the West. Los Muñequitos spend a lot of time abroad, though if you're lucky you might catch a performance in their home town. Clave y Guaguancó and Los Flacos del Guaguancó are also worth looking out for.

The National Folklore Group (Conjunto Folklórico Nacional) was created after the Revolution to keep African traditions alive in Cuba. Though dismissed by some as a gimmick, the group has done much to help popularise the purest forms of black music, including rumba and ritual yorubá music. They run courses for foreigners and their weekly 'Rumba Saturdays' are a well-known event in Havana. They are located at Calle 2 between Calzada and 5, Vedado.

Carnival: the carnivals of Cuba are a fusion of the best of European and African festivities, a celebration of life. They took off in Cuba last century, when street parties to mark the end of the sugar harvest or *zafra* turned into processions, known as *comparsas*, in which troupes of dancers would compete. Private companies sponsored different neighbourhoods during the Republican era, but after 1959 these same groups found themselves promoting trade unions and government policies rather than consumer goods. The economic crisis that followed the break-up of the Soviet Union meant that most annual celebrations were suspended at the beginning of the Special Period, in 1990, but reduced versions are now being held once more.

Carnival in Cuba takes place in July or August, most famously in Santiago, where it is celebrated amid great high spirits and general lawlessness; see page 323. The celebrations held in the capital are more stage-managed, partly for the sake of the tourists, but are still well worth seeing. A small carnival, aimed specifically at overseas visitors, is held in Varadero in January and February.

If you miss the real thing, it is possible to watch rehearsals at other times of year. Your best chance of seeing a practice session is to make friends with a Cuban who is directly involved or who knows where and when the musicians and dancers meet. Alternatively, try asking at the local Casa de la Trova or Casa de la Cultura.

Jazz. The country's African associations are demonstrated vividly in Cuban jazz, of which there is a strong tradition on the island. Indeed Cuban musicians have played a fundamental role in the development of Latin jazz.

The fusion of jazz and popular music took off in the United States in the 40s, when American and Cuban musicians first got together and created an intoxicating blend of jazz sounds and Latin rhythms. The pioneer of this fusion was Mario Bauzá, who is also credited with having introduced another Cuban, Chano Pozo, to Dizzy Gillespie — which was to become one of the most important collaborations in the history of jazz. What began as Cubop or 'jazz afrocubano' later became known as 'Latin jazz' because of the influence of bosanova, merengue and other Latin American rhythms.

Cuba's most famous jazz group is Irakere, led by the pianist Chucho Valdés. One of the first bands to blend jazz with Cuba's traditional and folkloric music, Irakere has been a breeding ground for some of the country's most talented musicians, including José Luis Cortés, flautist and leader of NG La Banda, and Arturo Sandoval, an inspirational trumpeter who now lives in the States. Other names to look out for in Cuba include Afrocuba, Quatro Espacio and Pucho López y su grupo. Perspectiva and Sintesis, both of whom blend rock and synthesiser jazz with traditional music, also have a big following.

Despite having some world class musicians at its disposal, the Cuban government does not promote jazz nearly as much as it does salsa. Irakere, for example, spends much of the year abroad, making regular appearances at Ronnie Scott's in London. As a result it is almost impossible to hunt down live performances in Cuba, though a jazz festival is held in Havana every two years, attracting top international musicians as well as the cream of the local talent.

Popular and Rock Music. A certain section of Cuba's youth is more interested in INXS and Led Zeppelin than in the Republic's own music. Hippies (known as *freakies*), rockers (*roqueros*) and heavy metal fans (*metálicos*) — once the target of persecution and prejudice in Cuba — are now generally tolerated by the authorities, which has encouraged the staging of rock concerts at political rallies. One of the most popular local groups is Máquina, led by Edesto Alejandro, which has fronted a campaign to raise awareness about Aids and safe sex. The home-grown rock movement, however, is very limited.

The only significant movement to have developed since the Revolution is *Nueva Trova*. The songs of Silvio Rodríguez and Pablo Milanés typify the genre, in which the syrupy melodies of the old *trova* (see above) are enhanced by poetic lyrics and injected with a political consciousness. Neither of these two artists went down well with the regime in the 60s (Milanés even spent time in a labour camp), but now they both cooperate with the authorities — particularly Rodríguez, who appears regularly at communist rallies. Pablo Milanés, who is by far the most popular of the two, has recorded some excellent reworkings of traditional Cuban songs; you are sure to hear local musicians singing *Yolanda*, one of his most famous works. The so-called 'Novísima Trova' is more a variation on a theme rather than a completely new movement, and is not widely recognised within Cuba. It exponents, such as Polito Ibañez and Gerardo Alfonso, are simply younger and bolder than the now aging members of Nueva Trova.

In the late 80s and early 90s, the role of protest singer was taken up by a long haired, thirtysomething singer-songwriter called Carlos Varela. His blend of Nueva Trova and rock, with lyrics voicing young Cubans' dissatisfactions with the regime, was banned for a time, circulating only on home-made cassettes bought on the black market. But he too is now tolerated by the regime, and has even been invited to perform in the presence of El Comandante himself. Although you don't often hear folc on the radio, his music is now available in hard currency shops.

Classical Music. The National Symphony Orchestra of Cuba, founded in 1960, is certainly the best in the Caribbean. In view of the limited competition this is perhaps no great achievement, but they give a more than creditable performance. This might be your once-in-a-lifetime chance to hear a live performance of the work of Cuba's top classical composers, Alejandro García Caturla (1906-40), famous for his evocation of Cuban dance music, and Amadeo Roldán (1900-39), who introduced Afro-Cuban elements into classical music for the first time.

Choral music is dominated by the National Chorus (Coro Nacional), though Cuba also has some excellent and more versatile smaller choirs, such as Havana's Coro Exaudi. Both these and visiting ensembles can be heard at the Varadero International Music Festival each November.

Music courses. If you want to learn to play an instrument, from the congas to the flute, you may like to enrol on a course. The average charge is $20 per hour. The main schools are as follows:

Conjunto Nacional Folclórico: Calle 4 between 5 and Calzada (tel 30-3060).
Elio Salvante Escuela de Música: Calle 8 between 13 and 15 in Vedado.
Conservatorio Estebán Salas: Santa Lucía no. 304 between San Pedro and San Felix, 90100 Santiago de Cuba.

NIGHTLIFE

If you are determined to see one of Cuba's top salsa bands, you'll have to stick around in Havana. Here, by far the best venue is the Palacio de la Salsa in the Hotel Riviera (see page 187), though some of the other large hotels stage concerts periodically. In general, whether you're in the capital or in a small country town, the best way to find out about concerts is to simply ask around. Some of the most enjoyable live performances to be seen in Cuba are the informal ones, where musicians — mostly amateurs — get together at the local Casa de la Trova. Found in every Cuban town, these music houses originated as a venue for ballad singers in the 19th century; although nowadays they are a forum for a broader range of music, boleros and traditional son are favoured over the more popular styles. The performances at the Casas de la Trova in Santiago and Camagüey are reasonably well organised, and a small admission fee is charged. In most provincial towns, however, people wander in and out, and everyone is free to join in.

Otherwise, most live performances are in the form of cabaret. Auberon Waugh once claimed that 'the visitor to Havana had better like them [cabarets] because they are all that is going in the way of entertainment'. Some Westerners find it sad that Cuba, with its generally good cultural intentions, should invest so much in the concept of cabaret. But while the essential ingredient to any cabaret in a dollar hotel seems to be an excess of female flesh, the titillation factor is much reduced in the shows laid on for local audiences. Most Cubans love cabaret, and have a tremendously good time. Many peso hotels put on a cabaret at weekends, as do some restaurants and night clubs. The evening's entertainment usually consists of a choice of bands (playing salsa or other traditional Cuban music), a crooning soloist and possibly a comedian. Dancing, however clumsily, is strongly recommended. Although you will never hope to compete with the Cubans' salsa footwork, well-meaning efforts will be appreciated. Admission is free or very cheap to local cabarets and there is usually alcohol of some sort available. Some clubs serve food, but don't expect anything appetising.

Most four or five-star tourist hotels have an in-house disco, admission to which generally costs $5-10. Many used to play just Western music, but nowadays the trend is to offer more of a mixture. Dress codes can be strict, particularly for men, who should wear long trousers. In practice, however, the doormen don't often turn away Western tourists, despite the fact that they usually look far scruffier than most Cubans, who are always well turned out. Prostitutes proliferate at many of these discos.

Havana's top discos, such as those in the Meliá Cohiba and Comodoro hotels, are not very different from clubs anywhere else in the world. Elsewhere, however, the quality of music varies enormously, being often loud and distorted. Drinks are overpriced (do as the Cubans do and take your own bottle of rum), the dance floor is small and sticky, and you emerge feeling that you've gone fifteen rounds with one of Cuba's top boxers rather than enjoyed a good night out. If you track down a local disco, at least the drinks will be cheaper and the atmosphere a touch seedier but more alluring. Go along on a Friday, Saturday or Sunday night and join the throngs of young Cubans queuing at the door; nothing much happens until 11pm. Note that you may have problems being admitted if you are not a couple (*pareja*). Even more fun are the open-air discos: a great night can be spent dancing under the stars on the Malecón in Havana or in Santiago de Cuba's main square.

SPORT

ajedrez	chess	*estadio, coliseo*	stadium
basket, baloncesto	basketball	*futbol*	soccer
boxeo	boxing	*partido*	match, game
campeonato	championship	*pelota, beisbol*	baseball
deportes	sport	*torneo*	tournament

Most young people are keen on sport, whether taking part in an impromptu game of soccer or cheering on their heroes in a televised baseball match. For a small country, Cuba has some outstanding sportsmen and women. Some of Cuba's greatest successes have been achieved in the field of athletics. The island's most famous athlete is Javier Sotomayor, the world record holder and Olympic champion in the high jump. As used to be the case right across Eastern Europe (and still is in some parts), top sportsmen and women are salaried by the state, and devote themsleves to sport full time.

Before the revolution, Cubans were known for their success in baseball and boxing, but little else; they had only ever one six Olympic medals. At the Olympics in Moscow in 1980 Cuba came fourth in the medal table. Cuba didn't participate in the Olympic games of 1984 or 1988, but performed creditably in Barcelona in 1992 and was tipped for great success in Atlanta in 1996. Its success has been most clearly demonstrated at the Pan-American Games, held every four years. In 1991, Cuba walked off with 140 gold medals, the first time a Latin American country had ever defeated the United States. Four years later, Cuba came second in the medal table after the USA.

Castro sees sport as an integral part of education, both physical and moral; the slogan 'sports are an antidote to vice' are the Cuban leader's own words. Sport is also a matter of great national pride and prestige. Despite its crippled economy, the Cubans kept to their commitment of hosting the Pan-American Games in 1991, for which it had to build a completely new stadium. The games were the most prestigious sports event ever to be staged in Cuba and one which the USA attended along with the rest of America, north and south.

Baseball. North Americans took baseball to Cuba in the 1860s. It caught on so quickly that by 1872 Havana had founded its own Baseball Club. Several decades later the Cubans were champions of the World Amateur Series, and top players were even making it into major-league baseball in the States. Cuban players still compete well at the international level. At the 1992 Olympic games in Barcelona, the Cuban team became the world's first Olympic champions.

Baseball is the national sport. Children play it in the street from the moment they can walk, and the country comes to a standstill during the climax of the National Series. The teams that usually end up battling it out during the national championships are Industriales (of Havana), Santiago, Pinar del Río and Villa Clara. Every large town has a huge stadium, the main purpose of which is to stage baseball games. Any young Cuban should be able to tell you when the next game is. Admission is just a few pesos. If you miss a league game, you may have to be satisfied with watching kids play in a local park — Sunday is the best day to observe these informal contests.

The rules are the same as in the United States, but the similarity ends there: you won't find a game in North America beginning with the cry 'Socialismo o Muerte'. There is more to baseball than rounders with a hard ball; the following is by no means a complete guide to the sport, but rather a brief guide to help you understand what is going on. After three fair throws by the pitcher, the batter is out. But if he hits the ball, he runs to the first of four bases, and further if he feels he can get away with it without being run out, i.e. a fieldsman throwing the ball to hit the base before the batter arrives. The equivalent of hitting a six at cricket is a 'home run'. Each of nine innings ends when a team has three 'outs' (in cricketing terms, loses three wickets). If scores are level after nine innings each, the game continues until there is an outright winner.

Cuban baseball has been hit recently by the defections of top players to the United States: in 1996, Olympic gold medal-winner Osvaldo Fernandez signed for the San Francisco Giants while his compatriot Livan Hernandez joined the Florida Marlins. Even with these losses, Cuba remained favourites to retain their Olympic title at the Atlanta Games.

Softball is also popular and has its own national league.

Boxing. The Cubans are something of a pugilistic race, and produce fine boxers. Some of the world's best amateur boxers are from Cuba, not least because the concept of 'amateur' is stretched a little. Teófilo Stephenson, three-time Olympic and world super-heavyweight champion and Cuba's most successful boxer in recent times, has all but retired from the international scene, but other big names such as Félix Savon and Roberto Balado are still competing with success at an international level.

Most towns have a gymnasium where matches are staged regularly, and occasionally makeshift rings are set up in streets or squares, where you can watch mini tournaments. The leading annual boxing competition is the Giraldo Córdova Cardín Tournament.

Basketball. While baseball is played avidly by both black and white Cubans, basketball (*baloncesto*) is dominated by black Cubans. The sport has a fanatical following, demonstrated both at matches and at streetside courts, which are seldom deserted.

Soccer. The government seems keen to encourage soccer, which is one of the few sports at which the island does not excel within Latin America. There are soccer pitches everywhere, but enthusiasm at a local level has yet to translate itself into success at top levels.

Few things amuse and entertain Cubans more than the sight of Westerners gamely trying to play soccer, so feel free to join a kickaround on the beach or in a park. More serious players might try to get a match with the Western diplomatic fraternity in Havana.

Rural Sports. In rural areas the favourite sport seems to be cockfighting, which is strictly illegal, particularly as it involves serious betting. This being a nation of cowboys, rodeos are also popular, though you'll be fortunate if your visit coincides with one. The most likely place you'll see a rodeo is at the Rancho King, in Camagüey province, where a show is laid on for tourists.

abierto	open	*librería*	bookshop
afiche	poster	*libretta*	ration book
artesanía	crafts	*mercado*	market
barbería	barber's shop	*muñeca*	doll
bolígrafo, pluma	pen	*película, rollo*	film (for camera)
cerrado	closed	*peluquería*	hairdresser's
cigarro	cigarette	*pilas*	batteries
cinta	cassette	*productos*	goods requiring ration
comprar	to buy	*normados*	coupons
disco compacto	compact disc	*pullover*	T-shirt
discoteca	record shop	*rebajas*	sale
dulcería	shop selling sweet and	*regalo*	present
	sticky cakes	*suave*	mild (cigarette)
empuje, hale	push, pull (a door)	*tabaco*	cigar
fuerte	strong (tobacco)	*tabaco rubio*	Virginian tobacco
gorra	baseball cap	*tienda*	shop
horario	(theoretical) opening hours	*vender*	to sell
joyería	jewellery shop	*venta libre*	free sale, i.e. not rationed

Revolutionary Cuba was not designed to be a consumer society and shopping is almost invariably disappointing for the Westerner with material aspirations. State control of the economy means that the range of goods available for local currency is strictly limited. Window-shopping is educational rather than entertaining, with a sad and shabby selection of objects that it is hard to imagine anyone wanting. The effect of the political and economic changes in the Eastern bloc on imports means that many shops now stand empty. Word spreads fast when shops receive new stocks, and queues are quick to form; the total supply of new goods is often snapped up within hours. Each Cuban has a ration card which in theory should guarantee a regular supply of essentials from toothpaste to clothes. In reality, however, the goods simply don't arrive or are of such dismal quality that people just don't bother to buy them. It is not unknown for a man to be offered women's underwear because it is all that is available. Some accept through desperation.

In the early 80s Castro allowed the establishment of private markets, where prices were determined by supply and demand rather than by government order. The vendors were predominately farmers who exceeded their official quotas. This first venture into real economic reform failed, since the President was alarmed by their success. There were accusations of profiteering among farmers selling sought-after produce, and the markets were closed or brought back under state control. Some observers have suggested that this was not so much because the idea of personal wealth offended his sense of egalitarianism but because he feared that the spread of free-enterprise ideology could create a challenge to his hard-line Communist dogma. After almost a decade, private markets and limited private enterprise have been re-introduced, albeit on a limited scale. This has brought new life to the streets of Cuba and has made life easier for those who can afford the inflated prices charged. The new developments have also made shopping a more entertaining experience for visitors, particularly in the search for food. See *Eating and Drinking*. The markets represent little competition when it comes to consumer goods, though in Havana there are markets where you can buy novelties such as santería paraphernalia and leather goods.

The hard-currency shops make life in Cuba tolerable for the visitor; as a foreigner you are far better placed than most locals, since you have access to goods available only for dollars. The very existence of these glittering emporia is a bitter reminder to Cubans of the failings in their economy and the oppression of tourism, which creates a two-tier society. Yet even in the dollar shops, you will be hard-pressed to find any gift more unusual than rum or a Che Guevara T-shirt to take home to your loved ones. Apart from the items described below, you won't find it easy to buy much in peso shops, for the simple reason that many goods are available only with ration coupons.

A few goods sold in hard currency shops, including records and Cuban cigarettes, are also available for pesos. The best value depends upon whether you obtain pesos at a favourable rate, i.e. on the black market. At official rates the peso shops represent poor value. A record might cost 20 pesos (the official equivalent of $20) in an ordinary shop, compared to $5-8 in a hard currency shop. But if you are changing at the rate of 20 pesos to the dollar, the former suddenly becomes better value at one dollar.

The limited legalisation of private enterprise has reduced the reliance on the black market, but the parallel economy is still alive and kicking. Since there is virtually nothing in the shops, most things are available only through the black economy — in Havana at least, where the supply network is now extensive. Many Cubans rely on the black market to survive. The main contact tourists are likely to have with it are through the hustlers who offer you cigars on the streets of Havana (see below). You also meet people offering PPG, an anti-cholestorol drug manufactured in Cuba and said to boost libido. It is popular as a recreational drug among Americans.

Opening Hours. Fixed opening times for shops don't exist, but the tendency for peso shops is to open at about 9.30am and close at 5 or 6pm, often with an hour's lunchbreak. The working hours of hard currency stores tend to be longer, with some stores trading until 10pm and open seven days a week; most shops close on Sundays. These hours are purely theoretical. Shops have a habit of opening later and closing earlier than the *horario* on the door might suggest, probably because there is not much to sell anyway. And quite frequently the proprietor decides to assess just how much stock he or she has. The sign *inventario* plagues the shopper in Cuba. It indicates that the shop will remain closed for an indeterminate period, usually an hour or more, in theory to allow an inventory to take place. There is rarely any sign of activity.

Hard currency shops. You can be walking along an ordinary, dowdy street in a provincial town and suddenly encounter a flashy, air-conditioned establishment which looks hopelessly out of place. Since dollarisation, the number of hard currency stores has grown rapidly. By the end of 1995, the Tiendas Panamericanas chain had 275 outlets, while Caracol had 161 shops. They accept only dollars and convertible pesos, and are referred to simply as 'shops' (pronounced '*shop*-ees') by Cubans. Those run by Caracol are usually attached to a tourist hotel, and sell essentials such as tampons and insect repellent alongside luxuries ranging from olives and chocolate to Complan and cannelloni, as well as Cuban trinkets and souvenirs. You may, however, take issue with the company's claim that they will be able to supply 'all your purchases in Cuba'. But since the legalisation of the dollar, other hard currency outlets have opened in town centres aimed at satisfying the needs of the local population. These include the Tiendas Panamericanas, which sells mostly imported goods. Everything is bar-coded, and priced in US dollars. Anything you might need, from a bottle-opener ($0.50) or camera film ($5) to the latest Italian fridge-freezer ($800), is available, in stark contrast to the range in the shops which deal only in pesos. Prices vary a great deal between shops, and prices are almost invariably higher in Havana. You can pay with cash, travellers cheques or credit card.

Books and Music. Most tourist shops have a small choice of books and music. In Havana, look out for the official outlets of ARTEX, the Cuban Art Export enterprise, which have a better choice than most. (Many of the products for sale in other shops are made by ARTEX.)

Books are among the few goods that are available for pesos. Many books look as though they've been sitting around for decades (don't expect to be able to get a discount if you choose a battered copy), with an inordinate number of political texts by Marx and Lenin, Castro and Guevara — great if you understand Spanish, are into that kind of thing and have lots of pesos to get rid of. Tucked amongst these heavy-duty tomes you may find a good selection of Latin American fiction in Spanish. Foreign-language books are restricted primarily to texts in Russian, long past their sell-by date, with the odd English and German novel thrown in. Children's books are quite attractive, and for adults with little Spanish provide good material to brush-up on the language. Some peso bookshops will try to charge tourists in dollars though this is not usual.

The authorities have cottoned on to the dollar-earning potential of books, and titles considered likely to be of interest to tourists — from Che's diaries to books about santería — are being diverted into hard currency shops. New editions of the works of José Martí, Fernando Ortíz and other well-known Cuban writers are also being reprinted. Few new books appear on the shelves, however. Most of the glossy guidebooks to Cuba, which gloss over the realities in the Republic, are published overseas.

Discotecas are among the most pleasing shops in Cuba, particularly if you like spending pesos. Their selection is limited, and is on vinyl only. Nevertheless, if you acquire a taste for Cuban music you can get reasonably well-pressed discs of leading artists for 10-20 pesos. Sometimes these are available from street vendors too, who rarely charge more than $1-2 per record. If you're in town for a while, let the vendor know what you're interested in and he or she will hunt it down for you.

Compact discs ($15) and cassettes ($5) are sold only in hard-currency shops (unless you delve into the black market); again the range is small and varies little between shops, but most recordings are unavailable abroad. The bigger stores also stock musical instruments. For a conga drum you should expect to pay around $150, for bongos about $70, but you can get a better price on the black market; local musicians are a good starting point for setting up these deals.

Postcards. One benefit of the boost in Cuba's tourist trade has been the improve-ment in the quality of postcards, though the uninspiring pictures of hotels or couples at sunset that were the norm a few years ago still abound. (It is sad to reflect that Cuba has to import even its worst postcards.) If you want to send your friends a vaguely artistic card, you should stock up in Havana, where extremely attractive photographs of the old city are now available. The cost is usually $0.30-$0.50. At peso news stands you can occasionally buy a limited range of badly printed cards. At only 10 or 20 centavos each, though, they are bargains if your friends are not too discriminating.

Clothing. Although you can't yet get T-shirts reading 'my campañero went to Cuba and all I got was this lousy T-shirt', you can get them with pictures of Che Guevara and revolutionary slogans. These are available only at hard-currency shops, for $5-8. If you're not into political statements, you might be happy with the 'Life's A Beach' style T-shirts for sale in the resorts.

Among the rows of terrible garments on the rails of the larger tourist shops, you can find the occasional bargain: e.g. genuine Levi jeans for $20. You can also pick up decent canvas shoes for a few dollars. Clothes in peso shops are mostly available only with a ration book. The traditional Cuban cotton shirt, called a *guayabera*, is rarely on free sale in local shops. You are more likely to find one in a hard currency shop, price around $20.

Cigarettes. Cuba claims to be the place where Europeans first tried *cohiba*, later known as tobacco. It now produces some of the worst cigarettes on the planet. Amidst all the shortages of essential items, the government has seen to it that cigarettes are available at all times, though they are rationed. A report some years ago revealed that the average Cuban adult still managed to smoke 4,000 a year, nearly twice the amount smoked in the UK and second in the world only to Cyprus, another tobacco-producing nation. While the number is sure to have dropped during the Special Period, many Cubans buy cigarettes before other essentials — for the simple reason that smoking kills the appetite.

Numerous cafés with no food or drink on offer remain open solely to sell untipped *Popular* cigarettes. These bear a health warning, but no mention about how rough they are. Any tourist who can smoke his or her way through one is sure to create a lasting impression.

For filter cigarettes, Cuban or foreign, you have to visit a hard-currency shop. Locally produced king-sized cigarettes, such as Upmann and Cohiba, cost about $1 a packet, while leading foreign brands such as Rothmans, Camel and Marlboro are $1.50. The range of mild cigarettes is poor. Cubans will accept mild (*suave*) cigarettes if they are offered, but they prefer them strong (*fuerte*). If you smoke roll-ups, take your own papers and tobacco and expect to cause fascination locally as you make your own cigarette.

Cigars. 'A woman is only a woman', claimed Rudyard Kipling in one of the most sexist remarks on record, 'but a good cigar is a smoke'. Cuba is claimed by many to be the source of the best cigars in the world. Groucho Marx no doubt came up with a good one-liner to describe his discontent when the new Marxist regime in Cuba meant that his favoured Havana cigars were no longer available in the USA (though US citizens may take 100 home). Other well-known ex-smokers of Cuban cigars include Winston Churchill, Ernest Hemingway and Fidel Castro himself, who gave up after a 'truly heroic struggle'.

Ordinary cigars, known as torpedoes, are about 10cm long and 1cm in diameter. Ignoring Fidel's good example in giving up, many Cuban men smoke them whenever they get the chance, savouring each for an hour or more. They are fairly disgusting. Branded cigars, such as Punch, Romeo y Julieta, Montecristo and H. Upmann, are most easily found in hard-currency stores. For a medium-size cigar you could pay $1, or $3 for the largest.

There is a well established black market in cigars, particularly in Havana where people approach you in the street offering to do business. Unless you have complete faith in the trader, such transactions are best avoided as the quality of the cigars is highly variable: one may taste like heaven, another like rags dipped in turpentine. A beautifully wrapped and sealed box is not without its perils either: one unfortunate tourist returned home to find that the box he had bought contained not high class cigars in aluminium tubes but a large stone and a few tatty panatellas.

Even if you do not smoke, note that some travellers subsidise their visit to Cuba by taking home their duty-free limit in cigars and selling them at a substantial profit. If you are buying cigars for speculation, try to go for the biggest and best-known (and make sure that the box has not been opened). Previous visitors have made good profits with Espléndidos (Cohiba) or Romeo y Julieta Churchills. A box of 25 can be bought for about $30 ($20 on the black market), and retails in the UK for over £300. Top-class restaurants are the best place to sell them, though to avoid being saddled with the cigars you would do well to approach your prospective buyers before your departure. You'll be lucky to make more than £50 profit on each box of 25 (the UK duty-free allowance is 50 cigars), but this is still a worthwhile way to offset the cost of your trip.

You can see Cubans making cigars at special stands in the lobbies of tourist hotels. For more background, visit a cigar factory on an organised tour. This is an interesting experience even for non-smokers. These places are the smoker's equivalent to working in a chocolate factory: employees can smoke as much as they like on duty, and take one or two cigars home each day. The Cuban health ministry does not cite the life expectancy of cigar workers.

Real aficionados might like to contact Special Places (01892 661157), which in 1995 launched a specialist cigar tour to Cuba.

GIFTS

Gifts to take home. Finding something good to take home to your nearest and dearest is a problem. Offering Popular cigarettes is a certain way to lose credibility. An album of Cuban music is a possibility, but your friends back home may not share your new-found enthusiasm for Los Van Van or Pablo Milanés. Rum and cigars are the obvious choices for smokers and drinkers. If you take booze back, wrap the bottle up well since the quality of the glass can be poor. Coffee is less intoxicating but also less messy to take home. The island's own make, Cubita, is very good and is available in most dollar shops.

Decent arts and crafts are hard to find. Wall-hangings that seem impressive in Caribbean surroundings may lose their appeal in a bedsit in Croydon or Cleveland. The Cuban flag, for sale in some tourist shops for $15, is a better option. You can occasionally find tasteful woodcarvings, but almost all goods sold in hard-currency shops are junk, from the cigarette lighters emblazoned 'Cuba' to straw hats, which fall apart as soon as you get them home. And such unappealing souvenirs are not necessarily a cheap joke: a mounted turtle head fetches $30. (Make sure that what you buy will be allowed into your home country; see page 58 for details of restrictions upon the export of items made from endangered species.)

Among the better buys are the political posters in which Cuba specialises. Also look out for *Cuba — La Fotografía de los Años 60s*, a marvellous collection of photographs of the revolution and after; it costs $10 and is available in some museums.

Gifts for Cubans. You are certain to meet locals who show you kindness and hospitality. Whilst you need not feel compelled to reciprocate, most Westerners are keen to offer presents as a way of showing gratitude.

Virtually anything you take will be accepted gladly. However, the kinds of gifts which go down especially well, among both men and women, are essentials such as soap, deodorant, toothpaste and shampoo. If you have room to pack just one thing, make it soap; in recent times most families have had to make do with just one bar of soap every few months. The above things are sold in hard-currency shops, as are less mundane treats such as chocolate and biscuits. Presents that you might want to take from home include novels and magazines, postcards, badges, etc. Baseball caps, cigarettes and razors go down well with the men, while make-up, perfume, underwear and fashion magazines are particularly popular among women. Clothes of any kind will be accepted willingly, even if they are T-shirts or shorts you decide to leave behind at the end of your trip.

aguja	needle	*jeringa*	syringe
analgésico	painkiller	*llame a un médico*	call a doctor
baño	bathroom *or* toilet	*paño higiénico*	sanitary towel
bendaje	bandage	*picadura*	sting, bite
brazo	arm	*pierna*	leg
calamina	calamine lotion	*píldora*	pill
calor	heat	*policlínica*	hospital
consultorio	surgery	*preservativo*	condom
estómago	stomach	*radiografía*	X-ray
estoy enfermo, a	I am ill	*roto*	broken
dolor	pain	*salud*	health
farmacia (de turno)	pharmacy (on duty)	*sangre*	blood
fiebre	fever	*Sida*	Aids
fumar	to smoke	*socorro*	help
insolación	sunstroke	*sol*	sun
inyección	injection	*tiburón*	shark

Cuba's welfare state is the envy of many countries even in the developed world, let alone other Third World nations. Before 1959, few people had use of the healthcare system. Now, however, Cuba has a vast army of doctors and a network of polyclinics which extends into the remotest corners of the island. Cuba's child mortality rate is among the lowest anywhere, below the level in the UK, and the average life expectancy is 73.5 for men and 77 for women — astonishingly high figures for a poor country. The top hospitals are extremely well-equipped, with everything for the most sophisticated of operations: people travel to Cuba from all over Latin America for hi-tech eye laser treatment, heart transplants and even cosmetic surgery. Castro once vowed that Cuba should become 'the greatest medical power in the world', and this is one ambition which has met with considerable success. As with everything else, however, the economic collapse that followed the withdrawal of Soviet support has had a disastrous effect. Basic shortages are now commonplace, and many patients must rely on their families to take in sheets, towels and even food. Without overseas donations, Cuba's health system would be in a much worse state. The government reserves some of its fiercest criticism of the US embargo for its effect on the health of Cubans. It has estimated that it wastes more than $4 million every year in buying medical products which could be transported from the States for a third of the cost.

In general, Cuba is a healthy place in which to be — much more so than most of Latin America. The main causes of death in Cuba are cancer, strokes, heart disease and asthma. There are no dangerous land animals such as venomous snakes and most infectious diseases have been eradicated. Vaccination drives over the last thirty years have completely eradicated malaria, polio and tetanus and have greatly reduced the incidence of other diseases from tuberculosis to meningitis.

You are extremely unlikely to encounter any but one or two of the hazards listed here. Few travellers fall ill, the most common complaint being a short bout of diarrhoea; in 1995, the Public Health Minister said the number of cases had increased because of a shortage of chlorine to purify water systems.

However safe Cuba is in relative terms, no-one should take their good health for granted. The advice below, coupled with sensible precautions, should ensure that illness does not spoil your visit. You should read an up-to-date book on the subject, such as *Stay Healthy Abroad* by Rob Ryan (Health Education Authority, £6.99) or *Travellers' Health: How to Stay Healthy Abroad* by Richard Dawood (Oxford University Press, £8.99). In either book, it is satisfying to be able to skip the pages dealing with diseases that afflict most other Latin American countries.

NATURAL HAZARDS

Heat. Those unaccustomed to the heat of the tropics must allow time to adjust. To avoid collapsing from heat exhaustion in the first week, wear suitable clothing and a hat to keep as much of the sun off as possible. Drink plenty of non-alcoholic fluids, and avoid over-exertion until you acclimatise. If you experience headaches, lethargy or giddiness after a long day outside, you probably have a mild case of heat exhaustion caused by a water deficiency; drink plenty of fluid and sit in the shade until the symptoms subside. Your body's requirements of salt also rise dramatically in the heat, so compensate for this by adding salt to your meals.

Heatstroke is the failure of your body's heat control mechanisms. This causes headaches and delirium, and must be treated immediately; remove all your clothes and cover yourself with a wet sheet in order to stop the body temperature from rising further. Seek medical help should there be no improvement: if the body temperature continues to rise the effects can be fatal. The same condition is often described as sunstroke, but this is misleading since it can occur when you haven't been in direct sunlight.

Prickly heat is the most common heat-related skin problem and can usually be prevented by having frequent showers, keeping your skin clean and dry, and by wearing loose, non-synthetic clothes. The best treatment is calamine lotion. Since the condition is caused by the blockage of sweat ducts avoid any exertion which would induce excessive sweating.

Sun. It is tempting for those escaping a cold European winter (or summer) to head straight for the beach as soon as they arrive. Visitors to Cuba at any time of year run the risk of being badly burnt. The most effective protection is to stay out of the sun between 10am and 3pm. The next best precaution is to expose yourself to the sun as gradually as you do to the heat, starting with less than an hour's exposure a day. Use a lotion with a high protection factor to screen the sun's rays. Sea water, perfume and after-shave increase the rate of burning.

If, like most sun-starved travellers, you ignore this advice and get burnt, apply calamine lotion or cold cream liberally, or soak a towel in cold water and place it over the most tender areas. Apply after-sun cream to the affected parts and drink plenty of non-alcoholic fluids; a cheap alternative to after-sun cream is vinegar, which effectively takes the sting out of sunburn and is available in some hard currency shops. For severe burns use a mild antiseptic and keep the skin clean and dry. Try to be kind to your skin, and do as the natives do, i.e. don't go out in the midday sun — known locally as *la hora del diablo* ('the hour of the devil').

Mosquitoes. Cuba is an insect's paradise. You'll just have to get used to the idea of sharing your room with a variety of creepy crawlies, particularly if you stay in the cheapest hotels.

Mosquitoes are the main menace, since they seem to like nothing better than to dine on fair-skinned visitors. While these hateful insects do not carry malaria in Cuba, their bites itch a lot and can make your nights a misery, above all in summer. Mosquitoes can bite at any time of day, but are a particular menace at dusk. At nightfall cover your limbs and apply insect repellent to exposed parts. Windows are rarely screened in Cuba, though most tourist hotel rooms have air-conditioning, which acts as a partial deterrent. In budget hotels you should remember to keep your windows closed during the day and at night smother yourself in yet more repellent and sleep with the fan on.

Most insect repellents contain a chemical called Deet. They include Jungle Formula, which comes in an aerosol, lotion or gel; the roll-on applicator is recommended. Repellents such as Autan are available in Cuban hard-currency stores, but you should ideally bring a supply from home. Eating copious amounts of garlic is also said to act as a repellent to mosquitoes, as well as to other people. Soap, calamine lotion or any of the sting relief creams on the market help to ease itching. Applying ice to the bites or taking a swim in the sea can also soothe irritation. Don't scratch bites since this only makes it worse and encourages other mosquitoes. If you plan to spend a lot of time in the countryside, take thick socks since mosquitoes love ankles and can easily penetrate thin cotton socks. Finally, avoid wearing tight clothing (loose shirts and baggy trousers are cooler anyway) and anything smelly, such as perfume and aftershave.

Sharks. These unfriendly fish are found in parts of the Caribbean. It is most unusual for sharks to attack near the shore, however. If you find yourself in shark-infested waters, it is better to do the breast stroke — which creates an impression of calm strength — than the crawl, which can make it look as though you are flailing helplessly. As a last resort, a sharp tap on the shark's nose may send it packing.

Ticks. These unpleasant arachnids sit about in the undergrowth and leap onto anything that moves. They burrow their mouths into your skin and stay there sucking your blood until their abdomen is full. At this stage they drop off, but it can take some time. Applying a lighted cigarette to a tick which has implanted itself sometimes works. Nail polish remover or strong liquor is more effective, as is smearing it with vaseline to suffocate the beast. Do not use tweezers as this can leave the tick's jaws in your flesh.

DISEASES AND OTHER HEALTH HAZARDS

Dengue Fever. This viral infection, endemic in Cuba, is transmitted by daytime-biting mosquitoes. It is most prevalent during the rainy season (summer), occurring mainly in urban areas. Dengue is a nasty illness, but complications are rare. The more serious form, known as dengue haemorrhagic fever, does not occur in Cuba.

The risk of contracting dengue remains tiny unless an epidemic occurs. The virus has an incubation period of five to eight days. Symptoms come on fast and include a high fever, severe headaches, photophobia (shrinking from light), loss of appetite, and severe joint and muscle pains (hence the nickname 'break-bone fever'). A skin rash of small spots may appear after a few days. There is no specific treatment, and the best prevention is to avoid being bitten in the first place. See above.

Gastric Problems. Much of Cuba's food is bland and boring, so you may conclude that the risk of gastric trouble is low. Any food, however dull, can carry bacteria, though the recent increase in the number of cases of food poisoning, giardia and amoebic dysentery are probably attributable to the water. The purification system is clearly not functioning as it should, and many Cubans now boil their drinking water. Unless you are very disciplined, it is hard to avoid drinking tap water completely. As a compromise, however, you may decide at least to purify the water in your hotel. The most common methods are purification tablets or iodine drops, but some other systems are worth considering; the Pentapure Travel Cup, available from more specialised shops, is recommended. Mineral water is available in dollar shops, but is not cheap.

Where the standards of hygiene are obviously low, avoid eating meat that appears to have been lying around in a fly-infested environment — this is more likely to be in a restaurant than in a private home. Be particularly careful about shellfish, which are a common cause of illness. In general, most upset stomachs in Cuba seem to be caused merely by the change of diet, the over-chlorinated water or the imbibing of too much rum.

Diarrhoea is likely to be the first clue that you have eaten something you shouldn't have. If left to its own devices it should clear up in a couple of days. Rather than take drugs, drink as much water as possible to avoid dehydration — ideally a mixture of water, sugar and salt — and eat only dry bread or rice. If the diarrhoea is particularly bad, rest in a cool, dark room. Lomotil, codeine and immodium, recommended by some doctors, alleviate the effects of the diarrhoea (and will block you up if you are going on a long journey), but do nothing about the cause. Antibiotics can have a detrimental effect, and they are best avoided unless you have picked up an amoeba or a more serious infection. In this case you should seek medical advice anyway.

Hepatitis. A viral infection of the liver, hepatitis comes in various types. The one which is most likely to affect travellers is Hepatitis A. It is easy to catch from contaminated food and water, though few visitors to Cuba fall victim to it.

Incubation takes two to six weeks, and symptoms include general malaise, loss of appetite, lethargy, fever, pains in the abdomen, followed by nausea and vomiting. The whites of the eyes and the skin turn yellow (this is difficult to detect if you have a suntan), urine turns deep orange and stools become white. Serious infection is comparatively rare but can lead to liver failure.

If you suspect infection, rest and seek medical advice immediately. Do not smoke or drink alcohol, nor eat fat. Some people are only mildly affected, but it can sometimes take six months for hepatitis to clear up; therefore, you are strongly advised to go straight home and recover in comfort.

The gamma globulin vaccine offers good protection against Hepatitis A, and every traveller should have it. The dosage can be varied, the maximum lasting for six months. Since the effect of the vaccine wears off gradually after it is administered, have the injection shortly before departure. A newer vaccine, Havrix, is more expensive than gamma globulin but gives immunity for ten years; it is administered in three doses, two a month apart before a trip, followed by a further one about three months later.

Rabies. An exceedingly dangerous viral infection, rabies (*la rabia*) is transmitted by mammals, notably dogs, bats and monkeys (you'll be lucky to see one of the latter in Cuba except in a zoo). If you are bitten, scratched or licked by an animal, wash the area with soap and water, encourage limited bleeding and cleanse with alcohol. Although the disease is rare in Cuba, anyone who plans to spend an extended period on the island should consider getting inoculated. The vaccine gives good protection, but does not make you immune; it means that any treatment you receive if you are bitten is likely to work more effectively than it would otherwise. The rabies vaccine is administered in two or three doses, usually one month apart.

Other Diseases. The other standard inoculations are typhoid, tetanus and polio. Typhoid, like Hepatitis A, is caught by consuming contaminated food or water. The typhoid vaccination is administered in two doses. The first should be about six weeks before your departure, with the second just before you leave. The injections can leave you with a sore arm and make you feel lousy for 24 hours. Travellers who have already had a course need only a booster injection. Polio and tetanus require a booster every ten years.

If you intend to travel elswhere in Latin America you should of course check which vaccinations are required or recommended. You may well need to take anti-malaria tablets, and yellow fever is a risk. Travellers who have visited a country where yellow fever is endemic within ten days of arriving in Cuba must show a valid certificate of vaccination against the disease.

Smoking. Cuba is cracking down hard on smoking. *'Fumar daña su salud'* reads the health warning on Cuban cigarette packets, and indeed the local smokes are so strong that your health will be damaged by the fumes from somebody else's cigarette. But a nation that produces arguably the best smoking material in the world (as well as some of the most noxious cheap cigarettes) is not collectively going to give up overnight, and smoking is still acceptable in most public and private places. Secondary smoking is almost compulsory in the hotels, buses and post offices of Cuba.

AIDS

The Acquired Immune Deficiency Syndrome or Aids (*Sida* in Spanish) is caused by a virus called HIV (Human Immunodeficiency Virus). This can damage the body's defence system so that it is unable to fight certain infections and other diseases. Aids is rampant in the Caribbean, with Cuba's neighbours having among the highest incidence of Aids on earth. In line with its remarkable record in other spheres of medicine, the number of people infected with HIV and Aids in Cuba is very low. The number of carriers of the HIV virus was 1,182 in December 1995 according to official figures, with 279 recorded deaths from Aids since the first case was detected in 1986. Despite the growth in both tourism and prostitution, the figures have not increased as dramatically as was predicted. The regime claims the slow spread of the disease in Cuba is a vindication of its stringent Aids policy, which has been much criticised abroad. The island has a rate of 0.8 reported cases per 100,000, according to WHO figures; the rate in the neighbouring Bahamas is 150 times higher.

Given the high incidence in neighbouring countries, it is perhaps not surprising that Castro's government has reacted so strongly to the disease. The greatest controversy has surrounded not so much the mandatory testing but the Aids sanatoria, where Cubans who are infected with Aids, ARC (Aids-Related Complex) or HIV are isolated; the most famous is Los Cocos in Santiago de las Vegas near Havana. There is no scientific evidence to show that restricting the activities of infected people protects public health, and various international organisations have denounced the policy as a violation of human rights. In its defence, Cuba claims that its policy of isolation has succeeded in extending the lives of those infected with the disease by up to seven years; and that by isolating patients they are defending the rights of the millions of Cubans who are not infected.

Probably in response to outside pressure, the restrictions placed on patients have been relaxed a little. Those Aids carriers considered responsible enough are allowed to go out to work and even live at home. Not all Aids sufferers have taken up the offer. Aids sufferers can live and eat better in the sanatoria than at home, and gay couples are accepted more than they would be in the outside world.

In 98% of cases, the virus is transmitted through sex. Publicity campaigns aimed at reducing the spread of Aids have warned that one way to become infected by the HIV virus is to have 'relations with foreigners'. Anyone going to Cuba for purposes other than tourism or business is required to have a blood test to detect the presence of HIV antibodies, and it is possible that people seeking medical treatment may be given a blood test. Foreigners discovered to be carriers will be deported.

Avoiding Infection. You cannot become infected with HIV through everyday contact with an infected person. For visitors who take sensible precautions against contracting the virus through unprotected sexual intercourse, risks are minimal. Education campaigns have concentrated on promoting the use of condoms, but still only about 6% of Cubans use what is known locally as *el quitasensaciones* ('killjoy'). You are strongly advised to take a supply of condoms if you might indulge in sex with people whose sexual history is unknown to you.

Infection through contaminated blood transfusions is a risk in many Third World countries. In Cuba, however, all blood donations are screened against the disease and the danger of being injected with a dirty needle is minimal. However, with resources stretched as never before, the temptation to re-use needles is high — though this is less of a danger for foreigners. Even so, you would do well to consider taking an Aids Pack. A normal kit should contain hypodermic needles, suture material (for stitches), intravenous drip needles and alcohol swabs. Your doctor should be able to make a kit up for you; ask him or her to supply a letter explaining that the kit is for medical use only — this will save you potential hassle at Customs among officials convinced you are a possible drug-user. It is also a good idea to label your pack with your blood group.

Sources of Information. For up-to-date information on the extent of Aids, contact the Panos Institute at 9 White Lion Street, London N1 9PD (tel 0171-278 1111; fax 0171-278 0345). It publishes various books, including *Aids and the Third World*, which contains the latest worldwide statistics and country-by-country reports. *WorldAIDS* is a bi-monthly magazine which has a section in each issue highlighting Aids in a particular part of the world. If you don't wish to pay for a year's subscription, you can order back copies individually.

The Terrence Higgins Trust is the UK's leading Aids charity. While it does not produce leaflets aimed specifically at travellers, THT offers good general information and advice on HIV and Aids. Write to the Trust at 52-54 Grays Inn Road, London WC1X 8SU (tel 0171-831 0330; fax 0171-242 0121), or call its Advice Centre on 0171-242 1010.

MEDICAL TREATMENT

Castro's government regards health care as a source of foreign exchange. There is considerable demand for Cuban medical services from nearby countries with poorer facilities; during the 80s, Castro's regime treated many of those wounded during the civil wars in El Salvador and Nicaragua. Capitalising on its reputation, Cuba has built up a sizeable 'Health Tourism' industry. More than 5,000 people a year visit Cuba for medical treatment, many of them from Latin America. The increasing number of tourists from Western countries means that the incidence of foreigners with broken ankles or sunstroke is also growing. Realising that Westerners are (or should be) heavily insured, the government gives good treatment and charges high fees. In the capital, the Cira García Central Clinic for Foreign Patients caters exclusively for foreigners, and the flagship Hermanos Ameijeiras hospital has two floors reserved for foreigners. In Havana, Varadero and the other main tourist centres, you will also find branches of Servimed, another clinic designed specifically for tourists, run by Cubanacán. Given the state of hospitals reserved for Cubans, you are advised to take advantage of your privileged position if you fall seriously ill or have an accident.

In Cuba, unlike in the USA, you will be treated first and questions about payment dealt with later. Emergency treatment is free, but any subsequent care and medicine must be paid for. The ambulance service is over-stretched, so try to make your own way to the hospital. If you are still conscious but you do not speak Spanish, get someone who can interpret to come with you.

For minor treatment, as an out-patient at a hospital or by the local doctor at a clinic, you are unlikely to have to pay except for the cost of prescribed medicine. As a foreigner you may also be given preferential treatment, e.g. by being allowed to jump the queue.

Pharmacies. You are advised to take your own supply of basic medicines, against headaches, indigestion, etc. Dollar shops have an increasing range of medicines, but prices are sky-high. With most medicines available only for dollars, the majority of Cubans must rely on local pharmacies. Many drug stores are charmingly old-fashioned — with elegant jars of medicines stored on shelves from the floor to the ceiling — but this aesthetic appeal is lost on most locals. The drugs even for the simplest prescriptions often aren't available. Donations from abroad that are distributed through local churches have provided an invaluable safety net during the Special Period. The shortage even of the most common of medicines like aspirin has encouraged people to turn to herbal remedies, traditionally the preserve of santería doctors. Some Afro-Cuban remedies have already been mass produced and conventional doctors are undergoing courses in traditional healing methods.

Even if pharmacists cannot sell you anything, they can be very helpful; indeed good ones can save you a trip to the doctor if all you have are minor and easily recognisable symptoms. If you require an inoculation, you can sometimes get this done at a pharmacy, though you would do better to go to a hospital.

Pharmacies are described according to their opening hours: *turno regular* (opening hours 8am-5pm daily), *turno especial* (usually 8am-10.30pm) or *turno permanente* (open continuously). Every town has an all-night pharmacy.

EVERYDAY HEALTH

Women's Health. If you are planning to travel while pregnant, check carefully the effects of any vaccinations you might require. It is advisable not to be inoculated with a live vaccine such as polio or yellow fever, especially during the first three months of pregnancy.

While you can buy tampons (*tampones*) and sanitary towels (*paños higiénicos*) in dollar shops, you are advised to bring all you need from home. Improve a Cuban woman's day by leaving anything you don't use behind.

Contraception. Locally produced condoms are available in pharmacies, but you are advised to opt for the imported versions sold in dollar shops. Other forms of contraception are difficult or impossible to obtain. Note that the effectiveness of the contraceptive pill is reduced if you have a stomach upset, or if you are taking a course of antibiotics.

Toilets. To distinguish between men's and women's toilets, look for a shoe symbol (a dainty high-heel signifying the women's, a butch boot for the men's), a fan (for women) and a hat (for men), or for one of the following:

women	damas	mujeres	ellas
men	caballeros	hombres	ellos

Public lavatories are hard to find in Cuban towns, but you can use the loo in a bar or restaurant without feeling obliged to buy anything. Some toilets are of the hole-in-the-ground variety, and almost all lavatories open to the public are filthy. Few have proper doors (they are usually chest-high saloon style affairs), or a proper seat; most loos do not have the required fittings. You'll either have to get used to the feel of cold porcelain, or develop strong thigh muscles. Carry your own paper, since it is rarely supplied; if you want to do as the locals do, throw the paper in the bin rather than the toilet bowl.

If you assume that all public toilets are disgusting, you will be pleasantly surprised when you find the odd one which is clean, has paper, a sink, soap and hand towels. Most of the good loos have an attendant waiting by the door, who expects to be given a tip.

INSURANCE

Some travellers go to Cuba with the naive view that insurance is unnecessary; firstly because of the Republic's celebrated health service, and secondly because crime rates have diminished since the revolution. Cubans indeed benefit from free health care, and for minor treatment foreigners are unlikely to have to pay. Westerners requiring hospitalisation, however, are charged fees comparable with those in the USA. Furthermore, while most Cubans are scrupulously honest, there is a small contingent of thieves who are never happier than when robbing foreigners. So insurance is essential for yourself and for your possessions.

The cover provided by most policies is fairly standard: delay and cancellation insurance of up to £2,000; £1 million for medical expenses; the same amount for personal liability; £20,000 for permanent disability; and lost or stolen baggage up to about £1,000 (sometimes valuable single items are excluded). Most now also offer an emergency repatriation service.

Every airline, tour operator and travel agent is delighted to sell you insurance because of their high commission (as much as 100%). Shopping around can save you money or get better cover for the same premium. Columbus (17 Devonshire Square, London EC2; 0171-375 0011) offers good rates for its worldwide insurance scheme.

If you are unfortunate enough to have to claim on your insurance, the golden rule is to amass as much documentation as possible to support your application. In particular, compensation is unlikely to be paid for lost baggage or cash unless your claim is accompanied by a police report of the loss (called a *denuncia*); see *Crime and Safety*. Thefts from tourists in Havana are sufficiently commonplace that the police usually issues a copy of the report to the victim as a matter of routine.

amarillo	slang word for marijuana	jinetero (-a)	somebody who tries to make money out of tourists
arma	gun		
asalto	mugging	ladrón	thief
bandido	bandit	metal	slang word for the police
bomberos	fire brigade	multa	fine
cárcel	prison	narco-traficante	drug-trafficker
cartera, billetera	wallet	nieve, cocaína	cocaine
clandestino	clandestine, underground	policía	police
		prohibido entrar	no entry
contrabandista	smuggler	seguridad	security, safety
drogas	drugs	testimonio	witness
ejército	army	trompetas	slang for secret police, literally 'trumpets'
herido (-a)	injured		
jefatura de policía	police station		

Levels of crime are lower in Cuba than in every nearby country, from the USA and Mexico to Haiti and Jamaica. This is a result of the harsh penalties imposed by the government, the large police force and, until now, the economic and social stability on the island.

The economic crisis has inevitably brought an increase in all types of crime, from black marketeering to robbery. Bag-snatching and pick-pocketing are a danger mainly in certain parts of Havana (see page 191), but are not unheard of elsewhere. The logic is simple. As a Westerner, you are probably carrying hard currency, perhaps $100, which for the average Cuban represents about 10 months' income. Therefore theft of a wallet or purse presents understandable temptation, particularly to poor young urban dwellers. Even so, most visitors feel safer in Cuba than in their home countries. The island could never be described as intimidating, and most travellers feel perfectly at ease walking through the streets at night.

By taking commonsense precautions the risks can be greatly reduced; this book warns of places to avoid and where you should take extra care. Finally, violent crime is rare, and against foreigners is virtually unknown; if you are unfortunate enough to have your bag snatched, it is most unlikely that you will be physically injured.

Most incidents of petty theft against tourists seem to be solved not by smart police work but thanks to the intervention of a passer-by, who either witnessed the crime or who managed to find out who was responsible. Even if the motive of this Cuban is to make a few bucks from a reward, it is worth following any lead since this will probably be your only chance of getting anything back.

How to Avoid Robbery. Western visitors displaying ostentatious wealth in darkened backstreets are asking for trouble — as is anyone who leaves their worldly goods on a beach while going for a swim. Leave as much money as possible in your hotel, and carry what you take with you in a moneybelt beneath your clothes or a pocket that can be buttoned or zipped shut. Do not carry around shoulder bags that can be easily swiped. Cameras symbolise gringo wealth and can be a major temptation too.

Some hotels have a bad reputation for security, and you are advised to put your funds in a safety deposit box *(caja de seguridad)*. Most hotels charge $1-1.50 a day for the use of the safe, so it's worth sharing a box with other travellers in order to split the cost. Rooms in the top hotels should have their own safe.

Reporting a Crime. The police are generally helpful and co-operative when it comes to dealing with tourists, though few speak English. Take along an interpreter if you can — the police certainly won't lay one on for you. You'll probably need to allow at least a couple of hours. After an initial verbal report, an *instructor* will be called, who will take down in writing your account of what happened (and the accounts of any witnesses you take with you). To reclaim losses from your insurers, you will need to provide evidence of the theft — the police should issue a duplicate statement (in Spanish), although they may try to palm you off with just a record of the case number. Make sure that the statement or *denuncia* is stamped.

If you lose air tickets, contact your tour operator's agent in Cuba or talk to the airline direct. Lost passports should be reported to your consulate. As well as obtaining new documents you will need to visit the immigration office to get a new tourist card: this is a formality as long as you have the police report of the robbery, and your new passport. If all your money is stolen, the consul can also arrange for funds to be sent from your home country or, as a last resort, repatriate you. Should the worst happen and you lose everything shortly before departure, ways and means can usually be found to get you home bereft of tickets and passport. As a rule, however, a deposit is expected prior to repatriation. The Cuban agency, Asistur, which now has branches across the island, was set up to help tourists in emergencies but in practice is of very limited assistance.

State Security and the Police. Bear in mind the possibility that you are being watched and heard — above all in Havana, the focus of political discontent in Cuba. Exercise discretion in what you do or say in public, if only because Cubans whom you befriend or deal with may be rendered suspect by so doing.

Talking confidentially in the middle of a public park (so that you can be fairly sure you are not being eavesdropped upon) may sound like a scene from a second-rate Cold War thriller. The reality in Cuba, however, is that there is a powerful state security apparatus with little to do except snoop on locals and visitors. Foreign journalists obviously attract the most attention. Those travelling on an official press visa may well be assigned a specific room in hotels, equipped with bugging devices, and checks may be run on Cubans whom they contact. Hotel lobbies have at least one plain-clothed spy, whose duty it is to report to the DSE (Department of State Security), and prostitutes are also said to be recruited as government informers. Any visitor, tourist or journalist, should be wary of getting involved in any dissident elements, since this will make your contacts potential targets for questioning. Most members of the opposition are under constant surveillance, whether by the DSE directly or by a contact in the local Committee for the Defence of the Revolution.

As far as tourists are concerned, the main duty of the police seems to be to 'protect' them from the attentions of black marketeers, *jineteros* and perceived delinquents. They maintain a heavy presence outside hotels and in the streets of central Havana, where they concentrate on questioning young male blacks — the people blamed for the country's petty crime problem.

Drugs. To some extent Cuba still retains the fiction that Eastern European countries maintained, i.e. that dealing in and using illegal drugs is unknown. While use of illegal drugs is lower than in more developed countries, narcotics are reasonably big business in Cuba. (The government is accused periodically by the United States of being involved in drug-trafficking.) Cuba is on the established route between the cocaine and marijuana producers of South America and the world's biggest narcotics market, the USA.

Marijuana is smoked by many young Cubans, particularly in Havana and Santiago. Much of this comes from Jamaica, though it also grows in abundance in certain areas, including around Guantánamo. The same people who try to get you to change money may also try to sell you marijuana.

The penalties for possessing illegal drugs are severe, and will at the very least involve deportation. Penalties for dealing are harsher still, with long prison sentences.

Photography. Foreigners are subject to a whole series of rules and regulations about what they may and may not photograph. It is forbidden, for instance, to take photographs of military installations, or anything with military connections: railways, ports, radio stations, bridges, factories and research institutes. You must not take photographs at airports or from an aircraft whilst in Cuban air space. It is probably wise to ask permission if you are in any doubt whatsoever, as it is not unheard of for the militia to confiscate a tourist's film. The authorities are also sensitive about photographs that can be seen to be harmful or embarrassing to the state, e.g. those of queues, beggars or confrontations with the police.

Like their country, most Cubans are highly photogenic. Many people adore having their photograph taken but others do not. It is good manners to always ask your subject for the go-ahead first. If you are in a busy tourist area such as

Old Havana or Trinidad, don't be surprised if people ask for money in return for a photo.

SPECIAL REQUIREMENTS

Travellers with Babies or Young Children. In many ways Cuba is an ideal destination for people with small children. It is relatively clean and free of disease, the weather is seldom excessively hot (except in the height of summer) and never too cold, and the locals can be incredibly kind and considerate towards Western children. Those with blonde hair are likely to become the subject of adoration.

One disadvantage if you're travelling from the UK is the long flight, which will involve a change of aeroplane unless you fly direct with Cubana (see page 47). Another problem is the lack of supplies for young children. Disposable nappies and jars of baby food are unobtainable except in a few dollar stores in Havana.

Babysitting is a problem that Cubans rarely face. Most families have a ready-made babysitter in the form of the grandparents, who usually live in the same house or flat. For tourists it may be possible to arrange a babysitter through the hotel, but this service cannot be relied upon. Cubans treat children indulgently, even to the degree of spoiling them, so if you do find a sitter you need have no doubt that children will be well looked after.

Travellers with Disabilities. Cuba is unpromising territory for travellers with disabilities — the average urban street is tough enough for the able-bodied. Blind and partially-sighted people will find Cuba particularly hard going. The help of an able-bodied companion is, unfortunately, essential.

Anyone with a sense of adventure who is keen to go to Cuba should contact the tour operators listed under *Getting There*, since these have some experience of circumventing the problems confronting the handicapped. The most useful source book is *Nothing Ventured: Disabled People Travel the World*, though it doesn't deal specifically with Cuba.

LOCAL QUIRKS

Electrical Equipment. You may wish to take a radio, hair dryer or other gadgets. Before you pack, make sure that they will work correctly on the Cuban electricity supply. This is usually the same as elsewhere in the Americas, i.e. 110 volts at 60 Hz compared to the European supply of around 240 volts at 50 Hz (though many hotels now have 220v supplies too). Some equipment is switchable between these voltages and frequencies, but other items will not work correctly at the lower voltage, and those with motors will run too fast.

Power cuts, voltage drops and frequency fluctuations are regular occurrences, so think twice before plugging in sensitive equipment such as a portable computer. Most Cuban electrical sockets accept plugs with two flat or round pins. Travel adaptors sold abroad should be able to cope with the sockets. Note that there is rarely an earth pin, and that the state of most Cuban electrical fittings is dreadful; an alarming number of hotel rooms have bare live wires showing. Take great care.

Youth and Student Concessions. Take an ISIC student card if it makes you feel better, but don't expect it to be of any use. Only those who are studying in Cuba are eligible for a student discount.

Complaints. Every enterprise in Cuba, from a neighbourhood bar to the plushest hotel, has a complaints book. This volume, marked *Quejas y Sugerencias*, is usually on display; if not you can ask for it. There's not much point complaining about missing bathplugs or lousy food, since things like these are part of Cuban life. The chief function of the book as far as Westerners are concerned is to help settle disputes. Suppose a hotel tries to charge you for telephone calls you haven't made, or a restaurant bill includes an item such as a salad which never materialises; asking for the complaints book often leads to the management backing down.

Weights and Measures. Cuba uses the metric system. Distances are measured in millimetres (25.4mm = 1 inch), metres (0.3m = 1 foot) and kilometres (1.6km = 1 mile). Volume uses the millilitre (550ml = 1 Imperial pint) and the litre (4.5l = 1 Imperial gallon). Weights are given in grams (27g = 1 ounce) and kilograms (0.45kg = 1 lb), though you sometimes hear the use of the *libra*, a hangover from the days when the pound was the unit of weight.

TOURIST INFORMATION

Prising out information such as opening times and places to stay is not the immense struggle that it once was in Cuba. The tourist information network that there is, however, still exists primarily to sell excursions, and is of limited use to the average independent traveller. If you want to find out about a bus route or a good place to eat, you'll do as well asking someone on the street as an official tourist information assistant. Most locals will be happy to help you out, and the extent of the average citizen's knowledge of his or her native town is impressive.

Bookings are most easily done at the information bureaux found in most tourist hotels. While some are worse than useless, others are very helpful and can, for example, help you get a grasp of the function of Cuba's various tourism agencies. There seems to be absolutely no communication between any of these organisations, as you'll find out if you complain to a Cubanacán rep that there's no soap in the bathroom of your Gaviota hotel.

If you arrive on a package tour, there's a good chance that you'll be looked after by Havanatur. This enterprise is devoted largely to organising ground arrangements for the customers of foreign tour operators. You should contact their representative if you need to change your flight times or want someone to negotiate on your behalf if the hotel room is infested with cockroaches. Independent travellers might also be wise to cultivate the friendship of the hotel's Havanatur rep, since he or she can prove invaluable in settling disputes, getting you a ride in a tour bus, etc.

Concerned primarily with selling excursions and hotel rooms, Cubatur used to be the island's only state organisation to deal with tourists. Ideally foreigners would use the services of Cubatur exclusively, paying in advance in hard currency or by credit card for everything from air tickets to museum outings. You are, of course, under no obligation to do so, but there are occasions when it can prove useful.

Cubanacán promotes international trade, joint ventures and also runs several hotels, has its own fleet of taxis and rental cars, etc. Its tourist interests tend to be more specialised, as are those of Gaviota, which is run by the Armed Forces Ministry.

Cuban Tourist Offices Abroad. The few countries in the world with a Cuban tourist bureau are listed below. In other places the Cuban consulate should be of some help. In general, however, the quantity and quality of tourist information is low and you'll find that independent travel agencies are a far better source: see *Getting There* for addresses.

Argentina
Oficina de Promoción e Información Turística
de Cuba
Paraguay 631, 2 piso
Buenos Aires
Capital Federal
Tel (1) 311-5820
Fax 311-4198

Canada
Bureau de Tourisme de Cuba
440 Blvd René Lévesque Ouest, 1402
Montréal, Quebec H2Z 1V7
Tel (514) 875-8004/05
Fax (514) 875-8006

Cuba Tourist Board
55 Queen St East, #705
Toronto, Ontario M5H 1R5
Tel (416) 362-0700/01/02
Fax (416) 362-0702

France
Office de Promotion et Information Touristique
de Cuba
24, rue du Quatre Septembre
Paris 75002
Tel 4742-5415

Federal Republic of Germany
Kubanisches Fremdenverkehrsbüro
Steinweg 2
D-6000 Frankfurt-am-Main 1

Italy
Via General Fara #30, terzo piano
20124 Milan

México
Oficina de Promoción e Información Turística
de Cuba
Insurgentes Sur #421, esq. Aguascalientes
Complejo Aristos, Edificio B, Local 310
Col. Hipódromo Condesa
México DF 06100
Tel (5) 574-9454/9651

Spain
Oficina de Promoción e Información Turística
de Cuba
Paseo de la Habana #28
Madrid 28036
Tel (1) 411-3097/3297

EMBASSIES

Foreign governments offer advice before you go about perceived problems in Cuba. In the UK, Foreign Office travel advice is available on 0171-270 4129; on BBC-2 Ceefax page 564 onwards; and on the Internet at http://www.fco.gov.uk/
If you get into difficulties, whether caused by theft, ill-health, running out of cash or involvement with crime, your first point of contact should be your

embassy (or the embassy of the country which represents you). The staff have a thorough understanding of the way things work — or fail to work — in Cuba; and they also have better lines of communication with home countries than you are likely to be able to organise. In a real emergency, the consul and other staff will do their utmost to help you out; however, if your problem is that you've sprained your ankle while drunk, or that you don't like the food, don't expect too much sympathy.

For details of Embassies and Consulates in Havana, see page 192.

SOURCES OF INFORMATION

Several groups exist to promote links between the West and Cuba. As well as providing invaluable background to the country, they also organise special trips. One such is the Cuba Solidarity Campaign, 129 Seven Sisters Road, London N7 7QG (tel 0171-263 6452, e-mail cubasc@gn.apc.org). It has regular meetings in regional centres in Britain covering a wide range of subjects, together with social events featuring Cuban food, drink and entertainment. The Centre organises an annual opportunity to spend a month in Cuba as part of the José Martí Work Brigade. The Centre says the scheme 'enables Western Europeans to express their solidarity with Cuba through the contribution of their manual labour, mainly building and citrus fruit picking'. Applicants, says the CSC, should be committed socialists. Several British trades unions sponsor individual members to take part in the Brigades.

For straight information, you should contact the Latin American Information Service, which compiles a weekly newspack with cuttings from national and international dailies and periodicals as well as radio reports. For further information and the latest subscription rates, contact the LAIS at PO Box 24, Manchester M7 0EX (tel 0161-228 7073, fax 0161-228 7071). Another possible source of information is the Latin America Bureau, which is an independent, non-profit making organisation, concerned with human rights and related social, political and economic issues in Latin America. As a supporter you are entitled to up-to-date information, discounts on books published by LAB, access to its library, invitations to events, regular mailings and so on. Through LAB you can also subscribe to *NACLA*, which is an English-language magazine on Latin America, published in the USA. Articles cover politics, economics, social affairs, culture, etc. For further information contact LAB at 1 Amwell Street, London EC1R (tel 0171-278 2829).

For a less objective view of events in Cuba, you can subscribe to the weekly issue of *Granma International*, published on the island (see page 69). Rates are $40 for one year or $10 for three months. Send a money order in US dollars or equivalent hard currency to Granma Internacional, Plaza de la Revolución, PO Box 6260, CP 10699, La Habana, Cuba (tel 81-6265, 81-7443).

Business Visitors. If you are travelling to Cuba on business and will need to be in regular contact with your office back home, you should choose your hotel with some care. Havana does not present much of a problem these days, though even here some of the big hotels have just one telephone operator, causing considerable delay at times for anyone trying to call abroad. It is worth checking to ensure that direct dialling is available. The top hotels, including the Nacional and Cohiba, have their own executive floors, with secretaries, translators, fax machines and photocopiers, etc. Staff in these hotels are also likely to have a greater command of the English language than in other places. Outisde the capital, facilities for business travellers are minimal, though the new resort hotels are better equipped than most, and at least have new telephone and fax lines. In Santiago, the best place to stay is the Santiago de Cuba hotel (see page 316).

If you want to be in constant touch, it is possible to hire a mobile phone.

Contact Cubacel at Calle 28 no. 510, between Avenidas 5ta and 7ma in Havana (tel 33-2222), though they also have outlets in some of the top hotels.

Sources of business information: in the UK, one of the best sources of information about doing business in Cuba is the West India Committee (Nelson House, 8/9 Northumberland Street, London WC2N 5RA; tel 0171-976 1495; fax 0171-976 1541), whose purpose is to strengthen commercial and other relations between Britain and the Caribbean. Members receive the monthly *Caribbean Insight* magazine, which keeps you abreast of the latest developments, and are also invited to special business lunches and seminars. The West India Committee incorporates Caritag, the Caribbean Trade Advisory Group to the British Overseas Trade Board, through which small and medium-sized export companies are provided with information and assistance developing their export potential in the region.

Additional information is available from Cuba Business at 254-258 Goswell Road, London EC1V 7EB (tel 0171-490 1997, fax 0171-253 7358) and also the Department of Trade and Industry. The latter commissions its own reports and also distributes reports issued by the Commercial Section of the British Embassy in Havana. For information write to the Cuba Desk, Exports to Europe and the Americas (EXA) Division, DTI, Kingsgate House, 66-74 Victoria Street, London SW1E 6SW (tel 0171-215 5000) or call the Caribbean desk direct on 0171-215 5040.

Two new publications available in Cuba are directed specifically at business visitors. *Opciones* is a weekly newspaper (price $1) whose national and international news coverage is geared to business interests, particularly Latin American. It has more details about exchange rates than *Granma* and also carries advertisements by Cuban factories looking for foreign partners. *Business Tips on Cuba*, a glossy monthly magazine available in Spanish, French, English, Russian and Portuguese, contains news and information about the Cuban economy, business, joint ventures and legal regulations. It sells for $5.

Anyone requiring legal advice regarding joint ventures may want to contact the international law office (known as the 'Bufete Internacional' — nothing to do with foreign food), which offers its services to individuals and foreign companies. It is based at Calle 47 no. 815, between Santa Ana and Conill, Nuevo Vedado (tel 33-5469, 81-3498; fax 33-5448).

Calendar of Events

Many public holidays were abolished after the Revolution, notably religious festivals, and new holidays were created to mark important events in recent Cuban history. Christmas is not recognised officially, but the New Year is enthusiastically celebrated. (December 31, while not officially a holiday, is usually treated as a day off as people prepare for parties.) Public holidays are shown in **bold** in the list below.

January 1	Anniversary of the Victory of the Revolution/ New Year
January 28	Birthday of José Martí
January/February	Carnaval, Varadero
February	Jazz festival (biennial)
February 24	Beginning of the 1895 Revolution
March 13	Anniversary of attack on Presidential Palace
April 19	Bay of Pigs Victory
May 1	International Labour Day
mid-May	Ernest Hemingway Marlin Fishing Tournament (Havana)
July 26	Remembrance of the 'National Rebellion' (Moncada Assault in 1953)
July 30	Martyrs of the Revolution Day
September 24	Festival of La Merced (Obbatalá)
October 8	Anniversary of the death of Che Guevara
October 10	Anniversary of the start of the 1868 War of Independence
November	Varadero International Music Festival
December	Latin American Film Festival
December 2	Anniversary of the landing of the *Granma*
December 8	Heroes' Day, commemorating death of Antonio Maceo in 1896
December 17	Diá de San Lázaro, Santiago de las Vegas, Havana

Havana: City and Province

The Malecón, City of Havana

The political and cultural heart of one of the world's strangest nations, the Cuban capital is unlike any other city in the world. In Havana, there is only the random roar of traffic. You might hear the odd wheezing lorry or a boy racer gunning his clapped-out Lada, but the most prominent sound is the background chatter and animated ambience of two million Latins living their lives on the streets. In the back streets of the old city, plumbing is poor or non-existent, and water is handed up in plastic buckets to the balconies of formerly magnificent houses. But Havana is still a city of great style and unrivalled atmosphere, a delightful confusion of Spanish colonial, neoclassical and Art Deco styles. These have been tainted by a few hideous high-rise hotels and apartment blocks, constructed in the 1950s, yet unlike most colonial cities in Spanish America, the Cuban capital has been little spoilt by modernisation. The brutalist architecture of the communists has largely been confined to the outskirts.

The preservation of Havana was never high on the list of Castro's priorities. This means that much of the capital is in a tragic state of decay. However, the last five years have seen a turnaround in the government's attitude to its heritage and it is directing much energy into restoration. Visit the city now and you can see it as it awakes gradually from a long hibernation.

Havana is about as representative of Cuba as New York is of the USA — it bears little relation to the country beyond. Yet taken on its own it is one of the most rewarding places in the world, with endless layers of colour and culture, and constant clashes of style and scale. Most visitors have to drag themselves away. Others capitulate altogether and spend their entire holiday in the capital.

History. Havana was founded in 1514 — as Villa de San Cristóbal de La Habana,

146

the last of the seven original Spanish villas — but 35 miles (55km) south of its present site. It moved to the north coast not long after it had replaced Santiago de Cuba as capital in 1553.

The new location was a fine natural harbour in close proximity to North America, and Havana was immediately the focus of activity on the island. It became the perfect gathering-point for Spanish ships heading from the mainland colonies back across the Atlantic to Europe. The city soon boasted one of the greatest assemblies of fortresses in Latin America, built to protect both the ships and city from attack. In 1674, construction of the city walls began, and by the mid-18th century these had defined what is now Habana Vieja or 'Old Havana'. This original, walled city was a great jumble of warehouses, churches and private dwellings, much as it is today.

Despite its fortifications, Havana could not withstand the British who, led by Sir George Keppel, Count of Albermarle, occupied the city in 1762. When the Cuban capital was returned to Spain in 1763, the Spanish resolved to take better care of their colony. The construction of new fortresses turned Havana into the most protected city in Latin America.

The British occupation gave Havana a new lease of life by loosening Spain's monopoly on trade. The late 18th century saw the start of major expansion in the city. The Marqués de la Torre, governor of the island at the time, set about redesigning the city, which included developing the area beyond the city walls and the laying of broad avenues such as the Prado. In the 19th century, Governor Miguel de Tacón carried on where de la Torre left off. As the city continued to expand, Havana could no longer be contained within the confines of the old fortifications, which were in any case obsolete in military terms by the mid-19th century. Demolition of the city walls began in 1863.

Old Havana was increasingly neglected as the city rapidly expanded westwards. The rich headed away from the crowded and increasingly unhealthy port area. They built themselves fine new mansions, the cream of which in the mid-19th century were in the Cerro district, south of central Havana. There was development west along the coast too, though the shaping of Vedado only really came about with the spectacular economic boom brought by the First World War. By 1920, Havana had already acquired an urban image above that of any other Latin American city, apart perhaps from Buenos Aires. The old mansions and palaces in Habana Vieja were left to deteriorate, as new public buildings were built around the Parque Central and smart new villas went up in the residential districts of Vedado and Miramar.

Following independence in 1902, the USA acquired tight economic and political control over its neighbour. While this association brought only misery to much of the Cuban population, to the capital it brought great prosperity. After the Second World War, Americans couldn't get enough of the place — or at least its casinos and prostitutes. The Mafia arrived too. By the late 1950s they were tearing down historic buildings to put up new hotels. Havana was one of the most exciting — and corrupt — places on earth.

The revolution affected the capital much more than other Cuban cities. Physically, Havana began a steady decline. Morally, the climate changed quickly, throwing thousands of pimps, prostitutes and croupiers out of work (though the first two categories have made a strong comeback). Financially, Havana went into recession as much-needed investment was directed to the provinces. This policy has been reversed in the 1990s, as Havana has shot to the forefront of Cuba's main tourist industry. Glossy 24-hour bars and newly restored hotels add unaccustomed colour to the neglected city streets. For tourists it is now possible to get a good meal, and also to enjoy the best and broadest range of entertainment in the Republic.

CITY LAYOUT

The boundaries of Havana are spread wide and include numerous places of interest. The centre of the city is divided into several distinct sectors, although you are likely to spend most time in just two of them:

Old Havana (Habana Vieja) is the spit of land which divides the harbour from the Atlantic, and stretches west from the water to the Parque Central and the Capitol building. It is on the list of UNESCO's 'heritage cities' due to its fine Spanish colonial architecture, and has the most of interest to visitors.

Centro Habana occupies the zone west of the old quarter as far as Calzada de Infanta and is the most densely populated part of the city. It is a largely residential area, disreputable in places (see *Crime and Safety*) and one you are more likely to pass through than explore. The main streets running through Centro Habana include Zanja, Neptuno and San Lázaro, all of which provide a good, fast route through the district.

Vedado is a more modern, spacious residential area, with a concentration of hotels and offices to the east. Activity here is centred upon La Rampa. It is officially part of Calle 23 from its junction with Calle M down to the Malecón, but in practice it is known as 'the ramp' in view of its profile, sloping down to the sea. This is the commercial heart of the city, with cinemas and airline offices, and is dominated by the high-rise Habana Libre hotel.

Plaza de la Revolución, also known less cumbersomely as Plaza, spreads south of Vedado. The area is named after the square around which the government and ministries are clustered. The main bus terminal is located in this district, but there is little else to drag you south.

Cerro, south of Centro Habana and Plaza, was where rich Habaneros came in the 19th century to escape from the social melting-pot around the port. They later gravitated west to Vedado and Cerro has remained on the fringes ever since. It is worth taking a ride along Calzada de Cerro to see the crumbling sophistication of a bygone era, but otherwise you are only likely to visit Cerro if you come to watch a baseball match at the Estadio Latinoamericano (see *Sport*).

Miramar, west of the Almendares river in the larger municipality of Playa, is a plush waterfront suburb. Huge villas and mansions that belonged to Havana's richest inhabitants before the revolution line Fifth Avenue ('Quinta Avenida'), the main route through the district; most are now in the hands of foreign embassies, joint ventures and government officials. Some of the capital's best restaurants are found in Miramar, and there is a narrow strip of sand that passes for a beach.

The *Malecón* is a wide promenade that runs from the mouth of the Almendares river, which marks the western boundary of Vedado, all the way along the seafront to the Castillo de la Punta, at the northern end of the Prado. It provides the fastest route between most points in Havana. The curving promenade is a delight to behold, with its multi-coloured façades and water crashing dramatically over the sea walls. During the day, kids play on the rocks and men fish, but the Malecón is at its busiest after sunset, when young people congregate to chat and share a bottle of rum. Constructed in the 20th century and being primarily residential, the Malecón is not a priority for restoration. Several buildings have already collapsed through neglect.

Street Names. After 1959, numerous names of main roads were changed. Some changes have caught on, but most pre-revolutionary names persist among the locals, even though the name plates have long since been changed. Do not be surprised, therefore, to be given apparently conflicting directions by the locals. The main changes are as follows:

New name	Old name
Avenida Galiano	Avenida Italia
Avenida Máximo Gómez	Avenida Monte
Avenida de Monserrate	Avenida de Bélgica
Avenida Menocal	Calzada de Infanta
Avenida Padre Varela	Avenida Belascoaín
Avenida Salvador Allende	Avenida Carlos III
Avenida Simón Bolívar	Avenida Reina
Avenida Agramonte	Avenida Zulueta
Paseo de Martí	Prado

Maps. The best map of Havana is the *Mapa Turístico: Ciudad de la Habana*, available for $2 from hard currency shops. The plan included in one of the tourist maps of the whole country (see page 73) is a reasonable alternative. A good pocket-size map of Habana Vieja is now also available.

ARRIVAL AND DEPARTURE

Air. *Arrival:* José Martí airport is about 15 miles (25km) south of Havana, just off Calle de la Independencia — the main road through the suburb of Rancho Boyeros. At present the set-up is a bit of a mess, and will continue to be so until Spring 1998 when a big new terminal is completed to the north of the runway. Until then, there are three terminals.

Terminal 1 is used for all Cubana flights, domestic and international.

Terminal 2 handles international services on other airlines, e.g. Viasa, Iberia, Aeroflot and charter services to Miami. It is within sight of Terminal 1, but in the unlikely event that you need to travel from one to another, you would do best to grab a taxi.

Terminal 3, also known as Terminal Caribbean, is the AeroCaribbean charter terminal, from where excursion flights to Cayo Largo and other destinations depart. It is south of the village of Wajay in a thoroughly unlikely setting. The departure lounge is a pleasant and shady garden. If you are driving to this terminal yourself, watch carefully for the signs pointing to your right; if you reach the signs for Terminal 2, you've gone too far.

Trying to travel from the airport into town by local bus could be a bad start to your trip. If you need to save money, though, it is possible to catch a bus on the main road to the centre of Havana. There is one bus, number 4, that runs (unreliably) between José Martí airport and the Parque Central for 40 centavos; it is supposedly supplemented by a 'taxi-bus' bearing the letter M and costing 1 peso, but sightings of either are rare. Otherwise, take any bus as far as you can towards the centre and then change.

Unless you have a transfer arranged as part of your tour, the easiest way to get to the city is by taxi. As you go through immigration at the airport, it's worth looking for people who might want to share a cab. The fare in a standard Turistaxi should be around $12 to Vedado, $14 to Old Havana. You can save a couple of dollars by looking out for a Panataxi — generally a red Lada — though these are scarce at the airport (see *Getting Around*). Allow about half an hour for the journey into town. Do not feel obliged to tip cab drivers at the other end, even if they are angling for a bonus.

If you have a pre-booked bus transfer, having passed through immigration and Customs you should look for the representative who will be there to greet those on package tours; you will probably share the same bus into town.

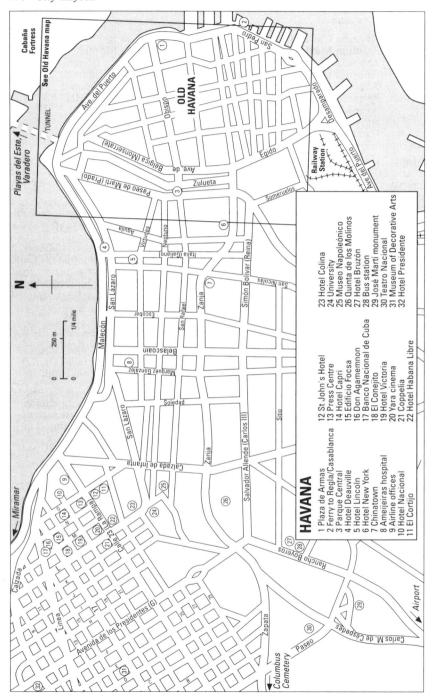

HAVANA

1 Plaza de Armas
2 Ferry to Regla/Casablanca
3 Parque Central
4 Hotel Deauville
5 Hotel Lincoln
6 Hotel New York
7 Chinatown
8 Ameijeiras hospital
9 Airline offices
10 Hotel Nacional
11 El Cortijo

12 St John's Hotel
13 Press Centre
14 Hotel Capri
15 Edificio Focsa
16 Don Agamemnon
17 Banco Nacional de Cuba
18 El Conejito
19 Hotel Victoria
20 Yara cinema
21 Coppelia
22 Hotel Habana Libre

23 Hotel Colina
24 University
25 Museo Napoleónico
26 Quinta de los Molinos
27 Hotel Bruzón
28 Bus station
29 José Martí monument
30 Teatro Nacional
31 Museum of Decorative Arts
32 Hotel Presidente

Cabaña
Fortress

See Old Havana map

OLD
HAVANA

TUNNEL

Playas del Este,
Varadero

Miramar

Columbus
Cemetery

Airport

Railway
Station

N

250 m

1/4 mile

After a long flight, cyclists are unlikely to feel like pedalling all the way into central Havana. Options include negotiating with a taxi driver, chartering a minibus, or sweet-talking a tour guide into letting you stow your bike in the hold of a tourist bus. If you decide to cycle into town, turn left onto Calle de la Independencia and head northeast until you reach the area covered by the map in this book.

Both terminals 1 and 2 have a car rental office, directly opposite the exit from the arrivals hall.

See page 56 for information on immigration procedures.

Departure: the best option for a cheap trip from the centre to the airport is on the 'taxi bus' marked *Aeropuerto*, which you can catch from the east side of the Parque Central. It serves both Terminals 1 and 2, supposedly every hour, and charges one peso. You cannot rely on this bus though, so set out early and be prepared to grab a taxi if nothing materialises.

Facilities for departing passengers are limited by international standards but adequate. Terminal 1 offers nothing in the way of facilities until you have passed through passport control, though the refurbishment currently in progress should bring some improvement. The international departure lounge, which is far superior to that for internal flights, has a decent snack bar, a reasonable duty-free shop and a selection of other stalls for last-minute gifts and souvenirs. Terminal 2 is much cleaner and better equipped, with good duty-free shops and an excellent selection of cigars at reasonable prices. All facilities are open 24 hours, in theory at least.

When several flights are scheduled to leave in quick succession, terminals become unbearably crowded. Checking in almost always takes an age. If you end up at the back of the queue, you would do as well to go and have a drink and return in half an hour. A better place to escape the crowds is the observation deck, though the mosquitoes are voracious in the evening. If you have excess baggage, go to the shop and stock up on chocolate and cigarettes with which to mollify the check-in staff.

A departure tax of $12 is levied on most tickets, though in some cases the cost is included in your fare. There are money exchange desks at the main terminals if you need to change travellers cheques at the last minute.

Airline Offices: almost all the airline offices are in the same block of La Rampa (Calle 23) in Vedado, between Calle P and Infanta. The Cubana office, at the bottom end, deals with both international and domestic flights. Don't bother with the information desk opposite the main door; go straight to one of the booking desks, even if all you need is information on flights or to confirm a reservation. No printed timetables are available. The office is open 8.30am-4pm Monday to Friday. For information on international flights call 7-4911 or 7-4916; 70-9391 to 96 for domestic flights.

Other airlines in the same block as Cubana are in the following order as you walk away from the Malecón:

LTU: Calle 23 no. 54 (tel 33-3524/25), open 8.30am-noon and 1-6pm Monday to Thursday, 8.30am-noon on Friday. This German airline serves Havana, Holguín, Varadero and Cayo Largo.

Aeroflot: Calle 23 no. 64 (tel 33-3200 or 33-3759), open 8.30am-12.30pm, 1.30-4pm Monday to Friday, 8.30am-noon on Saturday.

Mexicana: Calle 23 no. 74 (tel 79-8100, 79-6615), open 8.30am-4.30pm Monday to Friday, 8.30am-noon on Saturday.

AeroCaribbean: Calle 23 no. 60 (tel 33-5016). Open 8.30am-4pm Monday to Friday.

Iberia: Calle 23 no. 84 (tel 33-5041/2, at the airport 33-5234), open 9am-4pm Monday to Friday, 9am-noon on Saturday.

Viasa has its office inside the Habana Libre hotel, open 9am-noon and 1-4pm Monday to Friday. The queue can be extremely slow. If you need just to confirm a flight or ask for information, wait until after 5pm and call the after-hours number (tel 33-5068). The daytime number is 33-3130, but the staff rarely have time to deal with phone enquiries.

The Celimar office, for tickets to Miami, is at Calle 24 no. 4314, on the corner of 45, in Playa (tel 33-2555/2281/2983; fax 33-2074). It opens 8.30am-4.30pm Monday to Friday, closing for one hour at lunch. There is a special office for foreigners, which is smarter and has a shorter queue than the one reserved for Cubans.

All the offices of foreign airlines are linked by computer to their home countries. These links depend upon the Cuban telephone system, however, so connections are often faulty and you may have to wait hours or days to do something as simple as changing a reservation. If you wish to contact the airport direct, phone 79-6081 or 70-7701.

Unless you have a non-changeable ticket, it is essential to re-confirm your return flight at least 72 hours before departure. If you neglect to do so, you run the risk of your reservation being cancelled automatically. In addition, schedules and flight numbers sometimes change, for no obvious reason and at perilously short notice; re-confirmation enables you to find out about them. If you are on a tour, then your rep should confirm your flight on your behalf, but it's always as well to check.

Train. Most trains head out of Havana from the Central Station at the southern end of Old Havana (tel 31-2392). Expectant travellers surrounded by mountains of bags and boxes fill the main entrance hall, spilling out onto the street. You'll find comparative tranquillity in the adjacent dollar café.

Tourists are supposed to buy all tickets in dollars from Ferrotur (tel 62-1770) on Calle Esperanza, which runs along the north side of the station. You can normally reserve a seat just an hour ahead of departure, though if your train leaves in the evening, you must buy your ticket within office hours (8am-5pm); for peace of mind you are advised to arrange your journey the day before you plan to travel. The staff at Ferrotur are generally very helpful, and can also book tickets from other destinations for you.

The office where Cubans reserve and buy long-distance train tickets is at Misión and Economia, across the square from the station. The area is in a perpetual state of chaos, and you face a daunting task if you want to try to pay in pesos. You will normally just be directed to Ferrotur anyway.

A timetable, as of December 1995, is shown below. Remember that all trains in Cuba are liable to cancellation or delay. All services except the No 1 to Santiago are *regular*.

Camagüey: No 5, departing daily at 6.35pm, arriving 4.55am.
Cienfuegos: No 11, departing 10.15am on Monday, Thursday and Saturday, arriving at 5.04pm. Be prepared for schedule changes, and cancellations: fuel shortages or engine problems seem particularly frequent along this line.
Sancti Spíritus: No 7, departing at 9.20am daily, calling at Matanzas, Colón and Santa Clara. Arrives at 4.55pm.
Santiago de Cuba: No 1 (*especial*), departing 4.25pm daily. Stops include Matanzas, Santa Clara, Ciego de Avila, Camagüey, Las Tunas and Holguín. Arrives 6.45am. There are no sleeping cars but the reclining seats in air-conditioned carriages are reasonably comfortable.
Pinar del Rio: a *tren especial* (for which seats can be reserved) leaves on uneven dates at 6.15am, arriving at 11.30am. There is also a *servicio regular*, departing at 3am, which is a free for all. The journey is notorious for delays, up to 10 or 12 hours on bad days.

Prices are as follows:

Camagüey	$22	Matanzas	$4
Ciego de Avila	$18	Pinar del Rió	$6.50
Cienfuegos	$11	Santa Clara	$12
Holguín	$31	Sancti Spíritus	$13
Las Tunas	$27	Santiago de Cuba	$35

Anyone travelling to Matanzas and with a little extra time to spare, should seriously consider taking the train from the Casablanca station, reached by ferry from Old Havana (see page 156). This station serves only the local line to Matanzas. Services from the Central Station are faster and more comfortable but not nearly as fun. Even if you don't have any particular inclination to visit Matanzas, a spin in Cuba's only electric train is highly recommended. The journey takes about four hours.

Trains run four times a day, currently at 4.10am, 10.20am, 2.55pm and 9.10pm. Try to turn up 30 minutes in advance if you want to be sure of getting a seat (ask for a reservation as well as a ticket). Bikes should be allowed on, but you'll have to check with the driver. See *Matanzas* for more information about this railway journey.

Bus. *Long-distance:* buses serving all the main towns and cities in Cuba depart from the Terminal de Omnibus Interprovinciales at the corner of Avenida Rancho Boyeros and Calle 19 de Mayo, just northeast of the Plaza de la Revolución. From the Parque Central (east side) the most convenient bus is number 265 — if you can get it.

Cubans after a long-distance bus ticket go to the Oficina de Reservaciones Pasajes at the corner of Calles 21 and 4 in Vedado (open 7am-2pm Monday to Friday, 7-11am on Saturday). There is always a mass of people outside and it is not hard to see why tempers get raw. You'll have to push your way in if you want to consult the timetables. To reserve a place, people put their name on a list that is compiled by somebody sitting under a tree outside. It soon becomes clear whether or not they have a chance of travelling to their chosen destination within the next few days, weeks or even months.

There is no point in the average foreign traveller going through this rigmarole. If you are desperate to travel by bus, you will be better off turning up at the terminal and trying to persuade the person in charge of letting people on the bus to sell you a ticket. Remember, however, that by doing so you will probably be doing a Cuban out of a legitimately reserved seat. If you prefer to do everything above board, try getting a standby ticket in the department dealing with returns (*fallos*), which is upstairs. Predictably enough, this is the most disorganised bus station in the country, and after an hour or two of queuing and pleading for a ticket you may draw a blank. If so, look for a private cab or colectivo outside or at the central railway station: see below.

Transfers: if you are determined to travel by bus, your best bet will be to buy a 'transfer' on a tourist bus (see page 80). Current rates for a selection of destinations are: $25 to Varadero, $30 to Viñales and $45 to Trinidad or Cienfuegos.

Local: buses to nearby towns leave from a variety of places, e.g. at the junction of Galiano and Dragones for Cojímar, corner of Glória and Agramonte for Guanabo, and the square south of the Capitolio for Guanabacoa. There is always a crush to get on any of these; the *último* system of queuing operates, but imperfectly. It is a good idea to ascertain where the service begins from, since if you wait several stops after the terminus, the bus is likely to be full. More information about services to destinations outside Havana are given in *Further Afield*.

Taxis. You won't find many collective taxis these days, but they are a viable option if you have no luck with trains or buses. Colectivos aren't accustomed to serving faraway destinations, although drivers are always open to suggestion. The best place to pick one up is near the central railway station. You can't miss the row of old American cars lined up in the square outside the terminal, their drivers slumped about passing the time of day. Others congregate a block away, at the corner of Agramonte and Glória, but these serve primarily nearby seaside resorts.

For longer distances, you are advised to go for a private cab. Drivers spend most of their time ferrying people around the city, but will happily take you almost anywhere in the country if the price is right. See *City Transport* below.

CAR

Car rental. The two main rental agencies, Transautos and Havanautos, have representatives in several of Havana's top hotels, including the Plaza, Inglaterra, Sevilla, Deauville, Nacional, Presidente and Comodoro. (Both agencies print a leaflet giving the location of their agencies, both within Havana and nationwide.) It is worth making the effort, however, to go to the Transautos office beside the Hotel Capri at Calle 21 between Calles N and O in Vedado (tel 33-4038); this is where the main garage is located, so any problems with the car can be sorted out on the spot. Being central, the Capri branch is in big demand and its cars get booked up quickly. The turnover is so fast, however, that you can normally get a vehicle if you're prepared to wait an hour or two.

If you don't intend to stay in Havana, you may find it easier to use one of the airport offices; there are good road links from José Martí airport to the autopistas leading to other parts of Cuba.

You can also rent cars from Cubanacán, whose most convenient agent is located inside the Hotel Comodoro at Avenida 3ra y 84 in Miramar (tel 22-5551/59).

Petrol. There are several Cupet stations on the road into town from the airport. In central Havana, the most useful petrol station is just down Calle L from Habana Libre Hotel.

City Driving. Driving around Havana takes a lot of nerve, not so much for the quantity of vehicular traffic as for the cyclists and pedestrians, the erratic behaviour of local motorists, the confusing traffic signals and the poorly signed roads. Note that it is possible to avoid the city altogether on the motorway-standard bypass that links the main radial routes to and from the capital, though this is still awaiting completion. To reach Old Havana, the best way in is under the tunnel from Habana del Este; this is true even if you approach from the west. Signposting from outside Havana is good — just follow the arrows marked 'Túnel'. The tunnel takes you straight into the old city, and has a link to the Malecón, the rapid seafront road to Vedado. Any other route into the capital involves ploughing through suburbs with endless malfunctioning traffic lights.

It is near-impossible to drive through Havana while simultaneously navigating from a map. Either get your passenger to do this for you, or ask another motorist for directions.

Parking. While you can adopt the local habit of parking your car wherever it suits you, you should be wary of abandoning your vehicle anywhere remotely official. The regulations which prohibit parking close to government buildings are strictly enforced; there is usually a soldier with a whistle who will move you on. Don't even think of trying to park anywhere near the Plaza de la Revolución. Try to leave your car in a guarded hotel car park overnight.

CITY TRANSPORT

Engineers and urban planners with nothing much to do and an over-active imagination have apparently spent the last few years designing an underground train system for the city. Outside in the real world, however, Cubans must make do with what they can find, jumping on any bus no matter how full, hailing anything that moves.

Bus. Havana has a wonderfully motley collection of buses, which come in all shapes, sizes and colour. Most of those donated from abroad still have their original destinations on the windscreen, giving you the chance to catch a bus to a suburb of Frankfurt or Toronto. However, the most amusing addition to the streets of the capital since the start of the Special Period is the *tren bus*, a local invention concocted by joining two buses together and nicknamed *camelo* or 'camel'.

The most rewarding aspect of travelling by bus in Havana is the sense of achievement it gives — not just in finding a bus that is headed roughly where you want to go, but also in getting on it. Once you've found the right stop or *parada*, you could be lucky and wait just 15 minutes. But you could wait an hour or more and then have to fight your way on board and then withstand an often frightful crush. While only the hardiest of travellers may like the sound of such a scrum, unless you never leave the downtown area or can afford to take taxis everywhere, you cannot avoid using the buses. And even if you don't plan to use the system much, it is worth travelling by bus at least once just for the experience. Buses travel at terrifying speeds along the city streets, though this tends to be scarier for pedestrians than for passengers. Services run 24 hours a day in theory, but you won't find many in the early hours. The cyclebus (see below) runs the only reliable 24-hour service.

To work out which bus to catch, your best bet is to ask the locals. The established network of buses has long since disintegrated, with routes changing all the time. Once you're on the bus, you'll probably need to rely on a fellow passenger to tell you when to get off. Such is the crowd at most bus stops that the driver should stop automatically; work your way to the nearest door in good time, ready to leap off. In the suburbs you may have to request a stop, in which case bash the white box above the exit, whistle or scream *Pare* ('Stop!'). Bus stops are a long way apart, so if you don't establish which you want (or are too bashful to shout), you could sail ten blocks past your destination. If you're heading down to Old Havana, beware of missing the right stop. Those who fail to get off at the harbourside might end up going under the tunnel to the toll booth on the far side.

The most useful buses in central Havana at the time of going to press are routes 264 and 232, which run between the central railway station (Ferrocarril) and Playa, crossing Habana Vieja, Centro Habana and Vedado en route. You soon get to know which are the good pick-up points for buses, e.g. in the square by the Capitolio, or a couple of blocks down from the Habana Libre on Calle 23.

The normal bus services are supplemented by *ruteros* — cream and red midibuses which charge higher fares (40 centavos) and are therefore less crowded. You also find the odd 'taxi bus', for which the fare is one peso.

Many bus stops in Havana now double up as official hitching posts, with reps of the Inspección Estatal making sure the traffic stops.

Taxi. *Official taxis:* given the difficulties in getting around by bus, it is almost impossible to avoid using taxis. Tourist taxis are not cheap, though competition from private cabs has forced prices down slightly. All official *Turistaxis* have a meter (*taximetro*), which most drivers should turn on automatically. If they choose not to, either insist they do or, if you are familiar with the going rate, negotiate a price in advance. You can expect to pay $3-4 for the five-minute ride between the Habana Libre Hotel to the Parque Central, for example.

Turistaxis can be found outside all the top hotels. If there are none free, somebody in reception can call one for you. Otherwise, do this yourself by dialling 79-1940, 79-5665 or 79-8613. Cubanacán has its own fleet of taxis, which can be ordered on 33-1446 or 33-1349.

A cheaper breed of cab, the Panataxi, is a Lada rather than a spanking new Nissan or Peugeot and is not allowed to use hotel taxi ranks. That you have to order one over the phone (tel 81-0153, 81-4142, 81-5753) is not always convenient, but the fares are about 25% cheaper than those charged by Turistaxis, and the drivers are invariably friendlier. While you rarely see Panataxis cruising the streets, they will usually stop if you hail, and occasionally you can pick one up in the car park between Plaza de la Catedral and the Malecón. Panataxis are metered, though if you want a cab for a few hours they charge a special fee, currently $30 per three hours.

Whether you take a Turistaxi or a Panataxi, the drivers are usually strict about not taking more than four passengers. If there are five or more in your party, say so when you order your cab and they will send a larger vehicle.

Private taxis: by taking a private cab it is possible to undercut official fares by up to a third. Make sure you agree a price in advance, and it is worth finding out from someone beforehand roughly how much you should charge for a particular run. The Parque Central to Habana Libre run, for example, should not cost more than $2, La Rampa to Miramar $3-4 if you drive a hard bargain. The fare to the airport is usually $10. If you wish to visit a series of sights, negotiate a fee for the whole trip.

The main concentrations of private cabs are outside the Habana Libre and in and around the Parque Central. Periodic clampdowns by the authorities mean that drivers sometimes make themselves scarce, but they are generally easily spotted and in fact will often approach you first. Given that this is an illegal trade, some drivers prefer to drop tourists off a short distance from their hotel (and the accompanying posse of policemen and doormen).

Should you find a likeable and trustworthy driver, try to use the same person again; most car-owners can be contacted by telephone.

Peso Taxis: as described in the general introduction, most attempts to hail peso cabs meet with failure. Few taxi drivers will pick up tourists and even if you are with Cuban friends, you can spend ages waiting for a cab. If you are travelling alone, your best bet will be to find somebody to hail a peso taxi for you, but it is easier to deal direct with an unofficial private taxi.

Colectivos serves a few main routes in the city, in particular the journey between Miramar and Old Havana. These vehicles bear no distinguishing marks, other than the fact they are mostly large American saloons or hilarious stretch Ladas. The fare is 1 or 2 pesos.

Boat. Havana's best ferry service, between Habana Vieja and Casablanca, came to an abrupt halt after the launch was hijacked during the troubles in the summer of 1994. Passengers en route to Casablanca must now head a little further south to Muelle Luz,· at the foot of Calle Santa Clara near the main harbour area, where armed guards keep a close eye on the proceedings. This is also the departure point for the ferry to Regla, also across the bay from Old Havana (see page 185).

These ferries are highly recommended as a harbour trip, particularly at dusk. The fare is 20 centavos. Departures run roughly every 30 minutes, 24 hours a day. Hiccups in the service occur only when the boat decides to break down or when there is a storm. Don't fall overboard; the harbour is one of the most polluted in the world.

Bicycle. Havana would grind to a halt if it weren't for the bicycles. You would do well to join them, particularly if you plan to explore beyond the boundaries of the immediate downtown area. The government has been swift in creating cycle paths (*ciclovías*), which now exist along the Malecón, Línea in Vedado and Avenida Rancho Boyeros towards the airport. If you wish to cycle east along the coast, a fleet of special buses (marked 'Ciclobus') take cyclists through the tunnel: the pick-up point is at the bottom of the Prado. Queues can be long at peak times, though you should never have to wait more than 20-30 minutes. The service runs 24 hours.

Bikes can be hired from Panaciclos, based near the main bus station at Avenida Rancho Boyeros and Santa Ana (tel 81-0153, 81-4142). This is affiliated to Panataxi, and if you order a bike over the phone, a cab will deliver it to your hotel. The rental charge is steep at $1 per hour or $14 per day, though you can negotiate a better deal if you take it for several days.

The main perils attached to cycling in Havana are some dreadful road surfaces and the cyclists' craze for having speed competitions along the streets of Habana Vieja. At night, bicycle thieves are another hazard. Most are content to swipe unlocked bikes, but there are more unpleasant characters whose favourite tactic is to ambush cyclists in dark streets. If you are forced to cycle at night, stick to the busier streets or try to cycle as near the middle of the road as is safely possible.

The accommodation situation in Havana has greatly improved since the start of the decade. Few new hotels have been built, but several decrepit places have been renovated. Still, there is a dearth of characterful places, and the best hotels fill quickly in high season. If you have your heart set on a particular hotel, make a reservation before you arrive.

OLD HAVANA

This is by far the most pleasant area in which to stay, placing you within easy reach of the capital's best sights and a reasonable choice of restaurants. You will also find Havana's best-value hotels here. Several old mansions in the heart of the old city are currently undergoing refurbishment and should be open for business in the next year or so. They include the old Hotel Santa Isabel, in a prime position overlooking Plaza de Armas.

Since this is the city's main tourist centre, the degree of attention from hustlers and beggars is concomitantly higher than elsewhere, and you should be careful where you wander at night (see *Crime and Safety*). However, this should not put you off opting to stay in Old Havana. The following list begins at the cheap end of the range and works upwards.

Caribbean: Prado 164, on the corner of Colón (tel 338233, 338210). This hotel is understandably popular with low-budget travellers. It is well situated on the Prado and has some of the cheapest rooms in town, charging about $25 for a single, $30-35 for a double. More modern than most other buildings on the Prado, the Caribbean has seen many better days and is not for those who insist upon every creature comfort. Most rooms are pokey and windowless, and there have been reports of thefts from rooms; it is worth paying to put your valuables in the safe. All rooms have radio, colour TV, cold water shower and toilet, but only 50% of these facilities are likely to work. Ask for a room on the fourth or fifth floor, where at least you can glimpse daylight and enjoy a degree of ventilation.

Staff are not particularly friendly, but the hotel lobby is a sociable area and a good place to meet both travellers and Cubans, who come to eat in the café or drink at the small bar. The café on the ground floor (open 7.30am-10.30pm) serves a tolerable breakfast and other simple meals, e.g. a plate of spaghetti bolognese for under $3.

You can receive international (but not make) telephone calls in your room, but the switchboard is not always adept at transferring calls from reception.

Lido: Consulado between Trocadero and Animas (tel 62-2046; fax 62-7000), a block west of the Prado. Until recently, the two-star Lido undercut the one-star Caribbean by a couple of dollars, but its prices are likely to be hiked up once the current refurbishment has been completed. Still, cost-conscious travellers should check it out, if only because the downstairs café serves as cheap a breakfast as you'll get in Havana: coffee and toast for $1.50. The lobby is popular among Cubans living in the neighbourhood, who gather to watch television here in the evenings, but otherwise the Lido doesn't see much action. Be careful when returning to the hotel at night; although close to the Prado, the Lido is located in an ill-lit back street on the edge of barrio Colón, one of central Havana's more notorious areas: see *Crime and Safety*.

Ambos Mundos: Calle Obispo 153, on the corner of Mercaderes (tel 61-4887, fax 62-2547). Famous for its connections with Ernest Hemingway (see *Exploring*), this hotel has been under renovation for so long that it has become a standing joke. As of early 1996, promises that it would be open for business by the time this edition is published proved impossible to fulfil. The quality of the rooms and restaurant remains an unknown quantity, but you can be guaranteed a great view from the roof terrace.

Hostal Valencia: Oficios 53, on the corner of Obrapía, just south of Plaza de Armas (tel 62-3801). Housed in a restored colonial mansion, the three-star Hostal Valencia is the kind of place that Havana needs more of. A measure of its popularity is that it is hard to get in without a reservation, though a few days' notice is normally enough. There are just eleven rooms, gathered around a delightful courtyard. All are different and most have original features, such as traces of a mural or an alfarje-style ceiling. The best rooms, including Jijona or Valencia (the rooms have names not numbers), overlook Calles Oficios or Obrapía. Most rooms are double and cost $40-50, though there is one single room (more like a broom cupboard) for $27 and a larger, more expensive suite for $57.

The supply of hot water seems to be more reliable than in some of Havana's four-star hotels, and the staff are infinitely more pleasant. The only disadvantage, for some people, might be the lack of telephones in the rooms; and you cannot make international calls from reception either. The breakfast menu is simple, but you can usually order toast and jam, and even bacon and eggs. The improved Paella restaurant does a reasonable lunch or supper, but is almost invariably empty. A better bet is the Bar Nostalgia upstairs, where you can hear live music and buy unheard-of delights such as Oraanjeboom lager.

Inglaterra: Prado 416, in the Parque Central (tel 33-8593, 62-7071; fax 62-6715). Built in the late 19th century, the four-star Inglaterra has been refurbished back to a state of colonial elegance and is one of Havana's most sought-after hotels. It is popular with independent travellers, journalists and business people alike and, given its name, inevitably draws a sizeable contingent of British tourists.

The rates for a double room are around $80 in high season ($70 in low), and for a single $60 ($51). The rooms are plush and comfortable, though some are a little pokey, and you will have to toss up between having a quiet and windowless room in the centre of the building or an airier but noisier one overlooking the street. The best compromise is to ask for a room on the south side, which overlooks San Rafael, a pedestrian street, and gives a close-up view of the splendid Gran Teatro next door. Even the rooms on this side, however, are unprotected from the sound of the music which emanates from the hotel's roof terrace at night. The entertainment usually winds up at about 11pm, but at weekends can go on until 2am. Joining in the fun is often the best option. The rooftop bar provides a smashing view of the floodlit Gran Teatro and Capitolio.

It is hard not to recommend this place because of its position overlooking the Parque Central, and because it's the cheapest of the more comfortable hotels. However, the staff are not particularly helpful, the hot water is unreliable for an establishment of such pretension, and the breakfast, a choice of $4, $5.50 or $8 menus each incorporating large quantities of dry cakes and cold toast, is to be avoided — you would be well advised to head across the road to the Plaza or the Sevilla. In 1994, it was announced that George Galloway, Labour MP, would be using the £100,000 he won in a libel case against the *Daily Mirror* newspaper to renovate the kitchen and restaurant, but there is no sign of this project getting off the ground soon. The best food in the Inglaterra is available in the small Louvre restaurant on the ground floor, which serves poor pizzas but passable pasta, including a decent spaghetti bolognese for $4.

If the Habana Libre is the main focus of prostitution in Vedado, the Inglaterra seems to have taken on that role in the old city. Before the revolution, the hotel's downstairs bar was a regular meeting-place for writers and artists, among them Federico García Lorca. La Sevillana bar is still a popular meeting-place, though most of those who gather here seem to have less intellectual pursuits in mind. In the evenings, any lone male intent on having a quiet drink is likely to be pestered to the point either of submission or desperation.

Plaza: Ignacio Agramonte 267, on the northeast corner of the Parque Central (tel 33-8583 to 90; fax 33-8592). This stylish hotel is a notch up from the Inglaterra — with double rooms for $90, singles for $70 (fixed rates) — and certainly gives better value for money. The rooms are pleasant and come with everything from satellite television to a hair-dryer and safe deposit box.

The downstairs bar, with its fountain and abundant greenery, is cool and a good place to relax between forays outside. It is always buzzing, and stays open 24 hours. The Los Portales restaurant on the ground floor serves à la carte meals, but most people make for the terrace on the fifth floor, which is where buffet meals are served. The breakfast is one of the better ones in Havana — with someone preparing fried and scrambled eggs on demand — and the views are fabulous.

The hotel has its own free car and bicycle park across the road.

Santa Isabel: Plaza de Armas. A luxurious and exclusive new 28-room hotel, scheduled to open in summer 1996.

Sevilla: Calle Trocadero between Zulueta and the Prado (tel 33-8560 to 69, fax 33-8582). Famous for its appearance in Graham Greene's *Our Man in Havana*, the Sevilla re-opened for its first season in 1993 having been left to crumble for decades. No expense was spared in the hotel's renovation, but no amount of money could disguise what — from the outside — is a rather ugly building. Its high-rise wing, painted a dull brown and topped by a pretentious and little-used restaurant, rises above the roofs of the Prado with unwarranted pride.

Even so, the Sevilla has provided much-needed extra beds in the old city and has earned itself a place on the map as a good alternative to the Plaza and Inglaterra. It is the most expensive of the three — $105 for a double in high season ($85 in low), $75 (and $65) for a single — but rooms are spacious and each has a bath, a rarity in Cuban hotels. Perhaps the Sevilla's greatest asset, however, is its swimming pool, which non-residents can also use for $3 (with towels provided). The huge lobby has numerous sofas, chairs and even writing desks, ideal for scribbling postcards while waiting for friends, and the terrace bar is pleasant, with live bands most evenings. The buffet restaurant, also on the ground floor, is on a par with that of the Plaza. Breakfast costs $5, other meals $15.

CENTRAL HAVANA

This area has little in the way of accommodation, but its two best hotels have the advantage of being within walking distance of both Habana Vieja and Vedado.

New York: at Dragones and Aguila (tel 62-7001), next to the Cuban Telephone Company building. One of the few pesos hotels in central Havana, the New York Hotel is not exactly used to travellers enquiring about a room. However, it is in an excellent location, behind the Capitol, and furthermore has the cheapest rooms in town, at $15-21. Rooms come with a fan and cold water (at certain times of day).

Lincoln: an old and comfortable place at Galiano 164, on the corner of Virtudes (tel 62-8061). It has double rooms for $40 ($33 in low season), singles for $35 ($25), including toilet and shower, tepid to cold water, air-conditioning and TV. The old-fashioned Colonial Restaurant has a pleasant, unpretentious atmosphere and there is a rooftop bar with frequent live music.

Deauville: overlooking the Malecón at the northern end of Galiano (tel 62-8051, 62-8081). Known as the 'Doo-*veel*' among Havanans, this hotel was once described by the writer and journalist (and Ernest Hemingway's widow), Martha Gellhorn, as 'a post-war, pre-Revolutionary blight on the Malecón . . . a cement Bauhaus-style tower'. She may have been right, but the three-star Deauville is relaxed and surprisingly friendly for a hotel that deals mainly with package tourists. In addition, the views are great and you can enjoy being lulled to sleep by the sound of the sea. The Deauville hit the headlines in August 1994, when it was damaged during the rioting along the seafront, but it has been fully repaired and seems to have been rejuvenated by the experience.
    Room rates depend upon the view but are roughly $40-50 for a double, $25-35 for a single. These are a touch steep given that the hot water is unreliable and the ground-floor restaurant positively awful, but the Deauville is very lively. The lobby bar and open-air café outside are buzzing day and night, and the basement disco is the only one to speak of in central Havana.

VEDADO

The hotels in this area are for the most part ugly high-rise blocks built during the tourist boom of the 1950s. Undoubtedly very stylish at the time, many are now soulless places. There are advantages to staying in Vedado, however. In particular, the spaciousness can come as a relief after the more claustrophobic streets of Old Havana.
    Most hotels in Vedado are four or five-star. The cheaper, three-star hotels hold little appeal, the best of a poor selection being the *St John's* (Calle O 216, between 25 and Humboldt; tel 32-9531), which charges $35-45 for a double, $25-30 for a single. The other options are the *Vedado* (Calle O 244; tel 32-6501), next door to the St John's, and the *Colina* (Calle L between 27 and Jovellar; tel 32-3535 to 38). The latter at least boasts a good location, opposite the university, but the rooms are grimey and the restaurant poor.
    If for some reason you need to be within spitting distance of the long-distance bus station or the Plaza de la Revolución, try the *Hotel Bruzón* (Calle Bruzón 217 between Pozos Dulces and Boyeros; tel 70-3531), which has rooms for $20 (double) and $15 (single). There is a salsa disco (with occasional live music) in the basement.

Habana Libre: Calle L between Calles 23 and 25 (tel 30-5011, fax 33-3145). The former Hilton, this is the best known landmark in the capital — not only because its 23 floors rise high above the surrounding buildings but because the rebel leaders made it their headquarters after their triumph in 1959.

Refurbishment, by a Spanish hotel group called Guitart, has done little to resurrect this flagship five-star hotel. It is a deeply unattractive and unsavoury place, easily outdone by newly renovated hotels nearby such as the Nacional. Rates are high at $130 for a double ($100 in low season) and $80 ($65) for a single. The superb views from the top floors provide the one possible justification for paying these prices. Don't ask to be placed in room 1624, which is rumoured to contain radios and other bugging equipment manned by the military.

The Barracón restaurant on the ground floor is rather gloomy but serves surprisingly decent food; the meat-oriented menu includes traditional Cuban dishes, such as marinated roast pork with rice and beans and sweet potatoes for $8. The nameless cafeteria next door is grim but cheap. If you just want a sandwich, head for the lobby bar, though here you'll have to endure the rather seedy spectacle of male tourists in search of sexual gratification — particularly in the evening, when the lobby fills with prostitutes.

Even if you are staying elsewhere, you'll probably find yourself at the Habana Libre at least once. Several airlines have their offices here (including Viasa), you can extend your visa at the tourism desk by the door, withdraw cash on a credit card in the BFI bank, and use the swimming pool; there is also an executive floor for business visitors. Staff at the Cubatur desk by the entrance are friendly and generally helpful.

Nacional: Calles 21 and O (tel 7-8980-89, 33-3564; fax 33-5054). This five-star hotel is the jewel in Vedado, unmissable with its twin towers and commanding position above the Malecón. Built in the 1920s, the Nacional is one of Havana's oldest hotels (it has been patronised by the likes of Winston Churchill and Marlon Brando), but recent refurbishment has made it sparkle, emphasising its extravagant grandeur. With rooms going for $125-150 (single) and $135-190 (double), the Nacional is too expensive for most travellers, but anyone can enjoy the oceanside gardens, which provide a relaxing retreat from the hassles of life on the streets; you can sit in the shade undisturbed for hours. Read the closing stages of Graham Greene's *Our Man in Havana* while sipping one of the house cocktails. The daiquiris are steep at $3.50 apiece but are among the best in Cuba. Breakfast is no bargain either at $13, but is so good that it's worth splashing out if you're hungry enough to make the most of it; lunch and supper are equally pricey at $25. These prices fall to $10 and $20 respectively if you are a guest. The Restaurante Internacional on the ground floor is predictably pretentious but has an excellent reputation. The menu has a strong bias towards fish and seafood. There are several bars and cafeterias, two (small) swimming pools, an executive floor, and plans for a mini-golf course. The rooftop terrace is breezy but the high parapet means that there's not much of a view.

One of the Nacional's lesser-known claims to fame is its pivotal role in aviation; the International Air Transport Association was founded here on 18 April 1945.

Capri: Calle 21 and M (tel 33-3747, 32-0511; fax 33-3750), up the road from the Nacional. The lobby has some wild 1950s décor and a surprisingly good restaurant, but the rooms vary greatly in quality and are mostly scruffy and rather depressing — ask to see a range if you aren't satisfied. Doubles cost about $65, singles $48, though prices range according to the floor and view. The Capri is in bad need of a refit.

Victoria: Calle 19 and M (tel 33-3510, 32-6531; fax 33-3109). Cushioned from the hubbub of Havana, but still in a prime location, the four-star Victoria is a good alternative to the Nacional or the Presidente if you want a smart place in Vedado. Rooms in this Thirties construction are on the small side but tastefully decorated; doubles cost $100 all year round, singles $80. The Victoria's small size means that the staff are friendlier than in most other hotels in the area, and the food is not bad at all. There is also a swimming pool, albeit tiny. Past residents include Marlon Brando, Errol Flynn and the Nobel Prize-winning Spanish poet Juan Ramón Jiménez.

Presidente: Avenida de los Presidentes at Calzada (tel 32-7521 to 27), opposite the Foreign Ministry. This 10-storey maroon and pink creation is set away from most of the action, but the sumptuous furnishings and overall sense of style makes up for this slight inconvenience. The Presidente charges $75-85 for a double room, $44-60 for a single, depending on the floor.

Morro: Calle D on the corner of Avenida 3 (tel 30-9954, 32-9790, 32-0530). A small hotel tucked away in a quiet part of Vedado, a stone's throw from the Malecón and four blocks west of Avenida de los Presidentes. Prices are reasonable for this part of town, $30 single and $40 double.

Meliá Cohiba: Paseo y Malecón (tel 33-3636, fax 33-4555). Finally opened in 1995, after years of construction, the Meliá Cohiba is the largest hotel to have been built in the capital since the 1950s. It has 462 rooms, 25 suites and two executive floors. Havana has never seen anything like it. The Cohiba boasts the only escalators in the city, touch-screen computers for the use of guests and smart cards that not only unlock your door but also activate the electricity supply in your room. For a taste of such luxuries you must pay $140 single/ $170 double for a room in low season, $30/$40 more in high. A buffet breakfast costs another $12. Guests enjoy free admission to the Aché disco, the most popular night club in town (see *Entertainment*).

Riviera: Paseo y Malecón (tel 30-5051, fax 33-1345). Currently undergoing a major refit, the 50s' Riviera will never look anything but tatty, out-dated and even rather puny alongside the brand new Cohiba. The ugly exterior, however, reveals a pleasant and spacious lobby, and at $90 for a double ($60 single), the rooms are not badly priced compared with other five-star hotels in the city. The 24-hour cafeteria on the ground floor serves more than decent hamburgers, pizzas and sandwiches. Buffet meals are on the dear side, though, with breakfast costing $9.

The two main attractions at the Riviera — for guests and non-residents alike — are the excellent swimming pool and the Palacio de la Salsa, the city's top live music venue: see *Entertainment*. The hotel's location on the Malécon will appeal to some, but in other ways the Riviera is badly situated, being too far west of most places of interest.

MIRAMAR

There is little reason to stay in Miramar unless you can't bear the thought of being in the city centre and have plenty of money to pay for taxis. Buses 32 and 132 link Vedado and Miramar, but are always overflowing. All the following hotels are four-star establishments, popular among business visitors and for those tempted by the idea of being by the beach — in reality a narrow, unappealing stretch of sand.

Nearest the centre and probably the best of the Miramar hotels is the *Copacabana* (Avenida 1a e/ 44 y 46; tel 29-0601, fax 33-2846), which charges $75-81 for a single room, $100-108 for a double, the higher rates being for rooms with a balcony. The hotel has a lively lobby area with a posh bar and excellent restaurant, and there is a clean swimming pool with another restaurant and a café that serves excellent coffee and good pizzas for $3-4. Down some steps, a 150-m swimming pool has been created out of the sea and is a joy for the serious swimmer. Other facilities include a popular disco, a weights room, 'beauty parlour' (full massage available for $10) and tennis courts, and you can also arrange scuba diving trips.

A bit further on is the *Chateau Miramar* (Avenida 1a, e/ 60 y 70; tel 33-2225/ 1951, fax 33-0224), a comfortable Cubanacán hotel, though the food could be better. Next along the seafront, close to the extraordinary Russian Embassy building, is the *Complejo Tritón-Neptuno* (Calle 3 at the corner of 70; tel 22-5531, fax 33-2343), twin high-rise buildings with little to recommend them. Better is the *Comodoro*, nearby at Calle 84 and 1ra (tel 22-5551 to 54, fax 33-2028), which is a teaching hotel. If you want sumptuous surroundings and a place to lounge around a pool, this is the hotel for you.

PRIVATE ACCOMMODATION

An increasing number of independent travellers choose to rent a room or a flat from a local family, particularly those planning to stay in Havana for a week or more. The average daily rate is $10-15, though you should be able to negotiate a lower price if you are staying for at least a week. A deposit is not usually required. People may well approach you in Old Havana, particularly along the Prado or outside the Caribbean Hotel, otherwise simply ask around. Some people may offer you a beach house in Guanabo, a popular weekend retreat in Playas del Este (see page 201).

Eating and Drinking

The eating and drinking scene in Havana has been revolutionised during the last few years. The prospective opening of a branch of Maxim's in 1997 is merely the latest of a feast of new restaurants and bars that have started up recently. Many of these new places offer similar fare but they have still made life a good deal easier for tourists. Make the most of the opportunity to eat outside your hotel; once out in the provinces, the options are much more limited.

The majority of restaurants listed here are in Old Havana and Vedado, though if you want to push the boat out there are some higher class places — catering mainly for diplomats and business people — a little further afield. Reservations are not generally necessary, whichever restaurant you choose.

OLD HAVANA

Most restaurants in the heart of Old Havana, around Plaza de Armas, shut by 10pm, by which time the streets are almost deserted. If you want to take a taxi home, get the restaurant to call for one, although you may find a couple of cabs hanging around by the harbour just west of Plaza de la Catedral, or outside the ever-popular Bodeguita del Medio. Restaurants nearer the Parque Central tend to keep going until later. The following selection is listed in alphabetical order.

La Bodeguita del Medio: Calle Empedrado 207 (tel 61-8442, 62-4498), a stone's throw from Plaza de la Catedral. La Bodeguita del Medio or the 'BDM', as it is better known, began life in 1942. It has thrived since the Revolution, not least because until recently it was one of the few places in the country to combine reasonable food and pleasant surroundings. The décor is indeed unique in Havana (though Cuban restaurants elsewhere on the island and abroad have attempted to recreate it), its arresting feature being the graffiti which smothers the walls and even the tables. Ernest Hemingway, who helped make the place famous, made his own contribution — 'My mojito in La Bodeguita, my daiquirí in El Floridita, ' — visible but out of reach behind the bar. Other autographs belong to the murdered Chilean leader, Salvador Allende, Errol Flynn and even Fidel Castro himself. Guests are encouraged to leave their own mark.

La Bodeguita milks its connections with past celebrities to the full, and the artists and writers of yesteryear have long since been replaced by camera-wielding tourists. During the day the already narrow entrance is blocked by a stall selling souvenirs, and you have little hope of reaching the bar let alone ordering a drink. However, you can usually find a seat in the main restaurant, where Cuban cuisine is the speciality. Be warned that meals are extremely poor value when compared with what you can buy elsewhere. A main dish costs at least $10, but helpings are small and accompaniments such as rice, plantains and salad are extra. If you are hungry after a hard day's sightseeing, go somewhere else, though the upstairs terrace is very pleasant for an evening drink. After 6pm there is often a band, which plays music at a reasonable volume and keeps away the *Guantanamera*-singing group that does the rounds downstairs.

Casa del Científico: on the Prado at the corner of Trocadero (tel 63-8103). Built in 1919 as the official residence of Miguel Gómez, one of Cuba's first presidents, this elegant mansion is now in the hands of the Academy of Sciences. It is used as a hotel for visiting scientists, but its first-floor restaurant is open to the general public. The intimate, wood-panelled dining room is charming and the staff extremely friendly and uncommonly polite. The small menu features mainly traditional Cuban food, with most main dishes costing around $4. Come here for lunch or an early supper. At weekends there is a cabaret on the roof terrace, the Mirador del Prado. Note that this place does not look remotely like a restaurant from the outside.

Castillo de Farnés: Calle Monserrate 361, corner of Obrapía (tel 63-1260). Popular among the rebels in the 60s (there is a photograph of Fidel, Raúl and the others by the entrance to prove it) and restored in 1994, this is one of the best new arrivals on the restaurant scene in Havana. At the front is a pleasant Mediterranean-style bar (open 24 hours) for coffee and other on-the-hoof drinks, with a small and friendly restaurant behind. This specialises in Spanish cuisine and has one of the most interesting menus in Old Havana. This may be your one chance to try pigs' trotters, and the bean dishes — including soups (*fabada* or *potage*) and casseroles — make a cheap and filling lunch for $2-3.

Castillo de la Fuerza Real: the roof of the 16th-century fortress overlooking Plaza de Armas (see *Exploring*) is given over to a café, pizzeria and grill house. The food is good without being extraordinary. Not many people seem to make it up here, so there is always room to sit (indoors or out), and you can enjoy relative peace and quiet. This is a reasonable alternative to the busy El Patio Colonial on the other side of the square. It closes at 5pm.

El Floridita: Calle Monserrate 557, at the western end of Calle Obispo (tel 63-1070, 63-1060). Like the Bodeguita, El Floridita plays on its connection with Hemingway, a bust of whom marks the writer's favourite corner of the bar. He described the place in his novel *Islands in the Stream*, and introduced it to the rich and famous who visited Havana in the 50s, including Gary Cooper and Tennessee Williams.

The recent refurbishment has reduced the bar and restaurant to a caricature of their former crumbling grace, but the outré style complements the clientele, which these days consists of not only tourists and business visitors but also Havana's new rich, who come to flaunt their dollars at central Havana's most expensive restaurant. Seafood (and lobster in particular) is the Floridita's speciality, but if you want to savour the atmosphere, you can do so equally well from the bar — though at $5 a go, the daiquiris cost double what you'll pay in most places. If you want to splash out, at least try Hemingway's own recipe (without sugar), known as a *Papa Special*. Finally, take warm clothes as the air-conditioning is set at somewhere near freezing point.

D'Giovanni: just off Plaza de la Catedral at Tacón 4 (tel 61-4445), in a beautifully restored 18th-century mansion. Like other restaurants in Habana Vieja, D'Giovanni tends to be invaded by tour groups at lunchtime, but there are sufficient rooms for you to be able to escape the crowds. By contrast, it is almost too quiet in the evening; to be sure of company you should go after 8 o'clock — but before 10pm, when things start winding down. Service is slow but the pizzas ($5-8) and pasta are tasty and there is an extensive wine menu. If you eat downstairs in the courtyard, the menu is more limited but cheaper, and you are more likely to have at least some Cubans for company.

Hanoi: Bernaza and Teniente Rey, at the corner of Plaza del Cristo (tel 63-1681). As in most Habaguanex restaurants, the emphasis here is on providing cheap food in pleasant colonial surroundings. The Hanoi is an unassuming and rather quaint place and serves exceedingly cheap meals, particularly if you choose one of the *combinaciones*, which consists of a small mound of rice and beans, a piece of meat and a vegetable and costs just $2. These 'combinations' would not satisfy a big appetite, in which case you should choose from the à la carte menu.

Al Medina: in the Casa de los Arabes at Oficios 12 (tel 63-0862). The menu — which offers roast chicken, pilaf and beef stew among other things — is not particularly Middle Eastern, but prices are low ($3-4) and the setting peaceful.

El Patio: Plaza de la Catedral (tel 61-8511). Housed in a glorious 18th-century mansion on Cathedral Square, El Patio probably wins the prize for most beautifully situated restaurant in Havana. The food does not live up to the location, but arguably it's worth eating here just for the luxury of sitting on an upstairs balcony overlooking the square. The ground floor terrace is ideally situated for watching the world go by, but the world will also be watching you — it is not the place to escape from life on the streets. The inner courtyard, with one of the few fountains in Old Havana and masses of foliage, is more relaxing; this is the only area open for meals in the evening, and you can watch the chefs in action beneath the arches. The menu offers a mix of Cuban and international dishes. If you want a full three courses, go for one of the set menus costing $16 (plus 10% service). The wine list is good but expensive, with a bottle of 1948 Palacio de Aganza costing $159.

El Patio Colonial: in the Plaza de Armas (and not to be confused with El Patio in Cathedral Square), this bar-cum-restaurant is one of the best places in Habana Vieja for lunch. It is open-air but shaded by trees and always buzzing. Background noise is provided either by a band, piped music, or by the cockerels that inhabit a collection of cages in one corner (the restaurant occupies an old cock-fighting ring). El Patio serves good and reasonably priced food, including the ubiquitous sandwich, pizzas and roast chicken for $5. It is open theoretically until midnight, but after 10pm the action shifts indoors to the adjacent video bar-cum-disco.

La Piña de Plata: next to El Floridita at the top of Calle Obispo. This small restaurant seems to be popular with tourist agencies, who can half fill it with a minibus-load of people at lunchtime, but La Piña del Plata is a cool and air-conditioned haven from the sultry streets. The menu includes hamburgers and surprisingly good salads. The main drawback is the slow and grudging service.

La Torre de Marfil: Mercaderes 115 between Obispo y Obrapía (tel 62-3466). Another Habaguanex restaurant, again offering good value for money. The cooks manage to combine the limited ingredients available to them to make surprisingly convincing Chinese meals. You can even wash it all down with Chinese beer. Chow mein or chop suey costs $4-5, other main dishes $6-10. As at the Hanoi, you can choose from several *combinaciones*, in the form of a main dish with accompaniments rather than a whole set meal. The oriental décor is decidedly out of place in the colonial setting, but it at least makes a change.

La Zaragozana: Monserrate 352, between Obispo and Obrapiá (tel 63-1062, 61-8350). The menu matches the rustic décor of tiles and terracotta, with Spanish bean soups and casseroles similar to those served at the Castillo de Farnés nearby. There's much else besides, from cheap egg dishes and spaghetti to beef and seafood dishes — though if it's good steak and seafood you're after, you'll do better elsewhere.

Bars and Cafés. These have been listed separately from restaurants since while bars and cafés often serve cheap food, such as fried chicken, pizza and sandwiches, there is little variety between them. They have been selected more as a pleasant place for a drink and a snack rather than for a proper meal. Several are the fruit of the new vogue for 24-hour bars, which at night stand out like beacons in the ill-lit streets of Habana Vieja. Many of these are run by Habaguanex, a new agency managed by the office of the City Historian, which is involved in the restoration of Old Havana.

One bar not included in the list below is Sloppy Joe's, just down from the Plaza Hotel. The haunt of Hemingway and other international celebrities prior to the revolution, this famous bar was abandoned years ago and is now awaiting restoration. All it needs is someone to put up the money. Watch this space.

Café de Paris: San Ignacio 202, corner of Obispo. This café, set up by Habaguanex in 1994, was the first to introduce several new concepts to the eating and drinking scene in Havana: 24-hour opening, draft beer and good value for money. The prices are still unbelievably low: a glass of beer for $0.80, roast chicken and chips for $2.50. The main drawbacks are the very loud music and the small number of tables.

Café O'Reilly: O'Reilly 203 between San Ignacio and Cuba. As a peso bar, Café O'Reilly had a lot of regulars, with a permanent gaggle of Cubans chatting outside. Located within just a stone's throw from Cathedral Square, however, it was only a matter of time before it was refurbished and transformed into a dollar café. It lacks the old atmosphere but is a pleasant enough place for refreshment between museum visits — though $1 for an espresso coffee is uncalled for. A spiral staircase, which is Café O'Reilly's most charming feature, leads to another bar where alcohol is served.

Al Cappuccino: corner of Obispo and Oficios. Pseudo-Italian café on the Plaza de Armas, with passable coffee and mediocre snacks.

Lluvia de Oro: one of the new 24-hour places on Calle Obispo (at the corner of Habana). The worn mahogany bar and high ceilings in this former peso bar are original, unlike the huge video screen and juke box. Avoid the poor pizzas and cold chips in favour of the draft beer.

Monserrate: at the corner of Agramonte and Obrapía, opposite Castillo de Farnés. Cheap snacks (roast chicken for $2) and cheap drinks (beer for $0.70) are the main attractions at this 24-hour bar, though the selection on the jukebox — including Sheena Easton and the Eagles — might appeal to some.

Oasis: Prado 258, between Animas and Trocadero. The Arab Cultural Centre runs both a restaurant and bar at the Oasis. While the restaurant is permanently empty, the bar is very popular — particularly with Cubans, who don't seem to mind the loud music or the resident photographer, who does the rounds of the tables armed with his polaroid. The fact that it is the only bar on the Prado (other than the hotel bars) may have something to do with it. The best thing about the Oasis is its 24-hour bakery. This is the only place in central Havana to sell fresh bread, and you can buy scrumptious hot chicken sandwiches for just $0.80.

La Taberna del Galeón just off the Plaza de Armas, behind El Patio Colonial. Run by Ernesto Rodríguez, an extremely astute and entertaining businessman who speaks excellent English, the Taberna is a combined shop and bar. Downstairs, shelves are filled with vintage rums and liqueurs you'll not find easily in other places (including vile Cuban whisky), as well as the usual Habana Club range. The Taberna is now firmly on the tourist guide's map of the old city, and is invaded by groups of tourists periodically. However, you can escape to the small bar upstairs and try the house speciality — the *puñetazo*, a lethal but wonderful mix of rum, coffee and mint invented by barman Pedro Fernández. With its heavy wooden doors, the Taberna always looks permanently shut, but it is open Monday to Saturday until 5pm.

VEDADO

There are more restaurants per hectare in Vedado than anywhere else in Cuba, yet the choice is disappointing. You may admit defeat and retreat to one of the hotels or to Old Havana. Restaurants in Vedado still seem to be relatively unaccustomed to serving tourists (who prefer to stick to their hotels). This does at least mean that you will have as many Cubans as foreigners for company. Most places are within easy walk of La Rampa.

El Conejito: Calle M at the corner of 17 (tel 32-4671). Rabbit (*conejo*) is the house speciality, but there are other things to choose from, mostly pork and chicken. Main dishes cost under $5, and there are set menus too. The décor is rustic but pleasant.

El Cortijo: corner of Calles O and 25. This basement restaurant is perfect for cheap, unsophisticated food served in quiet and unpretentious surroundings. Most dishes cost just $2-3, the predominant cuisine being Cuban.

Don Agamemnon: Calle 17 no. 60, between N and M (tel 33-4529, 33-4062). Occupying an elegant early 20th-century villa in the shadow of Edificio Focsa, the Don Agamemnon is a welcome addition to the restaurant scene in Vedado. There is an open-air bar and grill at the back, serving pizzas and sandwiches, but the main reason to come to Don Agamemnon is to eat inside. Here, in addition to the usual mix of fish, chicken and seafood dishes, you can eat more unusual traditional dishes such as *boliche mechado* (beef stuffed with chorizo); main dishes cost around $10.

Makara: Calle O, next to St John's Hotel. A popular fast food restaurant. Displays by the entrance of the sandwiches and other simple meals on offer are rather off-putting, but the fresh orange juice is wonderful. A diner-style bar across the road serves similar fare.

Mesón La Chorrera: Malecón 1252, corner of Calle 20 (tel 34504). Occupying the 17th-century fort at the far end of the seafront, this is a real hub of activity in the evenings. Roast chicken is the thing they do best (you can eat half a chicken for $3.50), though most people just come for the bar and the cabaret, which kicks off at about 9 o'clock and is cheap by Havanan standards at just $2.

El Rápido: Línea y M. Given that it was originally billed as a 24-hour drive-in hamburger bar with rollerskating waitresses, El Rápido is now rather a disappointment. The rollerskates were abandoned soon after the restaurant opened because the Public Health Ministry decided they were bad for the staff's backs. What is left is an old parking lot, where a few people sit in their cars but most sit on uncomfortable plastic seats beneath the trees. Curiosity is more likely to bring you here than hunger, though a hot dog, chips and a drink for $1.50 is not a bad deal.

La Torre: Calle 17 no. 55, between M and N (tel 32-4630). The main appeal of La Torre is its location on the top floor of the boomerang-shaped Edificio Focsa (the entrance is opposite Don Agamemnon), though you must admire the view through dirty windows. This is a training school for waiters, so the service is usually infinitely more entertaining than in your average restaurant, and the staff are very friendly. This is a good place to escape the heat and bustle of the streets of Vedado, and the menu reveals several surprises, such as beef in beer sauce.

Bars and Cafés. The Malecón ought to be ideal territory for bars and cafés, but there are only a few, none of which are very appealing. In the evening, there aren't many alternatives to the hotel bars. You have to pay $3 admission to the rooftop Turquino bar of the Habana Libre, but this does buy you a complimentary mojito.

The Coppelia ice-cream park, set out among trees near the Habana Libre, is officially a venue in which to enjoy the sweet fruits of socialism, in reality a 1960s monstrosity with unbelievable queues and confusion. But this is where Havanans go for an afternoon out — one of the comparatively few places where Cubans socialise together. If you are an average Cuban with pesos, you can spend literally hours queuing for an ice cream. If you have dollars you can progress immediately upstairs, though up here, away from the hubbub below, you will miss out on the Coppelia experience. People queue because the ice cream served at Coppelia is far superior to the sweet and watery sorbet sold at the more common Tropical shops.

FURTHER AFIELD

La Cecilia: Avenida 5 no. 11010, between Calles 110 and 112, Playa (tel 33-1562, 22-6700). This restaurant, run by Cubanacán, serves some of the best food in Havana. Ignore the international dishes and go for traditional fare such as roast pork with all the trimmings. The prices are more than reasonable, particularly if you compare them with those charged by somewhere like the Bodeguita — though you will probably have to add the cost of a cab: La Cecilia is some way west of the centre and you won't get much change from $10 if you take a Turistaxi. Nevertheless, it is well worth the trek. The garden setting is delightful and the service excellent.

La Divina Pastora: located beneath the Cabaña fortress (tel 62-3886). Given its prices and location, the Divina Pastora is usually half empty, but it offers superb views across the bay, and the food is better than average. Fish and seafood are the speciality, including unheard of delights such as *ceviche*. Main fish courses cost $10-15, seafood more than $20. A good excuse to come here is to treat yourself before watching the firing of the cannon at nine o'clock: see *Exploring*.

Las Ruinas: Calle 100 esq. Cortina Presa, Parque Lenin (tel 44-3336). Las

Ruinas boasts an extraordinary setting inside a 1960s building that incorporates the crumbling, lichen-covered walls of an old plantation house. Alongside antique mirrors and mahogany cabinets, pride of place is given to a stained glass screen done by René Portocarrero, one of Cuba's best loved artists. Las Ruinas is one of Havana's most exclusive restaurants, complete with string quartet, and is popular among expats. The huge menu, however, caters to all budgets and tastes. If you aren't up to a full blown dinner, you can stop off for a spaghetti or pizza lunch for $5.

Tocororo: Calle 18 no. 302, corner of Avenida 3ra, Miramar (tel 33-2209, 33-4530). Another excellent Cubanacán restaurant, the Tocororo is the best place to come if you want to push the boat out. A lot of trouble has been taken to decorate this old Miramar villa, the most dominant feature being the abundance of Art Nouveau lampshades. The menu mixes international and Cuban dishes and there is a good choice of European and South American wines. Be sure to book in advance for dinner.

PRIVATE RESTAURANTS

The full impact of the legalisation of private restaurants (see page 103) has still to be seen, but in Havana it has already resulted in open advertising and even the writing out of menus in some cases. The greatest concentration of *paladares* has always been in the Colón district, west of the Prado. This area is best explored in the company of other Cubans, but you are sure to come across private restaurants in other districts, including Old Havana.

MARKETS AND SHOPS

There are two food markets in Central Havana. The liveliest and most entertaining is the one in Chinatown (Barrio Chino), off Zanja in Centro Habana, which has the best choice in terms of refrescos, snacks and other prepared foods. At the market on Egido, between Apodaca and Corrales in Old Havana, the emphasis is more on fresh produce and meat.

In addition to these formal markets, you find people selling snacks, such as ham-filled rolls or home-made pizzas, in the street. These casual traders tend to gather in certain streets, such as Calle Obispo and at the eastern end of Calle Neptuno, but wherever you see someone eating what looks like a home-made snack, it's worth asking them where they got it.

If you are bored by the small range of tinned and packet food available in the hard currency shops, you'll have to head out to the *Diplomercado* on Avenida 3ra, just beyond the huge T-shaped Russian Embassy in Miramar. Here you can buy fresh cheese, meat, vegetables as well as imported delicacies, but this is where expats come to shop for their dinner parties so prices are higher than average. Saturday at the Diplomercado is like a Saturday at any supermarket in the West, i.e. busy. Checkout 1 is for six items or less, while Checkouts 2 and 3 are reserved for diplomatic staff. Next to the main shops is a smaller one selling sweets, cigarettes, razors and fancy goods. There is also an electrical shop around the corner.

You'll probably decide that your day is best occupied just walking around, Old Havana being the best area in which to roam. There are plenty of museums and other sights, but don't set yourself a vigorous schedule or rigid itinerary, since it's hard not to be waylaid by people you meet or simply by life on the street.

HABANA VIEJA (Old Havana)

The streets of Habana Vieja were laid out in the 16th and 17th centuries and numerous buildings of that era have survived. Although many were expanded or altered subsequently, they retain features typical of the mudéjar architectural style of that early colonial period (see page 108). You will also see Cuba's finest examples of Baroque architecture from the late 18th and early 19th centuries, as well as several remarkable buildings erected after independence.

Under the auspices of UNESCO, Old Havana is being painstakingly restored. The years of neglect have taken a heavy toll and every year over a dozen or so buildings collapse. Viewed from one of the city's high-rise hotels, Habana Vieja seems part of a post-war scene. The parts to have received most attention from restorers include the Cathedral Square and Plaza de Armas, though work is gradually extending southwards. But these are islands of elegance in a sea of crumbling masonry, where families live in overcrowded and tumbledown apartment blocks, with decaying balconies and electric wires that extend like matted hair from ranks of fuse boxes in dark hallways. While conservation is clearly vital, a complete renovation cannot be contemplated; a terrifying number of apartment blocks could face demolition, and rehousing the inhabitants would be impossible.

Most of the newly-renovated colonial mansions have been turned into museums, but the chief interest often lies in the building itself rather than the exhibits. Museums traditionally close on Monday, but the opening hours of several have been changed to give more flexibility to tourists. Admission is usually $1 or $2, so it is useful to have plenty of change.

The following description of the sights of Old Havana begins in Plaza de la Catedral and moves south, then continuing with the area around the Parque Central.

Plaza de la Catedral. At the time of the founding of Havana, the area now occupied by the Plaza de la Catedral was little more than swamp. Nowadays, it is the focus of the tourist scene in Habana Vieja — with all that means in terms of souvenir stalls, tour groups, hustlers, police, musicians and people just being friendly. It's worth coming here as early as possible in the morning or, even better, as the light fades in the evening. Virtually enclosed by buildings, the tranquillity and intimacy of this place at such a time is unbeatable. Plaza de la Catedral boasts the most perfect assembly of colonial buildings in Havana, with a coherence and harmony absent in other squares. All but one of the buildings date from the 18th century, and restoration work means that you now have a good idea what the square was like during that period.

Occupying the north side of the square is the broad façade of the **Cathedral**. Dedicated to the Virgin of the Immaculate Conception, it is better known as the Catedral de San Cristóbal since it once housed the bones believed to be those of Christopher Columbus (these were later returned to Santo Domingo in the Dominican Republic). Construction of the church began in 1748, commissioned by the Jesuits, but was abandoned when the Order was expelled from Cuba in 1767. When it was finally completed a decade later, it became Havana's parish church (replacing the old Parroquial Mayor in the Plaza de Armas) and was then made a cathedral soon afterwards. The building is considered the supreme example of the Cuban Baroque style, most clearly visible in the distinctive curved cornices of the façade. The towers look as though they were tacked on as an afterthought; nothing can explain the sudden abandonment of symmetry, otherwise followed so rigidly. After the flourishes of the façade, the Neoclassical interior — remodelled in the early 1800s — seems positively austere. The cathedral is open Monday to Friday (9-11am and 2-6pm) and Sunday morning, when mass is held.

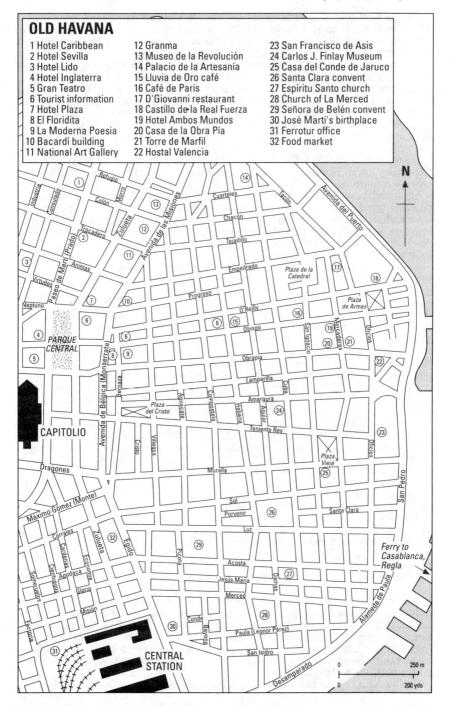

OLD HAVANA

1 Hotel Caribbean
2 Hotel Sevilla
3 Hotel Lido
4 Hotel Inglaterra
5 Gran Teatro
6 Tourist information
7 Hotel Plaza
8 El Floridita
9 La Moderna Poesia
10 Bacardí building
11 National Art Gallery

12 Granma
13 Museo de la Revolución
14 Palacio de la Artesanía
15 Lluvia de Oro café
16 Café de Paris
17 D'Giovanni restaurant
18 Castillo de la Real Fuerza
19 Hotel Ambos Mundos
20 Casa de la Obra Pía
21 Torre de Marfil
22 Hostal Valencia

23 San Francisco de Asis
24 Carlos J. Finlay Museum
25 Casa del Conde de Jaruco
26 Santa Clara convent
27 Espíritu Santo church
28 Church of La Merced
29 Señora de Belén convent
30 José Martí's birthplace
31 Ferrotur office
32 Food market

On the west side of the square is the **Casa del Marqués de Aguas Claras** (1751-75), a more sophisticated building than the other mansions in the square. It has a gorgeous courtyard with a fountain (a rarity in Havana), slaves' quarters still visible on the roof terrace and Art Nouveau glass panels above the windows. It is now occupied by El Patio restaurant. The **Education Museum** (Museo de Alfabetización) opposite, housed in the 18th-century Palacio del Conde Lombillo, has displays about José Martí, the literacy campaign and other achievements in the field of education. It is open 8.30am-5.30pm Tuesday to Saturday. The adjacent **Casa del Marqués de Arcos** (1741), under restoration at the time of going to press but previously an art gallery, was Havana's main post office in the early 1800s; an old letter box, in the form of a Greek mask, is inset into the wall.

If your time is limited, the most important place to visit is the **Museo de Arte Colonial** (closed Tuesday), housed in the Casa del Conde de Casa Bayona. As well as containing some fascinating exhibits, this is the oldest structure in the square and a superb example of a colonial residence. Built around 1720, it changed hands several times (Havana Club rum had offices and a warehouse here earlier this century) and underwent numerous alterations. The house was in a serious mess by the time the building was requisitioned by the state in 1963, but it has been beautifully restored. Another more recent restoration has left it looking perhaps a little too pristine.

There is a charming central courtyard, but the most outstanding feature of this building are the wooden *alfarje* ceilings upstairs, the trademark of the mudéjar craftsmen of the early colonial period (see page 108). While these are original, other features such as the panelled doors and coloured glass windows *(medios puntos)* date from the 1800s. The upstairs rooms have been furnished to give an idea of how a colonial family residence would have looked in the 19th century. The heavy mahogany furniture, made in Cuba, includes two magnificent armchairs, especially designed for the men to enjoy their post-prandial cigar and forty winks; the leather has been worked smooth and hard with use. Most other objects originated in Europe, such as the Baccarat glass candelabras, the family porcelain (made to order and shown off in glass-fronted cabinets) and the numerous spitoons or *escupideras*. These rooms provide an excellent vantage point for views over the square, but you will have to ask nicely for one of the attendants to open the shutters. Other rooms contain collections of miscellaneous objects, including a fine assembly of *mamparas*, the saloon-style swing doors which were very popular in the 19th century.

On the corner of the nearby cul de sac, the **Callejón del Chorro**, an inscription above a small fountain in the wall recalls the inauguration of the first branch of the Zanja Real (the 'Royal Ditch'), which was built to provide water for the city dwellers and the ships in port. It reached the square in 1592, and provided the city's water supply for around 300 years.

The **Wilfredo Lam Centre** (open 10am-5pm Monday to Saturday) occupies the building on the corner of Calle Empedrado by the cathedral. Founded in 1989 in memory of the artist, Wilfredo Lam (see page 110), the centre's main role is as a venue for exhibitions of foreign art. There are plans to set up a permanent exhibition of Lam's own work, but problems with security and lighting means that these have been shelved for the moment. The small shop sells a selection of books and videos on Cuban art.

A stone's thrown further up Empedrado is **La Bodeguita del Medio**, the famous old haunt of Hemingway (see *Eating and Drinking*), and next door the Casa de la Condesa de la Reunión (1809), now the **Alejo Carpentier Foundation**. Carpentier, the country's most famous literary figure of the 20th century, used the house as the setting for his most famous novel, *El Siglo de las Luces*. Display cases exhibit mostly photographs, facsimiles of manuscripts and copies of his works in different languages.

San Ignacio, which runs south from Plaza de la Catedral, is for one block a pedestrian area busy with people hawking souvenirs. Café O'Reilly is just around the corner if you need a drink. Otherwise, you can continue to Calle Obispo.

Calle Obispo. Always the main commercial thoroughfare of Old Havana, Calle Obispo is still the district's busiest street, being everyone's favourite route between the old city and Parque Central. It is in theory pedestrian, but watch out for erratic cyclists weaving their way through the crowds and careering across intersections.

The street has seen better days but there is still plenty to take in. There is no continuity in terms of architectural style, with the hideous 20th-century Ministry of Education, for example, standing alongside some of colonial Havana's oldest houses. Another monumental building erected with no regard for the surroundings is the Neoclassical pile on the corner of Calle Cuba — once the National Bank of New York and now the State Finance Committee. The **Museo de las Finanzas** in the basement (open 8.30am-5.30pm Monday to Friday, 8.30am-noon on Saturday) traces the nation's financial history from colonial times onwards, with displays of old banknotes, etc.

A couple of blocks further east, an arresting sight all in pink, stands the **Ambos Mundos** or 'Both Worlds' hotel. One of the key stops on the Hemingway Trail, this is where the American author reputedly began *For Whom the Bell Tolls* in the 1930s. He stayed here on and off for 10 years before taking up residence at Finca Vigía (see *Further Afield*). At the time of publication it was still an empty shell; if, once renovation is finally completed, 'Room 511' goes on show, the writer's supposed room is likely to be a reconstruction. The bell opposite tolls for no-one at present.

On the other side of Mercaderes from the hotel, one of Havana's most intriguing museums is hidden away up a staircase. The **Sala de la Revolución** (Tuesday to Saturday 10am-5pm, Sunday 9am-1pm, free) is an offshoot of the City Museum. It takes a refreshingly different approach to most revolutionary museums by placing Cuba's rebellion in an international context, with particular reference to French and Colombian revolutions. The national struggle itself is charted with displays of the trajectory of the *Granma* in 1956, Fidel Castro's Soviet revolver, and the front page of *El Mundo* dated 1 January 1959, with the headline 'Batista en Fuga — Cayó la Tiranía!'. A disproportionate amount of space is devoted to Lenin — including a copy of his desk and holograms of his spectacles.

Also on Mercaderes, an old pharmacy has been preserved as a museum, though the still-functioning chemists' shops further along Calle Obispo — with their original shelving and upstairs galleries but depressing lack of medicine — are of far greater interest.

The last block of Obispo before Plaza de Armas has been beautifully restored. Calle Obispo 117-19, with a delightful balcony hung with plants, is one of the oldest houses in Havana, built around 1648.

Plaza de Armas. This is about the best place in Old Havana in which to sit and watch the world go by. Settle down on one of the stone benches that line the square, and let the shade from the trees and the breeze from the harbour gently dispel the hassle and the heat.

Plaza de Armas, the oldest square in Havana, was the centre of government in Cuba throughout the colonial period. Following a major facelift, instigated by the Marqués de la Torre in the late 18th century, it also became Havana's most elegant square, where wealthy Habaneros gathered to stroll and converse.

The **Palacio de los Capitanes Generales** or the Palace of the Captains General (the 'captains' concerned being the old colonial rulers of Cuba) is considered Cuba's greatest architectural achievement of the 18th century. Built during the early flowering of the Cuban Baroque style, it greatly influenced architecture in Havana. This monumental building, which occupies an entire block, is solid and functional but beautifully proportioned. The sinuous cornices above the windows are restrained by comparison with the exuberant lines of the cathedral. While begun in 1776, the palace was remodelled in 1834 as the restraining influence of Neoclassicism was taking hold. Note the wooden paving outside the palace, said to have been laid to muffle the sound of carriage wheels so as not to wake the Captain General from his sleep.

The construction of the palace was ordered by the Marqués de la Torre, who is said not to have liked living in the nearby Castillo de la Real Fuerza. The first man to move in was his successor, Don Luis de las Casas, who took up residence in 1790, even though the building had not been completed. Until 1898, the palace was the seat of national and municipal government as well as a jail. After independence it became first the president's official residence and later the City Hall. It now houses the Office of the City Historian and the Museo de la Ciudad or City Museum (open daily 9.30am-6.30, admission $3, plus $2 for cameras).

One of the most outstanding features of the palace is the courtyard, with its elegant galleries and cascading vegetation. Dwarfed in such surroundings stands the figure of Christopher Columbus, sculpted in 1862. A medley of exhibits dating mainly from colonial times compete with the building for your attention. Downstairs, the highlights are the original bronze sculpture of La Giraldilla (see the *Castillo de la Real Fuerza* below), and an interesting exhibition of religious relics found during excavations in the palace — including objects from the original parish church (demolished by the Marqués de la Torre) — and from other churches in the old city. Upstairs, the lavish state apartments include the Throne Room (which was never used) and the Hall of Mirrors, with its original Venetian mirrors, Baccarat chandeliers and Sèvres vases; this last room witnessed the inauguration of Tomás Estrada Palma, the first president of an independent Cuba. In the other rooms, much weight is given to the independence struggle, with numerous portraits of the main participants and miscellaneous memorabilia including the death mask of Máximo Gómez. Don't miss the 'Sala de la República', where a montage incorporating Coca Cola bottles, busts of presidents and other symbols of the United States represents the rejection of North America during the Revolution.

The nearby **Palacio del Segundo Cabo** provided the model for the Palace of the Captains General, but it is a much more modest building. The most decorative feature are the lovely Baroque arches, embellished by the use of wrought-iron. Designed as the first headquarters of Cuba's postal service, it became the vice-Captain General's Palace in 1854 and after independence was used by the Senate. The Supreme Court moved here in the 1920s but the palace is now the seat of the Cuban Book Institute, with the Bella Habana bookshop on the ground floor.

Also on the north side of the square, but separated by a small moat, is the **Castillo de la Real Fuerza**. Built from 1558-77, this is one of the oldest military constructions in Latin America, and indeed its design was a prototype for other early forts in the New World. While the small fortification, long overshadowed by the Cabaña fortress across the harbour, has lost its prestige, it remains an image of durability, with walls 10ft (3m) thick. Perched atop the rather cute round tower is a bronze figure of a woman, known as **La Giraldilla**. It is said to represent Doña Ines de Bobadilla, the wife of Hernando de Soto, who was Governor of Cuba in the early 16th century and died on the Mississippi River while trying to conquer Florida. The weathervane — the 17th-century original of which is in the City Museum — is the symbol of Havana, and you will see her proud posture reproduced on numerous postcards and souvenirs.

There is nothing of historical interest inside the fortress (open 9am-5pm Thursday to Monday), which houses a collection of 20th-century pottery and is used for exhibitions by young Cuban artists. The roof offers a quiet respite from the bustle down below as well as a good view over the harbour. An enormous figure of Christ looms across the bay in Casablanca; it was inaugurated by Batista on Christmas Day in 1958, just six days before the triumph of the revolution.

The most unexpected sight in Plaza de Armas is **El Templete**, a Greco-Roman temple complete with Doric columns and a decorative frieze. It was built in 1828 to commemorate the founding of Havana and mark the site of the first Mass, said to have taken place beneath a *ceiba* tree in 1519. The tree you see today is not the original but it still has an important place in the hearts of Habaneros. The ceiba is endowed with magical powers and each 16 November, on the anniversary of the city's founding, people queue up to walk around the tree three times and make a wish.

The last building of any note in the square is the **Casa del Conde de Santovenia** which was one of the most prestigious hotels in Havana during the late 1800s. Converted later into offices, the building is under restoration and destined to revert to its former use as a hotel. The hideous modern building nearby houses the **Museo de Ciencias Naturales**, with the usual array of stuffed animals.

South of Plaza de Armas. The southern reaches of Habana Vieja remain a largely tourist-free zone. A lot of money has been spent restoring the first block or two south of the Plaza de Armas, but beyond that restoration work has mostly been focussed on just a handful of individual buildings.

Heading down Oficios towards Obrapía, on the right you pass the **Casa de los Arabes** (open 9am-6pm daily), occupying a charming 18th-century building that was a religous college in colonial times. The exhibits, most of which were gifts to the Cuban government from visiting Arab diplomats, are of only passing interest, but you may want to try the upstairs restaurant: see *Eating and Drinking*. There is also a prayer room, where Havana's small community of Arabs come to worship. Across the road is the **Car Museum**, with a predictable but enjoyable collection of Cadillacs and other motors. Non-fanatics will probably be satisfied with the view from the street.

Turning right up Obrapía and then right again onto Mercaderes, you'll find yourself outside the Torre de Marfil restaurant. Up a staircase on the opposite side of the street is the **Casa del Tabaco** (open 10am-5pm Tuesday to Saturday, 10am-12.30pm on Sunday), a fascinating little museum — and one of the few in Havana not to charge admission. Much of the cigar paraphernalia on display was donated by Fidel Castro (after he kicked the habit) and includes several cigar boxes, one in the form of the house in Oriente where the Cuban leader was born, and a fabulous collection of lighters. You can buy cigars in the shop downstairs.

Back around the corner is the **Casa de la Obra Pía** (open 8.30am-4.30pm, closed Monday). Don't be misled by the rooms facing onto the street, which contain various Alejo Carpentier memorabilia, including the Volkswagen Beetle he used to drive around Paris. Through the magnificent doorway lies one of the finest houses in Habana Vieja. First built in around 1665 and then enlarged in the late 18th century, the house centres on a courtyard where a profusion of greenery cascades from the galleries above, against walls painted in the rich golden yellow that you find all over Old Havana. There is not much to see on the ground floor, so head straight upstairs to the old living quarters. The staircase itself, with a painted floral border known as a *cenefa*, is a delight. The other highlight is the dining room, which occupies the space between the main courtyard and a smaller patio behind; the open-sided design provided diners not only with a view but also much-needed ventilation. Lift your eyes upwards, and you will see the old slaves' quarters on the roof terrace — a rare sight in the city.

The **Casa de Africa** (open 10.30am-4.30pm Tuesday to Saturday, 10am-noon on Sunday) opposite is a theme museum like the Casa de los Arabes but of far greater relevance to its environment. The main interest lies on the top floor, which is dedicated to the three main Afro-Cuban cults, Santería, Palo Monte and Abakuá (see page 32). The collection of ritual objects and costumes is small but well presented, and there is a room dedicated to the late Fernando Ortíz, the first Cuban anthropologist to take Afro-Cuban culture seriously. The lack of any in-depth explanations is disappointing, though, and for a greater insight into this fascinating subject you should visit the excellent museum at Guanabacoa: see *Further Afield*. The Casa de Africa is a lively cultural centre and stages performances of Afro-Cuban dance most weeks.

As you walk south along San Ignacio, you can make a short diversion to the **Museo Histórico de la Ciencia Carlos J. Finlay**, on Cuba between Brasil and Amargura (open 8am-5pm Monday to Friday, 8am-3pm on Saturday). Named after the man who discovered that yellow fever is transmitted by mosquitoes, the building was the first seat of Cuba's Academy of Sciences, founded in 1867. The Academy has since been moved to the Capitolio, but scientists still address their peers in the Neoclassical lecture theatre where Einstein himself once gave a paper; the original lecture theatre has been preserved as a museum piece. On the second floor is a 19th-century pharmacy, originally in Plaza Vieja and moved here to save it from demolition. The $2 admission fee includes a guided tour.

From the Carlos Finlay museum it is only a couple of blocks south and then east to **Plaza Vieja**. When the Plaza de Armas was taken over for troop drills following the construction of the Castillo de la Real Fuerza, Plaza Vieja became Havana's main public square — a busy marketplace and the focus of commercial and social life. Nowadays, it is hard to imagine how it was the centre of anything. The square was hit badly by Havana's expansion westwards in the 19th century, and then in 1952 its heart was cut out to make way for an underground car park, which remains in place to this day and devastates the aesthetic appeal of the square. Despite some interesting architecture, Plaza Vieja lures few tourists — or anyone else for that matter — into this part of the old city. The square is almost always deserted, bar the odd kid playing about on the concrete.

A number of 18th-century mansions recall Plaza Vieja's heyday, the **Casa de los Condes de Jaruco** (1733-37) being by far the finest. The most notable feature of this building is the loggia, which has some of Havana's biggest and best *medio puntos*; the central panel's floral design is particularly unusual. Now occupied by the Fondo Cubano de Bienes Culturales (closed Sunday), several rooms have been converted into exhibition space for the work of local artists and crafts people, providing a good excuse to explore the interior. Walking along the west side of the square you pass a delightful house with external murals that are unique in Havana. Beyond lies the **Casa de las Hermanas Cárdenas**, which has hardly altered since its construction (1736-1805); notice the lovely Baroque arch on the ground floor. The Centro de Desarrollo de las Artes Visuales, which has its seat here, stages art exhibitions on the second and third floors (open Tuesday to Saturday). The speciality at Fototeca, on the opposite side of the square, is photography. The first floor balcony provides lovely views of the square, with comfy chairs making this a good place to take a break. On the nearby corner is Plaza Vieja's finest modern building, an Art Nouveau high-rise block built as a hotel in 1906; it is in bad need of restoration.

Walking east along Teniente Rey brings you face to face with the **Convento e Iglesia de San Francisco de Asis** (open 9.30am-6.30pm). Built in 1738, this was one of Havana's most important monasteries during the colonial period. Its tower was the tallest in the city for some time and provided not only a landmark for sailors but also a lookout against pirates. Hurricanes, neglect and its use as a refrigeration plant have done plenty of damage to the church's appearance over the centuries, but the recent restoration reveals what a remarkably solid structure it is. The interior is almost completely unadorned and is well suited to its use as a concert hall. During the day, the authorities open the church as a museum, which means that they can conveniently charge admission; you may be satisfied with the view from the north entrance, but the attendants won't let you stand there long without paying.

Across Plaza de San Francisco, a rather characterless space despite the activity spilling out from the nearby harbour buildings, stands the former Commodity Exchange building (Lonja del Comercio); this is currently being remodelled by a Spanish group in one of the first real estate deals to have been agreed in Cuba. Walking south again along Oficios, at the corner of Muralla is the house where Alexander von Humboldt, German explorer and scientist, lived and worked at the beginning of the 19th century while trying to establish the meridian of Havana; hopes to turn it into a museum seem to have been rejected in favour of a more pragmatic decision to convert the building into a hotel. Across the street (at Oficios 211) is Havana's first National Assembly building, a bizarre blend of Neoclassical and Art Nouveau styles concocted in 1911. Now the seat of the local Poder Popular, you'll be lucky to poke your head through the door, though you should be able to get a glimpse at some of the ornate plasterwork in the immense hallway.

Taking a right turn along Sol you reach Calle Cuba and the **Convento e Inglesia de Santa Clara**. Behind the plain exterior walls lurks one of the highlights of this part of Habana Vieja. The oldest convent in the capital, begun in 1638, it is also one of Cuba's largest, occupying four entire blocks. Since the 1980s, it has been the home of the Centro Nacional de Conservación, Restauración and Museología, which oversees some of the restoration work being carried out in Old Havana. Partially funded by the UN, its laboratories are among the most advanced in Latin America. The labs and conservation workshops are mostly off-limits but the guided tours of the rest of the convent (available 9am-3pm Monday to Friday, price $2) should not be missed. The huge main cloister is a delight with its riot of greenery, and the convent boasts several superb alfarje ceilings. The small museum includes a small reconstruction of the original convent, which the restored complex now closely resembles; there are also a few religious objects, though the nuns took almost everything with them when they left in 1922.

One block south along Cuba is the **Iglesia del Espíritu Santo**. Erected in 1638, it is usually described as the oldest church in the city, but little remains of the original — except possibly for the alfarje ceiling. The most unusual feature is the chest tomb with an effigy of a certain Fray Gerónimo Valdés, who lived 1646-1729. You are most likely to find the church open after 3pm. The same goes for the nearby **Iglesia de la Merced**, though in every other way this elaborate church could not be more different. The European Baroque style of La Merced is unexpected in Old Havana, but its profusion of *trompe l'oeil* murals are considered the best of their kind in Cuban religious architecture. The church is much frequented by santería believers, who come to pray to Obbatalá, the Afro-Cuban equivalent of the Virgen de la Merced. On the saint's feast day, 24 September, people come dressed all in white — the colour associated with Obbatalá.

Walking west along Merced and then north up Compostela, at the corner of Luz stands the **Iglesia de Nuestra Señora Belén**. The church and adjacent convent are largely derelict, but the Baroque façade, with its two kneeling figures, is a photographer's delight. The largest religious house still existing in Old Havana, with a staggering six cloisters, the convent was devastated by fire in 1992. Restoration work has begun but is likely to take many years. There are rumours that nuns may be invited back to live there, though it is hard to imagine them settling down in a convent that some say will also include a hotel, restaurant and shops. As you head south notice the Arco de Belén, an arch that linked the convent, European-style, to the adjacent block.

Near the very southern edge of Old Havana, at Leonor Pérez 314, is the **Casa Natal de José Martí** (open 10am-5pm Tuesday to Saturday, 9am-12.30pm on

Sunday). The birthplace of Cuba's great independence fighter, this modest 19th-century house has been a museum since 1925. It traces Martí's life from childhood in a middle-class family to death in battle at Dos Ríos on 19 May 1895. Among the contents are letters, manuscripts, photographs and other memorabilia.

Havana's central **Railway Station** looms just around the corner, its twin towers and handsome clock rising high above the surroundings; notice the striking resemblance between these, built in 1912, and those of the Hotel Nacional, constructed two decades later. Inside you can see what is claimed to be the oldest engine in Latin America, La Junta, built in Baltimore in 1843. Near the station are remnants of the old city walls, most of which were demolished in the second half of the 19th century. You can follow the line of the original defences by walking north along Calle Egido. As you near the Parque Central, past one of Havana's main food markets (see *Eating and Drinking*), take a right along Teniente Rey to the Plaza del Cristo. A decrepit and little visited square, the main attraction here is the **Iglesia del Santo Cristo del Buen Viaje** (1640). The façade is Baroque, but the lovely 17th-century alfarje ceiling in the nave is original. Despite the peeling paintwork, the latter is in a good state of preservation — unlike the rest of the church; at the time of going to press the roof at the east end had collapsed comletely, leaving the high altar open to the skies.

From here it is just a short walk to the Parque Central.

Parque Central and Prado area

It was during the late 18th century, following the brief occupation by the British, that major expansion of the Cuban capital began under the governor Marqués de la Torre. While his main achievement was the redesigning of the Plaza de Armas, he also set his sights on the area beyond the city walls. In the 1770s, he laid the foundations of what was later known as the Prado. It was Miguel de Tacón, however, who was largely responsible for the shape and direction of developments outside the harbour area. New public spaces were created for a new age.

During the 1800s, the Parque Central and the Prado became the focus of the buzzing cultural and social scene in the capital. The introduction of Neoclassical architecture injected a new, more sophisticated style to the city, and by the turn of the century, Havana had become one of Latin America's classiest capitals. The boom that followed independence and the US occupation put paid to restraint, resulting in the construction of ostentatious buildings like the Capitolio and old Presidential Palace — symbols of the so-called 'pseudo Republic' which still dominate the area.

Parque Central. Unlike the Plaza de la Catedral and Plaza de Armas, and despite the presence of the Inglaterra and Plaza hotels, the Parque Central is dominated by Cubans rather than tourists. Havanans gather under the trees to wait for buses, to chat, and in one particular spot — known as the *Esquina Caliente* — to shout about the latest baseball results. At the centre, flanked by palm trees, stands a monument to José Martí, the first of its kind to have been erected in Cuba. Paid for by public subscription, it was inaugurated in 1905 in the presence of Máximo Gómez and President Tomás Estrada Palma. The figures around the bottom represent Cuba and various elements of the Cuban people, including soldiers of the liberation army.

Martí gazes towards the Parque Central's most imposing buildings, on the east side. To the right is the former **Centro Asturiano**, now the Court of Supreme Justice, to the left the **Manzana de Gómez**. This huge shopping mall was unique and the epitome of chic at the time of its construction at the turn of the century. Nowadays, all that's left is a depressing selection of tatty or empty shops. The **Plaza Hotel**, built in the late 1800s, occupies the next block. Take the lift up to the fifth floor restaurant for one of the best views in Old Havana. Don't fail to walk around to the back of the terrace to have a look at the **Edificio Bacardí**, which is best viewed from here rather than at street level. Built in 1929 for sugar and rum magnate, Emilio Bacardí (whose monogram features strongly), it introduced the Art Deco style to the city and marked a siginificant change in the architectural image of central Havana. Terracotta from the USA was used to decorate the upper façade and the tower, and has survived the ravages of the 20th century almost intact; the plaques of female figures are clearly visible from the roof of the Plaza. The interior has fared less well, with ceilings being lowered and other alterations made when the building was requisitioned following the revolution. Restoration is imminent, however. Eusebio Leal, the city historian, announced in 1995 that it would be done up as offices to be leased to foreign companies.

Heading back across the Parque Central, behind the Martí monument stands the Hotel Inglaterra, once a popular meeting place among Cuban intellectuals. Along one side runs **Calle San Rafael**, which from the 1920s replaced Calle Obispo as Havana's main commercial street. It still has the capital's biggest concentration of shops, though these are mere shadows of their pre-revolutionary selves. Still, San Rafael is always bustling, and remains a largely dollar-free zone.

Gran Teatro. One of Havana's most outstanding buildings, this ornate blend of Neoclassical and Art Nouveau styles is a monument to Cuban eclecticism. The first theatre on this site, Teatro Tacón, was built in 1837. At the beginning of this century, the Spanish Galician community bought it and incorporated it into the huge Centro Gallego, which is the building that you see today.

Even if you decide to see a performance here (see *Entertainment*), you should also treat yourself to a daytime tour (10am-7pm Tuesday to Sunday, price $2). Seen up close, the Gran Teatro is clearly in bad need of a lick of paint, but it remains supremely impressive, with its magnificent staircase and rotunda and the ornate ballroom, where you can still see the gallery where the orchestra once played. A room on the first floor has been reclaimed by the Galician association, one of several Spanish clubs still to exist in Havana.

The Gran Teatro is the seat of Alicia Alonso's Ballet Nacional de Cuba, which performs in the elegant García Lorca theatre. One of the appeals of the tour is the opportunity to watch dancers rehearse. Try to visit during the week, when the building fills with music and the buzz of dancers' chatter. There are often other rehearsals going on too — from opera to contemporary dance — so give yourself plenty of time to dawdle.

Capitolio. The Capitol has to be one of the most impressive sights in Havana if only for its sheer bulk. A loose copy of the State Capitol in Washington DC, built in the 20s, it is the most visible relic of American imperialism in Cuba. Begun as a presidential palace for the dictator Gerardo Machado, it ended up as the seat of Parliament.

The Capitol used to be off-limits but is now open for tours (9.15am to 4.40pm, Monday to Saturday). If you think the $3 charged for a full guided tour seems steep, you'll have to be content with seeing just the entrance hall for $1 or with taking in as much as you can from the doorway for free. A view of the entrance hall alone is enough to demonstrate the scale and opulence of the place, with its ranks of lamps and marble pillars beneath the high vaulted ceiling. Lording it over the scene stands a huge bronze statue of a woman representing the Cuban Republic. She is 11.5m high and weighs almost 30 tons.

The planetarium to the left of the main entrance caters mainly for families with children and normally opens only at weekends.

Pártagas Cigar Factory. Directly behind the Capitolio, this is the oldest cigar factory in Cuba to have been in continuous use since its foundation. Note that the date 1845 on the façade corresponds to the founding of the company rather than the building, which went up during the boom in the cigar industry in the late 19th century.

The Pártagas factory, now firmly on the Old Havana tourist trail, is open for tours 9am-3pm Monday to Friday, price $5. The workers are by now old hands at smiling for the cameras (especially for a tip), but the tour is still worthwhile for an overview of the whole cigar-making process. One of the most fascinating traditions, which pre-dates the Revolution, is the employment of someone to read to the staff while they work.

If you are travelling independently you may have to wait until a larger group turns up before being taken around, though the factory is better than it was at catering for individual tourists. The shop downstairs (also open on Saturdays) serves wonderful espresso coffee and has a good selection of cigars, which are also cheaper than in most other cigar shops.

Cigar factories are dotted all over the area. The only other one open for tours on a regular basis is the Corona factory, opposite the Museo de la Revolución at Zulueta and Refugio; it opens for tours between 9am and 5pm.

Palacio de Aldama. The Aldama Palace, at the corner of Amistad and Reina, across the Parque de la Fraternidad from the Capitol, doesn't make it onto many people's itineraries. Yet it is considered the most important residence to have been built in Havana last century. The palace was sacked during the Ten Years' War (1868-78), barely two decades after it was built, after which it was used as store rooms and offices. Nowadays, the Instituto de História de Cuba occupies the building. The palace is not officially open to the public, but if you have a quiet word with the staff by the entrance on Amistad, they should give you a short tour of the place. If enough visitors turn up, the authorities may even be induced to open the building to the public in a more organised fashion.

Palacio de Aldama fills a complete block and has no less than three façades. An austere building from the outside, nothing quite prepares you for the exquisite decorative ceilings that are the real attraction here. Embellished with both paint and plasterwork, they are thought to have been done by Italian craftsmen; you will not see such rich interior decoration anywhere else in Cuba. There are particularly fine examples in the Sala de Aldama (with a painting of Poetry, a lyre in one hand and a laurel crown in the other) and the Sala de don Domingo Delmonte, with a more delicate composition of allegorical figures enclosed within floral motifs.

El Prado. Known officially as the Paseo de Martí, everyone refers to the street that connects the Parque Central to the Malecón as 'El Prado'. Laid in the late 18th century alongside the city walls, it neatly marks the outer limit of Old Havana. With a raised tree-lined pavement running down the centre, this is the most elegant street in the city — once reserved for the privileged classes but now enjoyed by ordinary people (including the odd bagsnatcher). On some days, teachers from nearby schools bring their pupils here for their physical education lessons. And about halfway down you can watch people swap houses in a kind of open-air estate agency; notices stuck onto the trees advertise properties up for grabs all over the city.

The Prado is perfect for people-watching. Architecturally, it is also full of interest, though not many buildings are open to the public. Most are best admired from the outside anyway — private residences built early this century, painted every colour of the rainbow and with decoration more befitting a wedding cake than a building. You can have a look around the **Casa del Científico**, a former presidential home at the corner of Trocadero (see *Eating and Drinking*), but the highlight of the Prado is the **Gymnastics Academy** across the street. Constructed in the early 20th century as the headquarters of the Asociación de Dependientes del Comercio, its upper floors boast staggering galleries that run the length of the building (i.e. the whole block). The cream of the province's gymnasts and fencers now use these huge halls to train. You can watch them at work, but photography is restricted since the teaching methods seem to be regarded as state secrets. You may be approached by someone offering you a sauna and massage (a bargain at $4); the academy, like every other Cuban institution, needs to generate as much hard currency as possible.

Rounding off the Prado is the **Castillo de San Salvador de la Punta**, built in 1589, at the same time as the Morro fortress across the bay. The two together were vital in protecting the city's harbour (though they failed to keep the British out in 1762), and from the 17th century a chain stretched between them to secure the entrance to the port. San Salvador de la Punta is being turned into a Naval Museum.

Nearby are scenes typical of everyday life in Cuba — kids playing baseball and people queueing with their bikes for the ciclóbus or standing by the road in the hope of a ride through the tunnel. Surveying the scene from atop his horse is one of Cuba's great independence heroes, Máximo Gómez. Nearby is the less august sight of the **Spanish embassy** — an extravagant Art Nouveau creation and classic architectural wedding cake; floodlit at night it is an arresting sight among the ill-lit streets of the old city.

Museo de la Revolución. It is no doubt fitting that a museum named after the revolution should occupy the official residence of Batista and several other unsavoury characters of the republican era. No expense was spared in the construction of the former presidential palace, built 1913-20, but it is striking more for its size than its beauty. Tiffany & Co of New York took care of the interior design of the original palace, though you wouldn't think so to see it now. Much of the original décor has gone.

The museum is vast. You would need a week to study each display in any detail. In its effort to explain the historical context for the revolution as well as the revolution itself, the museum traces everything from the iniquities of the Spanish conquistadores to Cuban activities in southern Africa — all from an unrelentingly communist stance, of course. Exhibits are densely but well displayed. The penchant for charts, maps and three-D models (mostly of battles) begins to pall by the end, however some are fascinating. Everything is in Spanish, but English-speaking guides are available for an extra $3. Normal admission is $3, plus a further $3 if you want to take pictures.

The top (second) floor is devoted to Cuba as a colony, the wars of independence and the republican era, while the first floor covers the revolution and the post-revolutionary period. Here you will find out everything you ever wanted to know about the struggle of Castro and Co to win and then stay in power. Among the memorabilia of numerous revolutionaries are blood-spattered shirts, Che Guevara's black beret and a pair of Castro's trousers. Best of all is the *mise en scène* of Che and Camilo Cienfuegos emerging from the undergrowth of the Sierra Maestra, with their actual horses, stuffed, behind. Things get duller as you hit the section devoted to the 'construction of socialism', with innumerable statistics and tables. You'll look hard for a date post-1990. On the ground floor, look out for the Rincón de los Cretinos ('Corner of the Cretins'), featuring ex-presidents Batista, Reagan and Bush.

The museum is open 10am-5pm Tuesday to Sunday.

Granma. If you pay an extra $1 at the Museo de la Revolución, you can have a close-up look at the cabin cruiser *Granma*, which sits encased in glass behind it; you can get a perfectly good view from the pavement though. Small and faintly ridiculous-looking, the idea of it being packed with 82 revolutionaries led by Fidel Castro and including Che Guevara is almost comical. Around it are some of the vehicles used to storm (unsuccessfully) the Moncada Barracks in Santiago de Cuba, plus miscellaneous aircraft and guns, including pieces of a

US planes shot down during the Bay of Pigs. Soldiers guard the collection around the clock.

Museo Nacional de Bellas Artes. The grey concrete 50s building behind the *Granma* looks deeply unpromising from the outside but contains the country's most important collection of Cuban art. The National Gallery (open 10am-5pm Thursday to Monday, admission $3) was undergoing major reorganisation at the time of going to press, but sections of it were still open.

On the first floor you'll find a surprising range of European art, from Greek, Roman and Egyptian antiquities to Italian Renaissance paintings and works by Rubens, Velásquez, Gainsborough and Degas. The next floor is devoted to Cuban art. This includes works by Cuba's greatest 20th-century painters, including Wilfredo Lam, René Portocarrero and Amelia Peláez. There are a few pictures dating from the colonial period. In aesthetic terms these are mediocre in comparison with the modern paintings, but are interesting as social and historical documents. The ground floor is used for temporary exhibitions and a range of other activities (see *Entertainment*).

Iglesia del Santo Angelo Custodio. The church alongside the Museo de la Revolución was founded 300 years ago, but its forest of pinnacles and other neo-gothic touches date from last century. The interior is sumptuous, with lavish use of mahogany and some delicate paintwork on the ceiling. Cuba's national hero, José Martí, was baptised here.

Museo Nacional de la Música. The Music Museum, in a turn-of-the-century mansion at the end of Avenida de las Misiones (Capdevilla 1), gives an excellent insight into the main facets of Cuban music. If you can't understand the explanations, there are plenty of instruments to look at. The shop has a small but interesting choice of cassettes and records. Opening hours are 9am-5pm Monday to Saturday.

CHINATOWN

Havana's 'Barrio Chino' doesn't bear comparison with its counterpart in London, let alone San Francisco. It covers just a few blocks between Reina and Zanja, a few blocks west of the Capitolio, and the streets are deserted after dark. But this unexpected part of Havana has undergone a complete metamorphosis since a private market was set up here. The area's main pedestrian street is now a mass of stalls selling hot snacks and drinks, the kind of bustling scene that disappeared from Havana's streets for years. A few of the stallholders are Chinese, but the oriental flavour is found more in nearby shops and pharmacies. The Mi-Ching-Tang Society, a Chinese brotherhood founded 400 years ago, has 300 active members and welcomes visitors to its headquarters at Manrique 511 (entre Zanja y Dragones) to expore and eat. Other points of interest are the home of *Kwong Wah Po*, the local Chinese newspaper (San Nicolás 520) and the Cuban headquarters of the Partido Democrata Chino. Overlooking the market, on San Nicolás, is El Pacífico restaurant, which opens during the day for soup and snacks downstairs and proper meals (including frogs legs and chow mein) upstairs.

VEDADO

University of Havana. The heart of the University of Havana, on Calle L near the Habana Libre Hotel, is well worth a visit for its space, coolness, peace and light. It makes a refreshing diversion to explore the nooks and crannies of this turn-of-the-century complex and to take in the the rather jumbled views of Central Havana beneath it. The elegant staircase that provides the approach from the east side was the scene of many a student protest during the republican era. Students are a more placid lot these days, and the university is a good place to meet them.

One of the main reasons to go to the university is to visit the **Museo Antropológico Montané**, in Edificio Varona, on the south side of the central courtyard. The museum hoards many of Cuba's finest archaeological artifacts, and there is no better place to get a picture of the island's pre-Columbian cultures — particularly if you can understand the illuminating explanations given by the staff. There are many fascinating exhibits, including tools made out of shell and sharks' tooth necklaces, but pride of place is given to the god of tobacco, a stylised wooden figure found in 1906 near Maisí, the easternmost point of Cuba. The museum opens 9am-noon and 1-4pm Monday to Friday.

Museo Napoleónico. An Italianate mansion across the road from the university, at San Miguel and Ronda, contains one of Havana's more surprising museums. The contents are the legacy of the building's original owner, Orestes Ferrara, who was obsessed by Napoleon and all things Imperial. Every room contains superb examples of Imperial-style furniture, while the Napoleon memorabilia includes a tooth, a lock of hair and the hat he is said to have worn on St Helena. The museum is open 10am-5.30pm Tuesday to Saturday and 9am-noon Sunday; guided tours are available.

Museum of Decorative Arts. Located at Calle 17 between E and D, this is one of the best museums outside Habana Vieja (open 9am-4.45pm Wednesday to Sunday). Originally constructed in the 1920s, the house was completely remodelled a decade later with the help of the House of Jansen of Paris, which imported the vast majority of the materials and furniture from Europe — though Cuban mahogany was used for the doors. It is above all the handiwork of the interior designers that you are here to admire. Nothing impresses quite as much as the vestibule, with its fine stairway and set of 19th-century Venetian lamps, but the Rococo salon and extravagant Regency dining room come a close second. There are displays of Meissen and Sèvres porcelain upstairs, and don't miss the Art Deco bathroom.

Quinta de los Molinos. Situated on Avenida Salvador Allende, south of the university, the Quinta de los Molinos draws few visitors. Built for Governor Tacón in 1837, the villa takes its name from the snuff mills (*molinos*) that once existed in the same spot. In the late 19th century the house became the retreat of the liberation army commander, Máximo Gómez, whose tent and machete (a present from José Martí) you can see indside. At the time of going to press, the Máximo Gómez Museum was being revamped; it should be greatly improved when work is completed.

While the house is not the most outstanding piece of architecture in Havana, its setting is unusual in the city, surrounded as it is by extensive grounds. These include a small formal garden and what is optimistically referred to as a 'botanic garden'. The bedraggled collection of trees and shrubs is in bad need of attention, and a few well located benches in the shade would be a welcome addition. Hidden amongst the trees is the headquarters of the Asociación Hermanos Saíz, a writers' and artists' association. Known as La Madriguera, this is a popular meeting place for students, and you often find bands or individual musicians practising under the trees. Exhibitions, concerts and other events are staged here periodically.

Just beyond the Quinta de los Molinos is the 18th-century **Castillo del Príncipe**, one of Havana's two inland forts (the other, Castillo de Santo Domingo de Atarés lies south of the train station). It is now the city prison.

Plaza de la Revolución. Few people leave Havana without paying a visit to the Plaza de la Revolución, but it is a disappointment unless you are lucky enough to coincide with a rally. In the centre of the square is the huge seated figure of José Martí, erected not long before Batista fell. Towering behind it is the monument to the revolution — an ugly, 112-metre concrete obelisk, which is meant to be shaped like a five-sided star but from a distance resembles a huge hairbrush. Visitors are not allowed anywhere near it, let alone to the observation deck at the top; nor to the offices of the Central Committee beyond. (Anyone lingering in the square is likely to be asked to move on, or whistled at.)

Ministries, mostly erected in the 50s, stand like sentinels around Plaza de la Revolución. Among them is the Ministry of the Interior, which until recently was decorated with an impressive mural of Che Guevara and Fidel Castro (and was about the only official building which you were allowed to photograph). Now just a portrait of Che hangs there. Also on the north side is the Ministry of Communications, which you can enter freely. The only reason to do so is to visit the **Postal Museum** (open 9am-4pm, Monday to Friday), which is fascinating even for non-philatelists. You can spend hours poring over the huge stamp collection, arranged chronologically and by country. It includes such gems as an 1840 penny black from England and a 5p stamp from the Falkland Islands commemorating the marriage of Princess Anne and Captain Mark Phillips.

Columbus Cemetery. The huge Columbus Cemetery (open 7am-noon and 2-6pm) lies west of Plaza de la Revolución, at the far end of Calle 23. As well as the tombs of independence fighters and revolutionary heroes, the Cementerio de Cristóbal Colón contains monuments established by particular professions. Some of the statuary and architecture is very stylish, some of it startling. The rows of marble sculptures against a deep blue sky make a good photograph, but try to go early or late in the day since there are few trees to provide protection from the sun. A map of the cemetery, available at the door, shows where the most important graves are. One that is not marked is that of General Arnaldo Ochoa, executed in 1989 for corruption charges following a controversial trial; his is grave number 46,672 in Calle K.

If you've ventured this far, you should also visit the **Chinese Cemetery** at Avenida 26 y Calle 31, across the road from the western corner of the Colón Cemetery.

MIRAMAR

Ministry of the Interior Museum. Located at Avenida 5a between 12 and 14, about six blocks west of the Almendares river, this museum should entertain anyone interested in the intrigues of the CIA and Cuba's efforts to foil them. The first section is devoted to commemorating the founders of the Ministry of the Interior ('MININT' for short) and the bravery of particular agents, with detailed accounts of various failed assassination attempts against Fidel Castro. The highlight, though, is the CIA room. Here, displayed with great pride, are all kinds of classic CIA agents' gadgets, from miniature cameras made to look like cigarette lighters to radio trasmitters hidden inside rocks. The museum opens noon-6pm Tuesday to Friday.

ACROSS HAVANA BAY

Castillo de los Tres Reyes del Morro. 'Whoever is master of this hill,' said Bautista Antonelli, 'will be master of Havana'. The architect of El Morro fortress was proved right when the English attacked the city in 1762. Unfortunately, his building proved useless in defending Havana against the occupation. After the Spanish regained control, some of Spain's top military engineers were sent from Europe to revamp this and the rest of the city's fortifications.

There is not a great deal to do at El Morro (open 9am-7pm daily), other than enjoy the views across the bay, but there are a couple of small exhibitions, including a display about the Conquest, and you may be allowed an unofficial look up the lighthouse (erected in 1844). Food and refreshments are available at the Doce Apostoles restaurant and café on the battery down below.

Fortaleza de San Carlo de la Cabaña. A short walk from El Morro, the Cabaña is in an altogether different league. Constructed during the second phase of the fortification of Havana, following the British attack, this is by far the largest fortress in the city. Formerly a prison, which was closed in 1988 following a visit by the UN Human Rights Commission, the Cabaña now doubles as a military academy and a museum (open 10am-9.30pm daily, admission $3). Renovation work has been so extensive as to destroy the historic atmosphere of the place, but there is an interesting exhibition tracing the history of fortifications around the world. More curious-minded visitors may like to investigate the old moat, scene of the notorious 'Fosos de los Laureles', where political prisoners were shot during the Cuban fight for independence. If you go down the steps near the entrance and walk clockwise, you may not find the spot where prisoners were shot, but you can't miss the two missiles pointed unmistakably towards Florida. While they are unguarded, you should be cautious about taking photographs.

The fortress's long battery, which provides a broad panorama back towards Old Havana, is also the location for an extraordinary piece of theatre. Every evening, Cuban soldiers dressed in reproduction 18th-century uniforms, march up to the battery and fire a cannon shot (*cañonazo*) on the dot of 9 o'clock. In colonial times this signalled the closing of the city gates but is nowadays laid on for the tourists. Prepared with comic formality, it makes an entertaining spectacle.

Regla. If you fancy a ferry ride across the harbour, the best place to head for is the old ship-building town of Regla. The launch, which departs from Muelle Luz in Old Havana (see *City Transport*), deposits you opposite the church of the Santísima Virgen de Regla. A black image of the Virgin of Regla holding a white baby is what draws the crowds here. Not only is she the patron saint of Havana, but her Yorubá counterpart, Yemayá, is one of Santería's most important *orishas*. Her saint's day, on 8 September, is well attended and well worth coming to if you happen to be in Havana; celebrations begin on the previous day. Regla is an important centre of Afro-Cuban worship, and there is a small museum attached to the church devoted to Santería. This is a branch of the **Museo Municipal de Regla**, the main seat of which is a couple of blocks away on Calle Martí (open 9am-6pm Tuesday to Saturday, 9am-1pm on Sunday). This has its own room on religious cults, but if you are seriously interested in Afro-Cuban religion, you should also visit the museum in nearby Guanabacoa (see *Further Afield*).

Entertainment

The best source of information about events in Havana is *Cartelera*, which comes out on Thursdays and is what most hotel tourist desks rely on. *Habana* (see *Help and Information*) also provides details about venues and forthcoming events, as does Radio Taíno (the tourist channel), but be sure to check all information since the details given are not always correct.

The news that the Havana carnival, held in July, is to be reinstated in 1996, means an extra injection of life during an otherwise slow and sultry summer.

CINEMA

A programme of films currently showing in the capital is given in the daily edition of *Granma*. The best cinemas are in Vedado. The **Yara** (tel 32-9430), opposite the Habana Libre hotel, is the biggest in Havana and has some of the most up-to-date films. **La Rampa**, a few blocks down the hill on Calle 23, between O and P, shows less mainstream movies, both on its large screen and in the video hall (*sala de video*). So too does the **Charles Chaplin** (Calle 23 between Calles 10 and 12; tel 31-1101), a magnificent 1930s picture palace which puts on seasons of foreign movies and previews of new Cuban films; the artier international films are usually shown in the Sala de Video Charlot. All the above cinemas show films during the December festival of new Latin American film (see page 116).

The main cinema in Old Havana is the **Payret**, opposite the Capitolio, where you can sometimes catch a good picture. It is also worth checking out the **Mégano**, at the corner of Industria and San Martín behind the Capitol, which shows more *recherché* movies. Another place to check out is the **El Hurón Azúl** video hall inside the headquarters of the Writers' and Artists' Union (UNEAC) at Calle 17 y H in Vedado (tel 32-4571 to 74, fax 33-3158). Films, a programme of which is listed on the board outside, are often shown in the afternoon. Strictly speaking you should be a member, but interested tourists can usually join in. Other regular events at UNEAC include poetry readings and 'bolero afternoons'.

CLASSICAL MUSIC, THEATRE AND DANCE

The **Gran Teatro** is the most important venue for the performing arts in Havana. It has several different auditoria, the biggest and grandest of which is the García Lorca Hall (Havanans often refer to the whole theatre as the 'García Lorca'). A variety of events are staged here, including plays, classical concerts and performances by the National Ballet of Cuba; posters on the pillars outside advertise what's on. Tickets are sold at the box office in the lobby, though any tourism desk should also be able to reserve you a seat; expect to pay $10 for the big performances. If you hang around outside the theatre before a performance, you can sometimes pick up black market tickets.

The newly restored **Church of San Francisco de Asis** in Old Havana has become one of the most popular venues for classical music in the city. Look out for the excellent Coro Exaudi, which sometimes performs here. By contrast, the **Teatro Nacional** (tel 79-6011, 79-3558), at the junction of Calle 39 and Paseo in Plaza de la Revolución, is a characterless venue. Music and dance of all descriptions is performed in the main Covarrubias Hall, from imitation American rock to concerts by the National Symphony Orchestra. The smaller Avellaneda is used mainly for children's shows.

The most innovative theatrical performances are staged at Havana's smaller theatres, all of which are in Vedado. Try the **Teatro Nacional de Guiñol** (Calle M y 19) or the **Teatro Trianón** (at the corner of Línea y Paseo), where the excellent El Público company often performs. Plays are put on at the nearby **Teatro Mella** (Línea between Calles A and B; tel 3-8696), where you can also see performances by the Danza Contemporánea de Cuba and the excellent Danza Abierta troupe. The patio of the **Museo Nacional de Bellas Artes** (see page 182) is a popular venue for smaller and more informal music and dance events, mainly at weekends.

Afro-Cuban Dance. Traditional Afro-Cuban dance troupes perform regularly at the Casa de Africa (see *Exploring*) and the Palacio de Artesanía (see *Shopping*). While the calibre of these performers is not to be sniffed at, for a really professional show you should try to see the *Conjunto Folklórico Nacional*, which features some of Cuba's top musicians and dancers. The group is based at Calle 4 between Calzada and 5 in Vedado (tel 30-3060), where they stage 'Rumba Saturdays' every other week at 3pm, though they appear at other venues too.

POPULAR MUSIC

Salsa. Very occasionally Cuba's top salsa bands play in one of Havana's large hotels, but the best chance to see the likes of Los Van Van or Issac Delgado is in the **Palacio de la Salsa** in the Riviera Hotel (tel 33-04501). A relatively new arrival on the scene in 1995, this club was all the rage at the time of going to press. There is only a small dance floor in front of the stage, but sufficient space exists around the tables for people to dance throughout the hall. And they certainly do. The Palacio de la Salsa is seriously popular with Cubans (those that can afford the $10 admission charge, that is), who usually outnumber the tourists. The band normally goes on at 11pm or later, but it's worth arriving at 10-10.30pm in order to get a table. Drinks are not cheap — a bottle of rum costs $15 — and most Cubans seem to smuggle their own booze in.

The better groups sometimes play more exclusively for the benefit of Cubans at the **Tropical** club (also referred to as the Salon Rosada), an open-air disco near the Tropicana in Marianao. It is open at weekends only, from around 9pm to midnight. Arrive in good time and be prepared to queue.

Jazz. Don't hold out too many hopes of catching any jazz while you're in Havana. The capital's most famous jazz club, Maxim's (at Calle 10 between 3 and 5), closed several years ago following a flood and shows no signs of re-opening. There are no other regular venues for jazz, though periodic performances are put on at the **Casa de la Cultura** at Calzada and 8 in Vedado (where gigs are held during Havana's biennial jazz festival). It's also worth enquiring at the **Café Cantante** in the Teatro Nacional (Plaza de la Revolución).

Rock Music. Cuban rock bands usually play in Havana's larger indoor concert halls, such as the Teatro Nacional or the Teatro Karl Marx (Avenida 1ra between Calles 8 and 10 in Miramar), where the likes of Carlos Varela have performed. Exponents of the latest Novísima Trova sometimes play at the **Patio de María**, near the Teatro Nacional.

Cabaret

Plenty of tourist-oriented entertainments are laid on in the hotels, including cabarets, 'Afro Shows' and discos. The problem is picking a good one. Several hotels, such as the Inglaterra and Lincoln, have roof terraces where salsa bands play several times a week. If all you want to do is have a dance, and don't mind the obligatory dancers in brief and gaudy costumes, these places aren't bad. Most charge $5 admission, but some are free; if you arrive late in the evening you should be able to get a discount. On special nights and in larger venues, there will be more variety in the entertainment, with mournful singers and offbeat comedians alongside the usual salsa band.

Tropicana: of all the tourist shows in Havana, the most famous is the open-air Tropicana, an old-fashioned, Folies Bergères-style extravaganza that has been going for over 50 years. In its heyday, before the Revolution, famous names including Josephine Baker, Nat King Cole, Frank Sinatra and Cuba's Rita Montaner performed here. It is at Calle 72 no. 4504 at Calle 43 in the district of Marianao (tel 33-7507, 33-0174).

Some people swear that the show is worth every cent of the $35-plus admission fee. The performances and glitzy surroundings are undeniably impressive and the quality of the music is excellent. The attempt to recreate the 'Fabulous Fifties' in Castro's Cuba was always doomed to fail, however, and the atmosphere simply isn't there.

A seat at the Tropicana will set you back $35-50 if you book through a hotel, including transport there and back. If you have less money to spare, just turn up on the night and ask about the $20 bar seats, of which there are only a small number but which provide a decent view and rarely get booked up. Note that the cost of your ticket will be refunded if it rains. To the price of admission you should add the cost of drinks ($4 a time) and, in some cases, the cab fare — which will be about $12 if you take a tourist taxi. If you wish to use a still camera, you will have to pay $5; for a video camera, $25.

Traditionally, there are two shows, one beginning at around 9.30pm and another at about midnight. In low season, the second show may be cancelled, so check in advance.

Cabaret Parisien: the show in the Hotel Nacional, called the Cabaret Parisien, is the next best thing after the Tropicana, and miles more convenient. Tickets cost $15-25 and there's no great distance to travel.

1830: the smart villa next to the Chorrera fort at the far end of the Malecón, contains a pretentious restaurant but also a charming garden terrace by the water's edge (with a grotto), where cabarets are staged every night, admission $5. The show, which kicks off after 10pm, usually includes comedy, a live band, even a fashion show, and rounds off with a disco. If you want to attempt catching a bus east towards central Havana at the end of the evening, walk one block inland to Línea. To hail a passing cab, however, you would do better to stay on the Malecón.

La Maison: located at Calle 16 no. 701, on the corner of 7ma Avenida in Miramar (tel 33-1543 or 48), La Maison is Cuba's only existing model agency. It has also become an upmarket duty free shop, where busloads of tourists are deposited periodically and expected to spend lots of money on clothes and accessories. There is a fashion show in the garden every night at 9pm, which is worth seeing if you don't mind paying $10 for a laugh. Hotels in town offer a package deal costing either $25, which includes transport and a mediocre meal as well as admission to the show, or $15, which includes transport and a bottle of rum between four people.

Discos

The biggest concentration of clubs and discos in Havana is in Vedado. The majority of these look like (and often are) dives — dingy, airless basements where it is hard to escape schmaltzy, romantic dance music. The dress code can be strict, and many of these Cuban-style places require you to be a couple, mixed of course. One of the few clubs that isn't like this is the **Rio Club** at Calle 3ra and O, just across the Almendares river in Miramar, which is popular among young Habaneros and plays mostly American music. It is open from 9pm until late.

The discos that charge in dollars are another kettle of fish. The **Aché** club in the Meliá Cohiba Hotel, which is the place to be seen at the moment, has the most advanced sound and light system in the city, and can accommodate 1,000 people. There is always a crowd of people hanging around outside, even though many of them don't have the money to get in. Inside, you can dance to a complete mix of music, from salsa and funk to hits of the 60s and 70s. Admission costs $10, unless you're staying at the hotel, in which case there's no charge. It is open from 10pm-5am. The **Havana Club** disco in the Comodoro Hotel, which was most people's favourite until the arrival of the Aché, has lost out partly because it is located some way from the centre, in Miramar. Still, the music is usually good, with plenty of salsa; admission costs $10. More convenient than both these two is the disco in the Hotel Deauville, where you pay just $5 to get in. It is a bit of a dive, though, and is often very crowded.

If you don't mind travelling a little way out of the centre, consider going to the **Arcos de Cristal**, which is attached to the Tropicana in Marianao. Here you can dance to a mixture of live and taped music until 6 o'clock in the morning. For something totally different, there's **El Galeón**, a small galleon ship that sails around the bay every night, lights flashing and music blaring. There are two dance floors, one devoted to salsa and another to other kinds of music. Admission costs $10. El Galeón docks below the Morro fortress, on the other side of the bay from the centre of town. If you pay in advance, transport will be laid on from your hotel.

SPORT

Cuba took its role as host of the 1991 Pan-American Games extremely seriously, building an impressive array of new facilities across the harbour in Habana del Este. They served their purpose, but the stadium, velodrome and other facilities have hardly been used since. Half of the athletes' village is now given over to tourist accommodation (the Villa Panamericana), the rest being used to house the Cuban workers who built the complex.

The main sports complex in Havana is the **Ciudad Deportiva** on Avenida de Ranchos Boyeros, near the junction of the Vía Blanca south of Plaza de la Revolución. You can watch a whole range of sports here, including volleyball, basketball and hockey. Important boxing matches take place here too, though you'll be lucky if your trip coincides with one; if you're keen to see Cuban boxers in action, go to the training centre at the corner of Cuba and Merced in Old Havana. The **Sala Polivalente Ramón Fonst**, across the road from the long-distance bus station on Avenida de Rancho Boyeros, is used mainly for basketball, while at the **Sala Polivalente Kid Chocolate**, opposite the capitol, you're more likely to see people doing martial arts.

No one should miss the chance to see a baseball game at the **Estadio Latinoamericano**, on the corner of Avenida 20 de Mayo and Calle Pedrosa in Cerro. Games usually take place on weekdays, beginning at 8.30-9pm. For the biggest crowd, go when Havana's own Industriales team is playing. Take your own refreshments and, if you don't fancy sitting on hard concrete for a couple of hours, something to sit on. If you cycle, feel free to take your bike with you to your seat; everyone else does.

Golf. Serious golfers may find it hard to resist doing a round at the Diplo Golf Club (tel 44-4836, 44-82227), used almost exclusively by expats. It lies about 5 miles (8km) southwest of the centre off Avenida de la Independencia, about a $12 taxi ride from the Parque Central. The course has 18 holes and is beautifully maintained, though the fairways are rough in places. For one-off games, the charge seems to vary according to the whim of the staff. To avoid being ripped off, refuse to pay more than $50 for two people, including the hire of the clubs; you must buy your own golf balls. There is a small but pleasant pool for cooling off afterwards as well as facilities for riding and playing tennis.

Havana is the best place to shop — or at least to window shop — in Cuba. Strolling along one of the city's main shopping streets, such as Calle San Rafael or Galiano can be a depressing business though. Drab interiors reveal a range of goods that is unimaginably sparse, though Galiano still bears traces of its former elegance. Notice the Fondon Joyería shop at number 91, near the corner of San Rafael, its façade a riot of colourful tiles, or the building near the Hotel Lincoln, at the corner of Virtudes. Shopping is best combined with people-watching. The markets are good for this — either the food markets (see *Eating and Drinking*) or some of those that sell clothes, leather goods, etc.

There is one in Parque Curita, at the corner of Reina and Galiano, where you can pick up Santería paraphernalia, including necklaces for $2

Arts and Crafts. The most popular store for arts and crafts is the **Palacio de la Artesanía**, on Tacón at the northern end of Calle Cuba in Old Havana. Formerly the mansion of the Pedroso family, this shady and atmospheric building has been disfigured with garish boutiques selling every kind of souvenir you could possibly think of, from cassettes to cigars. The dollar emporium is firmly on the package tour itinerary, but is at least convenient for buying a whole range of gifts under one roof. Opening hours are 9am-6pm daily.

There are craft stalls on most days in the Plaza de la Catedral, but the art galleries are more interesting. In the **Taller Experimental de Gráfica** (open 8.30am-5.30pm Monday to Saturday), just off the square in Callejón del Chorro, you can watch lithographic prints being made and then buy them in the attached shop. There are a few shops selling arts and crafts along Calle Obispo, but you'll find more unusual things in the galleries in Plaza Vieja, which at least lies a little off the beaten track (see *Exploring*). **La Travesía**, across Plazuela de Albear from El Floridita, specialises in artifacts related to Santería; it is the main outlet for the work of Lydia Aguilera, whose large figures of orishas painted on wood dominate the shop.

At **La Exposición** in Manzana de Gómez, in the Parque Central, you can pick up reproductions of works by Cuba's top artists, including Wilfredo Lam, Amelia Peláez, Portocarrero and Víctor Manuel (a fine landscape painter), as well as photographs by Osvaldo Salas, most famous for his pictures of Che Guevara. Ask to see downstairs, where the bulk of the stock is kept. While not top quality, these prints are more attractive than the tat available in most shops and good value at $3-10. A much more modest shop called **Bazar**, on the corner of Galiano and Zanja, also stocks a few posters, which they sell for pesos. You can sometimes pick up a bearable woodcarving or piece of pottery in one of the peso shops along San Rafael, but on the whole the local shops have nothing that you'd consider giving a loved one back home.

Books and Music. Havana's most famous bookshop has long been **La Moderna Poesia**, at the top of Calle Obispo. It has a larger stock than the average peso shop, but you'll be hard pushed to pick up something you really want to buy. Still, it's worth a browse, since you can occasionally stumble across a good title. Nowadays, the *Librería Internacional* across the road is more of an attraction. It stocks a mixture of classics, including the works of Fernando Ortíz, José Martí and Che Guevara (some in English translation), as well as books about Cuba. All for dollars, of course. The shop opens 12.30-7.30pm, Monday to Saturday. There is an even better selection in the **Librería Bella Habana** in the Palacio del Segundo Cabo in Plaza de Armas, which is one of the few places to sell the Penal Code, price just $2. The best dollar bookshop in Vedado is in the International Press Centre (Centro de Prensa Internacional) on La Rampa. Since the CPI is geared for journalists, most books deal with politics. You can also pick up magazines, such as *Business Tips* and *Sintesi*, a digest of Prensa Latina reports covering foreign events.

The best books are almost invariably found in the street. You find second-hand book stalls dotted all over central Havana, but the largest concentration is in Plaza de Armas, where a dozen traders spread their wares beneath the trees in front of the Palace of the Captains General. Stalls often have the same titles, so it's worth doing the rounds to compare prices, but it's not hard to get a good price with a bit of haggling. You'll pay three times the price at the **Librería El Navio**, a second-hand bookshop around the corner on Calle Obispo, though this last place usually has some excellent pre-1959 titles. If you're after something special, it's also worth trying **Librería La Fijeza**, at Calle Concordia 57 between Galiano and Aguila in Centro Habana (tel 79-8254), which opens 10am-5pm daily. Again prices are high, but you'll find leatherbound books the likes of which you won't see in any other shop.

Havana badly needs a good music shop. Tourist outlets always have a few cassettes and CDs, but there is not one place that stocks the full range. The choice in the Palacio de la Artesanía is better than most, and there is a small but interesting selection of cassettes (as well as sheet music and instruments) in the Museum of Music on Avenida de las Misiones. If you're looking for (or don't mind) cheap records, keep an eye open as you stroll through the streets. There are usually a couple of record sellers along Calzada de Infanta, on the pavement or inside ground-floor apartments.

The shop in the Chaplin Cinema (Calle 23 between 10 and 12) sells posters, videos and books connected with Cuban film and art, and also music; it is open 2-9pm Monday to Saturday. Some tourist shops sell videos too, not only films and music, but also of religious ceremonies, etc. The shop behind the Yara cinema stocks just such a range.

Rum and Cigars. No tourist shop is worth its salt if it doesn't stock a few bottles of rum, but you rarely find a good choice. For the best selection, go to the Taberna del Galeón (see page 167) or the Casa del Ron, above El Floridita; both these places allow you to taste what you buy.

As for cigars, unless you know someone you can trust to acquire the real McCoy on the black market, you'll do best to stick to the official outlets. The shop in the Pártagas factory is recommended, as is that in the Casa del Tabaco in Old Havana (see *Exploring*). Otherwise, plenty of hotels have their own cigar shops.

Photo-processing. Publifoto is responsible for most photo-processing in Havana. Its most convenient branch is in the International Press Centre on La Rampa, where you can even get slide film developed, though the main shop is down the road in Edificio Focsa on Calle M between 17 and 19 (tel 32-3584/85). Several hotels act as an agent for Publifoto and can organise the processing for you.

Crime and Safety

You are more likely to be robbed in the capital than anywhere else in Cuba, and the heavy police presence in the city centre is largely a reaction to the rise in crime against tourists. However, if you take a few precautions only a stroke of ill luck is likely to spoil your stay. Some people warn against walking around the city at night, but it is not necessary to limit your movements so drastically. Even so, you should make judicious use of taxis and avoid deserted or ill-lit streets. After a day or two you'll get to know which are the brightest, busiest — and therefore safest — streets.

For general advice on the precautions you can take, see page 138. Never carry your passport, tickets or excessive amounts of money when you go out. Avoid carrying a handbag with a long strap, or sling it around your neck rather than just your shoulder. Bag-snatching is the favourite occupation of Havana's petty criminals, by day or night. They often work in pairs — with one to snatch the bag, and another waiting on a bike around the corner for the getaway.

There are several parts of the city where tourists are particularly vulnerable. The narrow streets of Habana Vieja are a favourite haunt of thieves and should always be treated with respect. The area south of Calle Obispo has been the scene of quite a number of bag-snatching incidents. The quiet streets around Plaza Vieja and beyond are lovely to explore, but they aren't well policed. When walking from Plaza de Armas to the Parque Central at night, take Calle Obispo, which is the best lit route between the two.

The other area to be wary of after dark is Centro Habana (between the Prado and Vedado), which includes the Colón and Cayo Hueso districts. Barrio Colón is the nearest thing central Havana has to a ghetto, predominantly black and with an apparently growing drug scene. It's the kind of place that's fun to experience if you're with people from the neighbourhood, particularly as there are lots of private restaurants in the area, but uncomfortable if you're on your own. It's reasonably safe during the day, however, and fine to cycle through. If walking from the Parque Central to Vedado at night, head along Neptuno (which is a bus route) or the Malecón — all of which are usually busy with people and safer than other streets. Be careful around the Hotel Deauville, which has become a favourite among bagsnatchers in recent years. Since the Prado is flanked along one side by barrio Colón, take care along here too. If you sit down, don't put your bag on the ground or beside you — keep it attached to your body at all times. The Prado is better policed than many areas, but the police aren't always in the right place at the right time.

Miscellaneous dodgy characters in addition to black marketeers hang around the areas most frequented by tourists. Most are not very persistent and can normally be got rid of with a stern 'No' or a cold shoulder. If people come up to you on the street whispering 'Pee Pee Hay', it's not a threat; they are trying to sell you locally manufactured anti-cholestorol tablets called PPG.

Embassies. British citizens, and those of Commonwealth countries except Australia and Canada, should contact the British Embassy at Calle 34 no. 708, between 7 and 17, Miramar, CP 11300 (tel 33-1771/2, 33-1286; fax 33-8104).

Most other diplomatic missions are also in Miramar. The Canadian Embassy is at Calle 30 no. 518, on the corner of Avenida 7 (tel 33-2516/7, 33-2527; fax 33-2044). Australia is represented by Mexico (see below). American citizens are looked after by the US Interests Section, a huge modern office block on Calzada between Calles L and M, near the Hotel Nacional. Despite the bad relations between the USA and Cuba, this office is just like a full-scale American Embassy but without an ambassador as the figurehead, and is in fact by far the largest diplomatic mission in Havana. Go along on any weekday and you will see the queues of Cubans in the nearby square queueing up for visas. The telephone numbers for the Interests Section are 33-3551 to 59, but it is virtually impossible to get through. Opening hours are 10am-4pm, Monday to Friday.

Representatives for some other countries are located as follows (in Miramar unless stated otherwise):

Argentina: Calle 36 no. 511, e/ 5 y 7 (tel 33-2972/2549/2573, fax 33-2140).
Austria: Calle 4 no. 101, corner of 1 (tel 33-2394/2825, fax 33-1235).
Belgium: 5ta Avenida no. 7408 (tel 33-2410/2561, fax 33-1318).
Bolivia: Calle 26 no. 113, e/ 1 & 3 (tel 33-2127/2426, fax 33-2739).
Brazil: Calle 16 no. 503, e/ 5 & 7 (tel 33-2021/2139/2786, fax 33-2328).
Chile: Avenida 33 no. 1423 (tel 33-1222/3, fax 33-1694).
Colombia: Calle 6 no. 106 (tel 33-1246/7/8, fax 33-1249).
Denmark: Paseo de Martí (Prado) no. 20 apto 4, Habana Vieja (tel 33-8128/ 8144, fax 33-8127).
Ecuador: Avenida 5A no. 4407, e/ 44 & 46 (tel 33-2024/2820, fax 33-2868).
Finland: Avenida 7B no. 6003 (tel 33-2132/2080, fax 33-2029).
France: Calle 14 no. 312, e/ 3 & 5 (tel 33-2308/2132/2080, fax 33-1439).
Germany: Calle 28 no. 313, e/ 3 & 5 (tel 33-2569, 33-2539; fax 33-1586).
Guyana: Calle 18 no. 506, e/ 5 & 7 (tel 33-2249/2094, fax 33-2867).
Italy: Calle Paseo no. 606, e/ 25 & 27, Vedado (tel 33-3334/3356, fax 33-3416).
Japan: Calle N no. 62, Vedado (tel 33-3454/55, 33-3507).
Mexico: Calle 12 no. 518, e/ 5 & 7 (tel 33-2498/2383/2634, fax 33-2719).

Netherlands (Paises Bajos): Calle 8 no. 307, e/ 3 & 5 (tel 33-2511/12, fax 33-2059).
Nicaragua: Calle 20 no. 709 (tel 33-1025, fax 33-6323).
Norway: see Denmark.
Panama: Calle 26 no. 109, e/ 1 & 3 (tel 33-1673, fax 33-1674).
Peru: Calle 36 no. 109, e/ 1 & 3 (tel 33-2477/2632, fax 33-2636).
Portugal: 5 Avenida no. 6604 (tel 33-2871/2593, fax 33-2593).
Russian Federation: 5 Avenida no. 6402 e/ 62 & 66 (tel 33-1085/1749).
Spain: Cárcel 51, corner of Zulueta, Habana Vieja (tel 33-8025/26, 33-8093; fax 33-8006/8015).
Sweden (Suecia): Avenida 31 no. 1411 (tel 33-2563/2831, fax 33-1194).
Switzerland (Suiza): 5ta Avenida 2005 (tel 33-2611/2729, fax 33-1148).
Uruguay: Calle 14 no. 506, e/ 5 & 7 (tel 33-2311/2040, fax 33-2246).
Venezuela: Calle 36A no. 704, e/ 7 & 42 (tel 33-2662/2612, fax 33-2773).

Visas. You can extend your tourist card at the tourist information desk inside the door of the Habana Libre Hotel (Calle L e/ 23 y 25), which is open 8am-3pm Monday to Friday. The fee is $8, payable in cash or with a credit card. There is an immigration office in the hotel for other enquiries. In extremis, you may have to resort to visiting the central immigration office at Avenida 3ra and Calle 20 in Miramar.

Tourist Information. An office of sorts is open to meet incoming international flights at Havana airport, but it does little other than sell postcards and the occasional map. In the city itself, the information desks in every tourist hotel are not usually well suited to giving information to independent travellers, though the desk in the Habana Libre is more helpful than most. For general enquiries, you'll do better at one of the Infotur offices, which are better at dealing with individuals and even have computerised information. Most are open until 7 or 8pm. Addresses of the main branches are as follows:

Habana Vieja: Calle Obispo 358 between Habana and Compostela (tel 61-4881); in Plazuela de Albear, across from El Floridita; and in the Manzana de Gómez, on the east side of the Parque Central (tel 63-6960).
Centro Habana: corner of Galiano and San Rafael (tel 63-5095).
Vedado: Calle 23 (La Rampa) at the corner of P (tel 70-7631/5284) and Calle 12 no. 570, corner of 25 (tel 33-3726).
Miramar: Calle 3ra, corner of 28 (tel 23-3376/2608, 33-1793; fax 31-8164), the head office of Infotur.
Regla: Calle Santuario 13 (tel 90-0182).

For 24-hour information, you can call 'Aquí Habana on 33-8383.

Publications: La Habana, published fortnightly and available from hard-currency stores and hotels, price $2, is a run-of-the-mill listings magazine. It has details of everything from beauty parlours to churches, in both English and Spanish. A better source of information about forthcoming events is *Cartelera*, which comes out on Thursday. Some people may try to charge you for it, but it should be free.

Guidebooks to Havana are either bland or non-existent. One of the few that is worth buying is *La Habana Colonial*, a specialist architectural guide published by the Dirección Provincial de Planificación Física y Arquitectura (Calle 25 and L). It contains (moderately technical) descriptions and photographs of more than 100 of Havana's best colonial buildings. The drawbacks: it costs $25, is in Spanish and can be purchased only directly from the DPPFA office near the Habana Libre.

Emergencies: Asistur (Prado 254, between Trocadero and Animas; tel 62-5519, 63-8284; fax 33-8087) exists to provide general assistance to tourists, including advice on dental and general medical treatment, repatriation and insurance. If you have everything stolen, this is a good place to come to send SOS faxes home. Asistur can arrange hotel and train reservations, and is also the only agency in Cuba to change American Express travellers cheques — though for a hefty 10% commission. The office is open 24 hours a day, seven days a week.

Communications. Several hotels have post and telephone offices, including the Plaza, Habana Libre and Riviera, but you can make telephone calls (local or international) and send faxes from most tourist hotels. In Old Havana, where both hotels and international telephone lines are scarce, you can call from the post office in the Plaza de la Catedral (open 10am-6pm) and the Seaman's Club, in Plaza San Francisco one block south of Hostal Valencia.

Most hard currency shops sell stamps, but these are one thing you can also buy in local currency. There is a handy post office next to the Gran Teatro in the Parque Central. If you have an important package to send, however, you should consider using DHL, which has its head office at Avenida 1ra and Calle 42 in Miramar (tel 33-1578, 29-0700), open 9am-6pm Monday to Friday, 8.30am-noon on Saturday, and agencies in several downtown hotels. The Cuban equivalent of DHL is EMS, based at Avenida 5ta and 112, Miramar (tel 33-6097).

Money. It is easiest to cash your travellers cheques at your hotel because this means you can avoid carrying your passport or large amounts of money through the streets. Some cashiers may refuse to change cheques on a Sunday or if you are not a resident, but this is not the norm. Hotel Nacional is a good place to exchange money, since not only can it cope with large sums (cashiers in smaller hotels have more limited supplies of cash), but staff will also break large bills down into small denominations without a murmur.

Hotels generally charge 4% commission. For the best deal (2%), go to the international branch of the Banco Nacional de Cuba at Línea 1, Vedado (tel 33-3003/3148, fax 33-3006). It opens 8.30am-1pm Monday to Friday. The queues are horrendous on Monday mornings, so either go early or wait until Tuesday. The Banco Financiero Internacional (see below) charges 3%.

Credit cards: you can withdraw cash on a credit card from the Banco Financiero Internacional in the Habana Libre Hotel (tel 33-3429, fax 33-3795). The minimum amount you can withdraw is $100, but there is no maximum. Banking hours are 8am-3pm. Don't forget your passport.

Medical Treatment. For minor treatment, ask your hotel to recommend a nearby clinic. More serious cases requiring hospitalisation will be taken to the Cira García Central Clinic for Foreign Patients, at Avenida 47 and Calle 18, Miramar (tel 33-2660). The care here is first-rate and extremely expensive. Another clinic specialising in the treatment of tourists is Servimed (specialised medical services for health tourism), at Calle 18 no. 4304 between 43 y 47, Miramar (tel 33-2658, 33-2023).

If you need surgery, you'll end up at the Hermanos Ameijeiras clinic in Central Havana (Calle San Lázaro 701 at Belascoaín; tel 79-8531 or 70-7721). Two floors are reserved for foreigners, where they can enjoy the hospital's best facilities, best food, and best-stocked pharmacies. All this costs a fortune to provide, of course, so fees are correspondingly high.

Laundry. The Alaska Laundrette is in Old Havana, on the corner of Villegas and Obrapia.

Other Useful Addresses. *Bufete Internacional:* an international law office offering legal services to individuals and foreign companies. It is located at Calle 47 no. 815, between Santa Ana and Conill, Nuevo Vedado (tel 33-5469, 81-3498; fax 33-5448).

Centro de Prensa Internacional: Calle 23 on the corner of O (tel 32-7491/2906/ 6755 and 32-0526 to 28; fax 33-3008/3139).

Federación de Mujeres de Cuba (Women's Federation): Paseo 260 on the corner of Calle 13, Vedado (tel 3-9932).

Unión de Jovenes Comunistas (Union of Young Communists): northern end of Avenida de las Misiones, near the Museo de la Revolución.

Casa de las Américas: Calle 3 y G, Vedado (tel 32-3587). Founded by Che Guevara as a centre for the promotion of Latin American art and literature, this is one of Cuba's best known institutes. Events held here include readings, exhibitions and music recitals.

Useful Numbers. *Police:* 30-1621, 30-3119.
Fire Brigade (Bomberos): 3-4511, 31-3158.
Ambulance: 32-8939.

Further Afield 61

Outside the city centre, but still within the boundaries of Ciudad de La Habana, there is plenty to see. If you have sipped cocktails at Ernest Hemingway's favourite bars, you can embark on what might loosely be described as the Hemingway Trail (in fact three scattered sites on the edges of Havana). Or, to feel the ambience which attracted the writer to Cuba, go to the small but atmospheric town of Santiago de las Vegas or the seaside village of Cojímar, both just a few miles from Havana. You can explore the historic town of Guanabacoa or, for a complete contrast, visit a post-revolutionary new town such as Alamar. And for those without the time to explore some of Cuba's more remote coastal areas, there are some fine beaches a short distance east.

Some of the places described below are accessible by public transport, but to visit several in a day by bus would require some perseverance. It is better to hire a cab or rent a car.

THE HEMINGWAY TRAIL

Hemingway Marina. 'Ernesto', as the locals called him, would have been dismayed at the sight of this ugly modern complex. Eight miles (13km) west of the capital, the Hemingway Marina is the largest yacht mooring in Cuba, but is remarkable only for how few yachts there actually are. Undaunted, the authorities are building hundreds of new chalets to cater for the sailors they clearly hope will one day come here. Only each May does the marina come to life, when marlin fishermen engage in a battle of wits during the Ernest Hemingway Marlin Fishing Tournament. The first post-revolutionary winner has not repeated his achievement since then; it was Fidel Castro.

There are two four-star hotels, Residencial Turístico Marina Hemingway (5a Avenida y 248, Santa Fe; tel 33-1150, fax 33-1831) and El Viejo y el Mar Hotel (5a Avenida y 248, Santa Fe; tel 33-1150 to 56, fax 33-1149). Cubanacán runs two restaurants, Papa's and Fiesta, but neither is worth a special journey.

For some Cubans this is a chic place to be seen, and it is also a mecca for prostitutes and jineteros in search of rich pickings. If you are lured to the marina by curiosity, take plenty of money — drinks are $5 at the hotel bars and an hour's fishing trip will cost $25. You would do better to explore the more pleasant beachside resort of Playa Baracoa, a few miles west.

Ernest Hemingway Museum. The Nobel prize-winning writer chose to live seven miles (11km) southeast of Havana in the suburb of San Francisco de Paula. His house, Finca La Vigía, just beyond the new ring motorway (Calle 100), is now

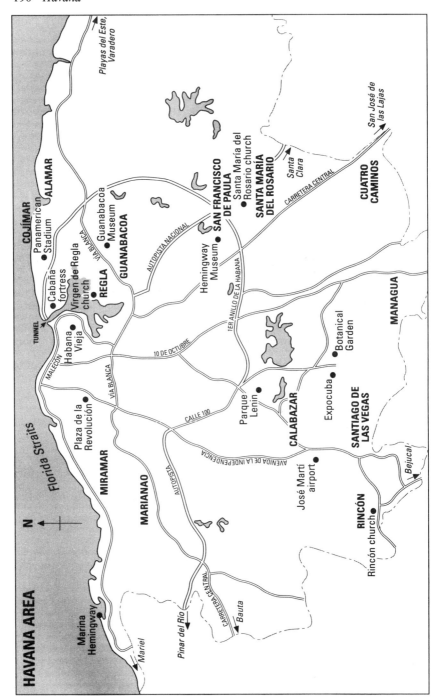

HAVANA AREA

Florida Straits

N

Marina Hemingway

Mariel

Pinar del Río

Bauta

CARRETERA CENTRAL

AUTOPISTA

MIRAMAR

MARIANAO

Plaza la Revolución

MALECÓN

VÍA BLANCA

CALLE 100

10 DE OCTUBRE

TUNNEL

Habana Vieja

Virgen de Regla church

REGLA

Cabaña fortress

COJÍMAR

ALAMAR

Panamerican Stadium

GUANABACOA

Guanabacoa Museum

VÍA BLANCA

AUTOPISTA NACIONAL

Playas del Este, Varadero

Hemingway Museum

SAN FRANCISCO DE PAULA

Santa María del Rosario church

SANTA MARÍA DEL ROSARIO

Santa Clara

CARRETERA CENTRAL

San José de las Lajas

CUATRO CAMINOS

1ER ANILLO DE LA HABANA

Botanical Garden

MANAGUA

Expocuba

Parque Lenin

CALABAZAR

SANTIAGO DE LAS VEGAS

AVENIDA DE LA INDEPENDENCIA

José Martí airport

RINCÓN

Rincón church

Bejucal

the Museo Ernest Hemingway. To reach it, take the Carretera Central to San Francisco de Paula and turn left opposite the post office. A short lane leads to the gates. Opening hours are 9am-4pm, until noon on Sunday and closed on Tuesdays. The museum may close on wet days — the staff say it is to avoid churning up the grounds.

The house, built by a Catalonian named Miguel Pascal Baguer in 1887-88, is set in extensive and well-kept gardens. Hemingway rented the house in 1939, and bought it outright in 1940. Finca La Vigía is a moving tribute to the man who championed Cuba, and contains some of his original manuscripts. With drinks and magazines left scattered randomly around, it is exactly as it was when he left the island in 1960 (the year before he shot himself in a cabin in Sun Valley, Idaho). Unfortunately, the closest you can get is to peer through the windows and doorways from the verandah. Due to earlier thefts by souvenir-seekers, a team of staff is devoted to keeping visitors out of the house itself, and you can't even take pictures of the interior. The layout of the house and the size of the rooms, however, is such that you can get a reasonably good view of the contents.

In the garden are the graves of his dogs, plus a pool (no swimming allowed). Best of all are the views, with Havana in the distance. The estate takes its name from the phrase *puesto de vigía* (look-out post), from the days when military commanders used the hillside for surveillance.

Cojímar. Six miles (10km) east of Havana, this small fishing village is where Hemingway spent much of his time and based his classic *The Old Man and the Sea*. A bust of the writer overlooks the harbour. Locally, Cojímar is more famous for the rafters who, over the years, have risked their lives in their attempt to escape Castro's Cuba; a strong current off the coast made Cojímar a favourite starting-point. The local people still talk about the shooting of two *balseros* in 1993 and the crazy scenes in September 1994, when thousands of Cubans set off across the Florida Straits. A small fort on the waterfront, now a military post, was once vital in deterring would-be rafters.

The odd coachload of tourists descends on Cojímar to visit the Hemingway haunts, but it remains an insuperably sleepy place — perfect for escaping the rigours of city life. Local kids swim off the small beach, while across the bay loom the high-rises of Alamar, not a pretty sight. The most striking structure is the huge pink mansion high above the town, which on Saturday nights functions as the Rockateca Metalica from 9pm to 3am.

La Terrazza de Cojímar restaurant (Calle Real 161) was a favourite haunt of Hemingway. You can sometimes follow the Hemingway tradition and enjoy *arroz con bacalao* (rice and salt cod), but you're more likely to meet other tourists and well-to-do city dwellers than local fisherfolk. One man you might encounter calls himself Gregorio Fuentes, and says he is the 98-year-old former skipper of Hemingway's boat, *Pilar*. He often lunches at La Terrazza, and at other times can be found at his home on Calle Pesuela number 209 — between Buena Vista and Carmen. From the pink mansion (see above), go left on Calle 5 for one block then right for three blocks. His is a small modern bungalow. He welcomes visitors, and talks animatedly about 'Papa' before asking for a hard-currency donation. The authors of this book have never seen so sprightly a nonogenarian, but are unable to specify his precise date of birth because Compañero Fuentes himself says he cannot recall it.

Bus 58 to Cojímar leaves from the square just west of Hotel New York, a couple of blocks west of the Capitol, though you can also pick it up at the top end of the Prado. The journey takes about 20 minutes, past the main Pan-American stadium and a string of firing ranges.

SOUTH OF HAVANA

If your visit is confined to Havana, at least try to make time to see a slice of 'real' Cuba. This can be found in several towns in the environs of the capital, including Santiago de las Vegas and Bejucal, described below. The places described below lie south and southeast of Havana, and can easily be combined in a day trip by car; by bus it would be difficult.

Parque Lenin. This huge park, reclaimed from marshland and larger than Havana's city centre, lies seven miles (11km) south of the city. It was at one time a highly popular place for rest and recreation, but the transport problem of recent years means that now it is often deserted. Many of the facilities barely function any more, though some areas spring to life at weekends. There are plans to revamp the whole place, but it will take some time to eliminate the aura of neglect.

The easiest way to get there is by car or taxi; the Parque Lenin is just south of the ring motorway, and is well signposted. An excellent map of Parque Lenin exists, but it has only ever been seen on sale in the kiosk at the Palacio de la Artesanía in Old Havana.

The northern part of the park is lovely walking or cycling territory. You could once upon a time hire a horse at the Escuela de Equitación, just past the Cafetería Los Ponies, but at the time of going to press no animals were to be seen. Another equestrian centre, the Club Hípico Iberoamericano, is aimed at more serious horsemanship. Nearby is a modest little amusement park, whose prime attraction is the (quite) big wheel. Further east is the drive-in cinema (Autokine), which might be a splendid place for a night out — one day. At the south end of the park is the Paso Sequito lake, where you can hire boats and explore other diversions, such as an art gallery and ceramics workshop. There is also a splendid aquarium, and one of the world's last monuments to Lenin.

Cafeterias are dotted around the park, but most have nothing to sell. If you are moderately hungry, you should make a beeline for Las Ruinas, in the southeast corner. Don't fail to have a wander round this extraordinary place, even if you don't want to eat: see page 168.

Just west of Parque Lenin and also well worth exploring is **Calabazar**. Despite having been swallowed up by Havana, this small town has a thoroughly provincial feel.

ExpoCuba and the Botanical Gardens. These places face each other across a road south of Parque Lenin. ExpoCuba is one of Castro's proudest achievements, a permanent exposition of Cuban successes in industry, along the lines of the Exhibitions of Economic Achievement once found all over the USSR. A cross between an industrial estate and a theme park, the exhibition has been rendered lack-lustre by the economic climate, but it is still interesting to tour the pavilions and play on some of the hands-on exhibits. There are frequent special events and visiting exhibitions.

A train used to run direct to ExpoCuba from Havana's Central Station, but now you must make do with the taxi bus, which departs from outside the same station at 10am, noon and 3pm at weekends. A private cab will charge about $10 for the journey.

Botanic Garden: the Jardín Botánico Nacional (tel 44-8334/8743) is the largest of its kind in Latin America, covering an area of 30 hectares and incorporating over 20 miles (32km) of road. It is clearly impossible to take care of such a huge park, and some of the trees and shrubs look positively forlorn. One visitor compared it to Kenyan scrubland (adding, mischievously, that it would make a wonderful golf course). However, certain parts have been well maintained, such as the Japanese garden, and there are many endemic species. The $3 admission fee will buy you the service of a guide, who will show you the best bits; there is an open-sided buggy for those without their own vehicle. If you'd like more independence, take your bike and a picnic. The gardens are open 8.30am-5pm Wednesday to Sunday. April and May are the best months to visit.

Santiago de las Vegas. This small town, a couple of miles south of the airport, has all the attributes of a Cuban town anywhere on the island. You can get one of several buses from the outskirts of the capital or the airport to Santiago. Walk a few blocks west from the crossroads on the main road to the town square (look for the church above the rooftops). Santiago's Parque Central is especially busy at dusk, when the locals gather to promenade. Along the pedestrian precinct which leads from the main square there are street stands selling trinkets and snacks, and you can buy delicious *guarapa* (sugarcane juice) at the market.

El Rincón: on the night of 16 December every year, El Rincón — a couple of miles southwest of Santiago de las Vegas — is the focus of an extraordinary procession. The Day of San Lázaro, dedicated to the patron saint of the sick and one of Cuba's most venerated saints, draws thousands of people. Some go for the spectacle, others simply to break the monotony of daily life; in recent years, the open expressions of frustration with the regime during the midnight mass have provided an added attraction. The police turn out in force, with water cannon and reinforcements at the ready, but there has never been any serious rioting.

Only a small minority of people express an intense religious fervour, but they do so in a startling way. Sick or troubled pilgrims drag themselves prostrate along the ground, often with chains or stones tied to their feet, all in an effort to persuade San Lázaro to answer their prayers. Most pilgrims embark on this grim journey in Santiago de las Vegas; although the distance to El Rincón is short, by the time they reach the church, many of them are in agony, their legs raw and bleeding.

The scene in the church, chaotic with people, flowers and candle smoke, is as bizarre as that outside. Spirits run high, with singing and cries of 'Viva Lázaro', 'Viva Cristo' blending with exhortations over the public address for people to remove their baseball caps and put out their cigarettes. Meanwhile, at the alter, pilgrims are blessed by the priest, often then to be carried away, exhausted, by friends. Elsewhere, people perform private acts of devotion, lighting a candle and quietly reciting a prayer.

Bejucal. This village, 5 miles (8km) south of Santiago and 20 miles (32km) from the capital, is well worth a visit if you aren't going to have much time to explore the interior. Bejucal's main square is thoroughly provincial, with the usual gaggle of men getting drunk in one corner. The museum in the old town hall doesn't have much to show, but it's an attractive building. There is more to look at two blocks away in the town's second square, including the 18th-century parish church, an old cinema and El Gallo restaurant. Housed in an attractive colonial building with fine furniture, El Gallo serves excellent and cheap food, and the staff are great. Wash your meal down with an infusion from the tea shop on the square.

San Antonio de los Baños. If you fancy a weekend break in the country, San Antonio de los Baños, about an hour's drive southwest of the capital, is not a bad place to choose. This is largely because you can stay at **Hotel Yagrumas** (tel 4460/63, fax 33-5011), which sits in a lovely spot just north of the town, overlooking a river with high wooded banks. It has a decent-sized swimming pool, the rooms are comfortable and the food not at all bad. Prices are fixed all year round — $45 for a double, $35 for a single, with buffet meals served in high season.

You can hire rowing boats ($1 per hour) or go on trips by motor boat, and there are also bikes for hire. Bejucal and Santiago de las Vegas, for example, are within cycling distance. This part of Havana province is also where some of Cuba's best tobacco is grown. The Santa Rosa and Sierra Maestra plantations are just south of San Antonio, along the Güira road and past the country's main air force base. While the plantations are not used to receiving tourists, the managers are generally very happy to show you around. Most of the workers in these *campamentos* are young people who have been mobilised from Havana. January or February is the best time to visit.

Santa María del Rosario. This is a delightful village in its own right, but the jewel of Santa María del Rosario is its 18th-century church which, along with the parish church in Remedios (see page 259), is one of the finest small colonial churches in Cuba. There are some fine Baroque altars in carved and gilded wood, a lovely pulpit and simple but attractive alfarje ceilings. The murals are the work of José Nicolás de la Escalera (1734-1804), Cuba's most accomplished Baroque painter. You need to time your visit carefully since the church is only open for mass, at 4pm on Thursday and Sunday.

Simple food and drink is available at El Mesón, in a restored colonial house across Santa María's leafy square.

GUANABACOA

Given the dreary surroundings of industrial complexes and suburbs, you may be pleasantly surprised by Guanabacoa's depth of history. The town, founded on the site of a thriving aboriginal community, is one of the oldest Spanish settlements on the island. It prospered on the back of the slave trade, processing hapless immigrants before despatching them to labour in the fields, and the town's wealth of fine churches attests to the fortunes made here. Its resistance to British occupation is still celebrated. While Guanabacoa has been swallowed up into the sprawling municipality of Havana, it manages to feel totally separate from it.

Guanabacoa's finest churches date from the 18th century. The **Parroquial Mayor**, which overlooks the main square, is rather plain compared with the other churches in the town. However, it has a magnificent gilded altarpiece that is one of the finest of its kind in Cuba, and a well-preserved alfarje ceiling. The church is open 8am-noon and at 8pm for mass.

The **Church of Santo Domingo**, near the corner of Calles Lebredo and Bertemati, about three blocks east of the main square, was constructed around the same time as the main parish church, but is altogether different. It has several exquisite altars, decorated with murals and painted woodwork, and an unusual alfarje that is split into many different sections, creating the effect of a cupola. The adjacent monastery has undergone substantial restoration, but the church itself is in excellent condition. Mass is held daily at 8am, but if you ask nicely, someone should be willing to let you in at other times.

The other church not to be missed in Guanabacoa is the **Church of San Francisco**, founded illegally by a group of Spanish missionaries in 1797. The huge monastery, recently painted an astonishing combination of pink and blue, is now a school, but the church continues to function. The highlight is the alfarje, more delicate and more decorative than the others you'll see in Guanabacoa. The church is four blocks southwest of Parque Martí, near where Calles San Francisco and Máximo Gómez meet. It is open 8am-noon, 3.30-5pm and 6-9pm.

Guanabacoa's other main landmark is the **Municipal Museum**, housed inside an old mansion at Calle Martí 108, between San Antonio and Versalles. Most of the exhibits concern the history of Guanabacoa, but of greatest interest are the rooms devoted to the Afro-Cuban cults. The guides are well-informed and will help you unravel the complexities of Santería, Abakuá and Palo Monte. The museum is open 10.30am-6pm Monday to Saturday (closed on Tuesday) and 9am-1pm on Sunday. The Afro-Cuban theme continues up the road at the **Bazar**

de los Orishas, a complex of shops selling art and crafts. The courtyard bar is a good place to take a break.

To reach Guanabacoa from Havana, try taking bus 3 from the square just south of the Capitol, though a couple of other services that stop at the northern end of the Prado also serve the town. There is an Infotur office opposite the Parroquial Mayor, but for a map of Guanabacoa you should ask at the museum.

ALAMAR

Many foreign dignitaries find this new town, nine miles (15km) east of the tunnel, a compulsory part of their visit. The Cuban government, and many of the people, take great pride in this post-revolutionary model settlement built entirely by micro-brigades of volunteer workers — the first of its kind to be built. As a tribute to single-minded determination by a people, it is indeed impressive. As a sight for visitors, however, you may be distressed by its bleakness. The blocks of flats look as though they were built overnight, and little thought has been put into enhancing the environment; you get from one hyper modern building to another on dirt tracks. Furthermore, little thought has been put into social and cultural amenities.

EASTERN BEACHES — PLAYAS DEL ESTE

Despite the aesthetic drawbacks of shabby beachside hotels and unimaginative apartment blocks, the Playas del Este have all the necessary ingredients for a seaside sojourn, including mosquitoes. The hotels are adequate, the beaches clean and the water clear. **Santa María del Mar,** just 30 minutes from Havana, has a fine beach and is the most popular among foreign tourists. But there is no residential area, so it is completely dead out of season. Nearby **Guanabo** is a proper community and is much livelier than Santa María del Mar, though the beach is not as good.

Lying beyond Alamar, the eastern beaches are easily reached along the Vía Blanca. If you can fight your way on, bus 400 from the junction of Agramonte and Glória (near the railway station) will take you to Playas del Este for 40 centavos; ask fellow passengers to tell you where to get off. Opting for a taxi is not a bad idea, and is not too expensive; colectivos can be hired across the road from the bus stop in Havana.

Santa María has a large but uninspiring selection of hotels, mostly three-star, charging $40-50 for a double room, $30 for a single. They are scattered the length of Avenida de las Terrazas, within a stone's throw of the beach.

Hotel Itabo: at the eastern end of Avenida de las Terrazas (tel 0687-2581), with a decent pool and reasonable restaurant. One reader, however, complains of 'truly dreadful evening entertainment and very high-profile prostitute activity in the bar — more akin to a Bangkok brothel'.
Hotel Atlántico: between Avenidas 11 and 12 (tel 0687-2551/2561). One of the better choices, close to the beach with a popular swimming pool and disco.
Villa Las Brisas: Calle 11 between Avenidas 1 and 3 (tel 0687-2469). A quieter option, set in pleasant gardens away from the seafront.
Villa Los Pinos: between 5 and 7 (tel 0687-2591). Quiet, close to the beach. A reasoable choice.
Aparthotel Las Terrazas: corner of Avenida de las Terrazas and Avenida de las Banderas (tel 0687-4910). A grim, five-storey block and best avoided.

The best hotel in Guanabo is the Hotel Miramar (Calle 480 y 9A), six blocks from the beach, which charges $30 for a double; facilities are simple but all rooms have balconies, and it has a pool and real live Cuban music. Among the alternatives, all on Avenida 5, are the Gran Vía (at 462; tel 0687-2271), Villa

Playa Hermosa and Cabañas Cuanda's, both at Calle 470, just south of Avenida 5 (tel 0687-2774).

The beaches stop beyond Guanabo, but then begin again. Beyond some rather unpromising countryside and, strictly speaking, the limits of the Playas del Este, is **Playa Jibacoa**. This consists of a series of inlets backed by verdant cliffs, with a reasonably rich coral reef offshore, and is the least spoilt of all those within easy reach of Havana. More popular, however, is **El Abra**, a short distance further east. In a cleft in the cliffs 40 miles (64km) from Havana, this is one of the country's best campsites (tel 83612), run by Cubamar and geared for the international market. The facilities are excellent, with horses, bikes and mopeds for hire, swimming pool, telephone service, etc.

PROVINCE OF HAVANA

Whoever mapped out the provincial boundaries of Cuba in 1974 left the Province of Havana with little of which to be proud. The city swallows up almost everything of interest to the traveller, from the Hemingway Marina in the west to the beaches of the east. The neighbouring provinces of Pinar del Río and Matanzas have better scenery and more charming towns. The Province of Havana is largely regarded as somewhere you have to pass through to get to the good parts of Cuba. Nevertheless, in between the grimy industrial complexes and road and rail links, there are some reasonable beaches and ordinary-but-pleasant towns. This section points out the highlights starting west of the capital and sweeping anticlockwise to the border with Matanzas. As you travel through, look for some of the intriguing placenames: settlements called Libre, Mango Dulce and Abraham Lincoln.

The provincial capital of **Bauta** lies astride the Carretera Central southwest of Havana. It is a scruffy little town whose only claim to fame is as administrative centre of the province. Due north, across the autopista to Pinar del Río and about 13 miles (20km) west of Havana, is **Baracoa**, a delightful seaside town with attractive wooden houses. Fringed by woodland, away from the bustle of the capital, this is a fine place to relax; there is a beach a short distance east.

Going west you cross the Banes river; just the other side is Playa Banes, rather too dirty a beach to be much fun. The highway continues to the port of **Mariel**. It was from here that the fleet taking thousands of disaffected Cubans sailed to Florida in 1980, in the so-called Mariel Boatlift (see page 20). There seems no reason to visit this ugly port, permanently covered in dust because of the nearby cement factory. Beyond Mariel the scenery gets more interesting, with the roads winding through hills and villages towards the province of Pinar del Río. **Cabañas** is a lovely spot on the bay of the same name, just before the provincial frontier. See page 220 for further details of what is a fine route west.

Guanajay, southeast of Mariel, is another fairly anonymous town on the Carretera Central. **Artemisa**, 8 miles (12km) south on the same highway, has a little more character, and you can visit the ruins of La Bellona, a 19th-century sugar plantation; the main house and slaves' quarters are still visible. Continuing south, you can turn off towards **Playa Majana** for perhaps your first sight of the Caribbean. Although this beach is only 30 miles (48km) south of the Atlantic beaches on the north coast, the water is noticeably warmer. Luxuriant vegetation makes the surroundings pleasant, but getting around is a problem. There is no road running along the lush south coast, as there is in the north.

Moving east through a series of small towns you might feel that you've gone forty years back in time to somewhere lazy, hot and Latin. The quality of light at dawn and dusk can make even the ordinariness of these flatlands look enchanting.

You would be hard-pressed to see any sign of old glories in the town of **Batabanó**. Yet early in the 16th century it was capital of Cuba for a while, before administration was moved to the harbour of Havana on the north coast. It is a truly unremarkable town, having slid into comfortable anonymity since its brief burst of fame. Most people just pass through Batabanó on their way to the port of Surgidero de Batabanó, 2 miles (4km) south. From here boats and hydrofoils sail to the Isle of Youth; see the following chapter.

The east of the province is dominated by **Güines**, a town of about 30,000. It is surrounded by industrial enterprises and ugly new districts for which the picturesquely crumbling old town centre doesn't quite make up. Güines, and the neighbouring towns of San José las Lajas and San Nicolás, are backwaters these days since the autopista has taken away traffic and people.

Along the north coast, there is little to attract other than the beaches at Playas del Este and El Abra, described in *Further Afield*. Around **Santa Cruz del Norte** there is little but industry and pollution, some of it pumped from the plant which manufactures Havana Club rum. Onshore oil derricks pump low-grade crude, while gas being flared off creates a pervasive and sickly stench. Go to Matanzas, half an hour further east, instead.

The Islands

Cayo Largo

Cuba provides opportunities for holidays-within-holidays, escaping from the main island. Among its numerous offshore islands are two which are easily accessible. For the visitor, they present the opportunity for a little island-hopping without leaving the republic. The choice is between the largest island, the distinctly uncommercialised Isle of Youth, and the purely tourist-oriented Cayo Largo. If you are happy just lazing in the sun for a day or two with nothing more taxing to do than decide on the most tolerable place to eat, choose the latter; but if you wish to meet interesting people and see unusual sights, go for the Isle of Youth. You should make the same choice if you're short of money; Cayo Largo is expensive to get to and expensive to stay on, whereas the Isle of Youth is one of the cheapest regions in Cuba.

ISLE OF YOUTH
(Isla de la Juventud)

Shaped like a comma, the Isle of Youth is a former US colony which is now a revolutionary showpiece. It is said to have served as the inspiration for Robert Louis Stevenson's *Treasure Island*, though there is nothing really to support the legend; the author certainly never went there. Cuba's biggest offshore island is about the size of Greater London, and is 60 miles (100km) south of the mainland. It has a population of 100,000.

The Isle of Youth has had a chequered history. Columbus discovered the

204

island in 1494, when he called it La Evangelista, but colonisation was slow; for a couple of hundred years it served mostly as a base for pirates, its caves and swamps providing perfect hideaways. Later renamed Isla de los Pinos (Isle of Pines), its name was changed once again in 1978. At one time it was little more than a penitentiary, housing Fidel Castro among others; the huge Model Prison is one of the strangest sights in Cuba.

Nowadays the Isle of Youth is young and lively, home to many foreign students, predominantly from Africa. The cosmopolitan atmosphere, combined with the feeling of detachment from the mainland with all its problems, makes the island a relaxed place to spend some time. The Isle of Youth is in some respects more affluent than the rest of Cuba because of the government's policy of encouraging settlement there, though the small number of tourists means that local people have scant opportunity to make extra cash.

The island is mostly low-lying, the highest peak measuring 310 metres (1,023 feet) above sea level. Most of the action is concentrated around the north of the island around Nueva Gerona, where the airport and several hotels are based. While the east coast is dominated by cliffs, the west coast has some fine sandy beaches. The south of the island is wild and unspoilt, difficult to explore but rewarding. The only place to attract a significant number of tourists is Hotel Colony — opened on 31 December 1958, just as the rebels were claiming victory over Batista. The wrecks and coral reefs offshore provide some of the best diving in the Caribbean. If you aren't a keen diver, the Isle of Youth is unlikely to reach the top of your list of priorities, but anyone with some time to spare and a desire to head off the beaten track, should consider making the short hop to the Island.

Arrival and Departure. You need a passport to travel between mainland Cuba and the Isle of Youth, so don't leave it behind at your hotel in Havana for safekeeping.

Sea: boats and hydrofoils depart from the port of Surgidero de Batabanó, on the south coast of the main island, 45 miles (70km) from Havana. Boats operate a day service outbound to the island, an overnight service back. The hydrofoil is much faster, taking just over two hours as opposed to seven or more hours, and is a cheap and pleasant way to travel from the mainland. The hydrofoils are Russian-built Kometas, a little rickety but large and comfortable. The Cuban name for them is *Lanchas Cometas* or *hidrodeslizadores.* The only catering on board is provided by attendants who bring round thirst-quenching refrescos and better-than-average rolls.

The views from the open-air section at the centre of the hydrofoil are good, passing through tree-covered cays as you near the island. But the final approach to Nueva Gerona is disheartening, through a river estuary lined with docks and industry. The boat or hydrofoil to Nueva Gerona drops you close to the centre of town, at Calle 31 between Calles 22 and 24.

Hydrofoil services are always oversubscribed, so it is best to book as far in advance as possible. If you intend to travel both ways by sea, reserve your return *(regreso)* trip at the same time as you book the outward *(ida)* journey. There is a lot to be said for travelling at least one way by air (see below), since it is much faster and also has good views.

Hydrofoils depart from each port four times a day, twice in the morning and twice in the afternoon. The fare is $8 each way, plus $3 for the bus link with Havana. The boat leaves Surgidero de Batabanó at 9am, arriving in Nueva Gerona at 5pm. The return journey departs the Isle of Youth at midnight, reaching the mainland at around 7am. There are no cabins; everyone stretches out on chairs or benches. The fare is $4 each way. Note that currently there are no boats back to the mainland on Saturday, Sunday or Monday, so be sure to check before you make your plans.

From Havana, connecting buses depart from the Terminal Aérea y de Ferries, a decrepit depot opposite the zoo on Avenida Kohly. They leave three hours before the boat or hydrofoil departure time. Information can be sought and tickets bought in advance from this terminal. At the time of going to press, it was rumoured that the venue was changing — so check in advance, or fly out to the island and return by sea.

If you want to return from Nueva Gerona by hydrofoil or boat and have no reservation, place your problem in the hands of the administrator of the port. Knock on the door marked *Admon* and ask there; travellers have in the past found that being foreign is sufficient reason for them to give you a seat. The official check-in time is one hour, and you must be sure to turn up at the port at least 40 minutes before sailing. After this time, places are given to those on the waiting list.

Air: there are two Cubana flights a day between Havana and Nueva Gerona, costing just $16 — the cheapest airfare in Cuba. The Russian Antonov aircraft used by Cubana carry only 44 people so, as with the hydrofoil, demand outstrips supply. Therefore do not risk turning up later than the check-in time specified on your ticket, and book your return journey before you leave the mainland. The Aerocaribbean service to Nueva Gerona is mainly for people on organised trips.

Sit on the left-hand side of the aeroplane for the best views. The flight takes you to Rafael Cabrera Mustelier airport, 3 miles/5km south of Nueva Gerona, a short bus ride from town. For information or reservations, go to the Cubana office in Nueva Gerona; it is next to the Hotel La Cubana at Calle 39 no 1415, between Calles 14 and 18 (tel 2531 or 4259). Office hours are 8am-noon and 1-4.30pm from Monday to Friday.

The town of Siguanea and the Hotel Colony are theoretically served by the airport at La Coloma, 25 miles (40km) southwest of Nueva Gerona, but because of fuel shortages the daily hop between the island's capital and La Coloma is presently suspended.

Getting Around. As elsewhere in Cuba, there is simply not enough public transport to meet the demand. To avoid interminable delays, hitch-hike, cycle or rent a vehicle — the road network is good and includes a short stretch of autopista between Nueva Gerona and La Fé. Havanautos and Transautos both have agencies at the Hotel Colony; try to book a vehicle before your arrival if possible.

There are no railways on the Isle of Youth. Buses radiate from the capital to the hinterland, and to the towns of La Demajagua, Siguanea and La Fé. To get any further south or east, you need to change buses at La Fé. It shouldn't be hard to find a taxi in Nueva Gerona, but elsewhere they are fearsomely difficult to find. In Nueva Gerona the central taxi station is at the corner of Calles 37 and 32. A despatcher works there during the day, ensuring that people heading in the same direction are squeezed into the same cab, and that pregnant or nursing women and the elderly get priority. Outside the capital, just flag down anything that moves.

NUEVA GERONA

The island's capital is not the prettiest town in Cuba, despite its riverside setting, but it is certainly an interesting place. Ranks of wooden houses give a strong sense of the American Midwest that stems from the influx of North American settlers at the beginning of this century. For a town of its size (around 30,000 inhabitants), Nueva Gerona has a remarkable amount going on. The Parque Central is as bustling as in anywhere in the country.

Accommodation. Unless you are travelling on an organised package, you will

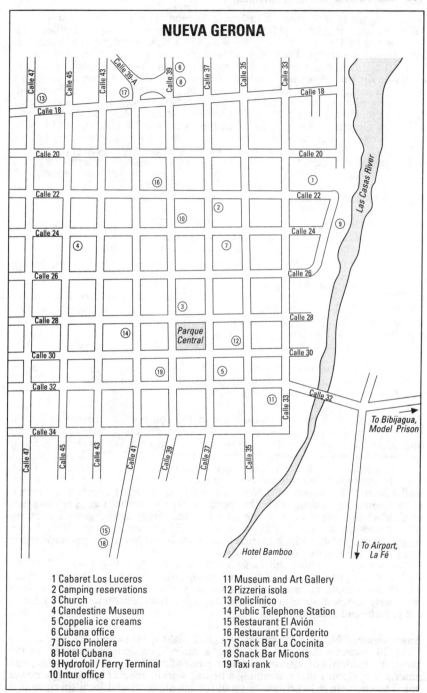

NUEVA GERONA

1 Cabaret Los Luceros
2 Camping reservations
3 Church
4 Clandestine Museum
5 Coppelia ice creams
6 Cubana office
7 Disco Pinolera
8 Hotel Cubana
9 Hydrofoil / Ferry Terminal
10 Intur office

11 Museum and Art Gallery
12 Pizzeria isola
13 Policlínico
14 Public Telephone Station
15 Restaurant El Avión
16 Restaurant El Corderito
17 Snack Bar La Cocinita
18 Snack Bar Micons
19 Taxi rank

certainly want to base yourself in Nueva Gerona. The best place to stay is the *Villa Gaviota* (tel 23290, 24486), a fairly new complex a couple of miles from town on the La Fé road. It charges around $30 a night (single) and $35 (double) for a room in a chalet. There is a bar and restaurant (serving decent meals), a post office, swimming pool, and even two ten-pin bowling lanes. Bikes are available for hire. The staff are laid back and friendly and the on-site tourist office is a good source of information and can organise trips all over the island.

The other hotels are peso establishments, most of which are not accustomed to taking tourists. In the town itself, try asking at *La Cubana*, at the north end of Nueva Gerona on Calle 39 between Calles 14 and 18, but you are likely to have more success at the rustic *Rancho del Tesoro*, about half a mile beyond the Villa Gaviota. A cabin for two at the Rancho (as it is known locally) costs about $15. The staff are friendly, the restaurant is passable. Another alternative is *Las Codornices Motel*, 3 miles (5km) from Nueva Gerona towards the airport.

There is a camping reservations office on the corner of Calles 37 and 22, which rents out tents at three or four campsites on the island.

Eating and Drinking. The best food on the Isle of Youth is sold for dollars at the Hotel Colony. Standards are lower in Nueva Gerona, but at least here you'll have the chance to eat outside your hotel. The capital's top restaurant is *El Corderito* at the corner of Calles 39 and 22. Queues are not too bad and the food is perfectly adequate. Of a similar standard is *El Cochinito* at Calles 39 and 24. The most gimmicky restaurant is *El Avión*, on the south side of town on Calle 41 between Calles 38 and 40. The tables are inside an old Cubana aircraft, but sadly the standard of catering is no higher than on the national airline. Nevertheless it makes for an interesting night out. Opening hours are 4pm to 11.30pm. The *Micons*, next to El Avión, is good snack territory; it serves refrescos which actually taste of fruit. The local branch of *Coppelia* is on Calle 37 between Calles 30 and 32.

Nueva Gerona is about the only place in Cuba where you might reasonably hope to put together a decent picnic. The block enclosed by Calles 24, 33, 26 and 35 contains a well-stocked market.

Exploring. Starting by Las Casas river in the southeastern corner of Nueva Gerona, there is a pair of lovely colonial houses on Calle 32 between Calles 33 and 35. One is an art gallery, the other a museum. The contents are less impressive than the surroundings, which are splendid. One block northwest is the main square, with the island's oldest church in one corner and the Town Hall, formerly the Spanish military headquarters. Continuing to the corner of Calles 24 and 45, you reach the *Museo de los Clandestinos*, a fascinating collection of memorabilia dealing with the build-up to the revolution. The museum establishes the importance of the island in the struggle, and gives context to other places on the island such as the Model Prison (see *Further Afield*). Down by the river, the boat which carried Fidel Castro and his fellow revolutionaries away from the Isle of Youth is on display.

You should also check out *Casa Marta* on Calle 22 between 43 and 45. As well as making papier maché dolls and clothes, which she sells in her small shop, Marta hosts santería ceremonies to which you may be invited. While these inevitably have an air of a performance rather than a ceremony, many locals are present and join in.

Entertainment. Nueva Gerona has two good night spots close to each other. On Calle 24 between Calles 35 and 37 is a disco. The doorman scrutinises the sartorial standards of visitors; shorts are not allowed. If you pass muster, you enter a low, gloomy hall resembling a British workingmen's club during a power cut. The clientele is largely made up of foreign students and local spivs, so it is a good place to meet people, and the choice of music is imaginative. It opens 6pm-midnight every evening but is liveliest on Fridays and Saturdays.

Better still is the *Cabaret Los Luceros*, by the river off Calle 20. This huge open-air venue stages a cabaret most evenings and attracts a predominantly young crowd (as well as large numbers of mosquitoes). Rum and sometimes food is served.

The *Casa de la Cultura*, on Calle 37 between 24 and 26, stages a mixture of events, including a regular salsa disco. For details of films, plays and and musical events throughout Nueva Gerona, consult page 2 of the local paper, *Victoria*.

Shopping. Local crafts are sold at a couple of places in Nueva Gerona. For ceramics, go to the workshop at Calles 34 and 55 or Tienda Juventud on Calle 39, next to the church; for jewellery made of semi-precious gems, there is another workshop on Calle 41 between Calles 18 and 20. The best bookshop in town is Librería Frank País on the corner of Calles 22 and 39.

Help and Information. *Medical care:* the Policlínico Comunitario at Calles 47 and 18 can treat most ailments; for more serious cases, go to the Héroes de Baire general hospital at the north end of Calle 39.

Post Office: corner of Calles 39 and 18.

Public Telephone Station: corner of Calles 41 and 28; note that it is difficult to get a line out from the Isle of Youth to the Cuban mainland, let alone to a foreign country. The highest chances are likely to be from the Hotel Colony.

FURTHER AFIELD

If you only have a couple of days on the island, you are advised to stay fairly close to Nueva Gerona. The best beaches on the island are in the southern half, but if you're desperate for a swim there is *Playa Bibijagua*, 5 miles (8km) east, to which there are buses and taxis. The prospect of enjoying a black sand beach may sound intriguing; but it is in fact more of a dirty grey, with lots of seaweed. The beach is unusual but, like the water, extremely uninviting. A bar provides refreshments and simple snacks.

Model Prison. Halfway between Nueva Gerona and Bibijagua there is a turn-off to the *Presidio Modelo*, a bizarre structure that is now a national monument. Commissioned as a high-security penitentiary by President Machado and built 1926-31, the design was taken from a similar prison at Joliet, Illinois, USA (as mentioned in Bob Dylan's *Percy's Song*). It was originally intended for common criminals, but later was used to house political prisoners.

Beyond the stylish guard houses and residences there are five huge circular buildings, rather like beehives, utterly incongruent with the surroundings. Gathered around the central store room and kitchen are the four prison blocks. Each consists of five storeys, with 93 cells per floor. In the 1950s revolutionaries such as Fidel Castro were imprisoned here with little hope of escape. For a time after the Revolution it continued as a prison for counter-revolutionaries, but has since become a museum. The complex is open to the public (Tuesdays to Saturdays 9am-5pm, Sundays 9am-1pm), and there is a fascinating museum, much of it devoted to the imprisonment of rebels involved in the attack on the Moncada barracks in Santiago de Cuba in 1953.

El Abra. Two miles (3km) south of Nueva Gerona on the road to the Hotel Colony (the continuation of highway 41) is a turn-off marked El Abra. A long avenue leads through orchards to a fine house on the edge of the Sierra Las Casas. It was home to the Sardá family, but its claim to fame is that José Martí lived here as an exile for nine weeks in 1870. Most of the contents, however, belonged to the Sardá family, and include a most impressive kitchen. Despite

ISLE OF YOUTH

the rather tenuous historical connections, it is worth visiting not least for its lovely position on the edge of the hills. It is open 9am-5pm from Tuesday to Saturday, 9am-1pm on Sundays.

HOTEL COLONY

The road southwest from Nueva Gerona leads past the new town of La Victoria to the village of Siguanea, which is effectively a dormitory town for employees at the tourist complex of the four-star Hotel Colony (tel 98181). The hotel is a grand structure, with excellent facilities, but is empty and depressing in low season. Double rooms cost $70 in low season, $85 peak.

The Hotel Colony is above all a diving centre, complete with hyperbaric chamber. The best diving area is around Cabo Francés, where there are over fifty marked sites. In addition to many varieties of coral, giant sponges and tropical fish, there are also a couple of sunken ships. Excursions are organised from the hotel to one or more of the 17 designated diving sites. Trips to the area can be arranged from Britain by Aquatours (0181-339 0040) and Scuba Cuba (01895 624100).

THE SOUTH

Most of the south of the Isle of Youth is uninhabited wood and swampland. The Lanier Swamp is the only other place in Cuba other than the Zapata peninsula where crocodiles are found; one of the few settlements in this area, Cocodrilo, is named after them. The residents of this small town are primarily fishermen, descended from immigrants from the nearby Cayman Islands who came here at the turn of the 19th century. Many of the older residents speak English as well as Spanish.

This region has some lovely white sand beaches, though only Playa Larga on the south coast and Punta del Este on the southeast are accessible; both are almost completely deserted, but chalets are starting to be built. You can snorkel or dive off the shore at Punta del Este, and also visit some caves nearby with decorations by Siboney Indians that are among the most important aboriginal paintings in the Antilles. Thought to date from around AD800, they were discovered only in 1910, by a shipwrecked French sailor. There are more than 200 pictures altogether. The circular and triangular shapes are probably representations of phases of the moon and the seasons, while the hieroglyphic-type signs may represent animals and faces. The caves are reached along a road from Cayo Piedra. The route is not well marked, so you might consider taking a guide; alternatively, trips are organised from the Hotel Colony.

CAYO LARGO

Measuring 15 miles (25km) by up to five miles (8km) wide, Cayo Largo is the most easterly of the Archipelago de los Canarreos. This strip of sand lies in the Caribbean 75 miles (120km) east of the Isle of Youth, and about 50 miles (80km) south of the Cuban mainland. Its southern coast consists of nothing but beach. There are three settlements on the island, each a self-contained tourist resort. Combinado, at the western end, is the port/marina/shopping complex, with occasional boats across to the beach of Playa Sirena. Cocodrilo, on the other side of the airport, is where most of the 'touristic installations' are located. The south-facing beach here is beautiful, and stretches east to the barren resort of Los Cocos, at the far end of the island's only road.

There are two ways of looking at Cayo Largo. From one point of view it is the ultimate idyllic tropical island, surrounded by clear blue waters and offering the chance to get away from it all and enjoy a pleasant antidote to the rigours of life in the rest of Cuba. If you are the sort of person for whom the chance to relax on the beach or enjoy watersports is a dream holiday, then Cayo Largo is a match for other Caribbean destinations. Lots of French and German holidaymakers seem content to spend a week or two at one of the hotels.

From another viewpoint, those in search of more intellectual stimulation may find the attraction wanes after a day. Any resemblance Cayo Largo might have had to an idyll ceased when hotels and bars started being built. You do not have to be of an overly cynical disposition to regard Cayo Largo as basically a big and uninteresting sand-dune littered with scrub, mangrove and the odd hotel.

As a device for extracting dollars from foreigners, it is extremely efficient. Some tour desks which sell excursions to the island are economical with the truth, and create the impression that all the sporting activities are free, but this is certainly not the case — everything from a sunbed to a jet-ski must be paid for.

The dollar is king on Cayo Largo. The only Cubans allowed on the island are those who work there. Access for foreigners is by air or private yacht only. The German airline LTU has a weekly flight from Düsseldorf via Holguín, while Aerocaribbean operates daily flights from Havana and Varadero. It is possible to buy the flight only (the one-way fare from Havana is $68), but it is cheaper to buy an all-in package. Such an excursion costs about $100 for a day, $175 for two days (one night) and $250 for three days (two nights).

The Day Trip. The standard one-day package trip to the island works as follows. Reservations need to be made at least the day before. The $100 fee covers most things apart from drinks and excursions. The pick-up from hotels starts at around 6am, and the flight is scheduled to leave at 8am. Upon arrival at Cayo Largo's airport, day-trippers are given a lobster cocktail snack together with an insipid fruit drink slightly contaminated by rum. You are then bundled onto a bus for a one-mile ride to Combinado, the island's harbour. It consists of a cluster of huts, shops and bars with a few old steamers dotted around. A boat takes you across an inlet to Playa Sirena, a beautiful strip of soft white sand. It is not ideal for children, however, as it slopes steeply away from the shore. Lunch is an expansive buffet, with barbecued main courses of steak or lobster. A free beer or soft drink is included.

Optional excursions include a boat trip to 'Iguana Island', a cay populated by big lizards. At $15 it seems rather extravagant given that iguanas can be seen ambling about on the main island anyway.

At about 3pm the boat returns to the port and passengers are consigned aboard a bus. A guide cheerfully advises that 'we are going to look at the hotels from the outside'. A quick drive around Cocodrilo, the main tourist complex, is followed by the return to the airport, where you sit around at the bar waiting for the flight. Tourists who have come from Varadero often feel rather unsatisfied, having exchanged one hotel/bar/shopping strip for another.

Some day-trippers have actually managed to return on a flight to a different destination, thereby using the day-trip as a means of getting from Havana to Varadero or even as far east as Las Tunas. You must expect to pay a good few dollars for the privilege.

Arrival and Departure. Few other airports double as discos, but Cayo Largo's terminal (code CYO) is also the Discoteca Blue Lake. Most arriving aircraft are greeted by a live band. The left-luggage facility at the airport charges $3 per item per day, but hotels and bars elsewhere on the island will look after baggage for a lot less.

The only other way for foreigners to arrive is aboard a private yacht. Skippers can moor at the island's main port of Combinado, which has adequate facilities.

Getting Around. Jeeps can be hired, though the attraction of renting for more than an hour palls on an island with only 10 miles (16km) of road. A free bus operates for the benefit of local workers; visitors can usually hitch a ride on it. Tourists are mostly ferried around on minibuses, or crammed on to tractor-hauled trailers — giving at least a brief taste of what life is like in the real Cuba.

Accommodation. On tours involving overnight stays most tourists will be billeted at one of the four-star hotels, such as the *Villa Capricho*, which resembles a series of jerry-built huts, or the *Hotel Pelicano*, both run by Gran Caribe. You can reduce the price of your package, however, by choosing to stay at one of the island's three-star hotels, such as the pleasant *Villa Iguana* or the *Hotel Isla del Sur*, which is rather like an upmarket timeshare development. If you want to try calling one of the hotels direct, note that they all share the same telephone number: 79-4215.

People don't usually come to Cayo Largo to paint the town red, but most hotels now have their own clubs or discos.

Eating and Drinking. You are never far from a lobster in Cayo Largo. Indeed, the quality and abundance of all sorts of food is much higher here than elsewhere

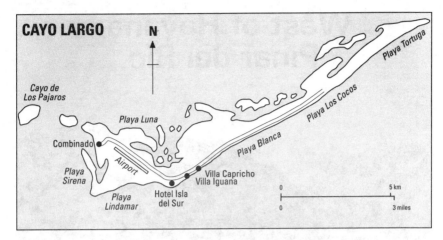

in Cuba, and it matches the quality of other Caribbean islands. So too do the prices for food and drink, about double those on the mainland.

Exploring. The days can be spent snorkelling, diving, fishing, windsurfing or simply lazing on the beach. A strenuous but pleasant day out is to walk the length of the island and back, or at least the nine miles (14km) of paved road between Combinado and Los Cocos. The most rigorous expedition around Cayo Largo is unlikely to take more than a day.

Wherever you are on the island, beware of voracious mosquitoes. Other wildlife is also plentiful. Playa Tortugas, towards the northeastern end of the island, is a breeding ground for sea turtles. Birdlife is also abundant and yachts can take visitors to the neighbouring Cayo Pájaros ('island of birds'). If you get the chance, take a trip to Cayo Rosario. This island, west of Cayo Largo, is about the same size as its neighbour but is completely undeveloped. It has a glorious beach and the calm water is lovely for swimming.

Cayo Largo is an excellent place for watersports. The waters which surround it are crystal-clear and usually calm. The best diving is off Cayo Largo itself and around nearby Cayo Ballenatos. The coral reef that skirts the southern shores of the island includes the protected black coral.

West of Havana: Pinar del Río

Tobacco Plantation

The finger of land pointing southwest from Havana towards Mexico's Yucatán peninsula is the province of Pinar del Río, a mainly agricultural province whose lush and undulating landscape is in places more reminiscent of South East Asia than of the Caribbean. The area is less developed than the eastern part of the island, and the sensation of living in a time warp has been enhanced by the greater reliance on oxen and horses as the principal source of power and transport. The standard of living is low compared to the rest of Cuba, and visitors should expect fewer creature comforts than in other parts of the island.

The population of the area is around 600,000, a small percentage of the total given that this is the country's third-largest province. Pinar del Río is devoted largely to the production of tobacco, with miles and miles of tobacco fields, thatched barns *(vegas)* where the leaves are dried, and factories where the dried leaves are rolled into some of the best cigars Cuba produces; it is claimed that the tobacco grown in Pinar del Río is the best in the world. The highest quality leaves grow around San Juan y Martínez and San Luis in the western part of the province, an area known as Vuelta Abajo.

The Guaniguanico mountains run like a twisted, humpy spine through Pinar del Río. They split into two ranges, the Sierra del Rosario in the east and the more picturesque Sierra de los Organos to the west. The hills are threaded with a network of caves and subterranean rivers, some of which can be visited. Most of the towns and villages in the province are clustered between the north coast and the Carretera Central, which skirts the southern edge of the mountains. The central highway penetrates furthest into Pinar del Río, though the Autopista, which extends as far as the provincial capital, is faster. The best approach, however, is along the coastal road or Carretera Norte. The scenery improves steadily beyond Cabañas, as the road runs along ridges overlooking tiny thatched cottages, sugar fields and landscapes dotted with royal palms. There is little going on in any of the small towns you pass through, though the weekend rodeo at Bahía Honda attracts people from all over the area; rodeos are not held every weekend, but are well worth watching if you get the chance. As scenic as the countryside is, be circumspect about taking pictures since this route crosses a military zone and photography is strictly forbidden. The north road is virtually traffic free, but look out for huge carts of sugar cane, which lurch around corners periodically.

The north coast of the province is sheltered by the collection of small islands which make up the Archipelago de los Colorados. The mainland coast is edged with sandy beaches, but most are completely undeveloped; they look set to stay that way since most development is taking place at the eastern end of the island. Cayo Levisa is pushed as one of the main attractions in the province, but the focus of interest in western Cuba still centres around Pinar del Río and the Viñales Valley.

SOROA

Soroa is about 90 minutes' drive along the Carretera Central, north of Candelaria. It is an interesting little complex, hardly a town, up in the hills of the Sierra del Rosario. Follow the signposts through the trees for a hilltop view over the surrounding countryside. There is a botanic garden, in which more than half the plants are endemic. Most famous is the orchid garden *(orquidería)*, with 700 types of orchids growing in it; of these more than a third are indigenous. Guided tours run every half hour from 9.30am-5.30pm (closed from 1.30pm to 4pm). Other attractions are a waterfall and Olympic-sized swimming pool, and there are horses for hire.

Up the hill from the orchid garden is the Castillo de las Nubes (Castle in the Clouds) restaurant. The quality of food is unpredictable, being better in high season, when the regular flow of visitors ensures a reliable supply of food.

If you want to stay in the vicinity, the two-star Villa Soroa (tel 82-2122, 2395/6) is 4 miles (6km) south of the complex, just off the Candelaria road. A newer and better alternative is La Moka Hotel, in a beautiful rural setting off the Carretera Central at Km 51, east of Soroa.

The forest around Soroa has Biosphere Hemisphere Reserve status.

MASPOTON

A track leads south over the mudflats from the town of Los Palacios on the Carretera Central to Maspotón, an area near the coast developed for tourists to go trout fishing and hunting. Visitors can shoot wild duck and pigeon from October to February. Guns can be hired from the Club de Caza at the resort by the day, and guides are available to take you to the best shooting areas. Be warned that by the time the cost of hire, guides and cartridges is added up, the bill is likely to be alarmingly high; you can get through $100 a day with ease. It is not suitable for late-risers, either, since your guide will encourage you to be in position to start shooting as early as 5am.

Accommodation at the Club de Caza is in bungalows which are basic but comfortable. Catering here is primitive even by Cuban standards, but if you have any ability at all at either hunting or fishing you can guarantee yourself a decent meal — anything you catch will be cooked for you in the hotel kitchen. The one-star Villa Maspotón in the nearby town of Los Palacios also has a few rooms (tel 96141).

La Güira National Park. By heading north at the Presa La Juventud ('Lake of Youth') to the spa village of San Diego de Los Baños, you can make a loop through pleasant scenery and look in on the **La Güira National Park**. This former estate is centred around an old mansion (now a museum) and some formal gardens. The whole place is in bad need of attention, but you can explore the woods and lakes, which are home to particularly rich birdlife. This is also one of the few places in Cuba where native deer are still found. On the edge of the park is **Los Portales Cave** which, in the heat of the 1962 missile crisis, Che Guevara used as staff headquarters for the western army, of which he was commander. It is now a campsite.

On Friday, Saturday and Sunday nights it is possible to stay at Cabañas Los Pinos, about 4 miles (7km) from the park entrance. The log cabins are very basic (i.e. no running water or electricity) but the setting is fantastic. The charge is $12 per night, including a meal at the equally basic restaurant. You would do well to take your own provisions. For more comfort, you should go to the recently refurbished Mirador hotel in San Diego de los Baños, which is next to (and run in conjunction with, by Servimed) the spa. It has excellent rooms and facilities, including a swimming pool.

If you return to the Carretera Central, the road runs through **Consolación del Sur**, with a fine Parque Central and gently crumbling colonial architecture. Alternatively, take the demanding route across the hills to the Viñales area.

CITY OF PINAR DEL RIO

The provincial capital was founded in 1774, considerably later than Cuba's other colonial cities, such as Trinidad. The buildings ranked along the arcaded main street are largely neoclassical. While not quite 'Paradise in the West,' as the tourist brochures would have you believe, Pinar del Río is a bustling place, with a pleasant, provincial feel.

City Layout. The usual grid system fails to work properly in Pinar del Río since too many roads meet at odd angles. The main street, José Martí, sweeps through the centre dividing north from south; its eastern continuation runs into the autopista to Havana. From west to east, the most important cross-streets are Rafael Morales, Isabel Rubio (which turns into the Carretera Central) and Avenida Comandante Pinares. Most places of interest are within a block or two of José Martí.

Tourist maps of Pinar del Río (city and province) are available for $1, most reliably from the tobacco factory: see *Exploring*.

Arrival and Departure. In a car or taxi, the motorway can take you the 110 miles (178km) from Havana to Pinar del Río in 2½-3 hours. The Carretera Central runs parallel, providing a slower but more interesting journey. In one direction at least, however, you should take the coast road from Havana via Baracoa, Cabañas, Bahía Honda, La Palma and Viñales. This route is virtually impossible to cover by public transport, even by stitching together a string of local services, so you'll either have to hire a car or hitch. Due to the dearth of traffic, be sure to set out early if you choose the latter option.

Buses arrive at the long-distance terminal on Calle Adela Azcuy between Cristóbal Colón and Pinares, a block north of José Martí. Most of these use the faster route along the autopista, taking about 3½ hours; buses along the Carretera Central take three or more hours. As usual, you'll be lucky to get on one though. To get anywhere east of Havana, you'll need to change buses in the capital.

Due to the demand for bus tickets, train is definitely the best way to travel between Havana and Pinar del Río, even though the daily service is one of the least reliable in Cuba. The journey can take anything from five to ten hours and

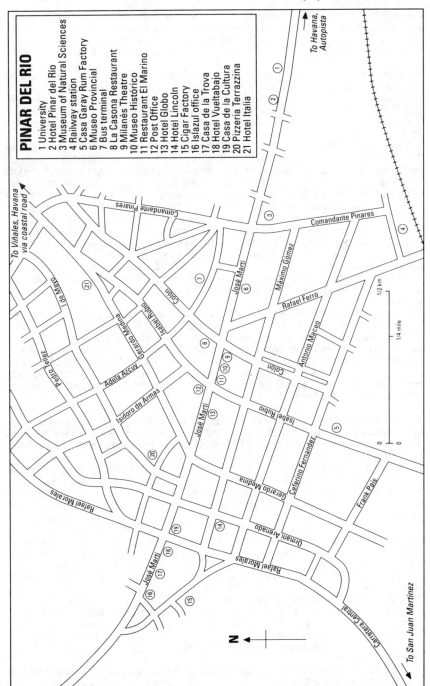

derailments are unusually common. Trains arrive at the railway station on Calle Ferrocarril between Rafael Ferro and Comandante Pinares. There are onward services to Guane, at the western extreme of Cuba's rail network. The town has just a couple of tourist taxis, based at the Pinar del Río Hotel.

Accommodation. The most expensive place to stay, and the one where package tourists go, is the three-star *Hotel Pinar del Río* (tel 5070/5077). It is dreary and inconveniently located on the main road at the eastern edge of town, although still within walking distance of the centre. A double room with hot water costs $30 ($24 in low season) and a single $23 ($20). The swimming pool was empty at the time of going to press.

The other hotels in Pinar, all of which deal in both pesos and dollars, are more central and altogether more authentic (i.e. strictly no-frills). One such is the *Hotel Globo*, on José Martí, next to the peppermint-coloured Poder Popular building. Originally built in 1917, the foyer and staircases are decorated in beautiful tiles. It is a little lacking in luxury (with water on tap only at certain times of day) and not particularly friendly. A peso establishment, rooms are rented to tourists for dollars: a double room with air-conditioning costs $22 (a single $15). The two-star *Vueltabajo*, on the corner of Rafael Morales and José Martí (tel 2303), offers similar facilities for $16 per double room; it has recently been renovated and is a pleasant and friendly place. The *Hotel Lincoln*, around the corner on Calle Ormani Arenado, is best left as a last resort. The only hotel to have a bearable restaurant (see below) is the *Hotel Italia* (formerly Occidente) on Calle Gerardo Medina. Expect to pay about $23 for a double room, $20 for a single.

If you prefer a rural setting, stay at *Camping Aguas Claras* (tel 2722), run by Cubamar. A former tobacco plantation, about 4 miles (6km) north along the Viñales road, it has a very pleasant setting, with chalets scattered around a swimming pool. Facilities are simple but good, ditto the restaurant; there are a couple of shops but these sell little in the way of food. The accommodation is cheap, with double chalets available for $18, $13 single. Day trips are organised, including on horseback, but be warned that you might feel isolated if you are without your own transport.

Eating and Drinking. The snakes and rats of the Viñales valley are said to be a local delicacy, but you are unlikely to find them on any menus in Pinar del Río. The restaurants serving the most edible food are the ones in the hotels, especially the Italia. Here, the main Florencia restaurant is overpriced (with main dishes for $5-7) but is at least a good deal less depressing than the adjacent Cafeteria Venicia, which has to be one of the gloomiest places in Cuba. Dinner is served from 6.30pm and to be sure of food and beer you should be punctual. Despite the existence of a menu there is unlikely to be more than one or two dishes available.

The best alternatives to the hotels are El Marino on Martí near the corner of Rubio and La Casona, nearby at the corner of Colón. Both are pleasant though the choice of dishes is small; turn up as soon as possible after 6.30pm. Otherwise try Pizzeria Terrazzina, on the corner of Calle 1 de Mayo and Antonio Rubio.

There are several cafés, which usually serve drinks of some kind and even a snack or two if you're lucky. Try the Coppelia ice cream parlour, on Gerardo Medina a block north of the main street, or the Esquinita bar (Isabel Rubio at the corner of Juan Gualberto Gómez), which is deliberately dark and conspiratorial — so much so that it looks closed even when it is not. Music is provided by the juke box (20 centavos for four plays, including some modern rock), but it is likely to be switched off if someone turns up with a guitar and feels like playing a few tunes.

The best place for snacks during the day is the market, which is south of the main street, off Calle Colón.

Exploring. The *Museo Histórico de la Ciudad* on José Martí provides a good introduction to the city without being particularly entertaining. Next door to it is the *Milanés Theatre*, constructed at the turn of the century like many of the finest buildings in the town. It is opulent, built entirely of wood, and has a seating capacity of over 500. A little further east is the *Museo Provincial*, which has the usual mixture of memorabilia, including some belonging to Enrique Jorrín, the creator of the cha-cha-cha. It also provides a place for exhibitions of regional art and holds evenings of music and poetry: a list of forthcoming events is posted outside. It opens 2-10pm Tuesday to Saturday, 6-10pm on Sunday.

One of the town's finest buildings is the Palacio Guasch, on the corner of José Martí and Pinares. Built between 1909 and 1914 for a wealthy citizen and given to the state by one of his descendants after the Revolution, it now houses the *Museo de Ciencias Naturales*. The eclectic Gothic-cum-Moorish building outshines the museum, but both are worth exploring. Don't miss the sculptures of prehistoric creatures in the courtyard. Opening hours are 2-10pm Tuesday to Saturday, 8am-noon on Sunday.

The provincial capital exists largely for the tobacco industry, but there is just one cigar factory. It is located below the handsome Plaza de la Independencia, near the western end of José Martí. A lot smaller than the factories in Havana, it has a much more intimate and relaxed atmosphere. As in tobacco factories across Cuba, the workers are read to from newspapers and books, but here local groups come and entertain them with music too. The cost of a tour is $2.

The other product for which Pinar del Río is famous is *guayabita*, a liqueur made by mixing a small fruit of the same name with spices and raw rum. *Casa Garay*, on Isabel Rubio between Ceferino Fernández and Frank País, is the only factory to make it, though it has been made in the region for over two centuries. Casa Garay is open for tours Monday to Friday and individual visitors will usually be accommodated. A small shop on the premises sells bottles of guayabita for $5 (as well as a bizarre range of other products, including Brillo pads and Spam). Fortunately, you are allowed to taste the drink before you buy any. Unfortunately, the sweet version (Guayabita Liqueur) is too sweet and the dry version (Guayabita Seca) is too dry, though both are more drinkable when diluted.

Entertainment. The best-known night spot in Pinar del Río is the open-air *Rumayor* nightclub and restaurant, on the Viñales road. The floorshow and music are second only to the top cabarets in Havana, and the restaurant boasts its own famous speciality — a spicy, grilled dish known as Chicken Rumayor. Try to go at a weekend, when the place is positively buzzing. Drinks are expensive, and the local habit is to sneak in your own bottle of rum. Buy one shot and a few soft drinks and try not to let the waiters see what you're up to.

La Cueva cabaret on Máximo Gómez, between Medina and Isabel Rubio, is not a patch on the Rumayor. More sedate musical evenings are held at the *Casa de la Trova* on José Martí between Comandante González and Rafael Morales, and you can even buy a bottle of rum to enjoy with the performance.

Sport. The local baseball team performs creditably at a national level. In the absence of much else to do in this corner of Cuba, the team is supported fanatically. Their home ground is the Estadio Capitán San Luis on the north-eastern edge of town, off the Viñales road.

Help and Information. The Isla Azul tourist agency has a surprisingly useful office at the western end of José Martí, which is open daily and even has maps. There is a late-night pharmacy at José Martí 50, adjacent to the Hotel Globo. The main post office is diagonally opposite.

THE VINALES VALLEY

With its dazzling scenery and incomparable tranquillity, the Viñales valley is one of the most beautiful places in the whole of Cuba. This part of the Sierra de los Organos range is scattered with large limestone formations, called *mogotes*, which date from the Jurassic period and are found in only a few places around the world, including Malaysia. One hundred and sixty million years ago they supported a plateau which long ago disintegrated, leaving only these rugged rock formations behind. They rise dramatically out of a dead flat landscape; in between the rich red earth is fertile and ideal for growing tobacco. And nestled amongst them, in the heart of the valley, is the spruce little town of Viñales.

This is a place to relax and do little. If you've been doing serious sightseeing in Havana, there is no better place to recuperate. You can spend all day admiring the views and enjoying the peace, and perhaps venturing out for the odd stroll. Walk along any country lane from Viñales and you'll come across a tobacco farm with its unmistakable thatched *vega*. The inhabitants of the Viñales valley are an incomparably gentle people, and most farmers will be delighted to show you around. The tobacco is sown later here than in Havana province, but since the sowing is staggered, harvesting lasts from January to March.

While you can visit Viñales as a day-trip from Havana, you should try to stay at least a couple of nights — not least because it has one of the best-located hotels in the country.

Getting There. The road from Pinar del Río is delightful, winding over hilltops for most of the 17 miles (27km) to Viñales. The bus service between the two towns is poor; tickets are issued on a first come, first served basis and you need to pick up a slip of paper with a number a couple of hours before the departure time. Hitching is good, however.

The journey from Havana via the autopista takes about three hours. If you follow the longer northern route, allow 3½-4 hours: the surface is generally good but there's much more to look at and the road is narrow. A private cab driver should agree to do the round trip from Havana for about $80.

Accommodation. In terms of facilities, there is not much difference between the hotels in Viñales; they are all three-star. The location is the deciding factor. Powercuts throw the valley into darkness on some evenings, but hotel rooms generally have an emergency light that runs off a generator.

Hotel Los Jazmines: off the Pinar del Río road a couple of miles south of Viñales (tel 82-93205/6). A handsome, pre-revolutionary hotel perched on a ridge above the valley, Los Jazmines is one of the main attractions of Viñales. The odd coachload of tourists apart (they are brought here to admire the view from the *mirador*), this is a blissfully quiet spot. You can while away hours simply watching life unfold in the valley below, taking the occasional dip in the glorious swimming pool. Rooms, each with a balcony, are a bargain at $25-30 for a single and $35-40 for a double. You can choose between the main building and the modern annex. The restaurant is adequate without being hugely exciting.

La Ermita: located on a hilltop east of Viñales, within easy walking distance of the town (tel 82-93204/08, fax 93294). La Ermita can't really compete with Los Jazmines, except in its proximity to the town. The views are pleasant, the staff friendly and the rooms reasonably comfortable, though the hot water supply is erratic. The swimming pool, which provides the focus of the hotel, is often murky and decidedly uninviting in low season. The food served in the dingy restaurant is thankfully not as bad as the surroundings. Double rooms cost $40 ($32 in low season), singles $30 ($22).

Rancho San Vicente: just north of the Cueva del Indio, a few miles north of Viñales (tel 82-93200/1). Unless Los Jazmines or La Ermita are full, there is no reason to stay in this badly located hotel; it is built by a rather gloomy stretch of road and has no view.

Eating and Drinking. There are two surprisingly decent restaurants in Viñales, *Las Brisas* and the *Casa de Don Tomás*, both on the main road; the latter, in a charming 19th-century wooden house, the oldest in the town, is the more congenial of the two. However, the paladar next to Las Brisas, at Salvador Cisnero 180, serves better food than both of these. This could be your one chance to eat guinea fowl or frogs' legs in Cuba. The restaurant by the Mural de la Prehistoria (see below) serves good traditional food, but caters mainly for tour groups.

Exploring. If you want to explore the area, ask around in Viñales or at the hotel about hiring a local driver, though there are few private cars in the town. Alternatively, you can hire a tourist taxi, of which there are several based in Viñales, usually to be found at Los Jazmines and La Ermita. They charge according to distance, plus $3 per hour — not bad value if you aren't travelling far.

Obtaining fuel in Viñales is almost impossible unless you buy it on the street from a local resident. The only reliable source is the Cupet petrol station on the eastern outskirts of Pinar del Río. Keep your tank topped up.

Cueva del Indio: just north of Viñales there are several caves which can be visited. Avoid the Cuevas de Viñales, which have been converted into a disco. By far the most impressive is the Cueva del Indio, 5 miles (8km) north of the town, which was used as a refuge by the Guanahatabey Indians following the Spanish Conquest, and much later by escaped slaves. You can explore the caves half on foot and half by boat, penetrating about a kilometre. Preparations are underway to open up a further 1,000 metres, thereby prolonging a marvellous but at present tantalisingly short experience. Admission is $2.

A farm next door to the cave has been set up for tourists, with guided tours laid on; the cock fights are not to everyone's tastes.

Mural de la Prehistoria: in Cuba you never know what awaits you around the next corner, and certainly nothing can prepare you for the sight of the 'Prehistoric Mural', hidden among a group of *mogotes* a mile or so southwest of Viñales. This gigantic evolutionary comic strip — beginning with an amoeba and ending with Socialist Man — was painted soon after the Revolution by Leovigildo González, a disciple of the well-known Mexican mural painter, Diego Rivera. Recently restored in lurid primary colours, it is a shockingly awful sight, particularly since the setting is so idyllic. The best way to enjoy this place is to visit early on or late in the day (before the tour groups arrive), and to turn your back to the hideous mural. If you want to join in the fun at lunchtime, the meals are excellent, usually consisting of pork, rice and beans, yuca and all the trimmings — washed down with Princesa, the local beer.

To reach the mural, follow the main road southwest out of town. After less than a mile a sign points off to the right.

Cayo Levisa: the pleasant white sand beaches on this small island off the north coast are the best in the area. They are not a patch on what lies further east but Cayo Levisa is still a good place to escape the crowds. Ferries serve the island twice a day from Puerto Esperanza, north of Viñales, the journey taking about 45 minutes. The three-star Villa Cayo Levisa, the only hotel on the island, is in bad need of renovation. At the time of going to press, the only way to visit was to go as part of an overpriced organised trip.

THE FAR WEST

Few travellers venture beyond the city of Pinar del Río, though a few cigar aficionados are attracted to the Vuelta Abajo area, Cuba's prime tobacco-growing region around San Juan y Martínez and San Luís. You don't have to be a cigar smoker to enjoy a visit to one of the plantations. The Meca del Tabaco cooperative in San Juan y Martínez is now well-geared to taking visitors around. They are most used to groups, but individuals are also welcomed.

As you continue west, the hills gradually peter out and the terrain becomes marshy. Guane is the end of the line as far as the western railway is concerned. Heading north, you reach Mantua, the site of an historic battle in the 1896 War of Independence. From here you could commence the return journey to Havana right along the north coast, but allow at least six hours driving time — the road is in a shocking state of repair.

Continuing west from Guane, beyond Sandino (with the two-star Villa Laguna Grande nearby), the Carretera Central reaches an end at the small town of La Fe. The distance from La Fe to the eastern end of the Carretera Central is 835 miles (1,340km). To the most westerly point in Cuba, the Cabo de San Antonio, is only 50 miles (80km).

The Guanahacabibes Peninsula, which juts out into the Gulf of Mexico west of La Fe, is one of the remotest parts of Cuba. It was the last refuge of the Cuban Indians as they fled the Spanish conquistadores, and is still almost completely covered in forest. Now part of Cuba's largest national park, and a UNESCO Biosphere Reserve, the peninsula is an important reserve for deer and wild pigs. The journey west to Cabo de San Antonio, skirting around the Bahía de Corrientes, is lovely. An unexpected find is the (three-star) hotel and diving centre at Playa María La Gorda, overlooking the bay. There is a fine beach here and the nearby coral reef and shipwrecks attract serious divers. There is little at the western extremity except a lighthouse, a couple of pleasant beaches, and the prospect of a long drive back.

Matanzas:
City and Province

Guamá

In the 19th century the province of Matanzas was the economic powerhouse of Cuba, the centre of sugar production and trade. As profits from the industry declined, the region hit upon hard times and fell under the shadow of Havana. More recently, the economic centre of the province has shifted east from the city of Matanzas to Cuba's largest resort, Varadero. But the province caters to a wide variety of tastes: with sun and sea at Varadero; history, art and architecture in the city of Matanzas; nature and wildlife in the Zapata swamp; and gloriously colourful inland towns.

There are three possibilities for the road journey east from Havana to the city of Matanzas. The old road is the Carretera Central, which takes you slowly (sometimes painfully so) on the inland route through numerous small towns. With a good map and a lot of luck, you could find a way through the sugar fields via Jaruco. Faster is the Vía Blanca, which skirts the north coast for the greater part of the journey and is a most enjoyable ride. Emerging from the Havana harbour tunnel, the road passes the turn-offs for Cojímar, Alamar and Santa María del Mar, all of which are described under *Havana: Further Afield*.

From the 60-kilometre marker the landscape becomes more attractive, as the Vía Blanca passes through rolling hills laced with streams, dotted with tall palms and thatched cottages. The frontier between the provinces of Havana and Matanzas is marked by a stunning viaduct, the highest in Cuba, where people often stop to take photographs. There is a broad valley on one side, the ocean

223

visible on the other. Less photogenic are the of oil derricks ranked along the shore further on. Inland from the city of Matanzas, there are dusty towns and villages where the horse is the dominant form of transport and the 20th century seems to be regarded as an irrelevance.

CITY OF MATANZAS

The nearest city to Havana, Matanzas provides many people with their first taste of the provinces and also a more accurate picture of what life in Cuba is really like. It is industrialised and run-down, but also thoroughly entertaining and rich historically and culturally. The approach from the west is stunning, as the Vía Blanca swings around the hilltop and the broad sweep of Matanzas bay stretches out before you. A billboard in the foreground of Castro looking heroic makes a good photo opportunity. Swinging down to the city and over the bridge, you encounter a grand wedge of an old palace which sets the scene for a crumblingly majestic city.

Matanzas means 'slaughter,' which probably stems from the town's early role as an abattoir and depot for meat awaiting shipment to Spain. From such unpromising beginnings grew a major sugar-trading port; in the mid-19th century, the area around Matanzas, Cárdenas and Colón produced more than 55% of the island's sugar. The city also became an important cultural centre and gathering place for intellectuals. Thankfully the title 'Athens of Cuba' is considered out of date, but Matanzas remains a lively arts centre. Past prosperity is evident in the heart of the city, though many buildings are in a sorry state of repair.

Matanzas is a manageable size, well-situated and with plenty to see — ideal for a stay of a few days. Furthermore, it is surprisingly free of tourists, though the odd group is bussed in to be whisked around a museum or two. Within Cuba, Matanzas has a bad reputation for crime, but few visitors encounter evidence of this. Most find only that the local people — known as *Mantanceros* — are very friendly.

City Layout. The San Juan and Yumurí rivers, which flow out into the Bay of Matanzas, divide the city into three districts: the main downtown area lies between them, with the district of Versalles to the north and Pueblo Nuevo to the south. The rivers are crossed by several handsome bridges; notice in particular the 19th-century rotating bridge near the mouth of the San Juan.

The street numbering system in Matanzas is bizarre. Odd-numbered streets run east-west, even-numbered ones north-south. But the starting point for the numbers must be some miles away since the centre of the city is at Calle 290 and Calle 83. To confuse matters further, every street has a name as well; those mentioned above are Calles Santa Teresa and Milanés respectively. Some streets have two names, pre-and post-revolutionary: Calle 79, the main shopping street, is now called Calle Contreras, but is also referred to by its pre-1959 name of Calle Bonifacio Byrne. To minimise confusion, in this chapter numbers rather than names are used. You can instantly pinpoint an address in Matanzas; the first three digits of the house number refer to the nearest cross street. For example, the Velazco Hotel at number 28803 on Calle 79 is near the corner of Calle 288.

For drivers, the nearest petrol station is on the road to Varadero, about two miles (3km) east of the city centre.

Arrival and Departure. *Train:* the coastal road from Havana is well worth taking, but another good way to and from the capital is on the Hershey train. It runs along the tracks laid by the American chocolate firm, Hershey, and is the only electric railway in Cuba. The journey in the ramshackle old train is terrific, taking you through plantations, numerous tiny villages, the lovely Yumurí valley and also Hershey itself, where smoking chimneys and water towers are visible

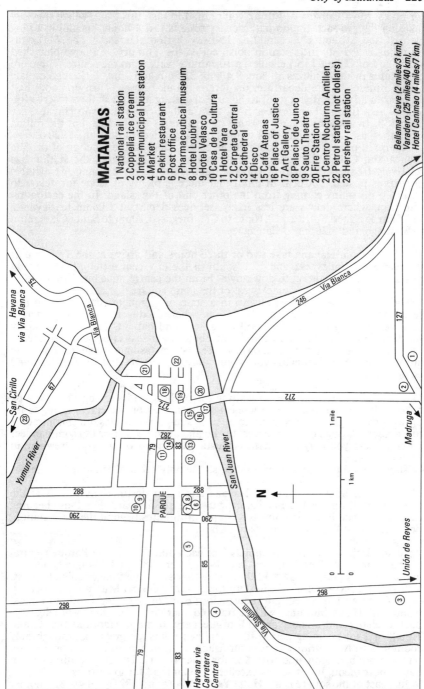

MATANZAS

1 National rail station
2 Coppelia ice cream
3 Inter-municipal bus station
4 Market
5 Pekin restaurant
6 Post office
7 Pharmaceutical museum
8 Hotel Loubre
9 Hotel Velasco
10 Casa de la Cultura
11 Hotel Yara
12 Carpeta Central
13 Cathedral
14 Disco
15 Café Atenas
16 Palace of Justice
17 Art Gallery
18 Palacio de Junco
19 Sauto Theatre
20 Fire Station
21 Centro Nocturno Antillen
22 Petrol station (not dollars)
23 Hershey rail station

Bellamar Cave (2 miles/3 km),
Varadero (25 miles/40 km),
Hotel Canimao (4 miles/7 km)

for miles. Most Cubans will think you're mad to take this train, which they say takes all day; in fact, the normal journey time is just 4 hours, including a long wait at the attractively crumbling halfway halt of Hershey. The Matanzas terminus is a dusty little station north across the Yumurí — a large blue shed at the end of Calle 67 in Versalles, a 10-minute walk from the centre. There are departures from Matanzas at 4am, 9.40am, 2.55pm and 9pm. Tickets go on sale 30-45 minutes before departure; the fare is about 5 pesos. Turn up about half an hour in advance if you want to be sure of getting a seat (ask for a reservation as well as a ticket). For services from the Casablanca terminus in Havana, see page 153. In addition, there are some tourist trains on the line, but the rolling stock they use appears identical to the normal service (built in the 1920s).

The main train station is south of the centre, close to the junction of the Vía Blanca and Calle 272. Astride the main line through island, the station has relatively frequent services to Havana, taking two or three hours. A timetable of sorts is posted, but bear in mind that there is plenty of scope for delays to build up on trains coming from the other end of the island. In the eastbound direction, where delays are less likely, services depart at 1.04am to Bayamo, 11.08am to Sancti Spíritus, 12.10pm to Cienfuegos, 4.10pm to Santa Clara, 6pm to Santiago and 8.20pm to Camagüey.

Bus: buses from Havana take two or three hours and arrive at the Terminal at the corner of Calles 298 and 127, south of the city centre (tel 7763). Several buses connect the station to downtown. From the centre, take bus 1 or 16 from the stop on Calle 79, one block west of the main square.

The bus station is almost always in a state of complete chaos, and no one seems to know when the next bus to anywhere is due to leave. In order to achieve anything you must be both persistent and patient. There are officially six departures a day to the capital, but obtaining a seat is not easy. In theory there are as numerous buses a day between Matanzas and Varadero, but these are irregular. For Cárdenas, you would do better to go first to Varadero and change there.

Colectivos: if you get fed up of waiting (or pushing and shoving), have a look outside the bus station, where there is usually at least one colectivo trying to fill up with passengers. Drivers tend to operate along fixed routes, most commonly to Varadero, though others run west to Havana. If you can afford to commandeer an empty car you may be able to persuade the driver to take you elsewhere in the province.

There are no turistaxis in Matanzas, so the only other alternative is to hitch.

Hitching: the hitching point for Havana and other destinations west is at the top of the hill on the Vía Blanca, near the Castro billboard. For those heading east, the official hitching point is a couple of minutes beyond the train station, near the turn-off to Colón and Santa Clara.

Accommodation. Two fine old hotels face each other across the Parque Central (Parque Libertad). The Velasco (Calle 79 number 28803; tel 4443), a handsome and cavernous building, sadly did not take tourists at the time of going to press. The **Hotel Louvre** (tel 4074), next to the Pharmaceutical Museum (see below), does. From an unmarked and inauspicious exterior, you step inside to a most wonderful 1850s building, with a fine old marble-topped bar, worn leather-backed chairs and a courtyard full of greenery. It masquerades as the 'Grand Hotel' in a forthcoming period film. The bedrooms are great too, though only room 4 is truly luxurious — it is furnished with French antiques. For this you pay $35 double, compared with $29 for other rooms. The elegant dining room has a short menu, but it serves excellent Cuban food for low prices.

Just east of the square is the **Hotel Yara** (Calle 79 no 28216; tel 4418), another glorious old building that has recently been renovated. Now a fully fledged tourist hotel, this is the most comfortable option in the centre of town.

If the Yara and Louvre are full, you'll have to try the three-star **Hotel Canimao** (Carretera Varadero 3.5km; tel 61014, 62415), a sort of Cuban Butlin's holiday camp 5 miles (8km) east of Matanzas. In fact this is not as bad as it sounds because the rooms ($35 for a double) and the food are reasonable, and the setting on the bend of the Canímar river is stunning. The river forms a dramatic gorge with limestone cliffs either side, and high above is one of Cuba's most impressive bridges. At the mouth of the Canímar is an 18th-century fortress called El Morrillo.

Eating and Drinking. The city-centre hotels serve an adequate breakfast, but they do other meals better. The Louvre, where *potaje de frijoles* and other traditional dishes are served for very reasonable prices, makes an excellent lunch stop if you're passing through. A good peso restaurant is the *Pekin*, just down the road on Calle 83, with good service, friendly staff and excellent main courses. The next best option for a sit-down meal is the *Años 30*, a moderately chic place on Calle 274 by the bridge across the Yumurí. On Saturdays it doubles up as a disco.

There are a couple of pleasant cafés on the main square, but the queues are too long for those without a whole day to spare. *La Viña*, in the southwest corner (Calles 83 and 290), usually opens 3-10pm and is a fine place for coffee or tea, but there is rarely any food available. Better still, head south to Calle 85, a pedestrian precinct where a string of kiosks sell all sorts of goodies such as ice cream, sandwiches and fresh fruit. Queues sometimes form but these are seldom long — note that the line tends to start about ten metres away from the relevant kiosk, so beware of pushing in. Nearby, at the corner of 87 and 298, is *La Gondola Cafetería*, a huge place with incongruous classical sculptures along the wall but never much in the way of food.

The *Café Atenas*, closer to the water in Plaza de la Vigía, is a good place to relax; it opens from 5pm, and takes dollars only. If you prefer to assemble a picnic then try the unmarked supermarket just around the corner from the main square (on Calle 288 between Calles 83 and 85). And for Coppelia ice-cream, head a mile south on Calle 272 to the branch at the junction of Calle 127, near the railway station.

Exploring. Matanzas is a pleasure to explore. The bustling main square and neighbouring streets are thoroughly entertaining, but it is equally rewarding to head into the quieter backstreets or along the river, where you find old men deep in a game of dominoes or young kids searching for crabs.

In terms of more conventional 'sights', the area between the Parque Central and the San Juan river is the centre of interest. Not to be missed is the *Museo Farmaceutico*, next to the Louvre Hotel at Calle Milanes 4951. This old pharmacy was founded in 1882 by a Frenchman called Triolet and was trading right up until the 1960s, when it became a museum. What remains is an extraordinary array of porcelain jars and bottles, many of which contain the original remedies, in addition to all the equipment used for preparing pills and potions. The museum opens 10am-5pm Tuesday to Saturday, 9am-1pm on Sunday. Admission is $1, which includes a guided tour (in Spanish).

Directly opposite on the far side of the square, the Liceo de Matanzas ('L de M' on the doors shows you where) is another breathtaking 19th-century treat. You can walk in and look around this elegant old music school, whose most notable feature is a huge mural of a chess-playing Che.

Vying with these two for 'most interesting sight in Matanzas' award is the *Cathedral of San Carlos* on Calle 83 at Calle 282. If the church is not open, go to the office at the side of the building (ideally in the afternoon) and someone should open up for you and even show you around. The first church was built in 1693, later destroyed by fire and replaced by this fine 19th-century structure. A German tourist was so impressed with the building that he has paid to have it restored. The interior is elegant and tranquil.

Clustered near the waterside at the *Plaza de la Vigía* (Calles 83 and 270) are several monuments; a plan of them appears on the wall of the Café Atenas. The bright blue *Palacio de Junco* is a beautiful old colonial home, built last century by a wealthy plantation owner. It is now the *Museo Histórico Provincial* and opens 10am-noon and 1-6pm Tuesday to Sunday. For a Cuban museum, a surprising amount of space is devoted to pre-revolutionary history: Matanzas' involvement with the sugar and slave trade is explored and there is a small archaeological display downstairs. Across the road is the *Teatro Sauto*, the graceful city theatre which is also a national monument. It was built through public subscription in 1863, at the peak of the city's economic fortunes, and is a convincing representation of a traditional European opera house. It opens 1-3pm Wednesday to Sunday for daytime visits; otherwise, go to a performance: see *Entertainment*. Adjacent to the theatre is the most handsome *Fire Station* in Cuba. Opposite is an art gallery and a craftshop, which deserve a browse; the shop has a surprisingly good selection, including locally-made clothes and ceramics.

If you'd like to do something different, seek out the *Casa de Abuelos* at Calles 91 and 288. This 'House of Grandparents' is a small day centre where the old people are incredibly welcoming and love talking to visitors. Take chewing gum or chocolate if you decide to go. For an alternative behind-the-scenes visit, head out to the *University*, on the western outskirts of the city. It is trying to promote links with Great Britain and Canada; a new Chair of Canadian Studies was created recently and the university is also keen to establish academic links with British universities. Anyone interested in visiting the university or in speaking to the students, can contact the Dean of the School of Languages, Profesor Zoe Domingues, in advance (tel 52-61647, fax 52-53101), or else just turn up.

Entertainment. The Plaza de la Vigía is the best place to go for evening entertainment. Close to the bridge is the city's main *Casa de la Trova*, where you can see some fine Afro-Cuban music. It is the home of the Muñequitos de Matanzas, Cuba's most famous rumba band (see page 120). Performances are usually just on Saturdays, either in the afternoon (2-4pm) or in the evening (9pm). Matanzas has another Casas de la Trova west of the Parque Central at Calles 83 and 304.

The Teatro Sauto hosts performances of classical and popular music, theatre, dance and comedy, mainly at weekends. Tickets are available either at the theatre itself or through ARTEX outlets in Varadero. Classical concerts are also held downstairs in the provincial museum, usually on Saturday evenings. Discos are held sporadically at the concrete shell on the corner of Calles 83 and 282. Down the road at Calles 83 and 268 (tel 2969), the *Centro Nocturno Antillano* serves up less high-brow culture in the form of cabaret. About once a week there is an event of some kind at the local branch of UNEAC, the writers and artists' union, at Calle 83 between Magdalena and Matanzas. This normally consists of music, poetry or maybe a talk.

Matanzas' main cinema is *Cine Velazco*, on the north side of Parque Libertad. If you prefer baseball to the movies, your evening would be better spent at the stadium, which is on Calle 127, east of the bus station.

Help and Information. *Post and telecommunications:* the main office is at Calle 85 number 64.
All-night pharmacy: Calle 85 number 123 (tel 2601).
Petrol station: one at Calles 270 and 85, and another on Calle 127 between the bus and train stations.

Cuevas de Bellamar

There are several cave systems in the area between Matanzas and Varadero. The most important of these are the Cuevas de Bellamar, 3 miles (5km) southeast of the provincial capital. People who have visited the Cueva del Indio near Viñales are likely to be disappointed, but the caves are still worth seeing — particularly if you can swallow the less than evocative names used to describe the various formations — from 'Ladies Room' to 'American Woman's Bathtub'. About 750m of the 2km cave system is currently open. Guided tours (in English) cost $2 per person and are available 9am-4.30pm. The tour lasts about 40 minutes, but you may have to wait a little while a group gathers. Expect to pay a couple of dollars for the ride in a private cab from the centre of town. Alternatively, try taking bus number 16 from Calle 79 near the main square. Alight at the turn-off a few hundred yards east of the main railway station, on the Varadero road, from where it is just over a mile uphill to the caves. There is a bar-restaurant at the site for drinks and emergency food.

If you are interested in seeing other caves, you can visit *Las Cuevas de Santa Catalina* near the town of Carbonera, 13 miles (20km) east of Matanzas. Once used as a tomb by Indians, there are five miles (8km) of subterranean galleries. Inside are strange mushroom formations and also some paintings. Much nearer Varadero are the *Cuevas de Saturno*, which are less extensive but perhaps more impressive than the Bellamar Caves, because of their sheer size, isolation and the lake in which you can swim. The location is unsignposted and a bit tricky, but the following directions should enable you to find them: turn off the main Matanzas-Varadero autopista at the Varadero airport junction; after about a mile you reach a large clearing on the left, where you should leave your car (or driver). With your back to the road, take the narrow footpath leading away to your right. This soon turns into a concrete stairway, which heads down into the caves. At the foot is a crystal-clear lake, where you can swim safely, as long as you are not perturbed by all the bats crashing around overhead.

A private 'taxi' should cost no more than $20 for the journey between Matanzas and Varadero, including stops at the caves.

VARADERO

Nowhere else in Cuba is so productive as this 12-mile sliver of sand dunes protruding northeast into the Atlantic. Varadero was where beach tourism began on the island, and the resort continues to be the main attraction for hundreds of thousands of holidaymakers. Official Cuban tourist literature describes Varadero as 'nature's masterpiece . . . a 20-km stretch of dazzling powdered sugar that dissolves into a limpid pool of turquoise'. More cynical visitors have described it as an unmitigated tourist trap, full of pink and peeling Canadians and troubled by groups of drunken Germans who seem to treat the place with the same lack of respect as British louts display to the Costa del Sol.

Varadero has been a resort since the turn of the century, when wealthy families from nearby Cárdenas built themselves summer houses here. The degree of development which followed fades into insignificance when compared with the surge of the 90s. Although the resort has some way to go before it becomes as over-developed as Benidorm or Corfu, the Cubans are pressing ahead with plans to milk the idyllic natural setting for all its worth. The gaps between buildings are being filled in by new luxury hotels, and the fringes of development are constantly extending eastwards along the peninsula. It seems likely that parts of Varadero will resemble a building site right up until the end of the century. Meanwhile, the real Cuba grows ever more distant. If you want to spend time getting to know the local people, this is not the place to do it.

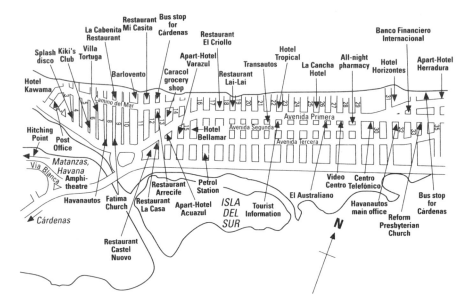

A rather more sinister development is Varadero's progress towards becoming the Bangkok of the Caribbean. Prostitution is open and increasing, and male tourists are approached daily by the prostitutes themselves or their pimps. The sexual undertone affects women too, since there is a school of thought among certain male tourists and Cubans that foreign women go to Varadero for sex alone.

Nevertheless, if you fancy the ultimate lying-on-the-beach-all-day-then-partying-all-night holiday, there are worse places to be. Varadero will meet your needs more exotically and less expensively than most other places in the Caribbean. The fine, white sand beach is clean and the water superb. The average winter temperature in the shade, and the water, is 25°C/77°F. Furthermore, Varadero is a popular base for divers. And should you choose to make the resort your base because of the attraction of a package holiday there, it is relatively easy to escape the clutches of your tour group and to go off and explore on your own.

Varadero occupies the Hicacos peninsula about halfway along Cuba's northern coast, jutting out into the Atlantic and cut off from the mainland by the Laguna de Paso Malo. The oil wells that litter the coast around Varadero skirt extremely close to the resort; these don't disturb the view, but the sulphurous fumes released during drilling are thoroughly unpleasant if the wind blows in the wrong direction — a fact not mentioned in any of the tourist brochures.

Resort Layout. The bridge from the mainland becomes the Autopista Sur, running the length of the peninsula along the southern coast. More or less parallel to it is Avenida Primera (written '1era'), which is the most useful through route, served by local buses 47 and 48. Avenida Kawama runs from the bridge to the western extremity of the peninsula, along a much narrower strip of land. The two other most important east-west streets are Camino del Mar, which runs close to the sea north of Avenida Kawama, and Avenida Playa, which skirts the northern shore further east.

Calles are numbered from 1 to 69. This last street marks the end of the town proper and the beginning of the zone with the newest and most exclusive hotel

VARADERO

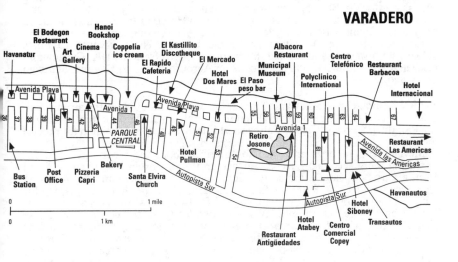

complexes. The west end of Varadero is the liveliest, with the main concentration of hotels, restaurants and other services. The stretch between Calles 23 to 64 has its fair share of tourist outlets, but along Avenida 1era you can still see fine old wooden houses where local families have been living for several generations — and which are a pleasant reminder that you are still in Cuba after all. Some are being developed as upmarket, characterful accommodation for tourists.

ARRIVAL AND DEPARTURE

Varadero is 85 miles (140km) east of Havana, linked to the capital and Matanzas by the Vía Blanca. The section of road between Matanzas and Varadero is the first toll road in Cuba — $2 for tourists' vehicles, 2 pesos for locals.

Bus services to the resort are poor — not surprising given that few Cubans live in or visit Varadero (the local population is only 18,000). But the Vía Blanca is one of the busiest roads in the Republic and hitching along it is comparatively easy. The bus station is at the corner of Calle 36 and the Autopista Sur, and is one of the most orderly in Cuba. Direct buses to Havana take three hours, with just two departures a day, at 8.20am and 6.30pm; these are usually booked up several days ahead. Other destinations have occasional direct services (e.g. one daily service to Santa Clara at 1.25am, 10 pesos), but there are more to Matanzas — look out for bus or truck number 410. In theory you can turn up just 10 minutes before the departure time and join the queue in the waiting room on the left of the entrance. But the bus doesn't always start in Varadero and may turn up almost full, allowing only a handful of passengers to get on. The return services from Matanzas tend to be much more crowded, so be prepared to come back in a private car ($10-15 negotiable) or to hitch. Tourist taxis are a rare sight in Matanzas.

If you fail to secure a seat on a bus for the capital, you will usually find a private cab or too under the trees outside the terminal; some function as colectivos, mainly for the run to Matanzas or Havana. Another alternative is to pay $25 for a transfer to Havana in a tourist bus. To do the same journey by tourist taxi will cost in the region of $80.

Hitching a lift west from Varadero is usually highly successful. The hitching spot is on the Vía Blanca, a five-minute walk over the bridge, past the Amphitheatre and across the lagoon from the Kawama Hotel. Lifts eastwards or inland are more difficult, with a straggle of hopefuls spread along the Cárdenas road. Just onshore from Varadero is the old airport. The new one, 10 miles (16km) southwest, has scheduled international flights from the UK, Canada and elsewhere, plus domestic charter flights on AeroCaribbean to Havana, Santiago and Cayo Largo.

Vehicle Rental. Havanautos and Transautos both have outlets at the airport (call 5-64185 and 5-63016 respectively) and in several of Varadero's hotels, including the Paradiso, Siboney, Cuatro Palmas and Internacional. See the map for precise locations.

Bicycles and mopeds are ideal for nipping about the resort area and for exploring more secluded beaches further up the peninsula. They can be hired from a variety of hotels, including Club Caleta, the Acuazul and the Kawama (see *Accommodation*). Rates are fairly standard, e.g. $1 per hour, $5 per day for a bike, $7.50 for one hour on a moped, $12 for two, etc. Most bikes and mopeds have been snapped up by midday so get there early for the best choice. Those that are still on the forecourt in the afternoon are probably being repaired or 'unavailable for hire' for no specific reason. You won't be given a lock, but you can buy one at the sports shop opposite the Cuatro Palmas hotel; this shop also sells puncture repair kits ($4.20) as well as pumps, bicycles and diving gear.

ACCOMMODATION

You should have no trouble finding somewhere to stay in Varadero, though finding a reasonably-priced room is not so easy. Most new hotels are three-star or higher, and many of the older and more lowly establishments are being renovated and upgraded. Accommodation generally comes in the form of mini-apartments — either in chalets or in conventional hotel buildings — with facilities such as sitting rooms and kitchens. Many hotels have both traditional hotel rooms and chalets, so if you are quoted a price, make sure you know what kind of accommodation you are being offered. Not many hotels have triple rooms, though a few will include an extra bed for an extra $20-25.

The accommodation described here is divided up into three categories: cheap (under $50 a night for a double room in high season), middle (under $90) and expensive (the rest). Addresses and telephone numbers of all hotels mentioned are given in the list at the end of each section.

Cheap Range. There are several two or three-star hotels at the western end of Avenida 1era. The *Aparthotel Varazul* is well-situated and quiet, and has double rooms for $45 in high season ($35 in low) and singles for $35 and ($28). You must check in at the Acuazul in the next block (see *Medium Range*), whose facilities you are also entitled to use (if you can stand the band in the evenings). The shop attached to the Varazul (entered off Calle 15) stocks all kinds of treats, such as fresh fruit, newly baked bread rolls and even butter. Further west the *Villa Barlovento* is particularly recommended. Behind the posh hotel of the same name are simple bungalows which are right next to the beach. It seems likely that one day these will be renovated and upgraded, but for the moment they remain one of the cheapest options, at $30-40 per night. The money saved can be blown on the Barlovento's superb breakfast; see below.

The other cheap options are the two-star *Villa Los Delfines* ($49 double, including breakfast) and *Villa Sotavento*, east of the Varazul in the old part of town. The *Herradura*, also two-star and in the same area, has benefitted from a full refurbishment and is excellent value with double rooms for $40-45 in high season ($30-35 in low), and singles for $25-30. Note that there is no sign outside, so look out for the cream and orange building with a big Coke machine outside.

If you prefer to stay in a place that feels closer to an ordinary, provincial hotel, then try getting a room in the Pullman or the Dos Mares. Both are in the old town and are free from the brouhaha that is part of life in most of the other hotels. Best is the stylish *Pullman*, with rooms for $40 (high) and $30 (low), singles $25-30; unfortunately it is difficult to get a room at short notice. A few hundred yards east is the *Dos Mares*, which is clean and charges $48 for a comfortable double room in high season ($42 in low) and $36 ($30) for a single, and serves one of the best breakfasts in Varadero. The Dos Mares is a hotel school, noticeable in the large number of staff; service in the attached El Istmo Restaurant is rather plodding, but the staff are very friendly and willing, and the food is good.

At the eastern end of the main strip, the *Siboney* and *Atabey* are formerly luxurious hotels which have fallen on hard times and have cut their rates accordingly. Expect to pay around $38-$50 for a double at the Siboney, while the nearby Atabey goes as low as $29 for an off-season double.

Atabey — Avenida 3 at Calle 61 (tel 667505).
Villa Barlovento — Calle 11 y Camino del Mar (tel 63910, 63721).
Dos Mares — Calle 53 y Avenida 1era (tel 62702, 62995).
Herradura — Avenida de la Playa e/ 35 y 36 (tel 63703, 63303)
Los Delfines — Avenida de la Playa e/ 39 y 40 (tel 667720, fax 667737).
Pullman — Avenida 1era e/ 49 y 50 (tel 667161).
Siboney — Avenida 3 at Calle 63 (tel 63012).
Sotavento — Avenida de la Playa e/ 12 y 13 (tel 62593).
Varazul — Avenida 1era e/ 14 y 15 (tel 337132/3/4, 62512, fax 337229).

Middle Range. If you want more facilities and a higher level of comfort, be prepared to pay over $60 for a double, around $50 for a single. Most hotels in this range lay on entertainments in the evening; while you are clearly not obliged to take part, anyone who goes to bed early might find it hard to get to sleep before the show is over, usually around 11pm.

The four-star *Club Kawama* is one of Varadero's oldest hotels, and consists of pseudo-colonial style chalets, scattered among palm trees close to the sea, just west of the bridge. The apartments are very comfortable, but are rented out only on a full-board basis: $140 for two in high season ($110 in low), $85 ($67) for a single; this isn't bad value if you don't mind being confined. The Kawama is one of the liveliest night spots in Varadero. There is a lovely beachside bar, but unfortunately this has become one of the resort's prime meeting-place for prostitutes, pimps and their customers. A much quieter option is the three-star *Villa Tortuga*, nearby, which consists of chalets and small apartment blocks and does not demand full board.

The three-star *Bellamar* is a good choice if you like high-rise hotels, excellent swimming pools and a central location. Its poolside areas are more spacious than at any of the other downtown hotels. The main drawback are the rowdy package tourists and the crass evening entertainments, which usually culminate with at least one or two people being thrown into the pool. A standard mini-apartment at the Bellamar costs $84 for two ($68 in low season), $65 ($50) for one. For a similar scene on a smaller scale try the *Acuazul*, which charges $86 for a double in high season ($70 in low) or $65 ($52) for a single, or the *Club Caleta*, a friendly and lively place with apartments ($70-80 per night) gathered around the pool. The restaurant at the back is good for a cheap lunch, e.g. spaghetti bolognese for $4.

The Tropical is a clean and comfortable package-tour hotel belonging to the Horizontes group, and is often used by British tour groups. A double room for walk-in customers costs $73, and a decent breakfast is a further $5.50.

Unusual for its location among the top range resort hotels east of the town centre is the four-star *Villa Cuba*, once part of the Du Pont estate (see *Exploring*). It is highly recommended for its location away from the hubbub of central Varadero and its friendly staff. The main hotel building is new and fairly small, but most accommodation is in three or four-bedroom houses. A room in one of these houses (with shared kitchen and sitting room) costs $65-75 ($55-60 in low season), which is excellent value. If you want a whole chalet to yourself, you'll have to pay nearer $150 ($120 out of season). The nearby *Caribe*, managed by the Gaviota agency, is another quiet place, with low-rise hotel rooms and bungalows for $85 (double) and $75 (single).

Acuazul — Avenida 1era e/ 13 y 14 (tel 5-63918, 33-7132, fax 33-7229).
Bellamar — Calle 17, e/ Avenida 1era and 3ra (tel 63014, fax 33-7246).
Club Caleta — Avenida 1era e/ 19 y 20 (tel 63513).
Caribe — Calle G y Avenida 1era (tel 63914, 63310).
Villa Cuba — Carretera Las Américas (tel 62975).
Club Kawama — Avenida Kawama y Calle O (tel 33-7155/6, 63015; fax 33-7334).
Tropical — Avenida 1 e/ 21 y 22 (tel 63915). Villa Tortuga — Calle 7 e/ Avenida 1era y Camino del Mar (tel 62243).

Top range. Hotels become more exclusive the further east you head. The change is noticeable by Calle 60, but the real tourist enclaves begin further out, where the beach begins to broaden. These mega complexes, most of which are joint ventures, make the rest of Varadero's hotels look positively small and humdrum. All of them are dominated by large groups of package tourists, mostly from Germany and Canada. They are ideal for those after a luxurious beachside holiday, but are badly situated for exploring Varadero town and travelling out of the resort: those who don't fancy catching the local buses into town will spend a fortune on taxis. Nevertheless, if you are based at a hotel in the town, you may choose to travel out to the resorts during the day to take advantage of their superior facilities, which include seafront swimming pools, outdoor fresh-water showers, etc.

The *Barlovento* is one of the few top notch hotels to be located in the centre of Varadero. A brand new hotel right by the entrance to the resort, it has comfortable rooms and excellent facilities, plus room prices that don't change between seasons. The cost of a double room is currently $98, a single $72. A good reason to stay at (or visit) the Barlovento is to be able to enjoy the breakfast, which is one of the best you'll get on the whole island: there is a seemingly unlimited selection of fruit (including mango), omelettes made to order, the closest rashers you'll find to real bacon, and even hot croissants.

Another good choice is the four-star *Cuatro Palmas*, well located near the junction of Avenida 1era and Avenida las Américas, and close to the sea. It charges $95 for a room in the main hotel building, $63 for a room in a chalet. Heading eastwards from here, along Avenida de las Américas, you start to hit the flash tourist enclosures, where you can more or less exist without venturing outside the hotel.

The four-star *Internacional*, built in the 50s, is one of the oldest hotels in Varadero and is cheap in comparison with the other top-range places. A double room with a seaview costs $100-130, without a view $80-100. The restaurant serves reasonable food, though the quality is not as high as at some of the newer joint-venture hotels beyond. Hotel *Riu Las Morlas*, just beyond the Internacional, is more low-key than most of the other new resorts, but has the drawback of offering only full board packages. Rates per person are $85 in high season, $65 at other times.

If you wish to stay in the most luxurious and modern hotels on the peninsula, continue east. The four-star *Tuxpán* charges $125 for a single room, $150 for a double. Yet the new *Bella Costa* next door, owned by the same German travel company LTI, is curiously much better value despite being five star; a single room costs $80, a double $120. The décor in both hotels is an aberration, but their restaurants serve some of the best food in Cuba. Beyond, the *Sol Palmeras*, is a massive horseshoe-shaped creation, with rooms, suites and bungalows and prices ranging from $80 to $120 per person. The *Melia Varadero*, also Spanish run, would never get five stars in Europe despite its glass lifts and water displays; it looks good at night, with dimmed lighting, but rather tatty in daylight.

The five-star *Paradiso-Puntarena* complex at the far western end of the peninsula is isolated from most of the action, which you will consider either an advantage or a major drawback. One of the older Varadero hotels, it has been revamped by the Spanish company Guitart, but it still lacks the class of the newer resorts. There is little to distinguish between the twin high-rise blocks, though the Puntarena has better shops and a pleasant cocktail bar on the first floor which shows satellite TV films.

Hotel Barlovento — Avenida 1era, corner of Calle 10 (tel 63721, 63910).
Bella Costa — Avenida Las Américas (tel 33-7010, fax 33-7205).
Cuatro Palmas — Avenida 1era e/ 60 y 62 (tel 63912, fax 33-7004).
Internacional — Avenida Las Américas (tel 63011, 63913, 337039, fax 337246).
Melia Varadero — Autopista Sur (tel 33-7013, fax 33-7162).
Paradiso-Puntarena — Final de Kawama (tel 63917, fax 52147).
Riu Las Morlas — Avenida Las Américas y Calle A (tel 33-7231 to 35, fax 33-7007).
Sol Palmeras — Carretera Las Morlas (tel 33-7013, fax 33-7162).
Tuxpán — Avenida Las Américas km 3.5 (tel 33-5241, 66219; fax 33-7205).

Mosquitoes: Varadero is notorious for its mosquitoes. Cold, air-conditioned rooms help keep them away, but you still need to slap on copious amounts of repellent.

EATING AND DRINKING

Varadero is second only to Havana in the variety of its restaurants, while the quality is generally better and prices lower; breakfast buffets are almost invariably superior to those offered in the capital. Cuisine is often 'international', but there is scope to enjoy some wonderful seafood and even some good creole dishes. As elsewhere, Italian food is good to fall back on if money is short. In addition, intense competition between restaurants means that complete meals are available for as little as $3.95 (though do not expect culinary miracles at this price).

Some of the best restaurants are in the hotels, but if you would like a change of scene there are plenty of places in town — particularly near the entrance to Varadero. Restaurants are listed below in order as you head east along the peninsula. Where no opening times are given, this is probably because the place advertises itself as '24 hours', a claim which should be taken with a pinch of sea salt.

Kiki's Club: Avenida Kawama e/ 5 y 6 (tel 33-7054). This restaurant was originally run by Canadians and known as Alfredo's Dive Club. Even though this part of the operation has closed, it still serves some of the best Italian food in town, particularly the pizzas; if you're feeling brave try the lemon pizza, a speciality of the house. Most main courses cost $7-8, though there are side dishes such as garlic bread for $1-3. The décor and atmosphere are very pleasant and it's a good place for a drink too, particularly towards the end of the evening when the crowds have left.

La Cabanita: On the shore at the top of Calle 9. Certainly cheap, not necessarily very cheerful. This is the venue of the sub-$4 lunch, comprising fruit juice, chicken, fried potatoes and coffee.

Mi Casita: Camino del Mar e/ 10 y 11 (tel 63787). Friendly and highly recommended, particularly for its seafood and steak. In addition, this is one of the few places to go out of its way to make a proper vegetarian meal, if requested. Mi Casita is open in the evenings only, from 7.30pm.

La Casa del Chef: Avenida 1era, opposite Calle 12. Watch for the specials being advertised outside this roadside dive — cheap lobster is a frequent attraction.

Restaurant Arrecife: Camino del Mar y Calle 13. Another aggressively marketed place, but tucked away from the main drag. Shrimp, lobster and lots of trimmings for $17.

El Dujo: Avenida 1era, in front of the Bellamar Hotel. The setting is pleasant but prices are rather high. The best deal on the menu is the mixed grill — prawns, lobster and fish for $15.

Lai Lai: Avenida 1era and Calle 18 (tel 63297), open from 7pm. This Chinese restaurant, which occupies a large house with a lovely balcony not far from the beach, should have plenty going for it. But while the food is good, the atmosphere is strangely lacklustre.

El Criollo: Avenida 1era and Calle 18. A small and unpretentious restaurant that is highly recommended. It serves traditional Cuban food, including black bean soup, grilled meat or fish ($6-8), with accompaniments such as fried plantain and sweet potato. The service is friendly without being particularly attentive.

El Bodegón Criollo: Avenida Playa and Calle 40 (tel 62180). Also specialising in Cuban food, this restaurant is associated with the Bodeguita del Medio in Havana. The menu and surroundings are very similar, with the smells from the kitchen pervading the restaurant, but the service and food are better. It is also relatively free from camera-wielding tourists, though the revolutionary decor is becoming an attraction. El Bodegón is open noon to midnight daily.

Casa de Queso: Avenida 1era and Calle 49. You can eat well if rather expensively at this 'house of cheese'. Fondues are the house speciality.

El Mesón del Quijote: Avenida Las Américas, on a small rise east of the Hotel Internacional. It is over-priced but at least has decent music; the food is much the same as elsewhere.

Las Américas: Avenida Las Américas (tel 63415, 61612), on the north shore. This mansion was built in the 1920s by a French munitions magnate called Irenée Du Pont, who then donated it to the Cuban government before he died (in 1963). The Moorish décor is oppressive and incongruous in a place like Varadero, but the views from the top floor bar are worth the climb. As is so often the case in Cuba, the food does not match the surroundings. The restaurant and bar are open daily noon-10pm. A taxi from the centre will cost about $7.

Peso Restaurants. These are thin on the ground, but there are a couple in the old town. They open briefly at lunchtime and again in the early evening. Despite the inconvenience, it's worth going if only to remind yourself what the world outside Varadero is really like. You should be able to pay in pesos, but check beforehand. Best is *Pizzeria Capri* on Calle 43 between Avenidas 1era and Playa, with a takeaway stall attached; there is invariably a queue. A few peso bars, each called El Paso, are scattered along the resort.
    The *Coppelia* is a huge place on the north side of the Parque Central. As in Havana, there's a special entrance for dollar-paying tourists.

Snack bars. These are establishing themselves all over the resort, with the familiar yellow and red of the El Rapido chain. Most sell cheap and nasty burgers, but they can be good locations if you intend to drink a lot of beer and do not wish to spend too much.

Picnics. There is nowhere better place in Cuba to try to assemble a picnic than Varadero. Starting at the hard-currency bakery on the corner of Avenida 1era and Calle 43, you can procure some fresh bread before checking out a peso shop, El Australiano (corner of 1era and Calle 26) which sometimes has fruit and vegtables on sale. At the Caracol grocery store (Calle 13 between Camino del Mar and Avenida 1era), you can find plenty of meat, cheese and other imported goodies.

EXPLORING

It doesn't take long to exhaust Varadero's cultural offerings. The **Museo Municipal**, housed in an early 20th-century building by the beach at Calle 57, is pleasant enough, but will occupy no more than an hour. On the other side of Avenida 1era from the museum is the **Retiro Josone**. These gardens have been cluttered with too many cafés and restaurants, but they are still a haven of tranquility. The centrepiece is a lake, the domain of a few birds including a number of flamingoes.

More unusual is the **Cueva de Ambrosio**, 8 miles (14km) east along the Autopista Sur from the bridge. These caves contain the most important aboriginal pictographs ever to have been discovered on the mainland. The native people who lived here centuries ago are sensitively commemorated in a series of displays, and this is one of the few places in Cuba where you can get a proper understanding of how they lived.

On your way back, you might want to stop off at the aquarium at km 8.5, where tropical fish are displayed. But frankly you'd be better off simply lying on the beach or — even better — seeing fish in their natural environment by snorkelling or diving.

SPORT AND RECREATION

Varadero has all the amenities you would expect to find in any Caribbean resort in terms of sports facilities. For example, you can play golf by the Las Américas restaurant, though the nine-hole course will disappoint most keen golfers. A round costs $55; the mini-golf at Avenida 1era y Calle 42 charges only $1. Most of the larger hotels have tennis courts, for which you pay $2-3 per hour. Other activities include horseriding, deep-sea fishing and yachting. You can also hire jet skis, catamarans, windsurfers and other watersports paraphernalia.

If you prefer spectator sports, find out when the next game is on at the baseball stadium behind the bus station.

Diving. The most rewarding pursuit on offer in Varadero is diving. Qualified divers can enjoy the clear waters and fascinating coral about a mile from the coast and 12-15 metres below the surface. There are about 25 marked scuba-diving sites around Varadero, including a number of old wrecks. Try to get recommendations for particular sites from other tourists before you approach one of the dive clubs.

Expect to pay about $30 for a trip several miles out, with one good long dive. For about $20 more you can go out for a full day with two dives. You can arrange a ten-dive package for around $300. Most people agree that the best diving is off the Caribbean coast, and all dive shops organise day trips from Varadero: expect to pay around $80, including dives. If you just want to snorkel, the same trip will cost around $40.

Serious divers might like to spend an hour at the Centro Médico Sub Acuático in Cárdenas, which has a decompression chamber and specialises in diving injury prevention and care.

The latest addition to Varadero's repertoire is *Varasub 1*, a submarine which takes daytrippers out for a price of $25. Those who prefer to sightsee rather than submerge themselves, can go on the 'Neptune's refuge tour', which takes you out to the reef and also to a cave with impressive stalactites and stalagmites. The cave contains a lake which is 80 feet (25m) deep in places.

Snorkelling. There are also opportunities for the safer and less expensive pursuit of snorkelling. A morning's outing with boat trip and equipment costs around $20. You can also snorkel straight from the shore. One of the best places to do this is at Coral Beach, 10 miles (15km) west of Varadero. If you haven't got your own wheels, then hitch or take a taxi; if you opt for the latter, arrange for the driver to come and pick you up later.

NIGHTLIFE

The nightlife of Varadero is at times a grotesque misrepresentation of Cuban culture. Many of the big hotels organise a variety of excruciating games and contests, whose success generally depends on how drunk the punters get. Only mildly less embarrassing are the fashion shows (*desfiles de moda*), advertised at some of the posher hotels. If you're in the mood for a floorshow, you'll do better to go to one of the cabarets, which are staged by most top hotels; that put on at the Melia Varadero is among the best. A more interesting setting, however, is the huge open-air amphitheatre of the **Cabaret Varadero** (tel 62169), just across the bridge on the mainland. The cabaret here is the closest thing you'll get to the Tropicana in Havana. It functions 10pm-3am, daily except Tuesday. Even if it's not your cup of tea, you can watch what's going on for free through the fence at the back. The main cabaret season is mid-January until mid-May. The amphitheatre is also where the International Music Festival is held in November.

Don't bother looking too hard for authentic Cuban music — recorded, let alone live — in Varadero. The best thing you can hope for is a good bop. Discos are usually attached to a hotel, and play a mix of music. The disco at the Kawama Hotel is popular, though you must head further along the peninsula for a flasher venue. La Bamba disco in the Tuxpán Hotel is a Western-style disco, with lasers, video screens, loud Spanish disco music and lots of young people. Admission costs $10, including a free drink.

You will find a more mixed clientele away from the hotels. Try La Patana, on a boat in the Paso Malo Lagoon by the bridge, which has reasonable music from 8pm to 3am; or El Kastillito at Avenida de la Playa and Calle 49.

Carnival. Varadero's carnival has little in common with the seasonal celebrations for which Santiago de Cuba is famous. There are processions along Avenida 1era, but the spirit is lost in the surroundings. There aren't enough Cubans to liven things up and the parties and competitions laid on for the foreign visitors are often embarrassing. This tourist extravaganza lasts from the second Monday in January to the second Sunday in February, most events taking place at weekends.

SHOPPING

The shopping complex at Calle 64 (not well signed) has a range of hard currency shops, as well as a swimming pool. You can buy coffee-makers for $4, useful if you are staying in an apart-hotel. Next door, on the corner of Calle 63 is Kawama Sports, with a good choice of equipment, including snorkels. It is open 10am-10pm. These touristy places are supplemented by El Encanto in the centre of the resort, which is a large supermarket. Customers are searched on the way out and their purchases checked, so retain your receipt.

The *Hanoi* is a small but excellent bookshop at Avenida 1era and Calle 44. It has a good selection of guides and maps to the province of Matanzas and an almost unrivalled stock of paperbacks in English, costing from $6 and including Penguin Classics and the latest Dick Francis novel. It has not turned its back completely on the past, and Che Guevara's *Ever Onwards to Victory* is on sale for $3. Posters are also available, plus the Cuban flag for $15.

A block away between Calles 46 and 46, an ARTEX shop has a reasonable stock of tapes and CDs, as well as books and more run-of-the-mill souvenirs.

HELP AND INFORMATION

Tourist Information: the closest approximation to independent advice can be obtained at the Information Bureau on Avenida 1era at Calle 23, which has a rudimentary selection of brochures and staff who will try to help you with travel advice even when you make it clear you do not want to be steered towards an organised trip. In addition, there is a tourist desk in virtually every hotel, geared solely to booking excursions. It is possible to organise trips all over the country, from day trips to Trinidad and Playa Girón to overnight stays in Santiago and Cayo Largo. In addition to hotel tourism bureaux, there are tour agency offices all over the place. Havanatur, for example, has offices by the Kawama Hotel and also at Calle 31 and Avenida 1era.

Money: the Banco Financiero Internacional (BFI) on Calle 32 between Avenidas 1era and Playa can arrange for you to withdraw cash on a credit card (minimum $100). It is open 8am-12.30pm and 1.30-7pm daily. Some hotels allow cash to be drawn on credit cards, but add an inordinately high surcharge, often 8%.

Post and Telephone Offices: the Centro de Comunicaciones Internacionales on Calle 64, just off Avenida 1era, is the main telephone and post office, with a DHL office (tel 62103) attached. It opens 8am-10pm daily except Sunday, when it closes at 8pm. You will have to pay in hard currency; the nearest places for stamps in pesos are Cárdenas and Matanzas. Telexes and telegrams can also be sent from this bureau. There are smaller telephone offices in a number of hotels, including the Internacional and Kawama; most hotels can arrange for you to call home from your room.

All-night pharmacy: Avenida de la Playa and Calle 44 (tel 6-2636). Also at Avenida 1era and Calle 28.

Hospital: Policlínico Internacional (Servimed) at Avenida 1era and Calle 64 (tel 6-2122) for the sole use of foreigners. A consultancy costs $20, while a call-out is $40.

Dentist: Avenida 1era and Calle 49 (tel 62767).

Police Station: the old one on Avenida 1era between Calles 38 and 39 was demolished in 1995, and there is no indication of when or where it might reappear. In the meantime, dial 116.

SOUTH OF VARADERO

Heading south and east from the Hicacos peninsula, you encounter some of Cuba's most fascinating towns. Despite the proximity of Varadero, places like Cárdenas are utterly unspoilt by tourism and barely touched by the 20th century. Travellers who are based at Varadero are strongly advised to venture deeper into the province of Matanzas, and — in order to get closer to the locals' way of life — to travel independently rather than on an organised tour.

Cárdenas. Only nine miles (15km) south of Varadero, this atmospheric, decrepit old town shares absolutely nothing in common with the overt commercialism of the island's biggest resort and, if only for that reason, is a pleasure to explore. Most of the action takes place along Avenida Céspedes, but the town has no real centre. The streets are blissfully free of vehicular traffic, the principal forms of transport are the bicycle and horse and cart. The standard fare for a ride in a horse-drawn cab is one peso, though enterprising locals offer tourists guided tours for dollars, typically $5 for four passengers.

Cárdenas has a surprising past. In 1850 this quiet port was invaded by 600 men, who had sailed from New Orleans under the leadership of a Venezuelan anti-colonialist called Narciso López. The occupation of the town didn't last long since the men (only six of whom were Cuban) failed to rally support among the local people, most of whom fled. After a bloodless but colourful gesture, López and his band left as they had arrived, on a steamship called *Creole*. A statue of López can be found at the entrance to the docks, at the northeast end of Avenida Céspedes.

Arrival and Departure: Cárdenas is cheap and easy to reach on local buses from Varadero (number 376); services are supposed to run roughly every 30 minutes. If you're staying in old Varadero, the most convenient stop is on Avenida de la Playa between Calles 35 and 36; further west, there is a stop on Avenida 1era between 12 and 13. Buses arrive in Cárdenas at the small terminal on the corner of Avenida 13 and Calle 13, a few blocks west of Avenida Céspedes. While the bus from Varadero is often half empty, it is usually full for the return journey; you should pick up a ticket from the booth, but this serves no useful purpose as there is normally room for everyone. If you need to take a taxi from Varadero, expect to pay $10-12 each way; arrange a time and place to be picked up for the journey back since there are no taxis in Cárdenas.

The main bus station is at Avenida Céspedes and Calle 21; horses and carts run people to and from the centre. Buses depart from here to Havana and to points around the province, but services are heavily subscribed. Buses to Matanzas (some of which stop at Varadero) depart mainly between 5am and 9am and then after midday, but there is no discernible schedule. Few buses from Cárdenas cover a great distance, and if you are heading into the interior you must try to piece together a series of local services. The most useful buses are those south to Jovellanos, Colón and Jagüey Grande. Several daily services head eastwards along the coast to the small communities of Martí, Itabo and Corralillo, an interesting area to explore.

Trains leave from the terminal at Avenida 8 and Calle 5 near the port. The light-blue castellated railway station is one of the town's finest buildings. The most reliable (and useful) services are the departures to Colón and Los Arobos at 2pm and 8.50pm. There are also trains to Guareira and Pedroso.

Cárdenas is not a great place to hitch from, and you may do better to get a local bus to a more convenient spot on the highway, e.g. Máximo Gómez, 15 miles (24km) east, where a road heads south to Colón; or Limonar, southwest of Cárdenas on the Carretera Central between Matanzas and Colón.

Accommodation: don't expect a high level of comfort in Cárdenas. The only option since the gorgeous Hotel Europa was demolished is the Hotel Dominica, an historic building but a poor place to stay. It is on the corner of Avenida Cespedes and Calle 9, facing the sad shell of the colonial mansion that was once the Europa. Formerly the governor's residence, the Dominica was occupied by Narciso López and his men in 1850. The rebels raised the Cuban flag for the first time in the country's history, an event commemorated by a plaque in the hotel (which is now a national monument). The Dominica has a variety of rooms, the average charge being $10 for a double. The food is terrible.

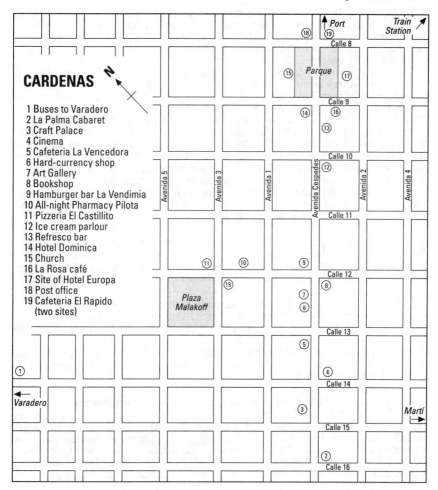

CARDENAS

1 Buses to Varadero
2 La Palma Cabaret
3 Craft Palace
4 Cinema
5 Cafeteria La Vencedora
6 Hard-currency shop
7 Art Gallery
8 Bookshop
9 Hamburger bar La Vendimia
10 All-night Pharmacy Pilota
11 Pizzeria El Castillito
12 Ice cream parlour
13 Refresco bar
14 Hotel Dominica
15 Church
16 La Rosa café
17 Site of Hotel Europa
18 Post office
19 Cafeteria El Rapido
    (two sites)

Eating and Drinking: it is hard to move in Cárdenas for snack bars. You can find burgers and soft drinks at several branches of El Rapido, or graze on snacks from a large number of private houses. For meals of a higher class, the only place in town is Las Palmas, on the corner of Avenida Céspedes and Calle 16 (tel 4762). This restaurant is housed in a lovely building, with a large and almost ecclesiastical hall. During the week getting a table shouldn't be a problem, but at weekends a reservation is essential. On certain nights of the week there is a cabaret of some description, sometimes combined with a disco. Las Palmas is closed on Monday and Tuesday.

Exploring: Cárdenas is above all a place in which to immerse yourself in ordinary Cuban life, but if you need a museum around which to structure your wanderings, there are a couple to choose from. The Museo José Echeverría (Avenida 4 and Calle 12) is housed in the former home of a student leader murdered during Batista's dictatorship. It is a general historical museum as well as a memorial to Echeverría. Much better is the Museo Oscar de Rojas (open 1-6pm Tuesday to

Saturday, 9am-1pm on Sunday), housed in an old mansion on Calzada at Avenida 4, also east of the main street. There are displays of coins, weapons, butterflies and archaeological relics belonging to the Taíno Indians, plus brief coverage of the history of Cárdenas. The museum's proudest possession is an extraordinarily ornate 19th-century hearse.

Don't miss Plaza Malakoff, with its extraordinary market building. This is a massive two-storey affair in the shape of a cross, with a dome at the centre and lovely wrought-iron balustrades. It is in a poor state and is closed off for restoration, though little progress has been made. Some of the buildings around Plaza Colón are also in serious need of repair, but the square is still the town's most elegant. It contains the first statue of Columbus to have been erected in the Americas, dating from 1862. The port is just a few blocks further north, but there is never much going on. Look out at the junction of Avenida Céspedes and Calle Sagua la Grande (Calle 5) for the extravagant façade of the Banco Popular, with imposing columns and a fine marble verandah.

The most touristy thing in Cárdenas is the Palacio de la Artesanía on Avenida Céspedes between Calles 14 and 15. It has a few interesting crafts, including a wide selection of wacky wall decorations.

Going south from Cárdenas, there are several similarly typical towns such as Périco, Colón and Jagüey Grande. In each you get the sense that nothing much is going on, nor is likely to in the forseeable future. These communities see few tourists and the people are extremely welcoming.

Jovellanos. Fifteen miles (24km) south of Cárdenas, this is one of the biggest towns in the area. While not enormously exciting, Jovellanos has a pleasant old centre, with a Parque Central overlooked by a church. The town is also notable for its Afro-Cuban music and dance, brought to the area by the Arará people of Benin, via Haiti, and found more commonly in the Oriente. If you're driving around, Jovellanos is a good place to fill up your tank with petrol and maybe have a drink and a snack.

Colón. Founded in 1837, this compact and dusty town was built with fortunes made from sugar, hence the amount of neo-classical architecture; even the shacks have colonnades. Colón, like Cárdenas, is well worth visiting for the street life and the flavour of 19th-century Latin America. The town is also famed for its *campasino* music, a rural Cuban style using guitars and improvised lyrics. With its unique and sleepy atmosphere, cheap hotels and better-than-average transport, Colón is a good base from which to explore the central Matanzas region.

Arrival and Departure: Colón is on the main railway line running east from Havana, and two or three trains pass through daily. There are also local services to Santa Clara and Cárdenas. The station is about a mile and a pleasant horsecab ride (1 peso) from the centre. Colón is also accessible on daily buses from Cárdenas, Jovellanos and Matanzas, but services are virtually non-existent from towns to the east or south, such as Cienfuegos. Buses to Cárdenas leave about three times a day from the Intermunicipal station. Those to Matanzas leave from the Interprovincial station, around the corner on Máximo Gómez, taking about two hours. Colectivos gather outside the intermunicipal bus station.

Accommodation: the Gran Caridad, a peso hotel on the corner of Calles Antonio Maceo and Máximo Gómez, has clean and spacious rooms with cold shower and toilet for about $12 a night. The restaurant doesn't serve breakfast, but does lunch and dinner, and there is an upstairs bar. The hotel's main drawback is the noise. A couple of blocks away, also on Máximo Gómez, is the newer Santiago Habana Hotel, which charges similar rates. Simple meals are available but are unlikely to satisfy a healthy appetite. You can fill up on beer and chocolate from the shop attached to the Cupet petrol station opposite.

South of Jovellanos and Colón, the countryside continues to be flat, scrubby and generally unexciting. Colour is brought by the extensive fruit orchards, where oranges grow in abundance. Almost equidistant from both towns is Jagüey Grande. Situated about a mile north of the motorway, this is a one-horse town that is anything but 'big'. Its most interesting part is centred around the old sugar railway.

Central Australia. Lying on the other side of the motorway from Jagüey Grande, at first sight Central Australia would appear to be little more than an oversized roadstop. The settlement's name and importance stems from the sugarmill (*central*), which looms above the trees a short distance south of the autopista. The railway which serves the mill crosses the highway a short distance east, unprotected by barriers; local people appear as if by magic when a train is due in order to flag down any oncoming traffic.

Central Australia's other claim to fame is that Castro directed the operation to repel the Bay of Pigs invasion from here. The Museo de la Comandancia, in the house used by the revolutionary armed forces, commemorates the affair and is open 8am-5pm Tuesday to Sunday.

Since Central Australia lies near an important crossroads, there are invariably lots of people waiting for lifts in all directions. Havana is 2-2½ hours away and Cienfuegos, Santa Clara and Matanzas are all within a 1½-2 hour drive; and the road running south nearby is the main route serving the Zapata Peninsula. Hitching a lift can be very successful, particularly as there are a lot of tourist buses passing through. To corner one of these, go to the Fiesta Campesina, a tourist complex where you can stay overnight in thatched wooden huts, eat reasonable food or just break your journey with a rest in the shade; it is also rather gruesome, with wretched-looking birds and animals in tiny cages.

ZAPATA PENINSULA (Ciénaga de Zapata)

The Zapata Peninsula is Cuba's prime wildlife area. Remote and inaccessible, it is almost entirely unspoilt. The peninsula bulges down from the island of Cuba, squeezed between the Bay of Pigs and the Cortés Inlet, due south of Matanzas. Like the Mississippi Delta region of the USA and the Kakadu area of northern Australia, it is largely swampland with lush vegetation, thick mangrove and lots of crocodiles (saved from extinction). The Spanish colonists flushed out the Indians who once lived here, but they then abandoned the area. Little development took place until after the Revolution, when the region was first earmarked for organised tourism.

There are numerous beaches to the east of the peninsula. Because of their relative inaccessibility, they are less busy than those in the north. Playa Larga and Playa Girón are the main resorts, being popular bases for diving trips. The interior is basically a flat swamp, and the part most easily visited is the **Laguna del Tesoro**, or 'Treasure Lake', which lies just east of the peninsula proper, but is well-endowed with wildlife. It is so-called because the indigenous natives reputedly threw their treasure into the lake rather than see it seized by the conquistadores. Its average depth is only 4 metres (13 feet). The surrounding land is thick with flora and fauna. Most tours of the area feature a boat trip out to the tourist complex of Guamá.

The main attraction in terms of wildlife, other than the crocodile, are the birds, some of which are unique to the area. There is a large number of warblers, as well as Cuban emeralds, green woodpeckers, hummingbirds and the trogon. You can also see Great and Reddish egrets, marsh hawks and the region's own specialities, the Zapata rail and Zapata wren. Non-specialists may have to make do with admiring the large number of ducks.

The main hazard if you are driving through the region, particularly between Playas Larga and Girón (see below) is the large number of crabs that wander in from the shore and across the road. They are large, red and suicidal, and however hard you try to avoid them you are doomed to crunch your way along the highway.

Guamá

Promoted as the Venice of the Americas, Guamá is a tourist resort built on a network of islands linked by bridges. It is on the eastern shore of Treasure Lake. Supposedly modelled on an Indian village, the complex is remarkable, having much more in common with a rich Florida resort than a socialist state. It was built after the Revolution, destroyed by fire and rebuilt. It is one of Cuba's biggest tourist traps, existing now almost solely for day trips by foreign visitors, although you can stay overnight. However long you stay, the large number of voracious mosquitoes will almost certainly make your life a misery.

Arrival and Departure: the only access to Guamá is along the 3-mile (5km) canal starting at the main road midway between Jagüey Grande and Playa Larga. This is a combined roadhouse/wharf with a service station, restaurant, cheap snack bar and shop, known collectively as La Boca. You may wish to look in at the crocodile breeding station just north of here, which features on all day trips to the area. Or you may prefer to eat a tortilla or hamburger at the snack bar and wash it down with a beer from the shop (where you can also buy much-needed insect repellent).

To reach the wharf, take a bus or hitch from Jagüey Grande or Playa Larga; you'll be lucky to find a taxi in either place. The official timetable for the 20-minute boat trip to the resort is as follows: depart La Boca at 6.30am, 8.30am, 3.30pm and 8pm; depart Guamá at 7am, 9am, 4pm and 9pm. The first departure in each direction does not operate at weekends or public holidays. You will not be allowed to board the last ferry from La Boca unless you convince the boatman you have an overnight reservation at Guamá. You pay the boatman $2 at his kiosk, but will not be issued with a ticket. You can take any boat back free.

There are additional services depending on tour group timings, which individual travellers may be able to join. The first one out from La Boca is around 10.30am, with the return journey at noon. Regular ferry services are supplemented by high-speed launches.

Accommodation: the three-star Villa Guamá (tel 059-2979) consists of thatched huts on stilts dotted around the island. Carrying your bags across a succession of precarious wooden bridges requires care and stamina, and is best achieved in daylight. Inside, the cabins are dimly-lit and consist of a bedroom, bathroom and living area. Don't be fooled by the mosquito screens; the huts are by no means mosquito-proof and the only safe treatment is lashings of repellent. A cabin for two costs $40 low season, $55 high.

Eating and Drinking: the resort has a huge thatched restaurant on the central island. Breakfast is miserable, even by Cuban standards. You might get a ham roll, overly milky coffee and — the saving grace — a small glass of freshly squeezed orange juice. Other meals are better. Instead of the standard lump-of-meat-with-rice, try the grilled fish with fried sweet potatoes. The omelettes are also above par. The food is best at lunch, since everything is shipped over by boat in the morning. A favourite offering of the barman is an early-morning heartstarter, rum and coconut milk served in a shell.

Exploring: it doesn't take tour groups long to exhaust the daylight activities of Guamá. A recreated Indian camp occupies one island, complete with sculptures of natives in 'Action Man' poses. Another houses a diminutive museum complete with shop. To enjoy the wildlife (the main reason for visiting Guamá), stroll around at dawn or dusk. There is more going on at dawn, and it also avoids the early evening hazards of mosquitoes and music; the evening tranquillity of the village is spoilt by the disco playing to nobody in particular.

You can hire rowing boats between 9am and 4pm. The lake is calm enough for you to row all around. The swimming pool is filled with the same murky water as the lake, plus added chlorine. Unless you're desperate for a swim, wait until you reach a beach.

The Bay of Pigs (Bahía de Cochinos)

The tongue of sea that protrudes northwards into the Zapata peninsula has attained prominence in the gazetteer of post-war intrigue. When the US decided to mount an invasion of Cuba in 1961, it chose to attack from the south rather than the more predictable approach from the north. The landing sites were chosen in this remote and lightly populated part of the island, and code-named Playas Roja, Azul and Verde — red, blue and green. The invasion, of course, was a disaster. Nowadays, the first two beaches (under their Cuban names of Larga and Girón) are tourist resorts which milk their military connections.

Playa Larga. Apart from the monument describing one of the decisive battles to put down the 1961 Bay of Pigs invasion, the rest of this resort is a collection of chalets with no proper centre, though the setting is lovely. Playa Larga is one of the main diving areas on the Caribbean, and you can walk to the reef from the shore. Most people are brought down on day trips from the north coast — Varadero is 80 miles due north — bringing little benefit to the local area.

If you need to stay overnight, see if the two-star Villa Playa Larga (tel 337542, 59-7219) on the beach is open and has a room. This collection of chalets has recently been taken over by Horizontes hotels and has been much improved. Note, however, that the same company owns the Villa Playa Girón, 20 miles/33km along the coast. And if bookings for the two properties are low, then the Villa Playa Larga closes.

When available, a cabin for two is $25 in high season, just $20 in low season and $18 ($15) for a single. These cabins have a lounge, bathroom, hot water (an immersion heater controlled from within the cabin), and bedroom with large wardrobes and air-conditioning; they are cleaned every day, with fresh towels and flowers provided. There is a well stocked tourist shop, two restaurants and a beach bar, and the swimming pool is a good alternative to the beach, which gets crowded at weekends in summer.

Playa Girón. As a place to stay for a two-week holiday, this resort is not a good choice, and you can meet numerous foreign tourists who are not enjoying their holiday as much as they might. Yet for independent travellers, or those on a day trip from another base, it makes a pleasant enough place to visit. The connection with the Bay of Pigs invasion is particularly strong here; the road between Guamá and Playa Girón is scattered with over 80 monuments erected to commemorate those who died or took part in repulsing the invasion.

Arrival and Departure: to or from Jagüey Grande, La Boca (for Guamá) or Playa Larga, take bus or truck 818, which runs several times a day. Truck 510 operates to and from Aguada, providing a useful link with the *autopista* for those heading east. Cienfuegos, 50 miles (80km) east, is linked with Playa Girón by two daily bus services. The roads hereabouts are also good for hitch-hiking, since there are few significant turn-offs where you might be dropped in the middle of nowhere.

Accommodation: cabañas at the two-star Villa Playa Girón (tel 337528, 59-4118, 59-4110) are sometimes fully occupied by tour groups. If not, a double will cost $30 off-season. The $3 breakfast is good value. Rooms may also be available at La Fermina Motel.

Exploring: whether or not you manage to get a place to stay at the Villa Playa Girón, you must visit the residence between cabañas 48 and 53. This was a house damaged during the invasion, and has been kept as a tribute to the armed forces that repulsed the attack; only Cuba would keep a wrecked villa in the middle of a holiday complex.

The Playa Girón Museum, 300m north of the resort, is a must. It is one of Cuba's best laid-out museums, and tells the story of the ill-conceived CIA operation to land a force of Cuban exiles at the Bay of Pigs on 15 April 1961, using bases in Guatemala and Nicaragua. Labelling of exhibits is in Spanish only, but even those who do not speak the language will get the gist.

The exhibition begins with pictures of life in the Ciénega region 'before the triumph of the revolution', and explains the political context of the Pluto Plan with which the USA aimed to defeat Castro. It reminds visitors that as well as organising the botched invasion, the USA also sent bombers to raid Havana and Santiago de Cuba.

Outside stands a British-built Sea Fury fighter, used by the Cuban air force to help repulse the invasion, plus the wrecked engine from a Cuban aircraft destroyed in a US bombing raid. Around the back, you can see a tank and the remains of an American B-26. The museum is open 9am-5pm Tuesday to Sunday, and admission is $2 for tourists.

The most thorough visit to the museum, however, won't make too much of a dent in your stay. Girón's other main attraction is its seaside location, but the beach is not the island's best. A concrete barrage has been built across the crescent of sand, either to keep the sand in or any future invaders out.

The resort pool is better than average, and is also a good place to learn the rudiments of sub-aqua diving. The pool is 10 feet (3m) deep, enough to pick up the basic technique, and the Dive Shop can arrange instruction and equipment. There are some interesting sites for diving and snorkelling nearby.

Cars and bicycles can be hired from the Playa Girón complex, but sadly there is nowhere very interesting within easy cycling distance apart from the Martires de Girón school of tourism.

Birdwatching. There are guides in both Playa Larga and Playa Girón that conduct special birdwatching tours into the swamp. If you are not an avid birdwatcher, at least go to La Salina, where there is a spectacular colony of flamingoes.

EAST OF CARDENAS

The road that runs close to the north coast is a useful alternative to the *autopista* and the Carretera Central, passing through a number of charming towns. There are also a number of places to stay overnight and break a journey, such as the Elguea Spa at the scruffy resort of Corralillo (tel 042-686290, 686367). Its thermal bath confers the term 'spa' on an otherwise unexceptional and isolated hotel.

Central Cuba

Old Town, Trinidad

Cienfuegos   **Villa Clara**   **Sancti Spíritus**

Many travellers seem to overlook the provinces of Cienfuegos and Villa Clara, making a beeline for the south coast of the province of Sancti Spíritus, where the delightful town of Trinidad has been preserved in all its colonial splendour. But it is inundated with visitors, and you would do well to explore the region's other highlights, such as the fine harbour city of Cienfuegos, and the historic towns of Santa Clara and Remedios. You will also find it hard to resist the lure of the lush mountains of the Sierra del Escambray, which rise majestically to the north of Trinidad.

CITY OF CIENFUEGOS

Some visitors can't find a good word to say about Cuba's principal port, finding it run-down, unattractive and with more than its fair share of unsavoury characters. Others can't praise it enough, finding a friendly and relatively prosperous town with all manner of delights from a handsome and bustling boulevard to a generous supply of cafeterias that actually have something to sell.

Cienfuegos (population 100,000) certainly boasts some distinctly unattractive features, including the Republic's biggest cement works and an ugly naval base. But while these affect the health of both the atmosphere and the water in the bay, they don't encroach upon the heart of the town. Unlucky visitors discover only the disadvantages of spending time in a maritime community, in the form of crime and drunkenness. Others enjoy conversations with Cubans who have worked at sea and like to reminisce about European ports they have visited. And the setting of Cienfuegos is magnificent, jutting out into a lovely bay. You won't necessarily agree with Cienfuegos's epithet — the Pearl of the South — but you can have a pleasant time here. Lisandro Otero, a well-known Cuban writer, wrote in 1960 that 'Cienfuegos is, without any doubt, a beautiful city. But when analysing the details there is nothing worthy of a special mention.' Even though there are few outstanding buildings or museums to visit, you can easily spend a day strolling around Cienfuegos or making small side trips in the vicinity.

History. The castle at the harbour entrance, the Castillo de Jagua, arrived before the city itself; the Spanish finished the fortress in 1745 to protect the communities living around the bay from pirates operating from Jamaica and the Isle of Pines. Cienfuegos was founded as Fernandina de Jagua in 1819 by a Frenchman called Louis Clement, who supposedly landed here with nine families after failing to make it to Florida. The name Cienfuegos, which means 'hundred fires' was adopted in 1820, in honour of the then Governor General of Cuba. The rapid growth of the new settlement had an adverse effect on its neighbour, Trinidad, with its inferior harbour. Merchants, businessmen and bankers switched allegiance, moving to Cienfuegos to invest money in the sugar mills that were being set up in the area. At one point in the 19th century, the port acquired the reputation of having the largest concentration of rich people in the country.

By the time of the Revolution, the port had more or less been abandoned. Like other ports, such as Nuevitas, Mariel and Matanzas, Cienfuegos has benefitted from industrial development since 1959, but has suffered equally since the onset of the Special Period. Even so, large amounts of sugar are still shipped from here.

City Layout. The fastest route between Havana and Trinidad is via Cienfuegos, but through traffic can bypass the town on the *circunvalación*, which links the roads to Rodas and to Trinidad. The main road from the north crosses the Inglés river on a couple of long bridges and runs straight as an arrow through the town centre to the Hotel Jagua on the Punta Gorda peninsula, the southern tip of the town. This road is officially Calle 37, but the northern half down to the seafront is universally known as Paseo del Prado or just the Prado. Life in the town revolves around this tree-lined boulevard (a poor imitation of Havana's own Prado), particularly in the evening when people venture out after supper to promenade.

At Avenida 46 the Prado becomes the Malecón, which runs along the waterfront down to the Jagua Hotel. Instead of a line of handsome colonial houses there are just a few open-air bars which are seldom open or busy; but the views over the bay are lovely, particularly at sunset.

Avenidas run north-south and are odd-numbered; calles run east-west and are even-numbered. The grid system is so regular that you can measure distances with precision; one city block is 80 metres. It breaks down in the northeastern part of town, but there is little to draw the visitor to this quarter. The oldest area of the city is known as Pueblo Nuevo and lies to the west of the Prado between Avenidas 46 and 62; this contains most places of interest, including the Parque Central.

Arrival and Departure. *Train:* the small railway station is seven blocks east of the Prado on Avenida 58 at Calle 51, at the end of a branch off the main line through Cuba. Trains run 10 times a week between Havana and Cienfuegos, taking eight or nine hours. There is a departure every day at 11.30pm, and on

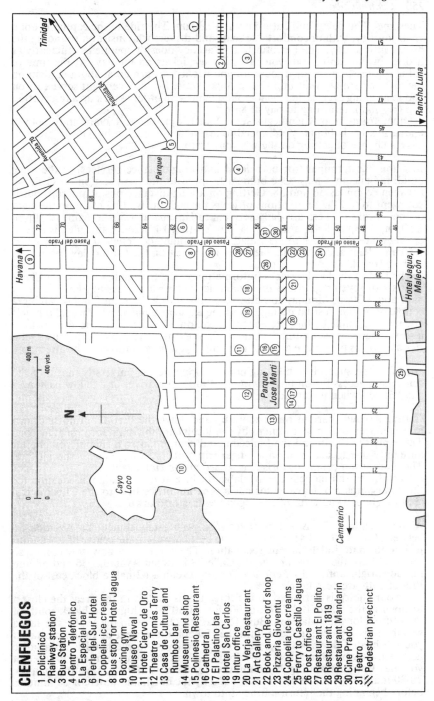

CIENFUEGOS

1 Policlínico
2 Railway station
3 Bus Station
4 Centro Telefónico
5 La Especial bar
6 Perla del Sur Hotel
7 Coppelia ice cream
8 Bus stop for Hotel Jagua
9 Boxing gym
10 Museo Naval
11 Hotel Ciervo de Oro
12 Theatre Tomás Terry
13 Casa de Cultura and
   Rumbos bar
14 Museum and shop
15 Polinesio Restaurant
16 Cathedral
17 El Palatino bar
18 Hotel San Carlos
19 Intur office
20 La Verja Restaurant
21 Art Gallery
22 Book and Record shop
23 Pizzeria Gioventu
24 Coppelia ice creams
25 Ferry to Castillo Jagua
26 Post office
27 Restaurant El Pollito
28 Restaurant 1819
29 Restaurant Mandarin
30 Cine Prado
31 Teatro
⁂ Pedestrian precinct

Tuesdays, Thursdays and Saturdays at 10.30am. The ride to the capital is not a great journey, with uncomfortable seats and drivers who insist on sounding the horn continuously. The Ferrotur tourist agency doesn't operate as efficiently as it does in the capital, but you can still buy tickets on the day. At the time of going to press, for the daytime train you needed to turn up at about 6.30am on the day and simply wait in line and hope, while for the overnight services, you had to go along even earlier — at around 6am — in order to pick up a reservation slip (*pre-tike*), returning to pay at 8am.

Other trains from Cienfuegos serve Sancti Spíritus at 4.39am and 2.34pm, taking nearly six hours. You'll need to arrive at the station by 4am in order to have a chance of getting on the weekday train.

Bus: the bus terminal (for both local and long-distance services) is the large building beneath a huge Che billboard, opposite the train station on Calle 49 between Avenidas 56 and 58. Getting on a long-distance bus is difficult, but if you want to try, the reservations office is through the waiting room on the right of the entrance. There are daily services to Havana at 1.50am, 6am, 12.30pm, 1.10pm, 3.15pm, 9.40pm and 11.50pm, costing 14 pesos. Camagüey is served on alternate days at 8am. Trinidad buses cannot be reserved, and depart at 6.50am, 10am and 12.15pm. Get your name put on the list the day before you wish to travel.

The best of the local services (information in the first hall) are to Santa Clara, with six or seven departures on a good day. There are buses to Playa Girón at 4am and 3.30pm Monday to Saturday, 5am and 3.30pm on Sunday, taking a couple of hours. Castillo de Jagua and the Rancho Luna and Pasacaballo hotels are also accessible by bus: see below. To get on a local bus, you need to pick up a slip of paper with a number (*tike*), wait, hope and then pay on the bus. Get a *tike* as early as possible, e.g. in the morning if you plan to travel in the afternoon.

Hitching: the supervised hitching point is opposite the university, north of the centre and accessible on bus 6 from the Prado; the driver or a fellow passenger will tell you when to get off.

Getting Around. Various buses zoom up and down the Prado, but horse-drawn cabs (referred to simply as *mulos* by the locals) are the main form of transport. These ply the Prado and the Malecón, and charge 1 peso a ride; if you charter an empty one to take you on a longer trip, you must negotiate a special fare. There are just a couple of turistaxis, based at the Hotel Jagua.

Cars, bikes and mopeds are available for hire at the Jagua hotel, location for the Transautos rep. Havanautos has a separate office next to the Cupet petrol station, about 1km north of the Jagua heading into town.

Accommodation. The *San Carlos Hotel*, a peso establishment on Avenida 56 between Calles 39 and 41, used to be the best bargain in the centre of town until it shut down for indeterminate renovation. The alternatives downtown (but also often full) are the *Ciervo de Oro* on Calle 29 between Avenidas 56 and 58 and the downright unfriendly *Perla del Sur*, on Avenida 62 half a block east of the Prado; both are peso hotels.

If your choice is narrowed to the three tourist hotels in the area, the closest to town is the *Jagua* (tel 7074, 6190; fax 33-5056), a high-rise block south of the centre along the Malecón. Built for Batista's brother in the 1950s, the Jagua was the most modern in Cuba until the Habana Libre went up in the capital. If you are loaded down with baggage, the easiest way to the hotel is on a horse and cart. City bus 9, marked 'Covadonga', serves the Jagua from the Prado, but you may find that waiting 30-60 minutes for a bus is more aggravating than the 20-30 minute walk. The bus turns around by the hotel, and waits for 10 minutes before beginning the return journey into town.

The Jagua is relatively cheap for a four-star hotel ($38 single, $52 double, $70 suite), but it abuses its monopoly as the only dollar hotel in Cienfuegos and is heavily overpriced in other respects, particularly when it comes to its buffet meals (which are poor and may be suspended if there is a shortage of guests). The main plus points are the views over the bay, the clean swimming pool and the poolside bar, which stays open until 3am.

Despite its size, the Jagua fills easily. At least there should be a Turistaxi handy if you are forced to try the other three hotels for foreigners, which are some way from the town. Closest is the three-star *Rancho Luna* (tel 432-48120/ 1/2/3, fax 33-5057), 10 miles (16km) east of Cienfuegos and backing on to a pleasant — if small — beach: see *Further Afield*. To find it by car from Cienfuegos, set off around the harbour and look out for signs reading 'Parqueo' around the 15km mark. Accommodation, in motel-style units or cabins, is cheap at $38 (double) and $28 single. The keep-fit lessons and the karaoke nights are off-putting, but there is no pressure to join in.

Half a mile east is the *Faro Luna* (part of the Cubanacán chain, tel 432-48162/ 5/8), which has neither location nor charm on its side and charges $45-$55 for a double room.

Five miles (8km) beyond the Faro Luna is the three-star *Pasacaballo* (tel 6212), which overlooks the mouth of the harbour. It is a huge Soviet monstrosity whose design is identical to that of a hotel in each of Trinidad and Santa María del Mar, so if you've mastered the layout of either of those you'll be able to find your way around the Pasacaballo. It is a dismal place in many ways but is beautifully situated opposite the Castillo de Jagua. A double room costs around $40 peak season, $30 low. The restaurant serves reasonable meals (the creole chicken and grilled fish are particularly tasty) and the service is fast.

The drawback with both these hotels (other considerations aside) is clearly the distance from Cienfuegos and the time spent waiting around for transport. So-called *pesetero* boats ferry tourists around and the Pasacaballo is on the route used by the public Castillo de Jagua ferry — but this runs just four times a day (see *Further Afield*). If you wish to travel by road, the taxi fare will cost about $10 one way from the Rancho Luna, a few dollars more from the Pasacaballo. Hitching lifts on tour buses can be fruitful, but is always unpredictable.

Eating and Drinking. The best restaurant in the town centre, for both surroundings and food, is *La Verja* at Avenida 54 number 3306. That the restaurant serves a hundred different dishes is an imaginative claim, but there is certainly a reasonable choice. The menu lists several seafood and meat dishes (from lobster stew to hamburgers), as well as side dishes such as steamed yuca and fresh fruit. Expect to pay $10-15 per person. The décor is lovely though shabby and the service rather disorganised. La Verja is one of the few restaurants in Cienfuegos which serves food after 7pm (its hours are 6-9pm), but the quality is undoubtedly better if you eat early. A reservation is essential on a Saturday night, which is cabaret night.

The other main restaurants are within a two-block stretch of the Prado. The *Mandarín*, on the corner of Avenida 60, is particularly popular among Cubans, though the kitchen is hard-pushed to serve authentic Chinese cuisine these days. Next best is *El Pollito* at Avenida 56, which specialises in beer and chicken (or 'chiken', as the sign outside promises). Between the two is *1819*, a beautiful building named after the year that Cienfuegos was founded. The interior is stylish and the food tries hard to match. The alternative is *El Polinesio*, on the Parque Central, which has a good reputation locally.

To be sure of a meal in one of the town-centre restaurants, you need to venture out soon after 6pm. Queues can be long and Westerners are not given priority. The best bet is to call in a few hours ahead and try to make a reservation (particularly at the weekends). Even those who have booked might have to wait up to an hour. The alternative is to queue for a gristly hamburger (not recommended) at the *Cafeteria Guamá* or a measly pizza at the *Pizzeria Gioventu.* If the prospect of failure depresses you, stick to the restaurants near the Jagua, which cater for tourists more than locals and open late. If you want quality, stick to the *Palacio Valle*, an early 20th-century palace built in an Hispanic-cum-Gothic-cum-Moorish style. The food is expensive but excellent, with seafood the speciality. For a romantic drink, sit on the rooftop terrace as the evening light fades over the bay. On the ground floor a modern day Carmen Miranda holds court, playing the piano (badly). Opposite the Jagua is the *Covadonga*, a more down-to-earth restaurant specialising in paella, which at least makes a change from rice and beans. The Cueva del Camaron, next door, does seafood.

The best peso bar in town used to be *El Palatino*, on the south side of Parque José Martí. It has since been converted into a dollar bar, catering mainly for tour groups. It is still pleasant, and is not a bad place to cool off during a hot day's sightseeing. It is open 10am-7pm, and serves various liquors, fresh lemonade and a few snacks.

Most of the town's cafeterias and snack bars are open only in the daytime. On good days the *Cafetería San Carlos* (on the Prado at 56) serves delicious coffee and hot chocolate. A couple of blocks down at Avenida 52 is *Coppelia*, though its stock of ice cream is unreliable. If you're prepared to queue, you may be able to pick up a hot dog at *Cafeteria Central* alongside the Cathedral. You must collect a ticket and then wait your turn.

Exploring. The main area of interest in Cienfuegos lies west of the Prado, around Parque José Martí. The city was founded here on 22 April 1819, and a statue to Martí marks the spot. Around the edge of the square are a variety of handsome buildings, dating mainly from the 19th and early 20th centuries. On the eastern side stands the impressive *Cathedral of the Immaculate Conception*, with its (unidentical) twin towers. As with most churches in Cuba, unless your visit coincides with a Mass — usually in the evening — you will find it closed.

On the north side is *Teatro Tomás Terry*, named after a man who on his death in the mid-19th century left a fortune of 20 million pesos — one of the greatest fortunes in the world at the time. The elegant auditorium is open to the public during the day (admission $1, pay in the adjacent ARTEX shop), but is best appreciated during a performance: see *Entertainment.* The art gallery next door has a small permanent display (of copies of famous paintings, from Leonardo da Vinci to Chagall), but more interesting are the rooms given over to temporary exhibitions. Opening hours are 9.30am-12.30pm and 1.30-4.30pm, admission $1.

On the other side of the square is the *Museo Histórico*, containing weapons and memorabilia of local patriots. You will probably find it more entertaining to spend another $1 to climb the small tower of the nearby *Casa de la Cultura* (ask downstairs first), or to browse in the adjacent shop.

The *Museo Naval*, at the top of Calle 21 northwest of the Parque Central, devotes much space to the role Cienfuegos played in the lead-up to the revolution of 1959. The museum describes the events of 5 September 1957, when Cuban sailors, supported by local students and other activists, rose against the Batista dictatorship. You can explore the grounds even while the rest of the museum is closed. The electric plant which was partially destroyed by the revolutionaries during the attack has been left as a memorial to the martyrs: you can see it on the corner of the Prado and Avenida 48.

Five blocks north on the Prado, on the corner of Avenida 58, the Casa de Cultura (no relation to the one in Parque José Martí) is a delightful place. An old *liceo*, it has a small exhibition of local heroes, but is well worth exploring for the quiet grandeur — especially on the upper floor, with its fine mirrors and elegant spiral staircase.

About 20 minutes walk along Avenida 48, west of the Parque Central and over the railway track, is *La Reina Cemetery*. The setting by the port is anything but picturesque, but the colonial burial ground is very much worth a visit — look out for the statue of the 'Sleeping Beauty' at the central crossroads of the cemetery. So too is the *Tomás Acea Cemetery*, on the Rancho Luna road, east of the Prado. It contains a reproduction of the Parthenon in Athens, as well as the graves of revolutionaries and a memorial to those who died in the 1957 uprising. Both cemeteries open 7am-5pm.

Entertainment. The *Casa de la Cultura* in Parque José Martí hosts live music about once a week and serves up a variety of rhythms. The *Casa de la Trova* is between the Malecón and the Jagua Hotel, but compared to the music houses elsewhere in Cuba the programme is disappointing.

Music is often on the menu in the Tomás Terry theatre, but the style is usually popular. Tourists should in theory pay in dollars. Once inside, you can help yourself to a seat in a box if the theatre isn't full. *Teatro Guiñol* on the Prado is another elegant venue, and offers mainly children's entertainment.

The most popular disco in town is the open-air *Tropizul*, on the Prado at Avenida 48. At weekends, throngs of young Cienfuegans hang around outside waiting for the doors to open — normally after 10.30pm. The music is Cuban, dancing compulsory. Two other popular discos are the *Aire Libre* (Calle 56, just east of the Parque Central) and the *Costa Sur* (near where the Prado and Malecón meet). The Aire Libre's admission policy is very strict and the heavies on the door are unfriendly; you'd do better at one of the other two. If you're with local people, you should be able to get in for pesos, though if they are full a few dollars might be required to twist the doorman's arm.

A much more low-key place than any of the above is the cafeteria on Avenida 62 (across the road from the Perla del Sur hotel), which is transformed into a bar-cum-disco in the evenings. Refreshment is normally in the form of rum, with free (and inedible) tapas thrown in. There is minimal décor and lighting and the music is loud, but it is cosy and you can sit back and admire (or join) the dancers. Closing time is midnight.

There are several cinemas and video halls, the best one being *Cine Prado* on the main street at Avenida 54.

Sport. The main stadium (*Estadio Municipal*) is southeast of the centre on Calle 45 near Avenida 34, clearly visible from the Malecón. If you prefer boxing to baseball, look out for the makeshift rings that are set up on the Prado, stopping most passing traffic in its tracks.

Shopping. The main shopping street is the pedestrianised Avenida 54. Many of the shops are dowdy but it's a pleasant enough place to stroll or sit. The most interesting store is one block north: the secondhand book and record shop on Avenida 56 between Calles 31 and 33.

The best shop for arts and crafts in Cienfuegos is the one adjacent to the historical museum in the Parque Central. It has some surprisingly good things for sale, including stylish straw hats for $10 and real Panamas from Ecuador for $25. In addition, there is an interesting selection of prints, textiles, jewellery and baskets. Opening hours are 9am-5pm Monday to Friday and 9am-noon on Saturday. There is a small ARTEX shop in the lobby of the Tomás Terry Theatre across the square, and some expensive new hard-currency stores.

Crime and Safety. Some visitors take against Cienfuegos because of the hassle they receive from young locals — either in the city centre or outside the Jagua. Would-be black market spivs seem to operate in teams of three or four, and prey mainly on male tourists. Fortunately, it is usually obvious from the start what they are after, enabling you to move off before the situation becomes too uncomfortable.

Help and Information. *Post Office:* corner of Avenida 56 and Calle 35, a block west of the Prado.
Car Hire: Transautos has a desk in the Hotel Jagua (tel 6184), while Havanautos is based at the Rancho Luna (tel 48120). There is a 24-hour Cupet petrol station a few blocks down from the Jagua.
Telephone Office: Avenida 58 between 41 and 43.
Medical care: an excellent policlínico is located just north of the railway station at Avenida 60 number 5101.
All-night pharmacy: on the corner of the Prado and Avenida 60.

FURTHER AFIELD

Castillo de Jagua. This small fort was built in the mid-18th century to protect the bay from pirates, but in fact it never came under serious attack; structurally, the fort has suffered more through neglect. Now, however, restoration work is almost complete. There is a small museum, but otherwise you'll not find much to do here except drink one of the house cocktails and admire the view, though the latter is marred by the hulk of the Pasacaballo Hotel looming opposite. To the west are the residential blocks of the Ciudad Nuclear, built for the people working on the nearby Juraguá nuclear plant. Cuba's only nuclear power station was begun in 1976 and abandoned indefinitely at the end of 1992. The government, however, has been looking for a foreign investor to take up the project, which it believes could generate 15% of the island's energy need. Discussions with experts from Russia and elsewhere about completing the reactor were held in 1995 — much to the dismay of the United States and Greenpeace, which believe the plant to be a safety risk.
   In contrast to the quasi-Soviet landscape around the nuclear site, the area immediately beneath the castle and along the shore looks entirely Mediterranean, with wooden houses tumbling down to the sea. There is little to disturb the tranquillity of the spot.
   The boat ride from Cienfuegos contributes to the fun of visiting Castillo de Jagua. Ferries leave at 6am, 7am, 3pm and 5pm, from the jetty at the bottom of Calle 25, west of the Prado and next to the Empresa Astilleros building (nip through the hole in the fence). There is no need to turn up in advance unless your heart is set on getting a seat, in which case arrive 30 minutes before; the fare has recently doubled, but is still only 50 centavos. The boat chugs along at a slow pace, and is a pleasant ride once you're past the evil-smelling waters of the harbour; you can catch glimpses of the Juraguá nuclear plant behind the hills across the bay. The boat calls at a couple of small fishing communities, at the Pasacaballo Hotel, Ciudad Nuclear and, finally, at the Castillo de Jagua itself. The journey takes about an hour. If you want to return by road, buses connect Castillo de Jagua and Cienfuegos twice a day.

Botanic Garden. Outside Cienfuegos is Cuba's first proper botanical garden, founded in 1912 by Harvard University. The gardens contain over 2,000 different species, including nearly 300 varieties of palms and 200 types of cactus. Unfortunately the location, between the villages of San Antón and Guaos, 9 miles (15km) east of the city, makes the gardens difficult to reach. A local bus serving Cumanayagua can drop you off. Otherwise hitch or pay around $30 (there and back) for a taxi.

Playa Rancho Luna. This is the nearest beach to Cienfuegos. It is pleasant but easily filled by the guests staying at the nearby hotel. There is a cleaner and bigger public beach five minutes' walk west. If you want chaises-longues and beach bars stick to the former, where you can also enjoy a variety of sports and other activities including boat and catamaran trips, waterskiing, windsurfing and diving. For more humble pursuits you can pay $5 for an hour in a rowing boat or on a horse.

Whichever beach you choose, watch out for the bothersome insects (known locally as *he-hin*), which are harmless but have an irritating bite.

From Cienfuegos you can strike north to Santa Clara, east to Trinidad, or west to Playa Girón and Havana. For anyone heading northwest towards the motorway, the drive is fairly uneventful, although **Rodas**, 20 miles (32km) from Cienfuegos, is a lovely place with a large main square overlooked by an old colonial church. Another 30 miles (48km) on is **Aguada de Pasajeros**, a buzzing town close to the Autopista. It has long taken its role as a roadstop seriously — its name means 'passenger watering station'. There is an important hitching point close by under the bridge, and a short distance west is a tourist roadstop. If you get delayed overnight, stay at Motel El Bosque in town.

SANTA CLARA

Experienced travellers regard anywhere described as a 'city of contrasts' with caution. Cubatur, which makes this claim on Santa Clara's behalf, presumably has in mind the contrast between the enormous Inpud factory (making domestic appliances) and the unspoilt charm of the inner city. There is not much specific to do in Santa Clara, but the main square is one of the best in Cuba and a pleasant time can be had simply watching the world go by. The large student population helps to make the town interesting and friendly, and the life injected on the streets by dollarisation has had a marked effect in Santa Clara.

City Layout. The absence of a decent map of Santa Clara (the one in this book is based entirely on personal observation) is especially irritating given the complexity of the road network. The *autopista* through the island passes to the south of the city — motorists should stay firmly on it if they do not wish to visit Santa Clara. The older Carretera Central approaches from Havana and the west. Upon hitting the city boundary, traffic is directed south around the *circunvalación*; if you miss the sign, you stay on the Carretera Central as it weaves around the city, clipping the southern edge of the centre. To confuse matters further, another ring-road passes around the north of Santa Clara. This is one place where arriving by train is worth the trouble — the station is eight blocks due north of Parque Vidal, the large central square. The main shopping street, Independencia, runs east-west one block to the north. Its middle section is a pedestrian mall, known colloquially as the Boulevard. West of the centre is a huge open area, the Plaza de la Revolución, where rallies are held.

Arrival and Departure. There are no air services to Santa Clara, which is reasonable enough since on the autopista you can cover the 180 miles (300km) to or from Havana in three hours. There has, however, been talk of Santa Clara becoming the new domestic air hub of Cuba: flights would arrive in waves from cities at each end of the island, enabling easy connections on any route.

Train: Santa Clara's fine station is already the rail hub of Cuba. The main daily departures at the start of 1996 were as follows.

  To Havana: train 8, dep 12.25am, arr 5.27am; train 2, dep 2.53am, arr 7.05am;
    train 6, dep 5.13am, arr 9.55am; train 18, dep 6.10am, arr 11.23am; train 4,
    dep 8.43am, arr 1.20pm.
  To Santiago: train 1, dep 8.48pm, arr 6.45am.
  To Camagüey: train 5, dep 11.27pm, arr 4.55pm; train 19, dep 3.28pm, arr
    9.55pm.
  To Cienfuegos: daily at 7.33am and 5.27pm, taking just over two hours.

SANTA CLARA

1 Station
2 Tren Blindado
3 Late-night pharmacy
4 Intermunicipal bus station
5 Cathedral
6 Hotel Santa Clara Libre

6 24-hour coffee shop
7 Hotel America
8 Revolution Museum
9 Revolution Plaza
10 Cupet service station
11 Palace of Justice

To Sancti Spíritus: daily at 7.18am and 5.29pm, taking nearly three hours.

For an example of a train which never quite made it to its destination, walk 15 minutes from the station to the Tren Blindado exhibition described in *Exploring*, below.

Bus: the Intermunicipal bus station is seven blocks west of Parque Vidal. It has comparatively frequent services to Remedios, Caibarién, Placetas amd Manicaragua.

If you're loaded down with luggage, don't try to walk to the Interprovincial bus station. It is over a mile beyond the other bus station, just past the curve in the road. There are usually one or two colectivos outside, which is just as well because of the thinness of bus services from Santa Clara. The four-hour route to Havana is served twice a day (at 2pm and 11.30pm).

There are two daily buses direct to Trinidad, usually leaving at 7am and 12.50pm. The alternative is to fight your way onto a bus to Manicaragua, midway between the two towns, and hitch or pick up a local bus (scarce) to

Trinidad from there. To reach Manicaragua's official hitching point, walk up the hill from the 'bus station', branch off to the right onto the Trinidad road and then walk a further kilometre to where there should be a few people waiting (plus a man in yellow). To increase your chances of getting to Trinidad in a day, leave Santa Clara as early as possible.

Colectivo: Santa Clara has one of the most organised colectivo services in Cuba. There is a colectivo station on the main road to the Intermunicipal bus station, from where cars set off to all parts of the country; destinations and fares are written up on a board.

Accommodation. Easily the most convenient place to stay is the three-star *Hotel Santa Clara Libre* (tel 27548/9, 27550) on Parque Vidal. This eleven-storey blight on the square is gloomy and crowded. But as part of the Isla Azul chain, it is cheap (a single costs $18, a double $24 in high season) and reasonably well equipped. Ask for an upper-floor room facing the square for a fine view of the city. The tenth-floor restaurant serves a good buffet breakfast, and the evening menu includes delights such as fish enchilada (stew) and yoghurt. Up one floor the bar is pleasant and offers good views.

If the Santa Clara Libre is full, you will be referred to the three-star *Motel Los Caneyes* (tel 422-4512/5, fax 33-5009), 3 miles (5km) west of the main square. It is on Avenida Eucaliptus beyond the Circunvalación Villa Clara. Supposedly resembling a native Indian village, it has features not normally associated with life in Cuba before Columbus, such as a disco, unisex hairdresser and air-conditioning. A single cabin costs $28, a double $38 in high season. The rooms are a bit dingy, but there is a fridge, hot showers and the surroundings and the pool are pleasant enough. Good buffet meals are also cheaper than average. The main drawback is its inconvenient location. Bus number 11 runs to and from the city centre every hour or so between 7am and 6pm. After that, you will have to rely upon the goodwill of local drivers if you do not have a car or bike.

Another option is the three-star *Villa La Granjita* (tel 26051/52), a mile or so out of town along the Carretera de Maleza. The newest of Santa Clara's hotels, run by Cubanacán, it has good facilities and is only marginally more expensive than the other two.

Eating and Drinking. Santa Clara is the centre of a fertile and productive area, and as a result has access to a relatively good supply of food. The liberalisation of recent years has been seized upon in Santa Clara, and street snacks have proliferated. More formal dining is still limited: the *Colonial 1878*, on Calle Máximo Gómez between Independencia and Parque Vidal, is the premier restaurant, but the quality of food is better at the Santa Clara Libre hotel.

Coppelia is on Calle Colón or, for a more substantial snack, try the nearby *Pizzeria Milán.* For serious drinking, join the locals at one of the two Casas de la Trova (see below).

Exploring. The most impressive sight in Santa Clara is the *Tren Blindado* — Armoured Train — exhibition. To reach it, follow Independencia east and cross the bridge, Puente La Cruz. Set in a small park off to the right is a collection of railway wagons in some disarray. This was a Batista troop train intercepted a few metres away by Che Guevara and a band of 17 revolutionaries on 29 December 1958. They had come into the town from their hiding place in the mountains to launch a surprise attack on the train, which was carrying 408 men. The Caterpillar bulldozer they used to derail the 18-coach train stands on its own heroic plinth. This incident was the decisive battle between the rebels and the forces of Batista; the dictator fled Cuba two days later. Displays inside a couple of the wagons tell the story (in Spanish). The exhibition opens 9am-noon and 3-7pm Tuesday to Saturday, 9am-noon on Sunday.

A more detailed exhibition covering the struggle between Guevara and Batista is on display in the *Museum of the Revolution*, out at the Plaza de la Revolución. Even if the museum is closed, it is worth making the trip up to the square, if only to take a snap of the towering bronze statue of Che Guevara in battle gear. In Parque Vidal itself, you should not miss the *Museo de Artes Decorativas*, which occupies one of the finest colonial buildings in Santa Clara, the former ancestral home of the Carta family. The furniture and other exhibits date mainly from the 19th century. Opening hours are 1-6pm on Monday and Wednesday to Saturday, and on Sundays 9am-1pm. Other fine buildings on the square include the *Provincial Palace*, a 20th-century replacement for the original colonial hall (and now used as a library, to which you can have free access), and the *Teatro Caridad*. Notice also the double pavements around the square; in colonial times these were split by a fence and provided two separate walkways for blacks and whites.

A particularly charming church, the Holy Sisters of Santa Clara, is a few blocks west of the square at the corner of Marta Abreu and Alemán. Another is the Iglesia de Nuestra Señora del Buen Viaje, which was first built in the mid-18th century. The later gothic touches are totally at odds with both the character of the original church and with the surroundings, but thankfully the interior was not touched; you can still admire the original alfarje ceiling.

Entertainment. Most weekend afternoons there are concerts in the bandstand in the middle of Parque Vidal. There are two Casas de la Trova which between them have music and dancing several nights a week. One is on the west side of the main square just along from the Hotel Santa Clara Libre, the other opposite Coppelia on Calle Colón. Try to catch a band called Los Fakires, the city's local musical heroes; call 5741 or 5872 to find out about upcoming performances. Informal performances of music, speech and dance are held at *El Mejunje*, a small cultural centre on Calle Marta Abreu, a couple of blocks from the main square.

Shopping. The relatively good resources of the area mean that there is a wider range of goods than you would expect in a place of Santa Clara's size. The distinction between hard-currency stores and peso places is blurred, with a surprising range of goods available for local currency at La Camp Ferretería, on Luís Estevez just south of the square. Top of the range is a good-quality leather saddle for 3,500 pesos. The dollar shops tend to be inexpensive — the one on the southwest corner of the square has the cheapest Che T-shirts in Cuba.

Help and Information. *All-night pharmacy:* corner of Luís Estevez and Julio Jover. *Telephone office:* between Calle Marta Abreu and the Boulevard, a block west of Parque Vidal.

Lake Hanabanilla

The road down to Trinidad through the Sierra del Escambray is spectacular; the southern reaches of this route are described on page 270. Beyond Manicaragua there is a road to the huge artificial lake at Hanabanilla, in a wonderful spot in the foothills of the Escambray mountains, 25 miles (40km) south of Santa Clara. Some visitors come here to fish for largemouth bass, but you can also go hiking through the woods, boating across the lake or simply admire the views.

The three-star Hotel Hanabanilla (tel 49125, 86932), part of the Horizontes chain, is on a hilltop on the east side of the lake. It has rooms with balconies, an excellent restaurant and great mountain views from the top-floor bar. It is best to book in advance if possible; expect to pay $20 for a single, $30 for a double. You can walk or take a boat to the Río Negro restaurant, in another fine position above the lake.

REMEDIOS

The other big attraction in the province of Villa Clara is Remedios, 26 miles (43km) east of Santa Clara. This is one of Cuba's oldest towns, a colonial gem with a rich cultural heritage and one of the finest churches in the country. San Juan de los Remedios, to give it its full name, was the most important settlement in the region in the early years of colonisation. The first settlement was founded in 1514, but the town's wealthiest families grew tired of constant incursions by pirates and so moved to a site further inland, founding Santa Clara in 1690. Remedios was devastated by a fire in 1819, but the town rose again from the ashes and indeed prospered during the sugar boom later that century. It now has a population of around 17,000.

That Remedios features on few tourist itineraries simply adds to the town's appeal. Unlike the rather precious museum town of Trinidad on the south coast, Remedios clearly has a life of its own. The large and leafy main square is a buzzing focus of the town, with with people engaged in animated conversation and music blaring from loudspeakers. Tourists remain a novelty but attract little hassle. No one should forego a gentle afternoon spent strolling around Remedios, preferably followed by an overnight stop in the Mascotte Hotel. And if you are in Cuba at Christmas, you could witness one of the country's top festivals.

Accommodation. The Mascotte Hotel (tel 395481) in the main square is the only place to stay in Remedios. It is a charming colonial building, with many original features and even the odd four-poster bed, which has been restored only recently. The charge of $20 per person is steep given the simple facilities, but the atmosphere and location provide ample recompense.

Eating and Drinking. The food in the hotel restaurant can't live up to the surroundings but is more than palatable and moderately priced. There are a couple of bars on the square, notably the China Café, La Fe ice-cream parlour and the adjacent Louvre café (open 9am-9pm). The Driver's Bar, hidden behind the Parroquial Mayor, serves yoghurt and cheese sandwiches from 9am to 8pm. This is a no-frills place without a great deal of ambience, but accepts Cuban pesos from tourists.

Exploring. All the principal sights are in or just off Plaza Martí. Dominating the square is the church of San Juan Bautista, often referred to simply as the **Parroquial Mayor**. This church is utterly breathtaking, and alone warrants a visit to Remedios. Do not leave without seeing it. Built in around 1620 and expanded at the end of the 17th century, the church's most striking feature is its alfarje ceiling (see page 108), a magnificent piece of craftsmanship which was discovered only during restoration work in the 1940s. It is unique among such ceilings for its painted decoration, with almost every inch of wood adorned with stylised floral designs. The main altarpiece is also one of the finest examples on the island. The work of a Cuban artist, Rogelio Atá, clearly no expense was spared in its creation. The exuberant carving glows with its rich layer of gold leaf. The side altars are more restrained but also feature ornate woodcarving and delicate paintwork.

Set back slightly from the square, on the west side, is the church of the **Virgen del Buen Viaje**. Very attractive from the outside, its plain interior can only disappoint after a visit to the Parroquial Mayor. The small art gallery on a nearby corner is usually worth a quick browse.

On the north side of Plaza Martí is the **Museo García Caturla** (open 9am-noon, 1-5pm Tuesday to Saturday, 9am-1pm on Sunday), named after one of the town's most famous sons. Alejandro García Caturla, a lawyer and composer, was a controversial figure, who shocked the local bourgeoisie by sympathising with the poor and by marrying a black woman, not once but twice. His colourful life came to an untimely end when he was murdered in 1940 after refusing to take a politician's bribe. Although he died at the age of just 34, Caturla earned himself a place in the history of Cuban music. A man who showed originality in almost everything he did, he is acknowledged as the first composer to incorporate African rhythms into classical music. The museum is housed in a colonial mansion, which belonged to Caturla's grandparents and provides an elegant setting for the collection of personal effects.

There is a Museo de Historia just south of Plaza Martí, but non-Spanish speakers will probably find the **Parrandas Museum**, on Calle Máximo Gómez close to the corner of Calle del Río, more rewarding. Labelling is still in Spanish, but Delvis, who works there, speaks good English and gives an enthusiastic guided tour. The museum traces the history of the *parrandas*, which are to Remedios what the carnival is to Santiago. The origins of the festival date back to Christmas 1835, when the town's Franciscan priest got local children to walk the streets banging cans together in order to keep people awake for midnight mass. What began simply as a spontaneous burst of noise, developed into a full-blown carnival with parades, music and fireworks. For most inhabitants of Remedios, the last Saturday of the year is the most important day in the calendar, though preparations begin months beforehand. While there is no official competition, the two neighbourhoods (*barrios*) of San Salvador and El Carmen vie with each other to produce the best show, which they plan amid great secrecy. Both districts erect a *trabajo de plaza*, an elaborate and colourful structure which can reach as high as 90 feet (28m). The bandstand in Remedios' main square was modelled on a *trabajo de plaza* made by El Carmen in 1903, and the museum has models of several others. There are also more traditional floats (*carrozas*), which on the night do the rounds of Plaza Martí, the focus of the whole extravaganza. During the night, the square disappears beneath a blaze of flashing lights and fireworks, accompanied by a cacophany of trumpets, trombones and drums along with the screams of exuberant (and often drunk) revellers. Congas follow the floats in traditional carnival style, but the most characteristic rhythm of the parranda is the polka — a musical style which doesn't exist in the folklore of any other part of Cuba. If you make it to Remedios for the last Saturday of the year, go prepared to stay up all night.

Further Afield. One of Cuba's less-celebrated but more pleasant resorts is Caibarién, just six miles (10km) beyond Remedios. A spit of land pokes out into the Buenavista bay, with some modest beaches on the eastern side, almost always empty. The town itself is run-down but friendly, and visitors approaching from the east are welcomed by a miniature Eiffel Tower.

From here, a good road runs southeast through Mayajigua (where the San José del Lago motel is beautifully located beside a lake) and Morón all the way to Nuevitas. It provides a good alternative to the Carretera Central, particularly for those who want to take a different route through the island in each direction. Just outside Caibarién, a causeway begins to Cayo Santa María — the first of the inhabited keys that stretch for miles along the north coast.

SANCTI SPIRITUS — the City

In *My Early Life*, Winston Churchill gives an account of his youthful visit to this city in 1895: 'a very second-rate place, and a most unhealthy place'. It is still tempting to dismiss Sancti Spíritus as a shabby, unattractive place, but it is one of Cuba's most historic cities. Founded in 1514 by Diego Velásquez, Sancti Spíritus was the fourth of the seven villas (garrison towns) established by Spanish colonists. The town prospered at the heart of a rich agricultural area, but its wealth provided a lure for pirates, who attacked Sancti Spíritus several times, almost destroying it on two occasions.

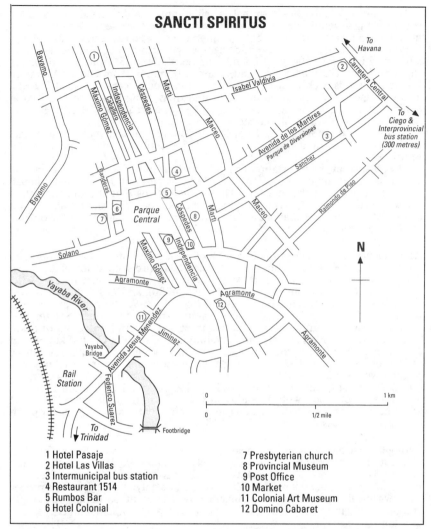

SANCTI SPIRITUS

1 Hotel Pasaje
2 Hotel Las Villas
3 Intermunicipal bus station
4 Restaurant 1514
5 Rumbos Bar
6 Hotel Colonial

7 Presbyterian church
8 Provincial Museum
9 Post Office
10 Market
11 Colonial Art Museum
12 Domino Cabaret

City Layout. The main street is Independencia. It crosses the central square, Plaza Cervantes, where it meets the Avenida de los Mártires, which broadens out into a boulevard a short way east of the square. The river Yayabo, which passes south of Plaza Cervantes, distorts the grid system; consequently Sancti Spíritus, like nearby Trinidad, is one of the hardest places in Cuba in which to find your way around.

Arrival and Departure. Sancti Spíritus is plumb in the middle of Cuba but just south of the main road and rail arteries through the island. Transport to and from the town is surprisingly difficult. The main train of note is the daily departure to Havana at 9.45pm, arriving in the capital at 5.27 the next morning; there are also two services daily to Cienfuegos via Santa Clara. The rail station is south of the Yayabo bridge at the end of Avenida Jeśus Menéndez.

The Interprovincial bus terminal is ten minutes' walk east from the main square along Avenida de los Mártires towards the Carretera Central. Unlike most Cuban bus terminals, all buses stop on the street outside and crowds surge forward onto them. Buses leave the terminal for Trinidad eight times a day, at 5.05am, 7.05am, 10.20am, 11.05am, 3.05pm, 4.05pm, 8.05pm and 10.05pm. Buses to Santa Clara depart at 5am, 10am, 2.05pm, 6.05pm and 10.45pm. To Havana, there is a daily bus at 9.30pm and one on alternate days at 7.20am. The Camagüey bus leaves on alternate mornings at 8am, and to Santiago at 8.40pm on alternate days; given the advance notice required these buses serve no useful purpose for most tourists.

Shorter bus journeys depart from the Intermunicipal terminal on the corner of Calles Sánchez and Carlos Roloff, a block south of the Avenida de los Mártires.

After a spell at the bus station trying to make sense of what is going on, you should start considering the alternatives. The cheapest option is to hitch, though this is best begun in the morning. The few colectivos that still operate gather across the road from the Interprovincial bus station. You should also find a couple of private cabs that should take you where you want to go for dollars; the fare to Trinidad, for example, is about $40.

Accommodation. In the centre of town, by far the best hotel is *La Perla del Sur* on the Parque Central, a lovely and recently refurbished colonial building. Alternatives are the *Colonial*, close to the centre at Máximo Gómez 23 (tel 25123), the *Pasaje* at Independencia 163 (tel 24280), and *Las Villas*, right next to the bus terminal at Bartolomé Masó 13 (tel 23958). All these are peso hotels, but accept dollar-paying tourists, each charging around $12 single, $16 double.

Tourists are encouraged to stay at two three-star hotels, located out of town. The *Villa Rancho Hatuey* (tel 26015, 26406) is at Carretera Central km 383, at the northern entrance to the city. Facilities are good but surprisingly expensive at $58 for a double and $38 for a single in high season. If you're watching your pennies, you would do better at the *Zaza Hotel* (tel 412 6012, 412 5334), 3 miles (5km) southeast of the city on the banks of Lake Zaza. This is a much quieter and more scenic spot, with double rooms for $35 in high season ($28 in low) and single rooms for $26 ($22). You can even hire boats and go fishing for perch or largemouth bass.

Eating and Drinking. There is a dearth of proper restaurants in Sancti Spíritus, although there are plenty of places for snacks. *Restaurante 1514* is on the corner of Laborí and Céspedes, just northeast of the main square. It has fair food for reasonable prices, but opens only 6-9pm daily. The only alternatives for a proper sit-down meal are the *Hanoi*, inconveniently located at Bartolomé Masó 401 and open only in the daytime, and the *Pío Lindo*, at the other (southern) end of the same street.

Cheap and cheerful options are the boisterous self-service restaurant *(autoservicio)* on the main square, and the pizza stall halfway along the Avenida de los Mártires.

Exploring. The *Colonial Art Museum*, just southwest of the main square at Calle Plácido 64, is one of the most atmospheric in Cuba. This old colonial house belonged to the Valle-Iznaga family, one of the most important in the region in the 19th century. It has been preserved in near-perfect condition, with sumptuously furnished rooms and elegant décor. Note how carefully everything is designed to allow for the circulation of air to keep the occupants cool. The museum opens 2-8pm from Tuesday to Saturday and 1-6pm on Sundays. The staff are friendly and helpful.

The *Parroquial Mayor del Espíritu Santo*, due south of the square on the corner of Avenida Jesús Menéndez, is one of several churches in Cuba to be described as the oldest in the country. Although founded in 1522, it was rebuilt in the 17th century following its destruction by pirates; the tower and cupola were later additions. Whatever its vintage, it is a lively and atmospheric place, and the proscenium arch over the altar makes it feel positively theatrical.

The small *Presbyterian church*, four blocks north on Calle Plácido, was built by a Scottish family at the turn of the century, and is dedicated to one James Glass. Sancti Spíritus' most picturesque sight, though, is the *Puente Yayabo*, which carries Avenida Jesús Menéndez over the river and is the only arched stone bridge in Cuba. It was erected in the 1820s.

Help and Information. *All-night pharmacies:* Bartolomé Masó 57, adjacent to the bus station (tel 25808); Independencia 19 (tel 25714); Independencia 123 (tel 24660).
Post Office: Guiteras 3; also adjacent to the bus station.

TRINIDAD

So highly is this town of 35,000 praised that you might reasonably doubt its ability to live up to the glowing tributes. Trinidad's reputation as a unique relic of the colonial era is well-deserved, however. For its cultural treasures, UNESCO placed Trinidad, like Old Havana, on the world heritage list in 1988. Within Cuba it is also a National Monument. The title is justified by the richness of Trinidad's colonial architecture which is mostly untouched by the trappings of the 20th century. Many of the streets are still cobbled, paved with the stone used as ballast in the ships of early Spanish traders. The town is full of interesting nooks and crannies and is the site of some of Cuba's best museums, but it is small and can be explored fairly thoroughly in a day. If you tire of the town itself, there is a good beach nearby and some glorious scenery inland in the Escambray mountains.

The only trouble with Trinidad is that nowadays it is awash with so many tourists in high season that it is hard to make the most of the place. Understandably, the local inhabitants are eager to reap some direct benefit from the flow of dollars through the town; as a result, behind every group of tourists a beggar or other hanger-on is sure to follow. The compactness of the centre means that it can be hard to avoid such attention.

History. The third of the seven Spanish colonial villas, Trinidad developed into a thriving port. The height of its prosperity was in the 19th century, built on sugar and slaves, with legal trade supplemented by a thriving contraband business. Being cut off by the Escambray mountains meant that Trinidad was free to indulge in all kinds of illegal trade, mainly with neighbouring Jamaica. Contact with this English colony and hence the industrial revolution helped transform the sugar mills around Trinidad into some of the most technologically advanced on the island. The 1840s, which saw the construction of 43 sugar mills in a matter of years, marked the peak of Trinidad's sugar trade. Decline came soon afterwards, however, a result partly of the silting up of the harbour and the rise in importance of the port at Cienfuegos. By 1860, Trinidad had virtually been abandoned by those who had built up fortunes in the area and was forgotten for almost a century. The first road to the town was laid only in the 1950s. During the War of Independence, the Liberation Army directed repeated attacks against the sugarmills and the wealthy Spaniards still living in the area. It is therefore all the more surprising to discover such fine examples of architecture from each of the 17th, 18th and 19th centuries.

Town Layout. The early settlers had no truck with the monotonous grid system, so the town centre is a maze of odd streets. The main ones are the two east-west thoroughfares of Antonio Maceo and José Martí, crossed roughly at right angles by Simón Bolívar. The historic centre rises northeast from Antonio Maceo, with the Plaza Mayor — dominated by the church — in the middle. The lower, newer part of town has its own Parque Central, a much less picturesque square.

Arrival and Departure. The principal route to and from Trinidad is the Carretera Sur, which links Sancti Spíritus and Cienfuegos. This road is anything but busy. Public transport is limited and hitching is not as fruitful as elsewhere, unless you are picked up by tourists. The scenic journeys go some way towards compensating for the difficulties in getting started. Allow about six hours if you are driving direct from Havana. If you hire a private cab, expect to pay around $100 for this same trip.

Trinidad is not a hitcher's paradise and your best bet will be to talk or pay your way onto a tourist bus leaving from one of the hotels on the coast. The local hitching points are not far from the edge of town and are marked on the map with a thumb symbol. You may well end up in the back of a jeep driven by other travellers: plenty of tourists drive around the region in hired cars, and are usually happy to give fellow foreigners a ride. (If you opt to drive through the mountains yourself, pick up local hitch-hikers to help guide you — there are many unsigned forks.)

The bus terminal is at the corner of Gustavo Izquierda and Piro Guinart. The timetable is scrawled on a blackboard, conveying the degree of uncertainty regarding departures. The bookings office is open 8-11am and 1-5pm. The one daily bus to *Havana* departs at 1.30pm, but it is booked up days or weeks in advance. The best service is to *Sancti Spíritus*, with eight departures every day: 3am, 5am, 7.30am, 11.30am, 1pm, 2pm, 7pm and 8pm. To try to get on the twice-daily *Cienfuegos* bus (7am, 3.30pm), you should go along the day before to put your name on the list; the journey takes two hours. You might also get a spot on the long-distance bus from the east, which departs for Cienfeugos at 9.10am and 2.45pm.

Santa Clara is surprisingly hard to reach, with just one unreliable service (theoretically at 5.15pm) per day. It takes the long route round via Sancti Spíritus. Doing the journey in stages via Topes de Collantes and Manicaragua isn't a breeze either. The buses into the mountains are converted trucks. According to how much comfort and speed you're after they are either painfully slow and overcrowded or a good way to meet the people and enjoy the scenery. To find out, clamber on to the daily departure at 10am to *Topes de Collantes*, or the Friday and Sunday service to *Manicaragua* at 3pm.

The local bus to Cabaiguán, a town on the Carretera Central 10 miles (16km) north of Sancti Spíritus, could be a good alternative to the over-subscribed services to the bigger towns. Finally, the port at Casilda (and on the way to nowhere much except the Ancón and Costa Sur hotels) is served by a half-hourly bus for much of the day. The crowds at the hitching spot show how inadequate this service is.

There used to be a fairly efficient collective taxi system, operating from by the bus station, but this has died a death. Miraculously, however, the railway has come back to life. Largely thanks to tourism, the fine old station is the terminus for regular services on the short journey into Sugarmill Valley, on the old route up to Sancti Spíritus. Trains depart at 5am, 9am, 1pm and 5.10pm. On Sundays at 11am, a steam-hauled tourist train plies the route, and costs $5. Even if you do not want to catch a train, the station is worth a visit. It is at the bottom of Calle Lino Pérez, south of the centre. Restoration work has turned most of the rambling, castellated structure into an art school, and visitors are welcome to wander around. The elegant Ionic columns and quadrangle create the impression of a cloistered college.

The airport is at the south of the town, close to the station and at the start of

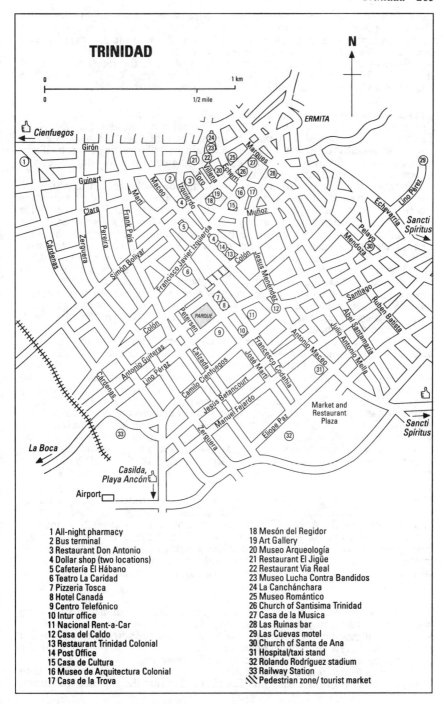

1 All-night pharmacy
2 Bus terminal
3 Restaurant Don Antonio
4 Dollar shop (two locations)
5 Cafetería El Hábano
6 Teatro La Caridad
7 Pizzeria Tosca
8 Hotel Canadá
9 Centro Telefónico
10 Intur office
11 Nacional Rent-a-Car
12 Casa del Caldo
13 Restaurant Trinidad Colonial
14 Post Office
15 Casa de Cultura
16 Museo de Arquitectura Colonial
17 Casa de la Trova
18 Mesón del Regidor
19 Art Gallery
20 Museo Arqueología
21 Restaurant El Jigüe
22 Restaurant Via Real
23 Museo Lucha Contra Bandidos
24 La Canchánchara
25 Museo Romántico
26 Church of Santisima Trinidad
27 Casa de la Musica
28 Las Ruinas bar
29 Las Cuevas motel
30 Church of Santa de Ana
31 Hospital/taxi stand
32 Rolando Rodríguez stadium
33 Railway Station
Pedestrian zone/ tourist market

the road to Casilda. As of January 1996 there were just two flights a week to Havana (at 3.30pm on Wednesdays and Thursdays), price $35 one-way; most of the remaining operations were joy-rides on a Russian biplane over the city and out to the beaches. The Cubana number at the airport is 2296.

Drivers can pick up a car at the Havanautos office in the Hotel Ancon, or at the Nacional Rent-a-Car office on Codahia between Peréz and Cienfuegos. The latter has a weekend special offering a Mitsubishi Lancer for $75.

Accommodation. The choice of accommodation in Trinidad is surprisingly poor. There are two old hotels in the Parque Central but one of these, the *Hotel Canadá*, has been closed for repair for years. The other, *Hotel Ronda*, is a very basic peso establishment but does normally take in dollar-paying tourists. If you hang around the Parque Central long enough, someone will probably offer you a room in a private house, by far the best option.

Foreigners are expected to stay in one of the tourist hotels, all of which are out of the centre. Most central and most popular among low-budget tourists is the two-star *Las Cuevas Motel* (tel 419-2013), in a lovely setting on the 'Finca Santa Ana' overlooking the town; any sign of a ranch has long disappeared. The 114 chalets, which scatter up the hillside above the main reception hut, are clean, have hot water and are well-priced at $19 single/double per night, with an extra $6 for 'especial' rooms. There is also a pleasant pool, with attached bar and shop. In theory, there is a sporadic free bus service to the beach. Disadvantages include the erratic water supply, an alarming amount of wildlife in the rooms (e.g. frogs emerging from the overflow pipe in your sink) and disappointing food. While you can avoid the food by eating in town, it is harder to ignore the groups of inebriated Germans that arrive on special holiday package deals with all food and drink included.

Whatever the drawbacks, Las Cuevas is considerably more congenial than the huge and impersonal beachside hotels that lie about a mile apart south of the town, on a spit of land that pokes out into the Caribbean. The Costa Sur and Ancón hotels, both geared to package tourism, have the advantage of being by the sea; but if you aren't interested in spending much time on the beach, they offer few benefits. They are often full in the peak high season, and both have appalling cabaret and all-night dancing sessions. Furthermore, the distance from Trinidad (7 miles/12km) is unlikely to appeal to all travellers. No public buses serve the hotels, though there is the special service from Las Cuevas, and the morning or evening workers' buses may give you a ride. Hitch-hiking is hard unless tourists stop for you. A taxi (difficult to find in Trinidad) will set you back around $10 each way. The best option is to hire a bike or a moped.

Costa Sur: tel 419-6100, 419-2480. This three-star Horizontes property is on the stretch of the beach known as Playa María Aguilar, marginally closer to town and cheaper than the Ancón. The rooms are also nicer — especially in the new block (Modelo Nuevo), where rooms 100-109, 200-209 and 300-309 are the best. A double room costs around $48. The catering facilities are not as good as in the Ancón, but the bar serves good grills. Be warned that the hotel has no sign outside, so you may overshoot — watch out for a modern block on the right by a bend in the road.

Hotel Ancón: tel 5-667424. Full of French, German and Canadian tourists playing ping-pong and learning to dance the lambada, the Ancón caters exclusively for 'sea and sand' holidays. A lowering of prices has made the hotel a more attractive prospect than a few years back, however. Single rooms cost $35-45 (those in the new wing being more expensive), doubles $55 upwards.

The ground-floor restaurant is charmless but lays on a better breakfast than either Las Cuevas or the Costa Sur. The alternatives are the à la carte restaurant beneath the lobby or the grim cafeteria in the basement. Out at the pool, you can swim up to Los Galeones bar and order drinks from the water.

Camping: there is a campsite between the Costa Sur and Ancón hotels; you may be allowed to stay here, but as a rule only if the hotels are full. If you don't mind being in the middle of nowhere, enquire about the *Guajimico Campismo*, a new site built recently by Cubamar and located midway between Trinidad and Cienfuegos.

Eating and Drinking. The increased level of tourism in Trinidad is most noticeable in the number of new dollar restaurants and cafés. The older establishments have survived, however, where Cubans can still eat for pesos alongside tourists.

At the corner of Colón and Antonio Maceo, is the *Trinidad Colonial*. Confusingly, half the locals refer to it simply as the Trinidad, the other half as the Colonial. The entrance has a shady courtyard ideal for a few sundowners, before you move inside for a meal. The food fails to live up to the surroundings.

The best of the new restaurants is *El Jigüe*, in a small square of the same name on Martinez Villena a block north of the Plaza Mayor. It is an elegant, airy place, and reasonable value. Pollo al Jigüe, the house speciality, costs $12. A block southwest of the square at Simón Bolívar 430, the *Mesón del Regidor* is a *parrillada* or grill house — not a great place for vegetarians unless you eat fish.

A passable stab at an Italian restaurant is made by *Don Antonio* on Izquierdo but it cannot escape giving the impression that it is purely a lunch-stop for tour groups; it opens only 12 noon to 5pm. The *Ristorante Via Reale*, on Calle Villena, has a bit more character. Pizzas start at $4, spaghetti Bolognese at $4.80 and Californian wine at $15. A much cheaper and probably more tasty option is offered by *Ricas Pizza*, dispensing pizza *con mucho queso* for 5 pesos from the private house next to the bus station.

At the time of going to press, the only place in Trinidad to serve an evening meal was the restaurant in the Fondación Santa Ana — formerly a prison and now a complex of shops and galleries — on Calle Lino Pérez down the hill from Motel Las Cuevas. The food is no better or worse than average, but the kitchen can rarely deliver the full range of dishes offered on the menu (particularly by the end of the day).

For drinks and light snacks you can't do better than *Café El Habano*, at the corner of Bolívar and Maceo, which serves great fresh fruit juices and tasty toasted sandwiches, and is friendly and unassuming. Also fun is *Las Ruinas*, a café created in the middle of a ruined property on Echerri, close to the cathedral. Cocktails are just $1 each, cappucino is available. Music starts at around 11pm and continues until the last customer goes home. In contrast, *La Canchánchara* on Martinez Villena, just down from El Jigüe, is a brash tourist trap. The old-fashioned bar and shady courtyard are pleasant, however, and a wide range of drinks is available, sometimes including sugar cane juice *(guarapo)*. The house speciality, after which the café is named, is a mixture of lime juice, honey, aguardiente (officially rum) and ice.

The cavernous *Pizzeria Tosca* on the Parque Central is one of the few peso places left in Trinidad, though the *Casa del Agro*, also in the square, sometimes has hot food for sale. You'll generally have better luck buying snacks for pesos from the stalls in the street. Finally, south in the port of Casilda, try the peso restaurant Santa Elena.

Picnickers can stock up at the town centre market, on the corner of Cienfeugos and Martí, or at the more expansive market on wasteground east of Eliope Paz.

Exploring. Rambling around Trinidad is highly recommended. There is next to no traffic (the cobbles deter most cyclists) and the town is laid out in such a way that one side of the street is always in the shade: a welcome feature on a hot day. Note that Trinidad's museums share the same opening hours: 9am-noon and 2-6pm Tuesday to Saturday, 9am-1pm on Sunday. While Monday is therefore not a great day for visiting museums, the streets will be emptier of tourists. Admission is standardized, too, at $1 for foreigners and 2 pesos for local people. Note that some museums prohibit the taking of photographs, whether of the interior or of the view from upstairs balconies. A little persuasion (and a tip) can sometimes bend the rules, however, particularly if you arrive at 9am before the busloads of tourists begin to arrive. Taking photographs of the local people can become an expensive business too, since these days many expect money in return.

The old town square, with its majestic palms and luscious bougainvillaea, is the symbol of Trinidad. Clustered around the edges are some delightful old mansions (now museums), but dominating the scene is the graceful church of Santísima Trinidad. Built in the late 19th century, with a few gothic touches, it is in good condition, but rather bare; the statues that were supposed to fill the niches never arrived. Catering for the interests of tourists, you can visit the church throughout the day and may be lucky enough to witness a service (and even the sight of the priest's Lada parked inside).

The main appeal of the *Museo de Arquitectura Colonial*, on the southeast side of the square, is that it demonstrates how little Trinidad has changed. The main thrust of the museum, however, is to trace the architectural development of the town during the 18th and 19th centuries, using pictures and maps. The *Museo de Arqueología Guamuhaya* across the road occupies an 18th-century house reputedly built on the site of the home of the famous conquistador, Hernán Cortés. Original Indian art and artefacts from the region are housed here, showing how life was before colonisation.

The best museum in Trinidad is undoubtedly the *Museo Romántico*, housed in the former palace of the Counts of Brunet and designed to demonstrate the lifestyle of Trinidad's sugar barons. Its name derives not from the elegant and romantic setting, but from the style of furniture displayed inside. Nevertheless, it is undoubtedly a romantic place, and newly-weds come here to have their photographs taken on the first-floor balcony. Ordinary visitors are not allowed to take cameras in.

Looking west along from the balcony of the Romantic Museum, you can't miss the yellow church of San Francisco de Asis, now home to the *Museo Lucha Contra Bandidos*. The museum contains mementoes, clothes and photographs of those killed fighting for the Revolution, but concentrates on the struggle against counter-revolutionaries in the Escambray mountains in the early 1960s. Among the exhibits is a gunboat used by the CIA to assist the 'bandits'. Once you've had your fill downstairs, climb the 121 steps to the top of the bell tower, from where there are wonderful views over the square and across to the mountains.

The other museum not to be missed in Trinidad is the *Museo Histórico Municipal*, in a restored mansion just south of the Plaza Mayor at Simón Bolívar 423. Displays provide a reasonable background on the sugar and slave trade, and there are also several fine pieces of furniture.

Don't neglect to explore the streets and sights away from the centre, such as the ruined church of Santa Ana (on the road up to Las Cuevas) and the hermitage of Nuestra Señora de la Candelaria above the old town. The latter is unfortunately bricked up, but remains thoroughly photogenic. It is most rewarding just before sunset, and you can stroll back down into town as the shadows cast magical shades on the pastel walls.

Outside the town, the *Museo Casa Alberto Delgado* is well worth a detour. It is 1km off the road from Trinidad to La Boca, the 'back route' to the Playa Ancón. At the end of the gravel track, you see a low adobe ranch-house, and a smaller yellow building close by where the keeper lives. Admission is free, and the story told is fascinating. Alberto Delgado was a rich farmer who became an

'Amigo de la Revolución'. He was assassinated by counter-revolutionaries at his home, the Finca Maisinicú, in April 1964. Subsequent books and a film *(El Hombre de Maisinicú)* turned him into a folk hero, and his home has been preserved as tribute to him. Everything from his cutlery to the stretcher that carried his corpse is on display, and feels as if it has remained unchanged for 30 years.

At the opposite end of the sublimity scale, tourists staying at the Costa Sur and the Ancón are invited to join a 'Rambo' day for $37. You get a trip in a Russian limousine, a day of hiking, swimming, swinging from ropes and shopping.

Entertainment. Trinidad's predominantly black population produces some fine music, and there is something going on most days. The newly opened *Casa de la Musica*, at the top of the town, is an impressive blend of original stonework and modern architecture, and offers performances most nights. These are openly equally to tourists and locals. The new development has stolen some of the thunder of the *Casa de Cultura* (corner of Francisco Izquierda and Martinez Villena; shows usually two or three times a week), and the *Casa de la Trova*, the blue building just south of the cathedral at Echerri 29. Beer and rum are available at all these venues. The best time to be in Trinidad for entertainment is the third week of November, for the Cultural Week which began in 1973 and has survived all the changes since then.

For the most authentic Afro-Cuban sounds, go to the *Cabildo de San Antonio de los Congos Reales*, a small religious-cum-social-cum-music club located well off the tourist circuit — at Isidro Armenteros 168, northwest of La Canchánchara. Go during the day (8am-noon and 2-6pm Monday to Friday and 8am-noon on Saturday) to find out about forthcoming events. More mainstream entertainment, in the form of cabaret, is put on in the cave near the Candelaria church.

The other main form of entertainment available in Trinidad is sport. Baseball games are held at the Rolando Rodríguez stadium on Calle Eliope Paz. During the day, you can watch young men train in the boxing gym next door.

Help and Information. The central telephone office is in the Parque Central. The main post office is at Maceo 418, between Colón and Izquierda. There is a 24-hour pharmacy on the western edge of town at Carretera Cienfuegos 200. The hospital is at the other end, on Antonio Maceo and Eliope Paz.

Beaches

The closest beach to town is Playa La Boca, 3 miles (5km) west, within possible walking or hitching distance. At weekends La Boca is a lively resort, with radios blaring at full volume and throngs of young Cubans. Further around the coast are a series of deserted rocky coves which are good for snorkelling; Cubans come here to catch conch and other shellfish.

The Ancón peninsula has by far the best beaches, which is why the Costa Sur and Ancón hotels are located here. The Costa Sur has good rock pools and is good for snorkelling. It is not ideal for swimming though; the beach has been 'improved' with broken coral, some of which is sharp. The sea and beach is better by the Ancón. You can arrange snorkelling, diving, water-skiing, boat trips, etc. at either. See *Accommodation* for details of how to reach the hotels from Trinidad.

ESCAMBRAY MOUNTAINS

Anyone with a day in hand should spend it exploring the Escambray mountains to the north of Trinidad. The range does not reach great heights, Pico San Juan at 1,140m being the tallest, but the shade and altitude can still produce a most un-Cubanlike chill. There are places you can visit in the mountains, but in truth all of them are simply an excuse to make some of the must stunning journeys in Cuba.

Topes de Collantes. The road to this mountain resort (2,600ft/790m) leaves the Trinidad-Cienfuegos highway three miles (5km) west of Trinidad. It winds up into the hills, with the first few miles providing a new and more spectacular view of Trinidad and the coast at every turn. The distance to Topes is only 12 miles (20km), but the journey takes 40 minutes by car, an hour or more by bus.

Topes de Collantes is a purpose-built health resort, dominated by a radio transmitter and a huge sanatorium. Built in the 50s to treat those suffering from tuberculosis, after the disease was eradicated it became a teachers' training school in the 60s. Now the whole complex is used for health tourism. The so-called *Centro de Descanso y Salud* (tel 40330, 40228) is a four-star resort-cum-sanatorium with surprising facilities, for anything from acupuncture to stress management. The number of clients is growing slowly, but Topes is normally almost eerily empty. Gaviota is trying to rejuvenate the whole place, but its campaign has yet to have a significant impact.

There is a collection of more conventional hotels in the valley southwest of the sanatorium. The *Hotel Los Pinos* is good for drinks or a meal, and the Caburni bar serves excellent fried plantain; but if you want to stay overnight, you will normally be directed to *Hotel Los Helechos*, beyond, which has excellent doubles ($30-40), with cane furniture, fridge, TV, contemporary Cuban paintings and even sporadic hot water. The cafeteria serves an excellent breakfast and evening meal.

Beyond the hotel are sports facilities of various kinds, including tennis courts, an indoor swimming pool and a sauna. At the far end, turn right out of the gates, then left beyond the Centro de Artesanías; this takes you on a one-hour walk through some spectacularly tall pines and deposits you on the main road close to the sanatorium.

In addition, Topes is the location of an environmental research station known locally as 'Fao' because of its association with the UN's Food and Agricultural Organisation. Visitors are welcomed, and can learn about the conservation and development work in the area. The rainforest is protected, with only dead or dying trees felled, but small-scale agriculture using the forest canopy is being promoted — shade-demanding crops like coffee and bananas are grown.

A few years ago it was easy to make round trips into the mountains from Trinidad. Nowadays it is much harder to piece together local buses, and you will almost certainly have to do at least some hitching. A public bus leaves Trinidad for Topes de Collantes only three times a week on Monday, Thursday and Saturday, but there is also a workers' bus, which should leave daily from the main square at 8am and 2pm. Once in Topes, ask staff at the hotels about when buses are due to leave for Trinidad. Hitchable traffic is scarce, particularly in the low season, though you may strike lucky and catch a taxi that has deposited tourists at one of the hotels.

From Topes you can either continue along the stunning road north to Manicaragua (and beyond to Santa Clara) or strike west to La Sierrita. This last route passes close to Pico San Juan, and provides breathtaking views of the sea and plains as you descend. The surface is poor and there are some very steep inclines, so take care if you are driving. Forget about hitching unless you have all the time in the world; traffic is almost non-existent along this route. Continue for a mile beyond La Sierrita to the main coastal road; at this point you are about 20 miles (32km) from Cienfuegos and 25 miles (40km) from Trinidad. With luck you will pick up a ride back to town.

Valle de los Ingenios

During the 19th century, over forty of Cuba's 100 odd sugarmills were built around Trinidad. Most of them were concentrated in 'Sugarmill Valley' between Trinidad and Sancti Spíritus, which is now a World Heritage site. There are plenty of ruins dotted about, from old mansions to slave cemeteries. Most striking is the 150ft (45m) Manaca Iznaga Tower, in the village of the same name 8 miles (13km) outside Trinidad. Resembling a cross between a folly and a church tower, it was built in as a lookout point from which guards could keep watch over slaves working in the fields below. The Cuban historian, Manuel Fraginals, once described it as the 'ultimate symbol of slavery in the sugarfields'. You can climb it for a view of the area. The restored hacienda down below contains a restaurant, and there are plans to develop the site further. Other smaller ruins are best located with the help of a local guide.

The Eastern Lowlands

1957 Chevrolet Nomad

Ciego de Avila   **Camagüey**   **Las Tunas**

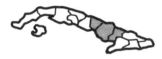

This part of Cuba has been rather unkindly described as 'Belgium with palm trees'. With a landscape almost as flat as a pancake, there seems little to distinguish one province from another nor one town from the next. Yet if you allow yourself the luxury of passing some time in these three provinces you could discover the most thoroughly Cuban part of the island — and indulge yourself at the new resorts on the offshore keys.

In the 19th-century War of Independence, Ciego de Avila province was literally central to the colonialists' defence. The Spanish army built a line of sentry towers across the slimmest part of the island, stretching just 30 miles (50km) from Júcaro up to Morón. The *Trocha*, as it was called, was designed to prevent revolution spreading to the west of Cuba, and was the scene of bitter fighting between colonial forces and the rebels.

Sugarcane and cattle dominate the plains of Camagüey, Cuba's largest and most sparsely populated province. During the colonial era, the region was almost totally isolated from the other main centres of population on the island — an isolation which only the opening of the Santa Clara-Santiago railway in 1903 (and of the Carretera Central in 1931) began to reduce. However, Camagüey was not poor. Cattle, and to a lesser extent sugar, brought great prosperity to the region — and in particular to the creoles who, unlike in other areas, came to wield more influence locally than the Spanish. Furthermore, the cattle trade lead to the development of a more liberal mentality than was found among the slavist sugar plantation owners of Havana. A deep rivalry developed between Camagüey and Havana which, in the 19th century, turned the former into one of the main focusses of rebellion against colonial rule. In the 20th century, the legacy of the province's history and isolation is a strong regionalism, for which Camagüeyanos are still famous.

The city of Camagüey — Cuba's third largest, after Havana and Santiago de Cuba — is the highlight of the region. Among Cubans, it is notorious for its harsh prisons, but Camagüey is also an oasis of culture in a land decorated with cowboys *(vaqueros)* and cattle ranches. Outside the city there is not a great deal to explore other than the beaches along the north coast, where the region's contribution to the tourism drive is concentrated. Camagüey's main resort, Santa Lucía, has a fine beach and offshore coral reefs, and nearby is the idyllic beach of Los Cocos. In Ciego de Avila province, the best beaches lie offshore, such as Cayo Coco, a strip of sand connected to the mainland by a causeway. The small province of Las Tunas, further east, has little to offer. There are plans to develop its northern beaches for tourism, but Las Tunas will never be able to compete with the neighbouring provinces. There are better places to spend your time.

CITY OF CIEGO DE AVILA

Before the creation of new provinces in the reorganisation of local government, Ciego de Avila was just a sleepy market town of 50,000. After 20 years as capital of a province of the same name, Ciego de Avila has become a sleepy little market city of 60,000. It has few attractions even as a stopping-off point; the neighbouring cities of Sancti Spíritus and Camagüey are much more interesting. Nevertheless, it is a place which many independent travellers find themselves visiting, if only to change rides, buses or trains.

City Layout. The bulk of traffic through the island uses the city's circunvalación,

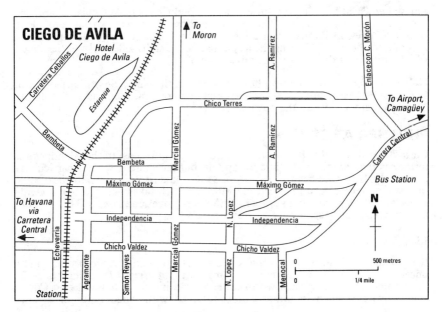

the bypass that swings north around Ciego de Avila. To see just a sample of the city take the Carretera Central, which runs straight through the middle and is known as Calle Chicho Valdés locally. The other main east-west streets are Independencia, a block north, and Máximo Gómez, three blocks north. This latter street should not be confused with the main north-south thoroughfare Marcial Gómez; parallel to this street, a railway line cuts through the city from north to south. The main square is Parque Martí, and the principal sight is its striking Art Deco church.

Arrival and Departure. The modest airport, named Máximo Gómez (tel 2525, 2291), is just three miles east of the town centre, adjacent to the Carretera Central. It is seeing an increase in international charter traffic because of the proximity of the Cayo Coco resort. Domestically, the only route is the Tuesday and Sunday service to Havana. The Cubana office (tel 5316) is at Calle Chicho Valdés no 83.

The Interprovincial bus station is just over a mile east of the town centre on the Carretera Central. Buses run to Havana (7 hours), Holguín (5 hours), Manzanillo (8 hours), Santa Clara (3 hours), Matanzas (6 hours), Cienfuegos (4 hours) and Camagüey (2 hours), but you'll be lucky to get on one. The private cars parked outside the bus terminal are a better bet.

Ciego de Avila is on the main east-west rail line, with two or three trains passing through every day. The station is on the south edge of the city centre, at the foot of Agramonte.

Accommodation. The three-star Hotel Ciego de Avila (Carretera de Ceballos km 2.5; tel 28013) is 2 miles (3km) north of the city centre, just beyond the small Estangua lake. It is nothing out of the ordinary, but like most modern hotels in Cuba it has air-conditioning, a swimming pool and a dismal restaurant. A double room costs around $40. The smaller *Hotel Santiago Habana* (tel 25703) in the city centre, on the corner of the Carretera Central and Honorato Castillo, is cheaper ($28), more central and rather run-down.

Eating and Drinking. The restaurant at the Hotel Ciego de Avila is probably the best you are going to get. The other options are mostly strung out along Independencia. El Paraíso, just along from the Hotel Santiago Habana, is the best of a mediocre lot. During the day a number of stalls sell snacks in the street, which you would do well to take advantage of.

Help and Information. The telephone office is on the west side of Parque Martí. For medical treatment, go to the Hospital General Antonia Luaces Iraola, on Máximo Gómez close to the bus station.

FURTHER AFIELD

Ciego de Avila is only 18 miles (28km) from the south coast of the island, closer to the sea than are the other inland capitals, but the shoreline is not particularly interesting. If you are heading east from Santa Clara or Remedios, the best route to take is the cross-country road via Morón, which takes you through a gentle landscape of rocky hillocks scattered with palm groves and *bohíos*. This is about as picturesque as Ciego de Avila province can get.

Morón

If the sole benefit of the new Cayo Coco resort is to entice more people to this once-elegant spa town, 25 miles (40km) north of Ciego de Avila, then the development will have been worthwhile. Morón is one of those classic Cuban small towns, steeped in atmosphere and laced with faded relics of a more grandiose era. The railway station, towards the south of the town, is a truly heroic building, with murals, marble and a momentous stained-glass roof. There is not much to do in Morón other than enjoy the gentle pace of daily life, but if you are passing through the province or heading for Cayo Coco, it is a far more pleasant place to stay overnight than Ciego de Avila. (You will also have the opportunity to take a photograph of your companion next to a sign reading 'MORON').

Arrival and Departure. The extraordinarily ornate railway station is also the bus station and horse-and-cart depot. Trains run to Ciego at 12.05am, 6.30am, 4pm and 7.13pm, and take about an hour. To Camagüey, there are departures at 3.13am and 1.32pm for the four-hour run. For Jucaro, the only option is at 4.50am (two hours). The train between Santa Clara and Nuevitas operates in either direction on alternate days. Finally, there is a daily train to Esmeralda at 8.10pm (arrives 10.33pm).

The most significant bus service is the hourly departure to Ciego de Avila between 5.30am and 12.30am (but not, unfortunately, precisely on every half-hour).

If you are driving to Morón from the Carretera Central, then watch out for the signs to Cayo Coco — the road to the resort goes past Morón, and is signposted considerably better. A by-pass sweeps through traffic off to the coast, while the main road into Morón continues as Avenida Tarafa; just past the station, it bears left and becomes Calle Martí, the main street.

If you need to fill up with petrol, there is a Cupet station at the edge of town on the Ciego road.

Accommodation. The Perla del Norte, opposite the station, is a peso hotel but the staff will normally let foreign visitors stay (for dollars) if there is room. Further north, the Hotel Sol de Madrid is in need of serious refurbishment before it can accommodate anyone. So most tourists end up staying at the three-star Hotel Morón (Avenida Tarafa; tel 3901/2/3/4/5), a Cubanacán hotel school on the edge of the town. The bronze rooster which stands at the entrance to the hotel is the symbol of Morón; at 6 o'clock every morning and evening, the recorded sound of a cock crowing is supposed to ring out from the small tower across the street, though like everything else this has been a victim of the Special Period. The hotel charges $45 for a double room ($39 in low season) or $36 ($30) for a single. The rooms are clean and there is a pleasant swimming pool with a bar.

Eating and Drinking. The restaurant of the Hotel Morón looks unremarkable but is surprisingly good; the shrimp dish that was the chef's special at the time of going to press was excellent. If you prefer a less formal atmosphere, try for a table at the rustic-style restaurant behind the swimming pool. This caters for Cubans, but the staff should let you in if there are spare tables. The poolside bar can fix a tasty but overpriced cheese and ham sandwich.

The options in town have proliferated recently. As well as a large number of street stalls selling coffee and snacks, the line up goes as follows (heading north from the Hotel Morón). The restaurant at the Perla del Norte is a bit tawdry but very cheap, and foreigners are welcome. Shortly after the handsome façade of the Cuban Telephone Company on the left, the Restaurant La Genovesa sometimes has pizzas. At the junction of Martí and Sergio Antuñas, El Oasis is a passable café. The Resturant Morón, a block and a half further north on the right, is the closest the town has to a 'proper' restaurant; hence queues can be long. Immediately across Callaja, the Morón branch of Coppelia is called La Milanesa. On the left, on the corner of Agramonte, is the 24-hour cafeteria La Diana. One block west and three north, the municipal market is on the corner of Castillo and Cisneros.

Exploring. The town was founded in 1543, and was named after the Andalusian settlement of Morón de la Frontera; it retains plenty of southern Spanish touches beneath its weary exterior. The population is also paler-skinned than usual. At the northern end, it also contains one of the first post-revolutionary structures, a huge concrete hyperbola looking uncomfortable in low-rise surroundings. While the town benefits from the flow of tourists to Cayo Coco, they provide only a passing trade. Most visitors who come specifically to Morón (including so many rich Americans that you'd be forgiven for supposing that the US embargo had ended) are lured by the swamps and lakes to the north of the town, which are among the best hunting and fishing grounds in the country. Even if you aren't an angler, you can enjoy the Laguna de la Leche, 3 miles/5km north of Morón and linked by both road and canal to the town. The lake gets its milky name because of the opaque whiteness of the water, which derives from the lime deposits on the lakeshore; storms whisk up a light greyish tinge. In reality, the tranquillity of the lake is more remarkable than its colour. You can chat to local fishermen, who will talk nostalgically about the fishing tournaments that took place here before the onset of the Special Period. Unless you can persuade someone with a boat to take you out on the lake, there is nothing much to do here, and the restaurant on the shore is badly neglected.

During the War of Independence, the *mambises* smuggled arms across the Laguna de la Leche to avoid the fortifications built by the Spanish between Morón and the Caribbean coast. The ruins of several of these sentry towers can still be seen along the Morón-Ciego-Júcaro road.

Ten miles (16km) north, on the road to Cayo Coco, you find just off to the left a settlement called Celia Sánchez. Castro's confidante decided to establish a Dutch village on the site, so the whole place is occupied by high-gabled, half-timbered houses that look entertainingly out of place in rural Cuba.

Cayería del Norte

The 'northern keys' that are scattered along the coast of Villa Clara and Ciego de Avila provinces are the great white sandy hope for Cuban tourism. Cuba's fourth-largest island, Cayo Coco is highly prominent on the tourism map — as is the neighbouring island of Cayo Guillermo. With a collection of pristine white sand beaches, the region has the potential to be bigger even than Varadero. While Coco and Guillermo are well on the way to saturation development, Cayo Santa María (east of Caibarién, Villa Clara) and Cayo Sabinal are just starting to capitalise on mile after mile of beach and virgin forest. The one possible brake on development is the need to protect the rich wildlife that inhabits the islands — particularly the birds, which include hummingbirds, flamingoes and white ibises.

Arrival and Departure. Cayo Coco is accessible along a 21-mile (34km) causeway, which leaves the mainland due north of Morón and is known as the Pedraplen. It opened on Moncada Day (26 July), 1988, and the environmental impact is a subject for much discussion; there are pipes allowing some water to flow from one side to the other, but there is evidence that the ecological balance has been badly disrupted. Noise from the construction frightened away birds, and impediments to the flow of water mean a kind of artificial lagoon has been created. At present, however, the flamingoes can still be seen, especially in October. A United Nations Development Programme (UNDP) project is aimed at protecting the area.

A smaller causeway links Cayo Coco to the diminutive Cayo Guillermo.

The tiny airport (tel 30-1165) on Cayo Coco can take only small aircraft, such as the Yak-40 used for tourist links to Havana and Varadero. Havanautos has a branch at the airport, and another on Cayo Guillermo.

Accommodation. The best beaches lie along the north coast, where you'll also find the main resort, the five-star Guitart Cayo Coco (tel 33-5388, fax 33-5166). This extraordinary development is designed to resemble a colonial town, with rooms in houses painted pastel shades and tiled in terracotta. It ends up looking like a complete mockery of Cuba, down to the plastic flamingos and pseudo-colonial architecture. The facilities are excellent, though, and the hotel breakfast is enough to demand a visit: honey-nut loops and white bread to salad Niçoise and doughnuts. After breakfast, the full range of watersports is available. Nevertheless, some visitors who just turn up for the day are relieved that they do not have stay any longer. If you want to try it, a room costs $92 off-season, rising to $132 over Christmas.

Touristically, Cayo Guillermo has much less to offer, though you will certainly find greater seclusion and it is a popular place for fishing. It features in Ernest Hemingway's *Islands in the Stream* ('Guillermo, see how green and promising it looks'), and the author is used as a theme throughout the four-star Villa Cojímar, next to the main beach (tel 30-1012, fax 33-5554). The adjoining three-star option is Villa Oceano. A larger beach, Playa Pilar (named after Hemingway's boat), is accessible by launch from here.

CITY OF CAMAGÜEY

Camagüey may lack the waterside charms of Havana and Santiago, yet it is one of the country's most historic cities and also one of its most cultured — providing a haven of refinement in a region otherwise characterised by its cattle-breeding culture. With tourism still in its infancy here, Camagüey remains as arguably the most authentic example of the classic Cuban city. The Camagüeyanos have a reputation within Cuba for being an educated but arrogant lot — they speak the best Castillian and they are proud of it. The Camagüeyanos are also extremely friendly, and it is hard to walk far without being engaged in conversation.

The sprawling outskirts of the 280,000-strong city reveal a rich colonial heart. Camagüey has more historic buildings than any other Cuban city after Havana, mostly dating from the 18th and 19th centuries. It does not possess the capital's wealth of grand mansions, but does have some of the country's finest colonial churches. The convent of Merced, for example, was one of the biggest in Cuba when it was built, and the cathedral is larger than Havana's. The past prosperity that enabled such buildings to be constructed is not as evident as in the island's other famous colonial cities. Apart from a small area around Plaza San Juan de Dios, little has been restored, and much of the city seems rather tatty. The atmosphere is gentle, with life moving at the same pace as the horses and carts and bicycles which ply the narrow streets of the centre. Cuba's tourism drive has barely touched the town, most visitors being bussed in for the day from the beach resorts, but Camagüey will certainly reward a stay of a day or two.

One thing it is impossible to miss in Camagüey are the *tinajones* — large terracotta urns made for storing water. The province is notoriously lacking in rivers, and in the 17th century the water shortage prompted Spaniards in the town to use local clay to make storage jars, which they modelled on those they'd had brought from Spain filled with wine or oil. Up to five feet high and almost twice as wide, the tinajones were placed outside — usually half-buried — as a means of keeping water cool. An elaborate system of guttering was evolved to feed the tinajones, and a side-effect was the development of a ceramics industry. Today, many buildings have a tinajón in the courtyard, although nowadays these vessels generally have an ornamental function. Most date from the 19th century, though their manufacture has recently been started up again.

History. Founded by Diego Velásquez on 2 February 1514, Camagüey was one of Cuba's first seven villas. The town started off with a different name and in a different place. Known as Santa María del Puerto Príncipe (later shortened simply to Puerto Príncipe), it was first located near the present site of the port of Nuevitas. Shortly afterwards the inhabitants later moved inland to escape the 'pirates and insects'. The city in its present location was founded in 1528 on the site of an Indian village called Camagüey, whose name was restored only early this century. The settlers may have escaped the insects but not the pirates, who followed them inland. The town was sacked by the Englishman, Henry Morgan, in 1668 and by a French pirate in 1679. Puerto Príncipe was rebuilt and by 1774 was the second biggest town in Cuba after Havana, with a population of more than 30,000. The trade in contraband, which took place on a greater scale than in either Bayamo or Trinidad, helped fund the city's early expansion. In the 19th century, however, the laying of the railway between Puerto Príncipe and the port of Nuevitas, boosted more legitimate trade, particularly with the United States.

Historically, Camagüey has always been a hotbed of rebellion. Many Camagüeyanos joined the first War of Independence against the Spanish, most famously Ignacio Agramonte (1841-73), the leading general of the war. He is still revered as one of Cuba's greatest national heroes. Another local man, Salvador Cisneros Betancourt, took part in both wars of independence, and in 1895 was chosen as President of the short-lived Republic in Arms. The city's rebellious nature persisted into the 20th century. In response to a series of strikes, the city was occupied by US troops in 1917, and there were numerous protests against Batista in the 50s. In the 60s, Camagüey became synonymous with the UMAP labour camps, where homosexuals, priests, intellectuals and other 'social deviants' were sent during the darkest era of the Revolution.

City Layout. The complex network of interlacing streets in Camagüey does not follow the usual neat grid pattern of most colonial towns. The labyrinthine street network is not simply a reflection of spontaneous rather than planned expansion of the old city — fear of pirates is said to have led to the development of meandering streets with just one exit, to facilitate the ambush of offenders.

Camagüey is most unusual for its lack of a large Parque Central acting as the main focus of the city. Parque Agramonte, more than any of the other small squares in the centre of Camagüey, functions to some degree as the main square, but while it is the place where locals gather to exchange gossip, it does not feel like the hub of a large city.

Camagüey is encircled by a ring road *(circunvalación)*. The Carretera Central sweeps through from west to east, skirting along the east bank of the Hatibonico river — more of an oversized ditch — just south of the city centre. There is not much to take you outside the colonial part of Camagüey, which is concentrated between the Hatibonico river and the railway line to the north. The main commercial street is Avenida República, which runs north-south through the whole of the old town and is your best reference point. Most places of interest lie towards the southern end, west of República. This is where Parque Agramonte is located — on Avenida Martí, another main street running east-west — and Plaza San Juan de Dios. North of the railway line, República becomes Avenida de los Mártires.

Arrival and Departure. *Air:* flights between Camagüey and Havana operate daily, arriving at the airport 8 miles (13km) northeast of the city. (A new terminal is under construction but has some way to go before completion.) The Cubana office (open 7.15am-3pm Monday to Friday, until 11am on Saturday) is at Avenida República no 400, just south of Hotel Colón (tel 92156, 91338).

Train: Camagüey is on the Havana-Santiago rail line and trains between the two cities pass through daily. Local trains serve towns off the main line, including Bayamo (7 hours) and Morón (3½ hours), and generally leave early in the

CAMAGUEY

1 Bus station
2 Museo Provincial
3 Railway station
4 Hotel Plaza
5 Hotel Colón
6 Cubana office
7 Teatro Principal
8 La Soledad church
9 Gran Hotel
10 La Merced church
11 Plaza de los Trabajadores
12 Casa Natal Agramonte
13 Plaza Maceo
14 Parque Agramonte
15 La Volanta restaurant
16 Casa de la Trova
17 Iglesia del Carmen
18 Cristo del Buen Viaje
19 Plaza San Juan de Dios
20 Market
21 Cupet station

0   300 m
0   300 yds

Havana

Av. de los Mártires
Avenida Carlos J. Finlay
Airport,
Santa Lucía

San José
Manuel Ramón

San Martín
Fidel Céspedes

Avenida República

Oscar Primelles
Oscar Primelles
Padre Olalo

Padre Valencia
Popular
Avellaneda
Agramonte

Carmen
Lugareño
Príncipe
Astilleros
Maceo
Enrique Villuendas

San Rámon
Agüero
Cisneros
General Gómez
Betancourt

Martí
Martí

Cristo
Hospital
Carlos M. de Céspedes
San Pablo
República
Río Hatibónico
Avenida Tarafa

La Bayamesa
Lamar
Castillo
P. Recio
Independencia
Cisneros
Hurtado
Carretera Central

N

Varona
Lugareño

Carretera Central
Bus station,
Holguín
Av. de la Libertad

morning. The railway station, located at the northern end of República, is within easy walking distance of all the city centre hotels.

The public relations person at the Hotel Plaza (opposite the station) can sell tickets for the Havana-Santiago *especial* train. Otherwise, you must go to the general reservations desk on the left as you enter the station.

Bus: the main bus station (Terminal de Omnibus Alvaro Barba) is 2km southeast of the city centre, on the Carretera Central. There are supposedly daily bus services to all major towns — including Cienfuegos, Santa Clara, Sancti Spíritus, Holguín, Bayamo, Manzanillo and Santiago — but you will have trouble getting on one unless you talk nicely to the person in charge of issuing tickets.

Buses to Santa Lucía beach, Nuevitas on the north coast and Santa Cruz del Sur on the south run from the Intermunicipal terminal on Avenida Carlos J Finlay, a stone's throw east of the train station.

Taxis: private, unlicensed vehicles gather under the trees opposite the inter-municipal bus station. Drivers will take you virtually anywhere you wish to go if the price is right. The trip to Santa Lucía will cost around $12. For a longer journey, such as to Bayamo, expect to pay around $40.

Driving: by road, Camagüey is 357 miles (571km) from Havana, 68 miles (108km) from Ciego de Avila, 77 miles (124km) from Las Tunas and 250 miles (400km) from Santiago. If you are approaching from the west, remember that the Ocho Viás motorway stops before you reach Ciego de Avila and is replaced by the Carretera Central, which has just two lanes and is in poor nick.

The narrow, one-way streets of Camagüey are a nightmare for motorists, and it is easy to get stuck behind horses and carts and bicycles. You see very few cars in the old town, where pedestrians seem to rule the roost. If you are just visiting for the day and want to park in the centre, aim for the Plaza de los Trabajadores (just north of Parque Agramonte), the Plaza Hotel (outside the railway station) or the Cupet station, which is just across the Hatibonico river. Horses and carts run from the park a short distance east of Cupet to the railway station, passing through the centre.

Accommodation. Camagüey has a good choice of hotels, including several in the city centre. Try for a room at the Hotel Plaza (tel 82413), a large graceful building opposite the railway station. The staff are very friendly and the rooms large and clean, with television, radio, fridge and even warm water. A double costs $30 ($24 in low season), a single $25 (or $20). Downstairs, the 24-hour Cafetería Vitral is extremely cheap. Toast and coffee costs less than a dollar, fried chicken is just $2, and there are special deals if you order a local Tinima beer with your meal: a steak sandwich with a bottle of Tinima costs $1.40. If the cafetería runs out of coffee, try the bar (open until 11pm) beyond the lobby — where a green perspex ceiling over the courtyard bathes punters in a rather unsavoury light. There are several dollar shops on the ground floor.

If atmosphere is more important than facilities, you should investigate the two hotels nearer Parque Agramonte, particularly Hotel Colón (tel 83369), on Calle República between Manuel Ramón and Fidel Céspedes. It is worth having a peek inside even if you aren't interested in staying here. There is a fine old-fashioned bar in the lobby, and walk through the high saloon doors at the back and you'll find an elegant courtyard with a restaurant. Room rates are $18 for a double ($14 in low season) and $14 for a single room ($12). Otherwise, try the three-star Gran Hotel at Calle Maceo 67 (tel 92093/4). Housed in a fine neo-colonial building, the Gran has more pretentions than the Colón, but it has the advantage of being right in the heart of the old town. The elegant Salon Caribe restaurant on the fifth floor (see *Eating and Drinking*) has the best views in Camagüey, with all the main landmarks nearby. A double room costs $22 ($20 in low season) and a single $18 ($17). Downstairs, there is a 24-hour snack bar and also a nightclub.

If you want greater levels of comfort, you will have to head out to the three-star Hotel Camagüey (tel 322-72015, 82490), which is the main tourist hotel, 2 miles (4km) southeast of the town, beyond the bus terminal on the Carretera Central (which at this point is also known as Avenida Ignacio Agramonte). The building itself is yet another 70s Soviet monstrosity, but is in reasonably good condition. As in so many of these hotels, there is a small swimming pool, a grim little cafeteria on the ground floor and a shop, restaurant and 24-hour bar (that is often closed) on the first. In high season, the restaurant can lay on a reasonable buffet. A double room costs $40 ($35 in low season) and $26 for a single. There are also *cabañas*, where three people can stay for $53.

If you can spend a little more money, you should consider Villa Maraguán (tel 72017, 721601). The address is Camino de Guanabaquilla, Circunvalante Norte — put more simply, close to the airport, north of Hotel Camagüey. Formerly a country club frequented by the American hunting fraternity, after the Revolution it became a hotel for members of the armed forces. Cubanacán converted it into a hotel in the early 1990s and did an admirable job. Rooms ($55 for a double, $43 for a single) are very comfortable, and other good reasons for staying at the Maraguán include the breeze, vegetation, swimming pool and tranquillity.

If you are determined to be in the centre and by some misfortune the Plaza, Colón and Gran hotels are full, you will have to try the Isla de Cuba (tel 91515), at the corner of Oscar Primelles and Popular, a gloomy place which charges $20 for a double and has dodgy plumbing, or the Puerto Príncipe (tel 82490, 82403) at Avenida de los Mártires 60, an ungracious peso hotel which rents rooms to tourists.

Eating and Drinking. Eating out in Camagüey can be a pleasure not necessarily for the food but for the glimpse it gives you of some of the city's finest colonial buildings. Best of all is La Volanta on Parque Agramonte, with its exquisite alfarje-style ceiling, grand chandeliers and antique mahogany furniture. The large windows give passers-by a good view inside and enable customers to watch the world go by too. Unlike the two restaurants in Plaza San Juan de Dios (see below), La Volanta is frequented primarily by Cubans. As a result the menu is limited, but this is a place to come for the surroundings rather than the food. Eat early (preferably 7-8pm) to avoid turning up after the kitchens have run out of food.

La Piazza, on the corner of Agramonte and Maceo, occupies the first floor of another fine colonial building, with a balcony overlooking the church of La Soledad. At the time of going to press it does not serve tourists, but it would be well worth asking whether they have changed their policy. There are already plans to turn a room on the mezzanine floor into a dollar bar, so it is probably only a question of time before the Cubans are pushed out from upstairs.

Just down the road, the Salon Caribe restaurant on the top floor of the Gran Hotel must win the prize for best location — there is a pleasant breeze as well as a fine panoramic view. Main dishes are perhaps overpriced at $5-8, but there is plenty of choice, from eggs in various guises to roast pork, chicken and fish. Hotel staff will try to persuade you to visit the 'mirador' on the roof terrace — for which you must pay $1 — but the view is just as good (and free) from the restaurant.

The main dollar restaurants in the old town are in Plaza San Juan de Dios. These cater mainly for daytrippers and are closed in the evening. La Campaña de Toledo is one of the few places in Cuba where you can eat *boliche mechado*, beef stuffed with chorizo, which is the house speciality. The large courtyard is pleasant for a drink if you don't feel like eating. The Parador de los Tres Reyes is housed in another 18th-century building, and has traces of original murals. The surroundings make up for any disappointment you might feel with the food. Another option is the Rancho Luna in Plaza Maceo, to which Cubans have access via their workplace and which rarely seems to have room for unexpected guests. For a younger crowd, go to Pizzeria Hatibonico, under the trees on the east bank of the river (between the two bridges), where you can eat pizza and spaghetti for pesos.

The Camagüeyanos love their food. The best place to see them in action is in the market on the west bank of the Hatibonico at the foot of Independencia. For 20 pesos you can enjoy a nourishing meal consisting usually of moros and cristianos, a pork escalope and salad. This is fast food at its best.

Exploring. The following tour of Camagüey begins in the north and heads south. The northernmost sight, the Museo Provincial Ignacio Agramonte (one block north of the railway line) is perhaps the least rewarding of all the sights. It contains an uninspired collection of objects related to local history and culture. Opening hours are 9am-5pm Tuesday to Saturday, 8am-noon on Sunday.

Heading south along República, past shops, peso eateries and the odd street vendor, you reach Iglesia de la Soledad. The peeling appearance of the exterior of this church does not prepare you for the treasures inside. La Soledad (built 1758-76) boasts a well-preserved alfarje ceiling, but the most striking aspect of the church are the painted designs on the arches and mammoth square pillars. The delicate, rather non-ecclesiastical floral designs add a pleasant sense of intimacy to the building. La Soledad is generally open in the morning; don't give up if it is closed first time — this is the finest church in Camagüey.

From La Soledad, Calle Maceo runs southwest. Spruced up recently and with music blaring from loudspeakers, this is the main shopping street for those with dollars. If you are short of time, you may want to head down Maceo and on to Parque Agramonte. Otherwise, take Avenida Agramonte west to Parque de los Trabajadores — more of a car park than a meeting place. On the left just before you enter the square is the Casa Natal de Ignacio Agramonte (open 10am-6pm Tuesday to Saturday). The independence fighter was born in this house in 1841 and it has been preserved as a museum. You will find the usual array of personal effects together some interesting art and a blow-by-blow account of the commander's brief life (he died in 1873). For non-Spanish speakers, the principal charm of the museum is the house itself — a lovely 18th-century mansion — and the beautiful period furniture.

Looming across the street is Iglesia de la Merced, built in 1748 and with an imposing tower that rises directly from above the main doorway. The church is currently being restored, but resources are so limited that only a tiny section is worked on at any one time. When first completed, this church was considered one of the finest in Cuba. The lighting is poor, but you can still admire the fine vaulted ceiling which is decorated with a sinuous, art nouveau-style design the exact date of which is unknown. You enter La Merced through the office on the west of the main entrance, and the receptionist will arrange for someone to show you around.

Calle Independencia or Cisneros will take you south to Parque Agramonte, a small but classic Cuban square, with benches on which to sit and gossip, trees to provide shade, a patriotic monument and a church. A mix of architectural styles runs from colonial to Neo-Classical and Art Nouveau. It's worth having a look inside the Casa de la Trova and La Volanta restaurant, both with attractive colonial interiors and period furniture. The dramatic statue of Ignacio Agramonte, mounted on a horse, was begun in 1902 during festivities celebrating the birth of the new republic, but took ten years to complete. Flanking the south side of the square is the Parroquial Mayor, referred to locally simply as the '*catedral*'. A church was built on this site as early as 1530, but this first wooden structure was destroyed by a fire that devastated the whole town in 1616. A new church, with just a single nave, was built soon afterwards. Subsequent changes mean that the cathedral has lost the purity of La Soledad, for example, but it boasts several original features, including an alfarje ceiling. At the time of going to press, the church was undergoing a complete restoration, which is likely to last some time.

A short walk south along Padre Recio takes you to a very different kind of square, Plaza San Juan de Dios. Fringed by charming 18th-century buildings, this is the only part of the city to have undergone a full restoration programme. The small church of San Juan de Dios is the most intimate in the city, with a simple mahogany alfarje and a high altar of mahogany and gold leaf. The old hospital next door is now the local heritage office. If you are interested in knowing more about the square or Camagüey as a whole, ask to see the city historian. In the courtyard there are posters with information about sights in and around Camagüey and photographs of the city as it was.

The farmers' market, a short stroll south of San Juan de Dios, carries you back to the reality of daily life in Cuba. This is Camagüey at its liveliest. People sell fruit and vegetables under the trees (sometimes off the back of a lorry), while the butchers gather under cover, flies buzzing furiously over their fatty and uninviting slabs of meat. Next door, you can eat a good lunch and revel in the convivial atmosphere. This is a good place to meet people.

There is not much to tempt you south of the Hatibonico river — though if you've got this far and can't be bothered to walk back into town, you can pick up a horse and cart from the other side of the bridge. (There are usually a couple of bicycle rickshaws by the market too.) If you want to explore, you can wander down Avenida de la Libertad, which has some interesting 20th-century architecture. Seven blocks down is the 18th-century Iglesia de la Caridad, dedicated to the patroness of Camagüey.

One thing you should not miss in Camagüey is the cemetery, seven blocks southwest of Parque Agramonte, behind the attractive 19th-century church of Santo Cristo del Buen Viaje. It is among the finest burial grounds in the country, and contains a number of interesting tombs; look out for the art nouveau-style chapel that shows an obvious Gaudí influence. Four blocks north, at the corner of calles Carmen and Martí, is Iglesia del Carmen, with its broad and beautifully-proportioned façade. Built in 1825, it represents a late flowering of the Baroque — it took some time for neoclassicism to penetrate the provinces from Havana.

Entertainment. For high culture in Camagüey you should go to the Teatro Principal, a couple of blocks northwest of Plaza de los Trabajadores. The theatre — a lavish confection of crystal and marble dating from 1850 — is used for all kinds of performances, including ballet. The Camagüey Ballet Company is the best in the country after Havana's National Ballet and performs modern dance as well as the classical repertoire. If the dancers are not performing at the theatre, it is sometimes possible to watch them rehearse at the ballet school at the junction of the Carretera Central and Calle 4, on the western edge of the city centre. You might want to call (tel 9-9215) before making the journey.

The Casa de la Trova in Parque Agramonte (admission 1 peso) is the place for traditional Cuban music, though for a serious dance you'll do better at one of the local cabarets. One of the most popular is El Colonial, on Calle Agramonte near the corner of República, which has a regular show. La Volanta restaurant sometimes puts on a cabaret at weekends, otherwise try the hotels, most of which lay on some form of live entertainment.

The Casa de la Cultura on Plaza de los Trabajadores puts on a range of evening events, from poetry readings to discos.

Help and Information. *Money:* Hotel Camagüey can cash travellers cheques for you. Or go to one of the banks on Avenida República or the BFI branch in Plaza Maceo.

Post Office: Plaza de los Trabajadores.
Car Hire: Transautos has an office outside Hotel Camagüey.
Petrol: the Cupet station is at the top of Avenida de la Libertad, just across the Hatibonico river.
All-night pharmacy: corner of Oscar Primelles and Avellaneda; also at the corner of José Martí and Torres Lasquetti.

EXPLORING CAMAGÜEY PROVINCE

Following a quick scoot around the city, most people head straight off to Santa Lucía on the north coast. You would do well, however, to resist the lure of the beach for long enough to at least get a flavour of what Camagüey province is about. If you have a car, just by taking a longer, cross-country route to the coast you will be able to appreciate the empty landscapes that are characteristic of the region.

At the heritage centre in Plaza San Juan de Dios in Camagüey, you can get information about all kinds of local sites, from old sugar mills (such as Ingenio El Oriente at Sibanicu, considered one of the best preserved in Latin America) to towns founded by North American colonists. One such place is **La Gloria** — originally Gloria City — about an hour and a half's drive north of the city across the Sierra de las Cubitas. Nothing much remains of the original settlement, except for its charming clapboard church, built in 1892. Local people will direct you to the house of the woman who nursed the last member of the American community to live in the town, a certain William Stokes, who is buried in the village cemetery. After his death in the 80s, the American's villa was dismantled and moved to the town, where his nurse still lives, surrounded by some of her old employer's belongings. *The Last American* by Enriques Cirules (published in 1987, in English as well as Spanish), is a novel based on William Stokes and the story of Gloria City. While there is not much to La Gloria, it has a history that will make the place appeal to those interested in the American involvement in Cuba.

North Americans were attracted to this northern part of Camagüey province because of its proximity to the port of **Nuevitas**, 50 miles (80km) northeast of Camagüey, and therefore to the US market. A labyrinth of railroads was built to connect the sugar plantations with the coast. The drive between La Gloria and Santa Lucía takes you across a land eerie for its flatness and emptiness, but the innumerable railway tracks recall the region's former prosperity.

Nuevitas is one of the ugliest coastal towns in Cuba. It is still a major port, however, responsible for shipping out sugar from the province's mills. The town's western district is disfigured by a huge power station, cement works and other heavy industry, while the southeast has a few beaches which you are strongly advised against using. The place is being done up for tourism, but Nuevitas will never be more than a stopping-off place en route to nearby **Cayo Sabinal** — accessible by boat but more easily by road. The beaches of Cayo Sabinal, of which Playa Bonita is the best known, offer a welcome alternative to Santa Lucía during the high season. There is also a wildlife reserve where visitors are taken on 'jeep safaris'.

SANTA LUCIA

With a fine sandy beach stretching for several miles, Santa Lucía is the main resort in the province of Camagüey. The best road in the region has been built to link the resort to the provincial capital and, more importantly, its airport, 65 miles (105km) southwest. There is clearly a fair amount of work still to be done at Santa Lucía, but development here is unlikely to ever reach the scale of that of Guardalavaca — let alone Varadero. There is nothing much to the resort beyond the five hotels and the obligatory Cupet station.

If you've come to Cuba to relax on one of the country's famous beaches, you will probably be disappointed when you first catch sight of the beach at Santa Lucía, which is perfectly pleasant but often disfigured by a blanket of seaweed. Do not despair. Playa Los Cocos, one of the island's finest beaches, is just a short drive away: see below.

One of the attractions of Santa Lucía is the scuba-diving. There is a small but interesting offshore coral reef and a couple of places can arrange trips ($30 for one dive, $50 for two and $150 for five); it is also possible to do a PADI course, which costs about $300. Other activities include windsurfing, horse riding and tennis. Day trips can be arranged to Cayo Sabinal and other nearby cays, as well as longer outings further afield — e.g. two days in Santiago for $180.

Evening entertainment may not satisfy those after a lively beachside holiday. In the low season, you may find yourself propping up the bar or nursing a bottle of rum on the beach, though most of the hotels have a games room, which invariably includes a pool and ping pong table.

Be warned that the mosquitoes are rabid during summer. The only consolation is that there are so many around and probably so full of blood that the beasts are gratifyingly easy to swat.

Accommodation. Apart from the dismal Villa Tararaco, Santa Lucía's hotels are modern, resort-style establishments, though they are generally more modest affairs than those you'll find at Guardalavaca in Holguín province. These are, from east to west:

Cuatro Vientos: tel 032-36493, 36317, fax 335433). The newest hotel, more tasteful and quieter than the others, with one of the best stretches of beach too. The name derives from the name of the aircraft used for the first non-stop flight from Spain to Cuba in 1933. This Cubanacán property charges $36 for a single room ($59 including food) or $60 for a double ($100 with food); meals on their own cost $8 (breakfast) and $15 (lunch or supper). Transautos has a desk on the ground floor.

Club Coral: tel 48302. This is one of the better organised hotels in Santa Lucía, with a choice between apartments and individual bungalows, and the food is good too. The current rate is $45 per single room, $65 for a double.

Caracol: tel 30402/03, 48302. Similar to the Coral, only smaller, the four-star Caracol offers *cabaña*-style accommodation at $46 for a double room, though there is usually some kind of special offer available if you take half board. The dance lessons, aerobic classes and similar pursuits are popular in high season.

Mayanabo Club: tel 36184 to 86. This three-star hotel is not somewhere that will appeal to many people since the hotel obliges you to take full board, at $75 per person. Even so, the Mayanabo has a good pool and looks onto one of the best parts of the beach.

Villa Tararaco: tel 36222, 36310. This two-star hotel is the cheapest place in Santa Lucía — $30 per double room, $25 for a single — but it has few other redeeming features. The Tararaco could do with a serious revamp. The rooms look fine on first glance, but the beds are so hard you may as well sleep on the floor. At least the rooms are separate from the soulless main hotel building and are just a few paces from the beach. The breakfast is horrifying, the only edible thing the kitchen seems able to prepare being scrambled egg.

Eating and Drinking. If you can be bothered to leave the main resort, the best place to eat is Lazo's Lobster House near Los Cocos beach: see below. In Santa Lucía, you must choose from the hotel restaurants. The best of these are in the Coral and Caracol. Nowhere in Santa Lucía is cheap. Main meals in the Caracol's grill restaurant cost $10-25, unless you opt for pizza or spaghetti.

Playa Los Cocos

Any disillusionment you might feel with Santa Lucía should disappear on seeing

Playa Los Cocos, just 5 miles (8km) west. A perfect crescent of fine white sand curves around a small bay of crystalline water. Nestled beneath palm trees at one end sits La Boca, a sleepy village of clapboard houses. You won't find many more heavenly places than this in Cuba. The atmosphere is so laid back that the harsh realities of daily life seem a million miles away; this is the perfect place to relax if you've been travelling around the island for a while. There is as yet no hotel at Los Cocos and no sign that one is being planned. For the moment, there are just a couple of small bars by the beach, which hire out snorkels and boats, and Lazo's Lobster House, where you can eat exquisite seafood and contemplate both the view and your good fortune to be in such a place. The impressive menu includes lobster, octopus and shrimps in many different guises.

To explore, you can hire a boat and go across to nearby Cayo Sabinal (see above). Nearer to base, flamingoes and other birds gather on the lagoon just behind La Boca.

King Ranch

This is the perfect place for anyone after something a bit different. The idea behind King Ranch is sound. Camagüey is cattle country after all, so what could be more logical than to have a ranch where people can watch a few local cowboys being put through their paces at a rodeo. Group trips are organised from Santa Lucía — lunch, a horse-ride and the rodeo for $20 — but if you're on your own and turn up on the off-chance you can watch free of charge if there's a show on. Some people may baulk at the idea of going to a rodeo laid on only for tourists, but it's hard to track down a real-life rodeo, and going to King Ranch does at least give you a small insight into the cowboy culture of the province. The place is run with enormous enthusiasm.

King Ranch lies 15 miles (24km) south of Santa Lucía — if you're trying to find it on a map, it's not far from a village called Camalote, just off the Camagüey road. The provision of accommodation has not been a priority, and at the moment there are just three rooms ($25 per room including breakfast). These are in the original ranch house, which until 1992 was a quiet country retreat for Fidel Castro and other members of the Council of State. The financial strictures of the 90s spurred the government to sacrifice the place to tourism, but some of the original furniture is still on show.

CITY OF LAS TUNAS

There is no particular reason why the traveller should want to spend any time in the capital of the province of Las Tunas, which rises on the edge of a large agricultural plain. The city reeks of neglect — the most attention Las Tunas has ever received was last century, when it was badly damaged during the independence war — and even the local hotel seems surprised when a foreign tourist turns up. It would not be the end of the world if you have to break your journey here, but quite honestly, if you are merely passing through it would be a waste of time and energy to dally long in Las Tunas. Places in the next three chapters are a lot more interesting.

The best time to see Las Tunas is in the early evening, when the church in the main square is open for mass. It is a squat little place with a lively atmosphere (and a Cuban flag sitting contentedly in a corner). The nearby Plaza de la Cultura, adjacent to the provincial museum, has an interesting relief mural of brick and clay.

Arrival and Departure. *Air:* if, for some reason, you decide to fly to Las Tunas from Havana, you will land at Hermanos Almeijeras airport on the northern edge of town, a 15-minute horse-drawn ride from the town. If you need a taxi you may need to call the Hotel Las Tunas where one usually resides. The Cubana town office is at the corner of Lucas Ortíz and 24 de Febrero (tel 4-2702).

Train: Las Tunas is on the main line between Havana and Santiago, and is served by daily through-trains in each direction; the journey from Havana takes about 12 hours. There are twice-daily services to and from Holguín.

Bus: the long-distance terminal is on the main road through town, about ten minutes walk southeast of the main square. It is not unheard of for tourists to talk their way onto a bus, but go prepared for disappointment.

Hitching: if you wish to travel by road, it is not unlikely that you will have to join the throng at the east end of the city, ten minutes' walk out from the bus station. The local Inspección Estatal has got organised hitching off to a fine art. You walk into a huge cage, collecting a ticket to your destination on the way in. Every time a truck stops, a block of numbers is called out and the lucky winners get on using a boarding ladder borrowed from Cubana.

Nearby destinations such as Holguín are regarded as too trivial to qualify for this sophisticated system, so you'll have to take your chances by the roadside with everyone else.

Driving: by road, Las Tunas is 77 miles (124km) from Camagüey, 49 miles (79km) from Holguín, 171 miles (274km) from Santiago and 434 miles (695km) from Havana. There is a 24-hour Cupet station on the western edge of town, on the road to Camagüey.

Accommodation and Food. The three-star Hotel Las Tunas (Avenida 2 de Diciembre; tel 45169, 45014) is a standard-issue Soviet-style atrocity located a mile east of the city centre. Perched uncomfortably on a hill some distance from anywhere of interest, it doesn't even offer a great view — apart from the weird water towers which look like huge flying saucers on sticks. It makes a change to be surrounded by Cubans rather than tourists, but the hotel is crying out for some attention. Rooms ($30 per night for a double, $25 for a single) come with TV and fridge but no hot water. You can at least get a cheap breakfast of coffee and toast in Cafeteria Las Delicias.

A much better option if you can do without a few three-star facilities is the Hotel Ferroviario, opposite the train station, with double rooms for $15 and singles for $10. This is a fine, atmospheric old place, with a restaurant, a courtyard where the occasional cabaret is staged, and welcoming staff. The farmers' market is nearby too. This is small by most standards, but you can pick up fresh fruit and treat yourself to a batido or a sandwich.

If you want somewhere to dance away your sorrows, try the Cabaret Taíno, on the Camagüey road.

Holguín and Granma

City of Holguín

Once you cross from the Eastern Lowlands into these provinces, suddenly life is more interesting. The landscape, which becomes steadily more lush and mountainous as you head eastwards, comes like a breath of fresh air after the plains. You are now well into Oriente, Cuba's eastern region and its richest historically and scenically.

Holguín province, which extends along the north coast of Oriente, figures large in the early history of the island. About a third of Cuba's archaeological finds, including the oldest, have been found in Holguín province. It was here too that Columbus first landed in 1492, in a lovely bay near Gibara on the north coast. Four centuries on it was the North Americans who landed, taking advantage of the chaos and devastation which resulted from the Ten Years' War. US business interests soon dominated the area, particularly after independence, when the United Fruit Company bought huge tracts of land around Mayarí, monopolising the region's most fertile land. Fidel Castro, who was born in the municipality of Birán, about 25 miles southwest of Mayarí, grew up in just such an atmosphere, a perfect breeding ground for a revolutionary.

The Americans were involved in nickel mining too, and the mines around Moa are still the region's main source of income. The second most populous province after Havana, Holguín has done comparatively well since the Revolution; industrial complexes and sprawling modern suburbs disfigure the provincial capital. The heart of the city is pleasant enough, however, and certainly worth visiting before heading deeper into the province. Further afield, the most vaunted attraction is the resort of Guardalavaca, Oriente's equivalent of Varadero. Antidotes to excess tourism can be experienced at sites of archaeological interest nearby and in the outstandingly pretty town of Gibara. While the scenery in Holguín is not as dramatic as that in neighbouring Granma province, it makes good touring country.

In few areas of Cuba will you find such contrasting landscapes as in Granma. The Rió Cauto, the country's longest river, which cuts a swathe through the north of the province, is flanked by flood plains where rice and sugarcane grow in abundance. While south of the provincial capital of Bayamo, and extending right down to the coast, rise the wildest and most remote peaks of the Sierra Maestra mountains. In the colonial period the area prospered largely thanks to rampant smuggling, which could flourish in this isolated corner of the island. Bayamo and Manzanillo, both developed on the back of contraband and remain Granma's most important towns. In Castro's Cuba, the province lives mainly off its sugar and coffee crops.

Of all the eastern provinces, Granma boasts the most associations with struggles against authority. It was the scene of Cuba's first known slave rebellion, which occurred in Jobabo near Bayamo in 1533. Three centuries later, a mill owner called Carlos Manuel de Céspedes launched the island's first war of independence in 1868 by freeing his slaves and announcing that Cuba intended to revolt against the domination of the Spaniards. His proclamation, known as the 'Grito de Yara', is commemorated throughout the Republic, and virtually every town in Cuba has a street named after its instigator. Many of the battles of that war were fought in the area. The region saw a lot of action during Second War of Independence too; José Marti himself was killed at Dos Rios, northeast of Bayamo, in 1898.

The province of Granma takes its name from the cruiser which carried Fidel Castro, Che Guevara and the other rebels to eastern Cuba in 1956. The mountains of the Sierra Maestra were a perfect haven for the revolutionaries during their campaign against Batista. Four decades on, the mountains are only marginally more accessible and are exciting to explore. Not many tourists make it to this corner of Cuba, but it is well worth the effort.

CITY OF HOLGUÍN

At first sight, Holguín looks thoroughly uninspiring, with its unremittingly ugly suburbs where apartment blocks and office buildings are dotted uncomfortably around the urban wasteland. While by no means the most interesting city in Cuba, the provincial museum is worth a visit if you are planning to explore the region. There is also some interesting architecture you can enjoy and fine views from a hill overlooking the city. Given that Holguín is the gateway to important tourist centres on the north coast, it is surprisingly short of good hotels and restaurants.

A settlement has existed on or near the site of present-day Holguín since before 1492, when Columbus first landed at Bariay on the north coast. Soldiers sent southwards to investigate the island found an encampment about 25 miles/ 40km inland, which the natives called Cubanacán. This meant 'the centre of Cuba' and was geographically inept; there are several existing villages with this name dotted around the Republic, none of them remotely near the middle of Cuba. Holguín itself was founded in 1525. It grew slowly but steadily over the next two centuries, thanks largely to the lucrative trade in contraband which filtered down from the port of Gibara. Only in the 18th century did Holguín begin to develop seriously.

City Layout. The centre of Holguín is a fairly regular grid but is unusual for the series of squares that are spaced at intervals on the north-south axis formed by Maceo and Manduley. The main city square is Parque Calixto García, usually known simply as 'El Parque'. No one seems to be able to agree on the names of the other squares: in case you get confused, Parque San Isidoro and Parque Julio Grave de Peralta are the same place, as are Parque San José and Parque Carlos Manuel de Céspedes.

The two main tourist hotels are located 2 miles (3km) east of the main square, near the Plaza de la Revolución, as unappealing and unattractive as any post-1959 parade ground.

Maps of Holguín are available in the Librería Pedro Rojena Camayid, an excellent dollar bookshop on the east side of Parque Calixto Garciá.

Arrival and Departure. *Air:* the Frank País airport, southwest of the city along the Carretera Central, has been served by charter flights from Germany and Austria for some time, and there are now charters from the UK too. There is a daily flight from Havana, which on Mondays and Saturdays calls at Varadero. The Cubana office is in the three-storey Policentro building at the southeast corner of Parque Calixto García (tel 5707). Buses to the airport run from Rodríguez, six blocks south of the main square, but allow plenty of time in case you have to improvise when it doesn't turn up.

Train: given that Holguín is an important provincial capital, its transport links are abysmal. It didn't even make it onto the trans-Cuba railway, the nearest station on this line being at Cacocum, 10 miles (16km) southwest. There is a branch line, however, so even if you can't hop on the Havana-Santiago *especial* service, there are daily trains from Holguín to both Havana (7.35pm) and Santiago (2.10pm). There are also several daily services to Cacocum, so you can pick up connections there too. Holguín's rail station, a chaotic affair, lies at the southern end of Manduley.

Bus: the long-distance bus station is by the Carretera Central, southwest of the centre. There are departures for Bayamo, Manzanillo, Santiago de Cuba and Las Tunas, but getting a seat presents the usual problems. You can always fall back on the taxis which congregate across the road to soak up extra demand.

Holguín has two Intermunicipal terminals. The one for points west is eight blocks southeast of the long-distance terminal, also on the Carretera Central, while buses for nearby towns to the east (including Gibara, Guardalavaca and Moa) depart from the station on Avenida de los Libertadores, east of the centre near the huge Calixto García baseball stadium.

Driving: the drive to Holguín if you are approaching from the west is not particularly interesting, unless you have the time to spare to take a cross-country route. If you are starting off from Santa Lucía, for example, you could take the road via Puerto Padre and Jesús Menéndez, the second half of which is particularly scenic. Note that the Carretera Central skirts the southwestern edge of Holguín city centre. If your eventual destination is Santiago de Cuba or Guantánamo, it is quicker to drive on the easterly road through San Germán and Mella than on the Carretera Central, which takes a sharp turn south to include Bayamo. The Cupet service station is at the western edge of the city.

Accommodation. The four-star Hotel Pernik (Avenida Jorge Dimitrov; tel 24-481011, 481667) has the usual characteristics of a large out-of-town tourist hotel in Cuba: ugly building, gloomy rooms, poor setting and a soulless restaurant; the large swimming pool might have water if you're lucky. The Plaza de la Revolución is just across the road, but the view over the square from the hotel is enough to satisfy most visitors. Despite the shortcomings, the Pernik's rooms are clean, well equipped and good value at $40 ($35 in low season) for a double and $30 ($26) for a single.

If your funds are more limited, a good solution is to stay at the two-star Motel El Bosque (also on Avenida Jorge Dimitrov; tel 48-1012, 48-1140), which is about ten minutes' walk up the hill, and use the facilities of the Pernik. The rustic look of the Bosque disguises a very ordinary hotel, however, and given the quality of the Pernik its rooms are overpriced at $30 for a double ($25 in low season), $24 ($20) for a single.

If you prefer to be in the thick of things, the best place to stay is the Turquino on Calle Martí at the corner of General Marrero. The friendly staff, bright and airy rooms and huge beds make up for the quirky water supply. Rooms ($15

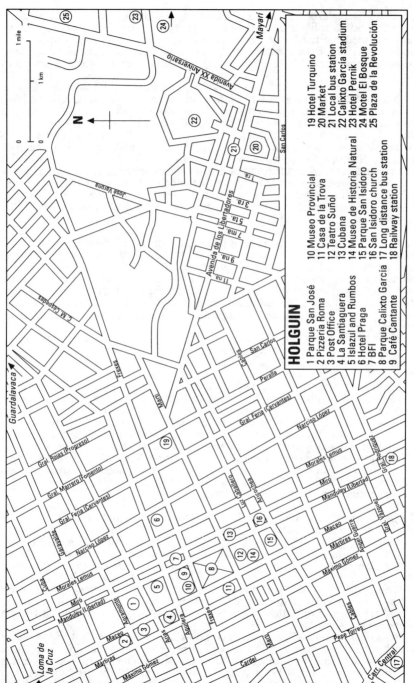

HOLGUIN

1 Parque San José
2 Pizzeria Roma
3 Post Office
4 La Santiaguera
5 Islazul and Rumbos
6 Hotel Praga
7 BFI
8 Parque Calixto García
9 Café Cantante
10 Museo Provincial
11 Casa de la Trova
12 Teatro Suñol
13 Cubana
14 Museo de Historia Natural
15 Parque San Isidoro
16 San Isidoro church
17 Long distance bus station
18 Railway station
19 Hotel Turquino
20 Market
21 Local bus station
22 Calixto Garcia stadium
23 Hotel Pernik
24 Motel El Bosque
25 Plaza de la Revolución

double, $10 single) come with air-conditioning, a fridge and radio. The restaurant is best avoided, unlike the top-floor cabaret. You can dance to a mixture of live and recorded music, though the local punters seem just as happy to sup beer and whisper in the dark. Alternatively, try Hotel Praga on Calle Narciso López between Frexes and Martí (tel 42-2665), which charges $12 for a double, $14 for a suite.

The alternative is to head right out of the city to Motel Mirador de Mayabe, 6 miles (10km) southeast of Holguín. The surroundings are lovely, and the swimming pool is dug into a huge terrace overlooking the valley, with Holguín reassuringly distant. The rooms, however, could do with some serious renovation, and the safari-style dining room needs a change of chef. The motel's chief claim to fame is its beer-drinking donkey, though the animal which earned this renown, Pancho, died in 1994 (possibly as a result of the nationwide beer shortage) and is on display, stuffed, in the restaurant. A younger donkey carries on the tradition but doesn't seem to share Pancho's penchant for lager. Accommodation is in cabañas (with air-conditioning but no hot water) and costs $19 for a double, $14 for a single. Another possibility is the three-star Villa El Cocal (tel 46-1902, 46-1924), near the airport.

Eating and Drinking. As far as most people are concerned, there's only one good place to eat in Holguín: the Hotel Pernik. Indeed, amid the mediocrity of Cuban cuisine the Sofia Restaurant is outstandingly good, with a long and appetising menu featuring steak in many forms, fresh fish and chicken and a wide range of vegetables. The typically cavernous Eastern European dining hall has been carefully disguised by tasteful décor and low lighting. The staff are are friendly and efficient. The Pernik also has a pleasant poolside bar, where you can enjoy cocktails and beer.

If you prefer to be out of a hotel environment, try the Tabernita de Pancho, next door to the Pernik, which is supposedly a Spanish restaurant but serves the usual fare. The outlook for diners who confine themselves to the city centre is bleak. After about 9 o'clock you'll be lucky to find anywhere still serving food, and nowhere can supply a satisfying meal. The Pizzería Roma on Maceo at Agramonte is a typical peso pizzeria, with a scattering of chairs and tables and unreliable supplies. There is more ambience in La Santiagüera, a tiny converted colonial house with just six tables, but they serve only beer and *entremeses* (e.g. spam on bread). There's more room at the Café Cantante (see *Entertainment*), but not much more in the way of food. For ice creams, go to the Cremería Guamá on the corner of Calle Luz Caballero and Manduley. During the day, meat-eaters can seek refuge at the market opposite the baseball stadium, where an array of stalls sell excellent pork sandwiches. You can buy fruit here and also at the farmers' market by the train station.

Exploring. Some historians date the foundation of Holguín to 1720, the year the church of San Isidoro, the town's first, was built. The square it overlooks has lost its early political and social prestige to Parque Calixto García, but San Isidoro remains the focus of religious life in Holguín; the status of the church was raised to that of cathedral in 1979. It is the finest church in the town, despite constant alterations. You'll probably have to make do with admiring the exterior, with its twin towers and elegant Neo-Classical doorway, but the early 19th-century wooden ceiling above the nave is worth seeing if you get the chance. There are a couple of statues of San Isidoro, whose feast day is on 4 April, when a special mass is held.

Walking north up Maceo, you pass a pink and white Neo-Classical mansion which should probably win first or second prize for finest building in Holguín, for character value if nothing else. While the Museo de Historia Natural inside would not win prizes, it has a certain dusty charm, and the exhibits include a collection of polymita shells, the brightly coloured snails which are endemic along the coasts of eastern Cuba — you see postcards of them everywhere and people in Oriente try to sell you bags of them.

You arrive next at Parque Calixto García, named after Holguín's local independence hero, of whom there is a statue in the centre. Architecturally, the mix of Art Deco and Neo-Classical buildings is most striking. The Teatro Eddy Suñol, a splendid monument to the Art Deco style, built in 1939, looks across the square at a more sedate row of mainly 19th-century buildings on the north side. Among the latter is the Museo Provincial, housed in a huge mansion that was built in the 1860s for a Spanish businessman. During the first War of Independence, soon after the house was finished, rebels attacked and confined the Spanish infantry here for two months. Making fun of the Spaniards' brightly-coloured uniforms, the *mambises* shouted 'Come out of your cage, parrots!', and the building has been known as La Periquera (the 'Parrot Cage') ever since. It is worth devoting some time to this museum, particularly if you are planning to explore the province. There are maps showing the location of the region's aboriginal settlements, its communities of escaped slaves (known as *palenques*) and the US-owned sugar mills. The museum boasts some excellent exhibits too. The pride of the archaeological collection is the so-called *hacha de Holguín*, a pre-Columbian stone figure found in 1860; it is now the symbol of the city. Among the abundant historical memorabilia, is a rusty razor blade used by Antonio Maceo's barber and unusual pre-revolutionary election campaign material, including publicity for Eduardo Chibás, an early hero of Fidel Castro who committed suicide in 1951. Even if you don't speak Spanish, you can enjoy the many illustrations, photographs and, in the 20th-century section, the political cartoons that cover the walls. When the planned refurbishment and expansion is complete, this will be one of Cuba's best museums.

A couple of blocks further on is square number three, Parque San José, the quietest and most attractive in the city. The square retains more colonial features than its counterparts in Holguín, and the early 19th-century church boasts some handsome Neo-Classical features, notably its portico and belfry. The plain interior could be described as 'neo-mudejar', the Moorish influence being most obvious in the style of the arches flanking the nave. Outside stands a monument to Céspedes, with a commemoration by Fidel Castro.

The last two of Holguín's five squares are of scant interest as you progress towards the Loma de la Cruz (Hill of the Cross), which closes the view at the north end of town. Tackle the flight of 461 steps and you can enjoy the 180-degree view from the top, and see how modest Holguín looks. Every year, on 3 May, locals celebrate the Day of the Cross, when a special mass is held at the top. There are usually a few bicitaxis in Parque San José, and horses and carts ply the route up to the base of the Loma de la Cruz too.

Unless you have a penchant for Cuban monuments to the Revolution or large open spaces empty of people and soul, you probably won't want to bother with the Plaza de la Revolución. The main feature of the square is the huge mausoleum of Calixto García, in the form of a modernist arch. A frieze along the top is an allegory of the struggle of the Cuban people, running from colonisation to the Revolution. In addition to the familiar faces of José Martí, Marx and Lenin, you can also pick out Che Guevara and Fidel Castro himself. Behind the monument, almost hidden by trees, is a monument to García's mother. Across the square is the local Communist Party headquarters and, of more interest to most local inhabitants, the city's huge baseball stadium. Holguín may not have the best team in Cuba, but it certainly has one of its best stadia. Sportslovers may be interested in visiting the small Sport Museum, ideally in combination with a weekend game.

Entertainment. For live music go to the Casa de la Trova on the west of the main square, or the Café Cantante near the Provincial Museum. This is one of the most exciting places to hang out in the evening, attracting a young clientele.

It opens 2pm-2am and offers beer, rum and the odd snack. There is also a cabaret at the Pernik.
The Suñol theatre on the main square shows films rather than live performances.

Help and Information. *Tourist information:* don't expect a lot, but Islazul and Rumbos have offices next door to each other on Calle Manduley between Aguilera and Arias. Staff can answer simple questions and you can usually pick up a few (fairly useless) brochures.
Post Office: corner of Calles Agramonte and Maceo.
Money: a branch of BFI was due to open on Manduley near corner of Aguilera at the time of going to press. Otherwise, you can change money at Hotel Pernik.
Car hire: Transautos in Hotel Pernik, Havanautos in Motel El Bosque.
Medical care: try the Policlínico Máximo Gómez at Agramonte and Pepe Torres.

Further Afield 61

The scenery all around Holguín is lovely, and gets better the further north or east you go. And these are exactly the directions in which you should go — north to Gibara and northeast to Guardalavaca and Banes.

GIBARA

Twenty miles/32km north of Holguín, the port of Gibara is cut off from the pulse of normal Cuban life and has retained its maritime charm with no trouble at all. Though founded only in the early 19th century, Gibara has the air of a town with a much longer history. In fact, a small port had already existed on the site for some time, and during the 1700s was the main sea access to this region. Gibara's official foundation date, 1817, is pegged to the construction of the small Fernando VII fort, which still overlooks the bay. Later, a defensive wall — second only to that of Havana — was laid to enclose the whole of Gibara. Only a few fragments of this remain, including at the entrance to the town.
    In the 19th century, Gibara was the main north coast port for eastern Cuba. A walk around reveals a place where immense fortunes were once made. The construction of the railway to Holguín gave a boost to the port and brought great affluence from the mid-19th century. Decline came in the 1920s, as for so many other coastal towns, with the construction of the Carretera Central. The train station has gone (the last service was in 1958), but you can still see the railway bridge which crosses the mouth of the Cacoyoquin river at the entrance to the town. Gibara hasn't seen much action this century, though in 1931 its inhabitants staged what is known as *La Guerrita* (or 'Little War') against the Machado dictatorship. It lasted just three days but has provided the town with good credentials in Castro's Cuba. The most notable figure to emerge from Gibara this century is the exiled novelist Guillermo Cabrera Infante.
    Don't let anything or anyone stop you coming here. Rather like Remedios (see page 259), Gibara is almost completely unspoilt. The odd busload of tourists from Guardalavaca arrives, catered to by one waterside restaurant, but you'll usually have the place to yourself. When you've had your fill of the waterfront, with its scattering of fishing boats and drunken fishermen, you can stroll through streets where rusting iron grilles, crumbling stucco and cracked azulejos provide rich terrain for photographers. The immense 19th-century mansions seem incongruous in such a small and sleepy place. One of the few buildings to have been restored is open to the public and alone provides reason enough to visit Gibara.

Accommodation and Food. The only functioning hotel at present is the Bellomar, on Calle General Sartorio, four blocks south of the Fernando VII fort. The clapboard building holds more charm than the staff, but the rooms are clean enough and cost just $10 for a double. A colonial mansion currently under restoration has been earmarked for a hotel, but it is unlikely to open in the very near future. It's always worth asking around for private accommodation.

To dine out properly, you will have to go to the El Faro restaurant on the waterfront. The dining room is airy and pleasant; there is a terrace if you prefer to be outside, but the view over the wall is of a small and dirty beach rather than Gibara's glorious bay. Depending on the day's catch, the menu offers a choice of seafood at good prices: grilled lobster for $14 or rice and lobster for $4.55 if you want to treat yourself without breaking the bank. Good options for a light lunch are the seafood cocktails or seafood soup, both for around $3. There never seems to be much action in the local eateries, though there is usually at least one person selling seafood snacks near the waterfront. Otherwise, enquire among the fishermen. If word spreads that there are fish-hungry tourists about town, something is sure to materialise. A popular fish round here is the *dorado* — literally 'goldfish' but fifty times the size of the fish that goes by that name in the West.

Exploring. When you arrive in Gibara, you are naturally drawn along the bayfront to the small square by the fort. This contains a dollar shop and is of scant interest, though there is a view of sorts from the ramparts. The main square is a couple of blocks inland. It is usually referred to simply as the Plaza de la Iglesia, after the Church of San Fulgencio which stands here. Built in the 1850s at the start of Gibara's economic boom years, the church expresses the confidence of the period. It is essentially neoclassical, but inside you find Moorish elements, including a simple alfarje ceiling of precious hardwood, and even neo-gothic touches. Among the various statues, notice in particular San José, a gilded statue of wood and plaster, brought from Seville.

Also in the square is the old Palacio de Gobierno, another fine neoclassical building and now the seat of the Poder Popular, but there is not a great deal to delay your progress along Calle Independencia, which runs along one side of the square and is the nearest thing Gibara has to a main street. Less than a block from Parque Calixto García are two understated entrances to two understated museums. The right-hand doorway leads into the Museo de Historia, which consists simply of one large room lined with dusty display cabinets. The old photographs are evocative of Gibara's days of former glory but for more enjoyment try to enlist one of the attendants. While they are not accustomed to having many demands made of them, the staff respond enthusiastically to visitors interested in Gibara's history.

Having placed Gibara in its historical context, head next door to the Museo de Artes Decorativas (also known as the Museo del Ambiente Cubano). Its opening hours are 8am-noon and 1-5pm Tuesday to Saturday, 8am-noon on Sunday, but they will normally admit anyone who turns up on a Monday. It is worth fighting to get in to this place. It occupies the first-floor living quarters of a fabulous 19th-century mansion, whose ground floor is occupied by the afore-mentioned history museum. The house was built by a Spaniard called Atanasio Calderón, though the building as you see it now is the legacy of José H. Buela, who made his fortune from the Gibara railway and who died in the 1930s. It has classic features of a 19th-century colonial home, including superb examples of the decorative swing doors known as *mamparas*, and *medio puntos* that are among the largest in the country. And few colonial homes in Cuba retain so many of the original furnishings. Much of these came from Europe, though there is some late 19th-century furniture in the so-called *perillita* style — a sort of Cuban imperial style gone bananas. The various art nouveau objets show that Buelas clearly kept up with the fashions; along with Havana and Cienfuegos, Gibara was one of the main entry points for the art nouveau style into Cuba. Finally, don't leave the building without going up to the roof terrace, from where you can view the whole town and fully appreciate the size of the house, which occupies almost an entire block.

For something a little different, you can take advantage of one of Cuba's few remaining ferry services. Small motor boats chug across the bay at regular intervals, and for 4 pesos you can do a round trip in less than an hour — a pleasant ride with good views back over Gibara.

Bariay Bay

Christopher Columbus' first documented landing in the New World was almost certainly in the small Bariay Bay east of Gibara. Although some Gibareños claim that his first landing was in Gibara itself, an international congress of geographers in 1936 concluded that Bariay was the first landfall. The principal clue given in Columbus' diary is the mention of a flat-topped mountain, which you can see not far from the shore. Even Baracoa, which in the past claimed that its famous Yunque was the mountain in question, has accepted that the explorer's first landing was on the northeast coast.

In 1992, a monument was erected to commemorate the 500th anniversary of Columbus's 'discovery' of America. This occupies the northern tip of Cayo Bariay, a small island linked to the mainland by a causeway, 4 miles/7km north of Fray Benitos. Most visitors come on boat trips from Guardalavaca, but if you are driving between Gibara and Guardalavaca it is only a short diversion from the route, lying roughly halfway between the two; allow about an hour from Gibara. While it is surprising that a Spanish colony should want to erect a memorial to its invaders, the monument is strangely moving. It consists of an arrangement of columns and idols, symbolising the meeting of the European and aboriginal civilisations. It is hard not to notice that while the 'European' columns are as sturdy as ever, the pre-Columbian idols are slowly crumbling away. The haunting sounds that emanate from loudspeakers amongst the trees are meant to give an impression of the noises that would have filled the air when Columbus landed. They don't necessarily conjure up images of ships and conquistadores, but they add plenty of atmosphere. The setting in a palm grove, with grazing goats and the sea a stone's throw away, is lovely. Looking east across the bay you can see the squared-off hill described by Columbus.

There are plans to build a café and no doubt eventually a hotel, but Cayo Bariay for the moment remains a haven of tranquillity, in contrast with what lies a little further east.

GUARDALAVACA

After Varadero, Guardalavaca is the most rapidly developing tourist resort in Cuba. But while the number of hotels has multiplied several fold over the last five years, Guardalavaca will never be a second Varadero. The beach simply isn't big enough, and despite lying just 35 miles (58km) northeast of Holguín, the resort feels surprisingly remote.

If you want a two-week break by the sea, you could be disappointed by the limited entertainment, though the newest resort hotels are better able to cope with the demands of package tourists — many of whom are Canadian or German-speaking, the latter brought by weekly charter flights direct from Düsseldorf and Frankfurt to Holguín. If you just want a break from the road, Guardalavaca is as good a place as any. The beach is not the most beautiful in the world — a dark band of seaweed near the shore ruins Guardalavaca's picture postcard potential — but the water is clear and the fringe of palm trees provides welcome protection from the harsh sun. The water locally is the perfect temperature (25°C) for marine life to thrive, and diving around the reef is rewarding. Ciego de Estero beach, overlooking Naranjo Bay a few miles west of the resort proper, is the best in the area. Beyond it is Playa Don Lino, quite a good place to escape the tourist hordes in high season; one possible point of interest nearby is the island's most scenic sugar railway, running from Rafael Freyre sugar mill towards Holguín.

There are coral cays only about 300m from the beach at Guardalavaca, and facilities for diving and other watersports are available. If you prefer to stay on land, you can hire bicycles and motorbikes. Guardalavaca is also well placed for some interesting trips inland.

Accommodation. There is no budget accommodation to speak of in Guardalavaca, so if you can do without a few comforts, it may be worth commuting from Banes. If you are travelling in low season, be sure to ask for a discount; this will normally be forthcoming. There is one main hotel strip in Guardalavaca, and the hotels mentioned below are listed in order from east to west.

Las Brisas: tel 30218. This is Guardalavaca's newest, best and most expensive hotel. It has most of the facilities you'd expect of a resort hotel, including swimming pool, dance classes, mountain bikes for hire, etc. The hotel overlooks one of the better sections of beach, which it has sought to keep for itself by building a barrier of rocks on either side. There is a choice of restaurants, including a grill by the pool and the smarter La Turquesa restaurant, where good buffet meals are served: $6 for breakfast, $9 for lunch, $15 for supper. If you aren't interested in exploring other possibilities, the room rates with food included ($108 for a double room, $84 for a single) represent reasonable value.

Villa Guardalavaca: tel 30121 to 24. Don't confuse this place with the cheaper cabin accommodation further west (see below). Double rooms in the main hotel building cost $75, or $63 in low season. Breakfast is a good deal at $3.

Villa Turey: tel 30195, 30295, at the western end of the hotel strip. Clean and new, with accommodation in bungalows, the Turey offers better value than the nearby Guardalavaca. A double room costs $65 ($51 in low season) and a single $48 ($39 in low season).

Villa Guardalavaca (cabañas): tel 30-144 or 30-212. Confusingly, these bungalows share the name of the hotel up the road, but are in every other respect completely separate. This place is the only hotel in Guardalavaca to offer travellers on a budget the chance to stay in the resort without breaking the bank, with double rooms for $40, and singles $30. Furthermore, the bungalows (which come with air-conditioning, television and hot water) are within spitting distance of the beach and the staff are very welcoming.

Rio de Luna: tel 30202. This is a four-star hotel by the fine Ciego de Estero beach west of Guardalavaca, with good facilities and watersports. Another resort hotel, the Río de Mares, is due to open nearby.

Villa Don Lino: tel 20-4443. Overlooking Playa Don Lino, about 15 miles (24km) west of Guardalavaca. This large complex of thatched huts was under repair at the time of going to press. When it reopens, it will hopefully be an improvement on the atrocious hotel that Villa Don Lino once was.

Eating and Drinking. There are scarcely any restaurants outside the hotels. The best is the Ancla, at the western end of Guardalavaca beach. Or try the simpler Pizza Nova, near Villa Guardalavaca, which is open-air and offers reasonable value.

Help and Information. *Fuel:* the Cupet petrol station is at the western end of the beach.

Medical assistance: Servimed, next door to the Villa Guardalavaca bungalows, has a pharmacy as well as a doctor.

Chorro de Maita

Just 3 miles (5km) south of Guardalavaca, a turning on the right leads to Cuba's prime archaeological site. Chorro de Maita, a burial ground dating from between 1490 and the 1540s, is the largest known aboriginal graveyard in the Antilles, and is of such importance that its discovery has shed new light on the culture of the Taíno Indians. A fascinating museum has been created out of one section of the burial ground, with more than 50 skeletons on display in the exact position in which they were found. Around the edge are cases of offerings found alongside the dead, including shell, bone and gold idols. Other offerings have been left in situ alongside the skeletons, with colour-coded arrows highlighting the different materials.

Chorro de Maita, where 108 skeletons have so far been discovered, is the only known collective burial ground of the Taínos, who habitually buried their dead individually in caves. The site also demonstrates that there was a certain cultural exchange between the aborigines and the Spanish. This can be seen in the style of some of the ceramics, and also in the manner in which the skeletons are laid out. While the Taíno dead are traditionally found lying in a foetal position, there are a number of skeletons at Chorro de Maita that are stretched out straight with their arms crossed on the chest — the Christian position. More interesting still, there is a Caucasian buried here, whom archaeologists presume to be a Spaniard and who appears to have lived in harmony with the Taínos.

The museum opens 9am-5pm Tuesday to Saturday, 9am-1pm on Sunday. Across the road, replica Taíno houses are being built, and will eventually contain displays to show how the aborigines lived. Below the museum, back towards the main road and then down a track to the right, is one of Che Guevara's command posts, used during the rebel campaign. There's nothing much to see, but Guevaraphiles will no doubt be interested.

BANES

A lovely drive through hills peppered with palm trees and *bohíos* (the traditional wooden houses of the Cuban countryside) separates Guardalavaca and Banes, 20 miles/32km to the southeast. At first sight, this small town seems like many off-the-beaten-track places in Cuba, where people go quietly about their daily lives amid a gentle air of decrepitude. Banes, however, has a particularly interesting history.

Banes once lay in an area with a sizeable Taíno population and the archaeological museum is the town's main tourist attraction. But Banes is also notable as a relic of US involvement in the region. It was founded in 1887 by a group of North American planters, who paved the way for the United Fruit Company to take over the town. From the turn of the century, the Banes region had closer links with the United States than with the rest of Cuba. This can be seen clearly in the North American influence on the town's architecture — the one or two-storey wooden houses, with a zinc roof and broad verandah being most characteristic. As you wander through parts of Banes, you can imagine the kind of luxury the North Americans enjoyed, with their own schools and hospitals, while most Cubans lived in comparative penury. The black population in and around Banes includes descendants of the Jamaicans brought in to work on the sugar plantations during the early 20th century.

Arrival and Departure. You may be able to find a bus from Holguín (these arrive at the terminal just off Los Angeles, on the east side of the bridge), but will have more chance of travelling to Banes by private car or colectivo. The road from Guardalavaca is good, but hitching surprisingly difficult.

Accommodation. Hotel Bani (Calle Céspedes 342) is the only place to stay in the centre of town. The staff are not very used to tourists, but should let you stay if pressed. Most people seem to end up staying at the Motel Oasis, which is half a mile west of the centre, on the Guardalavaca road. The chalets are not as well kept as the surrounding garden, but are at least spacious and cheap at $16 for two. The water supply is erratic, and guests normally have to make do with buckets filled from an outdoor tap. The restaurant is a grim and depressing place, and a rip-off if you're paying in dollars. The food is dreadful too.

If you don't mind being slightly further out of Banes, you should head straight for Motel Bani, a couple of miles north of the town on the Guardalavaca road. It consists of a small collection of cabañas on a hillock overlooking a lake. The accommodation ($17 per night) is simple but the setting beautiful.

The eating out possibilities in Banes are virtually non-existent, so in the evening you'll have little choice but to eat at your hotel. At least for breakfast or lunch you can make the most of the stalls in Avenida Cárdenas, the main street, where people sell pork sandwiches, *tamales* and other snacks.

Exploring. The Museo Montané in Havana (see page 183) has managed to acquire the cream of the archaeological finds made in the Banes region, but the Museo Indocubano still has a superb collection; this is simply but clearly displayed, with some explanations in English. All the objects on display come from the surrounding area, including Chorro de Maita and Farallones de Seboruco, a large cave near Mayarí which was discovered only in 1945 and contained important evidence of habitation dating back more than 5,000 years — estimated to contain one-third of Cuba's entire 'archaeological potential'. The finest objects are from the Subtaíno or *agroalfarera* culture, the first to use ceramics and gold. Most famous is the gold idol of a woman, with a feather headdress and holding a bowl, which seems to show the clear influence of Mesoamerican culture. There are well-preserved shell necklaces and utensils, and notice the *espátulas vómicas*, with which the aborigines made themselves sick before taking hallucinogenic drugs. The museum is at Céspedes (also known as General Marrero) 305, one block from Plaza Martí, the main square. It opens 9am-5pm Tuesday to Saturday, 8am-noon on Sunday and charges $1 admission.

Many visitors to Banes do the rounds of the archaeological museum and then move on. However, it is worth exploring the districts of the original town, designed by the United Fruit Company to distribute inhabitants according to their racial or social category. The heart of Banes — now referred to as the Centro Histórico — was dedicated largely to commercial activity, though there was also some private housing. Some of the best examples of these middle class homes are in Plaza Martí, which also has a curious art deco church (looking more like a 1930s cinema). Heading east, across the River Banes, you enter the old 'Barrio Americano', where most Americans and the top creole employees lived. It was conceived as an imitation of a North American town, with wooden villas, well-paved streets, a golf course, hospital and club. One of the finest houses still standing is a huge two-storey mansion that is now the Palacio de los Pioneros. Further east, the so-called Barrio Antillano or Barrio Jamaiquino (in an area known as La Güira) was for English-speaking employees, who enjoyed separate and slightly better conditions than the Cuban workers because of an agreement with the British government.

EAST TO BARACOA

If you let your eye travel eastwards along a map of Cuba, beyond Holguín it inevitably follows the line of the main road south towards Bayamo, Santiago and on to Guantánamo. This is the route that most travellers take too. Few people, Cuban or otherwise, venture along the road that skirts the north coast. Remote though this area may be, it is vital to the economy of Cuba. This is nickel country. The nickel deposits that stretch for more than 60 miles (96km) along the coast between Nicaro and Moa are said by some experts (particularly Cuban) to be the largest in the world. They are certainly among the largest. The high laterite content gives a deep ochre colour to the soil and to the dust that is scattered over the region from the nickel mines and refineries, and also publicises the damage being done to the environment: bright orange fumes are spewed out into the atmosphere, while rivers have been turned into stagnant pools the colour of rust. It can only be hoped that foreign investment in the nickel industry will help rectify past ecological devastation.

Unless you have a specific interest in environmental disasters, the only real reason to travel east along this road is to reach Baracoa. If the nickel is your motive, the main centres to aim for are the two largest nickel refineries, one near Nicaro, and the other — opened by Che Guevara in the 1960s and named after him — just beyond Moa.

Allow about six hours for the journey from Banes to Baracoa, a little more from Holguín; this allows for the odd rest stop. Set off early and with a full petrol tank, to give yourself plenty of time and to avoid getting stranded in Moa (three hours' drive from Banes). The road is good for most of the route. East of Mayarí the slopes are as straight as ski jumps as you progress across the northern fringes of the Sierra del Cristal. Raúl Castro led a column of rebels into this area in the 1950s, and in **Sagua de Tánamo** an armoured car from the Sierra campaign still sits on the main street. Sagua is the most attractive town along the route, and if you want somewhere to stretch your legs, this is a far more congenial place to stop than **Moa**. The largest settlement in the area, this scruffy town's only redeemable features are its seaside location and its food market (near the hospital), where you can stop off for sustenance. If you do need to stay overnight, Hotel Miraflores is a standard Cuban hotel providing standard accommodation, with double rooms for around $35, depressed staff and depressing food.

From Moa, motorists can reach Baracoa in three hours. If you are hitching, start early: the level of traffic decreases dramatically beyond Moa. After about an hour one of the best roads in Cuba reverts to one of the worst roads in Cuba. Most of the potholes and ruts are avoidable, but the rough surface makes the drive frustratingly slow, and you should avoid doing the journey in heavy rain. At least there is ample opportunity to admire the scenery of lush hills and scattering of small villages.

Moa's small airport, named after one Capitán Orestes Acosta (tel 7370), is connected to Havana, Holguín and Santiago de Cuba. Given the terrain, any of these flights will save you considerable time. But it seems a shame to fly anywhere in Oriente, where journeys are among the most memorable trips in Cuba.

PROVINCE OF GRANMA

Granma has more than just a silly name. The province takes its title from the name of the vessel that bore the revolutionaries ashore on 2 December 1956, but it has much besides first-rate revolutionary credentials. In some ways Granma is the archetypal Oriente province: lush, sometimes dramatic countryside populated by friendly and hospitable people. Furthermore, much of it is sufficiently off the main tourist trail to be almost virgin territory for travellers.

BAYAMO

This city of 100,000 has played a prominent role in the history of the island. It has the distinction of being the second villa (after Baracoa) to have been established in Cuba. Diego Velázquez founded San Salvador de Bayamo in 1513 in a cleverly selected spot. Its position on the banks of a navigable tributary of the Río Cauto, meant that the town had access to the region's main transport (and smuggling) routes while also being far enough away from the action to be free from pirate attack. The town grew rich not so much through agriculture as through contraband.

Carlos Manuel de Céspedes launched the first war of independence in 1868 from his plantation at Demajagua near Manzanillo, but he was born in Bayamo, and it was here that he conspired with friends, using masonic lodges and chess clubs as a cover. The city was also the first to fall to the rebels, who captured it on 20 October 1868 and declared it capital of their new republic. They later preferred to burn it down than hand it over to Spanish troops. Bayamo returned to the forefront of the people's struggle on July 26 1953, when a group of young men attacked the local army barracks to coincide with the assault on Moncada in Santiago.

'Bayamo, to arms in battle — write a proud page in Cuba's story' runs the Cuban national anthem. It is not surprising that Bayamo is proud of its history, and proud of the role Bayameses played in the island's fight for independence from Spain. Half the buildings in the centre seem to carry a plaque proclaiming an association with the struggle. There is not a great deal to see in the city since many historic buildings were destroyed by the fire in 1869, but you can spend a leisurely day here, seeing the main sights and enjoying the people. Sit for a few minutes in the main square and you are sure to attract a crowd. The Bayameses are very friendly but also quite demanding — go well supplied with pens, sweets or small change.

Bayamo doesn't make it onto many tourist itineraries. By not coming here, however, you will be missing out not only on Bayamo, but also on Manzanillo and the chance to explore the wilderness of the Sierra Maestra.

City Layout. The city lies high up on the east bank of the Río Bayamo, but the river is some distance away. You are likely to become aware of it only from a couple of good vantage points, such as the Bodega de Atocha or Parque Nico López. There is not much to take you away from the vicinity of the main square, Plaza de la Revolución. Jose Martí and García are the two main axes through the centre. A town map is available from the shop in the Céspedes Museum.

Arrival and Departure. *Air:* Carlos M de Céspedes airport is three miles northeast of the centre on the road to Holguín. The only available destination is Havana, three times a week. The Cubana office is on the corner of Martí and Parada (tel 3916).

Train: Bayamo is only on a branch line. A train departs for the 14-hour haul to Havana at 11.10pm every day, at least in theory, with a service to Manzanillo each morning and afternoon. The station is a ten-minute walk east of Plaza de la Revolución.

Bus: the main bus station is one kilometre south of the city centre, on the Carretera Central to Santiago at Avenida Jesús Rabí. There are relatively frequent shuttle services from Bayamo to Santiago and Holguín, and you may be able to make it onto one of these. Buses to more local destinations leave from the near the rail station.

Taxi: private cars congregate outside the bus station and rail station.

Driving: The road from Las Tunas is good and the journey should not take much over an hour; allow about the same for the trip from Holguín. The Carretera Central skirts the centre of Bayamo, sweeping down in a loop southeast of the centre, past the bus station, Cupet and the Sierra Maestra hotel.

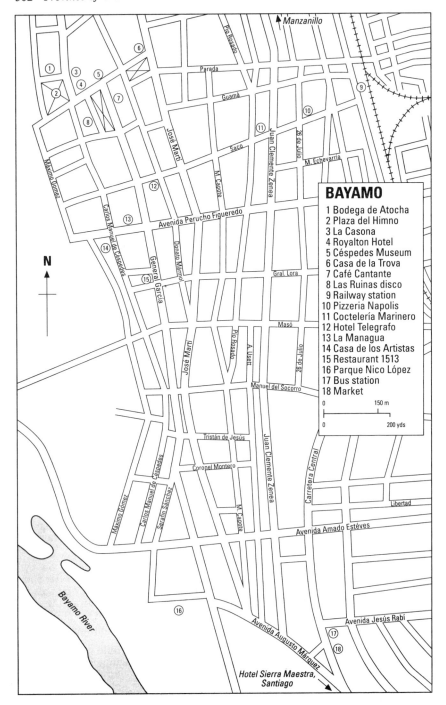

BAYAMO

1 Bodega de Atocha
2 Plaza del Himno
3 La Casona
4 Royalton Hotel
5 Céspedes Museum
6 Casa de la Trova
7 Café Cantante
8 Las Ruinas disco
9 Railway station
10 Pizzeria Napolis
11 Coctelería Marinero
12 Hotel Telegrafo
13 La Managua
14 Casa de los Artistas
15 Restaurant 1513
16 Parque Nico López
17 Bus station
18 Market

0   150 m

0   200 yds

Getting Around. Bayamo has a highly efficient system of horse-drawn *coches* — recalled in a famous Cuban song. The most valuable for the visitor is the constant stream of carriages linking the train station with the bus terminal and the Hotel Sierra Maestra. The pick-up points are next to the shoe-shiners opposite the rail station; at the vehicle exit from the bus terminal; and across the road from the hotel.

Accommodation. It is odd to arrive at the four-star Hotel Sierra Maestra (tel 48-1013), a massive modern complex, on the back of a horse and cart. It lies on Avenida General Manuel Cedeño (the Carretera Central), 2km northeast of the centre towards Santiago. A room costs about $35 single/$50 double. The hotel's huge suite has a bed with a feather mattress and is recommended if you're feeling extravagant or in need of a lot of space; it has its own roof terrace the size of three normal rooms. The hotel has a vast pool, and the restaurant is good and reasonably priced. The furniture in the lobby was apparently a present from Daniel Ortega when he was president of Nicaragua.

A new hotel is being built nearby, but there is no sign of when it might open. The only alternative at present is the no-frills Hotel Telegrafo, a peso hotel at the corner of Saco and Marmól that takes dollar-paying tourists. The Hotel Royalton on the main square was under repair at the time of going to press.

Eating and Drinking. Bayamo doesn't have a bad choice of restaurants for a short stay. The following all stay open until about 10pm. The two main options are La Casona, on Plaza del Himno Nacional, and La Managua on Calle Figueredo between García and Céspedes. The latter, named after the capital of Nicaragua, is the larger of the two and occupies a fine colonial house which has been restored and done up for tourism. The creole food is good and the ambience pleasant. The main alternative is Restaurant 1513, around the corner from La Managua on García at General Lora; this is an old-style Cuban place but serves decent food if you can get a table. For a younger clientele try Pizzería Napolis, at the corner of Saco and 26 de Julio, an open-air place.

Don't call it a day without paying a visit to La Bodega de Atocha in Plaza del Himno, which is a must for its fabulous fruit wines and the view over the river. They also serve rum and tapas, until 10 o'clock or according to demand. Another good place for drinks (they don't serve food) is the Café Cantante, on the east side of Plaza de la Revolución: see *Entertainment*.

For snacks during the day, try the Casa de Queso on Plaza de la Revolución, where drinks and cheese sandwiches are served from 1pm; or, if you can brave it, Coctelería Marinero, at the corner of Saco and Pio Rosado. Even if you don't fancy the oyster cocktails *(coctel de ostiones)*, this is a very photogenic place. You will also find snack vendors along García east of the main square. By the bus station, stalls under the trees sell delicious pork sandwiches or hot pork with *cassabe* (yuca pancakes) for pesos. For a shot of caffeine in the morning, try Café Oriente on the main square.

Exploring. As in most Cuban towns, life in Bayamo revolves around the main square. There is much pride attached to the fact that this was the first square in Cuba to be called Plaza de la Revolución — and unlike others in the country this name commemorates the uprising against the Spanish in 1868 rather than Castro's revolution of 1959. Every year on 20 October, the arrival of the rebels in Bayamo is remembered. The two most famous figures in the town's history face each other across the centre of the square. The first is Céspedes himself. The other is Perucho Figueredo, famous throughout the island as the author of the Cuban national anthem. A plaque on the nearby church of San Salvador recalls that the anthem was sung there for the first time on 20 October 1868, when the rebels took the town.

On the north side of the square is the Céspedes Museum (open 9am-5pm

Tuesday to Saturday, 9am-noon on Sunday), in the house where the independence campaigner was born — and one of the few buildings in Bayamo to have survived the 1869 fire. The exhibits include the press used to print Cubano Libre — the first independent newspaper to circulate in Cuba after the capture of Bayamo — but mostly cover the life of the man for whom it is named. The son of rich plantation owners, Céspedes became a lawyer, but he was also an accomplished composer and poet. Having launched the rebellion of 1868, he was named President of the Goverment in Arms, but later wranglings within the rebel movement forced him out. He retired to San Lorenzo, in the Sierra Maestra southwest of Bayamo, where he was eventually killed by the Spanish in 1874. The house is an attraction in its own right, and the first floor is furnished as it would have been in the period — though none of the contents is original.

Next door, the Provincial Museum contains the usual variety of exhibits, in this case including colonial relics that survived the fire and the original score of the national anthem. The museum was under restoration at the time of going to press. Also in the square, on the east side, is the Poder Popular building, where a plaque records that in this very place Céspedes signed a document abolishing slavery on 27 December 1868.

Plaza del Himno, adjacent to the main square, is taken up almost entirely by the church of Santísima Salvador de Bayamo, founded in 1516 and said to be the second oldest church in Cuba. While it was gutted in 1869, the 18th-century Dolores chapel survived, and you can still admire its fine mudejar ceiling and baroque gilded alterpiece. A painting above the main arch over the nave shows the blessing of Céspedes' rebel flag at the church door, and you can also see the font where Céspedes was baptised. The church is open 3-5pm Tuesday to Friday and also for mass in the evening. Some of Bayamo's oldest houses surround the church. One of them has been converted into the Casa de la Nacionalidad Cubana. This is a small research centre, but the staff are happy for you to have a look around. Two of the city's finest houses, however, lie a few blocks from the square. One is now the Casa de los Artistas (some locals refer to it simply as 'UNEAC', the name of the artists' and writers' union which runs it), near the corner of Céspedes and Figueredo. A plaque outside recalls that this was the birthplace of Tomás Estrada Palma, who was Cuba's first president after independence. It is now used as an art gallery, but the works of art have to compete with the fine surroundings for your attention.

The other must-see in Bayamo is the Casa de la Trova, in the small square two blocks east of Plaza de la Revolución, on the corner of Martí. The opening hours of this place are infuriatingly unpredictable, but it is quite often open during the day for the benefit of the odd coachload of tourists that turns up here. The building is worth a look, and you might be treated to your own private performance by the semi-resident band; if you don't like the kind of singing and dancing they have perfected for the tourists, put in your own requests. Around the corner at Martí 20 is the Asociación Nacional de Orquestas Charangas de Cuba. This is a good place to find out about live music performances, and you might be able to watch a local charanga orchestra rehearse.

The main reason to venture any distance south of the main square is to visit Parque Nico López, site of the Rural Guard barracks which was attacked by Castro's colleagues in 1953. The small building is now a museum (closed Monday), of course, recalling the event and later triumph. Even if you've had your fill of sights connected with the Revolution, the small park is pleasant and provides a good view over the river.

Entertainment. The Casa de la Trova sometimes has events in the evening. You should also check out the Café Cantante on the east side of Plaza de la Revolución. This place has been designed with some care and an uncharacteristic amount of imagination, and is buzzing at night. Across the square is Las Ruinas, one of Cuba's whackiest discos. It consists literally of a ruined house, whose façade is more or less intact but which has no roof. You can sit or dance amongst the remains of old columns. There are a couple of other night clubs around, but this is the place to be. It opens daily except Thursday.

Dos Ríos

If you are a serious follower of José Martí or Cuba's fight for independence, consider visiting Dos Ríos, near Cauto Cristo northeast of Bayamo. This is where Cuba's national hero was killed in battle on 19 May 1895. There is a monument here and a ceremony takes place every year on the anniversary of his death. In 1995, Fidel himself came to pay his respects.

SIERRA MAESTRA NATIONAL PARK

You can drive to Manzanillo in about one and a half hours, but you would do well to add a day or two to your itinerary in order to explore the Sierra Maestra. Yara is 22 miles (35km) west of Bayamo, and is where (legend has it) that the rebel Indian, Hatuey, was burnt at the stake. From Yara a road runs 20 miles (32km) south into the Sierra Maestra National Park, the largest protected area in Cuba and one of the most beautiful.

The road from Yara is steep but reasonably good and takes you up to **Santo Domingo** (via Bartolomé Maso) in about an hour. Santo Domingo was a rebel camp during the guerrilla campaign of the late 1950s. It is now a tourist complex, with cabins scattered amongst the trees. You can swim in the river, go horse riding, and hike up **Pico Turquino**, Cuba's highest peak at 6,390ft (1,974m). The trail through the hills is lovely, lined with rare cedar and mahogany trees, orchids and other tropical plants, though not much wildlife. And you will be rewarded by a glorious view from the top of Turquino, over the mountains and the Caribbean. You may encounter young and energetic revolutionaries along the route, particularly around New Year, when they climb the mountain in memory of the rebels who gathered here during the campaign. The Sierra is scattered with rebel bases, including Castro's own headquarters, which you can also visit.

MANZANILLO

The second largest town in Granma, Manzanillo feels more like an overgrown village. Flyblown and dusty though much of it is, Manzanillo has a colourful history, and its detachment from the main drag makes it feel perhaps a little wilder than most towns in the region.

Manzanillo grew up as a cosy little smugglers' port, slightly too far out of Spain's control for the mother country's liking. Entrepreneurs developed its potential in the 18th century. In a curious parallel of today's Cuban black market, they traded behind Spain's back in sought-after goods such as livestock, leather and tropical hardwoods. By avoiding the heavily controlled official channels of exchange, they met a need by providing scarce goods and selling Cuba's rich resources for more than the Spanish were prepared to offer.

Manzanillo's port was opened officially only in 1829, after which date sugar and slaves passed through in large quantities. British traders in particular exchanged slaves for precious wood, including cedar and mahogany, which at one time grew in abundance in the Sierra Maestra. There was a lot of British capital invested in the area and it was a British company, Beattie Brooks, which owned the Isabel sugar mill near Ceiba Hueca, south of Manzanillo, and controlled the local sugar trade (and, in effect, the port) from 1885 to the 1930s.

This century, the people of Manzanillo were in the van of the struggle for workers' rights. They formed Cuba's first communist cell in 1925, and for a time in the 1940s Manzanillo had Cuba's only communist mayor, Paquito Rosales, who was democratically elected before Batista's crackdown. In the local railway station, there is a monument to Jesús Menéndez, leader of the sugar workers' union in the 40s and one of Cuba's most eminent black figures of the 20th century; he was assassinated here in 1948. Celia Sánchez, who organised the underground movement in Manzanillo in support of Fidel Castro's 26 of July Movement, played a key role in the rebel campaign to topple Batista.

The history of Manzanillo revolves around its port, but the town curiously seems to turn its back on the waterfront. Activity in the harbour has long since come to a halt and, as in most Cuban towns, life revolves around the main square, Parque Céspedes. This is a gorgeous open square with just the right amount of greenery and an enchanting Moorish gazebo — another quirk in this thoroughly quirky town. Few visitors can resist the quiet charm of Manzanillo, nor the warmth of the local people, who have to be among the friendliest you could hope to meet. While there is not much to do, Manzanillo is one of the best places in Cuba to simply hang out a while. The musical tradition is strong too; along with Santiago and Guantánamo, the town professes to be the birthplace of *son*. La Orquesta Original de Manzanillo is one of the country's best exponents of traditional Cuban music. Furthermore, facing west across the gulf of Guacanayabo, the sunsets are often more stunning in Manzanillo than anywhere else in Cuba.

Arrival and Departure. It would be wonderful to arrive by boat, but the more usual approach to Manzanillo is by rail on the branch line from Bayamo. There is a daily service to and from Santiago via Bayamo. Trains run to Havana every other day. Manzanillo railway station, 13 blocks northeast of the main square, feels as though it's in the middle of nowhere. The walk to the centre is an interesting one, through a poor district of rickety wooden dwellings that give way to colonial mansions whose grandeur is so faded they are on the verge of collapse.

Manzanillo lies 35 miles (56km) west of Bayamo, about an hour by car along a good flat road. The local Cupet petrol station is on the Circunvalación, at the junction with the southbound road to Niquero close to Hotel Guacanayabo. Manzanillo is not a great place for hiring a local car plus driver — though if you're not in a huge hurry, one will eventually be found. The only place you'll find a tourist taxi is at the Hotel Guacanayabo.

To gauge the prospects of getting a flight out, try the Cubana office at Maceo 70, between Villuenda and Merchán (tel 2800). In January 1996, the only destination was Havana, on Monday and Saturday.

Accommodation. Most foreign visitors end up at the three-star Hotel Guacanayabo (tel 54812, 54012), a large block of a building on a hill southwest of the centre. It enjoys a more scenic position than most out-of-town tourist hotels. Furthermore, a double room costs only $24 off-season ($30 peak), and a single $18 ($22 peak). There is the usual selection of restaurants and cafeterias, including a small bar by the pool. If you don't want to take a cab into the centre, you can always walk down the hill to the seafront and jump on one of the horses and carts that ply the Malecón periodically.

You will get a much better feel for Manzanillo if you try one of the hotels in town, though don't expect too much in the way of comfort. The Casa Blanca, an unmarked white three-storey hotel at Loynaz 101, on the corner of Merchan, charges tourists $9 for a double and $6 for a single room. Don't expect a very warm welcome, but there is at least air-conditioning. The Hotel Inglaterra, at Villuendas and Codina, could have featured in a Graham Greene novel and is a much more characterful place to stay. The staff aren't very used to tourists, so expect a certain amount of discussion as to the price of a room.

Eating and Drinking. The lobsters and prawns brought ashore at Manzanillo are excellent, at least before they are frozen and shipped off to Havana or overseas.

MANZANILLO

1 Railway station
2 Casa Blanca hotel
3 Hotel Inglater
4 Cabaret Costa Azul
5 Parque Céspedes
6 Las Américas Restaurant
7 Museum
8 Celia Sánchez memorial
9 Parque Masó
10 Brisas del Mar
11 Hotel Guacanayabo
12 Cupet station

0   100 m

0   100 yds

By the time the seafood has reached the dowdy restaurant in the Hotel Guacanayabo, it has somehow lost much of its appeal. A fish popular locally is the *liseta*, and sometimes people approach you in the street offering to prepare it for you in their own home. There are a couple of seafood restaurants on the Malecón, but the supplies are erratic. Las Brisas del Mar, right at the water's edge about half way along, has a splendidly kitsch façade decorated with giant seafood. The décor inside is disappointing by comparison, and the fishermen don't always deliver, but this is a fun place for a rum or a beer and sometimes there's a cabaret. The nearby Liseta restaurant is a more basic open-air affair which opens for lunch only. At the other end of the Malecón, just four blocks north of the main square, the Costa Azul functions mainly as a cabaret but also serves meals.

The most reliable place for an evening meal is Las Américas in the main square. It has a pleasant ambience, friendly staff and a reasonable choice of creole food, including chicken and steak as well as lobster and prawns. Live music is laid on most evenings too. Across the square is the Zen Restaurant which, like most 'Chinese' restaurants in Cuba, has retained its original décor but long since stopped serving oriental food. This is where most privileged workers come to eat, so you'll need to book. Most people end up at Las Américas.

During the day, the top of Avenida Gómez, known as the 'Bulevar', is taken over by stalls selling not very appetising snacks and refrescos.

Exploring. The gazebo in Parque Céspedes, built in 1924 and known locally as the *glorieta*, is the main architectural curiosity in Manzanillo. It no longer serves any useful purpose in the town, but the local people seem very fond of it and it is maintained in immaculate condition. The nearby Edificio Quirch, also of Moorish design and built around 1916, could do with some renovation. On the other side of the square, the Museo Histórico is a modest affair, with just a couple of rooms — the first room devoted to the aborigines and the Conquest (with what is purported to be the original bodyplate of a Spanish conquistador) and the second to local people who distinguished themselves either during the guerrilla campaign or since. The curator, Angel, is a mine of information about the history of Manzanillo and well worth talking to.

Local groups perform on a small stage in one corner of the square, and if you are lucky, you will witness an *organo oriental* in action. This type of hand-operated organ was originally brought from Paris, and was first used to accompany popular dances at the end of the 19th century. The use of the so-called 'eastern organ' later spread to other parts of Cuba, but it remains most characteristic of Manzanillo. Some of the earliest versions of *son* were heard here (some citizens call it the birthplace of *son*) and the use of the organ certainly gave it a distinctive style. If there's no music in the square, ask at the Casa de la Trova, just off the square.

Seven blocks southwest of Parque Céspedes is the Memorial to Celia Sánchez, who was born in Media Luna near Manzanillo and became Fidel Castro's personal assistant in the Sierra and was his constant companion until her death of cancer in 1980. The memorial, consisting of a staircase with tiled murals of sunflowers and doves, is one of the most imaginative and moving of the hundreds of monuments in Cuba. On the anniversary of her death, crowds gather here to pay their respects, just as they do at her grave in the Colón cemetery in Havana. Whatever the Cubans may think of their leader, they reserve a very special place in their hearts for Celia Sánchez, a courageous woman who managed to remain untainted by the shortcomings of the regime.

Calle Caridad runs down to the sea from the Sánchez memorial and deposits you neatly at the start of the Malecón. The Parque Masó, which stretches eastwards along a muddy beach, has been closed for renovation for as long as anyone can remember, and you'll do better to head west. Forget the Havana malecón, there's not much life along here. The jetty is derelict and the water dirty. However, you can sit on the seawall and take in the view. If you walk the length of the promenade and can't be bothered to walk back, horses and carts trot along the seafront.

South from Manzanillo

The sights south along the coast from Manzanillo can make a leisurely day's excursion, or provide stopping-off points along an adventurous cross-country route to Santiago.

It is hard to believe that Cuba's first war of independence began in the spot designated as the **Parque Nacional de Demajagua** just south of Manzanillo. Little remains of Carlos Manuel de Céspedes' sugar mill, except a few rusted remains of mill machinery which over the years have become curiously entwined with a cluster of trees. There is a small museum, but the main feature of the memorial is the large wall where the bell that Céspedes rang to launch his rebellion in 1868 now hangs. Opposite is a plaque with quotations by Céspedes himself, José Martí and Fidel Castro. The latter's belief that his Revolution was simply a continuation of the struggle begun by Cuba's 19th-century independence fighters helps explain the arrogance of his words uttered in 1965 and quoted here: 'If we had lived then, we would have been like them. They, if they were living now, would have been like us.' There's nothing else to do or see except admire the view of grazing horses and the sea beyond. If you're driving to Demajagua from Manzanillo, turn south along the Niquero road by the Cupet station. After about 15 minutes, start looking out for a large board on the right with the moustachioed face of Céspedes. If you reach the village of Calicito, you've gone too far.

Continuing southwards, past Media Luna (there's a museum devoted to Celia Sánchez if you're interested) and then about 12 miles (20km) beyond Niquero, you reach the turn-off to **Playa de los Coloradas**, forever immortalised as the disembarkation point of the guerrillas yacht, *Granma*, on 2 December 1956. This is really a thankless and remote spot that even arch devotees of revolutionary sites might find hard to praise. A long walk along a wooden pathway leads through mangrove swamp to a jetty — following roughly the route taken by the rebels. A monument marks the actual landing place of the famous yacht. Serious revolutionary tourists can also brave the road south from Niquero, which leads up into the mountains to **Alegría de Pio** where, on 5 December 1956, a handful of guerrillas, including Fidel Castro, had their first encounter with Batista's troops.

Most people will probably want to head back up the coast after Las Coloradas, though if you have the energy you could continue down to **Cabo Cruz**, where a lighthouse really does mark the end of the road. **Guafe** is an archaeological zone nearby, with caves where Siboney Indians lived before the Conquest, but there's not much to see. The alternative is to continue over the hills to **Marea del Portillo** — about 25 miles (40km) from the turn-off midway between Media Luna and Niquero, and about 65 miles (110km) from Manzanillo.

Most visitors to Marea del Portillo seem to be Canadian, who fly over on special charter flights to Manzanillo and get bussed down en masse to the resort's two luxury hotels. It's hard to fathom why they should have picked this particular spot, apart from the fact that it is so remote. There is a beach, but it is black and by no means one of Cuba's best. Other attractions are the diving and excursions to offshore keys, and a park boasting century-old oaks, extravagant ferns, nightingales, woodpeckers and wild pigs. You can also hire horses or a vehicle to explore the mountains. There are two hotels at Marea del Portillo. The newest and best is the four-star Farallón del Marea, set on a low hill overlooking the beach. It charges about $65 a double ($45 single), compared with the $50 and $40 charged by the three-star Hotel Marea del Portillo (tel 59-4201/02, fax 59-4134).

If you have a sense of adventure, don't hesistate to drive the 125 miles (200km) east from Marea del Portillo to Santiago. The first half of the journey is very difficult — the road has been washed out by severe storms, and you must be prepared to cross fords and cope with generally appalling surfaces — but is still possible in a normal car (even a Peugeot 205). Towards Chivirico, you reach one of the newest tarmacked roads in Cuba, which serves a couple of new hotels (see page 325). The difficulties are well worth bearing for the stupendous views. You pass other sites associated with Fidel, Che and the others, including **Uvero**, the location of a bloody encounter on 28 May 1957. If you are making straight for Santiago, allow six hours.

Santiago de Cuba: City and Province

Moncada Barracks

Cuba's second-largest city (with a population of around 400,000), Santiago is also second only to Havana in historical and cultural importance. In revolutionary terms, it has primacy, and this is acknowleged by the titles 'Hero City' or 'Capital of the Revolution'. If you are accustomed elsewhere to having candid conversations with people about the regime, you won't find it so easy here. Santiagüeros are known for their hospitality but also for their loyal support for Fidel Castro.

Santiago de Cuba is also one of the most successful and complete 'melting pots' to be found anywhere in the Americas, its blend of African, Spanish, French and even elements of Chinese culture being expressed most vividly during the carnival. The predilection of the Santiagüeros for merrymaking has helped turn the city's carnival into one of Latin America's most famous festivals.

Santiago has had a chequered history, which shows in its architecture. Marginalised politically and economically for most of the first 300 years of its existence, and troubled by earthquakes and constant pirate attacks, few significant buildings date from the early colonial period. The undulating and seismically-prone terrain discouraged the construction of grand mansions, but while you don't find the variety of architecture that you do in Havana, there are streets of considerable charm, with old gas lamps, fancy ironwork and other interesting features. There is much to be said for simply strolling through the streets, but you should also make time to see some of the city's impressive museums.

The apparent absence of tourists surprises many visitors to Santiago. Most package tourists head straight for the resort hotels west of the city, perhaps venturing into Santiago just for a daytrip. And those tourists staying in Santiago itself are mostly confined to the dollar hotels located some way from the centre; you see few foreigners downtown in the evening. The reopening of the Casa Granda hotel in the main square could change all that, but for the moment Cubans easily outnumber visitors in most city-centre restaurants.

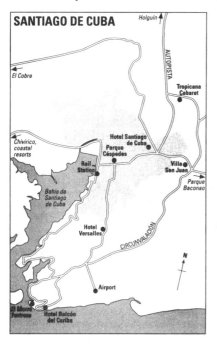

Some people simply don't take to Santiago. The heat may have something to do with it. The city's physical setting amongst the foothills of the Sierra Maestra and overlooking a magnificent bay is scenically marvellous but climatically terrible. The surrounding hills prevent the city from benefitting from any cooling breezes, and even the winter can be uncomfortably warm. The hot climate is exacerbated by the number of steep hills, which means that most people move at a snail's pace; don't overestimate the amount of sightseeing you can do in a day.

The province of Santiago de Cuba is one of the smallest in the country and does not require a great deal of time to explore; Granma province is in fact a better place from which to explore the Sierra Maestra mountains (see page 305). The main source of interest in this area lies east of the city, where you'll find a strange medley of revolutionary monuments, beaches, quirky museums and the virtual desert landscape of Parque Baconao.

History. The city of Santiago de Cuba was established in 1515 by Diego de Velázquez. The fifth villa to be founded by the Spanish, it was named the capital of Cuba almost immediately. Velázquez became the first Governor, and his beautiful house, which still stands in Céspedes Square, is marketed as the oldest building in Cuba. Another conquistador, Hernándo Córtez, used the town as a base for his forays into the mainland of Central America.

Havana replaced Santiago as capital in 1553, and the eastern city was abandoned to its fate. The copper and gold mines in the surrounding hills had brought a degree of prosperity to Santiago, but where there was wealth, pirates were sure to follow. It was in response to successive attacks by pirates that the Santiagüeros built the awesome Morro castle, though even this could not prevent the British-sponsored pirate, Captain Henry Morgan, from sacking the city in 1662. Ironically, profitable dealings with pirates and smugglers also funded much of Santiago's early expansion.

Perhaps the single most important event in the entire history of Santiago was the revolt by slaves in Haiti in the 1790s, which caused a sudden influx of 27,000 French settlers. During the early colonial era, Santiago had more links with Hispaniola than with Havana, so it was not a surprising destination for the French plantation owners. They founded coffee and sugar estates, which gave a significant boost to the local economy. They also had a profound influence on the culture and architecture of Santiago.

The people of Santiago played an active role in the war of independence at the end of the 19th century, and many of the leaders of the liberation movement, including Carlos Manuel de Céspedes and José Martí, are buried in the city's impressive Santa Ifigenia cemetery. Santiago figured even larger in the revolution of the 50s. Fidel Castro was born in Holguín province but he went to school in Santiago. It was here that on 26 July 1953, he and a small band of rebels attempted a surprise attack on the huge Moncada Barracks. Although Castro was captured, he succeeded in gaining increasingly widespread support for what became known as the 26 July Movement, which ultimately brought the revolutionaries to power. After Batista fled on January 1 1959, Castro appeared in Parque Céspedes and gave his first speech as leader of Cuba. Plaques on buildings all over the city recall associations with the campaign.

Santiago has grown considerably since 1959. Development has been focussed around the harbour, where industrial complexes belch large quantities of black smoke into the atmosphere. Thankfully, the heart of Santiago is some way from the port, and strolling through the streets of the old city it is easy to forget that the harbour even exists.

CITY LAYOUT

The city spreads east into the hills from the beautiful Bahía de Santiago de Cuba. Most places of interest are concentrated in the twenty blocks closest to the harbour, the original site for the city. Life centres on Parque Céspedes, the main square bounded by Félix Pena and Lacret (running north-south) and by Aguilera and Heredia (running east-west). The twin towers of the cathedral, which overlooks the square, provide a useful landmark.

It is quite possible to spend a week in Santiago without venturing down to the port. The southern end of Avenida Jesús Menéndez, known as the Alameda, was once a fashionable promenade and is still the focus of the carnival, but the rest of the harbourside road is dusty and unattractive, lined with delapidated warehouses. An area where you are likely to spend more time is east of the centre, around the junction of Avenida Las Américas and Victoriano Garzón, where the city's main tourist hotels are concentrated.

Streets in Santiago have names, not numbers, and most have two. In some cases the old name is used more than the new one — as with Enrramada, the old name for Calle Saco. Most maps give both the old and the new versions, but the most important changes in the city centre are as follows:

Old	New
Marina	Aguilera
Catedral	Heredia
Enrramada	José A Saco
San Basilio	Bartolomé Masó
San Pedro	Lacret
Santo Tomás	Félix Pena
Carnicería	Pio Rosado
San Félix	Hartman

Maps. You should be able to get a map at the bookshop beneath the cathedral — there is a good one which includes a map of Parque Baconao and costs only about $1. The *Santiago de Cuba Guiá Turística* (see *Help and Information*) has an A-Z style map that is better than nothing, but the single-sheet map is better for finding your way around the city.

ARRIVAL AND DEPARTURE

Air. Santiago's airport, Antonio Maceo, is 4 miles (6km) south of the centre. It

SANTIAGO

1 Santa Ifigenia cemetery
2 Proposed rail/bus station
3 Rum factory
4 Railway station
5 Tobacco factory
6 Museo de la
   Lucha Clandestina
7 Parque Céspedes
8 Plaza de Dolores
9 Hotel Libertad
10 Plaza de Marte
11 Hotel Rex
12 Moncada barracks
13 Local bus station
14 Long distance bus station
15 Plaza de la Revolución
16 Heredia theatre
17 Hotel Santiago de Cuba
18 Ferreiro market
19 Hotel Las Américas
20 M. E. S. Hotel
21 Tocororo restaurant
22 Casa del Caribe
23 Villa San Juan

Siboney,
Gran Piedra,
Baconao

Autopista

Tropicana,
Holguín

Avenida de Las Américas

Avenida de los Libertadores

Patricio Lumumba

J. G. Gómez

R. Ramos

Corrales

Marina

Paseo de Martí

Crombet

Jesús Menéndez

See Central Santiago map

Aguilera

Saco

Heredia

Masó

Félix Peña

Padre Pico

Céspedes

Garzón

Aguilera

Trocha

Miniel

Manduley

Pujol

VISTA
ALEGRE

24 de Febrero

E. Chivas

Hotel Versalles, Airport,
Balcón del Caribe

El Cobre

N

500 m
500 yds

was expanded to meet the extra demands of the Party Congress held in 1991, and now resembles a modern terminal — ten times nicer than Havana's, though facilities are still limited.

A cab into the city should cost about $7, but there is also a Cubana bus, which runs about once an hour. When leaving Santiago, you can catch this bus from Plaza de Marte or outside Casa Velázquez in the main square (though you'll have a better chance of getting a seat if you choose the former); the fare is one peso. You can find out when the bus runs from the Cubana office on Félix Pena, just south of the main square (open 9am-5pm Monday to Friday, 9am-2pm on Saturday, tel 22290, 20616) — you can't miss the crowd outside, and you may have to swallow a principle or two as you barge your way in.

In addition to the frequent daily flights between Havana and Santiago, there are also flights between Santiago and Montego Bay in Jamaica ($120 one way), which are used for day excursions (price around $180). Note that since this is simply an excursion, visa regulations are waived for one day.

Train. The No 1 *especial* service to and from Havana is by far the most comfortable way to travel to Santiago by land. The journey takes about 16 hours and costs $35 one way.

The railway station was supposed to have moved to a new site near the junction of Avenida Jesús Menéndez with Paseo de Martí in preparation for the 1991 Party Congress, but it never happened. The massive structure, designed to combine Santiago's bus and rail stations under one roof, still remains only half built. It seems likely that for some years to come rail passengers will continue to alight at the old station, some five or six blocks further south.

Foreign tourists must buy tickets from the Ferrotur office, which is on the first floor of the main station building and opens 9am-6pm. The main daily departures, with fares given in brackets, are as follows:

Havana ($35): 4.35pm, arriving at 7.05am the next morning.
Holguín ($5): 8.05am, arriving at 11.25am.
Camagüey ($13): 8.55am, arriving 5.50pm.
Manzanillo ($8): 5.45am, arriving at 11.55am.

Note that you need to book a seat on the Manzanillo train the day before (the office will be closed prior to departure), while for the others an hour or so's notice will do.

You are unlikely to find a taxi outside the station, and the horses and carts aren't much use since they cannot negotiate the steep hill that separates you from the centre of town. You have little choice but to walk.

Bus. Only Havana has a more chaotic bus station than Santiago. The Interprovincial terminal for long-distance services is located northeast of the city centre, on Avenida de los Libertadores close to the junction with Avenida Las Américas. There are daily services to Havana, Holguín, Las Tunas, Manzanillo, Bayamo, Baracoa and Guantánamo, but these are invariably heavily booked, and you normally need to make a reservation seven days in advance. Unless a Cuban acquaintance helps you arrange a seat, you'll probably have to hitch or negotiate with one of the drivers who hang around the station looking for business.

Transport — by bus or old cattle truck — to most other parts of the province departs from the Intermunicipal terminal, also on Avenida de los Libertadores but closer to town. There are also a few colectivos and private cabs. Arrive early in the morning for the best chance of getting anywhere.

Driving. Santiago is 75 miles (130km) from Bayamo, 110 miles (190km) from Holguín and a mighty 605 miles (970km) from Havana. Access to Santiago from the west is spectacular, as you descend from the hills along the Carretera Central or the new autopista; the topography means that you leave the city heading northeast, even if your eventual destination is west.

The narrow, one-way streets in the old town provide the usual nightmare for motorists, and you would do best to leave your car at one of the suburban hotels. The Cupet station is near the two bus stations below Moncada. See *Help and Information* for car rental outlets.

Boat. For some years the *Caribbean Queen* has sailed between Montego Bay in Jamaica and Santiago, but the service has rarely offered a regular or reliable service. There are also boats from Port Antonio. The best place to find out about these services is the tourism desk in Hotel Santiago de Cuba (tel 42612).

ACCOMMODATION

Santiago has a fairly impressive supply of hotels, but the majority are away from the centre. If you prefer to be at the heart of the action, you will have to make do with basic accommodation in peso hotels or splash out on a room in the newly restored Casa Granda hotel in the main square. Note that you may have difficulty in finding a room in July, when the carnival and Moncada anniversary celebrations can attract large crowds. The addresses and telephone numbers of the hotels described below are listed (in alphabetical order) at the end of the *Accommodation* section.

The main concentration of hotels is a couple of miles east of the main square around the junction of Avenida Las Américas and Victoriano Garzón. **Hotel Santiago de Cuba**, a red, white and blue high-tech, high-rise block is undoubtedly one of the most striking modern buildings in Cuba, but it is completely out of sorts with its surroundings — and is thankfully nowhere near the historic centre. The 15-storey, five-star Santiago was the flashest hotel in Cuba when it opened a few years ago, but the island's new joint venture hotels have already succeeded in making it look dated and rather drab. The prices are still up there at the top of the range though, with double rooms for $113 ($90 in low season) and singles for $100. The breakfast buffet costs $7, other meals $20. It is still the favourite hotel among business visitors, but most tourists are nowadays billeted in one of the new beachside hotels. In the low season, the Santiago is as empty as the Marie Celeste during the day, when the tourist information, car rental and other service desks are often unstaffed.

The three-star **Hotel Las Américas**, opposite the Santiago, does not compare favourably with most other dollar hotels in and around the city, but probably offers the best compromise between location (it's a 25-minute walk to Parque Céspedes) and comfort. Double rooms cost $40 ($35 low season) and singles $31 ($26). The food is poor and the swimming pool tiny, but you can always head across the road to the Santiago, where non-residents can use the pool free of charge. The Américas disco and poolside cabaret are popular locally, so you can expect company in the evenings. The **M.E.S**, in a quiet street not far from the Américas, is the cheapest hotel in this area. It has no sign — look out for two flights of steps and an awning leading up to reception. The hotel charges $15 (single) and $20 (double) for a clean though rather dingy room with shared bathroom. The staff are helpful and the restaurant serves good breakfast and dinner.

Villa Gaviota, a three-star hotel ten blocks east of the Américas, is well worth considering. Its location on Avenida Manduley, a blissfully quiet and leafy street, more than makes up for the fact that the walk into the centre takes a good 40 minutes. A double room is reasonable value at $40 ($28 in low season), and there is a swimming pool up the road for use by residents. The three-star **Hotel Villa San Juan** (formerly the less-enticing Motel Leningrado) is a similar distance from the downtown area, but feels much more isolated. Still, it is set in beautiful gardens and has a good restaurant and swimming pool. A double room goes for

$35, a single for $26, for which you can expect both hot water and air-conditioning. San Juan Hill (Loma de San Juan) was the scene of the final battle in the War of Independence and there is a memorial above the motel, consisting of a few cannons, a statue of a mambí soldier and a plaque saying that the 1895-98 conflict should have been known as the Spanish-Cuban-American War and not the Spanish-American War. Quite right too.

While it is possible to walk to the centre from any of the above hotels, do not over-estimate your energy levels, and you will almost certainly end up taking taxis, unless you have your own hired car of course. You will have no choice if you opt for one of the following two places. **Motel Versalles**, 3 miles (5km) southwest of the centre, has little going for it, though being located almost at the end of the airport runway it is convenient for an early flight. They charge a surprising $63 for a double and $45 for a single room. You'd do much better at **El Balcón del Caribe**, 5 miles (8km) southwest of the centre (about $10 in a taxi). Unfortunately, the hotel lies under the flight path for the nearby airport, but it is beautifully situated on a clifftop looking out to sea, and rooms are good value at $28-35 for a double. The Balcón del Caribe is still Cuban-run and of the old school, so don't expect too much from the restaurant. The pool is lovely though.

Travellers who choose to be in the centre of Santiago will not have much problem deciding where to stay. The downtown hotels may not offer the comfort of the suburban ones, but they are infinitely more convenient and charactered. It will be worth checking out the **Casa Granda**, which was undergoing major refurbishment at the time of going to press, but should be functioning by 1996. The city's best hotel earlier this century, it has easily the best location of any hotel in Santiago, overlooking the main square. If you can't afford the four-star rooms, treat yourself to a drink on the verandah.

There are five or six peso hotels in the Santiago, but the Bayamo, for example, does not take tourists. You can try the **Imperial** (two blocks north of the square), where a double room with a fan costs $10. For a degree of peace and quiet, however, you should head for Plaza de Marte. Directly on the square, **Hotel Libertad** offers rooms with a fan and cold water for $9 single, $12 double. **Hotel Rex** around the corner charges the same price for similarly no-frills accommodation, though rooms have air-conditioning. Its connections with the assault on Moncada in 1953 provide added appeal. The rebels ate their last supper here before the attack and some even stayed overnight. Room 36 has been turned into a museum, but there isn't much to see.

If you can't stand the heat of the city, you might consider staying in one of the hotels strung out along the coast. See *Further Afield.*

Las Américas: Avenida de las Américas y General Cebreco (tel 226-42011, 42695).
Balcón del Caribe: Carretera del Morro km 7 (tel 91011).
Casa Granda: Parque Manuel de Céspedes.
Villa Gaviota: Avenida Manduley 502 y Calle 19, Vista Alegre (tel 41368).
Imperial: Calle Saco 251 (tel 8917).
Libertad: Plaza de Marte (tel 23080).
M.E.S.: Calle L y 7, Reparto Terrazas (tel 42398).
Rex: top of Avenida Victoriano Garzón, just off Plaza de Marte (entrance on first floor).
San Juan: Carretera Siboney (tel 226-42478, 42490, 42434, fax 33-5015).
Santiago de Cuba: Avenida de Las Américas y Calle M (tel 42612, 42654, 42702; fax 41756).
Versalles: Altura de Versalles (tel 91014).

EATING AND DRINKING

For a city of over one-third of a million people, Santiago is poorly provided with restaurants. The choice for tourists is clearly better than for local people, and the options double if you don't mind eating in a hotel. The **Las Columnas** restaurant on the first floor of the Hotel Santiago de Cuba has three unlimited buffets a day. Lunch and dinner at $20 are overpriced unless your appetite is unusually large and indiscriminate. Breakfast, costing $7, is a much better deal. If you are staying in this part of town and feel like treating yourself, try the **Tocororo**, an expensive but intimate restaurant on Avenida Mandeley. Tables are scattered through various rooms in the elegant old villa, inviting you to imagine that you are eating in someone's private home. There is no menu, but the waiters will reel off a choice of seven or eight dishes. Despite the pretentious tendencies the food is good — mostly Cuban, with main meals costing $8-10. While a little sedate, the Tocororo is an ideal place to push the boat out or have a romantic meal for two.

Nowhere downtown can offer the class of the Tocororo, however the **1900** restaurant (on Bartolomé Masó, between Pio Rosado and Hartmann) at least has fine décor. It occupies what was once the Santiago home of the Bacardí family, a beautiful white building with giant chandeliers, fabulous mahogany furniture and a delightful courtyard. The surroundings make up for the chef's shortcomings, though the cooking has improved in recent years. The food is mostly creole. Prices are a little high, so for a cheap lunch you'll probably have to make do with an omelette. The 1900 stays open late, but turn up before 9pm to have a good choice from the menu.

The appeal of eating downtown is that in most places tourists are easily outnumbered by Cubans. The one restaurant in which this is unlikely to be the case is the **Miguel Matamoros**, on Plaza de Dolores, a new and smart place which is an increasingly popular venue for package tour lunches. It is large and has an extensive menu catering for all budgets, from omelettes and spaghetti for around $3 to lobster for $21. For livelier company, head for the popular **Taberna de Dolores** across the street. The chatter and music that emanates through the large windows of this fine colonial building make it hard to resist. Most punters stay downstairs, where you can eat (simply) as well as drink. The upstairs bar offers a fine view down over the square, but has less ambience.

The tourism drive has so far not led to a burgeoning of new cafés and bars as it has in Havana. **Cafeteria La Isabelica**, a Santiago institution in Plaza de Dolores, has existed for years. It has seen few changes during that time — the flagstones get a little dirtier, the tables and chairs a little more worn, but the range of coffee on offer is not what it was and the dollar prices are excessive. Furthermore, foreigners are meant to sit at two tables slightly apart from everyone else, though this at least means that Cubans are guaranteed seats. Most other cafés in Santiago make convenient refreshment breaks without deserving a great detour. **Apisun**, in Calle Lacret beneath the cathedral, is a popular place for coffee or *canchánchara* (a mixture of aguardiente, honey, lemon and ice), and it also sells honey. Around the corner, on Heredia, the **Casa de Vino** serves Cuban refrescos and sandwiches and is open 24 hours. The **Pico Real** bar on the 15th floor of the Hotel Santiago offers fine views, and the powerful air-conditioning makes this an excellent place to cool down during the day.

The main market (known as Ferreiro) near the Santiago hotel is one of the biggest and best in Cuba and is an excellent place for a cheap daytime snack. Here, and elsewhere in the city, you will see people selling *rallado* — ice shaved off a block to which a very sweet syrup is added, similar to the *granizada* sold in other Cuban towns. You can buy fruit at the small covered market at the corner of Heredia and Padre Pico.

EXPLORING

Parque Manuel de Céspedes is the heart and soul of Santiago. It is never quiet, and local people while away hours on end watching the world go by; rarely will

CENTRAL SANTIAGO

1 Maceo Museum
2 Placita Santo Tomás
3 Santísima Trinidad church
4 Parque Céspedes
5 Ayuntamiento
6 Casa de Velásquez
7 Claqueta Bar
8 Cathedral
9 Casa Granda Hotel
10 Bank
11 Casa de la Trova
12 Casa de Vino
13 Bacardí Museum
14 Carnival Museum
15 La Isabelica Café
16 Miguel Matamoros restaurant
17 Taberna de Dolores
18 Dolores concert hall
19 1900 restaurant
20 Museo de la Lucha
   Clandestina

0   250 m

0   250 yds

you cross the square without being approached. Towering over the action is the
Cathedral, raised up on the south side of the square. The Santa Iglesia Basilica
Metropolitana was consecrated in 1524, an example of how quickly Santiago
prospered after colonisation. The original church was destroyed by fire only a
few years later, however, and the building that replaced it was also subjected to
all kinds of calamities, from pirate attacks to hurricanes. Earthquakes hit the
third cathedral, inaugurated in 1690, and also the fourth, consecrated in 1818.
The building you see today combines the surviving 19th-century features with

alterations made in the 1920s, when the façade and much of the interior decoration were added. Its best features include the Angel of the Annunciation over the entrance, the carving in the choir and the unusual stuccowork on the Italianate ceiling. Diego Velázquez was buried in the very first cathedral, but excavators have never found his remains.

From the balustrade in front of the cathedral you can get the best view of the **Ayuntamiento.** Don't be fooled by the colonial look of this building, which was constructed in 1952 — though to an 18th-century design. It was from here that Fidel Castro gave his first victory speech on 1 January, 1959, and from where he orates on special anniversaries. Today it is Santiago's city hall and the door attendant refuses to let tourists even poke their head in for a glimpse of the courtyard.

Better things await you, however, in the **Casa de Velázquez,** also known, less romantically as the Museo de Ambiente Histórico Cubano, on the west side of the square. Reputedly built for Velázquez in 1516-30, this is one of the oldest buildings not only in Cuba but in Latin America, and should on no account be missed. The 16th-century building was extensively rebuilt in the 1960s, but it retains some of the original ceilings — superb alfarjes made of cedarwood. Restorers added certain features which it is thought were part of the original house, including the Moorish-style wooden grilles along the exterior balcony and around the inner courtyard, designed to hide women from public view and protect them from the sun.

The upstairs rooms are by far the most interesting, but there is superb furniture throughout. The most striking examples date from the boom years of the late 18th century, substantial mahogany pieces that look as good as new after 200 years. Providing an interesting contrast to the Velázquez house is an adjacent 19th-century building that forms part of the same museum. The house includes typical features of the period, such as the coloured glass *medio puntos*, the use of wrought-iron and the decorative friezes on the wall (*cenefas*), though the latter are not original.

You should allow at least one hour to visit this museum, which opens 9am-6pm and 9am-1pm on Sunday. The staff who conduct the guided tours are friendly, helpful and very well informed; they also speak English. Admission is $1, with an extra $1 charged for each photograph taken.

Calle Heredia, which runs east off the square, is Santiago's most perfect colonial street. Most buildings are open to the public as art galleries or museums. You may find this area overrun with tourists on days when cruise ships are docked, particularly in high season. The focus of their attention is generally the **Casa de la Trova** which, unlike in most Cuban towns, is a hub of activity throughout the day and not just in the evenings. A stream of musicians provide constant entertainment to locals and tourists alike. Refurbishment, under way at the time of going to press, threatens to change the atmosphere of the place and admission is already being charged; but not to visit this Santiago institution is like going to Athens and missing the Parthenon. Also well worth a visit is the **Museo del Carnaval** (closed Monday), near the corner of Calle Pio Rosado, for the background it gives to the country's most important festival. One block north, in a grand neoclassical structure at the corner of Pio Rosado and Aguilera, is the **Museo Emilio Bacardí,** another of Santiago's best museums that has only recently emerged from years of closure. It takes its name from the principal benefactor, the industrialist Emilio Bacardí Moreau — one-time patriot, mayor of Santiago and son of the famous rum magnate. The museum gathers together an eclectic historical collection, including an Egyptian mummy from Luxor, Indo-American relics, as well as one of the best collections of colonial paintings. One of the strangest exhibits is the home-made torpedo made by *mambises* to attack Spanish vessels. It also incorporates Callejón Bofill, a narrow alley of preserved colonial façades.

A few blocks east is **Plaza de los Dolores,** a pleasant square that makes a good stopping-off place for refreshment (see *Eating and Drinking*). You are also close to **Calle Saco**, Santiago's main shopping street. The shops are predictable and unappealing, but the street also surprises with its portfolio of architectural styles, from Italianate to Art Deco (the shop at number 418 is like a pink and white wedding cake). If you head north along Lacret or Felix Pena, the theme is more strictly colonial. This quiet area comes as a relief after the hectic streets around the main square. **Placita Santo Tomás**, six blocks along Felix Pena, is a delight, surrounded by one-storey, colonial buildings and barely a soul in sight. Overlooking the square is the 18th-century church of Santo Tomás, but you'll have to come in the late afternoon or evening to find it open. The same applies if you want to see inside the **Iglesia de la Santísima Trinidad** further east, built in the 1780s and the most attractive of Santiago's churches. The arches that flank its broad nave have an unusual delicacy, and there is a gorgeous alfarje, decorated with 12-pointed stars. Mass is generally held at 8pm.

The only other sight in this area is **Casa Natal de Antonio Maceo** (closed Sunday), at Los Maceo 207 between Delgado and Corona, back towards the harbour. The independence fighter was born in a cute colonial house, but the display of photos, documents and memorabilia will probably appeal only to serious students of Cuban history. Even so, if you're headed for the cemetery, you might consider stopping off.

The following sights are all within reach of the centre, but are scattered in different directions so are described individually.

Tivolí. When the French arrived in Santiago at the end of the 18th century, many settled in the quarter now known as Tivolí, which extends southwest from the main square. It is a picturesque and atmospheric area of steep streets and higgledy piggledy houses. Carnival is particularly colourful hereabouts.

The Padre Pico steps — a famous Santiago landmark featuring on many postcards — lead up to the Museo de la Lucha Clandestina. On 30 November 1956, members of the local 26 July Movement led by Frank País attacked the headquarters of the Santiago police. (This was timed to coincide with the landing of the *Granma*, only the yacht that was bringing Castro and the others from Mexico was late in arriving.) Many of the insurgents were killed, some of them gunned down on the Padre Pico staircase, but they had succeeded in almost completely destroying the building. For years after the Revolution it was left in its ruinous state, but was finally rebuilt in the 1970s. It is now a virtual replica of the original and houses a museum dedicated to the underground struggle in Santiago. If the minutiae of the rebellion begins to pall, just look out across the city from the upper floor — the museum occupies a prime spot high on a hill south of the main square. Opening hours are 9am-5pm Tuesday to Sunday.

Moncada Barracks. For many people it would be inconceivable to visit Santiago without seeing the Moncada barracks. This is where it all began, at 5.30am on 26 July 1953, when Fidel Castro and a handful of rebels launched their first attack against Batista. The huge barracks now house a school, but of course there is also a museum, the Museo Histórico 26 de Julio. The entrance to the barracks is at the corner of Portuondo and Moncada, off Avenida de los Libertadores (follow the signs for the 'Centro Escolar 26 de Julio'). Enormous bullet holes pepper the dirty yellow walls either side of the entrance — a certain amount of artistic licence was used in the 'reconstruction' of the original holes that Batista had filled in.

The first rooms provide a history of Cuba in pictures, accompanied by uplifting quotations from Cuban revolutionaries of this and last century, but this museum is designed for those in search of a blow-by-blow account of the 1953 assault and the aftermath. Explanations are in Spanish only, but certain concessions have been made to the internationalist audience: the walls are covered floor to ceiling with photographs, and many of the exhibits are self-explanatory. A model shows how the rebels reached the barracks (some of them by taxi), and other diagrams plot the progress of every stage of the subsequent campaign, from the landing of the *Granma* onwards. There is also the usual array of blood-spattered uniforms and weapons, including some very primitive looking grenades.

The museum opens 9am-6pm from Monday to Saturday, 8am-noon on Sundays.

Vista Alegre. The district of Vista Alegre, beyond Hotel Santiago de Cuba,is where many of the city's rich lived prior to the Revolution. Well-preserved mansions from the turn of the century onwards flank the tree-lined Avenida Manduley and surrounding streets, many of them now occupied by some institute or other. These include the Casa del Caribe (corner of Calles 13 and 8; tel 42285), a research centre dedicated to the study of Caribbean culture. Anyone interested in Afro-Cuban culture should make a point of coming here. Its library is open to the public (by appointment) and every Saturday afternoon scholars, poets and artists gather for readings and discussions; everyone is welcome. The centre publishes a tri-monthly magazine called *Caribe* as well as books. The Casa del Caribe also organises an annual Caribbean festival, which takes place in June and has a different theme every year; in 1995, for example, it focussed on the Anglophone Caribbean. (Do not confuse the Casa del Caribe with the Centro Cultural Africano Fernando Ortíz, around the corner at Manduley 106, which carries out much smaller-scale research and charges you $1 to see a tiny collection of African artifacts.)

Plaza de la Revolución. The brutalist monument to General Antonio Maceo, fittingly made of bronze for the 'Titan of Bronze', is an audacious scar upon the townscape, dominating Plaza de la Revolución. It protects an extraordinary museum. The Sala de Holografía is a revolutionary concept; it contains nothing but holograms of ideologically correct artifacts. Revolvers which changed the course of Cuban history are shown in convincing 3D, as well as belt buckles, binoculars, etc. It opens 10am-5pm from Tuesday to Saturday, 1-5pm on Sunday. Nearby is the huge Teatro Heredia, a bold modern structure which displays an awesome sense of space and hosts all manner of dramatic productions, from traditional opera to Communist Party congresses.

East along Avenida Las Américas, two blocks from the Américas hotel, you'll find the Bosques de los Héroes, a mound dedicated to revolutionaries, notably Che Guevara.

Cemetery of Santa Ifigenia. If your time in the city is severely limited, you should see the main downtown attractions and then head out to the Santa Ifigenia graveyard, with its mass of ornate tombs. The spirit of the Revolution lives on here, with the black and red flag of the 26 July Movement decorating the graves of those who served with the rebels. The highlight is the octagonal mausoleum (built in 1951) containing the grave of José Martí — to the left of the entrance. The six women around the exterior wall represent the six provinces of Cuba (as they were then). Inside, Martí's tomb is so placed as to catch the sun throughout the day, and is a moving and simple tribute. Nearby is the grave of Tomás Estrada Palma, the first president of an independent Cuba. Other notable tombs include those of Céspedes and Emilio Bacardí Moreau (both near the entrance) and a mausoleum for the heroes of the Moncada attack. Tourists must now pay an admission fee of $1, plus an extra $1 if you want to take photographs; in return, it is worth asking for a guide to show you around.

The cemetery is a good 30-minute walk northwest of the city centre, taking you beyond the railway line and through one of Santiago's poorest barrios. En route you pass the tiny Fuerte de Yarayó (at the corner of Crombet and Yarayó), erected last century. Looking back towards the centre of the city on leaving the cemetery, the cathedral looks miles away. If you're on foot, you could shorten your journey back by jumping on one of the horses and carts that ply Avenida Crombet en route to the railway station.

Factory Tours. Before 1959, the Caney rum factory founded by the Bacardí family in 1862 was about the only important industry in Santiago. Not today. After the Revolution, the Bacardís moved to Puerto Rico, where they launched the rum for which they have won worldwide fame. The Santiago factory continued to function, but with rather less commercial success. You used to be able to go on a tour of the factory, a few blocks north of the train station, but in 1995 the factory had ceased production. At the time of going to press, you could visit only the shop next door (somewhere worth bearing in mind if you need a drink while waiting for a train).

There is a tiny tobacco factory (Fábrica de Tabaco César Escalante) opposite the Customs (Aduana) building at the northern end of the harbourside Alameda. Factory visits are available between 9am and 5pm Monday to Friday. The adjacent cigar shop also opens on Saturdays.

ENTERTAINMENT

The locals won't hesitate to point out that the roots of Cuban music were first developed in Oriente, in particular in Santiago de Cuba, birthplace of great troubadours such as Sindo Garay and Miguel Matamoros, who did much to popularise *son* in the 20s. From the 40s, the era of the big band, many musicians were drawn to the bright lights of Havana, but nowadays Santiago is probably the best place in the country to enjoy authentic traditional music.

The other musical genre to have spread throughout the country from Santiago is the so-called *conga*, a rhythm that is inextricably linked with the carnival and that demonstrates so clearly the multi-ethnic roots of the city's music.

The Carnival. With the onset of the Special Period in 1990, Cuba's carnivals were either cancelled altogether or reduced to mere shadows of their former selves. For the Santiagüeros, whose year revolves around the July carnival, life just wasn't the same. The five-day celebration staged in 1995, however, hopefully heralds a full revival of one of the best cultural events in Latin America. In the past, people arrived from all over the island and beyond to submerge themselves in the high spirits, mesmerising rhythms and drunken chaos of Santiago's carnival, though lawlessness never quite reached the scale known in Brazil. It was not by chance that Fidel Castro timed the Moncada attack to coincide with the carnival. He knew that most of the city would be dancing or drunk or both.

The carnival evolved out of processions organised by social and religious groups during the colonial era, though it began to crystallise into its present form only at the turn of this century. The various barrios in the city would each organise a *comparsa*, a procession in which members would dress up in costume, often allegorical, according to the theme that had been chosen. These themes were usually of public interest, related to actual events of national and international importance.

Groups known as *congas* make up the core of the comparsas, with drums, trumpets, trombones, clarinets and other instruments all contributing to the din. They are perhaps the most popular element of the carnival — not something to watch as much as join in with. The tall conga drums provide the beat, but two other instruments are even more characteristic of Santiago's carnival. One is the *tumba francesa*, the straight cylindrical 'French drum' brought by the slaves of French planters who fled from Haiti in 1791. These African slaves had absorbed elements of their masters' formal contredanse into their own rhythms and produced the tumba francesa, a musical style with a drum to go with it. The other essential component in a Santiago conga is the Chinese cornet (*corneta china*), brought by contract labourers from China in the middle of last century.

The shrill sound of this last instrument gives a very distinctive character to the congas.

The carnival, held in July, takes over the whole of central Santiago, but the Alameda, which runs along the waterfront, is where the main procession *(desfile)* takes place. Huge floats *(carrozas)*, featuring papier mâché figures and dancers, are judged by a jury, the prizes usually going to those that are most popular with onlookers. There is an area with seats reserved for tourists, but this is a time to join in with the crowds. Another focus of activity is in Parque Santamaría across the road from the Moncada barracks.

Live Music. Despite the concessions made to tourism, the best place to listen to traditional music in Santiago is still the Casa de la Trova on Calle Heredia. On weekend nights, the music spreads out on to the street — an organised event advertised as 'Noches Cubanas' and well worth attending. The whole population seems to take to the streets around the main square, and often a stage is set up in the square for live music.

It is also well worth checking out the Claqueta Bar, set back from the street on Félix Pena between Heredia and Bartolomé Masó. Here you can sit beneath the trees and enjoy live music from around 9pm to the early hours. Bands may be interspersed with the odd comedian or other cabaret-style act, but the emphasis is very much on the music. Admission is free. Usually just drinks and snacks *(entremés)* are available, but sometimes they lay on something more substantial, such as roast chicken with rice. Until now the clientele has been almost exclusively Cuban, but this may well change with the reopening of the Casa Granda hotel in the main square. A place that is more obviously geared to the tourist trade is the newer Buró de Información Cultural in Plaza de Marte, where local groups play in a small courtyard from about 10.30pm.

At weekends you might find something going on at the Club de Jedrez (the Chess Club), just down from the Claqueta Bar. (There are photos of Che and Fidel playing chess inside.) This is a cracking little venue, if not necessarily for the quality of the performances — although among the aging crooners who sing along to a tape recording there is usually at least one good band. You pay just three pesos to get in and can then choose between rum and wine.

The best place to hear classical music is in the church in Plaza de los Dolores, converted many years ago into a concert hall. Performances are generally confined to the weekends — the Buró de Información Cultural should be able to tell you when the next concert is on. Santiago's best choir, the Coro Madrigalista, is based opposite the Bacardí Museum. You can sometimes hear them rehearsing during the day.

Discos and cabarets. Many young Santiagüeros frequent the disco adjoining the Las Américas or Santiago de Cuba hotels, but another popular place — and much more Cuban — is the Ciroa disco on Avenida Manduley (near Calle 13) in Vista Alegre. The cabaret show is a real laugh and is followed by dancing.

Santiago doesn't try to compete with Havana in many respects, but it does have its own Tropicana, northeast of the centre. While similar to the version in the capital, Santiago's is less over the top and with a lot more Cubans in the audience. The going rate booked from a hotel is $35 with transport. The only alternative is the rather dismal floorshow of the San Pedro del Mar cabaret, next to the Balcón del Caribe Hotel.

SHOPPING

Shopping is a dismal occupation in Santiago. Benetton, beneath the cathedral, sticks out like a sore thumb in a city with surprisingly few dollar shops. Calle Saco is Santiago's main peso shopping street, with several bookshops and craft shops. La Flor de Asia has the best range, including ceramics. The craft shop on

Félix Pena, beneath the Cathedral, offers an astounding range of tat for dollars. Nor does the dollar-only bookshop on Parque Céspedes have much of interest, though it is the best place to look for local guidebooks or maps; for Spanish books, you'll often do as well in the peso shops or from the street vendors. You'll find the best selection of tapes, CDs and records in the Egrem shop in Saco, near the corner of Hartmann, and in the Casa de la Trova.

One shop you should certainly avoid is the 'Expo and Sale' run by the Asociación Nacional de Ornitológica de Cuba. Signs in English outside this building at Saco 512 invite you to 'Take a living souvenir back now! Don't miss this only one chance!'. Do not transgress international controls on the movement of animals by buying a canary from here.

HELP AND INFORMATION

Tourist information: aside from tourism desks in the hotels, information is also available from the Buró de Información Cultural in Plaza de Marte (tel 23302, 23267). It opens 9am-8pm and can offer information on cultural events, museums, courses and guided tours. Hotels are the best place to look for the *Guía Caribeña*, a monthly newspaper in Spanish and English which has a few bland articles but not much hard information. There is also a Santiago de Cuba tourist guide in Spanish, English, French and German ($6.20), which describes the main sights and has a listings section.

Telephone Office: you can make international calls from the office on the main square (below the Cathedral), but opening hours are infuriatingly erratic. Should you need such a thing, you can rent a mobile phone in the Hotel Santiago.

Money: there is an international branch of the Cuban National Bank on the corner of Aguilera and Lacret, in Parque Céspedes, which opens 8am-noon Monday to Friday. The Asistur office in Hotel Santiago (open 9am-5pm Monday to Saturday) may be of use in an emergency, but charges its usual extortionate 10% commission for changing travellers cheques.

Medical care: the city-centre Policlínico Camilo Torres (Heredia and Valiente) can treat minor ailments; more serious cases are sent to the Hospital Saturnino Lora on Avenida de los Libertadores.

Car rental: Cubanacán in Hotel Santiago, Transautos in Villa San Juan and Havanautos in Hotel Las Américas.

Further Afield 61

Santiago province is small enough that you don't have to travel great distances to explore. Most sights lie east of the city. The coast road west of Santiago makes for a stunning drive, with the mountains extending right down to the shore. There are no real sights as such, but there are two resorts which boast far better locations than the coastal resorts in Baconao Park east of the city. The four-star **Hotel Sierra Mar** (tel 48-1013), 40 miles (64km) west of Santiago and opened in 1994 by Fidel Castro, is the flasher of the two. It overlooks a white sandy beach which is gorgeous but requires a lot of maintenance for the simple reason that it is manmade. The laying of rocks and digging of channels has so far been successful in preventing the beach from being washed away. The smaller **Hotel Los Galeones** (tel 26160), in a less dramatic but still pleasant setting by the sea, specialises in diving activities. The pristine tarmacked road deteriorates beyond the resorts; anyone fancying a dramatic but arduous back route to Manzanillo, see page 309.

If you head inland from Santiago, towards Bayamo, the scenery beyond El

Cobre (see below) is beautiful, but gradually flattens out as you move towards Bayamo province. Look out for spectacular river crossings, straddled by viaducts. The town of **Contramaestra** is a pleasant place to stay, if you can persuade the staff at the Hotel Praga on the main square, or the Hotel Luanda a few blocks west, to give you a room.

MORRO CASTLE

An easy and highly recommended trip from Santiago is to the Morro castle, which guards the entrance to the harbour 4 miles/7km southwest of downtown. Begun in the 1630s, it was designed by Bautista Antonelli, who was also responsible for the Morro castle in Havana. Henry Morgan virtually destroyed it in 1662, but the fort was rebuilt and then continually enlarged and remodelled until the end of the 18th century. Although much renovated, it is much more fun to explore than any other Cuban fort, with its labyrinth of stairs and passageways connecting the four different levels. Plus there are great views over the bay and out to sea. The somewhat sparse interior (all polished wood and glass rather than crumbling stone) houses the **Museo de la Piratería**, which covers the activity of pirates throughout the Caribbean and even includes Cuba's modern-day enemy, the CIA. It and the castle are open daily, 9am-5pm Monday to Friday, 8am-5pm at weekends.

EL COBRE

According to the locals, if you haven't seen El Cobre you haven't seen Santiago. This village, 10 miles (16km) west of Santiago, is one of the most stunning places in Cuba. It lies in a fertile valley, over which floats the serene Sanctuary of the Virgen de la Caridad, the patron saint of Cuba, making this the most sacred place in Cuba. The cream church with its three red-tiled towers looks miraculous among the lush mountains.

The village of El Cobre was founded soon after the conquest, thanks to the discovery of copper (*cobre* in Spanish) in the surrounding hills. The mines, the oldest in the island, are still there and functioning, but do not provide the wealth they once did.

Arrival and Departure. If you turn up at the Intermunicipal bus station in Santiago, you should be able to pick up a bus or truck heading for El Cobre or, failing that, a colectivo. Try to go early to give yourself plenty of time to get back. A dollar taxi will charge $12-15 for the trip. If you are driving, take Avenida Las Américas to its westernmost conclusion; it deteriorates into a rough road which winds through the hills to the turn-off for El Cobre.

Accommodation. The cheapest place to stay in the province — and possibly the whole of Cuba — is the hotel at the back of the Sanctuary. The *hospedaría* is intended mainly for visiting pilgrims, but when there is room foreigners are accommodated. The setting could hardly be bettered. A graceful old mansion presides over two valleys, with fine views from its creaking old verandah. The interior is cool and airy. Rooms are spartan, but with the location added to the low price — 10 pesos a night — it is churlish to complain. If possible you should book in advance with Hermana (Sister) Carmen Robles, Hospedería El Cobre, Santiago de Cuba (tel 36246). During religious festivals, all rooms are likely to be taken. The hospedaría also does filling meals.

Exploring. The church is formally called the Santuario Nacional a Nuestra Señora de la Caridad del Cobre ('National Sanctuary to Our Lady of the Charity of El Cobre'), known as Virgen de la Caridad for short. The lady in question is the one-foot tall statue of a mulatta virgin which, so the story goes, was found floating in the sea off the north coast in 1608, with an inscription at her feet that read 'I am the Virgin of Charity'. Kept first in the cathedral in Santiago, and later moved to El Cobre, the virgin was worshipped by slaves working in the nearby mines and constantly invoked in times of difficulty to provide consolation or protection. She was declared the patron saint of Cuba by the Pope in 1916.

The original church has been much altered over the centuries, and what you see now dates from the 1920s. Following the breathtaking view as you approach, the church is rather disappointing close-up, its cream exterior suddenly appearing dirty. Inside, the church itself is simply furnished, though with some intricate marquetry on the confession boxes and a lavish marble altar. A fascinating exhibition can be found in the chapel behind the main altar. El Cobre is a place of pilgrimage, and Catholics send gifts in thanks for favours granted by the Virgin. The collection includes crutches, a wheelchair, rum, soil from abroad and even a chunk of the Berlin Wall. Ernest Hemingway brought his Nobel Prize medal here, but it has since been removed for safekeeping. There is also a display case containing military insignia — including an M26.7 flag — perhaps surprising given past relations between the state and the church, but a reflection of the great importance of this sanctuary in the hearts of many Cubans.

From the exhibition, you can climb the stairs to see the Virgin herself, a tiny figure in a glass case swathed in a cape of yellow satin encrusted with copper and gold, and holding the infant Christ. She is deeply revered not only by Catholics but also by followers of Afro-Cuban religions. In Santería, the Virgin of Charity corresponds to Ochún, the goddess of fresh water and love. If you are in the area, do not miss the Virgin's saint's day celebrations, which falls on 8 September and attracts a huge and colourful crowd. At other times, the church is open 6.30am-6pm daily. Mass takes place each day at 8am.

El Cobre is a far cry from Lourdes but has the inevitable souvenir sellers. These specialise in trying to persuade visitors to buy glittering stones they claim to be gold but which are, in fact, pyrites — also known as 'fool's gold'. The same small boys who pester visitors to buy worthless bits of rock have also been known to rob them. Be careful.

PARQUE BACONAO

A large chunk of eastern Santiago province falls within the boundaries of Parque Baconao, one of the largest in Cuba. The landscape ranges from lush forest around Gran Piedra mountain to the rocky, cactus-strewn coastline. The park has suffered from years of neglect — it is virtually dead in low season and only mildly busy at other times. Efforts by the Cuban authorities to correct this situation are already visible in some refreshed museums and new hotels, but there is some way to go before Baconao Park draws large crowds. The beaches are fine for a cooling dip but cannot begin to compete with those west of Santiago, let alone those on the north coast. Even so, sights within the park are varied — including revolutionary shrines and a mini Jurassic Park — and provide plenty to fill a day trip.

It is virtually impossible to reach most places by public transport, and you'll probably have to rely on tourists for a lift if you're hitching. Hiring a car will enable you to pick and mix the attractions available in the park. The road is reasonable, allowing you to sit back and enjoy the lovely views along the coast. Maps of the park are available in Santiago.

Gran Piedra. A trip up this 3,980-foot (1,226m) peak, 16 miles (26km) east of Santiago, can offer a much-needed respite from the stifling heat of the city. La Gran Piedra, 'the big rock', is said to be a remnant of an ancient volcano. Whatever its history, the huge boulder perches atop the mountain in a most curious fashion. From it the views stretch for miles along the coast, out to sea

328 Santiago de Cuba

(they say you can see Jamaica on a clear day), and inland towards a distant arm of the Sierra Maestra. You can drive almost to the top, but it is worth taking time to explore a little. The park around the Gran Piedra provides some of the most accessible high walking territory in Cuba. The scenery is lush (you may be lucky and see hummingbirds) and is scattered with remnants of old French coffee estates — one of which, La Isabelica, has been restored (see below). Of course no maps exist, but if you're happy to follow your nose there are lots of old trails and roads weaving all over the hills. If all you want to do is the usual tourist thing of climbing the boulder, then be warned it is about 700 feet (225 metres) high, and the approach on a steep flight of steps can be demanding — not least because of the altitude.

The easiest way to the Gran Piedra is by rented car or taxi: if you take a private cab, expect to pay $10-15 for the round trip — but note that not all taxis will take you because the climb is tough on aging motors. If you're travelling by bus or truck, or hitching, you'll probably get to the turn-off to La Gran Piedra, 8 miles (13km) east of Santiago (just before Siboney), without too much difficulty, but don't rely on any help with the 8-mile climb from here. There is a minimal amount of traffic. The advantage, of course, is that you'll have plenty of time to enjoy the splendid views on the way up and to chat with the people you will inevitably meet en route — this is popular walking territory for young Cubans.

If you're tempted to prolong your stay, the two-star **Villa La Gran Piedra** rents rooms near the top for about $45 a night (double), and there is also a reasonable restaurant and bar. During the day, the restaurant is invaded now and again by tourists on a coach trip, but business is generally slack.

La Isabelica: the hills around the Gran Piedra were once an important coffee-growing area; old French haciendas — with names like La Henriette and Marseillaise — are dotted all over the place. Little remains of these relics from the colonial era, but La Isabelica, a mile or so along a dirt track beyond the Gran Piedra, has been restored and turned into a museum. It provides a fasinating insight into what life on such an estate was like. The house, reconstructed in 1961, was originally built by a Frenchman called Victor Constantin in the 19th century. It lies in a superb spot and contains some fine pieces of furniture. The large flat area in front of the house was used for drying coffee beans. Admission is free.

Granjita Siboney. The first thing you notice as you head east from Santiago is that along the roadside are numerous tributes to little-known revolutionaries — simple monuments bearing the names and professions of those who died fighting against Batista. This is the highway to the Siboney farmhouse, from where the 1953 assault on the Moncada Barracks was launched. On 25 July 1953, about 100 men gathered the night before the assault, most of them being briefed for the first time about the plan of attack.

The Granjita Siboney, 10 miles (16km) east of Santiago, is a revolutionary shrine and a museum (closed Monday). The former farmhouse contains a fairly predictable display of photographs and memorabilia, but you can examine the bill for the rebels' last supper at the Hotel Rex, which consisted of improbably large quantities of chicken, rice and beer. In the grounds you can see the well in which the weapons for the raid were concealed. The bullet holes around the front door are, like those at the Moncada barracks, reconstructions. Admission costs $1.

Siboney. The seaside resort of Siboney itself is a mile off the main road. It is a Cuban resort, as opposed to the many on this coast which cater for foreigners. The beach makes a lazy arc and looks lovely, but below the water it is extremely rocky. Don't go in without shoes or flippers. There are better beaches to come.

Arroyo de la Costa. Next along, the Arroyo de la Costa beach is blissful, except when occupied by the full complement of guests from the nearby Hotel Bucanero (tel 7126, 7293). The resort is thankfully low-rise, and its presence means that there are all sorts of recreational facilities available, including horseriding, watersports, sub-aqua diving, etc. The Bucanero caters for package tourists and offers only all-in deals, currently priced at $126 per night.

Valle de la Pre Historia. About 16 miles (24km) east of Santiago, people heading east on the coast road suddenly find themselves surrounded by concrete dinosaurs. No doubt you will have already seen the postcards, but the real thing is not a disappointment. This is kitsch at its best. The 'Valley of Prehistory', created in 1983, is a hilarious Flintstone-like park where you can pose among life-size models of brontosauri, tyrannosauri and other prehistoric creatures. You don't need more than half an hour, unless you stay for a drink in the 'cave' above the car park. There is no admission charge, but motorists are expected to pay a $1 parking fee. This will also secure you admission into the natural history museum across the road, but there's a much better museum just up the road.

Museo Nacional de Transporte. At the next turn-off for Daiquirí, a road leads off to the left to La Punta information point. Here, as well as a café and restaurant, you'll also find the Transport Museum. Under the trees is a collection of old cars, including what is said to be the Cadillac of the famous Cuban singer, Beny Moré. But given that you can see handsome old Lincolns and Cadillacs any day of the week in Cuba, the second part of the museum is far more interesting. This indoor section is made up of 2,070 miniatures that trace the history of transport from prior to the invention of the wheel right up to the 1990s. Even people who would normally run a mile from a transport museum should make the effort to come here. You can have fun looking for the prototype of the car you may have left behind at home.

Daiquirí. It would be nice to think that the daiquirí cocktail was invented in a more romantic spot than this run-down resort. Some people would indeed have you believe that the renowned blend of rum, lime and sugar was first prepared in El Floridita bar in Havana. But while it was El Floridita's daiquirís that Ernest Hemingway made famous (he writes about them in his novel *Islands in the Stream*), Cubans swear that although the Floridita refined the drink, the original was invented by miners in Santiago province. It would seem that when American soldiers landed at Daiquirí during the US occupation of the island in 1898, they adopted the local habit of mixing rum with sugar and water and then took it with them to Havana, where it took on the name daiquirí.

There is not much to Daiquirí, the place. The sandy, palm-fringed beach is very pleasant, the nearby **Villa Daiquirí** (tel 24849) less so. There are rumours that the hotel is to be closed down — it seems that even the flow of Canadian package tourists can't keep it going — but at the time of going to press it was still functioning. With rates at $60 for a double room ($45 low season) and $45 for a single ($31 low season), it is perhaps not hard to deduce why the hotel is so short of customers — particularly given the higher quality of those further east. Redeeming features include the reasonable (in all senses of the word) food and the live music in the evenings.

Eastern beaches. Rejoining the main route through Baconao Park and continuing eastwards, the road soon clings more closely to the coast, and passes a number of decrepit Cuban holiday camps and amusement parks. The beaches along here are not among the best on the coast, but Playa Verraco is not bad. Further on, however, you reach Baconao's two newest hotels. These are full-scale tourist resorts, both joint ventures run by the German group LTI and used predominantly by German and Canadian package tour operators. Hotel Carisol, which offers only all-in deals, is not a patch on the Hotel Los Corales next door (Carretera de Baconao Km-54; tel 226-27191, fax 335429). This is an altogether much friendlier place, with congenial surroundings, plenty of shade and rooms with no strings attached, though special half-board deals are offered. A double room costs $56, $40 in low season. Playa Cazonal, a stone's throw from the hotel, is Baconao's prettiest. The water is too shallow to provide much scope for serious exercise, but there is always the pool.

Laguna Baconao. At the end of the paved section of road, just one hour's drive from Santiago, lies Baconao Lagoon. The calm waters of this small lake enclosed by forested hills are best seen at the end of the rainy season. In the dry season, the water near the shores is dirty and stagnant, and there are few signs of life apart from a few morose-looking pelicans. This is a peaceful spot at any time, however, and you can go on boat rides, have a look around the tiny crocodile farm or simply have a drink in the bar.

The Road to Guantánamo. Few maps show the existence of a road direct from Baconao to Guantánamo, but a rough track over the hills can be negotiated with care, even in a standard Nissan Sunny (though this may cease to be the case after heavy rain). The dirt section runs for 15 miles/25km; halfway along this extremely scenic journey, you encounter a huge hoarding reading 'Capitalism is humiliating and degrading to human dignity'.

The Far East: Guantánamo

Baracoa

In some ways Guantánamo is the most fascinating province in Cuba. The city after which it is named is at first sight a rather squat and ugly place, but turns out to be lively and welcoming. Guantánamo also has one of the world's strangest geo-political oddities, on a par with Berlin before the Wall began to come down. Over forty square miles of the province and inshore waters are occupied by a US navy base, 17 miles (27km) outside the provincial capital. It (or rather a good Hollywood replica of it) features in the film *A Few Good Men*. It brushes against the Cuban town of Caimanera, out-of-bounds to most Cubans but accessible to lucky tourists who stay in one of the country's best hotels.

Further east, the terrain becomes less hospitable. The south coast of Guantánamo province is the nearest Cuba comes to being a desert, where the land supports cactuses that would look at home in a spaghetti western. Then the road turns dramatically inland and winds up and over the mountains to Baracoa, connecting the driest part of the island with the wettest. You can't get much more scenic or more dramatic than this.

Baracoa was where Europeans first settled in Cuba, but it was the last place to have a road. Until the 1950s, access to Baracoa was mostly by boat. To get away from it all and enjoy some glorious and lush scenery, fascinating history and uncrowded beaches, there is nowhere better in Cuba. The pace of life seems to have slowed almost to a halt and the people are even more laid back than elsewhere. The feeling is of a tropical paradise gone to seed.

Guantánamo province is the remotest there is in Cuba (and also probably the poorest). The mountains provided perfect shelter for the aborigines fleeing the conquistadores and later for escaped slaves; their descendants still live in the virgin forests.

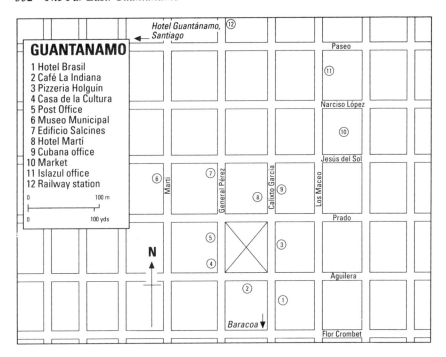

GUANTANAMO

Hotel Guantánamo,
Santiago

1 Hotel Brasil
2 Café La Indiana
3 Pizzeria Holguín
4 Casa de la Cultura
5 Post Office
6 Museo Municipal
7 Edificio Salcines
8 Hotel Martí
9 Cubana office
10 Market
11 Islazul office
12 Railway station

Paseo
Narciso López
Jesús del Sol
Prado
Aguilera
Flor Crombet
Baracoa

CITY OF GUANTANAMO

The city and the province of which it is capital are immortalised in the song 'Guantanamera'. It is an unofficial national anthem in Cuba as well as being beloved by British soccer fans — though the latter are almost certainly unaware that one of their favourite tunes was written in the 1930s as a tribute to a Cuban peasant girl. The city, however, is not as smooth and syrupy as the song.

No one seems to like Guantánamo much. Tourists often dismiss it as downright unattractive, while Cubans often comment that it is full of drunks and dopeheads. The poor image of the town nationally is not totally unrelated to its large black population (which says something about lingering racism in the island); a sizeable proportion of Cuba's Jamaican population resides here, and there is also a sizeable community of Haitian descent. Guantánamo's seedy image also stems from the days when the Marines stationed at the US naval base flocked to the town for gambling and sex. All this came to a rapid halt with the Revolution, but the reputation seems to have stuck. In reality, however, Guantánamo is not without charm. It is buzzing during the day and has some unexpectedly eccentric architecture.

Arrival and Departure. *Air:* Los Canos airport at Guantánamo is served by air from Havana daily except Tuesday. The Cubana office (open 8-11am and 2-4pm) is on Calixto García just off the main square and between Aguilera and Prado (tel 4789).

Train: the station lies six blocks north of the main square along Calle Pedro Agustín Pérez. And what a fine place it is. The faded neoclassical entrance leads into a tropical garden, in which you might be lucky enough to find a timetable and even a train. There is a local train every other day to Santiago (for which you must book a seat the day before) and a fast train to Havana (for which tourists can buy a ticket in dollars one hour before departure).

Bus: the main bus terminal is very inconveniently situated 3 miles (5km) west of town on the road in from Santiago. It is, however, the most modern and best equipped bus station in Cuba. The main interprovincial services are to Santiago, Holguín, Baracoa and Camagüey, but tickets are a virtual impossibility at short notice. There is only one heavily booked bus every two days to Baracoa. Guantánamo is not a good place to hitch from either. Your best hope may be to buy a transfer on a tourist bus, which stop periodically at Hotel Guantánamo — ask the doorman.

Driving: by road Guantánamo is 53 miles (86km) from Santiago, 99 miles (158km) from Baracoa, 131 miles (211km) from Bayamo and 653 miles (1,051km) from Havana. There are two alternative routes from Santiago: the fastest takes about one and a quarter hours. This is a very pleasant route along the N-1 via La Maya and Yerba de Guinea. The last stretch of the journey is along a motorway so out of place that people speculate it was designed as a landing strip for the Cuban airforce in the event of an assault by the Americans. A much longer route from Santiago runs along the coast via Baconao Park (see above); parts of this route are unpaved, but it should present no problem in fine weather.

Accommodation. The two hotels in the centre of town are on Calixto García, adjacent to the main square. Hotel Martí is a peso establishment but rents out rooms to tourists for $6. Hotel Brasil was undergoing a refit at the time of going to press, but it should be the better option once work is completed.

The only alternative is the monolithic Hotel Guantánamo (Calle 13 norte e/ Calles Ahogado y 1 oeste; tel 36015) in the north of the city. Although it is quite as ugly as any other quasi-Soviet monstrosity in Cuba, it is comfortable and cheap (a double room costs $25), and is frequented mainly by Cubans. Across the road is Plaza Mariana Grajales, the local revolution square with the usual monuments and billboards.

Eating and Drinking. Restaurants are few and far between in Guantánamo, and generally closed at night, when the town is almost completely deserted. The Siboney restaurant in the Hotel Guantánamo offers a limited menu but seems to do a roaring trade with local spivs and can be an entertaining place to eat. The best option downtown is the Bodeguita del Paseo (on Paseo, a few blocks west of the railway station), a rather quaint place where the polite staff manage to lend an aura of class not supplied by the dusty décor of plastic flowers and tourism posters. Although open until 10 o'clock, go early to have any hope of a hot meal. Latecomers may have to make do with a sandwich. Alternatively, head for the main square, where you might find a local youth selling pizzas or (inedible) hamburgers. In the daytime, you may get something to eat at the Pizzeria Holguín or at Café La Indiana, a smart new place with tasteful décor and photographs of old Guantánamo on the walls.

Exploring. If you have gone to the trouble of stopping off at Guantánamo, it is worth spending a couple of hours downtown. The main square, Parque Martí, is pleasant enough, with a small church and a bizarre stage which doesn't seem to get much use. There are a few interesting houses along Pérez and Calixto García, though some of the surrounding streets are more lively. Los Maceo, one block east of the main square, is where most Guantanameros do their shopping. The old market, a pink, vaguely neoclassical building with four red domes, occupies an entire block between Prado and Jesus del Sol, and is being restored to its former extraordinary glory. Another of several buildings downtown to have benefitted from a new restoration programme is Edificio Salcines, on the corner of Prado and Perez. Built in 1919, it has a strong Art Nouveau flavour but is typical of the eclectic architecture of the city. The rooftop figure of the woman, La Fama, is the symbol of the city. Formerly occupied by offices of the Ministry of Communications, it is to be turned into an art gallery. One block west on Calle Martí is the Museo Municipal, which has the usual assortment of memorabilia of revolutionaries past and present, but gives a useful insight into the town's history. The 1902-59 era is given more space than usual, with a lot of photographs and a few exhibits, including truncheons used by the Machado and Batista police.

If you have time in hand, you might consider visiting the Stone Zoo (Zoológico de Piedra), a short ride east of town. The large collection of limestone animals is made more curious by the fact that their creator, an amateur sculptor called Angel Iñigo, had only ever seen his subjects in pictures, but nothing can beat the Valle de la Pre Historia in Baconao Park (see page 329) for humour.

Entertainment. You might find some event going on in the Casa de la Cultura, in the main square, but try the Casa de la Trova first. The *changüi-son*, one of the oldest versions of son in Cuba, was created in Guantánamo, and you would do well to hear it in its hometown. Elio Revé, a native of Guantánamo, is a well-known performer of traditional music.

Help and Information. *Tourist information:* Islazul, at Los Maceo 663, can answer questions about local sights and has a leaflet or two.
Money: Hotel Guantánamo does not change money but, like some other hotels, it will let you pay your bill with a travellers cheque.

US Navy Base

The American base occupies the two promontories at the mouth of Guantánamo Bay, along with the sea and the islets between them, covering a total area of 45 square miles. The USA has use of the base until 2033 (or before, if both sides agree to abrogate it) under the terms of a lease signed in 1934, though the bay was first granted to the Americans under the Platt Amendment of 1901.

Each year the US government sends a rent cheque of $4,085 to the Cuban government, but Fidel Castro has not cashed one of these cheques; he is said to keep them in a drawer, a memorial to his immovable principles. The naval base has long since lost any strategic purpose, and is rather a symbol of the crazy state of US-Cuban relations. While the presence of the base is a constant source of aggravation for the Cuban regime, for the Americans the cost of running the base — an estimated $40 million a year — must far outweigh its usefulness. Officially, its principal uses are as a refuelling stop, and as a training centre for the Marines, but it is also used as a key communications and intelligence centre. It has also proved a useful detention centre for the thousands of Cuban and Haitian boatpeople, though most of these have now left the base. During the 80s and early 90s, a steadily increasing number of Cubans risked their lives in attempting to reach the base — usually by swimming, but sometimes by crossing on foot what is purported to be one of the densest minefields in the world. The fact that after August 1995 some Cubans were driven by the overcrowded conditions in the camps to risk their lives once more by escaping back into Cuba is just one of the tragedies to result from the inability of both the Washington and Havana administrations to solve a problem long past its expiry date.

The complex includes two airstrips, docking for forty ships and most of the amenities found in a small American town: a golf course and other sports facilities, cinemas, churches and the only McDonalds in Cuba. There is a population of about 7,000 Americans, including Marines, civilians and their families. After 1959, all contact and trade between Cuba and the base was stopped, and all supplies have to be shipped or flown in. Americans are not permitted to go outside the base, and the Cuban government refuses to supply electricity and water. Nevertheless, about 20 Cubans go to work at the base every day, each one of them undergoing a rigorous daily search before they are allowed in.

Viewing the Base. It would seem that the Cuban government will stop at nothing to earn some hard currency. A few years ago, an observation point was set up within the Cuban military zone that surrounds Guantánamo Bay in order for tourists to observe the naval base. You can arrange the trip at the Hotel Guantánamo (tel 36015), preferably a day or two in advance. Ask for Peter Hope, a charismatic man of Barbadian descent who acts as guide. For just $6 per person, he will take you into the military zone for an experience that is unforgettable as much for the fact that you are there at all as for the view over the base. If you don't have your own car, you will need to rent some transport, which will of course push the price up. Allow at least four hours for the whole trip.

The lookout, known as Los Malones, is off the Baracoa road, about an hour from Guantánamo. About 15 miles (24km) east of the city, you reach a small military post, where your passport will be checked. From here, the road winds 6 miles (10km) through a forest of cacti to a military command post on a hill northeast of the base. (The road becomes increasingly rough, so go with care and don't attempt the trip in wet weather.) Having been shown a model of the base and given a brief talk, you climb to the top of the hill for the view. Peter, who speaks perfect English, can point to all the interesting features inside and outside the base. Off to the left is a vast area of salt beds (most of Cuba's salt is produced in Guantánamo province), while nearer the lookout you can make out the American flag fluttering tauntingly at the entrance to the base. Through the telescope, you can watch the Americans going about their daily business. While young Americans probably looked forward to a posting to Guantánamo before the Revolution, life trapped in an inhospitable area of swamp and desert with no chance of escape must be a grim prospect in the 1990s.

Los Malones provides travellers with the best chance of seeing the base, though some have managed to get as far as Caimanera, a sleepy village in the military zone on the western side of Guantánamo Bay. It is off-limits to all Cubans, except those who live there and those with a special pass. Tourists will have the best chance of being let in if they have proof of a reservation — preferably pre-paid — at the three-star Hotel Caimanera (tel 99414). But be warned that even this doesn't always work. If you manage to get through the two checkpoints, you will be able to enjoy one of Cuba's best hotels, with a swimming pool, an excellent restaurant and even a a tower for observing the base. You won't see much, but in Caimanera you are a good deal closer to the action than at Los Malones.

If you fail to reach Caimanera with a hotel reservation and are determined to explore every avenue, you might try getting official permission. Call at the Immigration Department office at 1171 José Martí (six blocks south of the main square), make out your case (you want to witness American imperialism, etc., etc.) and hope that the *jéfe* acquiesces to your request.

East of Guantánamo. The scenery along the road by the south coast is beautiful, taking in wide palm-fringed bays and sleepy little towns. There are black-sand beaches along much of the coast, but this is not a great area for swimming — though there is a popular resort at Yateritas, 10 miles (16km) southeast of Guantánamo. At the village of Cajobabo you can continue along the south coast to the extreme east (see page 343), or turn left across the mountains of Baracoa. Playitas, near Cajobabo, is where Martí, Gómez and other mambises landed in 1895, at the start of the second war of independence.

The first half of the journey from Guantánamo to Cajobabo is plain sailing, but from here the road turns inland and upwards as it embarks on the climb over the mountains to Baracoa. This mountain road, known as La Farola ('The Beacon'), allegedly incorporates 203 bends. You should make the journey during daylight not so much because it is dangerous — the road is well-surfaced and there is little traffic — but because it is one of the most scenic and dramatic drives anywhere. The truly stunning ride takes around an hour. Allow three hours for the whole journey from Guantánamo.

BARACOA

The oldest colonial town in the Americas, Baracoa retains a considerable amount of charm. You won't spend much time sightseeing, but there are few better places to chill out for a few days. The town's geographical isolation is clearly conducive to a leisurely pace of life, and you won't feel any pressure to do anything very strenuous; taking in the atmosphere and meeting the people are the perfect pastimes in Baracoa. This is also a great place to enjoy nature. In contrast with the arid south coast, the forests around Baracoa are lush and rich in wildlife, and local rivers and beaches provide plenty of opportunities for swimming.

Baracoa makes all kinds of false claims to historical fame, chiefly that in October 1492 Columbus landed here rather than at Bariay up the coast near Gibara. The Baracoans' excuse for this misapprehension is that the flat-topped mountain, El Yunque ('the anvil'), is a perfect candidate for the 'high, square mountain that looks like an island' described by Columbus on his arrival off the Cuban coast. This landmark is visible from almost everywhere in the area, but a similar geological phenomenon can be seen at Bariay. No doubt, however, surrounds the fact that Baracoa was the first of the seven villas established in Cuba by the Spanish. From its foundation by Diego Velázquez in 1512, Baracoa also functioned as the island's capital until 1515, when this title passed to Santiago. Having started off as the departure point for the conquest of the rest of the country, the importance of Baracoa diminished as other parts of Cuba were opened up. This forgotten corner of the island was a haven for the aborigines, who sought the protection of the nearby mountains, where their descendants still live. Taíno ceramics and shell objects found in the area show that there were once numerous aboriginal settlements in the area.

There was little development in the region until the late 18th century, when more than a hundred French families came to Baracoa from Haiti and settled in the town. But the town was never more than an outpost. It was accessible only by sea right up until the 1950s, when a road was built across the mountains for the first time. Even then, this was little more than a dirt track, which was paved only after the Revolution. Nowadays, Baracoa lives mainly off tourism and agriculture. Despite being a port, there has never been much fishing in Baracoa, and the livelihood of the local people revolves largely around the abundance of cocoa beans, bananas and coconuts.

Town Layout. Baracoa extends along the coast from the eastern lip of the small harbour. The Malecón, which runs the length of the seafront, has none of the bustle, none of the class of Havana's waterfront and instead is a decrepit promenade which doesn't do justice to the town; few people come here, least of all at night. Parallel to the Malecón are the main streets of José Martí and Antonio Maceo. José Martí, where you'll find most shops (such as there are), becomes the highway to the south coast, which crosses the Río de Miel and then turns inland. In the evenings, the bustle of Martí shifts to Plaza Independencia, the focal point of the town and also known as the Parque Central.

Maps of Baracoa (combined with a plan of Santiago de Cuba) are available for $0.90 from the Castillo and Porto Santo hotels.

Arrival and Departure. *Air:* it is thrilling to arrive at Baracoa by air. There are great views on the approach, and you appear to be landing on water as you touch down — the short airstrip stretches across the width of the promontory at the western mouth of the harbour. There should be a couple of cabs waiting to take you the short distance into town; otherwise walk the 100 yards to the Porto Santo Hotel and take a taxi from there.

There are flights to Baracoa from Havana at dawn on Tuesday and Friday, both calling at Varadero. In the reverse direction, the Tuesday flight calls additionally at Guantánamo. On Tuesdays you can also fly to and from Santiago. On other days there is not a lot happening at the airport.

You can make bookings from Baracoa at the Cubana office at Calle José Martí 181 (tel 42171).

Driving: see page 300 for a description of the drive to Baracoa along the north coast via Moa. You would be ill-advised to undertake this journey after dark. The southern approach from Guantánamo, described above, is a little easier.

Bus: most buses, including those to and from Moa and Guantánamo, serve the dusty yard which serves as the intermunicipal terminal at the junction of Coroneles Galano and Rupert López, a couple of blocks east of the main square. If there is no hope of getting on a bus, this is as good a place as any to find out about alternative transport. There is never much action at the long-distance terminal (Omnibus Nacionales) at the western end of town near La Punta fortress, though there is supposedly one bus a day to Guantánamo.

Getting Around. You won't need anything other than your feet to get around the town. In terms of exploring, however, transport is a real problem around Baracoa. There is very little traffic, so hitching is difficult and the buses packed. You can hire cars at the Porto Santo Hotel, though you would do well to phone in advance to reserve one.

Accommodation. The favourite hotel among independent travellers to Baracoa has long been La Rusa (tel 43011), three blocks north of the Plaza Independencia. It is often referred to locally as the Hotel 'Miramar' — logical given that it overlooks the sea, but confusing if you've just arrived in town. And the whole point of the hotel is its name, which commemorates a Russian woman called Magdalena Menases, affectionately known as 'Mima', who was active in the 26 of July Movement. She lived in this building, which was converted into a hotel after her death in 1978; her portrait hangs over the reception desk. Mima used to entertain the Castro brothers, Che and other revolutionaries, and the hotel likes to encourage guests to think they are sleeping in a room used by one of them. Prices have gone up since La Rusa was requisitioned and refurbished by the Islazul tourist agency. While still eminently affordable at $16 for a single and $20 a double in low season, the rooms are small and poor value when compared with the alternatives (see below). Mima's foster son, René Frometa, lives across the street from the hotel and has plenty of stories to tell. He will show you his shelves of dusty memorabilia (including a revolver that was supposedly given to Mima by Raúl Castro) as well as his own paintings. His connection with the Russian is clearly a good way to get visitors into his small studio, but his naive pictures of Baracoa make cheap and very portable souvenirs.

The hardest-to-resist hotel alternative to La Rusa is El Castillo (tel 214-2103, 2115, 2147), in one of Baracoa's three 18th-century forts, where a double room for $25 in the low season is a positive bargain. (In peak season the price rises to nearer $40.) The hotel perches on the clifftop, providing wonderful views over the harbour, out to sea, back towards El Yunque and down over Baracoa's terracotta rooftops. A pleasant breeze fans the large terrace and the swimming pool is a great bonus after a hot day's exploring. Rooms are spacious and more

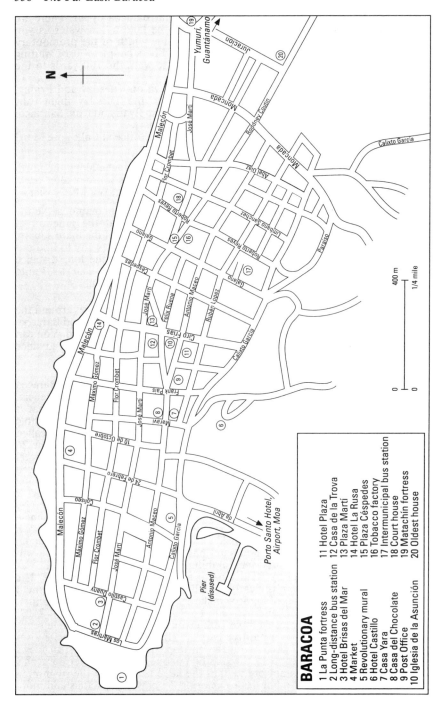

BARACOA

1 La Punta fortress
2 Long-distance bus station
3 Hotel Brisas del Mar
4 Market
5 Revolutionary mural
6 Hotel Castillo
7 Casa Yara
8 Casa del Chocolate
9 Post Office
10 Iglesia de la Asunción
11 Hotel Plaza
12 Casa de la Trova
13 Plaza Martí
14 Hotel La Rusa
15 Plaza Céspedes
16 Tobacco factory
17 Intermunicipal bus station
18 Court house
19 Matachín fortress
20 Oldest house

than usually comfortable, and the satellite television might appeal to some. The Duaba restaurant is also excellent (see below).

The new four-star Porto Santo Hotel (tel 214-3578, 3590), next to the airport, offers a similar standard of accommodation to the Castillo and similar value, with double rooms for $35 in high season ($28 in low) and $26 ($21) for a single. Its location away from the centre might appeal to some people, and whilst sipping your coffee or beer on the terrace you can enjoy the sight of Baracoa across the harbour.

If you're after the cheapest bed in town, head for the Hotel Brisas del Mar (tel 42222), a peso place at the corner of Martí and Castillo Duany. Double rooms are a snip at $6, but the hotel's location behind the long-distance bus station means that it is often fully booked. You could also try the Hotel Plaza, up an unmarked flight of stairs above the Encanto theatre in Plaza Independencia.

Eating and Drinking. Anyone with a penchant for coconut will be in their element in Baracoa, since the use of it in both sweet and savoury dishes is one of the main characteristics of the local cooking. Coconut oil is now used consistently for frying simply because of the shortage of normal cooking oil, lending a distinctive flavour to many dishes. And Baracoa is famous for *cucurucho*, a horribly sweet local delicacy made with chopped coconut, ripe fruit and honey that comes wrapped in palm leaves; the best place to buy it is at the factory along the road towards Finca Duaba (see below), where you will also find the local chocolate factory. On restaurant menus, the most common use of coconut is in the preparation of savoury dishes, such as fish or crab in coconut milk (*lechita*). Although fishing is not an industry around Baracoa, there is no shortage of fish to eat. If you are in Baracoa between August and December, ask around for *tetí*. A week after the August full moon, these tiny red fish appear en masse at the mouth of the Toa, Miel and Nibujon rivers. They arrive in a gelatinous ball that disintegrates on contact with fresh water, releasing thousands of fish that proceed to swim upstream; the process continues until December. The locals traditionally eat tetí raw, fried or in an omelette.

The best place for a slap-up meal is the Duaba Restaurant in the Castillo Hotel. The chef knows everything there is to know about local food, and there are several specialities on the menu. Try the *pescado Santa Bárbara* (fish in coconut milk) with traditional trimmings such as *plátanos chatinos* (fried plantain). Main meals cost $5-7, but there are plenty of cheaper dishes too, such as *ajiaco*, a traditional Cuban soup which is a meal in itself and costs just $1.80. Fruit also features more than usual on the menu; ask what fruit is available for fruit salads or a fruit shake.

No one at La Rusa hotel seems to care that their food is more expensive than the Duaba's but not even half has good. You would do better to try the Guamá restaurant in La Punta fortress, where at least you are more likely to be surrounded by Cubans, and the creole food is reasonably cheap. Another place worth checking out is the pizzeria on Ciro Frías, by Parque Martí, a no-frills, no-choice kind of place.

You used to be able to buy delicious ice cream sundaes and the locally made chocolate and coconut delicacies at the Casa del Chocolate, on Calixto García, but nowadays all that is available is sweet and watery hot chocolate. However, the reason to come here is not so much for the hot drink as for the ambience. This is the social hub of Baracoa. It is the only café open in the centre of town in the evening, and there is a constant stream of people to and fro between it and the nearby Plaza Independencia. It closes at 10pm but is already past its best by 9.30pm.

You can buy fruit at the market on the Malecón, but there is nothing in the way of prepared food. The streets of Baracoa are strangely devoid of people selling snacks.

Exploring. Plaza Independencia is the social centre of the community, and locals gather beneath the trees to exchange gossip, have their shoes polished or just sit and watch the world go by. At the eastern end stands the **Iglesia de la Asunción**. Founded in 1512, it is considered Cuba's oldest church, although the original building was destroyed by pirates in the 17th century. The present church dates from the early 19th century. Some restoration work has been carried out with the help of German money, but it still needs a lot of work doing to it. The most interesting thing inside is the so-called Cruz de la Parra, a wooden cross which Christopher Columbus is supposed to have brought with him on his second voyage of discovery — the only one of the 29 crosses Columbus carried to have survived. It was discovered under the branches of an old vine (hence the name: 'Cross of the Vine') near the home of an early settler. Cynics dismiss the claim out of hand, but carbon-dating has shown that the wood does indeed date from the mid-15th century. Catholics have never had much trouble believing the story. For centuries worshippers (including several presidents) have carved off bits for themselves as lucky charms. Some has also been removed for carbon dating. The cross has consequently shrunk from 2.6m to 1m, and now has its edges encased in metal and is protected in a glass case. You are most likely to find the church open in the evening (Mass is usually at 6pm) or on weekend mornings. At other times, if you ask around enough, the local priest or one of his helpers may come and open up for you. Padre Valentín Sanz, speaks excellent French and English, and will provide you with a fascinating insight into the building's history.

Almost smothered by foliage opposite the church door is a bust of the Indian chief Hatuey, described as the 'first rebel of America'. It is also recorded that he was 'sacrificed in Yara, Baracoa', but it has now been conceded that Hatuey was almost certainly burned to death at Yara in Granma province (see page 305). Another civic lie from Baracoa. The monument was erected by the local Masonic lodge, apparently as a snub against the Catholic church (Hatuey preferred to die than to be converted to the religion of his Spanish captors).

One block north of Plaza Independencia is Calle Martí, Baracoa's busiest shopping street. There is not much fun to be had from window shopping, but on the corner of Galano, in Plaza Céspedes, you can poke your head into the local **Tobacco Factory**. Just beyond the square, between Reyes and Sánchez, is the local **Court House** (*tribunal*), which can provide a fascinating insight into the administration of justice. The doors are usually wide open and anyone can wander in and watch.

It is only a short walk east to **Fuerte Matachín**, which has been restored and turned into one of Cuba's better local museums. The Museo Municipal (open 9am-5pm Tuesday to Saturday, 9am-1pm on Sunday) gives the usual overview of local history, but this is done well and focuses less than usual on the post-Revolutionary era. There is a good collection of aboriginal artefacts, a display of 98 types of wood found in the forests around Baracoa and cases devoted to several local characters, including La Rusa and the hirsute Pelu, who is blamed for having placed a curse on Baracoa. The museum also acts as a research centre, and if there is anything you want to know about Baracoa this is the place to come. The museum director, Alejandro Hartman, is well-known in the town and is a mine of information, but all the staff are helpful.

One block south, at Calle Juración number 49 on the corner of Calle Coutin, is what is claimed to be the oldest house in Cuba (history and local folklore are rather vague), though there is a far more attractive building in Santiago that makes the same claim. It is identifiable by the payphone bolted to the outside wall. There is no sign outside to tell you that it is anything special, and its concrete exterior makes it look considerably more modern than it is. The present occupant is generally quite willing to open the door to visitors and show them inside. The original house consisted of a single room, which has been added to considerably but whose antiquity is still discernable. Across the road is another local landmark, the Torreón de Joa, a tower which seems large, round, and pointless. It was built so that Spanish officials could keep an eye out for people smuggling arms and supplies to independence fighters in the mountains.

The western end of town is much quieter. It is worth strolling along to **La Punta** fortress, from where you get a good view across the harbour, with El Yunque rising in the distance. (The rusting hull of a ship beneath the fort wall was placed there to protect the boats at anchor in the harbour.) If you wish to add another picture to your portfolio of revolutionary icons, there is a good mural on Calixto García, about four blocks east of La Punta, with the usual pantheon of heroes from Céspedes to Che.

Finally, east of El Castillo, a staircase cut into the cliff leads up to a statue of a Taíno Indian, placed there in 1992, the 500th anniversary of Columbus' arrival on the island. A cross in the park near Fuerte Matachín marks the spot where he is said to have landed.

Nightlife. Don't expect to burn the candle at both ends unless you decide to prop up the bar at your hotel. The Baracoans seem to enjoy a close family life, and socialising in the evening doesn't extend beyond Plaza Independencia. The **Casa de la Trova**, an unmarked building on the north side of the square (José Martí 149a), is a small run-down affair with nothing in common with its counterparts in Santiago or Camagüey, for example. The entertainment, however, is also more informal than elsewhere, and is very much a free for all. Any visitor who joins in should go down a storm. For a more organised cabaret, go to the Castillo or Porto Santo hotels, or try the 'noche cubana' cabaret at the Guamá restaurant. For more sedate entertainment, head for the cinema in the main square.

Shopping. One place not to miss in Baracoa is **Casa Yara**, opposite the Casa del Chocolate. This is the main outlet for local artists, some of whom produce some interesting work. Alberto, who works here, will take you to visit the artists personally if you are eager to see more of their work. The sculptures of an artist called Domínguez, who takes his inspiration from aboriginal traditions, are among the most interesting. Casa Yara also organises performances of aboriginal ceremonies, which are usually staged in a forest clearing outside Baracoa.

For a more-interesting-than-average souvenir, look out for people selling the indigenous polymita shells. René Frometa (see *Accommodation*) usually has some to sell. Or just ask around. People sell them by the bagfull.

Help and Information. *Tourist Information:* the best source of information is the Casa Yara. Alberto makes an excellent guide if you want to get that bit extra out of your visit; he knows everyone there is to know in Baracoa and can fix anything from a visit to a santería priest to a trip into the virgin forest along the River Toa (see below). He relies on visitors tipping him rather than charging a fixed daily fee, though this may change if tourism takes off in a big way. The staff at the Museo Municipal are also a good source of information.

Medical care: there is a pharmacy by the main square and a Policlínico opposite the Matachín fortress.

Post Office: opposite the pink Poder Popular building in Plaza Independencia.

Money: you can change travellers' cheques at Hotel Porto Santo; the commission seems to vary from 2% to 4%, according to the mood of the counter staff. At the Hotel Castillo, staff will only give you dollars cash as change if you pay your room bill with a travellers' cheque. Local youths may offer to change dollars into pesos but can't help with travellers cheques.

Car hire: Havanautos has an agent in Hotel Porto Santo.

Petrol: Cuba's easternmost petrol station, the 24-hour Cupet facility, is on the eastern edge of town, on the Guantánamo road.

FURTHER AFIELD

There is enough to keep you busy for days if you are interested in exploring the wilds around Baracoa. But even those with just one day to spare, can get a taste of the natural beauty of the region. You don't need to set aside more than a morning to climb **El Yunque** (1,800 feet/560m), which lies temptingly close to town. The route to the top starts near Campismo El Yunque, about 2 miles/ 3km off the Moa road, though to do the thing properly you should go to Finca Duaba (at the top of the turn-off to the campsite), where you can hire a guide and horses. You will be advised to start as early as possible in the morning to avoid the midday sun. It's a short, sharp climb which takes less than two hours. From the top you can see right to Punta de Maisí, the easternmost point of the island (see below). Finca Duaba has been set up to demonstrate to tourists how cocoa, coconut and bananas are cultivated, and there is a restaurant, but it doesn't seem to do a roaring trade.

To cool off after the climb or after a morning's wander around town, you can head to one of the local beaches. Beaches extend west along the coast to the mouth of the Toa river and also east to the mouth of the Yumurí (see below). **Playa Maguaná**, about 8 miles (12km) northwest of Baracoa, is the only vaguely white sand beach in the area and is one of the best; Villa Maguaná offers accommodation and food. At **Playa Duaba**, closer to Baracoa, you have the luxury of choosing between salt or fresh water. The turning, just beyond the turn-off to El Yunque, is easily missed, so you'll probably need to ask someone. The unpaved road descends suddenly and then cuts across a lovely palm grove before veering right through a small hamlet right on the shore. There is room to park under the trees at the end of the road (near a monument recalling that Antonio Maceo and a small group of *mambises* landed here in 1895 at the start of the War of Independence), from where it is a stone's throw to the beach — or rather the two beaches. The Duaba river flows into the sea here, but a sandbar steers it parallel to the Atlantic for several hundred yards before letting the two meet. You can swim either side of the sandbar, enjoying the freshness and calm of the river or the salt and waves of the ocean.

The most popular spot east of Baracoa is **Yumurí**, named after the river which flows into the sea here. It's a delightful one-hour drive, along a good road which winds through the hills and then descends to the shoreline. The views are particularly good on the return — back towards El Yunque and along some idyllic little beaches. The village of Yumurí is rather like that by Playa Duaba, with simple wooden houses gathered beneath the trees, women washing clothes on the rocks in the river, people strolling about barefoot or chatting quietly in the shade. The village has never been anything but peaceful, but since the bridge across the river collapsed in 1994, passers-by have been few and far between. Yumurí lies on the road from Baracoa to La Máquina and Punta de Maisí, but now the traffic has all but stopped. One bus a day brings a few passengers from Baracoa, who are ferried the 50 yards across the river by local boatmen and then taken on to La Máquina by another bus. These same boatmen also take visitors into the gorge for which Yumurí is so famous. (Apparently, they are not supposed to give rides to foreigners, but they seem only too happy to oblige). In the dry season you can wander along the river bed, with forested cliffs towering either side, and swim when the water level is high enough. There are even a couple of houses here, where people have returned to escape the stresses of life outside. Back in the village, people sell polymita shells (*polimites*) — pay a dollar a bag, or barter what you've got.

If you are into serious exploring, you should enquire about going up the **River Toa**, which flows northwest of Baracoa: it is 120km long and is flanked by virgin forest which has been designated a biosphere reserve by UNESCO. The region has long been so isolated that in colonial times it was a haven first for aborigines and later for escaped slaves, who lived in communities known as *palenques*, some of which still exist. Deep into the interior is the village of **Caridad de los Indios de Yateras**, where direct descendants of Taíno Indians survive, though many of them are old and by no means of pure aboriginal descent; some suffer the deformations that result from inbreeding. If you wish to explore this area, talk to the staff at the museum or at Casa Yara. The rafting potential of the Toa river is considerable, but so far no-one has seen fit to realise.

THE EXTREME EAST

Easternmost Cuba is accessible — just. The only road to the edge was washed away some years ago, but you can make the journey with care. From the ragged little town of La Máquina — which can be reached from Yumurí, if you're lucky, or Cajobabo on the south coast — a track leads to the **Punta de Maisí**, Cuba's 'Land's End', which has a lighthouse, a tiny and thoroughly isolated village and a military base. If you like end-of-the-world, windswept places, this is for you. A four-wheel drive vehicle is recommended if you're driving.

At this point you are closer to Venezuela than to the western edge of Cuba, and much nearer to Haiti — just 60 miles (100km) east — than to Guantánamo. Havana is 800 miles (1,280km) distant, and it feels like a world away.

INDEX

Vacation Work also publish:

	Paperback	Hardback
The Directory of Summer Jobs Abroad	£7.99	£12.99
The Directory of Summer Jobs in Britain	£7.99	£12.99
The Teenager's Vacation Guide to Work, Study & Adventure	£6.95	£9.95
Work Your Way Around the World	£9.95	£15.95
Working in Tourism – The UK, Europe & Beyond	£9.99	£15.99
Working on Cruise Ships	£7.99	£12.99
Working with the Environment	£9.99	£15.99
Teaching English Abroad	£9.95	£15.95
The Au Pair & Nanny's Guide to Working Abroad	£8.95	£14.95
Working in Ski Resorts — Europe & North America	£8.95	£14.95
Kibbutz Volunteer	£7.99	£12.99
The Directory of Jobs & Careers Abroad	£9.95	£15.95
The International Directory of Voluntary Work	£8.95	£14.95
The Directory of Work & Study in Developing Countries	£7.95	£10.95
Live & Work in France	£8.95	£14.95
Live & Work in the USA & Canada	£8.95	£14.95
Live & Work in Australia & New Zealand	£8.95	£14.95
Live & Work in Scandinavia	£8.95	£14.95
Live & Work in Germany	£8.95	£11.95
Live & Work in Belgium, The Netherlands & Luxembourg	£8.95	£11.95
Live & Work in Spain & Portugal	£8.95	£11.95
Live & Work in Italy	£7.95	£10.95
Travellers Survival Kit Lebanon	£9.99	–
Travellers Survival Kit: Russia & the Republics	£9.95	–
Travellers Survival Kit: Western Europe	£8.95	–
Travellers Survival Kit: Eastern Europe	£9.95	–
Travellers Survival Kit: South America	£12.95	–
Travellers Survival Kit: Central America	£8.95	–
Travellers Survival Kit: USA & Canada	£9.95	–
Travellers Survival Kit to the East	£6.95	–
Travellers Survival Kit: Australia & New Zealand	£9.99	–
Hitch-hikers' Manual Britain	£3.95	–
Europe – Manual for Hitch-hikers	£4.95	–

Distributors of:

Summer Jobs USA	£9.99	–
Internships (On-the-Job Training Opportunities in the USA)	£15.99	–
Sports Scholarships in the USA	£12.99	–
The Directory of College Accommodations USA	£5.95	–
Emplois d'Ete en France	£7.99	–
Making It in Japan	£8.95	–

Vacation Work Publications, 9 Park End Street, Oxford OX1 1HJ
(Tel 01865-241978. Fax 01865-790885)